EIGHTH EDITION

SOCIAL WORK SPEAKS

NATIONAL ASSOCIATION OF SOCIAL WORKERS POLICY STATEMENTS
2009–2012

JAMES J. KELLY, PHD, ACSW, LCSW, *President*

ELIZABETH J. CLARK, PHD, ACSW, *Executive Director*

National Association of Social Workers

Published by

NASW PRESS

National Association of Social Workers
Washington, DC

Cheryl Y. Bradley, *Publisher*
Sarah Lowman, *Senior Editor*
Lisa M. O'Hearn, *Staff Editor*
Rebecca Tippets, *Proofreader*
Bernice Eisen, *Indexer*

Cover design by Metadog Design Group, Washington, DC
Typeset by Xcel Graphic Services, Forest Hills, MD
Printed by VictorGraphics, Inc., Baltimore, MD

Printed in the United States of America

ISBN 978-0-87101-384-2

Contents

Policy Statement Topic Areas

Adolescents

Adolescent Health
Adolescent Pregnancy and Parenting
Education of Children and Youths
Juvenile Justice and Delinquency Prevention
School Dropout Prevention
School Violence
Youth Suicide

Aging

Aging and Wellness
Client Self-Determination and End-of-Life
    Decisions
End-of-Life Care
Health Care
Hospice Care
Long-Term Care

Behavioral Health

Mental Health

Child Welfare

Child Abuse and Neglect
Family Policy
Family Violence
Foster Care and Adoption
Physical Punishment of Children
Public Child Welfare
Welfare Reform

Community

Community Development
Disasters
Housing
Social Services

Discrimination and Equity Issues

Affirmative Action
Civil Liberties and Justice
Correctional Social Work

Cultural and Linquistic Competence in the
    Social Work Profession
Gender-, Ethnic-, and Race-Based Workplace
    Discrimination
Genetics
Immigrants and Refugees
International Policy on Human Rights
Language and Cultural Diversity in the
    United States
Lesbian, Gay, and Bisexual Issues
Peace and Social Justice
People with Disabilities
Poverty and Economic Justice
Racism
Transgender and Gender Identity Issues
Women in the Social Work Profession
Women's Issues

Education

Early Childhood Care and Services
Education of Children and Youths
Physical Punishment of Children
School Truancy and Dropout Prevention

Employment

Drug Testing in the Workplace
Employee Assistance
Gender-, Ethnic-, and Race-Based Workplace
    Discrimination
Genetics
Homelessness
Housing
Poverty and Economic Justice

Ethnicity and Race

Affirmative Action
Civil Liberties and Justice
Cultural and Linguistic Competence in the
    Social Work Profession
Gender-, Ethnic-, and Race-Based Workplace
    Discrimination
Immigrants and Refugees

International Policy on Human Rights
Linguist/Cultural Diversity in the
   United States
Racism

Families and Children

Adolescent Pregnancy and Parenting
Child Abuse and Neglect
Early Childhood Care and Services
Family Planning and Reproductive Choice
Family Policy
Family Violence
Foster Care and Adoption
Genetics
Homelessness
Housing
Parental Kidnapping
Physical Punishment of Children
Public Child Welfare
Welfare Reform
Women's Issues
Youth Suicide

Family Planning

Adolescent Pregnancy and Parenting
Family Planning and Reproductive Choice
Genetics

Gender Issues

Affirmative Action
Civil Liberties and Justice
Family Violence
Gender-, Ethnic-, and Race-Based Workplace
   Discrimination
International Policy on Human Rights
Lesbian, Gay, Bisexual Issues
Poverty and Economic Justice
Transgender and Gender Identity Issues
Women in the Social Work Profession
Women's Issues

Health

Adolescent Health
Adolescent Pregnancy and Parenting
Aging and Wellness
Alcohol, Tobacco, and Other Drugs

Client Self-Determination in End-of-Life
   Decision
Early Childhood Care and Services
Family Planning and Reproductive Choice
Family Violence
Genetics
Health Care
HIV and AIDS
Hospice Care
Long-Term Care
Mental Health
People with Disabilities
Sovereignty and Health of Indigenous People

Macro Issues

Capital Punishment and the Death Penalty
Crime Victim Assistance
Environmental Policy
Family Policy
Genetics
Health Care
Housing
Immigrants and Refugees
International Policy on Human Rights
Peace and Social Justice
Poverty and Economic Justice
Role of Government, Social Policy, and Social
   Work
Social Services
Sovereignty and Health of Indigenous People
Technology and Social Work

Political Action

Civil Liberties and Justice
Crime Victim Assistance
Deprofessionalization and Reclassification
Electoral Politics
Role of Government, Social Policy, and
   Social Work
Voter Participation

Social Work Professional Statements

Confidentiality and Information Utilization
Cultural and Linguistic Competence in the
   Social Work Profession
Deprofessionalization and Reclassification

Employee Assistance
NASW Code of Ethics
Professional Impairment
Professional Self-Care and Social Work
Public Child Welfare
Rural Social Work
Women in the Social Work Profession

Substance Abuse

Alcohol, Tobacco, and Other Drugs
Drug Testing in the Workplace
Professional Impairment

Violence

Child Abuse and Neglect
Crime Victim Assistance
Family Violence
Physical Punishment of Children
School Violence
Youth Suicide

Policy Statements Approved by the 2008 Delegate Assembly

Adolescent Pregnancy and Parenting
Aging and Wellness
Civil Liberties and Justice
Correctional Social Work
Deprofessionalization and Reclassification
Drug Testing in the Workplace
Economic Policy
Environmental Policy
Family Planning and Reproductive Choice
Family Policy
Genetics
Health Care
HIV and AIDS
Housing
Immigrants and Refugees
International Policy on Human Rights
Language and Cultural Diversity in the
    United States
People with Disabilities
Professional Impairment
Professional Self-Care and Social Work
Prostituted People, Commercial Sex Workers,
    and Social Work
Slavery and Human Trafficking
Technology and Social Work
Transgender and Gender Identity Issues
Welfare Reform

Title Changes from the 7th Edition

Commercial Sex Workers and Social Work
    Practice is now Prostituted People,
    Commercial Sex Workers, and Social Work
    Practice
Economic Policy is now Poverty and
    Economic Justice
Linguistic/Cultural Diversity in the United
    States is now Language and Cultural
    Diversity in the United States
Senior Health, Safety, and Vitality is now
    Aging and Wellness
Temporary Assistance for Needy Families:
    Welfare Reform is now Welfare Reform

Statements Deleted

Managed Care
Volunteers and Social Services Systems

Foreword

The policy statements contained in this book set the parameters for National Association of Social Workers (NASW) positions and actions on a broad range of public and professional issues. *Social Work Speaks* is a comprehensive collection of policies adopted and revised by NASW's key policy-making body, the Delegate Assembly. This edition includes all of the new and revised policies approved by the 2008 NASW Delegate Assembly, as well as those approved by previous assemblies.

Since its inception in 1955, NASW's policy statement adoption has been a part of its governance process. The Delegate Assembly, a body of 277 professional social workers representing NASW's diverse membership, meets at regular intervals (every three years since 1981) to set broad parameters for the association's programs, to determine bylaws issues, and to agree on policy statements that guide advocacy efforts in public policy. In 2008, for the first time, the Delegate Assembly was conducted virtually. Only a few individuals—the president, the facilitators, the parliamentarian, legal counsel, and necessary national staff—were together in Washington. The delegates from all 50 states and U.S. territories logged in from their home computers or from a location arranged by their coalition or chapter. Delibeation and voting followed the customary Delegate Assembly process and used *Robert's Rules of Order*. New policy statements were approved, bylaws changes were adopted, and program priority goals were set. It was an efficient and exciting way to conduct the business of the association.

The involvement of social workers in policy development continues to be important. Increasingly we participate in a global community, where what happens in one country has repercussions around the world. The population of the United States is more culturally, ethnically, and racially diverse. There is a rapidly aging population and a widening gap between affluent and poor people. At the same time, the recent economic crisis is creating new challenges for human services agencies and organizations. Effective programs are being re-evaluated, and in some cases eliminated, due to decreasing revenues from fundraising and earnings on investments. Our social work value systems and our expertise lend themselves to creating and advocating for policies that provide effective solutions in the current context of our world.

THE PROCESS

The 2008 Delegate Assembly process built upon technology innovations used at the Delegate Assembly in 2005. All of the new and revised policy statements were available online for comment by the membership twice before being adopted by the delegates. This allowed members to make suggestions to improve the policies. Hearing panels met via online meeting software and teleconferencing, taking comments into account and making necessary revisions. These technology innovations allowed for greater involvement and input from the membership and from the delegates. Delegates could meet when it was convenient for them and focus solely on crafting the statement rather than having to meet during a full Delegate Assembly agenda.

All of the revised policy statements were voted on prior to the actual Delegate Assembly meeting. Only the new policy statements required agenda time at the virtual meeting. Consequently, these policy statements represent the collective thinking of thousands of experienced social work practitioners.

LEGISLATIVE ACTIVITY

Before taking a position on any federal legislation, the NASW national office compares the proposed legislative policy with policies in this book. If the proposed legislation is consistent with the thrust of an NASW policy statement or if it contradicts the statement, NASW's position will be readily apparent. However, in many cases, the proposed legislation contains some provisions that support NASW's policies and some that are inconsistent with, or only partially support, the NASW recommendations. In these cases, a decision is not made easily, and other factors must be taken into consideration. NASW then weighs the potential for revising the proposed legislation, the overall value of possible policy gains, political concerns, and other factors before a decision to support the legislation is made. When chapters make decisions on legislative action at the state level, they also review the NASW policy statements to ensure that action taken is not in conflict with NASW policy.

For social workers to be heard as one voice on federal policy, the national office coordinates action on federal legislation at the national, chapter, unit, and member levels. Action may include endorsements for, or opposition to, a bill before Congress, letters to Congress requesting action on a bill, or participation in coalition actions for or against a piece of legislation. Chapters coordinate action on state legislation.

LEGAL ACTION

NASW also initiates or participates in a number of amicus curiae (friend of the court) briefs on critical social and professional issues. For example, NASW was a major participant in *Kennedy v. Louisiana* (U.S. Supreme Court, No. 07-343, 2008), in which the Supreme Court ruled against the imposition of capital punishment in a child rape case and cited the NASW brief. In deciding which cases to support with a brief at the federal or state level, NASW looks to policy statements for guidance. The policy statements also provide a foundation for comment on federal regulations or proposed federal legislation.

POLICY STUDY AND ANALYSIS

Social Work Speaks may be used as a text or as supplementary reading for overview, intro-

ductory, or macro courses in public policy. The book may also serve as an adjunct to a wide range of specialty courses because so many of the policy statements address specific fields of practice.

As an articulation of what one Delegate Assembly viewed as an ideal policy, individual statements are useful for analysis and review. They are excellent resources for classroom discussion and debate, and they can be used to raise questions such as the following:

■ What important issues have practitioners raised in the subject area?

■ Are the issues ones I deem critical?

■ In my opinion, are there major issues that were not considered?

■ Do I concur with NASW's policy stance?

■ What documentation did NASW provide for the conclusions?

■ On what course work, research, other readings, or practice experience do I base my stance?

■ How do the positions compare with the public positions of other groups and organizations on the same subject?

■ How might the statements be amended?

■ What purposes might the statements serve?

■ How can I use the statements to become a more effective advocate?

For lobbying or analysis, policy statements should be considered in the context of their purpose and the time in which they were adopted, keeping in mind that each policy statement is the product of a specific Delegate Assembly. Social workers developed the statements to serve as broad parameters for advocacy work and to help professionals who are concerned with social issues focus their thinking. Nonetheless, because of the breadth of issues and the constantly emerging new information, readers may find that they need more specificity than the statements contain. Contemporary professional literature will serve as an important extension of the policy statements, and NASW national and chapter offices may also provide updated information in many areas (www.socialworkers.org).

As readers use these statements, they may also want to consider new or revised statements that could be presented to the 2011 Delegate Assembly. Social workers who want to be informed and involved in policy analysis, advocacy for social policies, or the formulation of future policy statements will find the eighth edition of *Social Work Speaks* useful.

James J. Kelly, PhD, ACSW
President, NASW

Elizabeth J. Clark, PhD, ACSW, MPH
Executive Director, NASW

PUBLIC AND PROFESSIONAL POLICY STATEMENTS

Adolescent Health

BACKGROUND

Adolescents often participate in risky health behaviors that ultimately contribute to the leading causes of mortality and morbidity among the youth population. The effects of risky behaviors, especially in conjunction with negative environmental and biopsychosocial influences, often extend into adulthood, are interrelated, and are preventable. Addressing the aspects of disease and dysfunction that are preventable can provide substantial economic benefits by reducing acute, emergency health care costs.

The Youth Risk Behavior Surveillance System is a program of the Centers for Disease Control and Prevention's (CDC) National Center for Chronic Disease Prevention and Health Promotion. One of its purposes is to determine the prevalence and age of initiation of health risk behaviors. With technical assistance from CDC, staff of state and local departments of education and health conduct a Youth Risk Behavior Survey (YRBS) every two years. The most recent school-based surveys were last conducted in 1999 among students in grades 9 to 12 in 42 states, 16 large cities, and four territories. According to the 1999 YRBS, approximately three-fourths of all deaths in the United States among people ages 10 to 24 result from only four causes: motor vehicle crashes, other unintentional injuries, homicide, and suicide. Survey results indicate that numerous high school students engage in behaviors that increase their likelihood of death from these four causes. Specifically, 16.4 percent of youths surveyed reported that they rarely or never wore a seat belt, 33.1 percent reported that they had ridden with a driver who had been drinking alcohol during the past 30 days, 17.3 percent had carried a weapon, 50 percent had drunk alcohol, 26.7 percent had used mari-

juana during the 30-day period preceding the survey, and 7.8 percent of respondents indicated they had attempted suicide during the preceding 12 months (National Center for Chronic Disease Prevention and Health Promotion, 1999).

A major contributor to morbidity and social problems among young people is sexual activity that leads to unintended pregnancies and sexually transmitted diseases, including HIV infection. The 1999 YRBS found that 49.9 percent of high school students surveyed had participated in sexual intercourse, with 42 percent of these sexually active students reporting that they had not used a condom the last time they engaged in sexual intercourse.

Two-thirds of all deaths among people 25 years of age or older stem from only two causes—cardiovascular disease and cancer. The majority of risk behaviors associated with these two causes of death are initiated during adolescence. In 1999, 34.8 percent of high school students reported having smoked cigarettes during the 30 days preceding the survey; 76.1 percent of high school students indicated they had not eaten at least five servings per day of fruits and vegetables during the seven days preceding the survey. Sixteen percent of respondents were at risk of becoming overweight, and 70.9 percent did not attend physical education class daily (National Center for Chronic Disease Prevention and Health Promotion, 1999).

Research concerning adolescent health indicates that substance abuse, truancy, delinquency, school failure, teenage pregnancy, and teenage violence all have a similar etiology (Hawkins, Catalano, & Miller, 1992; Hawkins, Lishner, Jenson, & Catalano 1987). Risk factors for poor adolescent health outcomes include severe economic deprivation; community norms that condone risky behavior; neighborhood disorganization; family mobility; lack of attachment for children with peers, family, school, and community; lack of commitment to school; rejection by peers; early and persistent behavior problems; family drug use; family violence; and poor family management. Because many of these risk factors can be identified during earlier developmental stages of childhood, prevention efforts directed at earlier antecedent behaviors may be more efficient and cost-effective when interventions are provided concurrently with the health or mental health diagnosis at secondary and tertiary treatment levels.

Although it is essential that social workers continue to advocate for social policy and political action that promotes healthy environments and social justice to mitigate external risk factors that lead to poor adolescent health outcomes, this type of political and social change is a long-term strategy. Research on resilience has provided a promising avenue for addressing adolescent health concerns in a timelier manner. The concept of "resilience" approaches health concerns with a "wellness" mentality that corresponds to the research on protective factors. Protective factors that increase the likelihood of positive health outcomes include the following:

■ *Protective factors in the family.* With information, encouragement, and support, parents can become more effective in demonstrating love and caring for their children, in becoming more involved in their children's activities, and in monitoring and supervising their children's behavior.

■ *Protective factors in the individual.* With age-appropriate information and support, youths can be empowered to develop more effective social skills, coping mechanisms, conflict resolution skills, problem-solving skills, and positive social values.

■ *Protective factors in the school.* Schools in which staff members create empathetic relationships with students and provide opportunities for youths to feel competent, valued, and

respected enable youths to resist and overcome negative influences in their lives more effectively.

■ *Protective factors in the peer group.* Youths with positive, effective interpersonal skills and supportive relationships create a healthy environment for their peers. These skills can be taught, modeled, and reinforced through health and life-skills education that uses evaluated curricula and other research-based interventions (Coordinating Council on Juvenile Justice and Delinquency Prevention, 1996).

Closely related to the research on protective factors is the Search Institute's development of a model that includes 40 developmental assets. On the basis of research conducted among more than 350,000 youths in 600 communities, the Search Institute found that the more developmental assets possessed by young people, the less the probability is that they will become involved in risky health behaviors (Scales & Leffert, 1999). Developmental assets fall into two major categories: internal and external. External assets include support, empowerment, boundaries, expectations, and constructive use of time, whereas internal assets involve a commitment to learning, positive values, social competencies, and positive identity. Parents, school personnel, human services agencies, voluntary organizations, religious institutions, and the community as a whole can deliver effective youth development activities that assist youths to enhance their developmental assets.

School-based health centers (SBHCs) are a particularly promising approach to increasing access by youths to prevention, to early intervention, and to medical treatment services. These health centers provide comprehensive medical and mental health screening and treatment for young people at their schools. SBHCs are designed to overcome barriers that prevent young people from obtaining health care—barriers such as lack of confidentiality, fear that confidentiality will not be maintained, transportation problems, inconvenient appointment times, costs, and apprehension about discussing personal information with strangers. SBHCs receive funding from a variety of sources. Close to 45 percent of SBHCs receive funds from Medicaid; 25.7 percent receive funding from Title V, the Maternal and Child Health Block Grant; 21.7 percent receive payment from students; and 20 percent receive funding through grants and private foundations (Fothergill, 1998).

Research conducted on SBHCs yields a number of promising results, including, but not limited to, the following:

■ Students with less access to health care, those who are uninsured, and those with greater health care needs (self-reported health conditions that limited daily activities) were more likely than other students to visit the SBHC (Kisker & Brown, 1996). SBHCs have been successful in coordinating care for adolescents and have improved access for the majority of students studied, particularly those lacking insurance or a source of health care (Hacker, Weintraub, Fried, & Ashba, 1997).

■ School-based mental health services have the potential for reaching disadvantaged children who would otherwise not have access to these services. Compared with youths served in a central community-based mental health clinic, the youth population served in SBHCs is more likely to have socioeconomic disadvantages or to be members of racial and ethnic groups and just as psychiatrically impaired as the central clinic population (Armbruster, Gerstein, & Fallan, 1997).

■ Adolescents with access to an SBHC were 10 times more likely to make a mental health or substance abuse visit (Kaplan, Calonge, Guernsey, & Hanrahan, 1998).

■ A total of 80.2 percent of adolescents with access to SBHCs had at least one comprehensive health visit compared with 68.8 percent of adolescents without access to such a center (Kaplan et al., 1998).

■ Adolescent users of SBHCs had a higher use of any health care provider than adolescents in the general population (Anglin, Naylor, & Kaplan, 1996) and were more likely to report seeing social workers and counselors (Santelli, Kouzis, & Newcomer, 1996).

■ Students who were treated showed a significant decline in depression and improvements in self-concept from pre- to postintervention (Weist, Paskewitz, Warner, & Flaherty, 1996), and fewer students in SBHC schools reported considering suicide compared with urban youths nationally (Kisker & Brown, 1996).

■ In SBHC schools a smaller percentage of seniors reported ever having had sexual intercourse compared with the national trend. In schools in which SBHCs focused specifically on family planning, there was a delay in the students' initiation of sexual activity (Kisker & Brown, 1996).

ISSUE STATEMENT

During the past four decades, the United States experienced a serious decline in the health status of adolescents, with a shift from communicable diseases to new causes of morbidity. These result from health-damaging behaviors such as depression; unintentional injuries; use of alcohol, tobacco, and other drugs; sexually transmitted diseases; and violence ending in homicide and suicide.

The increase in community violence is producing an increasing number of youths exhibiting signs of posttraumatic stress syndrome, with the resulting need for service programs that emphasize strengths, resilience, and wellness. Many youth programs lack cultural competence and remain "prescriptive and judgmental" in the approach to providing services to high-risk adolescents.

Recent proposals to limit Medicaid eligibility for adolescents ages 13 to 18, to redefine disability, and to eliminate resources for independent living are likely to increase the health problems of U.S. youths. Health statistics already indicate that there are critical problems in the adolescent population with increased rates in sexually transmitted diseases, substance abuse, and injuries resulting from youth violence. As many as 2.3 million of the 3.7 million medically uninsured adolescents who are not enrolled in Medicaid could be eligible for such coverage under the State Children's Health Insurance Program (CHIP) passed by Congress in 1997 (Center for Adolescent Health and the Law, 2000). CHIP made available $48 billion in federal funds over 10 years to help states expand health insurance coverage to low-income children and youths. Uninsured youths will benefit from Medicaid and CHIP only if the states in which they live choose to extend eligibility to them and if states then work to enroll them.

The number of youths experiencing severe health and mental health problems is also continuing to rise because of the barriers to care for youths who are living on their own and lack eligibility for primary health care services. This includes youths who are runaways and homeless, those who have aged-out of foster care, "throwaways," and gay and lesbian youths who are estranged from their parents.

Research and policy initiatives continue to rely on a "deficit model" with minimal or no grounding in prevention, youth development, or self-efficacy and responsibility. However, the social work profession is uniquely qualified to promote adolescent health and wellness by changing policy and advocating for and designing population-based, strengths-based, school-based, and clinically based program initiatives.

POLICY STATEMENT

NASW's position is to support and advocate for the following:

■ making youths a national, state, and local policy priority

■ improving adolescent health services and service systems

■ developing programs that create supports and opportunities for all youths with the following 10 key guiding principles:

1. Comprehensive, quality health care services must be universally available to and accessible by all youths. Services should include a continuum of prevention, early intervention, and treatment options available to youths at no cost to participants.
2. Communities should assess the internal and external developmental assets of youths who reside there. Schools and communities should be encouraged to

provide a variety of opportunities for youths to build developmental assets in those areas found most seriously lacking. Approaches selected for enhancing developmental assets should be research based.
3. Schools and communities should provide prevention and early intervention services for all youths in the least intrusive manner possible, using such modalities as student assistance programs, school-based health services, youth mentoring, and peer-facilitated health and life skills education curricula.
4. Youths with identified, research-based risk factors for physical, emotional, or behavioral problems should have the opportunity to participate, with their families or peers, in programs designed to provide education, skill building, guidance, support, and treatment. This should be done in a way that avoids labeling the youths in a negative manner.
5. Youth health services should be provided in a professional and confidential manner with strict adherence to the concepts of self-determination and client confidentiality. Health services for youths must be provided in the context of the youth's peer group, family, and community.
6. States must expand eligibility for Medicaid and CHIP coverage for uninsured children to the maximum federal allowance. They must work aggressively to enroll all eligible youths and to address the diverse and complex needs of young people with a comprehensive set of benefits that includes preventive care as well as diagnostic and treatment services.
7. Medicaid and behavioral health managed care organizations must recognize the need to fund prevention and early intervention services that may not meet the current definitions of "medical necessity." The definition of *medical necessity* should include research-based risk factors for disease and dysfunction in addition to traditional diagnoses.

8. Public funding sources should make equitable, ongoing funding available to all communities to provide prevention and early intervention services based on the unique needs of each locale. Funding should be provided on a universal rather than a competitive basis.

9. A minimum of 25 percent of all physical health, mental health, and substance abuse dollars should be allocated to research-based prevention and early intervention services for youths and their families.

10. Health services for youths must use a multidisciplinary approach because of the interplay among individual characteristics, environmental factors, and social pressures that influence youth behavior (NASW, 1999). Social workers should use multiple intervention strategies grounded in the public health, population-based approaches of epidemiological assessment, social planning, community organization and development, and social marketing principles to
   - inform and educate the public, families, and youths about adolescent health issues
   - mobilize community collaboration to identify, prioritize, and solve adolescent health and related social problems; these collaborations should be made up of key stakeholders and be as broad based as possible
   - empower adolescents, families, and communities through capacity-building activities to become active participants in the identification of adolescent health concerns; the creative resolution of these issues; and the advancement of adolescent, family, and societal well-being
   - promote and adhere to the legal requirements that protect the health and safety of adolescents, families, and communities
   - ensure public accountability for the well-being of all, especially vulnerable youth populations
   - develop primary prevention strategies that promote the health and well-

   being of adolescents, families, and communities
   - develop secondary and tertiary prevention strategies to alleviate health and related social and economic concerns.

REFERENCES

Anglin, T. M., Naylor, K. E., & Kaplan, D. W. (1996). Comprehensive school-based health care: High school students' use of medical, mental health, and substance abuse services. *Pediatrics, 97,* 318–329.

Armbruster, P., Gerstein, S. H., & Fallan, T. (1997). Bridging the gap between service need and service utilization: A school-based mental health program. *Community Mental Health Journal, 33,* 199–211.

Center for Adolescent Health and the Law. (2000). *Adolescents in public health insurance programs: Medicaid and CHIP.* Chapel Hill, NC: Advocates for Youth.

Coordinating Council on Juvenile Justice and Delinquency Prevention. (1996). *Combating violence and delinquency* (National Juvenile Justice Action Plan Full Report). Washington, DC: Author.

Fothergill, K. (1998). *Update 1997: School-based health centers.* Washington, DC: Advocates for Youth.

Hacker, K. A., Weintraub, T. A., Fried, L. E., & Ashba, J. (1997). Role of school-based health centers in referral completion. *Journal of Adolescent Health, 21,* 328–334.

Hawkins, J. D., Catalano, R. F., & Miller, J. Y. (1992). Risk and protective factors for alcohol and other drug problems in adolescence and early adulthood: Implications for substance abuse prevention. *Psychological Bulletin, 112,* 64–105.

Hawkins, J. D., Lishner, D. M., Jenson, J. M., & Catalano, R. F. (1987). Delinquents and drugs: What the evidence suggests about prevention and treatment planning. In B. S. Brown & A. R. Mills (Eds.), *Youth at high risk for substance abuse.* Bethesda, MD: National Institute on Drug Abuse.

Kaplan, D. W., Calonge, B. N., Guernsey, B. P., & Hanrahan, M. B. (1998). Managed care and school-based health centers: Use of health services. *Archives of Pediatrics and Adolescent Medicine, 152,* 25–33.

Kisker, E. E., & Brown, R. S. (1996). Do school-based health centers improve adolescents' access to health care, health status, and risk-taking behavior? *Journal of Adolescent Health, 18,* 335–343.

National Association of Social Workers. (1999). *Partners in program planning for adolescent health* (PIPPAH) [Brochure]. Washington, DC: Author.

National Center for Chronic Disease Prevention and Health Promotion. (1999). *Youth Risk Behavior Survey.* Atlanta: Author.

Santelli, J., Kouzis, A., & Newcomer, S. (1996). School-based health centers and adolescent use of primary care and hospital care. *Journal of Adolescent Health, 19,* 267–275.

Scales, P. C., & Leffert, N. (1999). Introduction. In E. C. Roehlkepartain, K. Tyler, & K. L. Hong (Eds.), *Developmental assets: A synthesis of the scientific research on adolescent development* (p. 7). Minneapolis: Search Institute.

Weist, M. D., Paskewitz, D. A., Warner, B. S., & Flaherty, L. T. (1996). Treatment outcomes of school-based mental health services for urban teenagers. *Community Mental Health Journal, 32,* 149–157.

Policy statement approved by the NASW Delegate Assembly, August 2002. For further information, contact the National Association of Social Workers, 750 First Street, NE, Suite 700, Washington, DC 20002-4241. Telephone: 202-408-8600; e-mail: press@naswdc.org

Adolescent Pregnancy and Parenting

BACKGROUND

The social work profession is in a distinctive position to respond to the issues of adolescent pregnancy and parenting. Because social workers assess problems and needs from an ecological perspective considering individual, family, and community factors, and use comprehensive approaches to solving problems, the profession can have a broad effect on issues regarding adolescent pregnancy and parenting. The issues of adolescent pregnancy and parenting are multifaceted and do not have a single root cause. As such, no single methodology exists for affecting adolescent pregnancy prevention, for supporting adolescent parents in parenting their children, or for overcoming the challenges adolescent parents face.

In looking at the issues of adolescent pregnancy and parenting, social work takes into account the medical, social, economic, familial, racial, ethnic, cultural, and all other ecological factors affecting and influencing the adolescent. To better understand the issue, it is valuable to look at where the United States ranks in comparison to other developed, industrialized countries. Despite a large decline over the course of the last 12 years, the United States continues to have the highest adolescent pregnancy rate of industrialized and developed countries (National Campaign to Prevent Teen Pregnancy, 2004). In fact, recent decreases have only moved the U.S. rates to where similar countries were in the 1990s (Darroch, Singh, Frost, & Study Team, 2001). As a point of comparison, the adolescent pregnancy rate of the United States is nearly twice that of Canada and Great Britain (Boonstra, 2002).

Although the rate of adolescent pregnancy in the United States has been declining over the past 15 years, each year almost 750,000 adoles-cent women become pregnant. Almost eight in 10 of these pregnancies are unintended (Alan Guttmacher Institute, 2006a; Boonstra, 2002). In the United States, about 57 percent of adolescent pregnancies result in a birth (Alan Guttmacher Institute, 2006a). The percentage of adolescent males who are involved in pregnancies is small, with only 3 percent of 15-year-olds to 19-year-olds being fathers and only 7 percent of the births each year involving adolescent males (Alan Guttmacher Institute, 2002).

Many teenage women reported that their early sexual experiences resulted from peer pressures, including efforts to sustain a relationship, and were not as pleasurable as had been antici-pated (Dodson, n.d.; Luker, 1996). Pregnancies of adolescents aged 15 years and under (approxi-mately 3 percent per year) account for the small-est number of adolescent pregnancies, and these pregnancies are frequently related to sexual ex-ploitation or sexual assault of the adolescent by the present partner or to sexual abuse of the ado-lescent by other adults in or outside of the fam-ily. Seven in 10 girls who had sexual intercourse before age 13 reported the experience was invol-untary. The younger the adolescent mother, the more likely that her male partner was 10 or more years older than she (Alan Guttmacher Institute, 1999a). There is also a strong link between ado-lescent pregnancy and sexual abuse not only for females but also for males (Saewyc, Magee, & Pettingell, 2004).

Like many social issues, adolescent preg-nancy and parenting affect minority popula-tions disproportionately. The decline in adoles-cent pregnancy has been sharpest in the African American population, with the pregnancy rate for 15-year-olds to 19-year-olds declining 40 per-cent between 1990 and 2002 (Alan Guttmacher

Institute, 2006b), although adolescent pregnancy rates are still highest among African Americans. In births to adolescent mothers, Latinas have the highest rate (83 births per 1,000 girls) compared with African Americans (63 per 1,000) and Caucasians (27 per 1,000) (Kaiser Family Foundation, 2006). Although adolescent Latinas had a slight increase in pregnancy rates from 1991 to 1992, by 2002 the rate was 19 percent lower than in 1990 (Alan Guttmacher Institute, 2006b).

Many factors account for the difference in the adolescent pregnancy rates among Western industrialized countries. Much attention has been paid to the success of countries such as France, Sweden, and Great Britain in preventing and lowering their rates of adolescent pregnancy. The United States could gain valuable knowledge about preventing and addressing the issue of adolescent pregnancy by examining the resources and methods that other industrialized countries use. A common misperception is that other countries have lower rates of sexual activity among their adolescents; however, an examination of rates of sexual activity among adolescents in the United States and other industrialized countries shows little difference in the rates of sexual activity. Indeed, abortion rates are lower in countries such as Great Britain, France, Canada, and Sweden despite having similar sexual activity as the United States. Because rates of sexual activity do not explain higher adolescent pregnancy rates in the United States, other factors must be considered and examined, particularly the significance of contraceptive use among adolescents (Darroch et al., 2001).

Other factors that contribute to the higher rates in the United States include a higher proportion of adolescents growing up in socially and economically disadvantaged situations; lower tolerance of adolescent sexual activity, coupled with limited comprehensive sexuality education for many youth; and challenges to accessing contraceptives and other reproductive health care services (Alan Guttmacher Institute, 2001).

ISSUE STATEMENT

The social work profession has long been concerned about the issues of unintended adolescent pregnancy and adolescent parenting. The implications of adolescent pregnancy and parenting are far reaching and affect not only adolescent parents but also their families and communities. Although there have been dramatic decreases in adolescent pregnancy across the country over the last 12 years, those adolescents and their families affected by an unintended pregnancy continue to face educational, economic, and health challenges. Even though declines in the rates of adolescent pregnancy include all races and ethnicities, adolescent pregnancy affects minority communities in a different and significant way. At times, changes in the political and cultural environment of the country may erode the support necessary to overcome the challenges surrounding adolescent pregnancy, and solutions become controversial, thus hindering professionals from having access to resources to prevent and address adolescent pregnancy.

Reproductive Technology

Advances in reproductive technology have had a major effect on the decline in adolescent pregnancy over the last 12 years. Methods of contraception, including delivery systems that last longer and encourage compliance with the administration of the contraceptive, are responsible for approximately 86 percent of the decline in adolescent pregnancy. This pattern of decline has been observed in other industrialized countries as well (Santelli, Lindberg, Finer, & Singh, 2007). Access to this technology is not without difficulty as more states are considering expanding required parental notification and consent to include birth control methods. Even with the advances in reproductive technology, many communities still lack access to affordable, confidential, publicly funded reproductive health care (Frost, Frohwirth, & Purcell, 2004).

Emergency contraception is an option for reducing adolescent pregnancy, and because it is taken after the act of sexual intercourse it is viable for those adolescents who did not plan to have sex. Although it is available over the counter for women 18 years of age and older, younger females must still access formal medical services to use this method.

Male Involvement

Programming and research on adolescent parents has traditionally focused on adolescent mothers. The stereotypes that adolescent fathers are not involved with their children, are irresponsible, and care only about sexual fulfillment often drive prevention and intervention programming, which may have negative effects on adolescent fathers who want to access resources. The limited data available about adolescent fathers indicate that adolescent fathers want to be and are involved in the lives of their children, even if the involvement does not include financial support (Kimball, 2004). These data suggest that programs must be more inclusive of fathers and that different methods of outreach and engagement are needed to involve them in services and programming

Maternal and Child Health

We know that adolescents access prenatal care later in the pregnancy or sometimes not at all (Child Trends DataBank, 2007). Often this is related to the fear and secrecy that might surround the pregnancy. The lack of prenatal care results in adolescents having negative birth outcomes, with a higher number of preterm births, low birth weights, and infants who die before the age of one (Reichman & Pagnini, 1997). All of these factors have a potential negative effect on the well-being of both the baby and the mother. The ability of adolescents to engage in confidential contraceptive, abortion, and prenatal services without parental consent is critical to the overall health of not only the adolescent but also the pregnancy and, if she chooses to maintain the pregnancy, the baby. When appropriate and acceptable to the adolescent, involvement of a supportive adult may be helpful.

Thirty-four states now require some sort of parental involvement in a minor's decision to have an abortion, up from 18 states in 1991 (Kaiser Family Foundation, 2006). Some states are also exploring consent or notification laws for minors' use of contraceptive services. These efforts would have a negative effect on the prevention of adolescent pregnancy and would create an increase in negative maternal and child outcomes.

Another factor in maternal health is repeat pregnancies. Second pregnancies are an issue for adolescent mothers, with 42 percent becoming pregnant within 24 months of the birth of their first child (Raneri & Wiemann, 2007). The implications of additional children stretch not only to the health and economic well-being of the adolescent mother but also to the potential effect on her ability to parent multiple children.

Educational Attainment and Poverty

The negative effect of an adolescent pregnancy on educational attainment and future employment and earning power is well documented. Adolescent mothers complete high school at much lower rates and go on to college less often than do their childless contemporaries (Hofferth, Reid, & Mott, 2001). Clearly, there is a link between completing high school and college and income stability. Adolescent parenting has a disproportionate effect on those already in poverty and can serve as a tie to that income status over the longer term. In the United States, adolescent mothers "are much more likely to come from poor or low-income families (83 percent) than [are] those who have abortions (61 percent) or teens in general" (Alan Guttmacher Institute, 1999b, p. 4). Adolescent mothers have an increased likelihood of ending up on welfare, with almost one-half receiving welfare benefits within five years of the birth of their first child (National Campaign to Prevent Teen Pregnancy, 2002).

Generational Impact

Adolescent pregnancy has long had a generational effect, with daughters of adolescent mothers being more likely to go on to become adolescent parents themselves—some estimate by 22 percent. The sons of adolescent mothers are also disadvantaged, with 13 percent more likely to end up in prison (National Campaign to Prevent Teen Pregnancy, 2002).

POLICY STATEMENT

Within the context of culturally appropriate and sensitive practice, and on the basis of NASW values and ethical principles, it is the policy of NASW to support and further the following:

■ services that are responsive to the needs and desires (including developmental, ecological, familial, biopsychosocial, mental health) of the client or clients (individual, families, groups, organizations, and communities) being served;

■ services and supports that are safe, legal, affordable, and confidential;

■ comprehensive health education and services for all adolescents;

■ a comprehensive approach to sexuality education for all adolescents, including but not limited to, physiology of sexuality and sexual relations, emotional aspects of romantic relationships, pregnancy prevention (including abstinence and contraception), realistic mock parenting activities;

■ comprehensive family planning services for all adolescents;

■ comprehensive services to adolescents who become pregnant, including but not limited to, health care, education (mainstream and alternative programs to meet all young parents' needs), parenting education and support, social and emotional well-being support (including infant mental health and other mental health services), legal services;

■ adherence to Title IX of the National Education Act that protects pregnant and parenting adolescents from discrimination in the public schools, denial of access to education, and exclusion from participation in school activities because of pregnancy or parenting;

■ comprehensive services to young males who father babies of adolescent mothers, including but not limited to, education (mainstream and alternative programs to meet all young parents' needs), parenting education and support, social and emotional well-being support (including infant mental health and other mental health services), legal services;

■ responsible and nurturing involvement of young fathers in their children's lives from the prenatal period all throughout their lives, when appropriate and possible;

■ comprehensive services to the children of adolescent parents, including but not limited to health care, education, services to promote social and emotional well-being; and

■ financial support that enables rather than hinders adolescent parents' engagement in their primary responsibilities of parenting and completing an education.

REFERENCES

Alan Guttmacher Institute. (1999a). *Teenage pregnancy: Overall trends and state-by-state information.* Washington, DC: Author.

Alan Guttmacher Institute. (1999b). *U.S. teenage pregnancy rate drops another 4% between 1995 and 1996* [Press release]. Washington, DC: Author. Retrieved June 15, 1999, from http://www.guttmacher.org/media/nr/newsrelease_teen_preg.html

Alan Guttmacher Institute. (2001). *Can more progress be made? Teenage sexual and reproductive behavior in developed countries.* Washington, DC and New York: Author.

Alan Guttmacher Institute. (2002). *Their own right: Addressing the sexual and reproductive health of American men.* Washington, DC and New York: Author.

Alan Guttmacher Institute. (2006a). *Facts on American teens' sexual and reproductive health.* Washington, DC and New York: Author.

Alan Guttmacher Institute. (2006b). *U.S. teenage pregnancy statistics national and state trends and trends by race and ethnicity.* New York: Author.

Boonstra, H. (2002). Teen pregnancy: Trends and lessons learned. *Guttmacher Report on Public Policy, 5*(1), 7–10.

Child Trends DataBank. (2007). *Late or no prenatal care.* Washington, DC: Author.

Darroch, J. E., Singh, S., Frost, J. J., & Study Team. (2001). Differences in teenage pregnancy rates among five developed countries: The roles of sexual activity and contraceptive use. *Family Planning Perspectives, 33*(6), 244–250, 281.

Dodson, L. (n.d.). *We could be your daughters: Girls, sexuality and pregnancy in low-income America.* Cambridge, MA: Radcliffe Public Policy Institute.

Frost, J. J., Frohwirth, L., & Purcell, A. (2004). The availability and use of publicly funded family planning clinics: U.S. trends, 1994–2001. *Perspectives on Sexual and Reproductive Health, 36*(5), 206–215.

Hofferth, S. L., Reid, L., & Mott, F. L. (2001). The effects of early childbearing on schooling over time. *Family Planning Perspectives, 33*(5), 259–267.

Kaiser Family Foundation. (2006). *Sexual health statistics for teenagers and young adults in the United States.* Washington, DC: Author.

Kimball, C. (2004). Teen fathers: An introduction. *Prevention Researcher, 11*(4), 3–5.

Luker, K. (1996). *Dubious conceptions: The politics of teenage pregnancy.* Cambridge, MA: Harvard University Press.

National Campaign to Prevent Teen Pregnancy. (2002). *Not just another single issue: Teen pregnancy prevention's link to other critical social issues.* Washington, DC: Author.

National Campaign to Prevent Teen Pregnancy. (2004). *Teen birth rates: How does the United States compare?* Washington, DC: Author.

Raneri, L. G., & Wiemann, C. M. (2007). Social ecological predictors of repeat adolescent pregnancy. *Perspectives on Sexual and Reproductive Health, 39,* 39–47.

Reichman, N. E., & Pagnini, D. L. (1997). Maternal age and birth outcomes: Data from New Jersey. *Family Planning Perspectives, 29*(6), 268–272, 295.

Saewyc, E. M., Magee, L. L., & Pettingell, S. E. (2004). Teenage pregnancy and associated risk behaviors among sexually abused adolescents. *Perspectives on Sexual and Reproductive Health, 36*(3), 98–105.

Santelli, J. S., Lindberg, L. D., Finer, L. B., & Singh, S. (2007). Explaining recent declines in adolescent pregnancy in the United States: The contribution of abstinence and improved contraceptive use. *American Journal of Public Health, 97,* 150–156.

Policy statement approved by the NASW Delegate Assembly, August 2008. This policy statement supersedes the policy statement on Adolescent Pregnancy and Parenting approved by the Delegate Assembly in 1999 and referred by the 2005 Delegate Assembly to the 2008 Delegate Assembly for revision, the policy statement on Adolescent Pregnancy approved by the Assembly in 1993, and the policy statement on Adolescent Pregnancy approved in 1984. For further information, contact the National Association of Social Workers, 750 First Street, NE, Suite 700, Washington, DC 20002-4241. Telephone: 202-408-8600 or 800-638-8799; e-mail: press@naswdc.org

Aging and Wellness

BACKGROUND

The aging of the U.S. population presents social and political implications for both the social work profession and society. Although ageism remains prevalent, the aging of the baby boom generation is challenging biases toward older people. Social workers, other professionals, and the public increasingly understand that old age is a time of continued growth and that older adults contribute significantly to their families, communities, and society. This shift influences gerontological social work practice, education, and research (Social Work Leadership Institute, 2007).

As the U.S. population ages, it is also becoming more racially and ethnically diverse (U.S. Census Bureau, 2005). The proportion of older people who are minorities will increase from 16.4 percent in 2000 to 23.6 percent in 2030 (Administration on Aging, 2006). In addition to race and ethnicity, cultural diversity among older adults is recognized increasingly in geographical location and living arrangements; national origin and civil status; sex, sexual orientation, and gender identity and expression; religious and political beliefs; and physical, psychological, and cognitive ability, among other factors.

Demographers attribute population aging primarily to declining fertility and mortality rates (United Nations, 2002). From 1950 to 2000 the proportion of adults 60 years of age and older increased from 12.1 to 16.3 percent of the U.S. population; this percentage is projected to rise to 26.9 percent by 2050. Similarly, the median age of the population rose from 30.2 to 35.3 years between 1950 and 2000, and is expected to rise to 40.7 years by 2050 (United Nations, 2002; U.S. Census Bureau, n.d., 2001). Globally, the "oldest old"—those 85 years and older—comprise the fastest growing segment of the population (National Institute of Aging & U.S. Department of State, 2007). By 2050 the world will experience a squaring off of the population pyramid: Ninety-four percent of the global population will survive to 60 years (United Nations, 2002; Wan, Sengupta, Velkoff, & DeBarros, 2005).

Although adults are generally living longer, gains in life expectancy are not equally enjoyed by all. For example, a study by Ezzati, Friedman, Kulkarni, and Murray (2008), of all counties in U.S. states, plus the District of Columbia, found that life expectancy actually decreased between 1983 and 1999 in almost 1,000 counties, primarily in rural and low-income areas; within those counties, women experienced the greatest increase in mortality rates (Ezzati et al., 2008).

Even among adults who are living longer, whether *healthy life expectancy*—defined by the World Health Organization (2002) as expected years free of illness, disease, or disability—is increasing remains unclear. In 2005, 42 percent of people 65 years and older reported they had at least one functional limitation, with women reporting higher levels of functional limitations than men (Federal Interagency Forum on Aging-Related Statistics, 2008). Although this number constituted a 7 percent decline from 1992, the overall levels of functional limitation among older adults remained fairly steady between 1997 and 2005. Moreover, percentages of disability increase with age. In 1997, 30.0 percent of people 65 years to 74 years of age reported an activity limitation, whereas 50.2 percent of those 75 years and older reported a limitation. Seven years later, 25.5 percent of the younger group and 43.9 percent of the older cohort reported any disability (Centers for Disease Control and Prevention, 2006).

Income security remains another primary concern for many older adults in the United States. The Social Security Act of 1935 (P.L. 74-271) moved a substantial portion of older adults out of poverty, providing a permanent, inflation-protected benefit (Social Security Administration, 2003). Without the Social Security program, the poverty rate among older adults would increase to more than half (National Committee to Preserve Social Security and Medicare, 2008b).

Even with the safety net of social security, almost one in 10 adults age 65 and older lives in poverty (U.S. Census Bureau, 2007b); poverty rates are even higher for older adults who are black, Latino, American Indian, or Alaska Native (U.S. Census Bureau, 2007a, 2007b). Older women, on average, are nearly twice as likely as men to live in poverty (Administration on Aging, 2008); poverty rates among older black and Latina women are especially high (U.S. Census Bureau, 2005). Kinship care also increases the risk of poverty for both women and men: Nineteen percent of the 2.4 million grandparents raising grandchildren who live with them—of which 29 percent are 60 years and older—live in poverty (AARP Foundation et al., 2007).

Aging frequently presents other serious challenges to older women, who comprise almost 60 percent of the population age 65 years and older. Older women constitute about 75 percent of the nursing home population age 65 and older; are more than four times as likely as men to be widowed; and are more than twice as likely to live alone (Administration on Aging, 2006). Because adult women, as a whole, still comprise the majority (61 percent) of unpaid caregivers in the United States (National Alliance for Caregiving & AARP, 2004), they disproportionately experience the financial, physical, and emotional consequences of caregiving as they age.

The growing importance of gerontological social work manifests in increased foundation investments in gerontological social work education, training, and research. In its 2008 report on the future of the professional health care workforce for older adults, the Institute of Medicine (IOM) affirmed both the increasing need for gerontological social work and the profession's initiatives to address that shortage. Social workers are well positioned to support and advocate for older adults and their caregivers.

ISSUE STATEMENT

Health and Behavioral Health Care

Social workers interact with older adults across the continuum of health and behavioral health care. Chronic illness and functional disability severely affect the health and quality of life of older people. Access to health promotion activities and disease prevention services throughout a person's life span can prevent functional limitations and is essential to healthy aging (United Nations, 2003). The ability to participate actively in, and advocate for, one's own health care is key to health promotion and especially important for older adults, the majority of whom have multiple chronic conditions (Vogeli et al., 2007).

Though frequently overlooked by health care providers and older adults alike, behavioral health promotion and treatment are also crucial to the well-being of older people. Depression is the most common mental health condition among older adults (Administration on Aging, 2004). The suicide rate for adults 65 years and older, especially white men, remains the highest for any age cohort (Adamek & Slater, 2006; Centers for Disease Control and Prevention, 2007). The Substance Abuse and Mental Health Services Administration (SAMHSA) considers substance abuse—particularly the use of alcohol and prescription drugs among older adults—an invisible epidemic and one of the fastest growing health problems in the United States (SAMHSA, 1998). Gambling addiction is also growing among older adults (Administration on Aging, 2007). The Medicare Improvements for Patients and Providers Act of 2008 (P.L. 110-275) eliminates, over a six-year period, the discriminatory co-payment for outpatient mental health services. This legislation, long sought by NASW, eliminates a severe obstacle to mental health diagnosis and treatment for older adults.

The growing need for long-term services and supports presents another challenge to older adults' well-being and quality of life. The Centers for Medicare and Medicaid Services (2007) estimated that 12 million people will need long-term care services by 2020. Medicare, Medicaid, and other insurance systems have not adequately addressed the need for home, community-based, and nursing home care for older people and their caregivers, and will continue to be challenged to meet this burgeoning need.

Housing

Housing that is compatible with the abilities and needs of older people promotes positive health outcomes and well-being. Government funding for assistive technology and home repair, modification, and redesign, combined with coordinated health and social service programs, can help people age in place, thereby preventing unnecessary and unwanted institutionalization (Cox, 2005). Moreover, an increasing number of housing options are available or under development to meet the needs of older adults in the community and in congregate settings. These include naturally occurring retirement communities (NORCs), shared housing, independent and assisted-living residences, and continuing care retirement communities (Cox; Gonyea, 2006). This continuum of options, if truly affordable and accessible, can enable older adults to live independently as long as possible in their communities based on individual preferences (Gonyea). Within nursing facilities and other long-term care sectors, the culture change movement—of which the Green House Project is one example (Rabig, Thomas, Kane, Cutler, & McAlilly, 2006)—strives to create a social model of care centered on the strengths and preferences of individual residents (Krugh, 2003).

Economic Security, Work, and Retirement

Public policy, employer practices, and societal attitudes affect both employment and retirement opportunities and, subsequently, economic security for older adults (Hudson & Gonyea, 2007). Many older people want or need to continue working beyond the traditional retirement age, at least on a part-time basis; employer bias and social security income restrictions limit their participation and promotion in the workforce, however. At the same time, efforts to privatize social security—which constitutes over half the retirement income for two-thirds of older adults and the sole source of income for at least 20 percent (Social Security Administration, 2003)—persist (National Committee to Preserve Social Security and Medicare, 2008a).

Whether their contributions to society are paid or unpaid, older adults committed to civic engagement increasingly serve as vital resources to their communities and simultaneously experience enhanced well-being as a result of their efforts. Growing recognition of the individual and societal benefits of older adults' volunteerism, lifelong learning, and political advocacy is transforming the notion of old age and retirement as a period of disengagement (Hinterlong & Williamson, 2006).

Caregiving

Caregiving for family and friends—including physical care, financial assistance, and emotional support—is a major intergenerational role for adults of all ages and has become increasingly common for older adults in later life (Montgomery, Rowe, & Kosloski, 2007). Older adults, especially older women, frequently serve as the primary caregivers for aging parents, aging children with disabilities, adult relatives living with HIV/AIDS, the children of those relatives, and the children of incarcerated relatives (Hooyman, 1999; McCallion & Kolomer, 2003; Poindexter & Boyer, 2003). The pressures of caregiving affect the quality of life of older adults, who often struggle to care for themselves while caring for others (Kropf & Yoon, 2006; Roberts, Allen, & Blieszer, 1999). Although the National Family Caregiver Support Program and other programs provide valuable assistance, many older adults provide care at great cost to their own physical, emotional, and financial well-being.

Elder Abuse and Mistreatment

Mistreatment of older adults includes physical, sexual, and emotional or psychological abuse (National Center on Elder Abuse, 2007;

United Nations, 2003); neglect, abandonment, and self-neglect; and financial or material exploitation (National Center on Elder Abuse, 2007). Early studies suggested that elder mistreatment by family caregivers was due to caregiver stress (Steinmetz, 1988); however, later studies have suggested abuser characteristics are more likely to be predictors of abuse (Brownell, Berman, & Salamone, 1999; Reis, 2000).

National efforts to address elder abuse and mistreatment include public education, passage of reporting laws, development of intervention strategies and models (notably interdisciplinary teams), and criminal prosecution of abuses that rise to the level of a crime (Tomita, 2006).

Diversity

Commitment to cultural competence underlies gerontological social work and reflects the core values of both NASW and the Council on Social Work Education (Chadiha, 2006).

Policies and programs frequently do not reflect the cultures and languages of either older adults with a migration background (such as Asians and Latinos) or indigenous older people; consequently, these groups may underuse or fail to benefit from needed services (Barusch, 2006; Min & Moon, 2006). Black older adults, who represent diverse cultures and interests (Chadiha, Brown, & Aranda, 2006), also experience disparities in service access, usage, and outcomes (see, for example, Barton Smith et al., 2007).

Gerontological social work practice reflects growing sensitivity to and knowledge about spirituality and religion (Murdock, 2005). Similarly, social work literature increasingly incorporates the experiences, strengths, and needs of lesbian, gay, bisexual, and transgender older adults and their caregivers (Butler, 2004; Coon, 2007; Hunter, 2005; Schope, 2005).

Ethical Issues

Advances in medical treatment have increased the ability to sustain life, bringing to the forefront ethical concerns regarding quality of life, cultural values, and death with dignity (Galambos, 1998). Questions of self-determination, end-of-life autonomy, and competency have gained increasing prominence among gerontological social workers. Complex issues of autonomy and protection arise in social work practice with older adults receiving protective and guardianship services (Brownell, 2006; Crampton, 2004; Kosberg, Rothman, & Dunlop, 2006; Linzer, 2004).

Professional Training

The social work profession, with its strengths-based, person-in-environment perspective, enhances older adults' quality of life in unique ways. The National Institute on Aging (as cited in IOM, 2008) estimated in 1987 that between 60,000 and 70,000 social workers would be needed by 2010 to provide services to the aging population. Since that time, the profession has undertaken multiple initiatives to promote education, training, and competence in gerontological social work. Nonetheless, a national workforce study conducted by the National Association of Social Workers (Whitaker, Weismiller, & Clark, 2006) found that the social work profession faces significant obstacles in recruiting new social workers to serve older adults, and that training of additional gerontological social workers is needed—a conclusion affirmed by IOM's Committee on the Future Health Care Workforce for Older Americans (2008).

POLICY STATEMENT

NASW supports the following policy principles that promote the well-being of all older adults:

■ continued development and promotion of gerontological social work content and practicum opportunities at the bachelor's, master's, and doctoral levels; expansion and promotion of continuing education, competencies, frameworks, and credentialing in gerontological social work.

■ promotion of optimal physical, mental, emotional, social, spiritual, and functional well-being of people as they age.

■ advancement of policies, programs, and professional behavior that promote self-advocacy, lifelong learning, civic engagement, and intergenerational compatibility.

- advocacy for the preservation and integrity of social security; expansion of public, private, and commercial systems of economic security for older adults, with special attention to the needs of older women.

- promotion of wellness, prevention, early intervention, and outreach services in health, behavioral health, and social service programs for older adults and their caregivers.

- advocacy for a comprehensive health care system (including prescription drug coverage) for all older adults, regardless of ability to pay.

- advocacy for parity in reimbursement for behavioral health services; support for policies and programs that address depression and substance abuse and reduce the incidence of suicide among older adults.

- advocacy for a comprehensive and affordable system of long-term services and supports that enables older adults to maintain maximal independence in the setting of their choice.

- expanded recognition of and reimbursement for the social work role in meeting the biopsychosocial needs of older people and their caregivers, including advance care planning and comprehensive care management.

- elimination of biases and policies that contribute to poverty, unnecessary nursing home placements, employment discrimination, and health disparities among older adults.

- recognition of and respect for the role and expertise of caregivers; continued development and funding of psychosocial and financial support programs for caregivers, including respite services.

- strengthening of government oversight, requirements, and funding for the protection of vulnerable older people in the home, in communities, and in institutions; passage of a federal elder justice act and federal funding for state-based programs to prevent and address elder mistreatment.

- expansion of policies and programs that address the transportation, housing, and service access needs of older people in urban, suburban, rural, and frontier areas.

- support for programs that enable older adults to become formal or informal care providers for children, including financial support and legal guardianship.

- participation of older adults and caregivers in the design, implementation, and evaluation of programs, policies, and research related to aging; continued intergenerational exchanges between new and experienced or retired social workers within NASW.

- promotion of policies that support death with dignity.

- support for additional governmental and foundation funding for research, professional publications, and communication of best practices in gerontological social work; continued development and use of gerontological evidence-based assessments and interventions.

REFERENCES

AARP Foundation, The Brookdale Foundation Group, Casey Family Programs, Child Welfare League of America, Children's Defense Fund, & Generations United. (2007). *Grand-Facts: A state fact sheet for grandparents and other relatives raising children*. Retrieved July 2, 2008, from http://www.grandfactsheets.org/doc/National%202007%20New%20Template.pdf

Adamek, M. E., & Slater, G. Y. (2006). Older adults at risk of suicide. In B. Berkman & S. D'Ambruoso (Eds.), *Handbook of social work in health and aging* (pp. 149–161). New York: Oxford University Press.

Administration on Aging. (2004). *Promoting healthy lifestyles: Mental health*. Retrieved April 21, 2008, from http://www.aoa.gov/eldfam/Healthy_Lifestyles/Mental_Health/Mental_Health.asp

Administration on Aging. (2006). *A profile of older Americans: 2006*. Washington, DC: U.S. Department of Health and Human Services. Retrieved July 21, 2007, from http://www.aoa.gov/prof/Statistics/profile/2006/2006profile.pdf

Administration on Aging. (2007). *Gambling and older adults*. Retrieved April 18, 2008, from http://www.aoa.gov/prof/notes/Docs/Gambling_Older_Adults.pdf

Administration on Aging. (2008). *Snapshot: A statistical profile of older Americans aged 65+*. Retrieved May 1, 2008, from www.aoa.gov/press/fact/pdf/ss_stat_profile.pdf

Barton Smith, D., Feng, Z., Fennel, M. L., Zinn, J. S., & Mor, V. (2007). Separate and unequal: Racial segregation and disparities in quality across U.S. nursing homes. *Health Affairs, 26*, 1448–1458.

Barusch, A. (2006). Native American elders: Unique histories and special needs. In B. Berkman & S. D'Ambruoso (Eds.), *Handbook of social work in health and aging* (pp. 293–300). New York: Oxford University Press.

Brownell, P. (2006). Departments of public welfare or social services. In B. Berkman & S. D'Ambruoso (Eds.), *Handbook of social work in health and aging* (pp. 435–443). New York: Oxford University Press.

Brownell, P., Berman, J., & Salamone, A. (1999). Mental health and criminal justice issues among perpetrators of elder abuse. *Journal of Elder Abuse and Neglect, 11*(4), 81–94.

Butler, S. S. (2004). Gay, lesbian, bisexual, and transgender (GLBT) elders: The challenges and resilience of this marginalized group. *Journal of Human Behavior in the Social Environment, 9*(4), 25–44.

Centers for Disease Control and Prevention. (2006). *Health with chartbook on trends in the health of Americans*. Hyattsville, MD: National Center for Health Statistics. Retrieved July 21, 2007, from http://www.cdc.gov/nchs/data/hus/hus06.pdf

Centers for Disease Control and Prevention. (2007, Summer). *Suicide: Facts at a glance*. Retrieved April 16, 2008, from http://www.cdc.gov/ncipc/dvp/Suicide/SuicideDataSheet.pdf

Centers for Medicare and Medicaid Services. (2007). *Long term care*. Retrieved April 24, 2008, from http://www.medicare.gov/LongTermCare/Static/Home.asp

Chadiha, L. A. (2006). Section IV: Cultural diversity and social work practice with older adults—Overview. In B. Berkman & S. D'Ambruoso (Eds.), *Handbook of social work in health and aging* (pp. 245–246). New York: Oxford University Press.

Chadiha, L. A., Brown, E., & Aranda, M. P. (2006). Older African Americans and other black populations. In B. Berkman & S. D'Ambruoso (Eds.), *Handbook of social work in health and aging* (pp. 247–256). New York: Oxford University Press.

Coon, D. W. (2007). Exploring interventions for LGBT caregivers: Issues and examples. *Journal of Gay and Lesbian Social Services, 18*(3/4), 109–128.

Cox, C. B. (2005). *Community care for an aging society: Issues, policies, and services*. New York: Springer.

Crampton, A. (2004). The importance of adult guardianship for social work. *Journal of Gerontological Social Work, 43*(2/3), 117–129.

Ezzati, M., Friedman, A. B., Kulkarni, S. C., & Murray, C. J. L. (2008, April). The reversal of fortunes: Trends in county mortality and cross-county mortality disparities in the United States. *PLoS Medicine, 5*(4). Retrieved April 23, 2008, from http://medicine.plosjournals.org/perlserv/?request=get-document&doi=10.1371%2Fjournal.pmed.0050066

Federal Interagency Forum on Aging-Related Statistics. (2008). *Older Americans 2008: Key indicators of well-being*. Washington, DC: U.S. Government Printing Office.

Galambos, C. (1998). Preserving end-of-life autonomy: The Patient Self-Determination Act and the Uniform Health Care Decisions Act. *Health & Social Work, 23*, 275–281.

Gonyea, J. G. (2006). Housing, health, and quality of life. In B. Berkman & S. D'Ambruoso (Eds.), *Handbook of social work in health and aging* (pp. 559–567). New York: Oxford University Press.

Hinterlong, J. E., & Williamson, A. (2006). The effects of civic engagement of current and future cohorts of older adults. *Generations, 30*(4), 10–17.

Hooyman, N. (1999). Research on older women: Where is feminism? *Gerontologist, 39*, 115–118.

Hudson, R. B., & Gonyea, J. G. (2007). The evolving role of public policy in promoting work and retirement. *Generations, 31*(1), 68–75.

Hunter, S. (2005). *Midlife and older LGBT adults: Knowledge and affirmative practice for the social services*. New York: Haworth Press, Inc.

Institute of Medicine (IOM). (2008). *Retooling for an aging America: Building the health care workforce.* Washington, DC: National Academies Press.

Kosberg, J. I., Rothman, M. B., & Dunlop, B. D. (2006). Advocacy and protection of older adults. In B. Berkman & S. D'Ambruoso (Eds.), *Handbook of social work in health and aging* (pp. 551–558). New York: Oxford University Press.

Kropf, N. P., & Yoon, E. (2006). Grandparents raising grandchildren: Who are they? In B. Berkman & S. D'Ambruoso (Eds.), *Handbook of social work in health and aging* (pp. 355–362). New York: Oxford University Press.

Krugh, C. (2003, May). De-institutionalizing an institutionalized system. *Aging Section Connection.* Washington, DC: National Association of Social Workers.

Linzer, N. (2004). An ethical dilemma in elder abuse. *Journal of Gerontological Social Work, 43*(2/3), 165–173.

McCallion, P., & Kolomer, S. R. (2003). Aging persons with developmental disabilities and their caregivers. In L. K. Harootyan & B. Berkman (Eds.), *Social work and health care in an aging society: Education, policy, practice, and research* (pp. 201–225). New York: Springer.

Min, J. W., & Moon, A. (2006). Older Asian Americans. In B. Berkman & S. D'Ambruoso (Eds.), *Handbook of social work in health and aging* (pp. 257–271). New York: Oxford University Press.

Montgomery, R. J., Rowe, J. M., & Kosloski, K. (2007). Family caregiving. In J. A. Blackburn & C. N. Dulmus (Eds.), *Handbook of gerontology: Evidence-based approaches to theory, practice, and policy* (pp. 426–454). Hoboken, NJ: John Wiley & Sons.

Murdock, V. (2005). Guided by ethics: Religion and spirituality in gerontological social work practice. *Journal of Gerontological Social Work, 45*(1/2), 131–154.

National Alliance for Caregiving & AARP. (2004). *Caregiving in the U.S.* Retrieved July 2, 2008, from http://www.caregiving.org/data/04finalreport.pdf

National Center on Elder Abuse. (2007). *Major types of elder abuse.* Retrieved February 25, 2008, from http://www.ncea.aoa.gov/NCEAroot/Main_Site/FAQ/Basics/Types_Of_Abuse.aspx

National Committee to Preserve Social Security and Medicare. (2008a). *Myths and realities about Social Security and privatization.* Retrieved April 22, 2008, from http://www.ncpssm.org/news/archive/myths/

National Committee to Preserve Social Security and Medicare. (2008b). *Social Security primer: History of the Social Security program.* Retrieved May 1, 2008, from http://www.ncpssm.org/ss_primer/

National Institute on Aging (National Institutes of Health, U.S. Department of Health and Human Services) and U.S. Department State. (2007). *Why population aging matters: A global perspective* (DHHS Publication No. 07-6134). Bethesda, MD: Author.

Poindexter, C. C., & Boyer, N. C. (2003). Strains and gains of grandmothers raising grandchildren in the HIV epidemic. In L. K. Harootyan & B. Berkman (Eds.), *Social work and health care in an aging society: Education, policy, practice, and research* (pp. 227–244). New York: Springer.

Rabig, J., Thomas, W., Kane, R. A., Cutler, L. J., & McAlilly, S. (2006). Radical redesign of nursing homes: Applying the Green House concept in Tupelo, Mississippi. *Gerontologist, 46,* 533–539.

Reis, M. (2000). The IOA screen: An abuse-alert measure that dispels myths. *Generations, 24*(11), 13–16.

Roberts, K. A., Allen, K. R., & Blieszer, R. (1999). Older women and their children and grandchildren: A feminist perspective on family relationships. In J. D. Garner (Ed.), *Fundamentals of feminist gerontology* (pp. 67–84). Binghamton, NY: Haworth Press.

Schope, R. D. (2005). Who's afraid of growing old? Gay and lesbian perceptions of aging. *Journal of Gerontological Social Work, 45*(4), 23–39.

Social Work Leadership Institute. (2007). *Looking for a long-term relationship: Integrating primary and long-term care delivery for older adults.* New York: New York Academy of Medicine.

Social Security Administration. (2003). *Income of the aged chartbook, 2001.* Retrieved May 1,

2008, from http://www.ssa.gov/policy/docs/chartbooks/income_aged/2001/

Steinmetz, S. (1988). *Duty bound: Elder abuse and family care.* Newbury Park, CA: Sage Publications.

Substance Abuse and Mental Health Services Administration. (1998). *TIP 26: Substance abuse among older adults* (DHHS Publication No. [SMA] 98-3179). Retrieved April 18, 2008, from http://ncadi.samhsa.gov/govpubs/BKD250/26d.aspx

Tomita, S. (2006). Mistreated and neglected elders. In B. Berkman & S. D'Ambruoso (Eds.), *Handbook of social work in health and aging* (pp. 219–230). New York: Oxford University Press.

United Nations. (2002). *World population ageing 1950–2050.* New York: UN Department of Economic and Social Affairs, Population Division.

United Nations. (2003). *Political declaration and Madrid international plan of action on ageing.* New York: UN Department of Public Information.

U.S. Census Bureau. (2001). *Census 2000 Summary File 1 (SF1) 100-Percent Data, Table PCT12.* Retrieved May 13, 2008, from http://factfinder.census.gov/servlet/DTTable?_bm=y&-geo_id=01000US&-ds_name=DEC_2000_SF1_U&-_lang=en&-_caller=geoselect&-state=dt&-format=&-mt_name=DEC_2000_SF1_U_PCT012

U.S. Census Bureau. (2005). *65+ in the United States: 2005.* Retrieved May 1, 2008, from http://www.census.gov/prod/2006pubs/p23–209.pdf

U.S. Census Bureau. (2007a). *The American community—American Indians and Alaska Natives: 2004.* Retrieved May 1, 2008, from http://www.census.gov/prod/2007pubs/acs-07.pdf

U.S. Census Bureau. (2007b). *Income, poverty, and health insurance coverage in the United States: 2006.* Retrieved May 1, 2008, from http://www.census.gov/prod/2007pubs/p60–233.pdf

U.S. Census Bureau. (n.d.). *General characteristics: Table 37—Age of the population of continental United States and of the population abroad, by sex: 1950.* Retrieved July 21, 2007, from http://www2.census.gov/prod2/decennial/documents/21983999v2p1ch3.pdf

Vogeli, C., Shields, A. E., Lee, T. A., Gibson, T. B., Marder, W. D., Weiss, K. B., & Blumenthal, D. (2007, December). Multiple chronic conditions: Prevalence, health consequences, and implications for quality, care management, and costs [Electronic version]. *Journal of General Internal Medicine, 22*(Suppl. 3), 391–395.

Wan, H., Sengupta, M., Velkoff, V. A., & DeBarros, K. A. (2005). *U.S. Census Bureau current population reports* (P23–209). Washington, DC: U.S. Government Printing Office.

Whitaker, T., Weismiller, T., & Clark, E. (2006). *Assuring the sufficiency of a frontline workforce: A national study of licensed social workers. Special Report: Social work services for older adults.* Washington, DC: National Association of Social Workers.

World Health Organization. (2002). *Healthy life expectancy (HALE) at birth (years).* Retrieved March 13, 2008, from http://www.who.int/whosis/indicators/2007HALE0/en/index.html

Policy statement approved by the NASW Delegate Assembly, August 2008. This policy statement supersedes the policy statement on Senior Health, Safety, and Vitality approved by the Delegate Assembly in 1999 and referred by the 2005 Delegate Assembly to the 2008 Delegate Assembly for revision, and the policy statement on Aging approved by the Delegate Assembly in 1990 and 1977. For further information, contact the National Association of Social Workers, 750 First Street, NE, Suite 700, Washington, DC 20002-4241. Telephone: 202-408-8600 or 800-638-8799; e-mail: press@naswdc.org

Affirmative Action

BACKGROUND

NASW's broad-based commitment to affirmative action incorporates diverse groups who have been historically or are currently oppressed, underserved and underrepresented, including people of color; people with disabilities; people who are gay, lesbian, bisexual, or transgendered; women; older people, and people who are disadvantaged or oppressed because of life circumstances. This list in no way, however, reflects all the groups who have been historically and are currently oppressed.

Mirroring society at large, NASW members have experienced a struggle regarding the support and acceptance of affirmative action, especially when we look at nominations and elections. Some members of the association believe that affirmative action has been successfully accomplished, and to this end, there is no need to continue addressing this issue. Other members, who are often in support of such inclusion policies, are still frustrated by the challenging process of meeting affirmative action guidelines.

At the federal government level, affirmative action originated in the 1930s. Affirmative action was not originally a civil rights effort. The 1935 National Labor Relations Act used the term "affirmative action" in a different context: ". . . an employer who was found to be discriminating against union members or union organizers would have to stop discriminating, and also take affirmative action to place those victims where they would have been without the discrimination" (Skrentny, p. 6).

President Roosevelt, responding to pressure from the prominent African American leader, A. Phillip Randolph, president of the Brotherhood of Sleeping Car Porters, as well the National Association for the Advancement of Colored People, issued Executive Order No. 8802 in June 1941 with the intent of fostering equal employment opportunities. That order created the Fair Employment Practices Commission to promote full participation in federal defense programs by all people regardless of race, creed, color, or national origin (Biermann, 2004). Since then, each president has continued some form of equal employment effort.

Affirmative action became a more widely used concept in the 1960s. Title VII of the Civil Rights Act of 1964 (P.L. 88-352) requires both public and private employers in traditionally segregated job categories to support the establishment of voluntary affirmative action plans. This law gives the courts the power to mandate affirmative action in cases of willful and intentional acts to deny equal opportunities. It also requires that the plans be flexible in application and temporary in duration. Employment issues have been further addressed through legislation, court interpretations, and additional executive orders. Notably, Presidents Kennedy and Johnson issued Executive Order No. 10925 (1961) and Executive Order No. 11246 (1965) respectively requiring government contractors to take affirmative action to ensure nondiscrimination and administratively strengthening compliance regulations through the creation of the Office of Federal Contract Compliance Programs (OFCCP) under the Department of Labor (Biermann, 2004). Presidents Nixon, Ford, and Carter continued enforcement of Executive Order No. 11246 and made significant changes with increased staff. The order specifically prohibits discrimination against workers on the basis of race, color, religion, sex, or national origin by government contractors receiving $10,000 or more in federal funds. Employers with 50 or more employees and who receive $50,000 or more in federal funds must have affirmative action plans, which are monitored by the OFCCP. The regulations implementing the order are found in 41 C.F.R. Chapter 60.

With Executive Order No. 12086 (1978), Carter consolidated enforcement of federal affirmative programs. Presidents Reagan, Bush, Clinton, and George W. Bush have continued enforcement of Executive Order No. 11246, but staff and budgets have been cut with each successive administration (Biermann).

Employment rules governing federal contractors and the Small Business Administration's Minority Enterprise Program have had some of the broadest impacts of any federal affirmative action program (Savage, 1995). An OFCCP study of 77,000 companies employing some 20 million people showed that minority employment increased by 20 percent and female employment by 15 percent after the implementation of affirmative action plans (National Council of La Raza, 1995). Some affirmative action programs in federal contracting have made initial attempts to resolve historic barriers toward advancement.

Executive Order No. 11063, issued in 1963 by President Kennedy addressed affirmative action in housing; it acknowledged that discriminatory practices in housing produce other forms of discrimination and segregation. The order directed all federal agencies to prevent discrimination based on race, color, creed, or national origin in the disposition of property, including sales, leasing, or rental, and in the lending practices of institutions with moneys insured or guaranteed by the federal government. The Fair Housing Act of 1968 (P.L. 90-284) and the Fair Housing Act Amendments of 1988 (P.L. 100-430) addressed housing discrimination and provided a basis for affirmative action policies in housing. The Housing and Community Development Act of 1974 (P L. 93-383), amended in 1981 (P.L. 97-35), required affirmative efforts by states and localities receiving community development block grants to strengthen fair housing practices. In January 1994, President Clinton issued Executive Order No. 12892, which retained the mandate to ensure fair housing and expanded President Kennedy's Executive Order No. 11063 to provide protection against discrimination in programs of federal insurance or guaranty to people with disabilities and to families with children.

Supreme Court cases *Grutter v. Bollinger* and *Gratz v. Bollinger*, decided in 2003, addressed affirmative action programs in university admissions, but their impact reaches beyond the educational arena. In *Grutter v. Bollinger*, the Supreme Court stated that race could be used as one factor for the University of Michigan's admissions, but in *Gratz v. Bollinger*, the Court indicated that points given to prospective students based solely on race were unconstitutional because this process violated the Equal Protection Clause. NASW participated in *amicus curiae* briefs supporting the University of Michigan's affirmative action principles.

NASW's rationale and position on affirmative action are well articulated in President Johnson's June 1965 speech at Howard University's commencement ceremony.

> Freedom is the right to share, share fully and equally, in American society—to vote, to hold a job, to enter a public place, to go to school. It is the right to be treated in every part of our national life as a person equal in dignity and promise to all others.
>
> But freedom is not enough. You do not wipe away the scars of centuries by saying: Now you are free to go where you want, and do as you desire, and choose the leaders you please.
>
> You do not take a person who, for years, has been hobbled by chains and liberate him, bring him up to the starting line of a race and then say, "You are free to compete with all the others," and still justly believe that you have been completely fair.
>
> Thus it is not enough just to open the gates of opportunity. All our citizens must have the ability to walk through those gates.
>
> This is the next and more profound stage of the battle for civil rights. We seek not just freedom but opportunity. We seek not just legal equity but human ability, not just equality as a right and a theory but equality as a fact and equality as a result. (Curry, 1996, pp. 17–18)

ISSUE STATEMENT

Despite equal protections that are supposed to be enforced under the U.S. Constitution, and regardless of laws and rhetoric, equal rights and just treatment have not been achieved in the United States. American history is filled with many examples of individual, organizational, institutional, and societal discrimination and disparities that adversely affected whole groups of people on the basis of their ancestral heritage, culture, ethnicity, skin color, primary language, age, class, gender, disability, sexual orientation, religion, spirituality, and other parts of their identity.

Persistent and ongoing discrimination and oppression early in our history has left an institutional base for inequality, and the residue continues to this day. Intended and unintended forms of discrimination abound, and without attention and corrective action, discrimination and the inequities that result from discrimination will continue. Affirmative action is one tool that our society has instituted to acknowledge past and current wrongs and to rectify actions.

Affirmative action is consistent with the social work profession's mission, which "is to enhance human well-being and help meet the basic human needs of all people, with particular attention to the needs and empowerment of people who are vulnerable, oppressed, and living in poverty. . . . Fundamental to social work is attention to the environmental forces that create, contribute to, and address problems in living."(NASW, 2000, p. 1)

NASW's *Code of Ethics* (2000) affirms the value of social justice:

> Social workers' social change efforts are focused primarily on issues of poverty, unemployment, discrimination, and other forms of social injustice. These activities seek to promote sensitivity to and knowledge about oppression and cultural and ethnic diversity. Social workers strive to ensure access to needed information, services, and resources; equality of opportunity; and meaningful participation in decision making for all people. (p. 5)

Opening access; promoting inclusive policies, programs, and practices; and working for equitable results are affirmative action components. Such focused affirmative action initiatives are needed to promote social work's equality and social justice agendas.

Affirmative action promotes mindfulness and action with regard to diversity. It has provided effective means for forcing changes in entrenched patterns of policy and practice, including those that were discriminatory and unjust. Furthermore, affirmative action programs have encouraged people to face and acknowledge factors related to unequal opportunities and access, including privilege, indifference, insensitivity, bias, and prejudice.

POLICY STATEMENT

Definition of Affirmative Action

NASW's definition of affirmative action is broad and inclusive. It reflects a firm commitment to actions leading to inclusive plans, processes, and results. Affirmative action seeks to address historical discrimination and the effects of such and to achieve substantially greater inclusion of and equity for diverse groups who have been historically or are currently oppressed, underserved, and underrepresented. These groups include people of color; people with disabilities; people who are gay, lesbian, or transgender; women; seniors; and people disadvantaged or oppressed because of life circumstances.

For the purpose of this NASW's policy statement, the following definition of affirmative action applies:

> *Affirmative action* is the mindful and deliberate steps taken to achieve an environment that values, respects, and reflects multicultural diversity. It includes efforts toward and achievements in:

- fair access
- equal opportunity
- just process
- equitable results.

NASW is firmly committed to affirmative action, and will vigorously pursue its development and implementation at all levels (organizational, local, state, and federal). Achieving an environment that values, respects, and reflects multicultural diversity will take deliberate and progressive actions.

Affirmative action is present-state oriented in that it is designed to address what is to transpire now and into the future. A policy cannot undo past wrongs, but it can acknowledge what happened and set into place proactive and preventive actions to ensure that unjust discriminatory practices are not repeated.

Affirmative action has been effective in a broad spectrum of domains, including, but not limited to, employment, education, housing, and government contracting. NASW strongly supports the inclusion of affirmative action principles and implementation of affirmative action programs in all arenas and contexts at all levels, including small groups, organizations, institutions, communities, societies, cities, and states, as well as implementation nationally. NASW supports affirmative action as a viable tool for upholding its ethical code to act to prevent and eliminate discrimination. NASW supports the following principles and actions:

■ Full endorsement of local, state, and federal policies and programs that give all people equal access to resources, services, and opportunities that they require—everyone should be given equal opportunity regardless of age, ancestral heritage, class, color, disability, gender, immigration status, language proficiency, national origin, race, religion, or sexual orientation.

■ Articulating recommendations and advocating for changes in local, state, and federal policies and programs to further open access and promote equality and social justice.

■ Supporting existing local, state, and federal policies and programs that open access and promote equality and social justice.

■ Joining forces with others to support affirmative action and social justice programs and counteract anti-affirmative action efforts or initiatives.

■ Creating, leading, and participating in coalitions for affirmative action and social justice.

■ Generating (or working with others in establishing) tactics and strategies for the pas-

sage of policies that strengthen affirmative action, civil rights, equity, and social justice.

■ Writing position statements, court briefs, and other documents in support of affirmative action, civil rights, equity, and social justice.

■ Publishing public information materials in support of affirmative action, civil rights, equity, and social justice agendas.

■ Conducting and supporting research about affirmative action and means to promote equity and social justice.

■ Identifying and supporting people running for public office who are proponents of affirmative action.

■ Being vigilant in upholding and promoting affirmative action and social justice initiatives.

■ Identifying measures to indicate what areas have been successfully or not successfully accomplished.

■ Supporting the development of policies that demonstrate accountability in working to achieve affirmative action in professional social work organizations.

■ Advocating for affirmative action practices within professional social work organizations to devise and implement plans to increase membership diversity reflective of the multicultural population demographics.

REFERENCES

Biermann, L. J. (2004). *Affirmative action basics: History of executive order program.* Denver, CO: National Employment Law Institute.

Civil Rights Act of 1964, Pub. L. No. 88-352, 78 Stat. 241.

Curry, G. E. (Ed.). (1996). *The affirmative action debate.* Reading, MA: Addison-Wesley.

Exec. Order No. 11063, 3 C.F.R., (1959–1963).

Exec. Order No. 12892, 59 C.F.R. 2939, (1994).

Fair Housing Act of 1968, Pub. L. 90-284, 82 Stat. 81.

Fair Housing Act Amendments of 1988, Pub. L. 100-430, 102 Stat. 1619.

Gratz v. Bollinger, 539 U.S. 244 (2003).

Grutter v. Bollinger, 539 U.S. 244 (2003).

Housing and Community Development Act of 1974, Pub. L. 93–383, 88 Stat. 633.

National Association of Social Workers. (2000). *Code of ethics of the National Association of Social Workers.* Washington, DC: Author.

National Council of La Raza. (1995). *Fact sheet on affirmative action and Latinos.* Washington, DC: Author.

Savage, D. (1995, April 2). Plan to boost firms owned by minorities is assailed. *Los Angeles Times*, pp. A14, A19.

Skrentny, J. D. (1996). *The ironies of affirmative action: Politics, culture, and justice in America.* Chicago: University of Chicago Press.

RESOURCES AND SUGGESTED READINGS

Web Sites

Affirmative Action Information Center
This site contains many articles, essays, and position statements related to affirmative action.
http://www.nationalcenter.org/AA.html

American Civil Liberties Union (ACLU)'s Supreme Court page
This section of the ACLU's site provides summaries of U.S. Supreme Court renderings, including discussions of affirmative action.
http://www.aclu.org/Court/CourtMain.cfm

American Association for Affirmative Action (AAAA)
This group addresses a range of issues in support of affirmative action.
http://www.affirmativeaction.org/ and see http://www.affirmativeaction.org/resources/

Chronicle of Higher Education
This publication has an archive replete with current articles, books, and other resources on affirmation action.
http://chronicle.com

Coalition to Defend Affirmative Action, Integration, & Immigrant Rights and Fight for Equality By Any Means Necessary (BAMN)

This organization provides activist perspectives and information about student efforts for equity.
http://www.bamn.com/literature/lit-um-case.asp

Cornell University Legal Information Institute
Cornell's LII provides fast references to court cases, including those involving affirmative action.
http://supct.law.cornell.edu/supct/cases/topic.htm

In Motion Magazine
This online publication provides a great deal of diversity and multicultural content, including a dedicated section on affirmative action.
http://inmotionmagazine.com/pr.html

National Organization for Women
NOW offers resources about affirmative action and court cases (some are dated).
http://www.now.org/issues/affirm/

National Public Radio
NPR lists some interesting diverse positions are expressed in articles.
http://www.npr.org/news/specials/michigan/

The Pew Research Center for the People and the Press
A Pew Research Center national study revealed that 63 percent of Americans favor and 29 percent oppose affirmative action programs to overcome past discrimination. This site reports the full results of the survey.
http://people-press.org/reports/display.php3?ReportID=184

Washington Post
The newspaper has archived its affirmative action special report on its Web site.
http://www.washingtonpost.com/wp-dyn/education/specials/policy/affirmativeaction/

Court Cases and Public Laws

Adarand v. Pena, 16 F.3d 1537 (10th Cir. 1994), cert. granted, 115 S. Ct. 41 (1994).

Brown v. Board of Education I, 347 U.S. 483 (1954).

Brown v. Board of Education II, 349 U.S. 294 (1955).

City of Richmond v. J. A. Croson, 488 U.S. 469 (1989).

Civil Rights Act Amendments of 1988, Pub. L. 92-318, Title IX, 86 Stat. 375, 20 U.S.C. §§1681–1688.

Civil Rights Act of 1991, Pub. L. 102–166, 105 Stat. 1071.

Fullilove v. Klutznick, 448 U.S. 448 (1980).

Freedman's Bureau Bill, 13 Stat. 507 (1865).

Local 28, Sheet Metal Workers' International v. Equal Employment Opportunity Commission, 478 U.S. 421 (1986).

Plessy v. Ferguson, 163 U.S. 537 (1896).

Public Employment Works Act of 1977, Pub. L. 95-28, 9 Stat. 116 (codified as amended at 42 U.S.C. §§6701, 6705–6708, 6710 1988 & Supp. V 1993).

Regents of the University of California v. Bakke, 438 U.S. 265 (1978).

Rehabilitation Act of 1973, P.L. 93-112, 87 Stat. 355.

Small Business Investment Act of 1958, P.L. 85-699, 72 Stat. 689.

United States v. Paradise, 480 U.S. 149 (1987).

Books, Journals, Pamphlets, Newspapers, Reports

Anderson, T. H. (2004). *The pursuit of fairness: A history of affirmative action.* New York: Oxford University Press.

Bergmann, B. R. (1996). *In defense of affirmative action.* New York: Basic Books.

Cintron, D. (1995, Fall). Hispanics' housing conditions: Poor participation in federal housing programs. *Fair Housing Report,* p. 12.

Cohen, C., & Sterba, J. P. (2003). *Affirmative action and racial preference: A debate.* New York: Oxford University Press.

Excerpts from Clinton talk on affirmative action. (1995, July 20). *New York Times,* p. A9.

Ezorsky, G. (1991). *Racism and justice: The case for affirmative action.* Ithaca, NY: Cornell University Press.

Fiscus, R. J. (1992). *The constitutional logic of affirmative action.* Durham, NC: Duke University Press.

Graham, H. D. (2003). *Collision course: The strange convergence of affirmative action and immigration policy in America.* New York: Oxford University Press.

Holmes, S. A. (1995, March 19). Past support for affirmative action haunts Republicans. *San Francisco Examiner,* p. A19.

Lemann, N. (1995, June 11). Taking affirmative action apart. *New York Times Magazine,* pp. 36–43, 52, 54, 62, 66.

Mills, N. (Ed.). (1994). *Debating affirmative action: Race, gender, ethnicity, and the politics of inclusion.* New York: Dell.

Myers, S. L., Jr. (1995, July/August). Equity, fairness, and race relations. *Emerge,* pp. 6, 48–52.

National Association for the Advancement of Colored People Legal Defense and Education Fund. (1995). *Fact sheet on discrimination and affirmative action.* Washington, DC: Author.

National Association of Social Workers. (2001). *NASW Standards for Cultural Competence in Social Work Practice.* Washington, DC: Author.

National Organization for Women Legal Defense and Education Fund. (1995). *Legal basics on affirmative action.* New York: Author.

National Women's Law Center. (1995). *Affirmative action and what it means for women.* Washington, DC: Author.

Schrag, P. (1995, April 10). Nixon the quota king. *San Jose Mercury News,* p. 7B.

Scotch, R. K., Schriner, K., & Smith, R. A. (2004). *Americans with disabilities and political participation: A reference handbook.* Santa Barbara, CA: ABC-CLIO.

Steinberg, S. (1995). *Turning back: The retreat from racial justice in American thought and policy.* Boston: Beacon Press.

Stone, J. H. (Ed.). (2004). *Culture and disability: Providing culturally competent services.* Thousand Oaks, CA: Sage Publications.

Supreme Court ruling imperils U.S. programs of racial preference. (1995, June 13). *Wall Street Journal,* pp. A1, A10.

Swain, J., French, S., Barnes, C., & Thomas, C. (Eds.). (2004). *Disabling barriers—enabling environments.* Thousand Oaks, CA: Sage Publications.

U.S. Commission on Civil Rights. (1977). *Statement on affirmative action* (Clearinghouse Publication No. 54). Washington, DC: Author.

U.S. Commission on Civil Rights. (1981). *Affirmative action in the 1980s: Dismantling the process of discrimination* (Clearinghouse Publication No. 70). Washington, DC: Author.

U.S. Commission on Civil Rights. (1995). *The legislative, executive and judicial development* *of affirmative action*. Washington, DC: Office of the General Counsel.

Yzaguirre, R. (1995, June 13). *Statement of Raul Yzaguirre on* Adarand Constructors, Inc. v. Pena [News Release]. Washington, DC: National Council of La Raza.

Policy statement approved by the NASW Delegate Assembly, August 2005. This statement supersedes the statement on Affirmative Action approved by the 1996 Delegate Assembly and referred by the 2002 Delegate Assembly to the 2005 Delegate Assembly for revision. For further information, contact the National Association of Social Workers, 750 First Street, NE, Suite 700, Washington, DC 20002-4241; telephone 202-408-8600; e-mail: press@naswdc.org

Alcohol, Tobacco, and Other Drugs

BACKGROUND

The U.S. government uses a two-pronged approach to address alcohol, tobacco, and other drug (ATOD) problems. One prong focuses on supply, the other on demand.

Supply

Attempts to reduce the supply of illicit substances include interdiction and enforcement of laws that criminalize the sale and possession of certain substances. Other supply-side efforts include regulation of the production and sale of alcohol, tobacco products, prescription drugs, and over-the-counter drugs. The Office of National Drug Control Policy (ONDCP), headed by a cabinet-level official, dubbed the "drug czar," coordinates both the federal government's supply- and demand-side efforts. Some special initiatives, such as the High Intensity Drug Trafficking Area Program, fall under ONDCP.

The federal government spends billions each year to control illicit drug production and distribution in the United States and other countries. Trial judges may use judicial discretion in sentencing opportunities when defendants are found guilty of drug offenses. Whether the offense is major drug (cocaine) distribution or street distribution of less than a gram of marijuana, federal government statutes mandate sentencing of the offender. Many inner-city minority youths, males and female, are imprisoned for lengthy mandatory periods, instead of receiving penalties appropriate for their crimes.

Demand

Federal government attempts to address the demand for illicit drugs were first widely addressed in 1970 with the passage of Comprehensive Drug Abuse Prevention and Control Act (P.L. 91-513), popularly known as the Controlled Substances Act, which expanded the definition of a "drug dependent person" to enable more people to obtain treatment (National Institute on Drug Abuse [NIDA], 2003). That same year, Congress also passed the Comprehensive Alcohol Abuse and Alcoholism Prevention, Treatment, and Rehabilitation Act (P.L. 91-616), establishing the federal National Institute on Alcohol Abuse and Alcoholism (NIAAA). NIAAA along with NIDA, established in 1974, became leaders in the federal fight against substance use on several fronts. The missions of the organizations were to focus on research and education and help establish community-based treatment programs. Today NIAAA and NIDA are part of the National Institutes of Health and maintain a strong research focus.

The Substance Abuse and Mental Health Services Administration (SAMHSA), established in 1992, is another federal entity vitally concerned with reducing ATOD problems through applied research, prevention, and treatment. SAMHSA administers the Substance Abuse Prevention and Treatment Block Grant, which channels money for services to the states. Single state agencies distribute the funds to community- and faith-based programs that provide prevention and treatment services. Many of these programs serve individuals who would otherwise be unable to obtain services because they lack health care coverage. Other federal agencies also have a role in ATOD prevention and treatment, including the Department of Education, which operates and promotes programming to keep schools drug free and provides mental health services to students and their families; and the Department of Veterans Affairs, which operates the country's largest substance use treatment program for veterans.

The federal drug control budget has favored law enforcement and interdiction over prevention and treatment approaches, although treatment funding has increased (ONDCP, 2004). The federal government's policy role is important, but states carry most of the responsibility for ensuring that services are delivered to individuals and families experiencing ATOD problems.

The self-help or mutual help movement also plays a major role in addressing alcohol and other drug problems in the United States. Alcoholics Anonymous (AA), the first 12-Step program, was founded in 1935 and predated many attempts by professionals to assist individuals with alcohol problems. AA has had an important influence on the philosophy of treatment programs in the United States. Narcotics Anonymous began in the 1950s. Al-Anon, a mutual-help group for families and friends of those who have alcohol problems, and Nar-Anon for those with family members and friends who have drug problems also developed through the movement. Other self-help groups have emerged to assist people with alcohol and other drug problems.

Social workers, too, are vital to preventing and treating ATOD problems. Although only 2 percent of NASW members cite ATOD problems as their major practice area ("72 percent work," 2001), ATOD issues are pervasive problems encountered in social work practice. Practitioners address ATOD problems in child welfare, health care, criminal justice, schools, nursing homes, and many other settings. NASW, therefore, must maintain a comprehensive ATOD policy statement.

ISSUE STATEMENT

Prevalence and Consequences of ATOD Problems

Significant numbers of Americans are affected by ATOD problems. In 2002, approximately 22 million people (9.4 percent of the U.S. population age 12 and older) met criteria for substance abuse or dependence (SAMHSA, 2003). Most (14.9 million) met criteria for alcohol use disorders alone, 3.9 million met criteria for drug use disorders alone, and 3.2 million met criteria for both alcohol and drug use disorders.

Alcohol, tobacco, and other drug problems have severe consequences for all members of the family system, especially children (Huang, Cerbone, & Gfroerer, 1998; National Center on Addiction and Substance Abuse [CASA] at Columbia University, 2005). Children affected by parental alcohol and other drug problems in this country are largely overlooked. Approximately one in four American children (19 million) is exposed at some time before age 18 to familial alcohol dependence, alcohol abuse, or both. More than one in 10 children (9.2 million) live with a parent or other adult who uses illicit drugs (CASA; Grant, 2000). Very few children from these families ever receive help for the psychological consequences of growing up under these circumstances.

In the 1970s and 1980s, several comprehensive reviews of empirical findings documented a wide range of problems encountered by children of alcoholics (COAs), such as emotional problems and hyperactivity in childhood, emotional and conduct problems in adolescence, and alcoholism in adulthood (El-Guebaly & Offord, 1977; Russell, Henderson, & Blume, 1985). There is strong consensus in the scientific literature that alcoholism runs in families (Chassin, Jacob, Johnson, Shuckit, & Sher, 1997; Cotton, 1979; Goodwin, 1979), and that male COAs are four to 10 times more likely to develop alcoholism than children whose parents do not have an alcohol problem (Heath, 1995).

Although there have been some indications of decreased incidence and prevalence of ATOD problems among youths, significant prevailing risk factors still exist. In 2003, 28 percent of high school students reported episodic heavy drinking, and 22 percent indicated marijuana use (Grunbaum et al., 2004). Also, among youths ages 12 to 17 in 2000, 9.7 percent had used an illicit drug within a 30-day period before their interview, and nearly 10.7 million adolescents ages 12 to 20 were underage alcohol drinkers.

Among the youths who were reported heavy drinkers in 2000, 65.5 percent of them were also current illicit drug users. Among non-drinkers, only 4.2 percent were current illicit drug users. In addition, 71.5 million Americans age 12 and older reported use of a tobacco product. Among youths who smoked cigarettes, the rate of the past-month illicit drug use was 42.7 percent, compared with 4.6 percent for non-smokers. These facts underpin evidence of alcohol and tobacco being gateways to the use of illicit drugs. More than 40 percent of people who begin drinking alcohol before age 13 will develop alcohol dependence some time in their lives (SAMHSA, 2001). Likewise, the younger people are when they begin smoking cigarettes, the more likely they are to become addicted to nicotine (Centers for Disease Control and Prevention [CDC], 1994). Cigarette smoking is the addictive behavior most likely to become established during adolescence. Several studies have found nicotine to be additive in ways similar to heroin, cocaine, and alcohol (CDC, 1994).

Barriers to Treatment

Most people with alcohol and other drug problems do not receive treatment. Of those who needed treatment for an alcohol problem in 2002, only 8.3 percent received help from a specialty alcohol treatment program (SAMHSA, 2003). Of those who did not get treatment, only 4.5 percent felt they needed care. About 35 percent of the latter group said they tried but were not able to get help; 65 percent did not attempt to obtain treatment. Of the estimated 7.7 million who needed help for a drug problem in 2002, only 18.2 percent received help from a specialty drug treatment program (SAMHSA, 2003). Of those who did not get treatment, only 5.7 percent felt they needed care: 24.4 percent of this group said they tried but were not able to get help; 75.6 percent did not attempt to obtain treatment.

In addition, managed care has taken a toll on the ability to obtain alcohol and drug treatment services through private health plans (Hay Group, 2001). Publicly supported services wax and wane depending on state and local budgets. Thus, people in need do not receive care because they cannot find help, they do not seek treatment, or they do not recognize that they have a problem. They also may be painfully aware of the stigma attached to being an "addict" or "alcoholic" or even being a person who seeks out help, particularly mental health services.

The labels, too, have become a significant obstacle to people seeking resolution. The focus shifts from the problem to the fear of the label and its stigmatizing consequences. "Disease first" language, as opposed to "people first" language, obliterates individual differences and depersonalizes those to whom the label is applied. Such terms as "alcohol abuse," "drug abuse," and "substance abuse" can be perceived as springing from religious and moral conceptions of the roots of severe alcohol and other drug problems. Continued use of these terms with their emotional overtones, may serve only to perpetuate misguided public attitudes about drug-using behavior. To refer to people who are addicted as alcohol, drug, or substance abusers misstates the nature of their condition and calls for their social rejection and punishment.

Although the inclusion of the terms substance abuse and dependence in the DSM-IV has had the positive consequence of allowing these conditions to be recognized as mental disorders deserving of reimbursed treatment, social workers should endeavor to drop such objectifying labels as "substance abuser" and "addict" for more respectful and less stigmatizing people-first language. NASW supports the rejection of "labeling language" and embraces a people-first language. Terminology that is more respectful and less stigmatizing and suggests that if a person's alcohol or drug consumption is creating problems, then the person should do something about it. Such a stance might help to focus on a more concrete and verifiable question of whether alcohol and other drugs are creating problems in a person's life for which he or she might seek help (White, 2001).

In addition, many individuals with ATOD problems have co-occurring disabilities and often encounter increased difficulties in accessing appropriate treatment. In 2002, about 20 percent of adults who met criteria for substance abuse or dependence also had a serious mental illness (SMI) compared with a 7 percent rate of SMI for those without substance abuse and dependence (SAMHSA, 2003). Individuals with co-occurring ATOD problems and SMI may not receive services that are appropriately integrated to meet their needs (DiNitto & Webb, 2005; Mee-Lee, Shulman, Fishman, Gastfriend, & Griffiths, 2001). Many people who have a cognitive or physical disability (for example, intellectual disability, spinal cord injury, traumatic brain injury, or who are deaf, hard-of-hearing, blind, or visually impaired) and a co-occurring ATOD problem also experience substantial difficulties in obtaining treatment that appropriately accommodates their needs, despite requirements of the Americans with Disabilities Act ([ADA], [P.L. 101-336], de Miranda, 1999).

Criminal Justice and Social Welfare

Many people are arrested and incarcerated for alcohol or drug offenses, and many incarcerated individuals have ATOD problems. In 2002 there were an estimated 1.5 million arrests for drug law violations (more than 80 percent were for possession), 1.5 million arrests for driving under the influence, and 573,000 arrests for drunkenness in addition to 654,000 liquor law violations (Dorsey, Zawitz, & Middleton, 2003). Between 1990 and 1999, 61 percent of the growth in the federal prison population was due to drug offenses (U.S. Department of Justice, Bureau of Justice Statistics [BJS], 2001). In 2002, 20 percent of men and 30 percent of women in state prisons were serving time for drug offenses (BJS, 2003). In 1999, 53 percent of the women in state prisons were using alcohol and drugs at the time of the offense for which they were incarcerated, and one in three women had engaged in the crime to obtain money to get drugs (Greenfeld & Snell, 2000). Alcohol and drug treatment in prisons and jails has increased, but many individuals do not get services while incarcerated or after release.

The economic costs of ATOD problems are high. Costs of alcohol problems were estimated at $184.6 billion in 1998, with two-thirds due to losses in current and future earnings (Harwood, 2000). Costs of drug problems in 2000 were estimated at $160.7 billion (69 percent in productivity losses, 22 percent due to criminal justice and social welfare costs, and 9 percent in health care costs) (ONDCP, 2001). Medical costs of smoking are about $75 billion annually and productivity losses are about $80 billion (National Center for Chronic Disease Prevention and Health Promotion, 2004). The greatest toll of ATOD, however, comes in the form of human suffering.

Confounding Issues

There is lack of agreement about how to define, prevent, and treat ATOD problems. Professionals in the ATOD field view alcohol and drug dependence as a brain disease (Leshner, 2001) or a chronic medical illness with treatment compliance and relapse rates similar to other chronic medical illnesses (McLellan, Lewis, O'Brien, & Kleber, 2000). The ADA and other public policies treat ATOD problems differently from other mental and physical illnesses (DiNitto, 2002; McNeece & DiNitto, 2005). Alcohol or drug disorders alone are no longer sufficient to qualify for Supplemental Security Income (SSI) or Social Security Disability Insurance (SSDI). Those who use illicit drugs or are convicted of drug law violations may be denied access to public assistance programs such as Temporary Assistance for Needy Families (TANF), food stamps, publicly sponsored housing, and student loans. People with other chronic illnesses or criminal convictions are not treated in this manner.

Evidence indicates that every $1 spent on alcohol and drug treatment results in about $12 saved in crime, criminal justice, and health care costs (NIDA, 1999). Yet much of the national, state, and local drug control budgets go to law enforcement or interdiction, although there is little to suggest that such efforts reduce alcohol and drug abuse or dependence (McNeece & DiNitto, 2005). In fact, the so-called "war on drugs" has escalated violence in the United States and other countries as "drug lords" compete for the lucrative drug trade and poor people succumb or are forced to produce, transport, or sell drugs to survive.

Congress and state governments are loath to try harm reduction approaches that other countries have adopted to reduce the consequences of ATOD problems. For example, Congress has failed to approve needle exchange, even though the U.S. Department of Health and Human Services (HHS) has recognized that appropriately conducted needle exchange programs can reduce HIV transmission and do not encourage injection drug use (HHS, 1998). Decriminalization of drug use has largely been rejected, although approaches such as drug courts and Proposition 36 in California, which provides treatment instead of jail for certain convictions of nonviolent drug offenses, attempt to divert individuals to treatment in lieu of incarceration.

Furthermore, people of color are often disproportionately affected by ATOD problems and the drug war. African Americans in particular are overrepresented among inmates serving time for drug sentences. In 2001, 57 percent of drug offenders in state prisons were African American (BJS, 2003). Penalties under the Controlled Substances Act are much stiffer for crack cocaine, which can be purchased more cheaply than powdered cocaine. This stratifying of penalties disproportionately affects people who are poor and people of color.

Among male adults and adolescents in 2001, 43 percent of all AIDS cases among African Americans and the same percentage among Hispanic Americans were due to injecting drug use, having sex with men and injecting drugs, or having sex with a heterosexual injecting drug user. Just 18 percent of cases were similar among white men (Centers for Disease Control and Prevention, 2002). In 1997, the alcohol-related cirrhosis death rate for white Hispanic men was 12.6 per 100,000, compared with 7.3 for non-Hispanic African American men and 5.1 for non-Hispanic white men (Stinson, Grant, & Dufour, 2001). Cirrhosis mortality is 2.8 times higher among American Indian men than among non-Hispanic white men and 1.5 times higher among American Indian women than among non-Hispanic white women (Singh & Hoyert, 2000). From 1995 to 1997, across Alaska, Arizona, Colorado, and New York, the rate of fetal alcohol syndrome per 1,000 population for American Indian/Alaska Natives was 3.2 compared with 1.5 for the general population of those states (Miller et al., 2002).

To address and bridge the gap between research and treatment (see Lamb, Greenlick, & McCarty, 1998), NIDA established the Clinical Trials Network to increase knowledge exchange between researchers and practitioners. SAMHSA established Practice Research Collaboratives to increase communication among treatment providers, researchers, policymakers, consumers, and other stakeholders. SAMHSA also funds 13 regional Addiction Technology Transfer Centers (ATTCs) and a national ATTC office to increase practitioners' access to state-of-the-art research and education.

Professional Directives

Social workers also experience ATOD problems, although prevalence rates are not well established (Elpers, 1992; Fewell, King, & Weinstein, 1993; Siebert, 2005). There is no reason to believe that social workers experience rates lower than the general population, and because they perform work that often exposes them to the effects of secondary trauma, there is reason to believe that social workers may be at higher risk (Stamm, 1999). For those in the helping professions, the issue of impairment involves the potential for impinging on patient care in addition to personal consequences. NASW recognizes that social workers have an ethical duty to help colleagues who are experiencing ATOD problems and other physical and emotional impairments (NASW, 2000). Social workers, however, are frequently reluctant to approach a colleague with an ATOD problem (Fewell et al.). A survey of social workers at high risk of ATOD problems showed that only 24 percent sought help for their problems (Siebert). Only a small number of NASW chapters provide assistance to members with ATOD problems.

POLICY STATEMENT

To improve the response to ATOD problems, NASW's position is that

■ Social workers must advocate for an approach to ATOD problems that emphasizes prevention and treatment.

■ Social workers must advocate to eliminate objectifying and stigmatizing language and labels and promote a more respectful, non-stigmatizing strengths-based language.

- The ADA, SSI program, TANF, and other federal, state, and local legislation, policies, and programs must treat ATOD disorders in the same manner as other physical and mental disabilities.

- More efforts are needed to eliminate health disparities that accrue from ATOD problems and discriminatory practices from the criminal justice system.

- Individuals with ATOD problems need access to appropriate treatment. The risk of relapse or continued ATOD use is too great to do otherwise. To accomplish this goal, private and public health care plans need to offer treatment for ATOD problems in parity with other physical and mental health problems. Systems of care should be made available for those lacking insurance coverage, and public and private care should be of equally high quality.

- Providers of ATOD prevention and treatment services need to assess their approaches and use those with demonstrated effectiveness.

- All reasonable avenues to address ATOD problems must be considered, including psychosocial treatments, medications, alternatives to incarceration, and harm-reduction approaches.

- Treatment for individuals with ATOD problems and co-occurring mental, physical, and other disorders must be offered in an integrated manner, and treatment programs must be fully accessible.

- Treatment for ATOD problems must be comprehensive given that patients, clients, and consumers often present with additional problems (health, employment, family, housing, legal, and other problems) that may impede recovery.

- Social workers in all settings need knowledge of ATOD problems and the skills necessary to screen for ATOD problems, to educate at-risk drinkers and tobacco users about the options available for reducing or eliminating consumption, to refer those who need ATOD treatment to appropriate services, and to motivate patients, clients, and consumers to take appropriate action. Social workers also need to be capable of offering family members and friends services or referrals to appropriate services, including mutual-help groups.

- Social workers need to work with other groups and professional organizations to identify and support efforts that are evidence based, grounded in best practices, and improve treatment outcomes.

- Schools of social work need to be encouraged to incorporate more information about the knowledge and skills needed to intervene with ATOD problems in all areas of the curriculum. The training received toward the BSW and MSW degrees needs to be promoted as providing sufficient knowledge for intervening with ATOD problems.

- ATOD prevention and treatment strategies must address the characteristics and needs of individuals with regard to gender, sexual orientation, ethnicity, culture, religion and spiritual beliefs, socioeconomic status, disability, and other factors.

- NASW must assist and encourage chapters to provide services for all social workers who are personally affected by ATOD problems.

REFERENCES

Americans with Disabilities Act of 1990, Pub. L. 101-336, 42 USC 12101 et seq.

Centers for Disease Control and Prevention. (1994, March 11). Preventing tobacco use among young people: A report of the Surgeon General (Executive Summary). *MMWR Recommendations and Reports*, 43(RR-4), 1–10.

Centers for Disease Control and Prevention. (2002). U.S. HIV and AIDS cases reported through December 2001. *HIV/AIDS Surveillance Report*, 13(2). Retrieved May 26, 2004, from http://www.cdc.gov/hiv/stats/hasr1302.htm

Chassin, L., Jacob, T., Johnson, J. L., Shuckit, M. A., & Sher, K. J. (1997). A critical analysis of COA research. *Alcohol, Health & Research World*, 21, 258–264.

Comprehensive Alcohol Abuse and Alcoholism Prevention, Treatment, and Rehabilitation Act of 1970, Pub. L. 91-616, 84 Stat. 1848, 42 U.S.C. 4501 et seq.

Comprehensive Drug Abuse Prevention and Control Act of 1970, Pub. L. 91-513, 84 Stat. 1236, 21 U.S.C. 801 et seq.

Cotton, N. S. (1979). The familial incidence of alcoholism: A review. *Journal of Studies on Alcohol, 40,* 89–116.

de Miranda, J. (1999, May/June). Treatment services offer limited access for people with disabilities. *Counselor, 17*(3), 24–25.

DiNitto, D. M. (2002). War and peace: Social work and the state of chemical dependency treatment in the United States. In S.L.A. Straussner & L. Harrison (Eds.), *International aspects of social work practice in the addictions* (pp. 7–29). New York: Haworth Press.

DiNitto, D. M., & Webb, D. K. (2005). Substance use disorders and co-occurring disabilities. In C. A. McNeece & D. M. DiNitto (Eds.), *Chemical dependency: A systems approach* (3rd ed., pp. 423–483).

Dorsey, T. L., Zawitz, M. W., & Middleton, P. (2003, December). *Drugs and crime facts.* Washington, DC: U.S. Department of Justice, Bureau of Justice Statistics. Retrieved May 26, 2004, from http://www.ojp.usdoj.gov

El-Guebaly, N., & Offord, D. R. (1977). The offspring of alcoholics: A critical review. *American Journal of Psychiatry, 134,* 357–365.

Elpers, K. (1992). *Social work impairment: A statewide survey of the National Association of Social Workers.* Indianapolis: NASW Indiana Chapter.

Fewell, C. H., King, B. L., & Weinstein, D. L. (1993). Alcohol and other drug abuse among social work colleagues and their families: Impact on practice. *Social Work, 38,* 565–570.

Goodwin, D. W. (1979). Alcoholism and heredity: A review and hypothesis. *Archives of General Psychiatry, 36,* 57–61.

Grant, B. F. (2000). Estimates of U.S. children exposed to alcohol abuse and dependence in the family. *American Journal of Public Health, 90,* 112–115.

Greenfeld, L. A., & Snell, T. L. (2000). *Women offenders* [Bureau of Justice Statistics Special Report]. Washington, DC: U.S. Department of Justice, Bureau of Justice Statistics. Retrieved May 26, 2004, from http://www.ojp.usdoj.gov/bjs/abstract/wo.htm

Grunbaum, J. A., Kann, L., Kinchen, S., Ross J., Hawkins J., Lowry, R., Harris, W. A., McManus, T., Chyen, D., & Collins, J. (2004). Youth risk behavior surveillance-United States, 2003. *Morbidity and Mortality Weekly Report, 53*(SS-2): 1-95.

Harwood, H. (2000). *Updating estimates of the economic costs of alcohol abuse in the United States: Estimates, update methods, and data.* Washington, DC: National Institute on Alcohol Abuse and Alcoholism. Retrieved May 24, 2004, from http://www.niaaa.nih.gov/publications/economic-2000/printing.htm#top

Hay Group. (2001). *Employer health care dollars spent on addiction treatment.* Chevy Chase, MD: American Society of Addiction Medicine. Retrieved May 26, 2004, from http://www.asam.org/pressrel/hay.htm

Heath, A. C. (1995). Genetic influences on drinking behavior in humans. In H. Begleiter & B. Kissin (Eds.), *The genetics of alcoholism* (Vol. I, pp. 82-121). New York: Oxford University Press.

Huang, L. X., Cerbone, F. G., & Gfroerer, J. C. (1998). *Children at risk because of parental substance abuse* [OAS Working Paper]. Rockville, MD: Substance Abuse and Mental Health Services Administration.

Lamb, S., Greenlick, M. R., & McCarty, D. (Eds.). (1998). *Bridging the gap between practice and research: Forging partnerships with community-based drug and alcohol treatment.* Washington, DC: Institute of Medicine, National Academies Press.

Leshner, A. I. (2001, Spring). Addiction is a brain disease. *Issues in Science and Technology.* Retrieved June 4, 2002, from http://www.nap.edu/issues/17.3/leshner.htm

McLellan, A. T., Lewis, D. C., O'Brien, C. P., & Kleber, H. D. (2000). Drug dependence, a chronic medical illness: Implications for treatment, insurance, and outcomes evaluation. *JAMA, 284,* 1689–1695.

McNeece, C. A., & DiNitto, D. M. (2005). *Chemical dependency: A systems approach* (3rd ed.). Boston: Allyn & Bacon.

Mee-Lee, D., Shulman, G. D., Fishman, M., Gastfriend, D. R., & Griffiths, J. H. (Eds.). (2001). *ASAM patient placement criteria for the treatment of substance-related disorders* (2nd ed.-rev., PPC-2R). Chevy Chase, MD: American Society of Addiction Medicine.

Miller, L., Tolliver, R., Druschel, C., Fox, D., Schoellhorn, J., Podvin, D., Merrick, S., Cunniff, C., Meaney, F. J., Pensak, M., Dominique, Y., Hymbaugh, K., Boyle, C., & Baio, J. (2002). Fetal alcohol syndrome-Alaska, Arizona, Colorado, and New York: 1995–1997. *Morbidity and Mortality Weekly Report, 51*(20), 433–435.

National Association of Social Workers. (2000). *Code of ethics of the National Association of Social Workers*. Washington, DC: Author.

National Center for Chronic Disease Prevention and Health Promotion. (2004). *Reducing tobacco use*. Atlanta: Centers for Disease Control and Prevention. Retrieved May 23, 2004, from http://www.cdc.gov/nccdphp/bb_tobacco

National Center on Addiction and Substance Abuse at Columbia University. (2005). *Family matters: Substance abuse and the American family*. New York: Author.

National Institute on Drug Abuse. (1999). *Principles of drug addiction treatment: A research-based guide*. Bethesda, MD: National Institutes of Health.

National Institute on Drug Abuse. (2003, April 11). *Congressional and legislative activities*. Retrieved May 25, 2004, from http://www.drugabuse.gov/about/legislation/Chronology/html

Office of National Drug Control Policy. (2001). *The economic costs of drug abuse in the United States, 1992–1998* (Publication No. NCJ-190636). Washington, DC: Executive Office of the President. Retrieved May 23, 2004, from http://www.whitehousedrugpolicy.gov

Office of National Drug Control Policy. (2004, March). *National drug control strategy, FY 2005 budget summary*. Washington, DC: Executive Office of the President. Retrieved May 25, 2004, from http://www.whitehousedrugpolicy.gov/publications/policy/budgetsum04/index.html

Proposition 36, Substance Abuse and Crime Prevention Act of 2000, California Penal Code 1210 et seq.

72 percent work for private organizations. (2001, January). *NASW News*, p. 8.

Russell, M., Henderson, C., & Blume, S. B. (1985). *Children of alcoholics: A review of the literature*. New York: Children of Alcoholics Foundation.

Siebert, D. C. (2005). Help seeking for AOD misuse among social workers: Patterns, barriers, and implications. *Social Work, 50*, 65–75.

Singh, G. K., & Hoyert, D. L. (2000). Social epidemiology of chronic liver disease and cirrhosis mortality in the United States, 1935–1977: Trends and differentials by ethnicity, socioeconomic status, and alcohol consumption. *Human Biology, 72*, 801–820.

Stamm, B. H. (Ed.). (1999). *Secondary traumatic stress: Self-care issues for clinicians, researchers, & educators* (2nd ed.). Baltimore, MD: Sidran Press.

Stinson, F. S., Grant, B. F., & Dufour, M. C. (2001). The critical dimension of ethnicity in liver cirrhosis mortality statistics. *Alcoholism: Clinical and Experimental Research, 25*, 1181–1187.

Substance Abuse and Mental Health Services Administration, Office of Applied Studies. (2001). *Summary of findings from the 2000 National Household Survey on Drug Abuse*. Rockville, MD: Author.

Substance Abuse and Mental Health Services Administration, Office of Applied Studies. (2003). *Overview of findings from the 2002 National Survey on Drug Use and Health*. Rockville, MD: Author.

U.S. Department of Health and Human Services. (1998, April 20). *Research shows needle exchange programs reduce HIV infections without increasing drug use*. Washington, DC: Author. Retrieved May 28, 2004, from http://www.hhs.gov/news/press/1998pres/980420a.html

U.S. Department of Justice, Bureau of Justice Statistics. (2001). *Prisoners in 2000*. Re-

trieved May 26, 2004, from http://www
.ojp.usdoj.gov/bjs/abstract/p02.htm
U.S. Department of Justice, Bureau of Justice
Statistics. (2003). *Prisoners in 2002*. Retrieved May 26, 2004, from http://www
.ojp.usdoj.gov/bjs/abstract/p00.htm

White, W. L. (2001). *The rhetoric of recovery advocacy: An essay on the power of language*. Peoria, IL: Behavioral Health Management Project. Available at http://www.bhrm.org/advocacy/rhetoric.pdf

Policy statement approved by the NASW Delegate Assembly, August 2005. This statement supersedes the statement on Alcohol, Tobacco, and Other Substance Abuse approved by the Delegate Assembly in 1996 and referred by the 2002 Delegate Assembly to the 2005 Delegate Assembly for revision. For further information, contact the National Association of Social Workers, 750 First Street, NE, Suite 700, Washington, DC 20002-4241; telephone: 202-408-8600; e-mail press@naswdc.org

Capital Punishment and the Death Penalty

BACKGROUND

Although more than half the countries of the world have abolished the death penalty in law or practice since adoption of the Universal Declaration of Human Rights over 50 years ago (Amnesty International, 1998), the practice of capital punishment persists in the United States. Between 1930 and November 2000, 4,890 people were executed and more than 3,500 people currently on death row await execution (Amnesty International, 1998; Death Penalty Information Center, 2000b; U.S. Department of Justice, 1997). Only China, Iran, Saudi Arabia, and the Congo execute more people than the United States (Amnesty International, 1998). To play a role in changing this reality, social workers need to be familiar with the following anti– and pro–death penalty arguments.

Anti–Death Penalty Arguments

Argument 1: The criminal justice system has sent innocent people to death row. Some have been executed (Friends Committee on National Legislation [FCNL], 2000). Between 1973 and 2000, 89 people were released from death row because of evidence of their innocence after spending an average of 7.6 years incarcerated and awaiting execution (Death Penalty Information Center, 2000b). Evidence that application of the death penalty is too arbitrary, too prone to error, and unfairly administered supports the argument that the system simply cannot be reliable enough to ensure the principle of life.

Argument 2: The death penalty is applied in a racially disparate fashion (FCNL, 2000). On the basis of a review of 28 empirical studies, the U.S. General Accounting Office (1990) reported a pattern of racial disparities at all levels—in charging, in sentencing, and in impos-

ing the death penalty. In 82 percent of the studies, race of the victim was found to be a factor in how the death penalty was applied, with those who murdered white people 4.3 times more likely to be sentenced to death than those who murdered black people even though people of color are the victims in more than half of all homicides. A study of death penalty sentencing in Philadelphia between 1983 and 1993 found that black defendants were nearly three times more likely to receive a death sentence than were all other defendants (Baldus, Woodworth, Zuckerman, Weiner, & Broffitt, 1998). Only two of the 20 people on federal death row in 2001 were white.

Argument 3: The death penalty unfairly penalizes those who are developmentally unable to understand the implications of their behavior or cannot obtain proper counsel. As of January 1, 2001, 73 persons were on death row under death sentences received for juvenile crimes. These 73 condemned juveniles constituted about 2 percent of the total death row population of about 3,700. Although all were ages 16 or 17 at the time of their crimes, their current ages ranged from 18 to 42. They were under death sentences in 15 different states and had been on death row for a few months to more than 22 years. Texas has by far the largest death row for juvenile offenders, now holding 26 (33 percent) of the national total of 74 juvenile offenders. There are currently 83 death row inmates (all men) sentenced as juveniles, constituting 2.24 percent of the total death row population (Death Row USA, 2002). Sixteen states (CA, CO, CT, IL, IN, KS, MD, MT, NE, NJ, NM, NY, OH, OR, TN, and WA) and the federal government have a minimum age of 18 for capital punishment. There is a problem in other states, where children age 14 or younger are tried as adults and subject to the death penalty.

On June 20, 2002, the U.S. Supreme Court ruled that the execution of people with mental retardation is contrary to the U.S. Constitution.

Finally, in relation to poor people, about 90 percent of people facing the death penalty cannot afford their own attorney, and no state has met standards developed by the American Bar Association (1989) for appointment, performance, and compensation of counsel for indigent prisoners.

Argument 4: The U.S. murder rate greatly exceeds European non–death penalty nations. Data released by the British Home Office reveal that the United States, which retains the death penalty, has a murder rate that is more than three times that of many of its European allies that have banned capital punishment. The data challenge the argument that the death penalty is a deterrent to murder. There are more than 110 nations around the world that have banned the death penalty in law or practice.

Pro–Death Penalty Arguments

Although this policy statement asserts that the reasons outlined fully justify rejection of the death penalty, four arguments that hold otherwise are assessed below (FCNL, 2000).

Argument 1: The death penalty deters violent crime more effectively than does imprisonment. Although recognizing that deterrent sanctions may be a valid and a necessary part of our system of criminal justice, statistics used to argue both sides fail to uphold the notion that the death penalty acts as a deterrent to homicide. In fact FBI reports show that, in general, homicide rates are lower in non–death penalty states. The South, which accounts for 80 percent of executions, repeatedly has the highest murder rate, and the Northeast, which accounts for less than 1 percent of executions, has the lowest murder rate (Death Penalty Information Center, 2000a). Although these figures do not disprove that individuals may be deterred from committing murder by the existence of the death penalty, they do suggest that the death penalty is not likely to be a more effective deterrent than an alternative such as life imprisonment.

Argument 2: Families of crime victims support the death penalty (FCNL, 2000). Crime victims' families respond to the death penalty in a variety of ways. Whereas some argue for vengeance or atonement, others argue against the death penalty because it continues the cycle of violence. There are organizations aimed at healing for crime victims that are congruent with social work values and ethics. For example, Murder Victims' Families for Reconciliation (MVFR) opposes the death penalty and supports the redirection of money currently spent on executions to victim-assistance programs. Restitution Incorporated helps death row inmates sell their artwork to support families of their victims or for crime prevention programs, and some groups seek actual reconciliation between murderers and victims' families (FCNL, 2000).

Argument 3: Murderers deserve to die (FCNL, 2000). Some people who hold this belief express a desire for revenge. Although this is an understandable emotion in those who have suffered, furthering vengeance is not a responsible role for the state. Social work values and ethical principles hold that a prisoner, regardless of the crime committed, is still a human being. Execution denies the inherent dignity and worth of such individuals by precluding the possibility of rehabilitation.

Argument 4: Keeping murderers alive costs society more than executing them (FCNL, 2000). Under a vigilante system of justice, whereby a person is caught and immediately hanged, this argument would be true (FCNL, 2000). However, in a society based on laws that are concerned with fairness, accuracy, equity, and justice, the argument is false. Numerous studies have shown that the criminal justice system would be less costly if there were no death penalty because the costs are higher in a capital murder case in terms of both the initial trial and appeals (FCNL, 2000). The most comprehensive study found that the death penalty costs North Carolina $2.16 million more per execution than the cost of a non–death penalty murder case, with a sentence of imprisonment for life occurring at the trial level (Death Penalty Information Center, 2000b). Thus, even with limits on appeals, the higher costs at the trial level would remain.

ISSUE STATEMENT

Social workers share the concerns of other citizens about the rise in violent crime. They are very aware of the terrible consequences to the families of the victims of criminal homicide, and indeed, many social workers have personally experienced the anguish caused to their own families when a loved one has been murdered. It is a premise of this policy statement, however, that punitive action by the state can never compensate for such losses and that the death penalty is neither a sufficient nor an acceptable solution to the problems caused by violent crime. The following broad professional values and their corresponding ethical principles and specific standards, as delineated in the *NASW Code of Ethics* (NASW, 1999), undergird social workers' responsibility to oppose the death penalty.

Dignity and Worth of the Person

NASW's broad ethical principle that social workers respect the inherent dignity and worth of each person prohibits support of the death penalty. Capital punishment is an officially sanctioned violent act of killing as a way to deal with lethally violent behavior. Although homicide is unquestionably an act that diminishes the value and worth placed on human beings, the legitimization of killing through capital punishment also diminishes their value and worth. Both forms of killing are thus contradictory to this social work principle.

This ethical principle also applies to efforts by social workers to enhance clients' capacity and opportunity for change. Although murder is a reprehensible crime, the infliction of the death penalty on people convicted of murder permanently forecloses their capacity for redemption and reform. Whereas returning individuals who have committed murder to the community may not serve the best interests of society, life terms served in prison create the potential for these incarcerated individuals to recognize and heal from the emotional wounds that fueled their addiction, violence, and criminal behavior (Casarjian, 1995).

Finally, this ethical principle and the corresponding *Code* (section 6.01) obligate social workers to be cognizant of their dual responsibility to clients and to the broader society and to seek to resolve conflicts between clients' interests and those of the broader society in a socially responsible manner consistent with the values, principles, and standards of the profession. Rather than being a deterrent to violent crime, capital punishment legitimizes and expands the cycle of violence in society at large by promoting violence as a solution to intractable human problems and behaviors. By opposing the death penalty, social workers seek socially responsible alternatives aimed at stopping the cycle of violence in society and the world that is damaging and destroying human capacities and relationships.

Social Justice

This broad NASW ethical principle states that social workers challenge social injustice and pursue social change on behalf of vulnerable and oppressed individuals and groups of people. Related to this principle, the *Code of Ethics* (1999, section 4.02) prohibits social workers from practicing, condoning, facilitating, or collaborating with any form of discrimination. Furthermore, the *Code of Ethics* holds social workers responsible for engaging in social and political action to prevent and eliminate domination of, exploitation of, and discrimination against any person, group, or class (section 6.04d) as part of their responsibilities to the broader society. These values, principles, and standards provide the grounding for social workers to oppose capital punishment in that the death penalty has always been and continues to be differentially applied to people who are poor, disadvantaged, of limited mental or intellectual capacity, and from ethnic or racial groups. In the United States where executions have increased rapidly over the past several years, studies have shown a marked racial bias in the defendants selected for execution (Baldus, 1994; Dieter, 1998; U.S. General Accounting Office, 1990).

POLICY STATEMENT

NASW, on the basis of the arguments stated and grounded in professional values and ethical principles and standards as delineated in the *Code of Ethics*, maintains that the integrity of human life and the promotion of human well-being are among the highest values to which a society aspires. The practice of capital punishment, which involves a deliberate act of execution by the state, is therefore at variance with the fundamental values of the social work profession. The death penalty is a violation of human rights that belong to every human being, even those convicted of serious crimes. In the United States its application is arbitrary, unfair, and prone to racial bias and targets people who are most vulnerable. Thus, it is the position of NASW that:

- The U.S. government and all state authorities, which have laws that provide for capital punishment, should abolish the death penalty for all crimes.

- Pending abolition, the U.S. federal and state governments should impose an immediate moratorium on executions.

- The states that allow for the use of the death penalty for crimes committed by those individuals under the age of 18 should raise the minimum age to 18, pending a moratorium or abolition.

- All states that allow the use of the death penalty against defendants who have mental impairments should enact legislation to prevent this practice.

- Federal and state authorities, pending abolition, should ensure that capital defendants are represented by attorneys who are adequately trained, funded, and experienced in the complexities of capital proceedings.

- In some cases NASW supports a life sentence as an alternative sentence to the death penalty.

REFERENCES

American Bar Association. (1989). *Guidelines for appointment and performance of counsel in death penalty cases.* Washington, DC: Death Penalty Representation Project, ABA.

Amnesty International. (1998). *United States of America: Rights for all.* New York: Amnesty International Publications.

Baldus, D. (1994). Reflections on the "inevitability" of racial discrimination in capital sentencing and the "impossibility" of its prevention, detection, and correction. *Washington & Lee Law Review, 51,* 359, 365.

Baldus, D., Woodworth, G., Zuckerman, D., Weiner, N. A., & Broffitt, B. (1998). Racial discrimination and the death penalty in the post-Furman era: An empirical and legal overview, with recent findings from Philadelphia. *Cornell Law Review, 83,* 1638–1770.

Casarjian, R. (1995). *Houses of healing: A prisoner's guide to inner power and freedom.* Boston: Lionheart Press.

Death Penalty Information Center. (2000a, July). FBI uniform crime reports: Murder rates per 100,000 population [Online]. Available: www.deathpenaltyinfo.org/murder rates.html

Death Penalty Information Center. (2000b, November 10). Facts about the death penalty [Online]. Available: www.deathpenaltyinfo.org/PressRoom.html

Death Row USA. (2002, April 1). NAACP Legal Defense and Education Fund [Online]. Available: www.deathpenaltyinfo.org/DeathRowUSA1.html

Dieter, R. C. (1998, June). *The death penalty in black and white: Who lives, who dies, who decides.* Washington, DC: Death Penalty Information Center.

Friends Committee on National Legislation. (2000). Responding to pro–death penalty arguments. *FCNL Perspectives, 3,* 15–29.

National Association of Social Workers. (1999). *NASW code of ethics.* Washington, DC: Author.

U.S. Department of Justice. (1997, December). *Capital punishment 1996* (Bulletin NCJ-167031). Washington, DC: Bureau of Justice Statistics.

U.S. General Accounting Office. (1990). *Death penalty sentencing: Research indicates pattern of racial disparities* (No. 5). Washington, DC: U.S. Government Printing Office.

Policy statement approved by the NASW Delegate Assembly, August 2002. For further information, contact the National Association of Social Workers, 750 First Street, NE, Suite 700, Washington, DC 20002-4241. Telephone: 202-408-8600; e-mail: press@naswdc.org

Child Abuse and Neglect

BACKGROUND

Assessing the scope of child abuse and neglect in our nation is challenging. Accurate statistics can be gathered only from formal abuse reports to child protective service (CPS) units. The Children's Bureau of the U.S. Department of Health and Human Services, which maintains the National Child Abuse and Neglect Data System (NCANDS), reported in *Child Maltreatment 2001* that 3 million referrals on behalf of approximately 5 million children were made to CPS agencies throughout the United States (National Clearinghouse on Child Abuse and Neglect Information [NCCANI], 2003c; U.S. Department of Health and Human Services, 2003). One-third of these reports were screened out of the investigation and assessment process, but 28 percent of the investigated reports were substantiated (NCCANI, 20003c).

In 2001 more than 903,000 children suffered from abuse or neglect, representing a rate of 12.4 maltreated children for every 1,000 children in the general population. Almost one-third of these children were younger than three. An estimated 1,300 children died from child maltreatment in 2001; 41 percent of the deaths were children 12 months or younger, and 85 percent were six years old or younger (NCCANI, 2003c). Many researchers believe that 50 percent to 60 percent of childhood deaths result from abuse and neglect, but are not included in these abuse and neglect rates because of pervasive underreporting of child maltreatment (NCCANI, 2003b). The prevalence of child maltreatment tends to decrease as children get older (NCCANI, 2003c).

Clarity about the prevalence of child abuse is complicated also by the difficulty of assessing environmental risk factors. African Americans and Hispanics are overrepresented in the statistics. Research has suggested that poor and racial and ethnic minority children and their families are disproportionately reported, labeled, and routinely mandated into the child welfare system by professionals who are socially and culturally distant from their actual family contexts (Wells, 1995). Despite the difficulties of tracking the extent of the problem, statistics clearly reveal a national crisis.

Historical Trends

Child maltreatment can be explored in the context of anthropology and its foundations in the study of the development of cultures (Bakan, 2001; Tower, 1996). Check (1989) asserted: "During the medieval times, for instance, there was neither a definition of childhood nor a vocabulary to differentiate it from adulthood" (p. 21). The most consistent belief was that children were the property of the parents without rights of their own (Tower).

Organized efforts to protect children are evident as far back as the Elizabethan Poor Laws in England in the mid-1550s, which sought to provide care and support to impoverished children and families. Novels penned by Charles Dickens ignited some of the first social protests against societal neglect of abused, abandoned, and crippled children (Tower, 1996), and since then movements emerged across western Europe and the United States, joining activists in the cause to stop the maltreatment of children.

The history of organized protection of children in the United States began with the case of nine-year-old Mary Ellen Wilson in 1874. The child had been through successive placements after the death of her parents. When church worker Etta Wheeler inquired, a neighbor in her New York City tenement reported the cruelties perpetrated on the child that she had heard through the thin walls. Wheeler turned to Henry Bergh, then well known as the first president of the American Society for the Prevention of Cruelty to Animals. With the help of an attorney, Mary Ellen was removed from the home, and Mary Ellen's caregiver was sentenced to a year of hard labor in a penitentiary (Tower, 1996). These landmark actions resulted in the establishment of the Society for the Prevention of Cruelty to Children and catapulted child maltreatment from the shadows of oblivion.

From then, activists made much progress in protecting children in the first half of the 20th century. The National Child Labor Committee was organized in 1904, and with the help of Jane Addams and others, the committee began working to reform child labor laws. In 1962, Kempe and colleagues published "The Battered-Child Syndrome," an article in the *Journal of the American Medical Association* about a pioneering effort to protect children from physical, sexual, and emotional abuse and neglect. For the first time, medical professionals presented epidemiological data about the frequency of physical child maltreatment and ignited a social movement (Leventhal, 2003). Leventhal concluded: "The authors' point was to inform the reader that physical abuse was not a rarely occurring phenomenon, but rather a common problem that was already recognized . . . across the country" (p. 545).

Legislation and Policy Development

The increasing awareness of the need to protect children in this country led to the establishment of the federal Children's Bureau in 1912. The Child Welfare League of America (CWLA) had its start in 1915 in efforts to create standards for services and aid to children (Tower, 1996). The Social Security Act, passed in 1935 (P.L. 74-271) sustained efforts to protect children, particularly those living in poverty. Described by Tower, the law mandated "child welfare services for neglected dependent children and children in danger of becoming delinquent" (p. 11). Public agencies began to implement child welfare policies and laws. Bakan (2001) described the radical shift, stating: "By implication, legislation making the reporting of child abuse mandatory indicates the protection of children is not the restricted province of parents but rather the larger responsibility of the society as a whole, which is to take over when the parents fail either by willful injury or by neglect" (p. 162).

Despite these efforts, legislation designed to protect children was often ineffective because of the continuing paternalistic values, particularly the philosophy that children were the property of parents. Political and societal beliefs and norms did not support efforts to intervene in the private affairs of families.

In 1974 key federal legislation addressing child abuse and neglect was enacted (NCCANI, 2003a). The Child Abuse Prevention and Treatment Act (CAPTA) (P.L. 93-247) established minimum definitions that serve as a baseline for intervention. *Child abuse* and *neglect* were described as (1) "any recent act or failure to act on the part of a parent or caretaker which results in death, serious physical or emotional harm, sexual abuse or exploitation" or (2) "an act or failure to act which presents an imminent risk of serious harm" (NCCANI, 2002b).

CAPTA also provided funding for prevention, assessment, investigation, prosecution, and treatment activities. Congress reauthorized and amended CAPTA several times to include adoption reforms, at-risk infants with life-threatening congenital impairments, children born with HIV or other life-threatening illnesses, and children who have been perinatally exposed to dangerous drugs (NCCANI, 2003d).

Public policy has also focused on what happens to children whose abuse and neglect investigations have been substantiated and whose custody issues must be decided. In 1980 Congress enacted the Adoption Assistance and Child Welfare Act (P.L. 96-272) . This law requires a six-month review while a child is in care and a "permanent plan" for the child within 18 months. Permanency planning and family preservation concepts developed as a result of studies demonstrating the negative effects of remaining in the foster care system long-term (known as "foster care drift") (National Association of Foster Care Reviewers [NAFCR], no date). This law also introduced the concept that "reasonable efforts" should be made to keep families together. In 1997, with great bipartisan approval, Congress enacted the Adoption and Safe Families Act (AFSA) (P.L. 105-89). It established funding for family preservation and support and added funds for adoption services. The law established time limits for making permanency planning decisions and initiating proceedings to terminate parental rights. ASFA requires that child safety be the paramount concern in making service provision, placement, and permanency decisions. ASFA initiated other significant changes in child welfare practice, including:

- Shortening the deadline for holding permanency hearing from 18 to 12 months

- Encouraging concurrent planning for adoption in all foster care placements

- Requiring agencies to file a petition to terminate parental rights when a child has been in foster care in 15 of the past 22 months

- Providing adoption incentives to states that increase their number of adoptions of foster children over a base year

- Clarifying what constitutes reasonable efforts and conditions under which a state is not required to work toward family reunification

- Requiring states to report track statistics reflecting the implementation and results of ASFA.

Current Status of Child Welfare

Today, the stories of children lost by social services, abused and neglected in foster care settings, and killed while in the custody of social welfare agencies fill the national news. Pear (2004) reported that "federal investigators have found widespread problems in child welfare programs intended to protect children from abuse and neglect" (p. 1). In a Dear Colleague letter drumming up support for increased funding for state CAPTA grants, Congressmen George Miller, from California, and Jim Greenwood, from Pennsylvania, ("Changes in the 2005 CAPTA," 2004) wrote: "The nation's child welfare system has long been stretched beyond capacity to handle the full scope of child maltreatment," and also pointed out that funding has been almost static for more than a decade.

ISSUE STATEMENT

Child maltreatment exists in a complex web of family interactions, and research has suggested serious, negative consequences for children that endure well into adulthood. According to NCCANI (2002a), "There is increasing awareness that child maltreatment and domestic violence co-exist in families" (p. 1). Brown and Bzostek (2003) reported that "recent research indicates that males exposed to domestic violence as children are more likely to engage in domestic violence as adults, and females are more likely to be victims as adults" (p. 4). Baldry (2003) demonstrated that a child witnessing violence is more likely to be involved in physical aggression, such as fighting, bullying, and threatening others, at school. Additional conflict arises when trying to protect women who are not only being abused by their partners, but also secondarily traumatized by having their children removed because of the dangerous home environment.

Furthermore, child welfare literature has suggested that "the link between substance abuse and child abuse has become stronger; parental substance abuse is highly correlated with child maltreatment and death" (Brissett-Chapman, 1995, p. 360). Some states take a highly punitive approach to parents who are substance abusers, and "this results in the substance-abusing mother not getting the treatment she needs for chemical dependency and inadequate medical care" (Alexander & McDougal, 2004, p. 5).

Childhood trauma has connections to heart disease, diabetes, obesity, unintended pregnancy, and alcoholism (Felitti, 2002). Childhood trauma can lead to significant mental health problems, such as posttraumatic stress disorder, depression, anxiety, and other disorders that impede an individual's ability to make healthy decisions concerning parenting, relationships, and health issues (Schnurr & Green, 2004). Hillis and colleagues (2000) found that being abused as a child may have long-term consequences for adult sexual behaviors that increase the risk of sexually transmitted diseases. Wyatt and colleagues (2002) warned that "the associations between child sexual abuse and HIV-related risks in adulthood have been well documented" (p. 661). The social costs of ignoring the effect of child maltreatment on physical health are enormous and impede our ability to break the cycle of family abuse.

While looking for the solutions in the United States, social workers also must advocate globally for coalitions designed to protect children around the world. More than 300,000 children worldwide are engaged as soldiers, abducted and forced to take up arms in bloody battles by political dissidents (Wadhams, 2004). Sexual exploitation of children occurs internationally with children being sold into prostitution and slavery. The United Nations Convention on the Rights of the Child (1989) is an important international child advocacy effort that "sets minimum international standards for the treatment of children to ensure their safety, survival and development" (Malcolm, 2000, p. 1). A total of 192 countries already have signed it. Somalia and the United States are the only member states that have not ratified this treaty.

Social workers have battled child maltreatment for more than 100 years, and to the battle they bring a unique body of knowledge. Concepts of working with people in their environments and of the primacy of the family help professionals understand that when dealing with child maltreatment, helping the child means working with the whole family and with other environmental factors in a culturally competent way. It means that they understand the devastating impact of poverty on children. Trained social workers understand the consequences of having natural and healthy developmental processes interrupted by traumatic events. As the United Nations Declaration on the Rights of the Child states, children "should grow up in a family environment, in an atmosphere of happiness, love and understanding."

Social workers are taught that prevention should be at the front end of all interventions. Prevention of child maltreatment is obviously a better strategy than dealing with the aftermath of child abuse and neglect. Miller and Greenwood (2004) pointed out that "if we could invest in proven prevention programs and strategies designed at the local level to meet individual, family and community needs, we could reduce the expenditure for costly back end crisis services."

POLICY STATEMENT

The National Association of Social Workers takes the following positions as an organization:

■ Children have the right to be treated with respect as individuals and to receive culturally sensitive services. Children have a right to express their opinions about their lives and have those opinions considered in all placement and judicial proceedings.

■ Immigrant children should have the same rights and protections as children who are citizens of this country.

■ Systems in place to protect children should be adequately staffed and fully funded, and they should provide service that reflects evidence-based or current best practices to address the problem of child abuse and neglect.

■ Communities, including extended family members, kinship networks, and neighborhoods must be involved in supporting children and caregivers to ensure a safe, secure, and consistently stable living environment.

■ All states must create and enforce laws that protect child witnesses of domestic violence and provide appropriate care for nonoffending parents and the children.

■ Authorities should leave nonoffending parents or guardians and their children in their own homes and remove the batterers to preserve the stability of children's caregiving and residence in domestic violence cases.

- Child abuse and neglect investigations and substantiations are best conducted using a specially trained, multidisciplinary team, including social workers, law enforcement, and health and mental health professionals.

- Policies and procedures should be developed in human services organizations to address and ensure the safety of social workers and other professionals working with abuse and neglect.

- Staff with social work degrees should be employed in schools, mental health programs, hospitals, and other human services organizations that deal with children and their families. All comprehensive medical assessments should address abuse and neglect issues.

- A bachelor's degree in social work is preferred for staff in child protective services. At the supervisory level, a master's degree in social work is recommended.

- Child maltreatment issues should be part of the curricula of all programs that train health professionals.

- Systematic changes are needed in child abuse reporting systems to ensure more standardized and effective intake assessments.

- Standardized definitions of child abuse and neglect must include identification of emotional and psychological abuse and risks and harm to children exposed to violence, and they must state the responsibility to provide intervention for such conditions no matter the etiology.

- Family-centered residential treatment programs for substance-abusing parents should be available to facilitate opportunities to help parents and children maintain the parent–child bond.

- Public awareness, media, and educational campaigns are needed to highlight the significance of child abuse issues and the related legal requirements of reporting systems.

- Sexual abuse and physical abuse prevention programs should be mandated in all schools from kindergarten to high school.

- The United States should ratify the United Nations Convention on the Rights of the Child.

- Funding should be dramatically increased for research, prevention, and services in all areas of child maltreatment.

- To truly help protect children by preventing child maltreatment, social workers and other professionals must also help families by identifying and addressing the individual, familial, and community challenges they encounter (NASW, 2004).

- Child maltreatment issues and concerns do not operate in isolation. To improve the service delivery in the area of child abuse and neglect, those systems that run parallel—mental health, substance abuse, domestic abuse, homelessness, and health care—need to be enhanced to effectively develop a service continuum directed at safety for children.

REFERENCES

Adoption Assistance and Child Welfare Act of 1980, Pub. L. 96-272, 94 Stat. 500.

Adoption and Safe Families Act of 1997, Pub. L. 105-89, 111 Stat. 2115.

Alexander, L., & McDougal, T. (2004). *Drug screening substance abusing parents*. Unpublished manuscript, University of North Carolina at Greensboro and North Carolina A&T University.

Baldry, A. C. (2003) Bullying in schools and exposure to domestic violence. *Child Abuse & Neglect, 27,* 713–732.

Bakan, D. (April, 2001). Slaughter of the innocents: A study of the battered child phenomenon. *Journal of Social Distress and the Homeless, 10,* 147–216.

Brissett-Chapman, S. (1995). Child abuse and neglect: Direct practice. In R. L. Edwards (Ed.-in-Chief), *Encyclopedia of social work* (19th ed., Vol. 1, pp. 353–366). Washington, DC: NASW Press.

Brown, B. V., & Bzostek, S. (2003). Violence in the lives of children [Child Trends Data-Bank Data Brief]. *CrossCurrents, 1,* 1–13. Child Trends. Available at http://www.childtrendsdatabank.org

Check, W. A. (1989). *The encyclopedia of health, psychological disorders and their treatment: Child abuse*. New York: Chelsea House.

Child Abuse Prevention and Treatment Act, Pub. L. 93-247, 88 Stat. 4 (1974).

Children's Defense Fund. (2000). Issue Basics, Adoption and Safe Families Act (ASFA). Retrieved October 10, 2004 from, http://www.cdfactioncouncil.org

Felitti, V. J. (2002). The relation between adverse childhood experiences and adult health: Turning gold into lead. *Permanente Journal, 6*(1), 44–47.

Hillis, S. D., Anda, R. F., Felitti, V. J., Nordenberg, D., & Marchbanks, P. A. (2000). Adverse childhood experiences and sexually transmitted diseases in men and women: A retrospective study. *Pediatrics, 106,* e11.

Kempe, C. H., Silverman, F. N., Steele, B. F., Droegemueller, W., & Silver, H. K. (1962). The battered-child syndrome. *JAMA, 181,* 17–24.

Leventhal, J. (2003). 'The Battered-Child Syndrome' 40 years later. *Clinical Child Psychology and Psychiatry, 8,* 543–545.

Malcolm, T. (2000, April 14). Advocates call for welcome for U.N. child rights document. Retrieved October 20, 2005, from http://natcath.org/NCR_Online/archives2/2000b/041400/041400l.htm

Miller, G., & Greenwood, J. (2004). Colleague letter in support of increased funding for fiscal year 2005 CAPTA appropriations. Washington, DC: 108th Congress.

National Association of Foster Care Reviewers. (n.d.). *Foster care review: past & present. Helping systems work for children.* Salt Lake City: Author. Available at http://www.nafcr.org./docs/foster_care_review.pdf

National Association of Social Workers. (2004, June). *"If you're right for the job, it's the best job in the world": The National Association of Social Workers' Child Welfare Specialty Practice Section members describe their experiences in child welfare.* Washington, DC: Author.

National Clearinghouse on Child Abuse and Neglect Information. (2002a). *Child abuse and neglect state statutes series, compendium of laws, child witness to domestic violence.* Washington, DC: U.S. Department of Health and Human Services.

National Clearinghouse on Child Abuse and Neglect Information. (2002b). *What is child maltreatment?* Washington, DC: U.S. Department of Health and Human Services.

National Clearinghouse on Child Abuse and Neglect Information. (2003a). *About the federal Child Abuse Prevention and Treatment Act.* Washington, DC: U.S. Department of Health and Human Services.

National Clearinghouse on Child Abuse and Neglect Information. (2003b). *Child abuse and neglect fatalities: Statistics and interventions.* Washington, DC: U.S. Department of Health and Human Services.

National Clearinghouse on Child Abuse and Neglect Information. (2003c). *Child maltreatment 2001: Summary of key findings.* Washington, DC: U.S. Department of Health and Human Services.

National Clearinghouse on Child Abuse and Neglect Information. (2003d). *Major federal legislation concerned with child protection, child welfare, and adoption.* Washington, DC: U.S. Department of Health and Human Services.

Pear, R. (2004, April 26). U.S. finds fault in all 50 states' child welfare programs. *New York Times,* p. A17.

Schnurr, P. P., & Green, B. L. (2004). *Trauma and health: Physical health consequences of exposure to extreme stress.* Washington, DC: American Psychological Association.

Social Security Act of 1935, Pub. L. 74–271, 49 Stat. 620.

Tower, C. C. (1996). *Understanding child abuse and neglect* (3rd ed.). Boston: Allyn & Bacon.

United Nations. (1989). Convention on the Rights of the Child (Resolution 44/25). New York: Author. Available at http://www.unicef.org/crc/fulltext.htm

U.S. Department of Health and Human Services, Administration for Children and Families. (2003). *Child maltreatment, 2001.* Washington, DC: U.S. Government Printing Office

Wadhams, N. (2004, January 20). United Nations seeks to end use of child soldiers. Retrieved October 20, 2005, from http://www.globalpolicy.org/security/issues/040120child.htm

Wells, S. J. (1995). Child abuse and neglect overview. In R. L. Edwards (Ed.-in-Chief),

Encyclopedia of social work (19th ed., Vol. 1, pp. 346–353). Washington, DC: NASW Press.

Wyatt, G. E., Myers, H. F., Williams, J. K., Kitchen, C. R., Loeb, T., Carmona, J. V.,

Wyatt, L. E., Chin, D., & Presley, N. (2002). Does a history of trauma contribute to HIV risk for women of color? Implications for prevention and policy. *American Journal of Public Health, 92,* 660–665.

Policy statement approved by the NASW Delegate Assembly, August 2005. This policy statement supersedes the statement on Child Abuse and Neglect approved by the Delegate Assembly in 1996 and referred by the 2002 Delegate Assembly to the 2005 Delegate Assembly for revision. For further information, contact the National Association of Social Workers, 750 First Street, NE, Suite 700, Washington, DC 20002-4241; telephone: 202-408-8600; e-mail: press@naswdc.org

Civil Liberties and Justice

BACKGROUND

Advancing social justice through the protection and preservation of individual civil liberties is a key tenet of the social work profession.

Beginning in the 1980s and into the 21st century, landmark, yet fragile, gains in civil liberties and social justice obtained by social movements of the 1950s, 1960s, and 1970s have been steadily eroded by executive order, legislation, voter referenda, and judicial decisions. Whereas the triumph of American freedom and democracy has been hailed by U.S. political leaders, it is ironic that in the United States the legal rights of women, people of color, people who are gay, lesbian, bisexual, and transgendered, and people with low incomes have been abrogated by federal cutback policies, judicial court decisions, and abridged by administrative neglect at all levels of government. Each of these groups is increasingly stigmatized as a means to distract attention from the socioeconomic and political issues that afflict the entire society. Under the guise of promoting family and cultural values, concerted political and ideological attacks have targeted immigrant groups, the changing roles of women in U.S. society, the growing acceptance of alternative sexual lifestyles, and the consequential evolution of diverse family constellations.

Simultaneously the civil liberties of many constituent populations—including people with AIDS or HIV-related illness, deinstitutionalized consumers of mental health services, recipients of public benefits, juvenile and adult offenders, union members, immigrants and refugees, pregnant women, terminally ill patients, and people with addictions—have been denied or severely limited by revisions of government policy or cutbacks in government programs. For example, the federal executive "gag" order issued in 1988 directed health care professionals in federally funded Title X family planning clinics to refrain from providing any abortion-related information to clients, including referrals for services, even when asked to do so by the client. If professionals failed to comply, their agency would lose Title X funding (Guttmacher Institute, 2000). The 1988 executive order not only denied women their reproductive rights, but also denied health and human services workers their right of free speech. The Supreme Court upheld the constitutionality of the rule in a 5-to-4 decision in *Rust v. Sullivan* in 1991. President Clinton suspended the rule in 1993, however formal repeal of the rule did not take effect until July 3, 2000.

■ The Constitution requires that habeas corpus shall not be suspended "unless when in cases of rebellion or invasion the public safety may require it" ("Brief Backs Habeas Corpus," 2007). Congress, the police, and the courts continue to abuse this constitutional check on abuses of power.

■ The purpose of the constitutional protection against self-incrimination is described in *Grunewald v. United States* (1957): "recent examination of the history and meaning of the Fifth Amendment has emphasized anew that one of the basic functions of the privilege is to protect *innocent* men" [italics added] (p. 353 U.S. 391).

■ There is no evidence that the death penalty serves as a deterrent to violent crime. In fact, an increase in homicides in the United States has occurred despite the reinstitution of capital punishment in most states. The abolition of the death penalty would bring the United States' penal system in line with other modern societies

In *Roper v. Simmons* (2005) the U.S. Supreme Court ended the death penalty for persons whose crimes were committed when they were juveniles. The Supreme Court cited the unique developmental forces at work, which affect the ability of juveniles to make judgments, solve problems, and control their behavior (Children's Defense Fund, 2005).

ISSUE STATEMENT

The profession vigorously pursues the attainment of the individual well-being of clients, and the achievement of the common good. Freedoms fundamental to the individual and society—freedom of speech, the press, and separation of church and state, the right to privacy, due process of the law, and freedom from self-incrimination and unreasonable search and seizures—are under attack at the local, state, and federal levels. A key question is how to balance the permissible exercise of government's executive power for the common good, with fundamental freedoms. Many political and religious leaders assert that the executive branch has authority to intervene to protect the safety interests of Americans, and may violate individual civil liberties and social justice goals to do so.

The assault on civil liberties also is demonstrated in the growing demands on censorship of books and other forms of cultural expression; restrictions on the rights of individuals to bring suit against the government and employers; persistent increases of police brutality, particularly in communities of color brought about, in part, by the absence of community oversight of law enforcement agencies; punishment of whistle blowers who expose government misconduct; and the criminalization of individual and social problems. These developments create a context conducive to the spread of harmful trends, as seen in racially or religiously motivated hate crimes, crimes against women, and restrictions on people's right to privacy. More than ever it is essential for social workers to take action to reverse these trends, in line with championing the cause of individual rights and social justice. If not, we risk losing the freedoms that social workers value and protect.

Although challenges to individual civil liberties and social justice are ever-present, the events of September 11, 2001, have spurred a significant imbalance in the concentration and abuse of government power, especially at the executive level. Those who criticize government policies are erroneously portrayed as "unpatriotic" or denigrating the "office of the presidency." Further, these events have led to concerted efforts to promote and protect the national safety through unconstitutional intrusions into the lives of persons in the United States. The far reaching powers of the Homeland Security Act (2002), the Patriot Act(s), and the myriad new "security measures" promoted by the executive branch of government are overly broad and in violation of civil liberty principles. For example, President George W. Bush authorized the National Security Agency "to eavesdrop without warrants on the international communications of Americans suspected of terrorist ties" (Lichtblau, 2008).

At minimum, setbacks to civil liberties and social justice continue in five major areas: (1) the criminal justice and penal systems; (2) access to justice, equal protection, and due process rights; (3) restrictions on First Amendment rights, particularly freedom of expression and the separation of church and state; (4) the right to privacy and its effects on social services; and (5) civil liberties and national security.

POLICY STATEMENT

NASW considers the protection of individual rights and the promotion of social justice essential to the preservation of our collective well-being as a society. Therefore, NASW urges social workers and other policymakers to focus on the following areas.

Criminal Justice and Civil Liberties

NASW supports

■ reduction of the disproportionate number of youth and adults of color within the criminal justice system;

■ expanding alternatives to detention and incarceration; and

■ development of an accessible, community-based, network of resources that affords preventive services, mental health assessments, and early treatment for both juvenile and adult offenders.

NASW opposes

■ the use of the death penalty as a method of punishment;

■ any legislation and prosecutorial discretion that permit children to be charged and punished under adult standards;

■ legislation that would permit no-knock entry by police into homes without a proper warrant, the use of preventive detention, or any other form of restraint that would erode constitutionally recognized Miranda rights against self-incrimination;

■ the use of mandatory sentencing requirements, particularly for first-time offenders.

Access to Justice, Equal Protection, and Due Process

NASW supports

■ the principle of habeas corpus, which safeguards people from unlawful imprisonment;

■ the establishment of civilian review boards to monitor police conduct and practices and to investigate allegations of excessive use of force by police officers;

■ restoration of full funding for comprehensive civil and criminal legal aid services;

■ the appointment of judges who are committed to the maintenance of civil liberties as guaranteed by the Constitution;

■ the appointment of judges who reflect the demographic diversity of the people of the United States, particularly women, people of color, people who are gay, lesbian, bisexual, and transgendered, and older adults;

■ the unimpeded application of individuals' civil rights through the courts in such areas as sexual harassment, employment discrimination, and housing bias.

Alternately, with regard to access to justice, equal protection, and due process, NASW opposes

■ threats to freedom of the press and due process;

■ mandatory drug and HIV testing on employees, prospective employees, and criminal defendants for actions with no direct relation either to drug abuse or HIV status, and which puts persons at risk of criminal prosecution;

■ any executive or legislative initiatives that would restrict the rights of individuals to file class action suits, either against the government or corporations.

First Amendment Rights

The right to dissent from prevailing opinions of the majority—in political and cultural arenas—is a fundamental principle of a democratic society. However, recent events have demonstrated that the existence of legislative or judicial rights does not guarantee their implementation by the executive branch of the government, particularly when the resistance of that branch is abetted by the judiciary. Therefore, NASW supports

■ the full implementation of existing civil rights legislation and its application to women, people of color, gays, lesbians, bisexual, and transgendered people;

■ the expansion of these rights to include immigrants and refugees, people who have mental illness (both hospitalized and in community settings), and recipients of public assistance and their families.

Furthermore, NASW supports

■ the right of all individuals to exercise their right to dissent responsibly and with respect for the opinions of others;

■ the right of all individuals arrested in the course of infraction of ordinary law to be fully informed of their rights;

■ pretrial treatment, trial activities, and sentencing on the basis of the province of the judicial system, following the constitutional principle of due process;

- the constitutional principle of separation of church and state;

- the right of workers to organize, to engage in collective bargaining to improve their working conditions, and to strike to draw attention to their grievances.

Using the same fundamental principle, NASW opposes

- the denial of funds from federal or state agencies, or access to services to which an individual would be otherwise entitled, on the basis of his or her participation in lawful protest and dissent;

- the arrest of any individual for the lawful exercise of his or her First Amendment rights of free speech and free assembly;

- the use of undue force by law enforcement officers;

- the alteration of the status of individuals participating in any acts of dissent, particularly in regard to employment, access to services, and other legal entitlements;

- the use of sanctions that discourage or punish whistle-blowers;

- the suspension of work or eligibility status of individuals before the institution of formal legal charges;

- all executive, legislative, or judicial actions that restrict freedom of speech, assembly, or cultural expression;

- all attempts to limit artistic freedom through the withholding of government grants (for example, National Endowment for the Arts);

- the imposition of any form of censorship by local authorities in regard to museum exhibits, library holdings, or school reading lists;

- any government restrictions on the rights of individuals or groups to protest policies or actions to which they are opposed;

- any abrogation of these rights by administrative regulation, legislation, or judicial action;

- the use of medical screenings to deny workers access to health benefits, imposition of mandatory drug testing in the workplace, and use of electronic or computer surveillance of employees to monitor job performance;

- all efforts to deny or retract these rights from any individuals or groups in the United States;

- the use of tax policy, administrative regulations, or distribution of government funds to support organized religion in any manner.

Right to Privacy and Effects on Social Services

NASW strongly supports the preservation of the constitutional right to privacy and entitlement to services, especially in health and human services settings, and strongly condemns the following:

- efforts by state legislatures, Congress, the executive branch of the federal government, or the courts to restrict access to information about abortion, contraception, or family planning, or to restrict access to any of these services; NASW specifically opposes the current ban on Medicaid funding for abortion and government efforts to erode and, ultimately, overturn the right of women to seek an abortion—established in *Roe v. Wade* (1973)—on the grounds that such actions constitute an unjustifiable invasion of privacy.

- mandatory HIV, DNA, or drug testing as a precondition for employment or the receipt of services for which an individual would be otherwise eligible.

- violation of the confidentiality of welfare case records of individuals who seek assistance because of drug or alcohol abuse or HIV-related illness.

- use of electronic information for purposes other than enhancement of services delivery to consumers.

- unannounced inspections of homes, made without warrants, at inappropriate times with the ostensible purpose of checking on continuing eligibility for public assistance or on the "desirability" of the home.

- use of degrading and humiliating methods to determine eligibility for public assistance or social services by investigators whose practices violate some of the basic principles of the profession.

■ state legislation to sterilize welfare recipients or deny them benefits if the number of children in a family exceeds a specified limit.

■ legislative or administrative actions that involve the imposition of punitive sanctions to deny the right of women on probation to become pregnant.

■ eviction of tenants determined undesirable in low-income public housing, without providing such tenants with clear expectations of residency, and administrative or judicial due process.

Civil Liberties and National Security

■ NASW supports government protection of the United States and its territories while upholding the constitutional rights of individuals, families, and communities.

■ NASW opposes overly broad use of executive power and electronic surveillance without court authorization.

REFERENCES

Brief backs habeas corpus reviews for detainees. (2007, October). *NASW News*, p. 5.

Children's Defense Fund. (2005). *The state of America's children: Yearbook, 2005.* Retrieved January 23, 2008, from http://cdf.convio .net/site/DocServer/Greenbook_2005.pdf ?docID=1741

Grunewald v. United States, 353 U.S. 391 (1957).

Guttmacher Institute. (2000, August) Title X 'gag rule' is formally repealed. *The Guttmacher Report on Public Policy*, 3(4). Retrieved January 16, 2008, from http://www.gutt macher.org/pubs/tgr/03/4/gr030413.html

Homeland Security Act of 2002, P.L. 107-296, 116 Stat. 2135.

Lichtblau, E. (2008, January 23). Democrats try to delay eavesdropping vote. *The New York Times*, p. A20.

Roe v. Wade, 410 U.S. 113 (1973).

Roper v. Simmons, 543 U.S. 551 (2005).

Rust v. Sullivan, 500 U.S. 173 (1991).

Policy statement approved by the NASW Delegate Assembly, August 2008. This policy statement supersedes the policy statement on Civil Liberties and Justice reconfirmed by the Delegate Assembly in 1999 and approved in 1993, which superseded the policy statement on Civil Liberties and Justice approved in 1967 and revised in 1971. The Delegate Assembly in 1999 also voted not to combine this policy with the policy on Drug Testing in the Workplace. For further information, contact the National Association of Social Workers, 750 First Street, NE, Suite 700, Washington, DC 20002-4241. Telephone: 202-408-8600 or 800-638-8799; e-mail: press@naswdc.org

Community Development

BACKGROUND

The development of strong communities has long been a tenet of the social work profession. A community where streets are safe to walk, the air and water are clean, housing is secure and affordable, human services and education are accessible, and community members work together toward common goals can be a source of strength and hope to its residents.

Early in the profession's history, Reynolds (1982) suggested that survival of the community depends on its ability to meet the social development and social welfare needs of its residents. It is social work's simultaneous focus on the interrelationship of the individual's and the community's development that sets it apart from other professions in the United States.

The emphases of community development have varied considerably in the past 40 years. In the 1950s the primary focus was on developing and coordinating agency direct services. In the 1960s, partially as a result of the civil rights movement and community action programs, emphasis shifted to community control and social reform. In the 1970s the focus was on the administration of agency programs in which citizen participation was mandated by federal legislation, such as the Economic Opportunity Act of 1964, the Model Cities Program, and Community Development Block Grants. In the 1980s and early 1990s, the focus was on helping communities survive economically and socially with decreased federal funding to state and local governments and the decline in the overall strength of the national economy. The present challenge is to advocate for meaningful social development policy and to engage in long-term planning while in a crisis management mode.

Recent decades have seen the development and dissemination of new practice models and theories of great relevance to community development (Mizrahi, 2001). Among these are neighborhood resiliency (Breton, 2001), the strength perspective (Saleebey, 1997), community empowerment (Cox, 2001; Lee, 1994), and collaboration and capacity-building strategies (Bowen, Martin, Mancini, & Nelson, 2000; Rothman, 2000). In addition social workers in the United States should be mindful of the rich community development literature by social workers and allied professionals throughout the world (Hokenstad, Khinduka, & Midgley, 1992).

Key Definitions

Community. According to Shaffer and Anundsen (1993), "a community is a dynamic whole that emerges when a group of people participate in common practices, depend on one another, identify themselves as part of something larger than the sum of their individual relationships, and commit themselves for the long term to their own, one another's and the group's well-being" (p. 10).

Community Development. Spergel (1987) referred to *community development* as "a deliberate intervention into the social network or structure of relations among people and organizations in a local area or interest community to facilitate social problem solving and improve patterns of service delivery and sociopolitical functioning" (p. 300). This definition was updated by Harrison (1995) in the most recent *Encyclopedia of Social Work* as

the process of working with communities to help them recognize how they can improve community life and welfare both in the present and in the future. . . . [C]ommunity development emphasizes both the achievement of specific goals and the development of less tangible qualitative aspects of social life in a community, such as the improvement of the capabilities—especially the leadership capabilities—of the residents. (p. 556)

Related Concepts

Community Building. Community building increases the community's capacity to effect positive change in community conditions by building, integrating, and connecting the community's social, human, physical, political, and economic resources through a planned and participatory process designed to meet community priorities and desired goals (Council on Accreditation of Services for Children and Families, 2001).

Community Practice. Community practice encompasses a wide scope of practice, ranging from grassroots organization and development to human services planning and coordination (Weil & Gamble, 1995).

The Role of Social Work, Social Workers, and NASW

The social work profession achieves the goal of community development by facilitating and participating with community stakeholders, residents, and all interacting institutions—political, economic, educational, religious, family, and the social welfare system—to find ways to improve the community's, and thereby the individual's, social, physical, and economic well-being. The methods used by social workers to reach the profession's goal include, but are not limited to, facilitating and participating in the community's work to identify its core values, belief systems, resources and strengths, and needs and problems; creating opportunities for community building or organizational mechanisms; helping the community to establish its goals, objectives, and strategies; collecting and analyzing data; studying alternatives; facilitating the community's selection of a course of action; facilitating and helping to implement this action; training and developing staff and community leadership; identifying

and developing funding sources; and establishing ongoing evaluations and feedback mechanisms.

These interventions are based on a profound respect for and understanding of cultural diversity and how it is expressed in multiple forms of social organizations and institutional life. Thus, social workers recognize the immense and historically unappreciated contributions, resilience, and strengths of diverse groups in our society.

NASW has a history of lobbying for policies and legislation that promote the development of strong communities characterized by equality and justice for all population groups. Undergraduate and graduate schools of social work education programs continue to be directed to instruct students in the area of community organization and development, keeping up to date with learning in this emerging, collaborative area (Council on Social Work Education, 2002).

The Context of Community

Social workers must help communities to continually renew themselves within the context of the following realities:

■ changing demographics, including the increasing presence and power of ethnic and other minority groups (including individuals with disabilities) and other disenfranchised and oppressed populations, the aging of the American population, the increasing diversity of the American family, the participation of women in work and political life, the need for medical and family leave, the need for youth development, and the removal of reintegration of incarcerated community members

■ the globalization of economic and information systems, including opportunities for empowerment; dangers of corporate control and exploitation; the often-ignored impact on local community life; and increasing partnerships between all nations in the global community, which are vital to the security of all people

■ environmental degradation, including urban sprawl, industrial pollution, inappropriate land use, toxic waste, and threats to the diversity of life on Earth

■ economic factors, including changes in the nature and function of work; the volatility of the economic market; the globally competitive nature of jobs and providing a living wage; the need for wages and policies that adequately support families; recognition of the interdependence of labor, management, and the worldwide economy; and unequal access to quality, affordable housing in integrated communities.

ISSUE STATEMENT

With communities undergoing significant economic, social, and environmental changes, community development is imperative to address these changes with positive, relevant solutions. Local communities and subpopulations (for example, farmers, women, black youths, Hispanic Americans, Native Americans, Asian Americans, elderly people and their caregivers, and adolescents) are directly and indirectly affected by world events, demographic changes, environmental changes, social attitudes, catastrophes, economic changes, and unique attributes of community life. These conditions can significantly affect the physical, economic, and social health of community residents.

Threats to community life include, but are not limited to, deterioration of neighborhoods; lack of affordable housing; homelessness; social disorganization; high crime rates; high rates of high school dropouts; underachievement among students enrolled in school from kindergarten through grade 12; increased domestic violence; unwanted teenage pregnancies; high infant mortality rates; increased racial tension; and increased discrimination against diverse groups, including people of color, gay and lesbian people, older people, and women. Instead of the community fostering social well-being, protection, and an enhanced quality of life, it has the potential either to foster disharmony and destructiveness or to allow them to prevail.

NASW believes that communities have inherent strengths and resources and the capacity to positively address their issues. "The goals of community development are to increase the community's capacity to create and sustain healthy families and to effect change in the community which improves the quality of life of families in the community and creates stronger and more stable communities in the long run" (Metropolitan Family Services, 2001). "[Community development's] viability and strength derives from diverse stakeholders who form alliances and further the community's interests. These stakeholders may include but are not limited to residents, associations, and institutions" (Council on Accreditation of Services for Children and Families, 2001, sec. S, p. 1). Community development "establishes a process that promotes people working together for a common purpose in groups and organizations. The process builds trust and sociability" (Naparstek & Dooley, 1997, p. 79). With community members' participation, focused planning, and commitment, communities can thrive in an increasingly complex and interdependent world.

Effective community social work practice is integrative, comprehensive, collaborative, participatory, strengths and asset focused, capacity building, sustainable, empowerment focused, focused on the present with an eye on the future, and inclusive. Effective community development demands flexibility. All social workers should have a foundation level of competence in working from "case" to "cause" (Schwartz, 1969), from individual needs to community issues. Furthermore, practitioners should have resource information and skills in making referrals to social work practitioners with advanced expertise in community development.

POLICY STATEMENT

In an effort to implement the social work goals and objectives of community development, NASW supports the following policy initiatives:

■ multiculturalism. NASW advocates the development and dissemination of best practices that support open communications, intergroup dialogue, and expanded educational curricula that honor and reflect the strengths of diverse groups in American society and promote participation of these groups within their communities.

- local, state, and federal legislation responsive to the needs of communities and diverse populations. NASW supports legislation related to supporting the self-identified need of communities and strategies that directly engage community residents in leadership and service provision.

- an increased federal government role in distributing funds more adequately to state and local governments. NASW supports renewed federal efforts in community development, social services, community empowerment, and coordination strategies. NASW believes that federal funding is crucial to supporting communities.

- the right of citizens to determine the destiny of their local communities to the fullest extent possible. Social workers should assist communities in gaining access to information and resources, develop local and participatory organizational mechanisms, and help citizens make socially responsible decisions and contributions.

- social work curricula related to community development. All social work students should be knowledgeable about the ways in which communities and populations with socioeconomic disadvantages can become more involved and competent in drawing on their strengths to solve problems and enhance the quality of their lives. Social work community developers should have a broad view of the community so that they can provide and develop local leadership and participate in the coordination of the multidisciplinary efforts of a variety of community groups.

- community development practice developed in conjunction with a strategic policy framework in which social workers can have an effect on both local and larger community interactivity. Clearly, social workers can learn from their efforts in partnering with citizens from low-income, minority communities through community development activities, which address community concerns within positive and systemic strategies.

As social workers practice locally within these principles and policies, they also must keep an eye to their responsibility as partners in the global community.

REFERENCES

Bowen, G. L., Martin, J. A., Mancini, J. A., & Nelson, J. P. (2000). Community capacity: Antecedents and consequences. *Journal of Community Practice, 8*(2), 1–21.

Breton, M. (2001). Neighborhood resiliency. *Journal of Community Practice, 9*(1), 21–36.

Council on Accreditation of Services for Children and Families. (2001). *Standards and self-study manual* (7th ed., version 1.0). New York: Author.

Council on Social Work Education. (2002). *Educational policy and accreditation standards.* Alexandria, VA: Author.

Cox, E. O. (2001). Community practice issues in the 21st century: Questions and challenges for empowerment-oriented practitioners. *Journal of Community Practice, 9*(1), 37–55.

Harrison, D. D. (1995). Community development. In R. L. Edwards (Ed.-in-Chief), *Encyclopedia of social work* (19th ed., Vol. 1, pp. 555–562). Washington, DC: NASW Press.

Hokenstad, M. C., Kinduka, S. K., & Midgley, J. (Eds.). (1992). *Profiles in international social work.* Washington, DC: NASW Press.

Lee, J. (1994). *The empowerment approach to social work practice.* New York: Columbia University Press.

Metropolitan Family Services. (2001, October). *Community development model.* Unpublished manuscript.

Mizrahi, T. (2001). The status of community organizing in 2001: Community practice context, complexities, contradictions, and contributions. *Research on Social Work Practice, 11*(2), 176–189.

Naparstek, A. J., & Dooley, D. (1997). Community building. In R. L. Edwards (Ed.-in-Chief), *Encyclopedia of social work* (19th ed., 1997 Suppl., pp. 77–89). Washington, DC: NASW Press.

Reynolds, B. C. (1982). *Between client and community: A study in responsibility in social casework.* Silver Spring, MD: National Association of Social Workers. (Original work published in 1934)

Rothman, J. (2000). Collaborative self-help community development: When is the strategy warranted? *Journal of Community Practice, 7*(2), 89–104.

Saleebey, D. (1997). Community development, group empowerment and individual resilience. In D. Saleebey (Ed.)., *The strengths perspective in social work practice* (2nd ed., pp. 199–216). New York: Longman.

Schwartz, W. (1969). Private troubles and public issues: One job or two? In *Social Welfare Forum: Proceedings of the National Conference on Social Work* (pp. 22–43). New York: Columbia University Press.

Shaffer, C. R., & Anundsen, K. (1993). *Creating community anywhere*. New York: Tarcher/Perigree.

Spergel, I. A. (1987). Community development. In A. Minahan (Ed.-in-Chief), *Encyclopedia of social work* (18th ed., Vol. 1, pp. 299–308). Silver Spring, MD: NASW Press.

Weil, M. O., & Gamble, D. N. (1995). Community practice models. In R. L. Edwards (Ed.-in-Chief), *Encyclopedia of social work* (19th ed., Vol. 1, pp. 577–594). Washington, DC: NASW Press.

Policy statement approved by the NASW Delegate Assembly, August 2002. This statement supersedes the policy statement on Community Development approved by the Delegate Assembly in 1993. For further information, contact the National Association of Social Workers, 750 First Street, NE, Suite 700, Washington, DC 20002-4241. Telephone: 202-408-8600; e-mail: press@naswdc.org

Confidentiality and Information Utilization

BACKGROUND

Problems involved in the use of information privacy, confidentiality, and privileged communication have commanded increased attention in both the public and private sectors of U.S. society in recent years. The emergence and rapid expansion of information and communication technology have made the development of a strong information policy a primary concern for social workers. This expansion has forced a reckoning with the fact that there is no longer a private domain. The availability of cellular telephones, answering machines, handheld personal computers, and convenience store facsimile machines requires that social workers specify through a policy statement how information will be protected within the bounds of professional relationships. Officially sanctioned government invasions of privacy, especially those resulting from 9/11 and the Homeland Security legislation, insurance company exchange of data, credit blacklisting, and countless other incursions into the personal affairs of virtually every citizen are cause for alarm. The danger of even greater abuses, deliberate or inadvertent, in the collection, maintenance, and use of personal data by government and industry poses a threat of unprecedented dimensions to Americans' basic civil liberties. Yet it is acknowledged that there is a need to transfer information, with the informed consent of the client, between and among professionals and professional agencies for the purposes of treatment and payment for services.

Issues of confidentiality and privacy are even more important now that the patient or client's record—which once consisted of writing on pieces of paper—may consist of thousands of electronic bits of information that include written, audio, and visual records and links to other files within the agency or to other locations and may also include personal, medical, financial, and other types of data.

The confidential nature of communications between social workers and their clients has been a cardinal principle of the social work profession from its earliest years and, indeed, is the framework of the social worker–client relationship. Legislative protection for social work information in adoption and juvenile court records dates back half a century: The Social Security Act of 1935 (P.L. 74-271), as amended in 1939, required state public assistance plans to "provide safeguards which restrict the use or disclosure of information concerning applicants and recipients to purposes directly connected with the administration of [the program]" [Title IV, section 502(a)(8)]. The Office of Vocational Rehabilitation issued regulations during the 1940s requiring similar safeguards. There are specific federal statutes in the practices related to alcohol and drug treatment (42 U.S.C. §§ 290dd-2 and 42 C.F.R. pt. 2). In 1975, when special education became a federal mandate under the Education for All Handicapped Children Act of 1975 (P.L. 94-142), the first federal requirements concerning students with special needs and pupil records, including confidentiality and parental consent, were codified. These mandates were expanded under the Individuals with Disabilities Education Act (P.L. 90-247) and were reauthorized under the Individuals with Disabilities Education Act Amendments of 1997 (P.L. 105-17). With the advent of the HIV/AIDS epidemic, many states have enacted statutes protecting the confidentiality of individual's HIV/AIDS records and providing civil and criminal penalties for unlawful release of information (see, for example, N.J. Stat. 26: 5C-7ff, 2001). Legislation, regulations, and guidelines dealing with sundry health, welfare, and educational programs in varying degrees have recognized the need for limiting and safeguarding the collection and use of personal data.

In both public and private agency practice, confidentiality has been a continual concern. Although pressures toward gathering, preserving, and, at times, revealing personal information are greater in the public sector, both public and private agencies have had to contend with the same basic issues and dilemmas: How is personal privacy to be balanced against the public's need for information, the need for accountability, and, at times, the need for protection? How does this translate to services by social workers in schools who work with students who are pregnant? How is the client's privacy to be maintained when there is a need to share information with third parties, obtain consultation, or otherwise divulge information in conjunction with professional purposes related to the client's interest? To what extent must the protection of individual privacy be balanced against the needs of research, the development of knowledge, and teaching?

Many of the same issues and dilemmas are present in private practice, although external pressures for sharing information are likely to be less on private practitioners than on agency practitioners. In schools, hospitals, and agencies in which there is a team approach to treatment, disclosure of information frequently is critical to treatment planning and individualized educational programs. Insurance carriers and managed care firms often demand detailed diagnostic and other personal data in the name of accountability, private practitioners as well as agency social workers are often subpoenaed to testify and reveal clients' confidences in divorce and custody proceedings and in other domestic lawsuits, and law enforcement agencies occasionally seek information from case records. In both public and private settings, social workers and other human services professionals must deal with the question of when legal protections of privacy—including statutory requirements for privileged communications—must yield to other legal requirements

such as protecting children from abuse or third parties from intended harm. The social work professional has a moral, ethical, and legal obligation to protect the confidentiality of clients.

In *Jaffee v. Redmond* (1996) the U.S. Supreme Court recognized a social worker–client privilege in the federal court system, protecting the confidentiality of patient and client communications to licensed therapists. Some federal legislation specifies confidentiality requirements for federal programs (such as Veterans Administration Medical Centers), other legislation contains requirements for programs that receive federal funding (such as substance abuse and education programs), and still other federal legislation specifies confidentiality requirements that states must include in their programs as a condition for receiving federal grants. The federal Health Insurance Portability and Accountability Act of 1996 (P.L. 104-191) has detailed regulations about confidentiality and informed consent for an individual's health information maintained by a wide range of health care providers and insurers, which comes into effect in 2003 or 2004, depending on the size of the health care provider (see 45 C.F.R. pts. 160, 164). Specific regulations for psychotherapy notes are included in these regulations.

The *NASW Code of Ethics* (NASW, 1999) provides strict guidelines for protection of confidentiality, informed consent, and maintenance and security of records [see 1.07, 1.08, 2.02, 2.05(c), 3.04(c, d), 3.09(d), and 5.02(e–m)].

ISSUE STATEMENT

In the most basic sense, the issue of confidentiality and use of information pits the individual's right to privacy against society's need to know. The issue involves an individual's and society's needs to ensure accountability; to protect other individuals; and to amass information for a variety of social welfare needs, such as disease control, research, and community planning. The social worker's central role as the recipient and custodian of personal information places a particularly heavy responsibility on the social work profession and on individual practitioners to know and keep abreast of legal requisites and then to weigh consequences, balance equities, and assume responsibility for actions taken.

By the end of the 20th century, social workers, agency administrators, clients, and legislators were beginning to be educated about the implications of the expansion of the world of technology and its beneficial and harmful potentials. Social workers must continue to be mindful of the threat to confidentiality posed by the development of electronic data processing and storage and the real-time availability of information through e-mail, chat rooms, and other communication technology. Precautions that once sufficed to ensure the safety of agency case records are no longer sufficient when correspondence is sent by telephone facsimile machines and data are fed into computer banks or linked to other information systems beyond the social worker's and client's control. The social work profession must reexamine its practices with regard to gathering information and maintaining, sharing, and using case records.

The profession also must reassess its policies and ethical base regarding privacy issues. It must consider the need to assume a more vigorous and active posture in this area, including the assumption of new advocacy roles. In addition, social workers must be aware of the protections and constraints on patient or client confidentiality, which may be legally imposed. Every state has extended the protection of statutory privilege to social work professionals, although what communications are protected and which social workers are included vary (Dickson, 1998). The privilege may be waived by the patient or client, as the legally recognized holder of the privilege, or may be legally required to be breached, as in the case of child abuse and at times to prevent harm to a foreseeable victim. Privacy laws vary by state, and it is critical for social workers to be aware of these laws and changes in them. Some laws apply to the federal government, such as the Privacy Act of 1974, which makes unauthorized release a federal offense, and some federal laws apply to records in specific settings, such as the Family Educational Rights and Privacy Act of 1974, which protects the confidentiality of student records in schools and colleges that receive federal funding. The confidentiality of other records maintained by state and local governments may be protected by other statutes and regulations in specific locales.

In addition, social workers are constrained to some degree by privileged communication. Whereas confidentiality is a professional mandate, privileged communication is a legal issue in which a client's right to privacy is protected by state law. Many courts have held that the right belongs to the client and that only the client can waive the protection (Perlman, 1988; Schwartz, 1989). Privacy laws, however, vary by state statute, and it behooves social workers to be familiar with the applicable laws in their states. Whereas the federal Privacy Act of 1974 renders unauthorized release of an individual's personal records maintained by the federal government a federal offense, records maintained by state and local governments are not governed by this act. Rather, they are governed by other statutes and regulations in specific locales. The enactment of the Health Insurance Portability and Accountability Act of 1996 (HIPAA) by Congress mandates the establishment of standards for the privacy of individually identifiable health information. The privacy rule became effective on April 14, 2001. Most health plans and health care providers that are covered must comply with the new requirement by April 2003. The privacy rule establishes a federal floor of safeguards to protect the confidentiality of medical information. State laws that provide stronger privacy protection will continue to apply over and above the new federal privacy standards.

POLICY STATEMENT

NASW policy addresses four sectors: (1) the government–regulatory agency–business sector, which includes the several levels of government, law enforcement agencies, insurance carriers, and other institutions and systems that collect, maintain, and use personal data banks; (2) the public and private social agency sector; (3) the individual social work practitioner; and (4) social work in schools. In many other areas of broad federal involvement, other than health, education, and welfare (for example, census data and tax return information from the Internal Revenue Service), restrictions are placed on usage and disclosure of personal information. NASW should be a support for timely member compliance to HIPAA and advocate that the rule protects patient privacy as intended without harming access to quality care and maintaining benefits.

Government–Regulatory Agency–Business Sector

For government units, agencies, and institutions that use automated personal data, the principles of a code of fair information practice should be adopted along the lines recommended by the Advisory Committee on Automated Personal Data Systems (U.S. Department of Health, Education, and Welfare, 1973) and HIPAA. Therefore, NASW recommends that, as appropriate, legislation should be enacted, regulations promulgated, and policies adopted to ensure the following:

■ No secret personal data record-keeping systems should be permitted.

■ Individuals must be able to learn what information is maintained about them and how it is used.

■ Information obtained about individuals for one purpose must not be used or made available for other purposes without the individual's explicit informed consent.

■ Individuals must have the right to and be provided with an approved process to enable them to correct or amend a record of identifiable information about them.

■ Efforts must be made to curb the proliferation of universal identifiers, including the use of social security numbers, whenever not currently mandated by law.

■ Any organization creating, maintaining, using, or disseminating records of identifiable personal data must ensure the reliability of the data for their intended use and provide standardized procedures for handling of the data to prevent misuse and maintain confidentiality.

Public and Private Social Welfare Agencies

NASW recommends that each social welfare agency develop and disseminate policies and guides that will cover at least the following 10 items:

1. what information is to be sought and from whom

2. what information is to be recorded and in what form

3. who has access to information about cases and under what circumstances

4. what is required to obtain informed consent before release or re-release of patient or client records (see, for example, 42 C.F.R. §§ 2.31ff, which sets forth the requirements for informed consent for the release of confidential information in federally funded substance abuse programs)

5. means for ensuring the accuracy of records and for noting differences

6. plans for disposing of records

7. social workers' responsibility to advise the client of the limits to confidentiality when more than one client is present, given that confidentiality by other clients cannot be guaranteed by the social workers

8. when and how the social worker has a "duty to warn" regarding danger to the public (refer to the *Tarasoff v. Regents of the University of California*, 1976, decision), including guidance about handling HIV-positive clients' information

9. in-service training to help social workers and other agency staff understand the policy *and learn how to address the dilemmas that arise when clients' wishes, needs, and safety* are jeopardized

10. a written agreement signed by all employees to protect the confidentiality of clients.

Certain kinds of data, such as political beliefs or opinions, should not be recorded at all, even if they are assumed to have some tangential relevance to the case. Process recordings, if used for teaching purposes, should be promptly disposed of—either summarized or expunged—as soon as they have served their purpose. In addition, the agency has the obligation to ensure that the client understands what is being asked, to determine why and to what uses will be made of the information, and to ensure informed consent for specific purposes and to specific parties in situations in which the client signs a release of information. Clients also must be helped to understand the possible consequences of refusing to give information required by government agencies under law. Therefore, NASW recommends the following:

■ Information about an individual client should not be shared with any other individual or agency without the individual's authorized informed consent unless state laws require the release of information, and in that case, the client will be informed about the legal process and what is to be released. Also, as required by NASW's *Code of Ethics*, concerns for the safety of a client must also be taken into account when the client does not want the information shared.

■ Case records and related files should not be transferred to another agency or individual without the authorized informed consent of the client or, when professionally appropriate and when such transfer will not cause harm to the client, the client's guardian or legal agent, and then only under rules requiring that the receiving agency provides the same guarantee of confidentiality as the transferring agency.

■ The concept of informed consent must be clearly explained to the client. The explanation and accompanying written statement must include the length of time for which the document is in effect, the person or agency and address to whom written material will be sent, and the type of records or information that will be shared. The client must be informed in writing of the right to have copies of any written information shared with another agency or professional.

■ Case records should be maintained in a safe and secure area and, when computerized,

appropriate security measures for access should be developed (see NASW, 1991).

Social Work Practitioners

Whether as independent or agency-based practitioners, social workers should have available for all new clients written information about records, release of records, information required by managed care and other insurers if applicable, and the legal and ethical limits of confidentiality or privileged communication and should ensure that clients understand these issues. Social workers should become familiar with HIPAA and plan to be HIPAA compliant by April 2003. The following five client principles should guide social workers:

1. Clients should be used as the primary source of information about themselves.

2. Only information that is demonstrably related to the solution of clients' problems should be received, recorded, or released.

3. Clients will be fully informed about the implications of sharing personal information, including the ethical and legal obligations of the social worker to respect privacy and protect the confidentiality and legal constraints and limitations that impinge on both the client and the social worker.

4. Clients' informed and authorized consent will be a prerequisite to transmitting information to or requesting it from third parties (see previous section on Public and Private Social Welfare Agencies).

5. Clients will be apprised of the kind of records maintained by the social worker or agency and should have the right to verify the accuracy of the records personally.

Social Workers in Schools

School social workers must be especially vigilant about the concepts of privileged communication and confidentiality, especially in the areas of special education and section 504 of the Americans with Disabilities Act of 1990 (P.L. 101-336). Whereas schools do not specifically talk about records compiled by social workers or verbal exchanges of communication by social workers, most school social workers work on multidisciplinary teams in which information sharing is expected to plan programming and assess progress. Furthermore, written reports, which are mandated to determine whether a student is eligible for special education, are open for review by those with responsibility for the student's education. It is incumbent on the school social worker to regularly inform parents of their children's right to a free, appropriate education; of parental rights to informed consent when they are asked to release records or agree to educational programming as written in an individualized educational plan; and of parental rights to review records and request removal of information that they do not believe to be educationally relevant.

Social workers in schools must also recognize that although the student is the identified client, the parents of a student younger than age 18 have certain rights, unless the student is an emancipated minor. This presents social workers in schools with a dual client situation, which can be especially complex if the student is pregnant and chooses not to inform her parents.

School social workers must be familiar with federal and state laws as well as the local education agency's policies and procedures for reporting child abuse and neglect and laws of confidentiality regarding HIV/AIDS and drugs and alcohol. School social workers are bound by a duty to warn if there is a danger to the student or another individual.

REFERENCES

Americans with Disabilities Act of 1990, P.L. 101-336, 104 Stat. 327 (1991).

Dickson, D. T. (1998). *Confidentiality and privacy in social work*. New York: Free Press.

Education for All Handicapped Children Act of 1975, P.L. 94-142, 89 Stat. 773.

Family Educational Rights and Privacy Act of 1974, 20 U.S.C. § 1232g.

Health Insurance Portability and Accountability Act of 1996, P.L. 104-191, 110 Stat. 1936.

Individuals with Disabilities Education Act, P.L. 90-247, 81 Stat. 804 (1968).

Individuals with Disabilities Education Act Amendments of 1997, P.L. 105-17.

Jaffee v. Redmond, 518 U.S. 1, 116 S. Ct. 1923, 135 L.Ed.2d 337 (1996).

National Association of Social Workers. (1991). *NASW guidelines on the private practice of clinical social work*. Washington, DC: NASW Press.

National Association of Social Workers. (1999). *NASW code of ethics*. Washington, DC: Author.

Perlman, G. L. (1988). Mastering the law of privileged communication: A guide for social workers. *Social Work, 33*, 425–429.

Privacy Act of 1974, 5 U.S.C. § 552A.

Schwartz, G. (1989). Confidentiality revisited. *Social Work, 34*, 223–226.

Social Security Act of 1935, P.L. 74-271, 49 Stat. 620.

Tarasoff v. Regents of the University of California, 551 P.2d 334, 131 Cal. Rptr. 14 (1976).

U.S. Department of Health, Education, and Welfare. (1973). *Records, computers and the right of citizens* (Report of the Secretary's Advisory Committee on Automated Personal Data System, DHEW Publication No. OS 73-94). Washington, DC: U.S. Government Printing Office.

Policy statement approved by the NASW Delegate Assembly, August 2002. This statement supersedes the policy statement on Confidentiality and Information Utilization approved by the Delegate Assembly in 1993. For further information, contact the National Association of Social Workers, 750 First Street, NE, Suite 700, Washington, DC 20002-4241. Telephone: 202-408-8600; e-mail: press@naswdc.org

Crime Victim Assistance

BACKGROUND

During the 1970s the harmful effects of crime and the often insensitive treatment of crime victims and witnesses by police, prosecutors, and judges were acknowledged by individual crime victims, research studies, and advocacy groups. Crime victimization studies identified a large gap between the number of crimes reported to police and the number of self-identified crime victims (Kilpatrick, Saunders, Veronen, Best, & Von, 1987). A major reason for not reporting a crime is fear of involvement with the criminal justice system. Domestic violence, sexual assault, and hate crime survivors often described their encounters with the criminal justice system as a "revictimization."

Crime victim assistance and advocacy programs are being developed to respond to the criminal justice system's historic lack of concern for victims. The criminal justice system began to recognize that by addressing victims' problems resulting from the crime, victims were more likely to work with police. This partnership hopes to increase the quality of evidence and lead to more convictions.

In 1984 Congress passed the Victims of Crime Act (P.L. 98-473), which established strong federal leadership in victim assistance. The act provided funding to qualified victim assistance and state compensation programs in all 50 states. Passed in 1994 and reauthorized in 2000, the Violence Against Women Act (P.L. 103-322) provides federal funding for shelters for battered women, sexual assault programs, and a variety of other measures to combat violence against women. All states have passed a "Victims' Bill of Rights," and 32 have enacted constitutional amendments requiring certain services for crime victims. The rights of crime victims vary from state to state. For example, elderly people may be compensated as a result of crimes that do not result in physical injury. In general crime victims' rights include the following:

■ the right to notification about the stages and proceedings in the criminal justice process, other legal remedies, parole proceedings, and the offender's release

■ the right to be heard through a victim impact statement and to provide information to the probation department conducting an investigation on the impact of the crime

■ the right to attend and participate in the criminal justice proceedings

■ the right to protection from intimidation and harassment, consideration of the safety of the victims and their families when bail is being set, and a safe waiting area before and during court proceedings

■ the right to confidentiality of records and a speedy trial

■ the right to general compensation and restitution for the crime, including prompt return of personal property seized as evidence

■ the right to the offenders' profits from the sale of stories of their crimes

■ the right to have expenses for a sexual assault forensic examination and counseling about AIDS and HIV infection and testing paid for by a law enforcement agency.

Research has shown that in states with strong victims' rights crime victims are more likely to participate in the criminal justice process, have better perceptions of the criminal justice system, and express better overall satisfaction with efforts taken on their behalf by agents of the system, including staff who assist victims and witnesses (Kilpatrick, Beatty, &

Howley, 1998). Victim assistance programs provide a full range of services that victims may need during the criminal justice process, from crime scene assistance to postsentencing help (Tomz & McGillis, 1997). Services for victims are provided by criminal justice institutions and by local community-based agencies. Criminal justice institutions may include local law enforcement agencies, prosecutors' offices, probation departments, and state correctional institutions. Community-based agencies include domestic violence and sexual assault programs, as well as organizations that assist all victims of crime. Community support groups also may be available to assist victims and their families. Two examples of such support groups are Parents of Murdered Children and Mothers Against Drunk Driving.

The Office for Victims of Crime (OVC) in the U.S. Department of Justice administers two major formula grant programs: Crime Victims Compensation (CVC) and Victims of Crime Assistance (VOCA; U.S. Department of Justice, 1998). The CVC program provides monetary assistance directly to victims to reimburse them for expenses incurred as a result of the crime. Reimbursement may be for medical expenses, mental health, loss of wages, and funeral expenses. Other expenses that may be covered are eyeglasses and other corrective lenses, dental services and devices, and prosthetic devices. Laws governing compensation vary from state to state, with each state responsible for establishing limitations on awards and guidelines and procedures to apply for benefits. Victims must report the crime to the police, cooperate with law enforcement and prosecutors, and apply for compensation within the stated time frame to be eligible for compensation, whether or not the offender is caught or convicted of the crime. Victims also must show that they did not in any way contribute to the crime.

The VOCA program provides financial support to community-based programs that provide services to crime victims. VOCA funds are allocated to each state and then competitively granted to local organizations. Recipients of VOCA funds include domestic violence shelters, rape crisis centers, crime victim centers, and statewide advocacy groups.

One of the more empirically grounded, widespread, yet initially controversial victim services is that of victim–offender mediation (VOM). VOM is the oldest and most internationally developed expression of restorative justice, a movement that elevates the role of crime victims in the justice process, offers a broader range of services to empower and serve crime victims, holds offenders directly accountable to the people and communities they have violated, provides opportunities for offenders to repair the harm they have caused, and engages the community in the processes of serving crime victims and holding offenders accountable (Umbreit, 2001). Based on ancient values that are deeply rooted in most indigenous cultures and in Judeo–Christian culture, restorative justice polices and practices are being developed in virtually all states, numerous European countries, South Africa, Japan, the South Pacific, and Israel. Social workers, both practitioners and scholars, have played active leadership roles in this international movement since its inception in the early 1980s (Umbreit, Greenwood, Coates, & Bradshaw, 2000).

In the early years of the crime victim–offender mediation movement, many victim advocates were skeptical. Today, numerous national and local victim services coalitions and agencies, including the National Organization for Victim Assistance, are active stakeholders in the movement. The Center for Restorative Justice and Peacemaking at the School of Social Work, University of Minnesota, has developed new victim-sensitive training materials and videotapes and provides training and technical assistance.

The Texas chapter of NASW has developed materials to promote professional awareness and training for social workers on the impact of violent crime and on crime victims' rights and services.

ISSUE STATEMENT

The social work profession has long been concerned with issues of crime and violence. Social workers' efforts often have targeted prevention and rehabilitation of offenders, but it is only recently that the profession and society as a whole have turned their attention to the effect of violent crime on victims and their families and communities.

The number of people affected by violent crime each year is significant. An estimated five of six people will become victims of either completed or attempted crimes at least once in their lives (Koppel, 1987). In 1998 an estimated one in seven U.S. residents age 12 and older were victims of crime (Rennison, 1999). On average, in each year between 1992 and 1998, 2.6 million of the 10.2 million victims of violent crime in the United States were injured in the victimization (Bureau of Justice Statistics, 2001). The National Violence Against Women Survey estimated that 5.9 million incidents of physical assault against women occur annually, with approximately 76 percent of those incidents perpetrated by current or former husbands, cohabiting partners, or dates. In contrast, men are more likely to be assaulted by strangers (Tjaden & Thoennes, 1998).

Each statistic represents a story of how violence changed the life of the victim, along with his or her family and friends. Victims of violent crimes suffer serious biopsychosocial, social, and economic injuries that may continue long after their physical injuries have healed. For example, the link between violent crime and posttraumatic stress disorder has been well established (Ochberg, 1988).

In their quest to transform themselves from crime victims to crime survivors, individuals may need a variety of social and mental health services at various times in their lives. Therefore, the likelihood of victims' contact with professional social workers is extremely high, whatever the practice setting.

To better assist these clients, all social workers should have basic knowledge of the effect of crime on individuals, the rights of crime victims, and the services and resources available to help them through the criminal justice system and to help them heal from the effects of the crime. Victims' reactions to violent crimes may vary by the type of crime committed; the crime scene; the perpetrator; and individual victim characteristics such as racial and ethnic background, age, gender, sexual orientation, immigration status, and disability. It is essential for social workers to be aware of cul-tural considerations when working with crime victims.

The crime victim assistance field has undergone rapid growth in the past 30 years. Policies and services for crime victims have emerged as an important and growing field of human services practice. Once considered radical, laws against domestic violence, sexual assault, and driving while under the influence of drugs or alcohol are now institutionalized in public policy arenas, along with social services such as shelters for battered women, rape crisis centers, and support groups for victims of drunk driving.

Public funding has facilitated the expansion of private nonprofit agencies and encouraged local and state criminal justice institutions to maintain units of professional crime victim assistants or advocates. Social workers who wish to enter this field will find that their generalist social work competencies—skills, knowledge, values, and abilities—provide an excellent foundation for crime victim assistance work (Danis, 2002).

Social workers who choose to practice in this setting may be at risk of secondary trauma. Listening to the stories of traumatized clients may cause vicarious trauma symptoms or compassion fatigue (Figley, 1995), which may lead to burnout, high agency turnover rates, and inconsistent services to clients.

POLICY STATEMENT

■ NASW encourages all professional social workers to practice universal screening for clients of all ages to determine whether the client has been victimized, or is currently being victimized, to provide better services and support.

■ NASW supports policy advocacy on local, state, and national levels to promote assistance for victims of crime and to ensure their safety and recovery from the crime.

■ NASW supports social work advocacy for individual victims of crime in overcoming the government obstacles, barriers, and loopholes that may complicate victims' efforts to obtain needed services or prevent them from obtaining services.

- NASW supports increased funding to assist crime victims, particularly underserved populations and historically oppressed groups that may be targets of hate crimes.

- NASW encourages all social workers to become familiar with the rights of crime victims and the services available to victims and their families.

- NASW supports continuing education about the field of crime victim assistance through activities such as workshops at conferences and information disseminated through the *NASW News* and chapter newsletters.

- NASW encourages schools of social work to develop curricula to prepare students to identify victims of crime in their chosen field of practice, understand the biopsychosocial effects of victimization, and acquire knowledge of services available to crime victims in their particular state. Furthermore, NASW supports the development of field placements for students to gain experience in this area.

- NASW supports research on the effects of crime on victims, including the psychological and financial consequences and the effects on secondary victims such as family, friends, and social services providers. NASW also supports research on the effectiveness of interventions to help victims heal from their trauma.

- NASW encourages social workers who offer victim services and referrals to be sensitive to differences in age; family supports; race and ethnicity; cultural, religious, or spiritual issues; immigrant status; sexual orientation and gender roles; disabling conditions; and attitudes toward trauma resolution, death and grieving, and the criminal justice system.

- NASW supports restorative justice practices as a preferable alternative to retributive justice. Providing opportunities for victims to share the impact of crime allows others to gain an understanding of the human consequences of crime. This process may reduce crime and achieve greater peace in communities. NASW encourages social workers to exercise extreme caution in responding to requests for mediation for crimes of severe violence.

- NASW strongly discourages routine use of mediation in domestic violence cases, by either family mediation or victim–offender mediation practitioners.

- NASW supports agency policies that are sensitive to the risk of secondary trauma for social workers and other advocates who work with victims of crime.

- NASW supports efforts to gain recognition for all same-sex and heterosexual domestic partners of crime victims by compensation and other assistance programs. All domestic partners should be entitled to the same benefits as married heterosexual partners.

REFERENCES

Bureau of Justice Statistics. (2001). *Injuries from violent crime, 1992–98*. Washington, DC: U.S. Department of Justice.

Danis, F. (2002). How victim assistance experts rate social work competencies for professional practice. *Professional Development: The International Journal of Continuing Social Work Education, 5*(2), 28–37.

Figley, C. R. (1995). *Compassion fatigue: Secondary traumatic stress disorders from treating the traumatized.* New York: Brunner/Mazel.

Kilpatrick, D. G., Beatty, D., & Howley, S. S. (1998). *The rights of crime victims—Does legal protection make a difference?* [Research in Brief] [Online]. Available: http://www.ojp.usdoj.gov/bjs/cvictgen.htm

Kilpatrick, D. G., Saunders, B. E., Veronen, L. J., Best, C. L., & Von, J. M. (1987). Criminal victimization: Lifetime prevalence, reporting to police, and psychological impact. *Crime and Delinquency, 33*(4), 479–489.

Koppel, H. (1987). *Lifetime likelihood of victimization.* Washington, DC: U.S. Department of Justice, Bureau of Justice Statistics.

Ochberg, F. (Ed.). (1988). *Posttraumatic therapy and victims of violence.* New York: Brunner/Mazel.

Rennison, C. M. (1999). *Criminal victimization 1998: Changes 1997–1998.* Washington, DC: U.S. Department of Justice, Bureau of Justice Statistics.

Tjaden, P., & Thoennes, N. (1998). *Prevalence, incidence, and consequences of violence against women: Findings from the National Violence Against Women Survey.* Washington, DC: National Institute for Justice and Centers for Disease Control and Prevention.

Tomz, J. E., & McGillis, D. (1997). *Serving crime victims and witnesses* (2nd ed.). Washington, DC: U. S. Department of Justice, National Institute of Justice.

Umbreit, M. S. (2001). *The handbook of victim–offender mediation: A guide for practice and research.* San Francisco: Jossey-Bass.

Umbreit, M. S., Greenwood, G., Coates, R., & Bradshaw, W. (2000). *Crime mediation collection.* Washington, DC: U.S. Department of Justice, Office for Victims of Crime.

U.S. Department of Justice, Office of Justice Programs. (1998). *Office for Victims of Crime fact sheet.* Washington, DC: Author.

Victims of Crime Act, P.L. 98-473, 98 Stat. 4792 (1984).

Violence Against Women Act, P.L. 103-322, 108 Stat. 1902 (1994, 2000).

Policy statement approved by the NASW Delegate Assembly, August 2002. For further information, contact the National Association of Social Workers, 750 First Street, NE, Suite 700, Washington, DC 20002-4241. Telephone: 202-408-8600; e-mail: press@naswdc.org

Cultural and Linguistic Competence in the Social Work Profession

BACKGROUND

Elements of cultural competence have received wide and far-ranging attention in social work literature. The discussion places major emphasis on the effective use of knowledge and skill application within an ecological context and transactional dimensions of motivation, skill, and empowerment (Breton, 1994). Cultural competence implies a heightened consciousness and analytical grasp of racism, sexism, ethnocentrism, class conflict, and cross-cultural and intracultural diversity. Furthermore, cultural competence contributes to efforts to address racial and ethnic disparities in health and mental health status and the disproportionate confinement in restrictive settings in the child welfare, juvenile justice, and criminal justice systems.

American society is constantly undergoing major demographic changes that heighten the diversity issues confronting social workers. The 2000 Census reported that the largest single ethnic minority group is the Hispanic population, who comprise 13 percent of the U.S. population (U.S. Census Bureau, 2001). Continued immigration and current birth rates are the factors propelling this growth and change in America's racial and ethnic makeup. Immigration to the United States by peoples from Asia, Eastern Europe, Russia, Africa, and Latin America can be expected to intensify the diversity social workers will witness in their practice settings. By 2050, population projections estimate that only 50 percent of the U.S. population will be "white alone, not Hispanic" (U.S. Census Bureau, 2004).

One dimension of cultural competence is the capacity to communicate. In the United States, the number of people for whom English is not the primary language has grown. The 2000 Census documented more than 380 language groups spoken in this country. More significantly, more than 18 percent of all families speak a language other than English in their households. Although many of these individuals are also fluent in English, 11.9 million people are linguistically isolated, meaning they do not speak English well or not at all (U.S. Census Bureau, 2003). As the country becomes more linguistically diverse, linguistic competence within the social work profession becomes more critical for effective service delivery. *Linguistic competence* is "the capacity of an organization and its personnel to communicate effectively, and convey information in a manner that is easily understood by diverse audiences including persons of limited English proficiency, those who have low literacy skills or are not literate, and individuals with disabilities" (Goode & Jones, 2003, p. 1). Individual practitioners and organizations are challenged to develop the capacity to use the verbal, written, and multimedia communications in a manner that supports effective practice.

Culture is not just an attribute of racial and ethnic groups. Cultural differences are often made manifest by belief systems founded in religions. The values, beliefs, and practices of particular faith groups can be the primary source of cultural identity and create a specific worldview that affects every component of a person's life. In addition, people who identify with a sexual orientation different from the dominant society also represent distinct cultural groups. Gay, lesbian, bisexual, *omnisexual* (people having or open to many forms of sexual expression), transgender, queer and questioning women, men, and youths have established their own cultural identity and demand fair treatment and inclusion in all aspects of American life. Social workers of all sexual orientations must be prepared to bridge the crosscultural experiences of people of different sexual orientations.

Another example includes people with disabilities who have established a cultural identity that demands more than empathy and accommodation. They wish to be recognized as bicultural people with the right to seek inclusion in both mainstream and their own cultures.

Professional interest in cultural competence among social workers is predated by a rich and varied history on the subject and many decades of discourse regarding the profession's response or lack of response to the service needs of diverse clients. The settlement house movement in the early history of the profession is an example of efforts to serve immigrants, many of whom were culturally different from the dominant population at the time. In retrospect, the practice at the time was designed to facilitate acculturation of immigrants into the dominant society. The Civil Rights movement of the 1960s marked the beginning of a shift in focus from promotion of acculturation and advocacy against the barriers to acculturation to greater affirmation of differences and recognition of the need to offer services attuned to the client's view of his or her life circumstances shaped by his or her cultural worldview.

In the 1960s, the Council on Social Work Education (CSWE) began to address the issues of racial and ethnic diversity in the recruitment and training of social work students and faculty, as well as in the content of social work curriculums. Schools emphasized the "dual perspective," or the concept that all people are part of at least two systems: the larger societal system and their immediate environment (Norton, 1978). Solomon (1976) defined *empowerment* as facilitating clients' connection with their own power, and in turn, being empowered by the very act of reaching across cultural barriers. Gallegos (1982) provided one of the first conceptualizations of racial and ethnic competence as "a set of procedures and activities to be used in acquiring culturally relevant insights into the problems of diverse clients and the means of applying such insights to the

development of intervention strategies that are culturally appropriate for these clients" (p. 4).

Green (1995) identified some culturally competent qualities and procedures: (1) clarification of the worker's personal values concerning "minority" people; (2) articulation of personal and professional values and ways they might conflict with or accommodate the needs of clients of color; (3) development of interviewing skills that reflect the worker's understanding of the role of language in racially and ethnically distinct communities; (4) the ability to relate to professionals of color in ways that enhance effectiveness with clients; (5) the capacity to use resources on behalf of communities of color; (6) the mastery of techniques for learning the history, traditions, and values of a racial or ethnic group; (7) the ability to communicate information on the cultural characteristics of a given group to other professionals; and (8) the knowledge of the effect of social policies and services on clients of color.

The concept of cultural competence has moved through a progression of ideas and theoretical constructs favoring cultural pluralism, cultural sensitivity, multiculturalism, and a transcultural orientation to social work practice (Gould, 1995). A brief review of the social work literature in the past few years reveals a range of content areas present in cultural competence, including racial identity formation; the interrelationship among race, gender, class, and ethnicity; HIV/AIDS among Hispanics and African Americans; work with poor families; work with poor African American or Puerto Rican families; sexual identity and sexual orientation; gay adolescents; acculturation and immigration; spirituality and religious diversity; biculturalism and multiculturalism; crossracial practice considerations; work with people with disabilities; outreach to American Indian and Asian American clients; empowerment; interracial marriage; racially mixed clients; biracial children; mental health services for Chinese, Cuban, Indochinese, and West Indian clients; sociocultural models of practice; and training of culturally sensitive practitioners.

Social workers must consider that cultural distinctions lie in many areas of life and even in abstraction. Cultural differences are evident in language; family lifestyle; roles of children;

treatment of and relations with elderly people, spouses, men, and women; religious beliefs and practices; orientation toward work; attitudes regarding justice and authority; social status; problem-solving methods; privacy; and attitudes toward the dominant group. Social workers need to consider the relationship among their own values, beliefs, and practices; the values, beliefs, and practices that guide the philosophy and administrative decisions of the organization that provides the auspice of their work, and the values, beliefs, and practices of the service population. This analysis may yield many areas of incongruence that must be resolved to achieve effective service delivery.

Diverse groups have differential experiences in American society. The differential treatment is a function of the dynamic interaction with the dominant culture of U.S. society, which in turns contributes to the values, beliefs, and practices adopted by the group. Social workers need sophisticated skills and abilities to advocate for clients against the underlying devaluation of cultural experiences based on difference and oppression. This mandate is addressed to social workers of all cultures, not just those who are members of historically and currently underserved, underrepresented, and oppressed groups. All social workers need to master culturally competent knowledge and skills because the pluralistic society is a social reality (Gould, 1995).

Cultural competence requires awareness. The quest for authentic cultural competence is a process of becoming more attuned to how clients experience their uniqueness, deal with their differences and similarities, and cope with a sociopolitical environment that is often unconcerned with the welfare of their people, however diverse their needs may be. Culturally competent social work practice starts with the driving assumption of individual uniqueness connected to humanness, and the individual experience of culture through which reality is seen and meaning is interpreted (Congress, 1994). Social workers' self-awareness of their own cultures is as fundamental to culturally competent practice as the informed assumptions about clients' cultural background and experiences. Just as the advocacy agenda is applicable to social workers of dominant groups, the

need to develop crosscultural skills is requisite for all social workers, including those from historically oppressed, underserved, and underrepresented populations. This expectation is important because of intragroup variability and the recognition that any given individual is a member of multiple cultures.

Although the discussion of culture often isolates people by virtue of race, ethnicity, religion, nationality, gender, class, sexual orientation, physical ability, and other attributes, in reality people represent intersections of these various cultural groups. Cultural competence requires the capacity to recognize the interaction of these multiple identities at the individual, family, group, neighborhood, and community levels and discern the salient cultural issues within any given helping relationship. Cultural competence requires a heightened consciousness of how clients experience their uniqueness and deal with their differences and similarities within a larger social context (NASW, 2001).

ISSUE STATEMENT

The complexities associated with cultural diversity in the United States affect all aspects of professional social work practice, requiring social workers to deliver culturally competent services to a broad range of clients. Cultural and linguistic competence requires knowledge, skills, and attitudes that promote and support respectful and effective crosscultural communication and practice. To that end, efforts are required at the micro-, mso-, and macropractice levels to affect direct practice and supervision, program administration, and social policy to achieve meaningful outcomes as defined by consumers, families, and communities.

Social workers using a person-in-environment framework for assessment need to include to varying degrees important cultural factors that have meaning for clients and reflect the culture of the world around them. Although in U.S. social work cultural diversity historically has been associated primarily with race and ethnicity, social workers are also aware of the need to develop culturally competent skills, knowledge, and values when working with people of a different gender, social class, religion or spiritual belief, sexual orientation, age, and disability. This kind of sophisticated cultural competence does not come naturally to any social worker and requires a high level of professionalism. This policy statement speaks to the need for definition, support, and encouragement of a heightened level of social work practice that encourages cultural competence among all social workers so that they can respond effectively, knowledgeably, and sensitively to the diversity inherent in the agencies they work in and with the clients and communities they serve.

Cultural competence is a vital link with the theoretical and practice knowledge base that defines social work expertise. Increasing cultural competence within the profession requires efforts to recruit and retain as diverse a group of social workers as possible, many of whom bring some "indigenous" cultural competence to the profession. In addition, cultural competence requires efforts to increase avenues for the acquisition of culturally competent skills by all social workers. Indigenous cultural competence is a result of absorbing positive and negative cultural memories through lifelong experiences, which can be an advantage as well as an obstacle when the workers confront the subjective qualities of sharing the same cultural experiences as their clients.

Cultural competence should not be equated with cultural identity or consciousness. For example, a Latino social worker is not inherently culturally competent when working with Latino clients; that is, it is not the social worker's ethnicity that makes him or her effective when dealing with clients of similar heritage. Rather, it is the combination of the worker's cultural history that is mediated through his or her social work training that makes for effective social work practice. This training emphasizes focus on the client context of socioeconomic status, race, gender, sexual orientation, religion, age, and abilities—all of which may vary among clients who share an ethnic heritage. When social workers have little contact with people who are culturally different, they must acquire cultural competence through cognitive methods to achieve affective insight. The profession needs to enhance culturally competent social work practice by

addressing the needs of both indigenous workers and those from different cultures struggling to acquire competence.

Cultural competence builds on the profession's stance on self-determination and individual dignity and worth, adding inclusion, tolerance, and respect for diversity in all its forms. Social workers know the importance of developing practices that are sensitive to different races, nationalities, language proficiencies, and immigration or migration experiences. Social workers are keenly aware of the deleterious effects of racism, sexism, ageism, anti-Semitism, homophobia, and xenophobia on clients' lives and the need for social advocacy and action to better empower diverse clients and communities. This policy statement reinforces this awareness but moves the discussion toward the development of clearer guidelines, goals, and objectives for the future of social work practice in which cultural diversity will increase in complexity.

POLICY STATEMENT

NASW seeks to promote cultural and linguistic competence in all areas of social work education, research, and practice. Social workers must honor the ethical responsibility to be culturally competent practitioners, as the NASW *Code of Ethics* (NASW, 2000) instructs. This policy statement adopts the definition of *cultural competence* proffered by Cross and colleagues (1989) as "a set of congruent behaviors, attitudes, and policies that come together in a system or agency or among professionals and enables the system, agency, or professionals to work effectively in cross-cultural situations" (p. 13). The word "culture" is used because it implies the integrated pattern of human behavior that includes thoughts, communications, actions, customs, beliefs, values, and institutions of a racial, ethnic, religious, or social group. The word "competence" is used because it implies having the capacity to function effectively. A culturally competent system of care acknowledges and incorporates at all levels the importance of culture, the assessment of crosscultural relations, vigilance toward the dynamics that result from cultural differences, the expansion of cultural knowledge, and the adaptation of services to meet culturally unique needs (Cross, Bazron, Dennis, & Isaacs, 1989; NASW, 2001).

NASW promotes and supports the implementation of cultural and linguistic competence at three intersecting levels: the individual, institutional, and societal. Cultural competence requires social workers to examine their own cultural backgrounds and identities while seeking out the necessary knowledge, skills, and values that can enhance the delivery of services to people with varying cultural experiences associated with their race, ethnicity, gender, class, sexual orientation, religion, age, or disability. Culturally competent practice is a critical component of professional social work expertise in all practice settings that include but are not limited to direct practice, community organizing, supervision, consultation, administration, advocacy, social and political action, policy development and implementation, education, and research and evaluation. Culturally competent practice is required in all geographic communities, whether urban, suburban, rural or frontier.

Culturally competent social work practice cannot occur within a vacuum. It requires an institutional and professional infrastructure that supports the efforts of individual practitioners to conduct themselves in a culturally competent manner. This means that the organization must have policies, procedures, and financial allocations that support and reward the growth and development of the staff. Furthermore, organizations must have the appropriate philosophy, policies, and procedures to ensure that the appropriate structures and practices are designed, funded, staffed, implemented, and evaluated to achieve the most effective and acceptable services to meet the unique needs and perspectives of a culturally and linguistically diverse service population. It is only through partnership with consumers, families, and cultural communities that social work institutions can successfully design the appropriate services.

It is the position of NASW that social policy be developed at the local, state, and national levels to promote cultural and linguistic competence. Such policies should assert the expectation of cultural and linguistic competence, institute the structures and financing to facilitate cultural and linguistic competence, and demand accountability of institutions and practitioners for cultural and linguistic competence. Such policies must address human resources and program factors that promote the recruitment and retention of a culturally diverse workforce, require appropriate educational preparation and continued professional development in cultural and linguistic competence of the workforce, and establish strategies to monitor and evaluate service outcomes for people of diverse cultures. Not only are these social policies needed to address the requirements of cultural and linguistic competence, but also such policies are needed to continue to work against the continued expression of racism, prejudice, and discrimination in this country.

NASW recognizes that the expertise required for the development of appropriate and effective interventions for diverse populations resides within that population. It is the position of NASW that collaboration with consumers, families, and cultural communities is a precondition for creation of culturally and linguistically competent services, reasonable accommodations, interventions, programs, and policies.

It is the position of NASW that practitioners and their host organizations ensure that services are offered in the language preferred by the consumers and families receiving service. In addition, NASW supports tending to the linguistic needs of social work's diverse workforce. Linguistic competence requires the growth in capacity to use the preferred language of the consumer and also to develop the skills to use appropriate strategies for interpretation and translation. Several strategies that organizations can pursue include modifications in staffing and operations, such as the inclusion of bilingual and bicultural staff; foreign language interpretation services; use of cultural brokers; provision of materials in alternative formats such as audiotape, Braille, enlarged print; and print materials in easy-to-read, low-literacy, picture, and symbol formats (Goode & Jones, 2003).

NASW recognizes that a policy statement alone cannot fully define the values, knowledge, and skills required for culturally and linguistically competent practice. Cultural competence is an important ingredient of professional competence, as important as any other component that forms the basis of the theoretical and clinical knowledge that defines social work expertise. This policy statement supports and encourages promulgation and adherence to the *NASW Standards for Cultural Competence in Social Work Practice* (2001).

NASW supports the advancement of practice models that have relevance for the range of needs and services represented by diverse client populations. It promotes the application of practices for which there is evidence of effectiveness for the relevant cultural group and the development of a knowledge base that emanates for the practice within and on behalf of cultural communities. As advocates for the providers and consumers of social work services, social workers need to promote cultural competence by supporting the evaluation of delivery models that are offered as culturally competent. Monitoring cultural competence among social workers should include establishing mechanisms for obtaining direct feedback from clients.

The social work profession is encouraged to take proactive measures to ensure cultural competence as an integral part of initial and continuing social work education and practice and to increase research and scholarship among its professionals. The social work profession should ensure cultural competence is an integral part of organizational practice and social policy.

REFERENCES

Breton, M. (1994). Relating competence: Promotion and empowerment. *Journal of Progressive Human Services, 5*(1), 27–44.

Congress, E. P. (1994). The use of culturagrams to assess and empower culturally diverse families. *Families in Society, 75,* 531–540.

Cross, T. L., Bazron, B. J., Dennis, K. W., & Isaacs, M. R. (1989). *Towards a culturally competent system of care: A Monograph on effective services for minority children who are severely emotionally disturbed*, Volume I. Washington, DC: Georgetown University Child Development Center, Child and Adolescent Services Program Technical Assistance Center.

Gallegos, J. S. (1982). The ethnic competence model for social work education. In B. W. White (Ed.), *Color in a white society* (pp. 1–9). Silver Spring, MD: National Association of Social Workers.

Goode, T., & Jones, W. (2003). *A definition of linguistic competence.* Washington, DC: Georgetown University Center for Child and Human Development, National Center for Cultural Competence.

Gould, K. H. (1995). The misconstruing of multiculturalism: The Stanford debate and social work. *Social Work, 40,* 198–205.

Green, J. W. (1995). *Cultural awareness in the human services: A multi-ethnic approach* (2nd ed.). Boston: Allyn & Bacon.

National Association of Social Workers. (2000). *Code of ethics of the National Association of Social Workers.* Washington, DC: Author.

National Association of Social Workers. (2001). *NASW standards for cultural competence in social work practice.* Washington, DC: Author.

Norton, D. G. (1978). *The dual perspective: Inclusion of ethnic minority content in the social work curriculum.* New York: Council on Social Work Education.

Solomon, B. B. (1976). *Black empowerment: Social work in oppressed communities.* New York: Columbia University Press.

U.S. Census Bureau. (2001). *Overview of race and Hispanic origin 2000.* Retrieved May 14, 2004, from http://www.census.gov

U.S. Census Bureau. (2003). *Language use and English-speaking ability: 2000.* Retrieved May 14, 2004, from http://www.census.gov

U. S. Census Bureau. (2004). *Projected population of the United States, by race and Hispanic origin: 2000 to 2050.* Washington, DC: Author. Available at http://www.census.gov/ipc/www/usinterimproj/

SUGGESTED READINGS

Child Welfare League of America. (2002). *Cultural competence agency self-assessment instrument* (rev. ed.). Washington, DC: CWLA Press.

Hogan-Garcia, M. (2003). *The four skills of cultural diversity competence: A process for understanding and practice* (2nd ed.). Pacific Grove, CA: Brooks/Cole—Thomson Learning.

Jackson, V., & Lopez, L. (Eds.). (1999). *Cultural competence in managed behavioral healthcare.* Providence, RI: Manisses Communications Group.

Lum, D. (2003). *Culturally competent practice: A framework for understanding diverse groups and justice issues* (2nd ed.). Pacific Grove, CA: Brooks/Cole—Thomson Learning.

Morales, A. T., & Sheafor, B. W. (2002). *The many faces of social work clients.* Boston: Allyn & Bacon.

U. S. Department of Health and Human Services, Substance Abuse and Mental Health Services Administration, Center for Mental Health Services. (2000). *Cultural competence standards in managed care mental health care services: Four underserved/underrepresented racial/ethnic groups.* Rockville, MD: Author.

Policy statement approved by the NASW Delegate Assembly, August 2005. This statement supersedes the statement on Cultural Competence in the Social Work Profession approved by the Delegate Assembly in 1996 and referred by the 2002 Delegate Assembly to the 2005 Delegate Assembly for revision. For additional information, contact the National Association of Social Workers, 750 First Street, NE, Suite 700, Washington, DC 20002-4241; telephone 202-408-8600; e-mail: press@naswdc.org

Deprofessionalization and Reclassification

BACKGROUND

Beginning with Abraham Flexner's paper presented in 1915, "Is social work a profession?" the issue of professionalism has been a prominent point of discussion. Some of the factors contributing to this question included the status of the earliest practitioners: upper class, women volunteers; and a lack of a professional code of ethics, professional schools of study, and research focused on social work issues. At the time of Flexner and Jane Addams, women rarely worked for pay. The only acceptable areas of "women's work" were caregiving and helping jobs such as teaching and nursing. Social work became part of this. Because women were not seen as equal in vocational arenas, work they did was rarely considered "professional."

Things changed after World War I for social work when there was a shift from apprenticeship training to university-based education and when there was more of a need for services. Although social work is still predominately a "women's profession" (NASW [2006] reports that 81 percent of all members are women), many concurrent trends have led social work to a clearer professional status. Some of the important trends include the national public service expansions in the 1930s and the 1960s, licensing, privatization of social services, the diversification of practitioners, and the growth of managed care. NASW and Council on Social Work Education (CSWE) now both define *professional social workers* as "individuals who have graduated from an educational program accredited by the Council on Social Work Education with at least a bachelors degree in social work" (NASW, 2006, p. 6). Unfortunately, once the answer to Flexner's question was "yes," then the stage was set for the current trend toward deprofessionalization and reclassification.

In 1983, Carol Meyer cautioned, "in every field of practice, on every level of government, and in the voluntary sector, the declassification of professional social work positions has become a dismal reality" (p. 419).

Gibelman and Schervish (1996) have documented similar phenomena where the public sector agencies have a great deal of difficulty attracting social workers. They identify causes for this as large caseloads, decrease in quality of service, insufficient personnel, and negative views of this area of social work practice.

With privatization often comes a decrease in accountability and regulation. As part of this shift, there is more of a separation between funders and practitioners, which in turn affects professional standards. As this shift occurred, agencies were left without accreditation, leaving them open for possible legal challenges. To protect themselves, agencies sought out accreditation from groups that "require agencies to use research and business models to analyze and improve policies and practices." (California Association of Deans and Directors, 2004). In addition, agencies that were once sure of funding now needed to raise their own capital. A by-product of these shifts included the hiring of non–social work executive directors. People trained in finance, business, and law are now frequently found in positions previously held by social workers (Healy & Meagher, 2004). They were also in a position to evaluate the services and the staff at these agencies.

Kahn (1981) described deprofessionalization as a trend that results in "reduction in educational requirements for entry-level jobs, assumption of interchangeability of bachelors degrees, reorganization of jobs to reduce educational requirements, nonrecognition of the exclusivity of bachelors (BSW) or master's of social work (MSW) skills, and equating education with experience" (p. 3). Healy and Meager (2004) saw the causes of deprofessionalization as "fragmentation and routinization of social work roles and tasks, a decline in professional categories of social work employment, and underemployment of social workers in paraprofessional positions" (p. 244).

At times, under various deprofessionalization and reclassification schemes, public and private agencies have created generic job classifications, such as clinical case manager, case management specialist, and social services worker that eliminated the title of social worker. The combined effect of the deprofessionalization and reclassification movement has been civil service systems that permit hiring of unqualified and uncredentialed individuals for social work positions.

Another consequence has been the eradication of chief social worker positions and functions in major agencies and departments. In addition, public and private agencies will often substitute in-service training for formal professional training. Several investigative reports support the position that social work education provides the beginning level practice knowledge and skills necessary for entry-level positions, and that experience alone is an unreliable indicator of job performance. A more recent NASW study concluded that graduate social work education is the best predictor of performance (NASW, 2006). Although the importance of social work education has been denigrated by the change in requirements for specific social service jobs, job performance requirements—such as psychosocial assessment, treatment planning, and discharge planning—have remained unchanged. Paraprofessionals, counselors, or human services personnel often are considered as trained "social workers" and are, at times, sanctioned to function under the title "social worker." As such, these noncredentialed personnel are held responsible for delivering social services although they lack the social work knowledge base, skills, and values necessary to perform such tasks.

Deprofessionalization and reclassification must focus on factors both external and internal to the social work profession, as well as on the value of social work education. Some external factors include relaxation of social services standards, at both the state and federal levels; reduction in federal and state funding for social services programs; radical changes in personnel policies; the diminished number of social workers in administrative and policy-making positions; and the changes in the insurance industry's payment for social services. Increasingly, people from other human services disciplines are competing with individuals who have BSWs and MSWs for jobs that once exclusively required social work education. Internal factors of the profession include the redefinition of tasks and responsibilities by specialty groups and a preference by social workers for employment in private agencies.

Trends in social work education indicate that students interested in social policy, social research, or social services administration choose other professional degrees, and workers with MSWs often must enroll in doctoral programs to specialize. As a result, non-social workers occupy decision-making and supervisory positions and make policies that affect the status of social workers and social work practice.

Since 1981, NASW has enhanced its capabilities to address deprofessionalization and reclassification. First, NASW has intensified legislative capabilities and lobbying activities at state and federal levels, resulting in the achievement of landmark legislative goals with the inclusion of social workers as payees under Part B and other sections of Medicare and the establishment of standards for social services staffing in nursing facilities. In addition, NASW has blocked legislation in some states that would have required social workers to obtain other professional licenses and certifications to practice in areas traditionally within their scope, such as family therapy.

Important research done in 2004 and published in 2006 through the Center For Workforce Study in collaboration with the University of Albany gives us a great deal of information regarding licensed social workers in terms of areas of concentration, gender, age, and pay among other characteristics. It enables the profession to better define itself and to work toward increasing awareness of and perceived perception of social workers by the public. This in turn helps further underscore professionalization in social work.

In 2001, NASW established the NASW Foundation, with the following goals:

■ to identify, develop and respond to social work policy and practice issues;

■ to assist with rapid response to social crises;

■ to support practice-based research, so that practice and research are directly linked;

■ to raise the visibility of social work and enhance public esteem for the profession;

■ to support the development of cutting edge continuing education that addresses critical issues;

■ to promote the appropriate application of new technology to the practice of social work.

As part of the Foundation's work, in 2004 NASW created "Help Starts Here," a public education campaign geared toward changing the public perceptions of social work and to improve the profession.

Finally, NASW increasingly has demonstrated its effectiveness in promoting the social work profession by assuming a leadership role in the social policy and political arena. In addition, NASW has supported national-level projects to increase the number of trained staff in child welfare, student loan forgiveness, and research and resources for major reinvestment initiatives. Since NASW designated social work licensing a high-priority action, all states have established some form of licensing or regulation. As insurance for high-quality social work services and maintenance of professionalism, it is necessary to evaluate our current licensing efforts and refine them accordingly. The focus now can move to providing stronger title protection and clearer, more universal licensing requirements for all social workers at all education levels.

ISSUE STATEMENT

Many legislators have failed to recognize the social work profession as a major contributor to effective social services and as an advocate for social welfare policies and programs in the United States. Systematically, social workers are being eliminated from direct services, supervision, policy making, and administrative positions. This elimination is being accomplished by deprofessionalizing and reclassifying traditional social work positions in the public and private sectors. Increasingly, public and private employers are hiring staff members who are uncredentialed as social workers and as such they are, inadequately trained, and not qualified to fill social work positions (Healy & Meagher, 2004). To help eradicate the issue, it is important to develop uniform national standards on all levels to define and regulate social work practice. NASW reports the number of practicing social workers to be 840,000, whereas only 310,000 hold state licenses (NASW, 2006). According to a 2007 survey of licensure boards conducted by NASW, all states regulate MSW social workers (NASW, 2007). Only 24 states refer to those with BSWs as licensed, though a limited number of other states certify them. Forty-nine states have advanced licensing requiring post master's supervised hours. In some of these states, only advanced practice is licensed. A handful of states have licenses for nonclinical social workers. This hodgepodge of licensing requirements only adds to the confusion over professionalism and leaves the door open for further deprofessionalization and declassification (NASW, 2007).

This trend is a result of the sociopolitical climate of downsizing; devolution of the role of government; cost containment in health and mental health services through managed care; and competition with allied professions for direct services, as well as supervisory and administrative positions. Many of these individuals, hired as a result of deprofessionalization and reclassification, lack social work practice knowledge, values, and skills, yet are required to perform such complex tasks as biopsychosocial assessment, treatment planning, interviewing, and acting as change agents. In addition, in many public sector agencies, work is being contracted out, again eliminating the assurance that these jobs will be filled with social workers with appropriate training and licensing. One way to change this trend is to make sure that title protection is in place not only in licensing professionals but also in job descriptions at the agency level. The term *social worker* should not be used unless the person in the position has had at least a minimal social work education and is licensed at that level. The California Master plan (California Association of Deans & Directors, 2004) includes a "Ladder of Learning" that comprises seven levels ranging from high school certificate, followed by an associate degree, and ending with the doctoral degree. This can be used as a national example. Through the use of this or some other such schema on a national level, the standards of professionalism through uniform requirements at multiple levels of licensing can be ensured. In addition to deprofessionalization, declassification remains an issue for social workers. Contributing factors to this include the following:

■ Because there are insufficient numbers of people with BSW or MSW degrees (currently 30,000 MSWs and BSWs graduate nationwide each year, with an overall ratio of 101 licensed social workers per 100,000 people) (NASW, 2006) or because of a lack of interest in employing these individuals in public services agencies, vacancies are filled by untrained staff with undifferentiated undergraduate degrees, causing agencies to emphasize on-the-job training.

■ Carework in this culture is generally assumed to be women's work, and it is implied women do not need an independent living wage. There is a discrepancy of 14 percent between the mean wages of men and women who are licensed social workers.

■ State employee unions have emphasized promotion on the basis of experience and do not support professional education.

■ Legislation and administrative rules have allowed other educational degrees and work experience to serve as the equivalent of social work education.

■ Fewer resources and budget cuts have led to a justification to lower social work standards and to fill jobs with less-qualified personnel who fit lower salary standards.

POLICY STATEMENT

Professional social workers possess the specialized knowledge necessary for an effective social services delivery system. Social work education provides a unique combination of knowledge, values, skills, and professional ethics that cannot be obtained through other degree programs or by on-the-job training.

Therefore, NASW supports

■ promotional opportunities for all social workers, including policy-making and administrative positions based on levels of social work education, experience, and competence.

■ service delivery that adheres to NASW's *Code of Ethics* (2000).

■ clients' rights to expect and to receive high standards of professional services. Under the equal protection law, clients served by both public and private organizations have the right to receive the same quality care provided by trained social workers.

■ the increased recruitment of high school students and early college students to the social work major in order to ensure an adequate number of social workers filling professional social work jobs.

■ efforts at the state level to implement regulations for the entire profession, including title protection, certification, and/or licensure.

■ organizational and public policies that promote the hiring of CSWE degreed social work practitioners and halt the general trend to hire less-qualified staff.

■ the promotion of social work as a distinctly different profession from other human services disciplines (such as counseling, clinical psychology, nursing, marriage and family therapy, and so forth) as it focuses on the intra- and interpersonal aspects of clients' lives.

■ the expertise, knowledge, and skills demonstrated by social workers with BSWs, MSWs and doctoral degrees should be actively communicated to clients, colleagues, and others at all times.

■ the identification of tangible social work skills gained through social work education such as bio-psychosocial assessment, treatment planning, interviewing, discharge planning, and so forth that are essential to the social services delivery system.

- the education of social workers in accredited programs with courses designed and taught by social work educators that will promote the culture, knowledge, and values and ethics of the profession.

- research and outcome studies that demonstrate the effectiveness and cost–benefit of hiring trained social workers. This research promotes the relevance of social work education to the tasks performed in public and private organizations.

- title and practice protection through regulation for social work in all practice settings on all practice levels.

- efforts to oppose legislation and policies that allow for the practice of social work by individuals without social work education, experience, and competencies.

- title protection in job descriptions so that the title "social worker" can be used only to refer to professionally prepared social workers.

REFERENCES

California Association of Deans and Directors of Schools of Social Work. (2004). *Master plan for social work education in the state of California.* Berkeley, CA: Author.

Flexner, A. (1915). *Is social work a profession?* Presentation to the National Conference on Charities and Corrections.

Gibleman, M., & Schervish, P. (1996). Social work and public services practice: A status report. *Families in Society, 77,* 117–124.

Healy, K., & Meagher, G. (2004). The reprofessionalization of social work: Collaborative approaches for achieving professional recognition. *British Journal of Social Work, 34,* 243–260.

Kahn, T. (1981). *Chapter action guide on declassification.* Lansing: National Association of Social Workers, Michigan Chapter.

Meyer, C. M. (1983). Declassification: Assault on social workers and social services [Editorial]. *Social Work, 28,* 419.

National Association of Social Workers. (1991). NASW: Relationships with other social work organizations and other human services disciplines. In *Social work speaks: NASW policy statements* (2nd ed., pp. 204–206). Silver Spring, MD: Author.

National Association of Social Workers. (2000). *Code of ethics of the National Association of Social Workers.* Washington, DC: Author.

National Association of Social Workers. (2007). Cross-state data. Retrieved March 12, 2008, from http://www.socialworkreinvestment.org/State/

Scheffler, R., & Kirby, P. (2003). The occupational transformation of the mental health system. *Health Affairs, 23,* 177–188.

Whitaker, T., Weismiller, T., & Clark, E. (2006). *Assuring the sufficiency of a frontline workforce: A national study of licensed social workers.* Washington, DC: National Association of Social Workers.

Policy statement approved by the NASW Delegate Assembly, August 2008. This policy statement supersedes the policy statement on Deprofesionalization and Reclassification approved by the Delegate Assembly in August 1999 and referred by the 2005 Delegate Assembly to the 2008 Delegate Assembly for revision, and the policy statement on Declassification approved by the Assembly in 1993 and 1981. For further information, contact the National Association of Social Workers, 750 First Street, NE, Suite 700, Washington, DC 20002-4241. Telephone: 202-408-8600 or 800-638-8799; e-mail: press@naswdc.org

Disasters

BACKGROUND

Disasters are collective, community-wide traumatic events that cause extensive destruction, death or injury, and widespread social and personal disruption (Freedy, Resnick, & Kilpatrick, 1992). The steadily changing global, political, and environmental climate has led to an increase in terrorism, random acts of violence, and catastrophic occurrences of nature. Federal laws, in particular the Disaster Relief Act of 1970 (P.L. 91-606), the Disaster Relief Act Amendments of 1980 (P.L. 96-568), and the Robert T. Stafford Disaster Relief and Emergency Assistance Act (P.L. 93-288), address disaster-related concerns.

A local emergency is declared when the governance of a city or county deems conditions to pose an extreme threat to the safety of people and property within that jurisdiction. When the disaster conditions threaten the safety of people and property within a state, the governor may proclaim a state of emergency, making mutual aid assistance mandatory from other cities, counties, and state authorities. When damage exceeds the resources of local and state governments, the president may declare a disaster, which activates federal assistance as provided for in the Stafford Act. Individual assistance may include low-interest loans, individual and family grants, temporary housing, assistance with basic needs, and crisis counseling.

In addition to Federal Emergency Management Agency (FEMA) and state and local governments, several volunteer agencies assume defined roles and responsibilities in disaster situations. Among these are the American Red Cross, Volunteer Organizations Active in Disasters (VOAD), and the Salvation Army. Other key organizations are involved in disaster response, including Volunteers of America, the United Methodist Church, the Southern Baptist Convention, the National Catholic Conference and Catholic Charities, the Mennonite Disaster Services, and the Christian Reformed World Belief (Myers, 1994).

NASW entered into the first of a succession of professional agreements with the American Red Cross in 1990 to facilitate social work participation in the planning, training, and provision of mental health services to disaster victims. In 1993, the California Chapter of NASW, Los Angeles County regions, developed a statement of understanding with the American Red Cross (NASW & American Red Cross, 1993). In 1994, after the Northridge earthquake, NASW, the California Chapter, and the American Red Cross' California Chapter formed a statewide statement of understanding. And in 2005 in response to the crisis caused by Hurricane Katrina, NASW engaged with the Red Cross to maintain a database—the Disaster Services Human Resources System—as a registry of trained disaster mental health professionals. The development of agreements with volunteer organizations and the delivery of disaster-related services continue to evolve. In the process, there is a need to understand the roles of the various organizations, to continue collaboration, and to have regular meetings to enhance cooperative service delivery and ensure comprehensive disaster management. In collaboration with the state mental health authority, social workers are among the professionals who make up the roster of volunteers being readied in New Jersey to be called in the event of a disaster. The phases of disaster management articulated by FEMA are (1) mitigation, (2) preparedness, (3) response, and (4) recovery. It is important to consider the commitment required in each of the phases of disaster in service delivery. Nearly three years after the events of September 11, 2001, local, state, federal, and international agencies continue with mitigation and preparedness activities. FEMA's (1996) *State and Local Guide 101: Guide for All-Hazards Emergency Operations Planning* assigns responsibility to carry out actions in emergencies and is the basis for government response to any disaster. Mental health planning is based on recommendations in the *Mental Health All-Hazards Disaster Plan Guidance* manual developed by Substance Abuse and Mental Health Services Administration (SAMHSA) (SAMHSA 2003). This manual helps state mental health program directors assess the status of mental health disaster plans throughout the country and provide guidance in the planning process.

In a community affected by disaster, in addition to people directly affected, several special populations can be identified. Among these groups of disaster survivors and victims are subpopulations historically of concern to social work: older adults, people with low incomes, people with preexisting mental illness, children, immigrants, refugees, people with disabilities, and people who are isolated, institutionalized, or otherwise at social or physical risk. These populations are among the most vulnerable disaster survivors and require special attention during preparedness, immediate relief, and recovery. People who have a history of trauma are also a group at risk. Virtually no one experiences or responds to disasters unscathed. Rescue workers and military personnel, witnesses to the event, first responders, people who are physically injured, mental health professionals, and the skilled workers on the scene all constitute at-risk populations. The makeup of the at-risk population group is determined by the nature of the disaster.

Whole communities warrant assistance, particularly in light of the constant stream of media coverage. Television also broadens the scope of the disaster. On one hand, covering a disaster is a public service, commanding the attention of the world to the needs of the people affected. On the other hand, the coverage deepens the wounds and intensifies the anxiety of people affected because of the constant repetition of the stories, the misinformation that breaking news is often fraught with, and the response of people and government as a result of the media coverage. Furthermore, media workers also constitute a population at risk because of their extended involvement in the areas affected.

Social workers from all fields of practice must have knowledge and understanding about disasters and the course of recovery. Effective interventions must be tailored to phases of recovery. There is a range of reactions to stress—reactions that are universal, normal for the situation, widely shared, and that abate naturally (Cohen & Ahearn, 1980; Weaver, 1995). The DSM-IV-TR states that "community-based studies reveal a lifetime prevalence for Posttraumatic Stress Disorder of approximately 8% of the adult population in the United States" (American Psychiatric Association, 2000, p. 466). Interventions models must be based on resilience and strengths rather than pathology and deficit.

Because of the chaos that ensues after a disaster, a well-ordered and coordinated mass response system is needed for effective disaster management. NASW has adopted a disaster policy at the national level for four primary reasons:

1.   Disasters are large-scale catastrophes that affect whole communities or multiple communities in geophysical, social, and psychological ways.

2.   The trauma and deprivation resulting from disasters often are magnified for those with few resources and reduced opportunities to rebuild homes and replace losses. As such, vulnerable populations are likely to be among those especially affected by disasters.

3.   Social workers are well suited to interpret the disaster context, to advocate for effective services, and to provide leadership in essential collaborations among institutions and organizations. Furthermore, compatible with social work epistemology, disaster assistance must be construed holistically, encompassing the physical, developmental, psychological, emotional, social, cultural, and spiritual needs of individuals and systems. Finally, respected disaster response modalities readily translate

to the language of empowerment and classic, generalist social work practice.

4. Social workers continue to respond quickly and effectively to need in the immediate aftermath of disasters. The importance of the potential contribution and role of social work warrants more than ad hoc, intuitive, spontaneous responses on a disaster-by-disaster basis. Effective disaster leadership and a proactive presence on the part of the profession require preparation, direction, training, and practice.

ISSUE STATEMENT

According to the Robert T. Stafford Disaster Relief and Emergency Assistance Act, as amended by the Disaster Mitigation Act of 2000 (P. L. 106-390) "major disaster means any natural catastrophe (including any hurricane, tornado, storm, high water, wind driven water, tidal wave, tsunami, earthquake, volcanic eruption, landslide, mudslide, snowstorm, or drought), or, regardless of cause, any fire, flood, or explosion, in any part of the United States, which in the determination of the President causes damage of sufficient severity and magnitude to warrant major disaster assistance under this Act to supplement the efforts and available resources of States, local governments, and disaster relief organizations in alleviating the damage, loss, hardship, or suffering caused thereby." (Title I, §§ 102, 5122).

Not all disasters meet the requirements for "major disaster," yet every disaster causes extensive destruction, death, or injury and produces widespread community disruption and individual trauma (Hartsough & Myers, 1987). Disasters occur from natural causes, human error, equipment or technological failure, and intentional human actions.

Inherent in social work policy is the recognition of individual as well as systems considerations. Incidents that affect individuals, such as rape or other violent crime, a serious home fire, or a tragic accident, may affect the family system and certain community members. These incidents are not "declared" disasters, but they create upheaval in communities. The financial resources to address them may

not be available. At times disasters are sudden, unexpected events; at other times they are slow, insidious occurrences allowing some degree of predictability.

A common language is essential to effective communication, policy, and planning. Quarantelli (1985) used the term "collective stress situation" to refer to a circumstance in which a social system fails to provide expected life conditions for its members. These extreme stress situations are divided into disasters and conflicts. Conflicts include war, riots, and terrorist attacks. Emergency services personnel experience the impact of an event through their response to the call for service as well as their membership in their family and community. Use of the term "critical incident stress" has proliferated. It is not uncommon to hear this phrase used to describe civilian stress responses. Traumatic stress differs from posttraumatic stress disorder. "Most people recover fully from even moderate stress reactions within 6 to 16 months" according to the *Disaster Mental Health Response Handbook* (New South Wales Institute of Psychiatry, 2000, p. 27). SAMHSA's service model calls for providing crisis counseling, including psychoeducation about reactions to disaster, in an attempt to prevent the onset of serious mental illness (SAMHSA, 2003).

The broad range of social work practice allows social workers to provide services in a variety of settings. Of necessity, social workers will follow the lead of the disaster response organizations in providing these services. Because of the increasing number and scope of disasters worldwide, multidisciplinary partnerships, training, research, and coordination of response efforts are needed.

POLICY STATEMENT

NASW supports participation in and advocates for programs and policies that serve individuals and communities in preparation for, during, and in the wake of disaster. NASW supports:

■ prevention or mitigation of the adverse consequences of disaster and effective preparation for disaster by individuals, families, social networks, neighborhoods, schools, organizations, and communities, especially where vulnerable populations are concentrated

■ enhancement of the efficiency, effectiveness, orchestration, and responsiveness of disaster relief and recovery efforts to prevent exacerbation of problems related to the disaster

■ policies and procedures that provide access to disaster relief services and resources to all (including relationship rights for gay, lesbian, bisexual and transgender people and undocumented immigrants

■ provision of behavioral health and social services to survivors in a context of normalization and empowerment, with sensitivity to the phases of disaster recovery and with understanding of the unique cultural characteristics of the affected community and its populations

■ attention to the long-term recovery phase of disasters

■ attention to the special training needs, stress management techniques, and support needs of first responders and other disaster workers

■ education of social workers and social work students in the specialized knowledge and methods of trauma response

■ continued research on the impact of disasters, effective interventions, and disaster management strategies

■ development of a cadre of well-trained, culturally competent disaster professionals committed to effective interdisciplinary and interorganizational collaboration in disaster planning and disaster response

■ provision of accurate and effective public information on the normal phases of disaster reaction, functional coping methods, and strategies for accessing and successfully using the disaster assistance systems.

REFERENCES

American Psychiatric Association. (2000). *Diagnostic and statistical manual of mental disorders* (4th ed., Text Rev.). Washington, DC: Author.

Cohen, R. E., & Ahearn, F. L. (1980). *Handbook for mental health care of disaster victims*. Baltimore: Johns Hopkins University Press.

Disaster Mitigation Act of 2000, Pub. L. 106-390, 114 Stat. 1552.

Disaster Relief Act of 1970, Pub. L. 91-606, 84 Stat. 1744.

Disaster Relief Act Amendments of 1980, Pub. L. 96-568, 94 Stat. 3334.

Federal Emergency Management Agency. (1996). *State and local guide 101: Guide for all-hazards emergency operations planning*. Washington, DC: Author.

Freedy, J. R., Resnick, H. S., & Kilpatrick, D. G. (1992). Conceptual framework for evaluating disaster impact: Implications for clinical intervention. In J. H. Gold (Series Ed.) & L. S. Austin (Vol. Ed.), *Clinical practice: Volume 24. Responding to disaster* (pp. 3–23). Washington, DC: American Psychiatric Press.

Hartsough, D. M., & Myers, D. G. (1987). *Disaster work and mental health: Prevention and control of stress among workers* (DHHS Publication No. ADM 87-1422). Washington, DC: U.S. Government Printing Office.

Myers, D. (1994). *Disaster response and recovery: A handbook for mental health professionals* (DHHS Publication No. SMA 94-3010). Washington, DC: U.S. Government Printing Office.

National Association of Social Workers, & American Red Cross. (1990). *Statement of understanding between National Association of Social Workers and the American Red Cross*. Washington, DC: Authors.

National Association of Social Workers, & American Red Cross. (1993). *Statement of understanding between the California chapter of the National Association of Social Workers, Los Angeles County regions and the American Red Cross*. Los Angeles: Authors.

New South Wales Institute of Psychiatry and Centre for Mental Health. (2000). *Disaster mental health response handbook*. North Sydney, Australia: Author.

Quarantelli, E. L. (1985). An assessment of conflicting views on mental health: The consequences of traumatic events. In C. R. Figley (Ed.), *Trauma and its wake: The study and treatment of post-traumatic stress disorder* (pp. 173–215). New York: Brunner/Mazel.

Robert T. Stafford Disaster Relief and Emergency Assistance Act, Pub. L. 93-288, 88 Stat. 143.

Substance Abuse and Mental Health Services Administration, Center for Mental Health Services. (2003). *Mental health all-hazards disaster plan guidance* (DHHS Publication No. SMA 3829). Rockville, MD: U.S. Department of Health and Human Services.

Weaver, J. (1995). *Disasters: Mental health interventions.* Sarasota, FL: Professional Resource Press.

SUGGESTED READINGS

American Red Cross. (1992). *Disaster mental health services I: Glossary of terms* (ARC Publication No. 3077-1A). Washington, DC: Author.

Austin, L. (Ed.). (1992). *Clinical practice: Responding to disaster.* Washington, DC: American Psychiatric Press.

Ayalon, O., Lahad, M., & Cohen, A. (Eds.). (1998). *Community stress prevention. Volume 3.* Upper Galilee, Israel: Tel Hai Academic College, Community Stress Prevention Centre.

Ayalon, O., Lahad, M., & Cohen, A. (Eds.). (1999). *Community stress prevention. Volume 4.* Upper Galilee, Israel: Tel Hai Academic College, Community Stress Prevention Centre.

Coarsey, C. (2004). *Handbook for human services response.* Blairsville, GA: Higher Resources.

Cohen Silver, R., Holman, E. A., McIntosh, D., Poulin, M., & Gil-Rivas, V. (2002). Nationwide longitudinal study of psychological responses to September 11. *JAMA, 288,* 1235–1244.

Farberow, N. L., & Gordon, N. S. (1986). *Manual for child health workers in major disasters* (DHHS Publication No. ADM 86-1070). Washington, DC: U.S. Government Printing Office.

Green, B. L. (1993). *Mental health and disaster: Research review* (Report to NIMH, Requisition 91MF175040). Washington, DC: Georgetown University Medical Center, Department of Psychiatry.

Green, B., Grace, M., Lindy, J., Gleser, G., Leonard, A., & Kramer, T. (1990). Buffalo Creek survivors in the second decade: Comparison with unexposed and nonlitigant groups. *Journal of Applied Social Psychology, 20,* 1033–1050.

Green, B., Grace, M., Lindy, J., Titchener, J., & Lindy, J. (1983). Levels of functional impairment following a civilian disaster: The Beverly Hills Supper Club fire. *Journal of Consulting and Clinical Psychology, 51,* 573–580.

Herman, J. (1992). *Trauma and recovery.* New York: Basic Books.

Holen, A. (1991). A longitudinal study of the occurrence and persistence of post-traumatic health problems in disaster survivors. *Stress Medicine, 7,* 11–17.

LeDoux, J. (2002). *Synaptic self.* New York: Viking.

Lima, B., Pai, S., Lozano, J., & Santacruz, H. (1990). The stability of emotional symptoms among disaster victims in a developing country. *Journal of Traumatic Stress, 3,* 497–505.

National Institute of Mental Health. (2002). *Mental health and mass violence: Evidence-based early psychological intervention for victims/survivors of mass violence. A workshop to reach consensus on best practices* (NIH Publication No. 02-5138). Washington DC: U.S. Government Printing Office.

North, C. S., Smith, E. M., & Spitznagel, E. L. (1994). Post-traumatic stress disorder in survivors of a mass shooting episode. *American Journal of Psychiatry, 151,* 82–88.

Pearlman, L. (1995). *Trauma and the therapist.* New York: W. W. Norton.

Phifer, J., & Norris, F. (1989). Psychological symptoms in older adults following natural disaster: Nature, timing, duration, and course. *Journal of Gerontology: Social Sciences, 44,* S207–S217.

Shore, J., Tatum, E., & Vollmer, W. (1986). Psychiatric reactions to disaster: The Mount St. Helens experience. *American Journal of Psychiatry, 143,* 590–595.

Stith Butler, A., Panzer, A. M., & Goldfrank, L. (Eds.). (2003). *Preparing for the psychological consequences of terrorism: A public health strategy*. Washington, DC: Institute of Medicine, National Academies Press.

U.S. Department of Veterans Affairs, National Center for Post-Traumatic Stress Disorder (n.d.). *Effects of traumatic stress in a disaster situation*. Washington, DC: Author.

Ursano, R. J., Fullerton, C. S., & Norwood, A. E. (Eds.). (2003). *Trauma and disaster responses and management* (Review of Psychiatry Series, Vol. 22, No. 1). Arlington, VA: American Psychiatric Publishing.

Policy statement approved by the NASW Delegate Assembly, August 2005. This policy statement supersedes the statement on Disasters approved by the Delegate Assembly in 1996 and referred by the 2002 Delegate Assembly to the 2005 Delegate Assembly for revision. For additional information, contact the National Association of Social Workers, 750 First Street, NE, Suite 700, Washington, DC 20002-4241; telephone: 202-408-8600; e-mail: press@naswdc.org

Drug Testing in the Workplace

BACKGROUND

The testing of employees for the presence of alcohol and illicit drugs is an area of concern for employers and employees, to the legal and social environment, and to professional practice. Increasingly, the idea of drug testing demands that social workers make professional, ethical, and even personal decisions. The abuse of alcohol and illicit drugs is common in our society.

Section 504 of the Rehabilitation Act of 1973 (P.L. 93-112) and the Drug-Free Workplace Act of 1986 (Federal Register, 1986) are federal laws. The former protects qualified individuals from discrimination on the basis of their disability. Examples of impairments include alcoholism and drug addiction. The latter applies specifically to workplaces that are a recipient of federal funds. To be certified as a drug-free workplace, a drug-free policy must be published and a drug-free awareness program must be in place.

The NASW *Code of Ethics* (2000) states that "the social worker should respect clients' rights to privacy. . . . Social workers should protect the confidentiality of all information obtained in the course of professional service, except for compelling professional reasons" (Section 1.07c). Recognizing the stigma associated with substance abuse, the social worker needs to be aware of the federal confidentiality regulations (42 CFR Part 2) (HHS 2004) in which, confidentiality has been the practice for substance abuse treatment programs across the country. Similar privacy rules also apply with the Health Insurance Portability and Accountability Act of 1996 (P.L. 104-191) standard.

Federal laws and the *NASW Code of Ethics* (2000) affect the profession's response to drug and alcohol policies in the workplace, directly and indirectly. Since the inception of the industrial–occupational social work field of practice, practitioners have been concerned about the lives of workers, their conditions of employment, the structures and cultures of their workplaces, and the relationships among these elements.

ISSUE STATEMENT

The social worker's response to workplace issues raised by drug-testing policies neither resolve nor explore all of the social, legal, scientific, and or ethical issues posed by drug testing in the workplace. As in all areas of professional work, the social worker facing drug-testing policies are guided by the *NASW Code of Ethics* (2000), in addition to reason and the law, while balancing the interests of the employer, the employees, and the public. Although the social worker is expected to observe the law, this expectation in itself does not mean that an employer's legal rights coincide with social work ethics. The social worker evaluates each situation and makes informed decisions on whether to promote drug-testing policies, acquiesce to them, challenge them, or even withdraw from the organization in protest.

Employers may be justified in implementing drug-testing policies to protect their organizations, their customers, other employees, or society. The profession is concerned with helping individuals who abuse alcohol and other drugs (AOD) to find successful treatment and preservation of employment consistent with the Rehabilitation Act of 1973 (P.L. 93-112) and other employee protection regulations.

Employers are entitled to maintain safe and healthy workplaces and to take steps to ensure that their products and services are not affected by employees' substance abuse. Drug testing is not required under the Drug-Free Workplace Act of 1986. Employees are entitled to expect AOD-abusing coworkers to be appropriately treated when it is probable that the person abusing substances will injure other employees or their interests. The public is entitled to expect protection from issues and problems that may result from substance abuse. Each situation compels the social worker to formulate his or her own ethical evaluation, abiding by the *NASW Code of Ethics* (2000). For example, Section 1.01 provides that "[t]he social worker's primary responsibility is to promote the well being of clients." However, Section 3.09 requires that "social workers generally should adhere to commitments made to employers and employing organizations."

A drug-testing policy that appears to promote the general well-being also may discriminate against substance-abusing individuals or vulnerable populations for whom services must be an ethical focus. The *NASW Code of Ethics* (2000) mandates that social workers "should not practice, condone, facilitate, or collaborate with any form of discrimination on the basis of race, ethnicity, national origin, color, sex, sexual orientation, age, marital status, political belief, religion, or mental or physical disability" (Section 4.02). When a drug-testing policy is the sole approach to substance abuse, the employer strongly risks punishing individual workers without helping them to obtain treatment. A health and wellness program that includes education, assessment, and employee assistance incorporated within a drug-testing policy may be more effective. Providing access to treatment is in accord with the *NASW Code of Ethics* (2000), which states that "social workers should engage in social and political action that seeks to ensure that all people have equal access to the resources, employment, services, and opportunities they require to meet their basic human needs and to develop fully"(Section 6.04a). Whenever possible, referral to an Employee Assistance Program (EAP) should be encouraged.

Drug-testing policies are considered punitive in workplaces where companies do not clearly communicate the rationale, procedures, laboratory methods, and consequences of a negative test. Positive results of drug tests have too often led to automatic dismissal or refusal to consider employment.

False positives are relatively uncommon if the laboratory is using the federal guidelines of the U.S. Department of Health and Human Services (DHHS) (2004). Although the potential of persons who do not abuse substances being stigmatized by the false positive is low, the consequences can be disastrous. The biggest source of inaccurate results is an interruption of the chain of custody, faulty protections, or contamination at specimen collection sites (DHHS, 2004). The employee should be given an opportunity for retesting following a positive test result.

Policies and practices should link the positive results of tests to assessment and referral to company EAPs or to treatment and other resources, when appropriate. AOD abuse is not restricted to any one group of employees but afflicts people at all levels of the organization. Any drug-testing policy should be bias-free to preclude resentment, morale problems, and discrimination.

POLICY STATEMENT

NASW supports

■ comprehensive and ethical approaches to the problem of AOD abuse at the work place, preferably as a cooperative labor–management initiative.

■ consideration of alternatives to drug testing, such as hand–eye coordination and response time performance tests.

■ an approach that includes education, prevention strategies, and treatment options for those who have been identified as abusing AOD.

■ confidential referrals to an EAP and encouragement of self-referrals. Sharing information with management must be consistent with federal laws and HIPAA on confidentiality.

■ health and wellness programs that include education, assessment, and employee assistance incorporated within a drug testing policy.

■ advocacy for clients' access to comprehensive treatment and insurance coverage.

- community treatment programs that anticipate obstacles to treatment, such as lack of child care for mothers, who are less likely than other groups to be treated for AOD abuse.

- the promotion of clearly defined policies and testing procedures that are consistent and fair to all employees, following the federal guidelines for workplace drug testing.

- education of all social workers on the issues of drug testing, including its effect on civil rights, etiology of AOD abuse, its course, and its effect on individuals and family systems.

- monitoring and publication of research, law, and practice on drug-testing issues.

- appropriate political action to challenge and change inadequate or inappropriate existing laws.

- the development of comprehensive curriculums on AOD abuse in schools of social work that include relevant theory, practice, and policy issues.

- the education of society at large about the nature of AOD abuse, its far-reaching effects, the importance of treatment, and the best ways to link clients with treatment.

- vigorous advocacy for improved AOD services for all socioeconomic groups.

REFERENCES

Federal Register. (1986). Drug-free federal workplace (Executive order 12564). Available at http://www.archives.gov/federal-register/codification/executive-order/12564.html

Health Insurance Portability and Accountability Act of 1996 (HIPAA), P.L. 104-191, Aug. 21, 1996, 110 Stat. 1936.

National Association of Social Workers. (2000). *Code of ethics of the National Association of Social Workers.* Washington, DC: NASW Press.

Rehabilitation Act of 1973, P.L. 93-112, Sept. 26, 1973, 87 Stat. 355.

U.S. Department of Health and Human Services. (2004). *Mandatory guidelines and proposed revisions to mandatory guidelines for federal workplace drug testing programs.* Washington, DC: U.S. Government Printing Office.

Policy statement approved by the NASW Delegate Assembly, August 2008. This policy statement supersedes the policy statement on Drug Testing in the Workplace approved by the Delegate Assembly in 1999 and referred by the 2005 Delegate Assembly to the 2008 Delegate Assembly for revision. The 1999 Delegate Assembly also voted to not combine this statement with the policy on Civil Liberties and Justice. This policy statement also supersedes the policy statement approved in 1990. For further information, contact the National Association of Social Workers, 750 First Street, NE, Suite 700, Washington, DC 20002-4241. Telephone: 202-408-8600 or 800-638-8799; e-mail: press@naswdc.org

Early Childhood Care and Services

BACKGROUND

Early childhood is a diverse field that is unified by a common core of knowledge: Children from birth through eight years of age require special attention to begin the developmental process in an optimal fashion. The growing awareness of the critical nature of experiences during these years requires the social work profession to be involved in setting policies that ensure the well-being of young children and their families. The United States remains the only technologically developed nation that lacks a national policy regarding the early childhood years.

Early and extensive enrollment in nonparental child care is the norm in the United States. In 1999, the National Household Education Survey (National Center for Education Statistics, 1999), which questions families about nonparental child care arrangements regardless of the employment status of the mother, reported that 61 percent of children younger than four were in regularly scheduled child care arrangements, including 44 percent of infants, 53 percent of one-year-olds, and 57 percent of two-year-olds. Although parents and relatives continue to provide vast amounts of early child care, reliance on child care centers outside the home has increased. An estimated 12 million children age six and younger spend some or all of their day being cared for by someone other than their parents (U.S. Department of Education, National Center for Education Statistics, 2002). According to Capizzano and Adams (2004), 73 percent of children age five and younger with working mothers are regularly in child care; 46 percent of children ages three and four from high-income families are in center-based care compared with 36 percent of children from low-income families.

Economic necessity often demands dual-earner families in the United States, and with the rate of marital disruption and single childbearing, many women have no choice but to work. According to the Whirlpool Foundation (1995), the majority (55 percent) of working women in the United States bring home half or more of the family's earnings. According to the Children's Defense Fund (2003), 6 million young children are living in single-parent families where working is necessary if these families are not to be dependent on welfare. The proportion of children age three and younger who are in child care centers, preschools, Head Start programs, and other early childhood education programs tripled between 1977 and 1994, from 8 percent to 24 percent of children with employed mothers (U.S. Census Bureau, 1982, 1997).

As many recipients of Temporary Assistance for Needy Families are entering the workforce to comply with federal and state work requirements, the demand for child care is growing. These families deserve access to the same quality of early childhood education and child care that higher-income families receive, and most need some form of child care assistance. Welfare reform must focus not only on getting parents to enter the workforce, but also on equity of access to high-quality child care for children living in poverty to have the optimal environment for learning and development.

It is important for children to have quality child care. High-quality early childhood programs provide important educational and nurturing experiences to young children. Findings from a study of by Peisner-Feinberg and colleagues (1999) revealed that children in high-quality child care demonstrated greater mathematical ability, greater thinking and attention skills, and fewer behavioral problems; these findings were particularly significant for at-risk children. However, many families experience difficulty finding quality and affordable child care. Parents pay most of child care costs— 60 percent; the federal, state, and local governments pay 39 percent; and private financing covers less than 1 percent (Mitchell, Stoney, & Dichter, 2001).

ISSUE STATEMENT

The National Association for the Education of Young Children (NAEYC) advocates for high-quality early childhood education and child care and provides accreditation to child care facilities that meet certain standards. NAEYC (2000) offers six statements that define its vision for excellence:

(1) that all young children deserve excellent early care and education;

(2) that high quality early experiences make a difference in children's lifelong academic and social success;

(3) that programs must be accessible to all families;

(4) that early childhood professionals must have excellent preparation, ongoing professional development, and compensation commensurate with their qualifications and experience;

(5) that effective early education must be both challenging and appropriate to young children's ages, individual needs, and culture and;

(6) that everyone needs to work together to build a successful future for our youngest children. (pp. 2–3)

The development of knowledgeable, competent, and culturally sensitive professionals to work with young children and their families is a continuous process. The revised NAEYC *Standards for Preparation of Early Childhood Professionals* (2001) requires closer partnerships among institutions of higher education and education settings in the community. These

guidelines require enhanced emphasis on linguistics and cultural diversity, inclusion, subject matter, and the communities in which children live. In addition, the standards call for attention to the complexity of assessment issues in today's educational settings, a "continuum of teaching strategies" and developmentally effective approaches, and field experiences for future educators. The revised standards emphasize that professionals in early childhood work in many diverse settings.

Early childhood care and services should be designed to incorporate the principles of infant mental health, which concern the optimal development of infants and toddlers within the context of secure and stable relationships with caregivers. For example:

Infant mental health is the developing capacity of the child from birth to age 3 to experience, regulate, and express emotions, form close and secure interpersonal relationships; and explore the environment and learn—all in the context of family, community, and cultural expectations for young children. Infant mental health is synonymous with healthy social and emotional development. (Zero to Three Infant Mental Health Task Force, 2002, p. 1)

A healthy parent–infant relationship is necessary for the competent physical, cognitive, social and emotional development of the infant. All early development takes place within the framework of interaction between the infant and adults partners. The parent's capacity to nurture the infant depends upon the extent to which she herself is supported and nurtured as well as her abilities to use the support that is available to her. (Weatherston & Tableman, 2002)

The quality of care is most important in child development. Young children who receive high-quality child care, including good verbal and cognitive stimulation, sensitive and responsive interaction with caregivers, and large amounts of attention and support, are more advanced in all areas of development compared with children who fail to receive these important facets of care (Lamb, 1998; Smith, 1998). These findings are applicable to infants, toddlers, and preschoolers and to all forms of child care, ranging from family to center-based programs (National Institute of Child Health and Human Development [NICHD] Early Child Care Research Network, 1998, 2000). Parental involvement and support are crucial factors in any good early childhood program. Parents must always be supported in their role as the primary educators and caregivers for their children. Parents provide the stimulation; emotional, social, and financial support; structure; safety; and interactions and learning experiences on a constant basis for their children. Family-centered care is an integral part of any high-quality early childhood and child care program. In essence, the basic elements of high-quality child care are similar to those of good parenting, and both promote positive developmental outcomes.

Social work is a critical component of a community system of early childhood care and services. A comprehensive system of care must incorporate a multi-disciplinary approach in which collaboration and coordination of care are essential components. Social workers bring a unique understanding of coordinated care and collaboration and are especially trained in identifying and addressing the special emotional and developmental needs of young children who have been exposed to environmental stressors, including neglect, social isolation, violence, substance abuse, and mental illness of primary caregivers.

POLICY STATEMENT

Early childhood is recognized as including a broad range of experiences from birth through 8 years (NAEYC, 2001). NASW supports effective early childhood programs and services that:

■ are offered in diverse settings: families' homes, public and private schools, family day care homes, and group child care centers. Programs should be designed to include children from various racial, ethnic, cultural, and socioeconomic backgrounds.

■ are integrated and include perinatal services, family support services, health and mental health services, educational services, day care (full- and part-time), respite care, culturally sensitive parenting education, and before- and after-school care.

■ include comprehensive prevention, intervention, and support services that are provided for infants and young children, with and without special needs, and their families.

■ are built on the belief that families, as the constant in their children's lives, should be supported in actively participating in the development and implementation of services and programs affecting their children.

■ are built on the belief that families, as the constant in their children's lives, should be supported in actively participating in the development and implementation of family-centered, multidisciplinary services and programs affecting their children, and social workers should be members of that team.

■ use the services of appropriately trained and culturally competent providers who receive ongoing training to ensure continuous learning and professional development.

Furthermore, NASW supports:

■ national, state, and local policies that use the principles of child development and early childhood education to meet the physical, social, emotional, and educational needs of young children and their families.

■ equal access to high-quality, culturally and developmentally appropriate, affordable early childhood services and programs.

■ programs and services that reflect the needs of a variety of family structures and have as their basis sound principles of child development.

■ parents as the first and primary educator and caregiver for young children, and the belief that all children benefit from a sustained primary relationship that is nurturing, supportive, and protective.

■ the co-location of early childhood services including health, education, and child welfare services.

- continuing implementation of existing legislation to ensure appropriate early childhood programs and services for all infants and young children, including children with special needs and their families.

- programs and services that conduct regular, periodic developmental assessments of children in care, provide universal parent education components, and address factors that place children at risk, including health and nutrition, environmental, psychosocial, economic, racial, ethnic, cultural, and linguistic factors.

- high-quality standards with adequate safeguards for very young children and their families in all settings.

- a living wage and adequate benefits for providers of early childhood care and services.

- efforts to ensure continuity for infants and young children receiving services.

- universal access to early childhood services and care including evidence-based home-visiting and preschool programs.

- family leave policies that are equitable, affordable, and universal.

- child care subsidy policies to ensure that all families who need it have access to assistance.

- a variety of equitable child care choices for all families. Those choices should be comparable in terms of quality, accessibility, and availability, and include other family support services such as health, education, and transportation services.

REFERENCES

Capizzano, J., & Adams, G. (2004). *Children in low-income families are less likely to be in center-based child care.* Washington, DC: Urban Institute.

Children's Defense Fund. (2003). *Quality child care helps parents work and learn.* Washington, DC: Author.

Lamb, M. (1998). Nonparental child care: Context, quality, correlates. In W. Damon, I. Sige, & K. Renninger (Eds.), *Handbook of child psychology* (5th ed., pp. 73–134). New York: John Wiley & Sons.

Mitchell, A., Stoney, L., & Dichter, H. (2001). *Financing child care in the United States: An expanded catalog of current strategies.* Kansas, MO: Ewing Marion Kauffman Foundation.

National Association for the Education of Young Children. (2000). *A call for excellence in early childhood education.* Washington, DC: Author.

National Association for the Education of Young Children. (2001). *Standards for preparation of early childhood professionals.* Washington, DC: Author.

National Center for Education Statistics. (1999). *National Household Education Survey, 1999.* Washington, DC: U.S. Department of Education.

National Institute of Child Health and Human Development Early Child Care Research Network. (1998). *Chronicity of maternal depressive symptoms, maternal behavior, and child functioning at 36 months: Results from the NICHD study for early child care.* Washington, DC: U.S. Department of Health and Human Services, National Institutes of Health.

National Institute of Child Health and Human Development Early Child Care Research Network. (2000). The NICHD study of early child care: Contexts of development and developmental outcomes over the first seven years of life. In J. Brooks-Gunn & L. J. Berlin (Eds.), *Young children's education, health, and development: Profile and synthesis project report.* Washington, DC: U.S. Department of Education.

Peisner-Feinberg, E. S., Burchinal, M. R., Clifford, R. M., Culkin, M. L., Howes, C., Kagan, S. L., Yazejian, N., Byler, P., Rustici, J., & Zelazo, J. (1999). *The children of the Cost, Quality, and Outcomes Study go to school.* Chapel Hill, NC: University of North Carolina Frank Porter Graham Child Development Center.

Smith, S. (1998, April). *The past decade's research on child care quality and children's development: What we are learning, directions for the future.* Paper prepared for the Child Care in the New Policy Context meeting of the Office of the Assistant Secretary for Planning and Evaluation, U.S. Department of Health and Human Services, Bethesda, MD.

U.S. Census Bureau. (1982). Trends in child care arrangements of working mothers. In *Current population reports*. Washington, DC: U.S. Government Printing Office.

U.S. Census Bureau. (1997). *Who's minding our preschoolers? Fall 1994* (Update). Washington, DC: U.S. Government Printing Office.

U.S. Department of Education, National Center for Education Statistics. (2002). *America's children: Key national indicators of well-being, 2002*. Washington, DC: U.S. Government Printing Office.

Weatherston, D., & Tableman, B. (2002). *Infant mental health services: Supporting competencies/reducing risks* (2nd ed.). Southgate, MI: Michigan Association for Infant Mental Health.

Whirlpool Foundation. (1995). *Women: The new providers*. New York: Families and Work Institute.

Zero to Three Infant Mental Health Task Force. *What is infant mental health?* Washington, DC: Zero to Three.

SUGGESTED READINGS

Brandon, P. (2000). Child care utilization among working mothers raising children with disabilities. *Journal of Family and Economic Issues, 21,* 343–364.

Children's Defense Fund. (2002). *Low–income families bear the burden of state child care cutbacks*. Washington, DC: Author.

Children's Defense Fund. (2002). *State developments in child care, early education, and school-age care 2001*. Washington, DC: Author.

Children's Defense Fund. (2003). *Quality child care helps parents work and children learn*. Washington, DC: Author.

Donahue, E. H., & Campbell, N. D. (2002). *Making care less taxing: Improving state child care and dependent care tax provisions*. Washington, DC: National Women's Law Center.

Gnezda, M. T. (1996). Public policy report. Welfare reform: Personal responsibilities and opportunities for early childhood advocates. *Young Children, 52*(1), 55–58.

Shonkoff, J. P., & Phillips, D. A. (2000). *From neurons to neighborhoods: The science of early childhood development*. Washington, DC: National Academies Press.

Policy statement approved by the NASW Delegate Assembly, August 2005. This policy statement supersedes the statement on Early Childhood Care and Services approved by the Delegate Assembly in 1996 and referred by the 2002 Delegate Assembly to the 2005 Delegate Assembly for revision. For additional information, contact the National Association of Social Workers, 750 First Street, NE, Suite 700, Washington, DC 20002-4241; telephone: 202-408-8600; e-mail: press@naswdc.org

Education of Children and Youths

BACKGROUND

Federal Legislation

The War on Poverty launched during the administration of President Lyndon B. Johnson arguably set the pattern for the significant involvement of the federal government in public education that we observe today. The original Elementary and Secondary Education Act of 1965 (ESEA) (P.L. 89-10) set standards for students, teachers, and most important, formulas for block grants to states. The landmark legislation was hailed as one of the most important components of the War on Poverty because it instituted large-scale resources to educationally deprived students, including those from low-income neighborhoods, those who were nonnative English speakers, and those with disabilities.

The passage of the Education for All Handicapped Children Act of 1975 (P.L. 94-142) brought a major shift in responsibility for educating people with disabilities. This landmark legislation guaranteed all children a free and appropriate public education (FAPE), the right to due process, and individualization of instruction according to need. Subsequent re-enactments of this legislation have broadened the coverage to include the educational needs of children ages three to 21 years, additional conditions that qualify people with disabilities for coverage, and greater encouragement for the implementation of local programs for children from birth to three years.

At first, this legislation ironically resulted in the segregation of children with disabilities from the regular education classrooms for some or all of the school day to receive specialized instruction and therapy. The Regular Education Initiative (McDonald, 1996) sought to rectify this situation by emphasizing "inclusion" for people with developmental disabilities. Schools are now encouraged to deliver services in the regular classroom with classmates who are not identified as students with special needs. Inclusion also refers to students with other problems, who can benefit from personalized instruction in small groups or with specialized co-instructors assigned to the regular classroom to support their specialized learning needs (McDonald, 1996). It remains essential, however, that accommodation of students with severe disabilities in pull-out programs continue to be available when their individualized education plan (IEP) identifies the need. This approach was mandated and reinforced with passage of the Individuals with Disabilities Education Act (IDEA) (P.L. 101-476), which mandated specific changes in IEPs to include measurable goals and clear intervention strategies.

Perhaps the most dramatic and far-reaching federal legislation affecting primary and secondary education has been the passage of the No Child Left Behind Act (P.L. 107-110). This act mandates specific testing of students on their proficiency in basic skills at various intervals. Because of this and other issues, the law has become a lightening rod of controversy with opponents questioning the reliability of standardized tests. Says Disability Rights Advocates (2001):

> It is a basic principle of test validity that a test must actually measure what the test is intended to measure. A test is not valid in itself, but is valid only for a particular purpose. A test that is valid for one purpose may not be valid for another. As noted in a recent

report by the National Research Council of the National Academy of Sciences, "tests that are valid for influencing classroom practice "leading" the curriculum, or holding schools accountable are not appropriate for making high-stakes decisions about individual student mastery unless the curriculum, the teaching, and the tests are aligned." (p. 14)

No Child Left Behind mandates teacher accountability on an unprecedented scale. Although supported by most parents, teacher unions continue to be increasingly disturbed by this legislation.

The No Child Left Behind Act, as well as many other educational issues, became highly politicized in the presidential campaign of 2004. Some of the issues included proposals for proficiency tests in math and reading for high school graduates, increased funding of private schools through vouchers for low-income families, increased funding for charter schools, Pell grants for regular course work assistance for high school students, and strengthened partnerships between employers and college students. The 2004 Individuals with Disabilities Education Improvement Act (P.L. 108-446), a revision of IDEA, calls on educational institutions to demonstrate improved outcomes for all students.

Federal and State Funding

Since 1980, most federal funds were disbursed to states through block grants and earmarked for mandated categorical programs. Over the years, this method has significantly changed in favor of unrestricted funding to individual states for disbursement. This change allows individual states to determine how this money is spent. As a result there has been a progressive decline in funds appropriated for educational services. Also, although many states have opted to pay for education through property taxes, this has shifted an unequal burden onto homeowners. Increased income taxes are proving to be unpopular, so many states are looking at sales taxes or gambling revenues to pay for increased school funding.

High-Risk Students

There is an urgent need to better identify and provide services to vulnerable student groups, such as children with disabilities, poor rural youths, children of migrant laborers, other economically disadvantaged children, children of color, pregnant adolescents, children of adolescent single parents, new immigrants, abused and neglected children, truant children, drug-dependent children, latchkey children, and children who move frequently. For example, children who have limited language skills have a four times greater chance of graduating from high school if they participate in bilingual programs, yet these programs are threatened constantly with cutbacks (Committee on Education and Labor, 1986). Specific legislation that mandates continuous services to transient or homeless students was established in 1987 by the Stewart B. McKinney Homeless Assistance Act (P.L. 100-77), which has been amended and later became known as the McKinney-Vento Act.

Many of the reforms of the 1960s and 1970s, such as the War on Poverty's attempts to raise family incomes and to provide school breakfasts and health programs, were based on the recognition that students who are hungry, sick, or worried about their families could not achieve as well in school as students who were free of these cares. These reforms have been continuously threatened by budget cuts. A movement to develop a full-ranging curriculum focused on children's health and mental health issues to be offered from kindergarten through high school is widely supported, but such a curriculum is hollow without the provision of concrete services, such as school breakfast and lunch programs and counseling for anxiety-producing problems in students' lives.

Potential dropouts and push-outs represent another significant high-risk group in the educational system. In too many cases, discipline involves suspensions or expulsions that deny access to school or placement in supervised atmospheres. Given that these students have already shown that their ability to maintain self-control and anticipate consequences is limited, their exclusion from school increases the risk of negative behaviors, such as crime and misuse of alcohol and other drugs.

Furthermore, students from racial and ethnic minority groups experience a disproportionately high incidence of suspensions and expulsions. Various alternatives to out-of-school suspension are being implemented in many districts around the country, but the results of these experiences have not been evaluated (Gay, 1989). In addition, children and youths who have been incarcerated must not lose their right to an equal education.

Safe, Positive, and Secure Schools

Fortunately, the use of corporal punishment has been declining in U.S. schools. Decreased public acceptance, increased litigation against school boards and educators, and legislative actions such as child abuse laws have contributed to this decline. Regretfully, however, many states continue to use corporal punishment as a disciplinary measure, even though research and experience prove it counterproductive and harmful in the long term (Strauss, 1991). As many studies have shown, showing expectations of success have a positive effect on how well students do. Students can be provided with a safe, positive, and secure school environment by valuing all students for the contributions they make, promoting the cultural sensitivity and competence of faculty and staff by ensuring a nondiscriminatory educational climate, establishing rational and humane disciplinary policies and alternatives to suspension and expulsion, and eliminating corporal punishment, intimidation, and scapegoating from public school education.

Alternative Education

Millions of youths are underserved or not served at all by the public educational system. About 30 percent of children who start first grade do not finish high school. Of those who complete 12th grade, many do not have the requisite skills and behaviors to enter the labor market successfully. Many become marginal participants in society and heavy users of public health, welfare, rehabilitation, and penal resources (Children's Defense Fund, 1990; Hare & Sullivan, 1996). Any reform in public education must include alternative routes to becoming educated and finding successful roles as adults. These alternatives, however, must not isolate "undesirable" students from the mainstream, but rather offer them sufficient support to meet their unique behavioral and situation needs.

The widespread availability of the computer, and the Internet in particular, has had a revolutionary impact in the classroom, and more significantly, on educational formats for learning at home. The 1999 Parent Survey of the National Household Education Surveys indicated that 850,000 parents are home schooling their children (Bielick, Chandler, & Broughman, 1999). No doubt, parents who are home schooling are sincere in their efforts and are providing an education that allows their children to be competitive in a rapidly changing and highly technical world. Home schooling arrangements, however, lack reasonable oversight by qualified school personnel to ensure that all children have access to the highest level of their educational ability.

Relationship of School to Home and Community

Parents and school personnel often have mistaken perceptions of each other because of problems in negotiating the bureaucratic maze of public school education and because of the blame and antagonism over students' problems. Effective communication among school personnel, families, and communities is vital to reach the goals set for each student. Coordination of services is critical to the efficient and effective use of resources and the attainment of goals. Making school buildings available for use as community centers and early childhood education sites is key to building schools' relationships with families and communities. Providing services to parents after school and at night gives the school a position in the community as not just a caretaker and educator of students. Most school buildings are underused during summer seasons and can be available for educational purposes.

Sex Education

Although more young people are sexually active at an earlier age than in the past, in general they lack adequate knowledge and motivation to protect themselves from the hazards of premature sexuality, including pregnancy and disease. Sexually active adolescents and preadolescents who are experimenting with drugs are particularly vulnerable. Although education in this area may be crucial, this topic is characteristically downplayed for fear of offending some constituent group.

In 1986, Surgeon General C. Everett Koop called for AIDS education to be included in sex education curriculums beginning in elementary schools (Koop, 1986). At the time, NASW commended Koop for this brave stand. The need still exists. Public schools have been loath to comply with Koop's call because of public dissent. A few exceptions have braved the path, but much still needs to be done to support young people dealing with their emerging sexuality.

Social Workers in Public Schools

School social workers are one of the few resources in schools for addressing personal and social problems that inhibit students' ability to learn. They constitute a stable and growing force within the field of education. Approximately 9,300 school social workers serve students in 37 education jurisdictions across the country (Torres, 1996). Sadly, the distribution of social workers is uneven and inequitable; school social workers tend to be clustered in greater proportions in industrial states and in school districts with greater resources. The skills and competencies of school social workers enable schools to carry out their primary functions of educating all pupils more effectively, by:

■ assessing and intervening in the social and emotional needs of students in relation to learning;

■ understanding, evaluating, and improving the total environment of pupils and thus contributing to a positive school climate;

■ strengthening the connections among families, schools, and communities by identifying and linking these components to create the best learning environment for the student and making education relevant to all constituents;

■ building mutual communication and support among all participants in the school system, including other professionals, parents, students, staff, and the community;

■ developing preventive and remedial intervention programs for systemic problems

■ providing meaningful and relevant consultation and in-service programs to teachers and school administrators concerning student needs and counterproductive school policies;

■ providing group and individual counseling for students and when necessary, for the family;

■ ensuring that students with disabilities receive appropriate educational services; and

■ providing training and support for conflict resolution programs and other student support programs, such as drug use prevention, sex education, alternative suspension programs, and parent education programs.

ISSUE STATEMENT

The education of our nation's children continues to be a top priority of NASW. NASW has been very active in advancing legislation to promote the role of school social workers, and many NASW publications have highlighted the role of school social workers in education. In addition, in 1995 NASW established the first Specialty Practice Section for School Social Work. School social workers continue to collaborate closely with school psychologists and other professionals in the school system. In fact, many policies identified and incorporated in this statement were collaboratively developed with other agencies and organizations.

Public education is a primary institution that shares with the family the responsibility for raising and training children and youths. Furthermore, public education is a vital socializing force that, with the family, promotes the total development of the child—intellectually, socially, and physically. To nurture the full potential of children and youths, our nation's public schools are an excellent forum to ensure equal opportunity and preparation. NASW believes that schools must pursue excellence and provide for the physical and emotional safety and growth, in addition to the education, of children. Schools must identify students with disabilities and disadvantages early and provide support to such students in accordance with federal legislation, such as the Individuals with Disabilities Education Improvement Act of 2004. Educational environments promote transitional learning in the areas of work, community living, and civic responsibility. Students with excessive truancy and who are at risk of dropping out must receive outreach services, and factual health information for students regarding sexuality, relationships, and sexually transmitted diseases must be provided within the context of a comprehensive health and family life education course.

POLICY STATEMENT

Components of Education

Education is a continuing maturation process that promotes the intellectual, physical, and social development of students in their environments. It is the position of NASW that the educational system has a responsibility to provide all students with free, appropriate, and high quality education. Through quality education, students should be able to attain full vocational and career skills and concomitant behaviors conducive to success and lifelong learning. In addition, students need educational opportunities that foster increased self-awareness and self-actualization, empathy for others, understanding and acceptance of differences in race, culture, ethnicity, and sexual orientation, and understanding of the personal realities of individuals with disabilities and how to help them to participate more fully in normal daily

activities. Finally, educators should facilitate an awareness that health-compromising behaviors, particularly sexual ones, substance abuse, and violence, can have lifelong and life-threatening consequences. The following are steps school districts can take toward achieving these goals.

■ **Pupil Services Teams.** The policy of NASW is that the model of collaboration used by multidisciplinary teams, including school social workers, psychologists, pupil services personnel, teachers, administrators, and families, in the identification and evaluation of students for special services is optimal for the delivery of services to all students. The school social worker provides expertise in coordinating home, school, and community resources to enhance learning objectives, in assessing students' adaptive behaviors, and in describing cultural history. The multidisciplinary team can also implement intervention and prevention strategies for at-risk students before a special education referral is made as a result of the diagnostic assessment team process.

■ **Least-restrictive Environment.** Every student has the right to a free, appropriate public education in the least-restrictive environment. NASW supports the least-restrictive environment concept as it is determined individually for each student. The school social worker on the multidisciplinary team plays a key role in determining the least-restrictive setting for each student and in helping parents and students become involved in the decision making process. NASW supports the regular education environment as the first placement consideration, and NASW strongly supports placement of students in the setting that best meets the student's needs, with the appropriate continuum of services, staffing, and assistive devices, and re-placement in a more restrictive setting if so determined by student need.

■ **Alternative Testing and Performance.** All students do not learn in the same fashion. Divergent learners may test poorly on standardized tests. This does not mean the student is not learning, rather the particular testing used may not adequately tap the student's knowledge. Therefore, alternate ways to measure academic growth is essential, especially among the learning disabled population of students and other educationally disadvantaged pupils in American public schools. There is a risk that educationally disadvantaged students held to the same standards as other students will be "responsible" for low test scores that districts receive and therefore will place school districts on various watch lists. This combination of circumstances can often result in discrimination toward the educationally disadvantaged population if the standards of achievement are not changed to reflect growth among divergent leaders.

■ **Family, School, and Community Linkages.** Strengthening the relationship among the families, schools, and communities is a fundamental principle of any educational policy. NASW encourages linking the school to community resources as sound public policy and encourages further policy development focused on bringing schools, families, and communities together for mutual support and problem solving as well as for cultural and celebratory events. School–community centers, which facilitate the participation of families and the wider community in school activities, allow opportunities for community-based social workers to collaborate with school social workers in working with teachers and families.

■ **Early Childhood Education.** It is the policy of NASW that early childhood education should continue to be expanded and made available to all children through federal and state support (Bishop, 1996; see also NASW policy statement on *Early Childhood Care and Services*). Significant research supports the position that early intervention for children with disabilities of all types benefits their later ability to succeed educationally. In addition, such programs promote total learning for all children through their emphasis on early stimulation of children within the home, recognition and use of parenting skills, provisions for adequate nutrition and medical care, and the introduction of important social skills needed for later school success.

■ **Career and Vocational Education.** NASW affirms that the primary function of education is to prepare students for life tasks, specifically the world of work. Preparation should include instilling the attitudes and behaviors that ensure successful entry into the labor market. American children must be prepared to compete in a global society that offers opportunities for all nations to share the resources of the world. It is the policy of NASW that transitional experiences and entry structures should be available throughout the educational ladder. To accomplish this, schools, postsecondary educational institutions, communities, and businesses should continue to form linkages that provide opportunities for entry into the labor market. Career and vocational programs should have the same economic and academic investment from school facilities and administrations as college preparatory programs have (see NASW policy statement on *School Dropout Prevention*). High schools should assist all students who are preparing for post-secondary education, and all students should be graduating with a high school diploma.

■ **Comprehensive Health and Mental Health Education.** It is the policy of NASW that educating students about their health and physical needs and about optimal health practices, including sexual conduct and HIV/AIDS education, is a necessary and appropriate function of public schools. Such programs should be developed by multidisciplinary teams that include, but are not restricted to, social workers, health care providers, educators, and parents. The programs should be evidence-based and use best practices. They should be offered in early childhood programs or kindergarten and should continue throughout students' formal public education. Naturally, such programs should be age and developmentally appropriate and provide information that enables students to make responsible choices about their bodies, behavior, relationships, and emotions. To make responsible choices, students need access to basic facts about human physiology and psychology, including information on reproduction, family planning, pregnancy prevention, responsible parenting, HIV/AIDS and sexually transmitted diseases, substance use, healthy eating, exercise, stress management, anger management, and general lifestyle decisions.

A comprehensive life education program should involve parents and should promote open communication among parents, students, and schools. With increasing attention to children suffering physical and sexual abuse, it is imperative that students are protected from violence and abuse. Social work services must be made available for the education and counseling of affected students. Prevention programs that build self-esteem, teach conflict mediation and bully prevention skills, promote positive decision making and help students develop protective behaviors to guard against victimization should be provided in schools.

■ **Nondiscriminatory and Integrated Education.** The right to equal educational opportunity requires a nonsegregated, nonsexist environment and a curriculum that reflects a pluralistic society. NASW views the optimal goal of integration as a requisite for a positive, pluralistic educational experience. Integration should provide for and facilitate interaction among students and faculty of diverse racial, cultural, religious, spiritual, and ethnic backgrounds. An integrated environment promotes understanding, knowledge, and acceptance of diversity in family composition (for example sexual orientation and same-sex families). To ensure nondiscriminatory education for all races, a policy prohibiting the use of discriminatory or stereotyping labels, for example by sports teams and mascots, should be established. Bilingual education programs promote greater understanding of the educational process of those experiencing language and cultural barriers.

■ **Discipline.** It is the policy of NASW that disciplinary practices in schools, including detention, suspension, and expulsion, must reflect the desire to shape students' behavior toward productive participation in schools and society. Many such policies are clearly punitive in intent and thus do not reflect the school's concern for retaining and successfully graduating students involved in their disciplinary system. The focus of school discipline should be to help students accept responsibility for their own behavior, rather than punishment, through a shared problem-solving process with parents and guardians. NASW subscribes to the following recommendations as policy initiatives related to disciplinary actions:

1. Students should be guaranteed due process in serious disciplinary actions;

2. Social workers should be used as advocates in promoting the best interests of the students and schools;

3. Alternative education programs should be developed based on students' unique educational needs; and

4. The use of corporal punishment in schools should be abolished in the remaining states that still approve of such practices, and social work services should be made available to train teachers to teach children conflict resolution techniques, including improved interpersonal communication skills.

■ **Full Funding for Education.** All legally mandated educational programs must be funded at a level that ensures their effective implementation. Such programs include IDEA; the Education of the Handicapped Act Amendments of 1986, including Part H; the Rehabilitation Act of 1973 (P.L. 93-112), especially section 504; the Americans with Disabilities Act of 1991; the No Child Left Behind Act; and Title IV, VI, and VII of the Civil Rights Acts of 1957 and 1964. Programs must not be weakened by changing or eliminating key rules and regulations because of politically shortsighted initiatives or economic recession. The rights of students and families should not be eliminated or reduced to foster a more controlling, and in some cases, more oppressive environment. Mandating educational programs without allocating the full cost of implementing such programs is not good public policy. Full funding for education should include safe and fully functioning educational facilities in addition to appropriate programming.

■ **Evaluation and Research.** Evaluation of school social work services is critical in documenting effectiveness. Federal, state, and local education agencies as well as school social workers should conduct research related to the effectiveness of social work services in the schools. Research that examines both the short-term and long-term effectiveness of innovative prevention programs must be supported.

■ **Role of School Social Workers.** NASW encourages legislation and funding at the federal and state levels to substantially increase the number of social workers available in schools to serve both students with identified disabilities and students in the general school population. Because of the inequitable distribution of social workers both nationally and within individual states, NASW recommends that pupil services teams in every state include school social workers on the elementary and secondary levels who graduated from a Council on Social Work Education–accredited program. Furthermore, school social workers are qualified to implement interagency agreements between school districts and human services agencies, both public and private, to promote collaboration in the provision of services to all pupils. Human services agencies include protective services, juvenile courts, mental health facilities, family services agencies, and rehabilitative resources. School social workers are the professionals who help ensure that students have access to necessary components of education. These components enable students to acquire the academic skills and the ability to function in and contribute to a multicultural society.

REFERENCES

Americans with Disabilities Act, Pub. L. 101-336, 104 Stat. 327 (1990).

Bielick, S., Chandler, K., & Broughman, S. P. (1999). Homeschooling in the United States: 1999. *Education Statistics Quarterly, 3*(3).

Bishop, K. (1996). Part H of the Individuals with Disabilities Education Act: Analysis and implications for social workers. In R. Constable, J. Flynn, & S. McDonald (Eds.), *School social work: Practice and research perspectives* (3rd ed., pp. 116–131). Chicago: Lyceum Press.

Children's Defense Fund. (1990). *Children, 1990: A report card, briefing book and action primer.* Washington, DC: Author.

Civil Rights Act of 1957, Pub. L. 86-387, Title IV, Sec. 401, 73 Stat. 724.

Civil Rights Act of 1964, Pub. L. 88-352, 78 Stat. 241.

Committee on Education and Labor, House of Representatives. (1986). *The report on bilingual education of the 99th Congress, 2d session.* Washington, DC: U.S. Government Printing Office.

Disability Rights Advocates. (2001). *Do no harm—High stakes testing and students with learning disabilities.* Retrieved March 12, 2005 from, http://www.dralegal.org/publications/do_no_harm.pdf

Education for All Handicapped Children Act of 1975, Pub. L. 94-142, 89 Stat. 773.

Education of the Handicapped Act Amendments of 1986, Pub. L. 99-457, 100 Stat. 1145.

Elementary and Secondary Education Act of 1965, Pub. L. 89-10, 79 Stat. 27.

Gay, G. (1989). Ethnic minorities and educational equality. In J. A. Banks & C. A. Banks (Eds.), *Multicultural education: Issues and perspectives.* Boston: Allyn & Bacon.

Hare, I., & Sullivan, K. (1996). The economic, political and social world of school social work. In R. Constable, J. Flynn, & S. McDonald (Eds.), *School social work: Practice and research perspectives* (3rd ed., pp. 66–84). Chicago: Lyceum Press.

Individuals with Disabilities Education Act, Pub. L. 101-476, 104 Stat. 1142 (1990).

Individuals with Disabilities Education Improvement Act, Pub. L. 108-446, 118 Stat. 2647 (2004).

Koop, C. E. (1986). *The Surgeon General's report on Acquired Immune Deficiency Syndrome.* Washington, DC: U.S. Government Printing Office.

McDonald, S. (1996). The trend toward inclusion. In R. Constable, J. Flynn, & S. McDonald (Eds.), *School social work: Practice and* research perspectives (3rd ed., pp. 147–155). Chicago: Lyceum Press.

No Child Left Behind Act of 2001, Pub. L. 107-110, 15 Stat. 1425.

Rehabilitation Act of 1973, Pub. L. 93-112, 87 Stat. 355.

Strauss, M. A. (1991). *Beating the devil out of them*. New York: Lexington Books.

Torres, S. (1996). The status of school social workers in America. *Social Work in Education, 18,* 8–18.

Policy statement approved by the NASW Delegate Assembly, August 2005. This policy statement supersedes the policy on Education of Children and Youths approved by the NASW Delegate Assembly, August 1996 and referred by the 2002 Delegate Assembly to the 2005 Delegate Assembly for revision, which superseded the statement on Preschool, Elementary, and Secondary Education, approved by the Delegate Assembly in 1987. The original policy statement was approved by the NASW National Board of Directors in June 1985 following recommendations by the Delegate Assembly in 1984. For additional information, contact the National Association of Social Workers, 750 First Street, NE, Suite 700, Washington, DC 20002-4241; telephone: 202-408-8600; e-mail: press@naswdc.org

Electoral Politics

BACKGROUND

Social workers have always participated vigorously in political processes. The social work profession grew out of the political activism of its founders, from Jane Addams and Jeanette Rankin in the early 1900s to Frances Perkins, Harry Hopkins, and Molly Dewson in the New Deal era, to current political office holders. Social workers now hold many prominent political offices, and, in recent decades, have moved toward greater participation in political activity (Weismiller & Rome, 1995).

In most representative democracies around the world, the electoral political system is the determining vehicle for expressing human values and for the provision of resources. As experts in the areas of human needs and services delivery, social workers' role in the political process is axiomatic. Since the early part of the 20th century, social workers have participated in national, state, and local political party campaigns and elections, and they have lobbied the legislative and executive branches of government, advancing policy recommendations and implementing new programs.

Beginning with Theodore Roosevelt's Progressive Party in 1912, social workers have been active in presidential campaigns, including those of Franklin Roosevelt, Lyndon Johnson, and Bill Clinton. NASW has been active in partisan federal and state elections since 1976. Social workers show a growing willingness to enter the political arena in all capacities—as voters, party officials, political professionals, candidates, and officeholders.

Two studies fortify the perception that social workers are active in campaigns and elections and that they vote at much higher rates than the general public. One conducted in 1984 replicated a 1968 survey designed to assess the level of activism by social workers (Reeser & Epstein, 1990). Among measures of electoral participation, this study found increases in specific behaviors, such as giving money to campaigns, volunteering for candidates, and encouraging political activity among clients. Reeser and Epstein's historical comparison of social workers' political behavior in the original survey and their own demonstrated fundamental increases in the profession's political activism profile.

The second study examined social workers' electoral participation in the 1988 presidential campaign (Sherradan & Parker, 1991). More than 92 percent of the 222 social workers who responded reported voting in that election, a turnout rate 1.62 times that of the general public. In the same study, social workers reported making campaign contributions, going to meetings and rallies, and working for candidates or political parties at a rate twice that of the general public. The authors concluded that these high participation levels provide a foundation from which the profession can exert increased political influence.

Throughout its 50-year history, NASW has promoted the broad concept of electoral political action in various ways. Political activity is encouraged in the *Code of Ethics* (NASW, 2000), and successive Delegate Assemblies have encouraged social worker involvement. On the practice level, valuable program initiatives have included:

■ operating federal and state political action committees (PACs)

■ organizing national, regional, and chapter training programs

- establishing a check-off system on annual membership renewal forms to enhance voluntary candidate contributions

- mobilizing Association support for political candidates whose stance on issues advances NASW's professional and program agenda

- encouraging social workers to seek public office

- promoting voter registration.

Furthermore, by supporting practitioners who spent decades securing legal and commercial recognition of the profession through licensing and vendorship campaigns in state legislatures, NASW steadily built elements of electoral political activity into its program.

Some social work educators and practitioners, however, have been more equivocal and cautious in their approach to electoral politics (Salcido & Seck, 1992; Weismiller & Dempsey, 1993). Educators' ambivalence is reflected in social work education programs with a dearth of either electoral political field placements or specific curriculum material about campaigns, elections, political parties, or other important electoral institutions and processes (Wolk, Weismiller, Dempsey, & Pray, 1994).

Electoral Political Institutions and Processes

Electoral politics are the formal and informal systems by which citizens and groups in a democracy contest for the power to run government (Plano & Greenberg, 1989). Primary electoral political institutions include political parties, interest groups and coalitions, candidate campaign organizations, PACs, the campaign industry (that is, businesses that provide management, polling, fundraising, and communication services to candidates), and the media. Electoral political processes encompass candidate nominations, party conventions, primaries, caucuses, campaigns, elections (including primary, general, and special), voter registration, voting (including absentee and special voting programs), ballot measures, and transitions.

Some aspects of electoral politics, including political parties, PACs, transitions, and political education require special attention by NASW. Participation in these processes often amplifies the political influence of a group.

Political parties are voluntary groups of voters with shared ideology, who organize to try to win elections, control government, and influence public policy. Political party activity increases organizational electoral power. A person who holds firmly to a party or its cause is a *partisan*, hence the term "partisan politics." Partisan politics are about working with, or within, major political parties to achieve desired public policy goals. Whatever partisan choices an individual or organization makes, it is still possible and often necessary to have civil and constructive relationships with partisans of other political parties.

Confusion often occurs about the terms "bipartisan" and "nonpartisan." *Bipartisan* means relating to, or involving, members of two parties. Republicans and Democrats presenting a united front in the face of a serious foreign threat to the country is a bipartisan action. *Nonpartisan* usually refers to elections in which candidates have no party designations, and political parties are prohibited from entering candidates.

Federal election law refers to a corporate political committee as a separate, segregated fund (SSF), although it is more commonly called a PAC. As the name implies, money contributed to an SSF is held in a separate bank account from the general corporate treasury. These accounts hold money voluntarily contributed by Association members, and can be used legally for candidate contributions (Plano & Greenberg, 1989). NASW maintains such an account, called Political Action for Candidate Election (PACE), in accordance with federal election law. Authority to make decisions about candidate endorsements and disbursements from the PACE fund has been delegated by the NASW National Board of Directors to the National PACE Board of Trustees.

Transition refers to the time between election to an office and the assumption of the office. Successful candidates use transition time to prepare to hold office. This presents an opportunity for organizations and campaign activists to shape the development of a new administration.

Political education is how an organization develops a sense of the framework in which its political activity will take place. It involves educating members about specific policy issues, candidates, parties, and electoral processes, and how these relate to the economic, political, and social situations in local, state, and national elections (Kahn, 1991). Political education also includes helping members develop an understanding of the relationship between politics and economics that they can explain easily to others. In asking rhetorically, "What makes politics so important?" Jesse Jackson answered: "The political order is the distribution system for the economic order. Politics determines who gets what, when, where, and how" (National Rainbow Coalition, 1994, p. 1).

NASW Involvement in Electoral Politics

Current tax and campaign election laws permit corporations such as NASW to use dues-generated funds to support all electoral activity of their members, except for direct contributions to candidates. Although these laws make much activity legally permissible, the availability of funds limits what is organizationally feasible. NASW has numerous demands on its resources and must balance many needs in its program planning and budgeting process.

National Level. Elections provide a vehicle for accomplishing diverse Association agendas. NASW has focused on electing progressive candidates to public offices for three decades. Since 1984, NASW and PACE have made it a priority to support the candidacies of women and people of color seeking election to federal offices whose agendas are aligned with those of the Association on the most significant issues. The composition of Congress shows some increased diversity, and social workers can be proud of the role NASW has played in that change.

Elections can also be used to gain power for the profession. The 1993 Delegate Assembly made support of social worker candidates for public offices a priority. Between 1991 and 1995 the Association published three editions of the directory, *Social Workers Serving in Elective Offices* (NASW, 1995).

State Level. NASW electoral activity in states originated primarily from chapter legislative initiatives on professional issues such as licensing and vendorship. Acquiring the means to support or oppose legislators spurred the creation of chapter PACs. Once they were in the electoral arena, chapters quickly realized the value of trying to influence the outcome of statewide office races, particularly the governor's office and capitalized on opportunities to do so.

Ballot measures are also an increasingly used electoral tool that chapters are using to spread their sphere of influence. NASW's interest in state ballot measures is mounting. These measures include the *initiative*, a mechanism by which citizens can propose legislation or constitutional amendments; the *referendum*, a mechanism by which voters can veto a bill passed by their legislature; and the *recall*, a procedure enabling voters to remove an elected official from office before his or her term has expired (Plano & Greenberg, 1989).

Recent election cycles have seen important referenda on abortion in Maryland (in 1992) and on public school financing in Michigan (in 1994). Initiatives on welfare reform in California, anti-gay and lesbian rights proposals in Oregon and Colorado, and tax limitations in Washington state went before voters in 1992. In the 1994 election cycle, several states authorized anti-gay and lesbian proposals, and California presented restrictive immigration legislation, an initiative on a single-payer health care system, and a recall vote on a state senator who supported gun control restrictions (Priest, 1994). Ballot measures present major threats and opportunities in the electoral arena (Pear, 1994).

Issues Raised by Electoral Political Participation

Candidate Endorsements. A candidate endorsement is a public statement of support and commitment to provide resources and mobilize members to promote, work, and vote for the candidate. NASW has authorized PACE to make such endorsements on behalf of the Association. Endorsement decisions are based on established process and criteria, including thorough research on the potential endorsees and their opponents and deliberations between NASW, PACE, and chapters (NASW, 1994).

Candidate Contributions. Through PACE, NASW provides financial support to endorsed candidates. Current federal law and state laws require that money given to candidates by corporations such as NASW come only from monies voluntarily contributed by members and disbursed by PACs. NASW may also make other campaign support available to candidates such as recruiting volunteers; mailing information to members; publicizing a candidate's record on policy issues; and using an endorsement by NASW, photo opportunities, letters of support, and assistance with position papers and issue development.

Fairness. The social work professional value of fairness requires that the Association maintain procedures for candidate endorsements that are open and even-handed. To maintain credibility with candidates and its own members, NASW and PACE follow a clearly defined endorsement process, with criteria that are applied fairly to all candidates who wish to go through the process.

NASW can promote inclusion of members in its political activities by respecting the diversity of political positions they hold. PACE is committed to endorsing political candidates only on the basis of their support for NASW policy positions, not on the basis of political party affiliation. It is PACE's responsibility during its endorsement deliberations to give fair consideration to all candidates (Kendall, 1994).

Communication with Power versus Exercise of Power. Having readily available communication with a public official is often confused with having power to influence that official. Having readily available communication with a decision maker is not synonymous with power. Social workers frequently view a friendly political relationship as a successful relationship, regardless of whether it advances the agenda

of the profession or of that professional. The goal of NASW is to build political relationships with elected leaders that will result in a favorable action on its policy priorities (Kendall, 1994).

ISSUE STATEMENT

Social work is inextricably linked to electoral politics in a variety of ways. The political authority of decision makers confers ability to determine access to, and distribution of, vital resources. Political power sets, limits, and defines quality of life for all citizens, affecting almost every aspect of their daily lives.

Social workers possess a continuum of knowledge about human needs and behavior, services delivery, systems that affect individuals and groups, and the effects of public policy. Therefore, they are in a unique position to participate in electoral politics, to advocate for candidates, laws, and policies that promote NASW's agenda. As a profession, it is imperative that social workers become informed about, and involved in, all levels of electoral politics.

Social workers frequently approach electoral politics with great caution because of its potential for divisiveness. The major cause for division occurs around the concepts of partisanship and political parties. Some members of the profession believe that NASW should be nonpartisan in terms of candidates for office or that NASW should take positions only on issues, not candidates. Other members think that NASW should be aligned with only one of the major parties, and still others favor a bipartisan or multi-partisan approach.

There are two practical difficulties with NASW adopting a nonpartisan approach to candidates or taking positions on issues instead of candidates. For most political offices in this country, partisanship is unavoidable. Only a few offices, such as those on school boards and some municipal and judicial positions, are contested on a nonpartisan basis. Virtually all other elective offices involve partisan contests. If an individual or group wants to be able to influence electoral outcomes, it has to make partisan choices. Campaigns and elections in the U.S. political system are, by and large, about choices among candidates, not issues. Social workers must be involved in the election of candidates who support NASW values and issues to advance the profession.

POLICY STATEMENT

1. NASW reaffirms that participation in electoral politics is consistent with fundamental social work values, such as self-determination, empowerment, democratic decision making, equal opportunity, inclusion, and the promotion of social justice.

2. NASW's ability to achieve public policy goals and other political objectives depends on participation in the full spectrum of legitimate electoral activities; these activities should be thoroughly integrated into other Association programs.

3. NASW's primary organizational strength lies in the involvement and mobilization of its members in all aspects of electoral politics, with particular emphasis on campaigns and elections, electoral coalitions, fundraising, and the seeking of public office.

4. NASW reaffirms that members seeking or serving in appointive and elective public offices are rendering community service consistent with the profession's *Code of Ethics*.

5. NASW encourages its members to participate in all facets of electoral political activity and recognizes the right of individual members to make their own choices about electoral participation and candidate support.

6. NASW seeks to work collaboratively with the Council on Social Work Education and social work education programs to develop appropriate curriculum material on, and field placements in, electoral politics, and to expand opportunities for political social work practice.

7. NASW cautions that members' vigorous participation in electoral politics and advocacy for NASW positions are bounded by

avoidance of conflicts of interest that would take unfair advantage of any professional relationship or exploitation of others to further their personal, religious, political, or business interests (NASW, 2000).

REFERENCES

Kahn, S. (1991). *Organizing: A guide for grassroots leaders*. Silver Spring, MD: NASW Press.

Kendall, J. (1994). *Report and recommendations: Midwest PACE project meeting and focus group*. Washington, DC: National Association of Social Workers.

National Association of Social Workers. (1994). *Candidate endorsements* (PACE Tip Sheet Series No. 4). Washington, DC: Author.

National Association of Social Workers. (1995). *Social workers serving in elective offices* (3rd ed.). Washington, DC: Author.

National Association of Social Workers. (2000). *Code of ethics of the National Association of Social Workers*. Washington, DC: Author.

National Rainbow Coalition. (1994, June 10). *Jax Fax, 2*(23).

Pear, R. (1994, November 7). Debate on whose voice is heard on initiatives. *The New York Times*, p. B11.

Plano, J. C., & Greenberg, M. (1989). *The American political dictionary* (8th ed.). Fort Worth, TX: Holt, Rinehart & Winston.

Priest, D. (1994, November 2). Ballot names may yield to ballot measures. *Washington Post*, p. A9.

Reeser, L. C., & Epstein, I. (1990). *Professionalization and activism in social work: The sixties, the eighties, and the future*. New York: Columbia University Press.

Salcido, R. M., & Seck, E. T. (1992). Political participation among social work chapters. *Social Work, 37*, 563–564.

Sherradan, M., & Parker, M. D. (1991). Electoral participation of social workers. *New England Journal of Human Services, 11*(23), 23–28.

Weismiller, T., & Dempsey, D. (1993). NASW becoming a dynamic political force [Letter]. *Social Work, 38*, 645–646.

Weismiller, T., & Rome, S. H. (1995). Social workers in politics. In R. L. Edwards (Ed.-in-Chief), *Encyclopedia of social work* (19th ed., Vol. 3, pp. 2305–2313). Washington, DC: NASW Press.

Wolk, J. L., Weismiller, T., Dempsey, D., & Pray, J. L. (1994, November 12). *Political practicums: Educating social workers for policy making.* Paper presented at the Baccalaureate Program Directors Meeting, San Francisco.

Policy statement approved by the NASW Delegate Assembly, August 2005. This policy statement supersedes the policy statement on Electoral Politics approved by the Delegate Assembly in 1996 and referred by the 2002 Delegate Assembly to the 2005 Delegate Assembly for revision. For additional information, contact the National Association of Social Workers, 750 First Street, NE, Suite 700, Washington, DC 2002-4241; telephone 202-408-8600; e-mail press@naswdc.org

Employee Assistance

BACKGROUND

Employee assistance (formerly known as occupational social work) has evolved into the practice of delivering social services in the workplace. Although social workers have been practicing in employment settings since the late 19th century, their history in this work has been sporadic.

With Bertha Capen Reynolds as a strong advocate for occupational social work through her work for the Maritime Seaman's service during World War II, the military (especially the U.S. Army) and the American Red Cross carved out specific arenas for practice (for example, mental health services and services for military families). Unfortunately, in the 1950s social work practice emphasized the private practice psychoanalytic model, which eclipsed the interest social workers might have had in the workplace as an arena for practice.

Occupational social work began to reemerge in the 1960s, particularly with the support of the National Institute of Mental Health for the Center for World of Work at Columbia University. However, the occupational alcoholism movement developed by the National Institute of Alcohol Abuse and Alcoholism emerged as the main delivery system in the workplace for treating troubled employees. When the programs expanded to include mental health counseling for employees and family members and changed their designation to "Employee Assistance Programs" (EAPs), these clearly became the primary system for the delivery of a variety of services.

EAPs operate through various models (for example, contract vendors, in-house programs, or consortiums of groups of employers who form a partnership to contract for services) and are financed by both profit and nonprofit employers. Large and small organizations provide or contract for programs. "EAPs and EAP providers vary enormously in size, cost, system of delivery, philosophy of assistance, and personalization of service" (LeFave, 2002).

The core services, which are primarily staffed by social workers, include assessment and referral, brief counseling, management consultation, personal and professional coaching, critical incident stress management (CISM), employee education, and management and labor union training. With the advent of managed behavioral care, social workers became the primary providers of mental health counseling in national networks. Some of these programs combined with employee assistance services to form integrated systems. Social workers who provide assessment and clinical counseling should have master's degrees.

Since the 1990s employee assistance systems have flourished and grown. As of 2002, 80.2 million people were covered (Oss, 2002). The programs have expanded to deal with "work–life" concerns and now include child care, eldercare, and educational referral services.

Recently, demand has increased for CISM programs, including counseling regarding disasters, death, and trauma. Again, social workers are the major profession staffing these as well as other workplace stress reduction programs. Social workers providing briefings for these services should have training in CISM.

ISSUE STATEMENT

Social workers are a major profession staffing EAPs. Social workers have tended to be identified with the Employee Assistance Professional Association (EAPA), which represents members from various professions. Social workers prefer their own identity and often express concerns about ethics, standards, and treatment restrictions imposed by for-profit systems. NASW could provide a base for activities of these occupational specialists.

The lack of professional training opportunities for occupational social workers is striking. Social workers are requesting appropriate credentials to work in this area. Recently highlighted in the *U.S. News and World Report* Graduate Schools Report (Spake, 2001), the University of Maryland School of Social Work's EAP specialization was cited as unique. It is 15 years old and graduates approximately 40 students a year. Continuing education is offered through EAPA programs rather than schools of social work. Over the past five years, the number of EAP specializations in schools of social work has decreased.

The social work field should address the lack of sophistication in the assessment of addiction problems as well as the need for social workers to provide brief treatment, to prepare social workers to staff EAPs, and to maintain their present majority status in the provision of mental health care in the workplace. Social workers involved in administration, policy, and research as well as clinical social workers need to understand the workplace system—with its organizational structures and its terminology—as well as the services already provided through social security, unemployment compensation, workers' compensation, and disability insurance programs. They also need to understand the many laws relevant to this area, such as the Confidentiality of Alcohol and Drug Abuse Patient Records (1996), the Knox-Keene Health Care Service Plan Act of 1975, *Tarasoff v. Regents of the University of California* (1976), the Anti-Drug Abuse Act of 1986 (P.L. 99-570; Drug-Free Workplace), and the Omnibus Transportation Appropriation Bill of 1991 (P.L. 101-336).

Social workers involved in EAP practice should develop and use specialized knowledge and skills about privatization, outsourcing, and the rise in the use of temporary workers. Studies about the impact of privatization should include the consequences of lost benefits on health and social welfare, in addition to economic consequences.

There is a major need for training social workers for new roles in the workplace. Account managers, management and benefit consultants, personal and professional development coaches, trainers for a wide variety of subjects, and CISM specialists are just a few of the new up-and-coming functions that social workers could and should fill.

The Council on Accreditation of Services for Families and Children is now providing EAP accreditation for stand-alone EAPs. A social worker acted as the chief author of the standards for the accreditation. Thus, social workers are in a center-stage position in forming the guidelines for the field. More social workers need to become involved in the accreditation process as peer reviewers and team leaders in this important effort. The federal government has contributed financially to the accreditation process. NASW should endorse these standards for accreditation.

Because homicide is the leading cause of workplace death for women (Anfuso, 1994), it is essential that EAPs address the impact of domestic violence in the workplace. Workplaces must create environments that promote self-disclosure of risk of workplace violence. Many batterers, restricted by protective orders, seek out their spouses—at their places of employment. Workplace violence is planned, premeditated, foreseeable, and preventable. Violent confrontations occur at doors, lobbies, and parking lots of workplaces. Policies, guidelines, and protocols will assist management and maintain a safe work environment and the personal safety of threatened partners as well as coworkers. Workplaces should be educated about and honor protective restraining orders. Social workers, as EAP professionals, are best suited to achieve these objectives.

POLICY STATEMENT

Most adults are now in the workplace. More than 50 percent of the workforce are women. Employee assistance has emerged as the major delivery system for addressing the mental health, substance abuse, and work–life concerns of employees. EAPs, staffed primarily by social workers, have evolved into an emerging and rapidly growing delivery system for all kinds of services. They have become the "in-house HMOs" for mental health as well as the "in-house family services" system.

NASW could be a major influence both nationally and internationally as these programs proliferate around the world (Masi, 2000). The International Federation of Social Workers also has shown interest in providing training for all its members. Together these two organizations can meet the challenge for workforces around the world. Schools of social work should investigate the feasibility of appropriate programs to train students and alumni to staff the many roles needed for this field.

The growth of EAPs is enormous. NASW and schools of social work should move rapidly to fulfill their responsibilities to their members and students. The opportunity is presently there. Employers want EAPs. They are willing to pay for them. They know their value. The events of September 11 have created an even greater demand. Social workers provide the best staff for EAPs. NASW is encouraged to consider the development of standards for EAP social workers. Both NASW and schools of social work face an enormous and challenging opportunity to provide the neces-

sary value base, knowledge, and skills for implementing the best and most culturally competent services to the millions of clients served by these programs. Social workers are presently providing CISM services. This is a critical competency for EAP professionals. Users of this policy statement are advised to seek further guidance from the following NASW policy statements: Family Violence and Alcohol, Tobacco, and Other Drugs.

REFERENCES

Anfuso, D. (1994). Deflecting workplace violence. *Personnel Journal, 73*(10), 66.

Anti-Drug Abuse Act of 1986, P.L. 99-570, 100 Stat. 3207.

Confidentiality of Alcohol and Drug Abuse Patient Records, 42 C.F.R. § 2 (1996).

Knox-Keene Health Care Service Plan Act of 1975, Health & Saf. Code §§ 1340 et seq.

LeFave, A. (2002, March–April). Competency-based coaching: Drawing on traditional EAP skills. *EAPA Exchange.*

Masi, D. A. (Ed.). (2000). *International employee assistance anthology.* Washington, DC: Dallen, Inc.

Omnibus Transportation Appropriation Bill of 1991, P.L. 101–336.

Oss, M. (2002). *Open minds.* Gettysburg, PA: Industry Statistics.

Spake, A. (2001, April 17). Social work returns to its roots. *U.S. News and World Report,* p. 55.

Tarasoff v. Regents of the University of California, 551 P.2d 334 (1976).

Policy statement approved by the NASW Delegate Assembly, August 2002. This statement supersedes the policy statement on Occupational Social Work approved by the Delegate Assembly in 1984 and reconfirmed by the Delegate Assembly in 1987 and 1993. For further information, contact the National Association of Social Workers, 750 First Street, NE, Suite 700, Washington, DC 20002-4241. Telephone: 202-408-8600; e-mail: press@naswdc.org

End-of-Life Care

BACKGROUND

Advances in health care technology have given physicians the ability to prolong life in ways that would have seemed impossible only a few years ago. Often, however, the psychosocial consequences of prolongation of life are not considered as an important part of end-of-life decision making and care. Advances in critical care medicine enhance physicians' and clients' opportunities to avoid discussions about death, quality of life, and suffering.

Decisions regarding end-of-life care should be considered at numerous junctures over the course of one's life, not just when diagnosed with a terminal illness or faced with an acute, life-ending event. End-of-life decisions encompass a broad range of medical, spiritual, and psychosocial determinations that each individual should make before the end of her or his life. A person may choose to delegate end-of-life decisions, with or without an advance directive, depending on an individual's capacity to do so. Ideally, individuals decide to address such decisions through advance care planning. In emergencies, when care consideration is not possible, difficult decisions may need to be made by family members and friends, who are often ill-prepared to decide what their loved ones might have wanted. Such decisions can include where a person plans to spend the final months before death and the degree of self-sufficiency and technological intervention she or he wishes during that time. The use of personal, family, and social resources to carry out these decisions may change, depending on the course of the particular illness, and are among some of the most important decisions individuals and their loved ones face (NASW, 2004).

Definitions

For the purpose of this position statement, the following are common terms and definitions associated with end-of-life care. It should be noted that many of these terms are interpreted differently, based on state laws and regulations, across the United States. Here, for the sake of clarity, we describe our specific use of the terms.

Advance Care Planning. Advance care planning encompasses all aspects of an individual's desires for end-of-life care, including living will, health care proxy, "do not resuscitate" orders, and funeral planning.

Health Care Directives. These are written statements that instruct family, friends, medical professionals, and others how an individual wishes to be treated at the end of life, including medical care preferences (resuscitation orders, surgeries, artificial feeding, and organ donation, for example) and how his or her affairs are to be settled. Advance directives include the Durable Power Of Attorney for Health Care and Living Will (also known as Directive to Physician) documents (see definitions below). The appointment only takes effect when individuals are no longer able to make decisions for themselves. It is a Medicare requirement that each client, on admission to a hospital, nursing home, or end-stage renal disease (ESRD) treatment facility be asked if she or he wishes to assign a health care power of attorney, or if she or he has an advance care directive or health care proxy (Patient Self Determination Act, P.L. 101-508).

Minors. Most states will not recognize a formal advance directive signed by a minor, even if he or she is living independently. In most situations, parents and legal guardians retain legal authority to make decisions about medical treatments for a child (Institute of Medicine, 2003).

Decisional Capacity. Decisional capacity is the ability of an individual to understand his or her medical condition, to participate in treatment planning in and out of hospital care, to understand the consequences of his or her decisions, and to meet all other criteria as defined by law (Last Acts, 2001). Decisional capacity can be determined by a psychiatrist or any other physician. The legal definition may vary based on state laws and regulations.

Do Not Resuscitate (DNR) or Do Not Attempt Resuscitation (DNAR). A DNR is an order written by a physician indicating that cardiopulmonary resuscitation is not to be performed. This may also include removal of medications that artificially maintain a blood pressure and the discontinuation of artificial nutrition (New York State and Missouri are exceptions on nutrition). A DNR or DNAR option is discussed with a client or health care agent or family member, but the recommendation not to resuscitate is a medical decision, thereby alleviating a client or family member from making this decision.

Double Effect. This term is related to the ethical principle of "the rule of double effect," which refers to medical treatment that can both produce a desired effect, such as pain relief, but also cause secondary adverse effects, including death. The logic, in effect, is that if the treatment is given only for the desired effect, to relieve pain, the treatment is ethical, even if one could reasonably expect the client to die from the treatment (Last Acts, 2001). Many experts cite morphine given in hospice care as an example. It has powerful pain-relieving properties, but also depresses respiration, which can lead to death.

Durable Power of Attorney for Medical Decision Making (Health Care Proxy). A durable power of attorney for health care decisions is a way to give another individual legal power to make medical decisions when the individual no longer can. The written form used to designate the proxy is also called a durable power of attorney for decision making in health care matters (Lynn & Harrold, 1999). Different states have different versions of this form.

Euthanasia. Euthanasia is the intentional act of ending the life of an individual who would otherwise suffer terribly from a terminal condition. This act is illegal in the United States and also referred to as "mercy killing" (Lynn & Harrold, 1999). It is not to be confused with physician-assisted suicide, described later in this statement.

Family. Anyone the client defines as her or his family, including spouses, partners, parents, siblings, and friends falls into this category. Friends and partners may not have legal status to make decisions for clients unless they are designated as such by a durable power of attorney for health care decisions, but their input should be sought and noted.

Medical Futility. Treatments and procedures provided near the end of life that offer little or no benefit are called medically futile (Bartlow, 2000). The underlying idea of futile care is that if an individual or family member wants life-sustaining treatment, but the physician does not believe the quality of the individual's life justifies the physical burdens of care on the patient, the doctor has the right to withhold any such treatments other than comfort care (Smith, 2002).

Hospice Care. Hospice care is care provided under eligibility guidelines, including diagnosis and prognosis, that focuses on caring, not curing, and in most cases, is provided in the client's home. The focus is on ameliorating physical, psychosocial, and existential suffering (National Hospice and Palliative Care Organization, 2003).

Incompetent. This is a legal term that can only be applied and decided by a judge. This term is often confused with diminished or lack of decisional capacity.

Life-Sustaining Treatment. Life-sustaining treatments are expected to extend life. In the context of end-of-life care, these may also be considered to be futile or death avoidant.

Living Will (Directive to Physician). A living will is a legal document that declares an individual's wish to die a natural death. The document informs the physician that, in the event of a terminal or irreversible condition, she or he does not wish to have her or his life prolonged by artificial or extraordinary means. These documents are not legally binding in all states.

Pain. Pain is the physical sensation resulting from physical illness or conditions that cause discomfort for a client. There are varieties of verbal and nonverbal methods to assess pain. Severity of pain is whatever the client tells the health care provider. Pain should be assessed for clients with and without consciousness (Joint Commission on Accreditation of Healthcare Organizations [JCAHO], 1999).

Palliative Care. Palliative care is an approach that improves quality of life for clients and families facing life-threatening illness (NASW, 2004). This approach is applicable early in the course of illness in conjunction with other therapies that are intended to prolong life and includes those investigations needed to better understand and manage distressing clinical complications (World Health Organization, 2003).

Palliative Sedation. This treatment involves the monitored use of drugs and other procedures intended to induce varying degrees of relief of unmanageable, intractable, and intolerable symptoms in imminently dying clients (Hospice and Palliative Nurses Association, 2003).

Physician-Assisted Suicide. In physician-assisted suicide, a client ends her or his life with the prescription requested of and provided by a physician for that purpose. As of 2005, the state of Oregon was the only state where this act is legally permissible. In all cases, the client must have decisional capacity and meet other criteria as defined by law (Oregon Department of Human Services, 1997).

Suffering. Although suffering can be both physical and psychological in nature, it can extend itself in the dying trajectory to the existentialist level. Depression or existential suffering refers to the feelings of misery, fear, and immobilization, as well as the search for meaning an individual may feel at the end of life. As soon as an individual begins the difficult work of grieving, including "struggling with," and through depression, the road to resolution, acceptance, and healing has started (Bartlow, 2000; Peck, 1997).

Terminal and Irreversible Condition. This phrase defines a condition with no reasonable chance of recovery or a condition caused by injury, disease, or illness, which, within reasonable medical judgment, would produce death within a short time, and for which the application of life-sustaining procedures would serve only to postpone the moment of death or be futile.

Withdrawal or Withholding of Treatment. These are acts that eliminate interventions that prolong death or that create further pain and suffering. Action is followed at the direction of the client or his or her health care agent. Withdrawal of treatment may include the following: removal of medicines that artificially maintain blood pressure, and extubation and withdrawal of ventilatory support. Withdrawal comes with assurances that the physician will provide enough sedating medication to avoid patient and family suffering.

Legislation

In recent years, a proliferation of state legislation has been introduced concerning assisted suicide, most notably Oregon's 1997 implementation of physician-assisted suicide. However, state legislatures across the country are debating similar "death with dignity" bills, many of which would authorize physician-assisted suicide. Legislatures and state ballot initiatives that recently have discussed death with dignity bills include those in Arizona, Florida, Hawaii, Maine, Wisconsin, Wyoming, and Vermont. In 2001 U.S. Attorney General John Ashcroft filed suit against Oregon to overturn the Death with Dignity Act and stop its proliferation to other states. In 2004 a federal appeals court ruled against the Attorney General and upheld the Oregon statute.

Political and social leaders are also attempting to influence personal choice and clinical practice in this area. State legislatures have become involved in such high profile cases as the Terri Schiavo case in Florida and the illegal Jack Kevorkian practice, in which he euthanized several patients. In 2004, the Vatican released an opinion that feeding tubes are medical therapy and cannot be withheld from a permanently unconscious person (Smith, 2004). It is not clear what impact the Pope's statement will have on the nation's Catholic hospitals or health care providers and clients.

The 1990 Patient Self-Determination Act mandated the requirement that hospitals, skilled nursing facilities, ESRD facilities, home health agencies, hospice programs, and HMOs maintain written policies and procedures guaranteeing that every adult receiving medical care is given written information concerning living wills, durable powers of attorney for health care, or advance directives.

A groundswell of new policies and practices in end-of-life care has been positive in recent years. The positive changes include state policies on pain and symptom management, the JCAHO's requirements for pain assessments, reconsideration of state-mandated advance directives, the use of out-of-hospital DNRs, and the increased practice of palliative care.

ISSUE STATEMENT

Social work practice settings addressing end-of-life care include health and mental health agencies, schools, courts, child welfare and family service agencies, correctional systems, agencies serving immigrants and refugees, military service agencies, substance abuse programs, and employee assistance programs. Social work is a broadly based profession that can meet the needs of individuals and families affected by end-of-life situations. Social workers require guidelines that are compatible with professional and personal ethics, legal parameters, and respect for client self-determination. Furthermore, other professionals may look to social work for guidelines on these complex issues.

Using the expertise in working with populations from varying cultures, ages, socioeconomic statuses, and traditional and nontraditional families, social workers help clients and families across the life span cope with loss, trauma, suicide, dying, death, and bereavement; they must be prepared to assess such needs and to intervene appropriately.

In acknowledging and affirming social work's commitment to respecting diverse value systems in a pluralistic society, we recognize that end-of-life issues as complex because they reflect the varied value systems of different groups. Consequently, NASW does not take a position regarding the myriad moral and value-laden questions associated with end-of-life decisions, but affirms the right of individuals to direct their end-of-life care.

We also recognized that de facto rationing of health care based on age, sexual orientation, religion, socioeconomic status, race, ability to pay, provider biases, and government policy differentially affect people's rights to choose among viable service alternatives and diminishes their ability to give truly informed consent. Social workers should advocate to minimize the effect of these factors when determining the care options available to individuals.

In examining the social work role with clients concerning end-of-life decisions, the following issues must be addressed:

■ potential conflict of social work values with those of the clients, clients' families, other health care professionals, or agency settings

■ limits of confidentiality, social work licensing laws, and state and federal laws and regulations

- emerging pressures for cost control and rationing of health care (for example, using health care institutions and insurers to encourage use of end-of-life practices to control costs)

- the possibility that individuals would feel the need to hasten their deaths and the social work role of exploring such feelings and discussion with clients

- the necessity to define, defend, and advocate for safeguards that protect individuals and society in the implementation of end-of-life practices

- lack of access to end-of-life care options for all persons.

POLICY STATEMENT

NASW's position concerning end-of-life decisions is based on the principle of client self-determination. Choice should be intrinsic to all aspects of life and death. Social workers have an important role in helping individuals identify the end-of life options available to them. This role must be performed with full knowledge of and compliance with the law and in accordance with the *NASW Code of Ethics* (NASW, 2000) and *NASW Standards for Social Work Practice in Palliative & End of Life Care* (NASW, 2004).

Often, social workers meet with clients who express a desire to talk about their thoughts and feelings about dying and death. Social workers play an important role in assessing desire-to-die statements; in providing appropriate knowledge, compassion, and skill; and intervening to ameliorate pain and suffering. Social workers can explore and assess all these issues with clients and can educate and direct them to appropriate resources such as pain management, palliative care, or hospice care.

The position of the National Association of Social Workers on end-of-life care provides several areas of consideration and specific action steps for social workers and other providers dealing with this issue.

Practice

- Facilitate client and family understanding of all aspects and options in end-of-life care.

- Provide emotional, psychological, social, and spiritual care and services along the end-of-life continuum.

- Be aware of cultural diversity in end-of-life care practices and beliefs so that culturally sensitive practices in end-of-life care can be used with clients and families.

- Provide access to information to facilitate informed consent for decision making.

- Be aware of client diagnoses and trajectories of illness to best prepare for future health care needs and decisions.

- Discuss and encourage advance care planning if appropriate.

- Be present (if the social worker is comfortable with being present) with the client and family at the very end of life (whatever the site) as appropriate, and when requested by the client or family.

- Be present (if social worker is comfortable with presence) with a client or family in assisted-suicide situations in states where this practice is legal and requested by the client.

- Strive to facilitate continuity of care across all care settings.

- Assess mental health functioning to include assisting in decisional capacity determinations, depression, anxiety, suicidal ideation, and facilitate or provide interventions or referrals for care.

- Be knowledgeable about institutional policies on capacity, advance directives, pain management, futile care, and DNR orders.

- Be knowledgeable about state specific policies on end-of-life care.

- Recognize the importance of an initial and ongoing assessment to provide the appropriate intervention(s) along the continuum of care.

- Be competent in assessing pain and other symptoms.

- Be able to differentiate between pain and existential suffering.

- Act as a liaison with other health care professionals to communicate clients' and families' concerns to the health care team to improve the quality of end-of-life care.

- Provide mentoring and consultation to other health care professionals and social work colleagues and students in the field of end-of-life care.

- Be self-aware of personal values and feelings about dying and death and obtain assistance for the best interests of client, as well as to meet one's own personal needs to resolve issues.

- Refer the client or family to another social worker if your own value system conflicts with your client's decisions.

- Prevent abandonment by care providers of the client or family facing an end-of-life situation.

- Obtain competent supervision when working in end-of-life care.

- Be knowledgeable about hospice care for cancer and non-cancer diagnoses, such as congestive heart failure, diabetes, and ESRD.

- Keep abreast of changes in end-of-life care by participating in continuing education and research activities.

Advocacy

- Advocate for adequate pain control and symptom management in institutional and agency committees and in state and national legislative and regulatory forums.

- Promote access to care for all people facing end-of-life situations.

- Participate in local, state, and national committees, activities, and task forces concerning client self-determination and end-of-life decisions.

- Include education and research on these complex topics in social work curricula.

- Support initiatives, both public and private, that seek to expand the hospice benefit.

REFERENCES

Bartlow. B. (2000). *Medical care of the soul.* Boulder, CO: Johnson Printing.

Hospice and Palliative Nurses Association. (2003). *Palliative sedation.* Retrieved May 11, 2004, from http://www.hpna.org/position_PalliativeSedation.asp

Institute of Medicine. (2003). *When children die: Improving palliative and end of life care for children and their families* (Summary). Washington, DC: Author.

Joint Commission on Accreditation of Hospitals. (1999). *Pain: Current understanding of assessment, management and treatment.* Retrieved May 11, 2004, from http://www.jcaho.org/news+room/health+care+issues/pain+mono_npc.pdf

Last Acts. (2001). *What does it mean? Common terms used in talking about end of life care.* Retrieved May 11, 2004, from http://www.lastacts.org/files/misc/glossary.pdf

Lynn, J., & Harrold. J. (1999). *Handbook for mortals: Guidance for people facing serious illness.* New York: Oxford University Press.

National Association of Social Workers. (2000). *Code of ethics of the National Association of Social Workers.* Washington, DC: Author.

National Association of Social Workers. (2003). Client self-determination in end-of-life decisions. *Social work speaks: National Association of Social Workers policy statements, 2003–006* (6th ed., pp. 46–49). Washington, DC: NASW Press.

National Association of Social Workers. (2004). *NASW standards for social work practice in palliative & end of life care.* Washington, DC: Author.

National Hospice and Palliative Care Organization. (2003). *What is hospice care.* Retrieved May 11, 2004, from http://www.nhpco.org/i4a/pages/index.cfm?pageid=3281

Oregon Department of Human Services. (1997). *Oregon's death with dignity act.* Retrieved May 11, 2004, from http://www.dhs.state.or.us/publichealth/chs/pas/pas.cfm

Patient Self-Determination Act (PSDA), Pub. L. 101-508, 104 Stat. 1388 (1990).

Peck, F. S. (1997). *Denial of the soul: Spiritual and medical perspectives on euthanasia.* New York: Harmony Books.

Smith, V. A. (2004) Pope's feeding-tube declaration pits religion, medicine. *Philadelphia Inquirer.* Retrieved November 17, 2004, from http://www.philly.com/mld/philly/

Smith, W. J. (2002). *Doctors deny some patients hospital care.* Detroit News. Retrieved June 1, 2004, from http://www.detnews.com/2002/editorial/0201/13/a13-389247.htm

World Health Organization. (2003). *Palliative care.* Retrieved May 11, 2004, from http://www.who.int/cancer/palliative/definition/en/

Policy statement approved by the NASW Delegate Assembly, August 2005. This statement supersedes the policy statement on Client Self-Determination in End-of-Life Decisions approved by the Delegate Assembly in 1993 and reconfirmed in 1999. For further information, contact the National Association of Social Workers, 750 First Street, NE, Suite 700, Washington, DC 20002-4241; telephone: 202-408-8600; e-mail: press@naswdc.org

Environment Policy

BACKGROUND

Evidence suggests that all elements of the global ecosystem are under attack and threatened in ways that may be reaching the point of irreversibility. The threats to the natural environment include damage to the ozone layer; unplanned, not "smart growth" land use that is based on private property and profit motives rather than any sense of collective good; the escalating use of nonrenewable natural resources; and the rapid extinction of whole species of plants and animals, along with the invasion of nonnative species; and an increasingly scarce and contaminated water supply (Shiva, 2002). For most of human history, estimated to be between 500,000 years and 1.5 million years, the effect of human activity on the biosphere has been negligible. In the final decades of the 20th century, and into the 21st, the human race in all areas of the globe has created technologies and lifestyles that threaten to alter irrevocably the habitability of the biosphere for all life forms (Berger & Kelly, 1993; Gore, 2006; Pruss-Ustun & Corvalan, 2006). Although human population growth is in and of itself a significant factor, those of us who live in highly developed regions on the planet have contributed disproportionately to environmental pollution and degradation.

The environmental crisis cuts across political, economic, cultural, and social boundaries. It will affect all countries, races, ethnicities and nationalities, classes of people, political parties, and economic interests (United Nations, 2007).

In the early 2000s, considerable focus was put on global warming as a major environmental challenge. Former Vice President Al Gore took a major and effective leadership role in educating the citizens of the world about the "inconvenient truth" of climate change (Gore, 2006). His essential argument, one that is well grounded in scientific data, is that the activities of human beings contribute to global warming such that the viability of the planet is now in danger. He presents information that demonstrates that global warming is a clear and present danger but that there is still time to take action to protect, restore, and save the environment. Data documenting global warming were first published in 1957, when Roger Revelle and chemist Hans Suess published an article in the journal *Tellius*. Five years later, Rachel Carson (1962) sounded a broader environmental alarm about the natural environment with her book *Silent Spring*. Colburn and colleagues' (1997) book *Stolen Future*, described by some as the *Silent Spring* of the 1990s, provided research on how human-made chemicals disrupt endocrine systems.

In the first decade of the 21st century, increasingly sophisticated methods are producing a rigorously examined, disturbing body of scientific documentation with regard to human exposure to and harmful health effects associated with industrial, commercial, agricultural, and household chemical use (Beyond Pesticides, n.d.; Centers for Disease Control and Prevention, 2005; Poppell, 2003). Techniques such as integrated pest management are identifying best practices in reducing and balancing human health risks from pests and pesticides (United States Environmental Protection Agency, 2007). The precautionary principle, as an alternative to traditional risk assessment methods, is used increasingly to apply research knowledge while protecting the most vulnerable citizens (Myers & Raffensperger, 2005).

Neighborhoods, communities, and countries that are poor, especially those that are populated by people of color, are at greater risk of environmental pollution and its effects (Morello-Frosch & Jesdale, 2006). Citing findings from various research studies, Rogge and Combs-Orme (2003) reported evidence that ethnic minority groups and rural communities in the United States and internationally are disproportionately exposed to the dangers associated with environmental degradation. Whether it is the location of a toxic waste dump, the locations of storage facilities for nonbiodegradable toxic substances, the exportation of banned pesticides, or the location of dangerous chemical manufacturing plants (for example, the Dow Chemical plant in Bhopal, India), people of color and poor people are often exposed to many more environmental hazards than the rest of the population. Often, residents feel they have no power to resist either having dangerous sources of contamination in their communities or accept the argument put forth by corporate and governmental agents that these sources attract desperately needed economic development (Bullard, Mohai, Saha, & Wright, 2007).

The inextricable links among poverty, environmental degradation, and risk to human well-being cannot be denied. Children have a particular risk. Developing cells are more susceptible to damage, and toxins concentrate more rapidly in smaller bodies. Pesticides may concentrate in sources of nutrition, including breast milk. Hand-to-mouth activity of children increases the likelihood of ingesting toxins. Pesticides and other toxins concentrate in or near the ground, where children play, particularly in developing countries (Healthy Schools Network, 2007; United Nations Environment Programme, 2002). The relationships and subsequent health disparities are clear in polluted inner city neighborhoods, where children of color suffer from high rates of asthma; in crop lands, where poor migrant workers carry agriculture pesticides home to their families on their work clothes; in low-income Louisiana parishes along the industrial "Cancer Alley" stretch of the Mississippi River; and in the unsanitary, crowded, and hastily and poorly constructed maquiladoras that house

Mexican plant workers along the U.S.–Mexico border. Air pollution is linked to asthma among U.S. children, which increased 118 percent from 1980 to 1993. Despite earlier legislation that reduced lead in the air by an estimated 98 percent, 35 percent of African American children living in inner cities are still estimated to have elevated blood lead levels (Children's Environmental Health Network, n.d.; Gorey, 1995; Rogge & Combs-Orme, 2003). Although most research examining the effects of toxic exposure on children occurs in industrialized countries, children's risk, exposure, and harm are global phenomena.

As Hoff and McNutt (1994) illustrated in the first edited volume on social work practice and the environmental crisis, all forms of social work practice are affected by environmental degradation. Park (1996) stated that "the violent threat to the Earth requires an emphatic response from social workers" (p. 320).

Social work is unique among the helping professions in its emphasis on the person-in-environment perspective. Until recently, much of our professional attention to the environment emphasized its social, cultural, and economic components, oftentimes to the exclusion of the natural or physical environment. Beginning in the latter two decades of the 20th century, a few social work scholars began to consider the implications of this exclusion by focusing attention on the natural environment as a critical component of the social work person-in-environment perspective.

The "ecological paradigm" and "life model" developed by Germain and Gitterman (1980) have been widely embraced by social workers as a practice perspective and strategy that encompasses the person and environment configuration. This model drew heavily from ecological thinking and opened the door for the profession to understand and consider the environment to both the social and natural realms. The use of the ecological metaphor for understanding the environment gave social workers the tool necessary to go beyond its traditional concentration on the social environment.

Berger and Kelly (1993) explored the idea that social workers at all levels and in all forms of practice have a role to play in the developing environmental crisis. In 1994, Hoff and McNutt published an edited book that laid out the reasons why the environmental crisis was an important issue for social welfare and social workers. Later, Berger (1995) argued that social workers needed to face up to and act on their awareness of the out of control "habitat destruction." Hoff and Rogge (1996) argued for the compelling need for the social work profession to develop and implement responses to the environmental crisis, particularly the omnipresent "environmental injustice."

ISSUE STATEMENT

Environmental justice is a concept that has gained currency in the public arena and has particular relevance for the social work person-in-environment perspective (Rogge, 2008). *Environmental justice* is defined as "fair treatment and meaningful involvement of all people regardless of race, ethnicity, income, national origin, or educational level with respect to the development, implementation, and enforcement of environmental laws, regulations, and policies" (p. 136). Fair treatment means that no population, because of policy or economic disempowerment, is forced to bear a disproportionate burden of the negative human health or environmental effects of pollution or other environmental consequences resulted from industrial, municipal, and commercial operations or the execution of federal, state, local, and tribal programs and policies" (U.S. Environmental Protection Agency, Office of Federal Activities, 1998, p. 2). Environmental justice is a fundamental principle embedded in the idea of sustainable development and is consistent with the principles of social work. Shorthand definitions of this complex construct often note the importance of attending simultaneously to the "three Es" of equity (social justice), economy, and environment to manage world resources for current and future generations (Rogge, 2000). For social workers, more fully integrating environmental, social, and economic justice means applying familiar social work knowledge, skills, and methods to new substantive areas and learning new applications for substantive expertise.

Social workers have a special concern for and responsibility to oppressed populations who suffer disproportionately with dangerous environmental conditions. Social workers have fought against "environmental racism." *Environmental racism* is defined in the *Social Work Dictionary* (5th ed.) as "The practice of operating hazardous businesses or storing toxic waste products in or near areas inhabited primarily by racial and ethnic minorities groups" (Barker, 2003, p. 145). Poor communities often are similarly affected disproportionately. For example, many landfills located in inner city areas are filled with refuse from wealthier suburban communities. Some poor communities have agreed to store hazardous materials as a source of much needed economic activity.

Although the social work profession has been gaining understanding of the importance of the natural environment and how this affects all populations, and particularly those who are already vulnerable, the environmental crisis has worsened. Thus, it can be argued that the more economically developed world carries a greater responsibility for facing up to and addressing the crisis that has resulted. For example, climate change created by global warming stems from the size of our individual and collective "carbon and ecological footprints," which are much greater for those of us in the developed world (Hoff, 2002; Natural Resources Defense Council, 2007). Social work, with its focus on political advocacy, can be an important force in addressing this problem.

It is estimated by some that we have a mere two decades to address global warming in a significant way or the damage to the earth's atmosphere will be irreparable (Gore, 2006). Current attitudes, practices, and lifestyles in developed countries that are based on the misguided notion that there is an endless supply of fresh water and other natural resources that can be exploited at will still predominate. In developing countries, growing populations who seek the industrial, commercial, and economic benefits of the Western world produce another potentially unprecedented strain on diminishing and nonrenewable natural resources. Our collective refusal to acknowledge and act on the perilous reality we face, in light of mounting evidence, is the result of more than collective ignorance. True understanding requires some sophisticated knowledge about the physical and biological working of the biosphere, yet requires knowledge of social and psychological dynamics as well.

Facing up to the needs of the natural environment requires change in how society organizes and sets priorities about community capital and means of production. It requires that we all alter, at least in some way, our current lifestyles, provoking great resistance among those who are happy with their lifestyles as well as those who aspire to become like those of us who have comfortable lifestyles. As a result, it is easier, with some notable exceptions, to collectively numb ourselves and otherwise ignore the needs of the environment while pretending that our collective destruction of it is not likely. Social workers and those we serve will benefit by the profession's increasing awareness of the reality of our current environmental situation as we educate ourselves and others to gain further understanding and to take action. Action in support of the environment should be included in all of the profession's public and private activities.

POLICY STATEMENT

Social workers need an environmentally responsible credo to which we can subscribe and that will influence our individual and collective actions. Social workers must become dedicated protectors of the environment. Together, we can model environmental awareness for those who come in contact with us in our personal and professional lives.

NASW supports and advocates for

■   policies that reduce environmental risks to poor, minority, and disadvantaged communities who have been disproportionately affected.

■   more rigorous and effective testing, regulation, and labeling of chemicals and products that contain them.

■   the elimination of fossil fuels, where feasible, to be replaced with clean energy, such as solar, wind, and water.

■   secure and affordable food systems that are free of toxic chemicals and pesticides.

■   the reduction of children's exposure to pesticides and other chemicals through approaches such as the precautionary principle and integrated pest management.

■   the protection of individuals who work in hazardous jobs by strict national and international environmental standards, including effective enforcement mechanisms.

■   interdisciplinary research, policy practice, and community-based actions to promote environmental health and justice.

■   strategies that will reduce our individual and collective "carbon and ecological footprints."

■   adequate funding of such agencies as the U.S. Environmental Protection Agency. State and local counterparts must have the necessary resources and authority to establish and enforce environmental protection in accordance with generally acceptable scientific standards and data.

■   the development and funding of environmental governing agencies throughout the world, with enforcement by the appropriate offices within the United Nations and other appropriate entities.

■   the reduction or elimination of all forms of environmental racism and injustice.

■   social work education at all levels, incorporating discussions of the natural environment, ideas of habitat destruction, chemical contamination, environmental racism, environmental justice, and sustainability.

■   social work practice methods and techniques broadened to consider the natural environment.

■   comprehensive training and development of social workers' skills in identifying difficult-to-detect workplace and environmental hazards to physical and mental health.

■   programs that enable social workers to achieve a deeper awareness and understanding of environmental dangers through the study of traditional perspectives and theories held by indigenous peoples in the United States and other countries.

■ community organizing, coalition building, social and economic development planning, case advocacy, and political action to improve the person–natural environment interface.

■ the inclusion of the natural environment as a routine part of the assessment and treatment planning activities of social workers in all settings with all clients, especially those clients who are most likely to be victimized by unsound and unsafe environmental practices.

■ social services agencies and organizations, including NASW, recognizing the need to protect the environment and acting accordingly.

In addition, NASW advocates against

■ policies that allow toxic waste to be relocated or exported from wealthy industrialized areas and nations to less economically favored areas and nations

■ government and corporate policies which further environmental injustice.

REFERENCES

Barker, R. L. (2003). *The social work dictionary* (5th ed.). Washington, DC: NASW Press.

Berger, R. M. (1995). Habitat destruction syndrome. *Social Work, 40,* 441–443.

Berger, R. M., & Kelly, J. J. (1993). Social work in the ecological crisis. *Social Work, 38,* 521–526.

Beyond Pesticides. (n.d.). Retrieved October 8, 2007, from http://www.beyondpesticides.org/

Bullard, R. D., Mohai, P., Saha, R., & Wright, B. (2007). *Toxic wastes and race at twenty: 1987–2007: Grassroots struggles to dismantle environmental racism in the United States.* Retrieved July 11, 2007, from http://www.snre.umich.edu/news/newsdocs/Toxic%20Wastes%20and%20Race%20at%20Twenty%20Rpt%20(2).pdf

Carson, R. (1962). *Silent spring.* Boston: Houghton Mifflin.

Centers for Disease Control and Prevention. (2005). *Third national report on human exposure to environmental chemicals.* Retrieved September 17, 2007, from www.cdc.gov/exposurereport

Children's Environmental Health Network. (n.d.). Retrieved October 8, 2007, from http://www.cehn.org

Colburn, T., Dumanoski, D., & Myers, J. P. (1997). *Stolen future: Are we threatening our fertility, intelligence, and survival?—A scientific detective story.* New York: Plume.

Germain, C. B., & Gitterman, A. (1980). *The life model of social work practice.* New York: Columbia University Press.

Gore, A. (2006). *An inconvenient truth* [Documentary]. Retrieved October 8, 2007, from http://www.climatecrisis.net/aboutthefilm/

Gorey, K. M. (1995). Environmental health: Race and socioeconomic factors. In R. L. Edwards (Ed.), *Encyclopedia of social work* (19th ed., Vol. 1, pp. 868–872). Washington, DC: NASW Press.

Healthy Schools Network. (2007). *Healthy schools network.* Retrieved October 8, 2007, from http://www.healthyschools.org/

Hoff, M. D. (2002). Effects of global warming on human cultural diversity. In *Encyclopedia of life support systems* (Chapter 3a). Retrieved November 3, 2007, from http://www.eolss.net/E1-04-toc.aspx

Hoff, M. D., & McNutt, J. G. (Eds.). (1994). *The global environmental crisis: Implications for social welfare and social work.* Brookfield, UK: Avebury/Gower House.

Hoff, M. D., & Rogge, M. E. (1996). Everything that rises must converge: Developing a social work response to environmental injustice. *Journal of Progressive Human Services, 7,* 41–57.

Morello-Frosch, R., & Jesdale, B. M. (2006). Separate and unequal: Residential segregation and estimated cancer risks associated with ambient air toxics in U.S. metropolitan areas. *Environmental Health Perspectives, 114,* 386–393.

Myers, N. J., & Raffensperger, C. (2005). *Precautionary tools for reshaping environmental policy.* Cumberland, RI: MIT Press.

Natural Resources Defense Council. (2007). *Global warming.* Retrieved October 8, 2007, from http://www.nrdc.org/globalWarming/gsteps.asp

Park, K. M. (1996). The personal is ecological: Environmentalism of social work [Commentary]. *Social Work, 41,* 320–323.

Poppell, C. (2003). *Bearing the burden: Health implications of environmental pollutants in our bodies*. Washington, DC: Physicians for Social Responsibility.

Pruss-Ustun, A., & Corvalan, C. (2006). *Preventing disease through healthy environments: Toward an estimate of the environmental burden of disease*. Retrieved October 8, 2007, from http://www.who.int/quantifying_ehimpacts/publications/preventingdisease/en/index.html

Rogge, M. E. (2000). Social development and the ecological traditions. *Social Development Issues, 22*(1), 32–41.

Rogge, M. E. (2008). Environmental justice. In T. Mizrahi & L. Davis (Eds.-in-Chief). *Encyclopedia of social work* (20th ed., pp. 136–139). Washington, DC and New York: NASW Press/Oxford University Press.

Rogge, M. E., & Combs-Orme, T. (2003). Protecting children from chemical exposure: Social work and U.S. social welfare policy. *Social Work, 48,* 439–450.

Shiva, V. (2002). *Water wars: Privatization, pollution, and profit*. London: Pluto Press.

United Nations. (2007). *The millennium development goals report 2007*. New York: United Nations. Retrieved October 8, 2007, from http://www.un.org/millenniumgoals/pdf/mdg2007.pdf

United Nations Environment Programme, United Nation's Children's Fund, & World Health Organization. (2002). *Children in the new millennium: Environmental impact on health*. Retrieved October 8, 2007, from http://www.unep.org

United States Environmental Protection Agency. (2007). *Integrated pest management (IPM) in schools*. Retrieved October 8, 2007, from http://www.epa.gov/pesticides/ipm/

United States Environmental Protection Agency, Office of Federal Activities. (1998). *Final guidance for incorporating environmental justice concerns in EPA's NEPA compliance analyses*. Washington, DC: U.S. Government Printing Office.

Policy statement approved by the NASW Delegate Assembly, August 2008. This policy statement supersedes the policy statement on Environmental Policy approved by the Delegate Assembly in 1999 and referred by the 2005 Delegate Assembly to the 2008 Delegate Assembly for revision. For further information, contact the National Association of Social Workers, 750 First Street, NE, Suite 700, Washington, DC 20002-4241. Telephone: 202-408-8600 or 800-638-8799; e-mail: press@naswdc.org

Family Planning and Reproductive Choice

BACKGROUND

The modern history of family planning in the United States began in 1916 when Margaret Sanger, a public health nurse in New York City, opened the first birth control clinic. She and two of her associates were arrested and sent to jail for violating New York's obscenity laws by discussing contraception and distributing contraceptives. Ms. Sanger argued that birth control must be legalized.

Government support of family planning in the United States began in the 1960s when President Kennedy endorsed contraceptive research and the use of modern birth control methods as a way to address the world's population growth. It was under President Johnson and the War on Poverty that family planning services became more widely available. The rate of unwanted childbearing among people living in poverty was twice as high as it was among the more affluent population. This difference was attributed to the lack of available family planning services for women living in poverty.

By 1965, with bipartisan support, federal funds were made available to support family planning services for low-income women.

Title X of the Public Health Service Act of 1970 provided the majority of public funding for family planning services until 1985. Because of fiscal pressures and political factors, such as the growing power and influence of the religious right (mobilized in opposition to the 1973 Supreme Court decision legalizing abortion), Congress has not formally reauthorized Title X since 1985. Appropriations have continued, but inflation-adjusted funding for Title X services decreased by 58 percent from 1980

over the next two decades. More recently, other federal sources—including Medicaid, social services, and maternal and child health block grants; state children's health insurance programs; and Temporary Assistance for Needy Families—as well as state and local funds—have become available to subsidize family planning. Nonetheless, Title X remains central to the national effort (Gold, 2001).

As a result of Title X funding, contraceptive use among American women increased considerably between the early 1980s and the mid-1990s, and the country's unintended pregnancy rate—and the abortion rate—declined. But as Title X funding decreased, the decline in the number of unintended pregnancies slowed sharply. According to research by the Guttmacher Institute in 2006, this progress has ground to a halt:

> The newest data paint a disturbing picture of two very different Americas—one in which middle- and upper-class women are continuing decades of progress in reducing unplanned pregnancy and abortion, and the other in which poor women are facing more unplanned pregnancies and growing rates of abortion. (Gold, 2006, p. 3)

Although progress on universally accessible family planning in the United States has stalled, international family planning efforts are also challenged. The World Health Organization (WHO) defines *family planning* as "the ability of individuals and couples to anticipate and attain their desired number of children and the spacing and timing of their births. It is achieved through use of contraceptive methods and the treatment of involuntary infertility" (WHO, 2007b, p. 1). WHO estimated that more than 120 million couples worldwide do not use contraception, despite wanting to space or limit their childbearing.

There are numerous economic and social benefits to good public family planning policies. In the United States, public funding for family planning prevents more than a million pregnancies each year. It has been estimated that each federal and state tax dollar spent on family planning saves three dollars in Medicaid costs for pregnancy-related and newborn care (Gold, 2001). Women who use family planning services are more likely to use prenatal services and thus have reduced infant mortality and fewer low-birth weight babies, in addition to reducing their own risk of death or health problems. Family planning also reduces infant deaths by helping women space pregnancies. The infant mortality rate is two times higher for a child born within two years of a sibling, a rate that is constant throughout the world (Pichler, 2007).

Emergency Contraception

The "morning after pill," or emergency contraception (EC), is a form of contraception that can be used shortly after sexual intercourse to prevent unintended pregnancy. Offered as a "second chance" for individuals who did not use contraception before intercourse, EC is equally valuable as a safeguard against method failure. EC pills are estimated to reduce the risk of pregnancy by up to 89 percent (Rodrigues, Grou, & Joly, 2002). When offered in a timely manner to victims of sexual assault, EC almost eliminates the fear of pregnancy resulting from this criminal act, helping to restore a sense of control to the victim.

Although this form of fertility control is safe, inexpensive, and easy to use, EC generates opposition by groups who oppose all forms of birth control or believe that it is an abortifacient. These arguments among policymakers threaten the accessibility of emergency contraception to those who might benefit from its protection.

Abortion

Research indicates that half of all pregnancies of American women are unintended and that four in 10 of these end in abortion (Guttmacher Institute, 2008). The correlation between high levels of unintended pregnancy and abortion cannot be discounted. As stated by Sharon Camp of the Guttmacher Institute (2006), "behind almost every abortion in the United States is an unplanned and unwanted pregnancy . . . [Abortion] . . . is a last resort for a woman who is faced with a crisis pregnancy" (p. 1). The United States has one of the highest abortion rates in the developed world, and it is estimated that 35 percent of women will have an abortion by 45 years of age. Although women of all backgrounds have abortions, abortion in the United States is increasingly likely to occur among single women, racial or ethnic minority women, low-income women, and women who have had at least one child (Boonstra, Gold, Richards, & Finer, 2006).

Abortion is a controversial medical procedure, but it has been performed over an average of a million times each year since 1973. The right of American women to terminate their pregnancy is founded on the Supreme Court decision in *Roe v. Wade* (1973) that has been under assault since the ruling was pronounced. A July 2007 national poll affirms, however, that a small majority of Americans, despite their ambivalence, still support the legal status of abortion. Looking at polls spanning the decade before, the percentages for all abortion questions have only fluctuated a few points over these 10 years, perpetuating an uneasy, but relatively stable tension (Polling Report, 2008).

Abortion rhetoric has always been highly charged, but only a tiny fraction of opponents have dedicated their lives to fight abortion on every level—from political activism to physical violence against abortion providers and patients. During the 1980s and 1990s, violence and physical, emotional, and social harassment forced many providers to abandon their practices. In addition, restrictions and regulations at every level of government have made it harder for women who need abortion services to access them. Consequently, one-third of

American women live in counties with no source of abortion services (Guttmacher Institute, 2003).

Men and Contraception

The primary methods of birth control before the 1960s were abstinence, withdrawal, and condoms, methods that depended on the cooperation of men. After the pill revolution, men have been largely left out of the area of reproductive choices (Ndong & Finger, 1998). However, men are important to reproductive health (Population Reports, 1998). The only effective ways to prevent sexually transmitted infections (STIs) are abstinence or condom use, both involving the cooperation of men. As research continues on male methods of contraception, fertility control and reproductive health are coming to be viewed through the wider lens of gender equality and shared responsibility.

Violence and Reproductive Health

Physical consequences of sexually violent acts may include STIs, HIV/AIDS, unwanted pregnancy, miscarriage, gynecological problems, sexual dysfunction, and injury. These wreak havoc on the victim's reproductive and emotional health (WHO, 1998).

ISSUE STATEMENT

Although contraceptive coverage in private insurance plans has improved in recent years, many women still lack coverage or have plans that do not cover the specific contraceptive they would like or face a prohibitive co-pay for their method of choice. As of 2004, only 20 states had comprehensive contraceptive coverage mandates, and employer self-insurance plans are generally not covered by these mandates (Moore, Finer, & Darroch, 2003).

The NASW *Code of Ethics* (2000) states that "social workers promote clients' socially responsible self-determination" (p. 5). Self-determination related to reproductive health means that without government interference, people can make their own decisions about sexuality and reproduction. As social workers, we sup-

port the right of individuals to decide for themselves, without duress and according to their own personal beliefs and convictions, whether they want to become parents, how many children they are willing and able to nurture, the opportune time for them to have children, and with whom they may choose to parent. Caring for children presents challenges for all parents, but for unwilling or unprepared parents, the economic, social, physical, or emotional challenges may be too great. Conversely, the right to parent should not be denied to capable people, regardless of gender or gender identity and expression.

Decisions about parenthood are crucial for individuals, their families, and their local communities, and multitudes of individual decisions even bear significant implications for the global community. Resolving personal issues of such importance should not be undertaken without access to reproductive health services that are based on the most current science and address the needs of a diverse population.

To support self-determination, these reproductive health services, including abortion services, must be legally, economically, and geographically accessible to all who need them. Medical research has advanced the prevention and treatment of HIV/AIDS and other STIs, the development of effective male contraceptives, wider choices of female contraceptive methods, and safer childbirth practices. Denying people with low income access to the full range of contraceptive methods, abortion, and sterilization services, and the educational programs that explain them, perpetuate poverty and the dependence on welfare programs and support the status quo of class stratification.

The United Nations' Fourth World Conference on Women adopted a platform statement in 1995 recognizing the importance of women's sexual and reproductive health (United Nations, 1995). The International Federation of Social Workers (IFSW) has adopted a policy statement on women's health issues, including sexual and reproductive health, and has identified this as an area of critical concern to social work (IFSW, 1999). WHO confirms that, despite tremendous advances in the development and accessibility of family planning services, there are still millions of individuals around the world who are unable to plan their families as they wish. In addition to lack of access, poor quality of services, and technological issues, the utilization of family planning practices is hampered by power imbalances within couples and families and broader social, cultural, and religious issues (WHO, 2007a).

In 1979, the United Nations Commission for Human Rights stated that unimpeded access to family planning and reproductive health services, including abortion services, is a fundamental human right that contributes to the advancement of women worldwide (United Nations, 1979). Women who defer childbearing have the chance to further their education, develop work skills, acquire broader life experiences, have fewer children, provide better for the children they do have, and improve the well-being of their families. Family planning and access to a full range of reproductive health services are basic to meeting family needs, as well as allowing individual self-determination in reproduction and sexuality to be realized. Adequate financing through a continuing partnership between the private and the public sectors is necessary to make family planning programs and professional services available to all, regardless of the ability to pay. Government policies and medical programs, as well as medical programs under private auspices, should ensure that individuals have full access to the technical knowledge and resources that will enable them to exercise their right of choice about whether and when to have children.

As part of the professional team operating these programs, social workers must realize their professional duty to promote self determination and assist clients in obtaining whatever help and information they need for effective family planning and for maintaining their reproductive health. Social workers also have a professional obligation to work in local, state, national, and international arenas to establish, secure funding for, and safeguard family planning and reproductive health programs, including abortion services and HIV/AIDS prevention and treatment, to ensure that these services remain legal, increasingly more effective, and available to all who need them.

POLICY STATEMENT

The NASW position concerning family planning, abortion, and other reproductive health services is based on the bedrock principles of self-determination, human rights, and social justice:

■ Every individual, within the context of her or his value system, must have access to family planning, abortion, and other reproductive health services.

■ The use of all reproductive health services, including abortion and sterilization services, must be voluntary and preserve the individual's right to privacy.

■ Women (in particular women of color, women in institutions, and women from other vulnerable groups) should not be unethically used in the testing and development of new reproductive techniques and technologies.

■ The nature of the reproductive health services that a client receives should be a matter of client self-determination in consultation with the qualified health care provider furnishing them.

■ Public policies and legislation, nationally and internationally, must support a woman's authority over her sexual life and reproductive capacity, free from coercion, violence, and discrimination.

■ Lesbians, gay men, and both male-to-female and female-to-male transgender people, as well as those who feel more comfortable living androgynously, are as capable as any other people of being good parents and should have equal access to parenting support services.

■ Social workers who choose to restrict their services to clients and the community in a way that deprives their clients or community of a comprehensive consideration of all legal reproductive health options have a responsibility to disclose the limited scope of their services and to assist clients in obtaining comprehensive services elsewhere.

Availability of and Access to Services

NASW supports

■ the fundamental right of each individual throughout the world to manage his or her fertility and to have access to a full range of effective family planning and reproductive health services, regardless of the individual's income, marital status, age, race, ethnicity, gender, sexual orientation, national origin, or residence; these services include, but are not limited to, contraception; and emergency contraception; fertility enhancement; prevention and treatment of HIV/AIDS, STIs, and the human papillomavirus (HPV); prenatal, birthing, and postpartum care; sterilization, abortion services, and adoption rights.

■ a woman's right to obtain an abortion, performed according to accepted medical standards and in an environment free of harassment or threat for both patients and providers.

■ reproductive health services, including abortion services, that are confidential, available at a reasonable cost, and covered in public and private health insurance plans on a par with other kinds of health services (contraceptive equity).

■ improved access to the full range of reproductive health services, including abortion services, for groups currently underserved in the United States, including people with low income and those who rely on Medicaid to pay for their health care, adolescents, individual challenges and needs, sex workers, single people, lesbians, people of color and those from nondominant ethnic and cultural groups, those in rural areas, and those in the many counties and municipalities that currently do not have providers of such services.

■ public and private adoption services that better address the needs of birth parents and that invite women and men, regardless of sexual orientation or gender expression, to consider adoption as a genuine alternative to abortion or parenting, contributing to a broader range of options.

■ national, state, and local public awareness campaigns and educational programs relating to reproductive health and choice.

Legislation

Recent years have seen many initiatives at the state and federal levels to challenge and thereby overrule or undermine the rights granted by the Supreme Court's *Roe v. Wade* (1973) decision and subsequent high court decisions. Federal and state legislative bodies have sought to restrict funding for abortion and other reproductive health care services and research and impose restrictions to impede the use of services, while Congress has restricted or eliminated funding to developing countries.

Therefore, NASW

■ supports legislation to facilitate a woman's access to contraceptives and emergency contraception.

■ supports legislation to ensure that women who have been sexually assaulted have access to emergency contraception.

■ supports legislation that ensures privately and publicly funded health insurance coverage includes access to all forms of reproductive health technologies, contraceptives, vaccinations, and medication equally for men and women.

■ supports legislation to permit women and couples to donate human tissue and frozen, living, or deceased embryos to legitimate research projects.

■ opposes government restrictions designed to limit access to reproductive health services, including abortion services.

■ opposes government restrictions on financing reproductive health services, including abortion services, in health insurance and foreign aid programs.

■ opposes any special conditions and requirements imposed on reproductive health care providers, such as the prescribed warning of unsubstantiated health risks resulting from abortion or mandatory waiting periods, which are not based on medical standards.

- opposes legislative or funding restrictions on medically approved forms of contraceptives and emergency contraception.

- opposes limits and restrictions on adolescents' access to confidential reproductive health services, including contraceptive and abortion services, and the imposition of parental notification and consent procedures.

- opposes legislative restrictions limiting access to parenting for lesbian, gay, bisexual, and transgender individuals.

Education and Research

For people to exercise self-determination in making choices related to sexuality and reproductive health care for themselves and their families, NASW supports

- public and private funding for research to develop and disseminate medically safe and effective methods of preventing, postponing, or promoting conception (including antiretroviral therapy), appropriate for women and men;

- academic and clinical education for students in the medical and health professions relating to the physical and psychological consequences of pregnancy and pregnancy loss and education for appropriate specialties on pregnancy termination techniques, postabortion care, contraceptive methods, and appropriate contraception counseling;

- school-based age-appropriate, culturally informed sexuality and reproductive health education programs that include information about the role of personal beliefs, culture, and values in individual and family decision making on these issues; prevention of STIs; range of reproductive health services and contraceptive methods; and introduction to skills for making healthy personal choices about sexuality and reproduction;

- funding for the development of sexuality education curriculums, as described earlier;

- development and funding of education and research programs to prevent the spread of STIs, to prevent unwanted pregnancies, and to reduce all forms of sexual violence and coer-

cion from which many unwanted pregnancies result; education that informs students, social workers, or others, about the normally occurring diversity of sexuality and of gender identity and expression, including the equal ability of all people to have their family planning and reproductive health care needs met.

REFERENCES

Boonstra, H., Gold, R. B., Richards, C., & Finer, L. B. (2006). *Abortion in women's lives.* Retrieved May 15, 2008, from http://www .guttmacher.org/pubs/2006/05/04/AiWL .pdf

Gold, R. B. (2001). *Title X: Three decades of accomplishment.* Retrieved September 27, 2007, from http://www.guttmacher.org/pubs/ tgr/04/1/gr040105.html

Gold, R. B. (2006). *Rekindling efforts to prevent unplanned pregnancy: A matter of 'equity and common sense.'* Retrieved May 15, 2008, from http://www.guttmacher.org/pubs/ gpr/09/3/gpr090302.html

Guttmacher Institute. (2003, January 15). *After three decades of legal abortion, new research documents declines in rates, numbers and access to abortion services* [Press Release]. Retrieved September 20, 2007, from http:// www.guttmacher.org/media/nr/2003/ 01/15/nr_011003.html

Guttmacher Institute. (2006, May 6). *A tale of two Americas for women* [Press Release]. Retrieved September 15, 2007, from http:// www.guttmacher.org/media/nr/2006/05 /05/index.html

Guttmacher Institute. (2008, January). *Facts on induced abortion in the United States.* Retrieved February 1, 2008, from http:// www.guttmacher.org/pubs/fb_induced_a bortion.html

International Federation of Social Workers. (1999). *International policy on women.* Oslo, Norway: Author.

Moore, K., Finer, L., & Darroch, J. (Eds.). (2003, October). *The unfinished revolution in contraception: Convenience, consumer access and choice.* Retrieved September 12, 2007, from http://www.guttmacher.org/pubs/2004/ 09/20/UnfinRevInContra.pdf

National Association of Social Workers. (2000). *Code of ethics of the National Association of Social Workers.* Washington, DC: NASW Press.

Ndong, I., & Finger., W. (1998). *Introduction: Male responsibility for reproductive health.* Retrieved May 30, 2008, from http://www.reproline.jhu.edu/english/6read/6issues/6network/v18-3/v18-3.htm

Pichler, S. (2007). *Griswold v. Connecticut—The impact of legal birth control and the challenges that remain.* Retrieved May 30, 2008, from http://www.plannedparenthood.org/files/PPFA/fact-griswold.pdf

Polling Report. (2008). *Abortion and birth control.* Retrieved May 30, 2008, from http://www.pollingreport.com/abortion.htm

Population Reports. (1998). *Reproductive health: New perspectives on men's participation.* Baltimore: Johns Hopkins School of Public Health, Population Information Program.

Rodrigues, I., Grou, F., & Joly, J. (2002). Effectiveness of emergency contraceptive pills between 72 and 120 hours after unprotected sexual intercourse. *American Journal of Obstetrics/Gynecology, 186*(1), 167–168.

Roe v. Wade, 410 U.S. 113 (1973).

United Nations. (1995). *Platform for action summary: Obstacles, strategies, actions.* New York: Author.

United Nations Commission for Human Rights. (1979). *Convention on the elimination of all forms of discrimination against women.* New York: Author.

World Health Organization. (1998). *Gender and health: Technical paper.* Retrieved October 19, 2007, from http://www.who.int/reproductive-health/publications/WHD_98_16_gender_and_health_technical_paper/WHD_98_16.chapter3.en.html

World Health Organization. (2007a). *Family planning: Promoting family planning.* Retrieved October 18, 2007, from http://www.who.int/reproductive-health/family_planning/index.html

World Health Organization. (2007b). *Working definition used by department of reproductive health and research.* Retrieved September 20, 2007, from http://www.who.int/topics/family_planning/en/

Policy statement approved by the NASW Delegate Assembly, August 2008. This policy statement supersedes the policy statement on Family Planning and Reproductive Choice approved by the Assembly in 1999 and referred by the 2005 Delegate Assembly to the 2008 Delegate Assembly for revision, the policy statement on Family Planning approved by the Assembly in 1967 and reconfirmed in August 1990, and the policy statement on Abortion approved by the Assembly in 1975 and reconfirmed by the Assembly in 1990. For further information, contact the National Association of Social Workers, 750 First Street, NE, Suite 700, Washington, DC 20002-4241. Telephone: 202-408-8600 or 800-638-8799; e-mail: press@naswdc.org

Family Policy

BACKGROUND

Strengthening families and providing family support are priorities of the social work profession. The family is the primary socializing agent and the primary economic unit in our culture. Families in the United States have undergone tremendous changes in composition, structure, and roles in the 20th century (Ooms, 1995). They have fewer children, and people are living longer. An increasing number of women, including women with young children, are in the workforce. In addition, families have been highly mobile, moving away from parents and other natural support systems. New immigrants and refugee families help expand the cultural, religious, and ethnic diversity on which this nation was built. Economic and political conditions around the world, particularly in developing countries, profoundly affect the conditions in which families in the United States live.

Contemporary American families are an amalgam of many different lifestyles and many different structures. Policy cannot be primarily based on the traditional nuclear family. Families can include a mixture of race, culture, religion, ethnicity, and sexual orientations. Family composition may cover a range of constellations, including traditional married parents with biological children; divorced, separated, or unmarried parents who have individual, separate, or shared responsibility for the care of children; intergenerational arrangements for child or elder care; gay and lesbian couples with or without the care of children; couples in which one or both partners is transgendered; and adoptive parents and foster families (U.S. Household and Family Structure, 2008).

The makeup of families is shifting in other ways. An elderly population provides new challenges and opportunities. Changing the dynamics of retirement and the concepts of extended family, baby boomers will soon become a significant part of the aging population. Baby boomers will inevitably "reinvent" aging, along with the types of care needed for older adults, and affect families' perceptions of aging. Grandparents are now raising grandchildren and facing many challenges as parents abdicate responsibility of their children. Often the grandparents are required to step in because of incarceration, economic hardship, teenage pregnancy, death, HIV/AIDS, unemployment, mental illness, domestic violence, divorce, substance abuse, and other issues. These grandparents provide a safety net for vulnerable children.

Elder abuse looms as a major issue for the 21st century (U.S. Department of Health and Human Services, 2008). The most common category of investigated reports involves self-neglect. Caregiver neglect, financial neglect, and financial exploitation follow. These issues will have a significant effect on how families perceive themselves in the later years and the policies that can affect a better outcome for the accommodation of those changes.

Baby boomers (people born between 1946 and 1960) have assumed leadership roles during their lives. They often find themselves as caregivers, squeezed in between caring for younger loved ones such as children and their elderly parents or other elderly family members. In 2005, 71 percent of baby boomers, then aged 41 to 59, had at least one living parent

(Pew Research Center, 2005). They now seek to influence ideas about retirement or semiretirement in a way older adults of past generations never thought possible. Their voices dominate public debate and make demands for changes to public policy. "Phased retirement" has become the watchword for baby boomers who seek to affirm family life yet still make contributions to the workforce. Such a lifestyle affects the various roles in the family.

Family social policy needs to recognize and respect a variety of family compositions and their respective specific needs. *Family* is defined in its broadest sense to include two or more people who consider themselves "family" and who assume obligations and responsibilities that are generally considered essential to family life. Families are first-line providers of such services as health care, counseling, education, dependent care, long-term care, and income support. Whereas, in general, families strive for financial and social independence, some families must depend on external support systems, such as social services or social insurance entitlements. Many, however, have no guarantee that they will receive assistance when it is needed. When families are unable to perform the roles expected of them, they may incur great stress and deep stigma before they can get the help they need. When help is received, it may be too little and not appropriate to address the families' needs.

ISSUE STATEMENT
Stress of the Caregiving and Provider Roles

Profound changes in family structure have been brought about by the increase in longevity, which has resulted in many four- and five-generation families. According to the U.S. Census Bureau (2000), 2.4 million of the nation's families consisted of grandparents raising their grandchildren. This represents a 19 percent increase over 1990 data. Adult family caregivers, usually women, may experience five or more episodic or continuous caregiving phases: caring for children, parents, grandparents, spouses, and siblings. Family caregiving has not been compensated in this society

except for families receiving Temporary Assistance for Needy Families, which provides income below the federal poverty level and is severely restricted and time limited. The caregiving role can be financially precarious, as well as emotionally stressful and physically straining. As women increase their participation in the workforce, and increasingly all two-parent families (whether gay, lesbian, or heterosexual) have both parents working, prioritizing and balancing home and work responsibilities become more challenging, especially for parents also caring for elders. Welfare legislation, which forces a parent to obtain employment without providing adequate quality child care, places additional hardship on the family.

Grandchildren in need of care by their grandparents pose other challenges for the family. According to the American Association of Retired Persons (2007), more than 6 million children—approximately one in 12—are living in households headed by grandparents (4.5 million children) or other relatives (1.5 million children). Nationally, 2.4 million grandparents are responsible for the basic needs of their grandchildren. These needs include child care, schools, child development, health, mental health, safety, and education, among others. These needs are being thrust on grandparents to respond to with little or no support from the parents. Some grandparents are the custodial grandparents with legal custody of their grandchildren. Other grandparents provide daily care for their grandchildren but do not have legal custody. A number of grandparents simply focus on helping the child's parent provide better care of the grandchild. Though the elderly and the disabled are protected in the United States, children and their families do not have the same universal social insurance entitlements or health care. Changes in the local, national, and world economies have brought about major shifts in livelihoods. Kammerman and Doverman (2007) utilize Census and Labor Department data to profile U.S. families (The Clearinghouse on International Developments in Child, Youth and Family Policies at Columbia University, 2007). The authors note the changing ethnic, racial, and gender landscape of the workforce that is due to immigration largely from Asian and Hispanic countries and female labor force participation. These families may encounter multiple job changes and the lack of financial security. The loss of jobs, underemployment, lack of health benefits, inability to obtain a job because of one's racial or ethnic identity, primary fluency in a language other than English, and sexual orientation are critical factors in many contemporary families. These factors may threaten the survival of a family unit. The lack of resources also threatens the fundamental biopsychosocial development of family members. Kammerman and Doverman (2007) also observe that the U.S. compares unfavorably to Europe in the development of family social policies. The lack of paid family and medical leave may create stress in the workplace and at home for U.S. families. Lack of comprehensive prenatal care is linked to low birthweight, developmental delays, and health problems. The lack of early childhood education or day care is linked to poor social development and poor performance in school. The lack of financial support for home-based care may leave a medically fragile child or adult unattended.

Family Violence

Family violence is growing in frequency and intensity in our society. Elimination of family violence is not dependent merely on better services, punitive judicial actions, and other protective approaches. Family violence must be seen in the context of root causes of violence in our society, including poverty, racism, sexism, unmet needs, and insufficient supports for child and elder care. Van Soest and Bryant's (1995) study supports this view, concluding that social workers have overlooked institutional and structural–cultural explanations for violence and have focused instead on interpersonal family concerns.

Culturally Diverse Families

The meaning of cultural diversity is changing in the United States. Hispanic and Asian American populations in the United States are expected to triple by 2050, making white peo-

ple only a slight majority. Black families have myriad within-group differences, with historically diasporic roots from Africa and the Caribbean. Today, communities are rich with people and families from all racial and ethnic groups and increasingly with people from around the world. Many families are now multicultural in composition, and this blending will undoubtedly characterize families of the future. This growing diversity in race and ethnicity brings strength to our communities and potential understanding, although it challenges the skills of social workers. Many families with members who are relatively recent immigrants face the effects of discriminatory legislation and policies.

Families with Gay and Lesbian Members

Families with gay and lesbian members face a multitude of challenges (Hunter, cited in Jordan & Franklin, 2003). They face discrimination that includes loss of employment, absence of domestic partnership rights, and lack of support from law enforcement agencies and the courts concerning civil rights. They are also the targets for residential discrimination, personal violence, and family prejudices in matters of child custody, foster care, or adoption decisions. Some human services organizations that provide enrichment programs for youths openly discriminate by prohibiting the participation of gay or lesbian young people in their programs and as staff members. Positive gains are beginning to be seen, for example, the United States Court of Appeals for the Fifth Circuit upheld an employer's job termination of a counselor who refused to counsel a lesbian client on relationship issues, stating that homosexuality conflicted with the counselor's religious beliefs (2001). In June, 2003, the U.S. Supreme Court ruled that homosexual sodomy laws are unconstitutional in the 50 states, Puerto Rico, and Washington, DC. The right to marry is gradually being afforded to gay and lesbian couples, though it promises to remain a state-by-state battle for many years to come.

Family- and System-Focused Services and Practice

Increases in substance abuse, school dropouts, teenage out-of-wedlock pregnancies, suicide attempts, family violence, and stress-related health disorders are as rooted in societal failures as in family dysfunction. Multiproblem families experiencing more than one stressful event need multi-level assessment (Jordan & Franklin, 2003). However, solutions often focus on single symptoms and families may have multiple service providers, each addressing a different facet of their family functioning. The fragmentation of services and symptom-focused practice cannot be eliminated unless service providers reframe the presenting problems as family- and community-systems issues.

Moreover, practice that focuses on the individual in isolation from his or her family and primary support network may be limited in scope and effectiveness. Thus, as in child welfare and care for the elderly population, the very protection of the child and elderly person depends on effective, evidence-based services with family members (Janzen, Harris, Jordan, & Franklin, 2006). In addition, individual problems must be understood in the socioeconomic context. Family-focused practice requires community mobilization to parallel the support network. Many times, change in the family system or community institution, such as the workplace, is a precondition for the growth and development of individuals or families.

Economic and Social Services Infrastructure

Families juggle numerous economic responsibilities. Supports to families should encompass a comprehensive array of economic and social services entitlements to enhance family functioning. Gaps in social services and economic resources are often the root of homelessness or family violence. Although the nation has developed a patchwork of services, according to Kammerman and Doverman (2007), no comprehensive family support system exists (The Clearinghouse on International Developments in Child, Youth and Family Policies at Columbia University, 2007). Adequate dependent care, flexible work schedules, and other family supports are essential. Companies and corporations need to be much more responsible in responding to the requirements of the families of their employees. Wages that allow families to live above the poverty line and benefits that include health care options, retirement plans, and paid family leaves will reduce family stresses.

Inequitable pay for women is another serious problem for families, because so many women are the sole supporters of their families. About 71 percent of women participated in the labor force in 2005, whereas 60 percent of married women with children and 75 percent of single mothers work (Kammerman & Doverman, 2007). Equal pay for equal work will allow women to support their families. Workplace policies and practices historically have been overlooked in debates about family policy despite their critical role in promoting or undermining family stability and functioning. Employee policies, wages, and work roles are critical to the stability of families and to the development and protection of both children and adults. Therefore, the role of private-sector policies in promoting family support policies in the United States warrants attention.

POLICY STATEMENT

NASW advocates a full range of comprehensive services to families from primary prevention to rehabilitation across the life cycle. Strengthening families also necessitates the creation of policies that recognize the family as an intergenerational system that includes biological, social, and psychological ties. Understanding what happens in families in terms of the flow of life over the generations, the impact of gender on family life, the family life cycle, and cultural variations in life cycle patterns is essential. Governmental programs and policies must recognize and support the family unit. Social workers can effectively develop a comprehensive national family policy by working together with other advocates, including other providers of human services and health care, law enforcement officials, criminal justice personnel, educators, and community groups. Social workers who, by virtue of their values and education, view strengths and problems in a family and larger systems context should take a leadership role in this effort. Social work professionals in the United States need to consult and collaborate with social work professionals in other countries to benefit from and build on the policy and practice experience of colleagues around the world.

NASW recommends that a comprehensive family support policy be built on the following principles:

■ Families are given a strong voice in all aspects of decision making that affect their lives.

■ Families are provided support that is flexible and targeted to meet the unique, diverse needs of family members.

■ Families are provided available and accessible services within communities and at flexible hours.

■ Support to families encompasses a comprehensive infrastructure of economic and social entitlements, including health care; income supports; family allowance; and access to employment, education, dependent care, housing, and social services.

■ Welfare policies that enable families to achieve self-sufficiency and contain national standards that ensure education and training opportunities, including school-based options for young parents to attain high-level skills; sufficient choices of high-quality day care for parents and other primary caregivers who are entering the workforce or undertaking training and educational programs; provision of transitional health and day care services; and adequate family income supports.

■ Opposition to profit-oriented ownership of the essential safety net services for families, such as welfare supports, job assistance, and schools.

■ Education of policymakers on the development of family policy legislation that includes cultural competency and the diversity of today's families.

■ Assistance to grandparents raising grandchildren.

■ Encouragement by the media of positive messages about families and sensitivity to the level of violence portrayed and its effect on families.

■ Affirmation of cultural diversity; elimination of biases by institutions or practitioners.

■ Services to families that are delivered by adequately trained professionals, including training on working with culturally diverse families.

■ Diverse families are supported in relation to their ability to function biculturally.

To support these principles, it is important that the social work profession advocates policies that will provide support to families. These policies include the following:

■ full and equitable employment, including initiatives that promote permanent part-time jobs with adequate wages and benefits for adults and youths.

■ early childhood and family life education addressing all aspects of caregiving, couple relationships, and problem solving throughout the life span.

■ affordable, accessible, and high-quality dependent care in a variety of settings to meet the needs of all families.

■ affordable, accessible, and high-quality housing available in all urban, suburban, and rural areas so that families may experience a high quality of life.

■ paid family and medical leave to provide time off from work for the birth, adoption, or illness of a child or the illness of a spouse or older or disabled relative.

■ comprehensive and available health, mental health, and family planning services, including strategies focused on prenatal and perinatal care for high-risk mothers.

■ comprehensive services that are designed to keep family units together and to preserve the quality of life, especially when families are faced with chronic and life-threatening illnesses, such as HIV or AIDS.

■ gender-equitable income supports or credits for people whose family caregiving demands impede their continuous participation in the labor force.

■ supportive programs in the workplace that provide education, flexible working hours, day care facilities, counseling, and assistance to working family members.

■ a comprehensive range of supportive and protective services that meet the needs of family members who are abused or neglected and also include corrective intervention services for the perpetrator.

■ policies that assist the public in understanding family violence, encourage citizens' involvement, and use multidisciplinary teams to find a solution.

■ same-sex marriage and second-parent adoption for gay- and lesbian-headed families.

In working with families, social workers need to be constantly aware of the social justice mission of the social work profession and of the empowerment goal in practice at all levels. This suggests that social workers become allies with families in their struggles for adequate resources and environmental supports, prerequisites for quality of life. As a profession, we know that taking significant initiatives will strengthen families and communities and will add vitality and meaning to the lives of people and to society. We must work to identify significant indicators that will demonstrate to the profession and to society that working to achieve the mission of supporting and strengthening families does produce significant results.

REFERENCES

American Association of Retired Persons. (2007). *State fact sheets for grandparents and other relatives raising children.* Retrieved December 18, 2007, from http://www .grandfactsheets.org/state_fact_sheets.cfm

Janzen, C., Harris, O., Jordan, C., & Franklin, C. (2006). *Family treatment: Evidence-based practice with populations at risk* (4th ed.). Belmont, CA: Brooks/Cole.

Jordan, C., & Franklin, C. (2003). *Clinical assessment for social workers: Quantitative and qualitative methods.* Chicago: Lyceum Books.

Kammerman, S., & Doverman, E. (2007). *The Clearinghouse on International Developments in Child, Youth and Family Policies at Columbia University.* Retrieved from http://www .childpolicyintl.org/countries/us.html

Ooms, T. (1995). *Taking families seriously: Family impact analysis as an essential policy tool.* Washington, DC: Federal Family Impact Seminar Reports.

Pew Research Center. (2005). *Baby boomers approach 60: From the age of Aquarius to the age of responsibility.* Washington, DC: Author.

U.S. Census Bureau. (2000). *Grandparents living with grandchildren: 2000.* Retrieved December 18, 2007, from http://www.census.gov/ prod/2003pubs/c2kbr-31.pdf

U.S. Department of Health and Human Services, Administration on Aging. (2008). *Elders & families.* Retrieved February 8, 2008, from http://www.aoa.gov/eldfam/eldfam .aspx

U.S. Household and Family Structure. (2008). *Census 2000 analysis by the Social Science Data Analysis Network.* Retrieved February 8, 2008, from http://www.censuscope.org/us

Van Soest, D., & Bryant, S. (1995). Violence reconceptualized for social work: The urban dilemma. *Social Work, 40,* 549–557.

Policy statement approved by the NASW Delegate Assembly, August 2008. This policy statement supersedes the policy statement on Family Policy approved by the Delegate Assembly in 1999, 1990, and 1981. For further information, contact the National Association of Social Workers, 750 First Street, NE, Suite 700, Washington, DC 20002-4241. Telephone: 202-408-8600 or 800-638-8799; e-mail: press@naswdc.org

Family Violence

BACKGROUND

Violence in family and primary relationships has existed throughout history, but only recently has it been documented clearly and considered a social problem of enormous magnitude (Blumer, 1971). Simply defined *family violence* refers to a pattern of injurious physical, sexual, or emotional acts knowingly or recklessly committed by and on family members for the purpose of maintaining power and control over them. In this context "family" refers to individuals related by blood, marriage, or legal status as well as to those who constitute primary associations, past or present. Family violence includes abuse; neglect; and exploitation of partners, parents, children, and elderly people and animals.

The scope of family violence has come to public attention issue by issue. Although the child protection movement began in this country more than 100 years ago, public attention was drawn to the problem of child abuse in the 1960s by the medical profession (Kempe & Kempe, 1978). In the early 1970s the women's movement was responsible for identifying partner abuse and developing the first shelters and services for battered women. Subsequently, child sexual abuse was identified as a major social problem. Only in the late 1970s was elder abuse uncovered in the field of gerontology (Gelles, 1997). Little attention has been given to partner abuse in same-sex relationships, sibling abuse, the correlation between animal abuse and its link to human violence (Flynn, 2000), and the abuse of parents by adolescent children.

Each type of family violence has had a similar historical development. Extreme cases were publicized, gained national prominence, and were then discounted as rare occurrences. Research later demonstrated the various gra-

dations and widespread nature of the phenomenon. Social services and public legislation have, in each case, struggled to balance competing values of protection, self-determination, and family privacy.

Family violence is present in all racial, ethnic, religious, geographic, economic, political, age, and educational groups. However, risk factors such as poverty and isolation may contribute to or aggravate the problem (Gelles, 1997; McKendy, 1997).

The correlation between family violence and alcoholism or substance abuse is frequently noted. Research suggests that 36 percent to 52 percent of men who are violent with their intimate partners also abuse alcohol (Brekke & Saunders, cited in Gelles, 1997). A similar correlation exists with child abuse (Gelles, 1997). However, it is not clear whether there is a causal connection between substance abuse and family violence. Gelles (1997) reported that extreme alcoholism is not associated with extreme violence, and, on the contrary, violence was found to be lower in situations in which someone was "almost always drunk" (p. 11). Because alcoholism is believed to be uninhibiting, drinking may be an excuse rather than a cause for violent behavior.

The National Center for Child Abuse and Neglect estimates that annually more than 1 million U.S. children are physically, sexually, and emotionally abused and that more than one-half million are seriously injured. Approximately 2,000 die each year as a result of abuse or neglect (Gelles, 1997). The shame and guilt experienced by victims of child sexual abuse, as well as the level of societal denial regarding this problem, are among the reasons it is the most underreported form of child abuse.

The incidence data on intimate partner abuse provide only a limited picture of the scope of the problem. Best estimates from national survey data in the United States and the Netherlands suggest that 25 percent of women will experience physical violence in an intimate relationship, and perhaps 10 percent will experience severe violence (Romkens, 1997). The National Violence Against Women Survey estimates 5.9 million incidents of physical assaults against women annually, with approximately 76 percent of those incidents perpetrated by current or former husbands, cohabiting partners, or dates (Tjaden & Thoennes, 1998). Women who die from the actions of their partners represent one-third of all reported homicides of women; about 11 percent of all murder victims are killed by someone with whom they are intimate (Bureau of Justice Statistics, 2001).

Because of the research problems in measuring other forms of intimate partner abuse and neglect, such as sexual, psychological, or emotional abuse, researchers have focused primarily on physical acts of violence. However, the other forms of intimate partner abuse and neglect are considered pervasive and serious problems that affect a broad sector of the population (Koss et al. 1994).

Violence often escalates in frequency and severity. Fear of bodily harm and loss of financial support as well as concern for children, fear of a pet being harmed or killed, attachment to partner, and social or religious pressures may contribute to a person's decision to remain in a violent relationship (Ascione, 1998). It is well documented that violence may escalate after the abused partner chooses to end the relationship. In fact, women are most at risk when they leave or threaten to leave a violent partner (Mahoney, 1991). Publicized cases in the 1980s demonstrate that some battered women and incest victims have resorted to the most extreme method of escape: murdering the perpetrator of the abuse.

National survey research on couples that measured the numbers of aggressive behaviors without considering context or consequences has been misinterpreted to conclude that men and women are equal participants in spousal violence. The authors of these studies have,

themselves, disclaimed this conclusion (Gelles, 1997). Injurious or hurtful consequence is part of the definition of family violence. It is primarily women who suffer the consequences of violence in heterosexual couples (Browne, 1993; Koss et al., 1994), although research on gay and lesbian couples suggests that the rates and dynamics of intimate partner abuse are similar to those in heterosexual couples (Stahly & Lie, 1995).

Practitioners have identified physical, psychological, financial, and medical abuse of elderly people. Estimates of incidence of abuse and neglect among people older than age 65 vary from 4 percent to 10 percent annually (Gelles, 1997). Although frail elderly people are at risk for abuse, recent work suggests that older adults living with and caring for impaired family members, such as mentally ill or substance-abusing adult children, are even more likely to become victims of elder abuse (Anetzberger, 1987, 2000; Wolf, Godkin, & Pillemer, 1984). In addition some research suggests that spouse abuse may be more common among elderly people than previously thought (Pillemer & Finkelhor, 1988). The recent National Elder Abuse Incidence Study revealed that approximately one-half million older people seen by service providers in 1996 suffered some form of elder abuse; however, only one-fourth of the situations had been reported (National Center on Elder Abuse, 1998). It is important for social workers to understand the challenges of working with mentally competent elder abuse victims who may refuse services to protect impaired loved ones or fear the potential loss of freedom with protective intervention.

The co-occurrence of child maltreatment and spousal violence and the effects on children of witnessing violence in the home have received increasing attention. About 50 percent of men who abuse their wives also abuse their children (Straus & Gelles, 1990). Women who are victims of domestic violence abuse their children at probably twice the rate of other mothers (Schechter & Edleson, 1994). About one-third of families in child protective services systems, and more than one-third of the most severe child abuse cases, are estimated to also involve abuse of the mother (Schechter & Edleson, 1994). Children who witness domestic violence may suffer psychological difficulties and be at increased risk for violence in their own future relationships (Holden, Geffner, & Jourlies, 1998; Jaffe, Wolfe, & Wilson, 1990; Kolbo, Blakely, & Engleman, 1996). Links have also been found between domestic violence and the use of public assistance (Brandwein, 1998a, 1998b; Raphael & Tolman, 1997) and homelessness (Browne & Bassuk, 1997).

ISSUE STATEMENT

The field of family violence has evolved from awareness first of child abuse, then woman and partner abuse, elder abuse, and most recently the effects on children of exposure to family violence. Additionally, committing violence against animals during childhood may likely serve as a signal for a troubled child and dysfunctional family relations (Boat, 1999). Each of these areas has grown with different service delivery systems, different theoretical analyses, and different ideological or political perspectives, resulting in fragmentation in both scholarship and services. For example, the fields of child and elder maltreatment may use family systems theory to understand abuse within a family. However, understanding of partner abuse has depended largely on gender analysis, which identifies sexism as a cause. Battering is placed within a continuum of violence against women that also includes the institutional status of women, psychological wounding, economic assaults, pornography and prostitution, sexual harassment, sexual assault, and "femicide" (Stout & McPhail, 1998). Domestic violence is considered a problem rooted in the structure of society rather than the pathologies of individual men. Community-based programs for batterers are called intervention, not treatment, as mental health treatment cannot be an adequate response. Criminal justice responses are also important in holding batterers accountable for their behavior.

Fragmentation in the field of family violence has inhibited the development of common definitions, comparable research on incidence and prevalence, and theories of causality. Practitioners and researchers are segregated by their expertise, which tends to focus primarily on a particular type of family violence, such as child, intimate partner, or elder abuse. Also, different orientations and the emotional and political nature of family violence contribute to sharp divisions among professionals who work in the field of family violence. For instance, agencies committed to protecting children and those dedicated to empowering women have frequently been in tension with each other.

As the various fields of family violence mature, efforts are being made to understand the tensions and to learn from the varied perspectives to provide more effective, inclusive, and coordinated services. These collaborative efforts are an area for social work leadership.

Despite a rich involvement with child and adult protective services, the social work profession has been lax in adequately preparing its members to address the problem of family violence in all its manifestations. Not only does the educational system have inadequate curricula, but also many agencies lack sufficient policy statements, staff development, and in-service training programs to address the multifaceted aspects of family violence. Without adequate training, professionals may blame the victims, believing that the wife, child, or elderly individual provokes or is in some way responsible for the violence. With increasing recognition that witnessing parental abuse can be emotionally damaging to children, the nonabusing parent, usually the mother, is often blamed for "failure to protect" rather than supported in her efforts to protect herself and her children. All social workers should recognize the complex economic, emotional, cultural, and societal factors that keep the family member in the violent situation.

Families, in many diverse forms, are the contexts in which most children grow and develop through their early years. Families are the primary safety net for most vulnerable adults. Families are also, too often, the locus of violence against their most vulnerable members. The acceptance of family violence as a normal way of life, particularly violence against women, children, and animals, is pervasive in

American culture. Violence is presented as an acceptable form of behavior in literature, video games, children's stories, advertising, and radio and television programs.

The complexity of family violence requires professionals to examine micro and macro issues in assessing, intervening in, and studying the problem in all its forms. Family violence harms individuals directly and may have long-term effects on the health and well-being of families, communities, and society.

POLICY STATEMENT

NASW supports educational strategies to address family violence:

■ NASW encourages schools of social work to develop and implement curricula and field experiences to prepare students adequately to meet the demands of work in the field of family violence. All social workers should be skilled in the assessment of risk and protective factors associated with family violence and appropriate reporting, referral, and intervention.

■ NASW promotes the development of in-service training and continuing education on all forms of family violence to increase the awareness and intervention strategies of social work practitioners.

■ NASW supports continuing education of practitioners and research related to the relationship among animal abuse, domestic violence, and childhood trauma.

■ NASW supports prevention programs to address family violence.

■ NASW will work to eliminate the social and structural injustices that perpetuate family violence, specifically all forms of gender-based exploitation and structural inequities, through articles in its publications and more detailed information about the systematic causes.

■ NASW will work toward the elimination of sexism, racism, classism, ageism, homophobia, and other prejudices within the social work profession and in society that have an effect on family violence.

■ NASW will work to end the portrayal of violence in the media, which normalizes family violence.

■ NASW supports the development of programs to teach children, teenagers, and adults about their right to a life without violence. These include programs for children about the integrity of their bodies, programs for teenagers about dating violence, and programs for people of all ages about alternatives to violence in resolving conflicts.

■ NASW will promote research on all forms of family violence to examine assessment procedures, dynamics, causality, treatment, and prevention.

■ NASW supports legislative and policy efforts that address family violence.

■ Each NASW chapter should work to strengthen and enforce legislation to protect individuals in the home and other environments as well; to provide for the legal rights of all family members; and to promote the removal of a perpetrator, rather than the victim, from the home.

■ NASW supports adequate funding for federal programs to provide grants; to serve as a resource for information on programs and research; and to provide leadership within the federal government for changes in national policies, attitudes, and programs on family violence.

■ NASW will work for legislation that funds needed programs and services for victims and perpetrators as well as prevention programs.

■ NASW supports expanding and improving services that address family violence.

■ NASW supports universal screening of all clients for domestic violence issues to identify the effects of cyclical family trauma.

■ NASW supports the use of emergency shelters and support services for undocumented women and children in family violent situations.

■ NASW promotes the creation of interdisciplinary training, education, and comprehensive services to link and coordinate programs with health, mental health, and protective services; the courts; schools; law enforcement agencies; the military; places of worship; workplace service providers; and social services systems for the effective treatment and prevention of family violence.

■ NASW will work for the expansion of agency programs to include services for victims and perpetrators of violence. Specialized treatment and preventive services should be developed in conjunction with other community resources to respond to and work to end family violence.

■ NASW is committed to learning from and collaborating with advocates and survivors in the battered women's movement.

■ NASW supports efforts to understand and ultimately bridge the philosophical and service gaps among agencies addressing the needs of different groups (children, batterers, women, gay men, lesbians, and elderly people).

■ NASW will work with the child welfare system to support efforts to assist rather than punish the nonoffending custodial parent for "failure to protect" when children have witnessed domestic violence.

■ NASW strongly encourages social workers employed in batterers' intervention programs to work closely with survivors of domestic violence and their advocates and to include "quality of life of survivors and their children" as one measure of successful outcome for batterers' intervention.

■ NASW supports that employers develop environments for self-disclosure of battered victims/employees; self-disclosure would result in employers accepting restraining orders, therefore creating a safe work environment and eliminating employment discrimination relative to wrongful terminations.

REFERENCES

Anetzberger, G. J. (1987). *The etiology of elder abuse by adult offspring.* Springfield, IL: Charles C. Thomas.

Anetzberger, G. J. (2000). Caregiving: Primary cause of elder abuse? *Generations, 24*(11), 46–51.

Ascione, F. R. (1998). Battered women's reports of their partners' and their children's cruelty to animals. *Journal of Emotional Abuse, 1,* 290–304.

Blumer, H. (1971). Social problems as collective behavior. *Social Problems, 18,* 298–306.

Boat, B. W. (1999). Abuse of children and abuse of animals: Using the links to inform child assessment and protection. In F. R. Ascione & P. Arkow (Eds.), *Child abuse, domestic violence, and animal abuse: Linking the circles of compassion for prevention and intervention* (pp. 83–100). West Lafayette, IN: Purdue University Press.

Brandwein, R. (1998a). Family violence and social policy: Welfare reform and beyond. In R. Brandwein (Ed.), *Battered women, children, and welfare reform: The ties that bind* (pp. 131–171). Thousand Oaks, CA: Sage Publications.

Brandwein, R. (1998b). Family violence, women and welfare. In R. Brandwein (Ed.), *Battered women, children, and welfare reform: The ties that bind* (pp. 2–16). Thousand Oaks, CA: Sage Publications.

Browne, A. (1993). Violence against women by male partners. *American Psychologist, 48,* 1077–1087.

Browne, A., & Bassuk, S. (1997). Intimate violence in the lives of homeless and poor housed women: Prevalence and patterns in an ethnically diverse sample. *American Journal of Orthopsychiatry, 67,* 261–277.

Bureau of Justice Statistics. (2001). *Homicide trends in the United States* [Online]. Available: www.ojp.usdoj.gov/bjs/

Flynn, C. P. (2000). Why family professionals can no longer ignore violence toward animals. *Family Relations, 49,* 87–95.

Gelles, R. (1997). *Intimate violence in families* (3rd ed.). Thousand Oaks, CA: Sage Publications.

Holden, G., Geffner, R., & Jourlies, E. (Eds.). (1998). *Children exposed to marital violence.* Washington, DC: American Psychological Association.

Jaffe, P., Wolfe, D., & Wilson, S. K. (1990).

Children of battered women. Newbury Park, CA: Sage Publications.

Kempe, R., & Kempe, H. (1978). *Child abuse.* Cambridge, MA: Harvard University Press.

Kolbo, J., Blakely, E., & Engleman, D. (1996). Children who witness domestic violence: A review of empirical literature. *Journal of Interpersonal Violence, 11,* 281–293.

Koss, M., Goodman, L., Browne, A., Fitzgerald, L., Keita, G. P., & Russo, N. F. (1994). *No safe haven: Male violence against women at home, at work, and in the community.* Washington, DC: American Psychological Association.

Mahoney, M. (1991). Legal images of battered women: Redefining the issue of separation. *Michigan Law Review, 90,* 1–94.

McKendy, J. (1997). The class politics of domestic violence. *Journal of Sociology and Social Welfare, 24,* 135–155.

National Center on Elder Abuse. (1998). *The National Elder Abuse Incidence Study: Final report.* Washington, DC: Author.

Pillemer, K., & Finkelhor, D. (1988). The prevalence of elder abuse: A random sample survey. *Gerontologist, 28,* 51–57.

Raphael, J., & Tolman, R. M. (1997). *Trapped by poverty, trapped by abuse: New evidence documenting the relationship between domestic violence and welfare.* Chicago: Project for Research on Welfare, Work, and Domestic Violence, Taylor Institute, and University of Michigan Research Development Center on Poverty, Risk, and Mental Health.

Romkens, R. (1997). Prevalence of wife abuse in the Netherlands: Combining qualitative and quantitative methods in survey re-search. *Journal of Interpersonal Violence, 12,* 99–125.

Schechter, S., & Edleson, J. (1994, June). *In the best interest of women and children: A call for collaboration between child welfare and domestic violence constituencies.* Paper presented at the University of Iowa School of Social Work and Johnson Foundation conference on Domestic Violence and Child Welfare: Integrating Policies and Practice for Families, Racine, WI.

Stahly, G., & Lie, G. (1995). Women and violence: A comparison of lesbian and heterosexual battering relationships. In J. Chrisler & A. Hemstreet (Eds.), *Variations on a theme: Diversity and the psychology of women* (pp. 59–78). Albany: State University of New York Press.

Stout, K. D., & McPhail, B. (1998). *Confronting sexism and violence against women: A challenge for social work.* New York: Addison Wesley Longman.

Straus, M., & Gelles, R. (Eds.). (1990). *Physical violence in American families.* New Brunswick, NJ: Transaction Books.

Tjaden, P., & Thoennes, N. (1998). *Prevalence, incidence, and consequences of violence against women: Findings from the National Violence Against Women Survey.* Washington, DC: National Institute for Justice and Centers for Disease Control and Prevention.

Wolf, R., Godkin, M. R., & Pillemer, K. A. (1984). *Elder abuse and neglect: Report from the model projects.* Worchester: University of Massachusetts Medical Center, Center on Aging.

Policy statement approved by the NASW Delegate Assembly, August 2002. This statement supersedes the policy statement on Family Violence approved by the Delegate Assembly in 1987 and reconfirmed by the Delegate Assembly in 1993. For further information, contact the National Association of Social Workers, 750 First Street, NE, Suite 700, Washington, DC 20002-4241. Telephone: 202-408-8600; e-mail: press@naswdc.org

Foster Care and Adoption

BACKGROUND

Foster care and adoption have long served as society's way of providing alternative care to children who—on either a temporary or a permanent basis and for a variety of reasons—cannot live with their families of origin. Although child placement institutions have provided needed assistance for many children, they have been subject to problems that have limited their potential for meeting children's needs.

During the past 20 years, the social services systems that provide alternative care to children have changed significantly. The Child Welfare League of America (CWLA) has estimated that there are approximately 500,000 children in foster care (CWLA, 1996). With the passage of the 1997 Adoption and Safe Families Act (ASFA; P.L. 105-89), state child welfare agencies were mandated to improve their foster care systems. ASFA emphasized the safety of children as a priority and established time lines relating to permanency and termination of parental rights after the first 15 months that a child is in placement. Additionally, ASFA mandated state child and family services reviews and program improvement plans for states that failed the federal review process. NASW supports the use of child and family services reviews to improve child welfare practice and adequate fiscal resources for states to improve systemic factors.

Legislative reforms include the Chafee Foster Care Independent Living Act (Foster Care Independence Act of 1999, P.L. 106-169) to address aging-out youths transitioning to adulthood. Every year in the United States approximately 200,000 youths transition from foster care to adulthood. Studies have shown that education is a significant factor in deter-

mining a successful transition. Social workers must take a proactive role to improve education outcomes for youths in foster care.

Today more than ever states are relying on alternatives to foster care. Twenty-six percent of children in foster care are in kinship placements. Despite the increase in the use of relative caregivers, many children continue to enter foster care or remain in foster care because of the lack of family resources and prevention services in their communities. State agencies need to promote more services to maintain children in the context of their extended families when parents are not able to take care of their own children. NASW supports public policies that encourage the development of legislative, administrative, and community efforts that support grandparents and kinship caregivers in the best interests of the child. NASW also supports subsidized adoption, guardianship, and financial support equivalent to foster care.

The foster care population has changed. There is an increase in the proportion of hard-to-place children and children with special needs, including children of ethnic and racial groups who are disproportionately represented in the foster care system, older children, sibling groups, developmentally disabled children, medically fragile children, children with AIDS or who are HIV positive, children with disabling conditions or difficulties, children born to substance exposure, and undocumented children. Each group presents unique challenges to systems designed to care for children.

The presence of gay, lesbian, bisexual, and transgender adolescents in the child welfare system, and their unique psychosocial needs, is often overlooked. They may be excluded from placement options because of a provider's discomfort with the youth's sexual orientation or gender identity. The lack of accurate information among child welfare professionals about sexual orientation, gender identity, and the challenges facing sexual minority youths undermines the provision of competent services delivery to youths, their families, and other caretakers.

Federal standards governing the removal of American Indian children from their families were implemented under the Indian Child Welfare Act (ICWA) of 1978. The act preserved the "existence and integrity of Indian Tribes" and their resources by protecting American Indian children and requiring placement of children in homes that reflect their unique culture and values and the rights of tribes and tribal courts.

Current federal legislation rests on a foundation of public policy that includes the Adoption Assistance and Child Welfare Act of 1980 (P.L. 96-272), which prioritized family preservation and permanency as major goals of child welfare, and ICWA, which acknowledged the sovereignty of children of federally recognized American Indian tribal governments and was designed to ensure the rights of American Indian children. The Multiethnic Placement Act (MEPA) of 1994 (P.L. 103–382; U.S. Department of Health and Human Services, Children's Bureau, 2001) was intended to remove barriers to permanence for children who are members of racial and ethnic groups. The Interethnic Adoption Provisions of the Small Business Jobs Protection Act of 1996 (P.L. 104–188, §1808; U.S. Department of Health and Human Services, Children's Bureau, 2001) clarified the intent of MEPA to eliminate placement searches to match by race or culture, decrease the length of time that children are in foster care, facilitate the recruitment and retention of foster parents, and establish specific financial penalties for noncompliance with MEPA.

Considering the major role that the social work profession plays in the development of foster care and adoption services, it has a responsibility to assist in assessing public social policy and best practice standards with regard to social services. Social workers should ensure that the services reflect the best and most current knowledge in the field to meet consistently the needs of children and the community. Social workers who participate in the development of foster care and adoption policy and in the delivery of services must be knowledgeable about national standards in foster care and adoption and must uphold professional standards of practice.

ISSUE STATEMENT

Poverty and racism profoundly affect the entire child welfare system. Consequently, children of racial and ethnic groups, particularly African American and American Indian children, are disproportionately represented in the child welfare system. In addition, the presence of gay, lesbian, bisexual, and transgender children and youths in the child welfare system and their unique needs are often overlooked.

Safety is the primary goal for children in out-of-home care. ASFA underscores the importance of safety and child well-being as outcomes. This not only implies keeping children safe from abusive parents, but also it acknowledges that children may be at risk in foster homes, group homes, or other placements. Social workers and agencies have an absolute obligation to monitor the safety of these vulnerable children and to provide resources that promote child well-being.

The "continuum of care" refers to a range of out-of-home placement options for children. Such options include kinship care with relatives or close friends of the child. Other placement resources include general foster family care, specialized foster family care, treatment foster care, group homes, residential treatment facilities, and supervised independent living programs. A continuum of care should be maintained to meet the diverse and unique needs of children in the foster care system.

Recognition must be given to children's needs for security, continuity of parenting relationships, education, and nurturing in foster care and adoption services systems. In addition, families must be strengthened and supported as the primary and preferred source for meeting children's physical and psychological needs. Therefore, societal intervention into the parent–child relationship must be considered carefully so that the intervention meets the child's needs, both immediately and over time. The child's enduring ties to a family must be recognized. Child welfare practice cannot be separated from a family systems approach.

Appropriate and adequate information regarding resources, rights, and responsibilities must be available to all parties in foster care and adoption proceedings. Specifically, it is society's responsibility to ensure comprehensive, high-quality services, with particular attention to the special needs of high-risk children and the resources necessary to meet them. A growing population of children in need of services is children with HIV/AIDS. The complex interplay of social and medical factors that are implicit in the care of these children presents particular challenges to foster care and adoption services. They require a renewed commitment to ensure children with HIV/AIDS the same opportunities to have permanent families as other children, without isolation and segregation. Comprehensive, high-quality services are of particular concern in the provision of services to children with AIDS-related conditions. All services provided to this special population must be grounded in a multidisciplinary approach and include well-thought-out medical treatment when needed.

State agencies and social work professionals must take a proactive role to improve educational outcomes for children in foster care by fostering communication with local school districts and school social workers in developing case plans that include services to help foster children achieve their educational potential. Research, training, and evaluation of foster care and adoption delivery systems and services must be funded and disseminated. A national information system is essential for providing information for policy development and the allocation of resources.

An emerging issue is the privatization and use of managed care in the child welfare arena. NASW can play a vital role in monitoring the quality of services in the transition to new models of services delivery through feedback from its members. The Child Welfare Section can take a leadership role at the state and national levels in reporting to the profession outcomes of children and family well-being.

POLICY STATEMENT

NASW supports a child welfare policy designed to provide the best care for all children in need of foster care and adoption services that is predicated on the following six fundamental principles:

1. Every child has the right to a permanent, continuous, and nurturing relationship with a parenting person or people who convey to the child an enduring sense of love and care. The child should perceive himself or herself as a valued family member. The paramount concern shall be the health and safety of the child. This concern shall supersede the right of birth parents to maintain legal custody when such custody is physically or emotionally harmful.

2. The opportunity to provide such a nurturing environment is the primary responsibility of the child's family. Thus, it becomes society's primary responsibility to provide the necessary services and supports required to safeguard and enhance, with every available means, the ability of all families to fulfill this essential role. Failing this, it becomes society's responsibility to provide for expeditious, alternative arrangements that are permanent and meet the child's physical, mental, emotional, and educational needs.

3. The termination of parental rights, whether voluntary or involuntary, should never be undertaken without due process. Societal intervention into the parent–child relationship is an extremely serious action, which should be pursued only when the child's right to a safe, secure, and nurturing home is seriously threatened. Services should be provided with sensitivity, professional skill, regard for the legal rights of the parties involved, and a sense of the limitations and potential outcomes of such an intervention.

4. The best interest of the child is the primary consideration when developing the permanency plan. When a child enters the foster care system there should be concurrent planning for family reunification or preparation for adoption through termination of parental rights.

5. Policy and budget leaders need adequate data and research based on a national information system that informs policy development and the allocation of resources.

6. The intensity and complexity of social work in the field of child welfare, including foster care and adoption, requires highly qualified personnel with specialized education and knowledge of both the micro and the macro systems associated with the delivery of services. Out of this knowledge must emerge accompanying skills for working effectively with the complex interaction of individuals; families—biological, nuclear, and extended; foster care, adoption, mental health, and private and public child welfare agencies; and educational and legal organizations with which the agencies are most closely involved.

A child's family should receive sufficient and timely support services to prevent the need for substitute care. Neither foster care nor adoption services should be used merely because they provide a convenient choice in a difficult situation.

All people should have the right to employment opportunities or income supports that enable them to meet basic family needs, including:

■ The objective of every child's placement is to provide a safe, nurturing, and secure alternative home when it is not possible for the child to remain with his or her family.

■ Placement decisions should reflect a child's need for continuity, safeguarding the child's right to consistent care and to service arrangements. Agencies must recognize each child's need to retain a significant engagement with his or her parents and extended family and respect the integrity of each child's ethnicity and cultural heritage. When placing children, agencies must first consider placing the child with kin.

■ Social work professionals must take a proactive role to enhance the educational outcomes for children in foster care. Child welfare agencies should work to develop collaboration and communication among the courts, the social worker, and the local school system to focus on the child's educational needs and stability.

■ People involved with the foster care system, adoption proceedings, or child and family services have the right to receive adequate information from the appropriate agency, court,

or community sources, especially regarding their rights, prerogatives, responsibilities, and adequate legal representation.

■ Ongoing research and evaluation, with input from clients, should be used by service providers to form and guide policies and practices in foster care and adoption.

■ Decision makers in child placement services always should be sensitive to the inherent trauma resulting from removing a child from family surroundings and family members. The child's need for an improved environment must be balanced against the possible damage that could result from the separation. The decision makers also must explore alternatives to out-of-home placement and actualize the concept of "reasonable efforts" to prevent removal from the home. The decision-making process must include the development and implementation of a permanent plan for the child. This permanent plan must include a timely decision to terminate parental rights when it is clear that the child cannot remain in or return to his or her family. For some children permanent planning would include preparation for independent living.

■ All efforts should be made to keep siblings together in placement. When children have been neglected, the bonds between siblings are often more significant than the parent–child bond. Separating siblings should be done only for the purpose of child safety. Sibling therapy can be used to repair sibling ties and to change dysfunctional sibling interactions. When siblings must be separated, regular sibling visits must be maintained. Lack of placement resources is not sufficient justification for separating siblings.

■ All independently made arrangements for children should conform to and be judged by the same principles of care established throughout this policy and should conform to national standards of foster care and adoption practices.

■ Barriers that prevent children from being placed in permanent homes must be removed. Financial barriers can be breached by the complete use and expansion of existing adoption subsidy programs. Barriers that are unsupported by tested experience—such as resistance to using single parents, foster parents (for adoption), and nontraditional family patterns (including lesbian and gay, bisexual, and transgender parents) as potential foster care and adoption resources—must be removed.

■ Legislation legitimizing second-parent adoptions in same-sex households should be supported. Legislation seeking to restrict foster care and adoption by gay, lesbian, bisexual, or transgender people should be vigorously opposed.

■ Child and Family Services Reviews should be used to improve child welfare practice, and adequate fiscal resources should be provided to states to improve systemic factors.

■ Professionals at various levels in the government must monitor aggressively and carefully foster care and adoption services, whether provided by the public or the voluntary sector. Professionals in both the public and the private sectors should have expertise in child welfare to ensure that caring, comprehensive, permanent planning, and services for children are provided.

■ Funding of foster care and adoption services should guarantee high-quality services to all children, regardless of their race, ethnicity, language, capabilities, religion, sexual orientation, gender identity, geographic location, or socioeconomic status. Additional recruitment alternatives are needed for gay, lesbian, bisexual, and transgender adolescents for whom existing resources are not accepting or are inadequate, such as family foster care using gay, lesbian, bisexual, and transgender adults as foster parents and group homes designed specifically for gay, lesbian, bisexual, and transgender adolescents. Recruitment efforts should be made to bring families in the child welfare system who are willing to be trained to work with this population and also who are willing to adopt.

■ Foster care and adoption agencies must be administered and staffed by trained social workers.

■ Caseloads should not exceed the ability of workers to provide reasonable, full, and careful attention to each child and his or her family.

■ Community services and foster care that enable children to remain in their neighborhoods and schools should be supported.

■ The long-range advantage to society in providing high-quality family services—including, but not limited to, foster care and adoption—should be promoted. This promotion means advancing the concept of community responsibility for all children's needs and seeking to improve the public image and understanding of foster care and adoption.

■ The social work profession stresses the importance of ethnic and cultural sensitivity. An effort to maintain a child's identity and his or her ethnic heritage should prevail in all services and placement actions that involve children in foster care and adoption programs, including adherence to the principles articulated in the Indian Child Welfare Act.

Foster Care

NASW supports principles related to foster care that include the following:

■ Research-based risk and safety assessment tools should be used as decisions are being made to remove children from or return children to their homes.

■ When foster care becomes the intervention of choice, services to reunify the child with his or her family should begin immediately. These services should work toward improving the conditions in the home and facilitating the child's return. Services should be limited by time and planned.

■ NASW supports public policies that encourage legislative, administrative, and community efforts to support grandparents and other kinship caregivers in meeting the needs of children in their care (Generations United, 2000). Those kinship caregivers whose children are part of the formal foster care system should receive the following supports, as needed:

　■ reimbursement equal to that received by nonrelative foster parents

■ initial emergency start-up funds to meet licensing and certification requirements or to provide concrete resources for care of the children

■ subsidies for guardianship or adoption

■ access to legal resources and representation for helping to obtain permanence

■ support groups, training, or both

■ kinship resource lines to provide support and information, counseling, and so forth

■ treatment resources to meet the special needs of the children

■ caseworkers trained in the unique aspects of kinship care.

■ Vigorous recruitment, mutual selection, initial and ongoing training of foster parents, and adequate financial support are seen as prerequisites to a successful foster care system. Foster parents need to be particularly sensitive to the special needs of children in their care and to be able to work with and support birth parents who are making appropriate efforts to ensure the return of their children.

■ Comprehensive and specialized training of foster parents should be required as a precondition to the licensure of foster homes, and in-service training should be required as a condition for continuing licensure.

■ Foster parents should be viewed as partners on the services delivery team. Therefore, resources are needed to assist the foster parents in providing care to the child. Resources for foster families should include day care, respite care, peer support counseling, and parent education.

■ Liability insurance for foster parents should be the responsibility of the placement agencies.

■ The full and prompt reimbursement of actual maintenance costs and fees for services provided by foster parents should be viewed as an essential part of the agency's plan of care for the child and an investment in both the child and society. The agency also should acknowledge that there are children with spe-

cial needs of all ages and establish a cost schedule accordingly.

■ A variety of foster care arrangements should be available to the child welfare agency, including family foster care, group home care, therapeutic foster care, day treatment foster care, and residential treatment, so that appropriate placements can be made for all children who need temporary, emergency, planned long-term, and specialized foster care. The spectrum of arrangements should include supervised independent living programs for children who are making the transition from foster care to living on their own.

■ Some of these services should include subsidized tuition from state colleges and universities for youths who are younger than 25 years, youths who are or were in the custody of a state agency for no less than 12 consecutive months, youths who were in the custody of a state agency because they were in need of care and protection, and youths who were never returned home or adopted.

■ Social workers must be knowledgeable and proactive about the services available to youths aging out of the foster care system under the Chafee Foster Care Independent Living Act. Social workers should advocate in their state for a full range of services such as state-supported tuition assistance for postsecondary education and vocational training.

■ Child welfare agencies should ensure that each child in foster care has a case plan. The plan should include the reasons the child was removed from the home; the special needs of the child while in and out of home care; and the services to be provided to the parents, child, and foster parents. This is the process of "concurrent planning." The plan will assist in reunifying the family or, if that is not feasible, will result in adoption or another form of permanence. The agency's six-month case-planning review or foster care review panel process should involve all parties, including the caseworker and supervisor, the birth parents and other relatives of the child, foster parents, and the child (if of an appropriate age). In addition, an objective party who is not involved in the management of the case or delivery of services may be involved in the review of the status of the child in care. An attorney or guardian ad litem should participate in the process to represent and advocate for the best interest of the child. Each party to the service-planning process should receive a copy of the initial case plan and subsequent revised plans and agreements. As mandated by ASFA, case plans must be reviewed by the court and adequate legal representation provided for all parties, including the child.

■ The placement of choice should be within the child's family of origin, among relatives (kinship placement) who can provide a more stable environment for the child during the period of family crisis. If no such relatives are available, every effort should be made to place a child in the home of foster parents who are similar in racial and ethnic background to the child's own family. The recruitment of foster parents from each relevant racial and ethnic group should be pursued vigorously to meet the needs of children who require placement.

■ Every effort should be made to maintain a safe, secure, stable, and caring environment for the child with the minimum number of placements.

■ NASW advocates policies that support the systematic involvement of child welfare agencies with foster parents. Foster parents should be trained and compensated and receive continuous support commensurate with their level of skills.

Adoption

NASW supports principles related to adoption that include the following:

■ All parties to adoption are individuals whose needs and rights should be respected and considered to the greatest extent possible. Full recognition must be given to a child's right to and need for ties to his or her birth family and to the right of the birth parents, regardless of their condition, to the services they may need to parent their child and prevent the need for adoption. The child must, nevertheless, be seen as the primary client whose need for a permanent plan must take priority.

■ Adoption policy and practice should recognize that services should be extended to all parties involved in the adoption and should be made available for as long as they are needed and desired.

■ Postadoption services should be provided, if needed, long beyond the legal consummation of the adoption.

■ Special attention should be given to children with special needs, including children of racial and ethnic groups, children who are older, children with disabilities, children who have been subjected to sexual abuse and other trauma, children who are HIV positive or medically fragile, and members of sibling groups, to ensure protection of their right to a caring environment. This care extends to the recruitment of appropriate families and professional services throughout the adoption process and beyond legalization.

■ Publicly funded subsidies should be available in all cases in which the cost of the child's permanent care becomes a barrier to appropriate adoptive placement. If adoption subsidies are needed throughout the child's minority years and transition into adulthood, the subsidies must be adequate to meet the child's special needs.

■ NASW supports social workers' compliance with state and federal statutes and best practice standards regarding confidentiality and sharing of information regarding adoption.

■ The needs and rights of adoptees to know their birth origin should be recognized and respected. This right extends to requests from adult adoptees for identifying information. Open adoption should be considered if it is in the best interest of the child.

■ Active and continuous recruitment of adoptive parents from diverse ethnic or racial groups should be aggressively pursued to ensure all the needs of all children awaiting placement are met.

■ NASW supports the need to protect the rights of the child. NASW opposes placements made by third parties who are not related to the child or who are not licensed as placement agencies and do not ensure the welfare of children through careful preplacement selection and early monitoring of placement by qualified professionals. However, in states in which placements by third parties, including international adoptions, are legally recognized, NASW advocates that the assessment and supervision of adoptive families and children be carried out by professionally trained social workers. In such states, NASW will continue to support appropriate legislation to eliminate third-party placement.

Education and Retention of Social Workers in Child Welfare

■ Foster care and adoption agencies must be administered and staffed by professionally educated social workers, licensed social workers, or both.

■ Child welfare agencies should actively recruit graduates from BSW and MSW programs.

■ NASW supports partnerships between schools of social work and child welfare agencies in working to promote BSW and MSW education for child welfare employees.

■ Child welfare agencies should provide ongoing professional training in cultural competence, changes in laws, policies, and new developments to uphold best practices that are based in research.

■ Child welfare agencies should provide competitive salary levels and professional opportunities to recruit and retain social workers.

■ Child welfare agencies should provide a healthy environment, competent supervision, and case consultation.

■ NASW supports partnerships between schools of social work and child welfare agencies in the development of child welfare curricula.

REFERENCES

Adoption and Safe Families Act of 1997, P.L. 105-89, 111 Stat. 2115.
Adoption Assistance and Child Welfare Act of 1980, P.L. 96-272, 94 Stat. 500.
Child Welfare League of America. (1996). *Standards of excellence.* Washington, DC: Author.
Foster Care Independence Act of 1999, P.L. 106-169.
Generations United. (2000, August). *Grandparents and other relatives raising children: Challenges of caring for the second family* (Fact Sheet) [Online]. Available: http://www.gu.org/factsheets.htm
Indian Child Welfare Act of 1978, 25 U.S.C., ch. 21.
U.S. Department of Health and Human Services, Children's Bureau. (2001). *A guide to the Multiethnic Placement Act of 1994 as amended by the Interethnic Adoption Provisions of 1996* (chap. 1) [Online]. Available: http://www.hhs.gov/ocr/mepaipp.htm

Policy statement approved by the NASW Delegate Assembly, August 2002. The 2002 Delegate Assembly also decided not to combine this policy statement with the policy statements on Public Child Welfare and Child Abuse and Neglect. This policy statement supersedes the policy statement on Foster Care and Adoption approved by the Delegate Assembly in 1979 and 1987. For further information, contact the National Association of Social Workers, 750 First Street, NE, Suite 700, Washington, DC 20002-4241. Telephone: 202-408-8600; e-mail: press@naswdc.org

Gender-, Ethnic-, and Race-Based Workplace Discrimination

BACKGROUND

Discrimination is defined as treating one person unfairly over another according to factors unrelated to their ability or potential, such as age, disability, sex, gender, or national origin (http://www.legal-definitions.com/discrimination.htm). Discrimination based on age, disability, gender, gender identity, national origin, race, religion, and sexual orientation continues to affect a variety of employable citizens in the workplace. New forms of discrimination such as genetics, size and body image, and discrimination based on credit are on the increase in the workplace. These practices occur at every stage of the employment process, from interviewing, hiring, training and promotion, through retention and times of lay off. Ethnic slurs, graffiti, and other forms of offensive conduct have become more pervasive in the workplace and can make the employment arena a hostile and abusive place to be. Most analyses of wage discrimination and other workplace-related issues analyze either gender or race and ethnicity separately. However, because patterns of employment discrimination by gender, race, and ethnicity intersect and reinforce each other, it is useful to consider them together. Doing so should not obscure the fact that African Americans, Native Americans, and Americans in each of the Spanish-speaking and Asian ethnic and cultural groups have their own unique histories of employment in the United States and have faced oppression and discrimination at different times in the history of this nation (Amott & Matthei, 1991; Glenn, 1985).

Men and women in each of these groups not only have shared many experiences of oppression but also have had experiences of oppression that have been unique. In employment, gender has affected patterns of work and employment-related discrimination in each of these groups. Most analysts agree that race, ethnicity, class, and gender together powerfully shape social and economic life in America (Amott & Matthei, 1991; Glenn, 1985; Rothenberg, 1995). "Differences in race, class and gender are very costly for some and very profitable for others" (Rothenberg, p. 117).

The civil rights protests of the 1960s brought to the forefront of America the injustices perpetrated on segments of U.S. society through racial segregation and discrimination. During the height of the civil rights protests and demonstrations, President John F. Kennedy went on television on June 11, 1963, to address the nation. He said, "We are confronted primarily with a moral issue. It is as old as the scriptures and it is as clear as the American Constitution. The heart of the question is whether all Americans are afforded equal rights and equal opportunities, whether we are going to treat our fellow Americans as we want to be treated."

Since the 1960s, several pieces of federal legislation addressed discrimination in the workplace: Equal Pay Act of 1963 (EPA) (P.L. 88-38), Title VII of the Civil Rights Act of 1964, Age Discrimination in Employment Act of 1967 (ADEA) (P.L. 90-202), and the American's with Disabilities Act of 1990 (ADA). Title VII of the Civil Rights Act of 1964 (P.L. 88-352) prohibits discrimination based on race, color, national origin, sex, and religion and prohibits retaliation. The Equal Pay Act of 1963 prohibits discrimination on the basis of sex in the payment of wages or benefits, where men and women perform work of similar skill, effort, and responsibility for the same employer under similar working conditions. The ADEA prohibits employment discrimination against people

40 years of age and older. The ADA prohibits employment discrimination against people with disabilities and requires employers to make reasonable accommodations for people with disabilities. There are also federal protections from discrimination on other bases, including status as a parent, marital status, political affiliation, and conduct that does not adversely affect the performance of the employee (U.S. Equal Employment Opportunity Commission [EEOC], 1964).

The EEOC, created in 1964, enforces statutes that make it illegal to discriminate against employees or applicants for employment on the basis of race, color, religion, sex, national origin, disability, or age. Despite more than four decades of legislation calling for nondiscrimination in employment, in 2004 the EEOC received more than 100,000 complaints of discrimination (EEOC, n.d.) and recovered more than $352 million in monetary benefits for complainants (EEOC, n.d.). In 2004, charges of discrimination based on race accounted for about 27 percent of all complaints filed with EEOC, followed by charges of discrimination based on gender (24 percent), age (17 percent), and disability (15 percent) (EEOC, n.d.).

Discrimination can occur at every stage of employment, from recruitment, application process, hiring, and remuneration to separation. Discrimination based on race is deeply entrenched in the workplace and remains pervasive. Forms of occupational segregation, subjugation, subordination, and violence are still with us. Although the extent to which earnings differentials by gender and race and ethnicity result from discrimination is disputed widely, research has repeatedly shown that the earnings gap between white American men and both white American women and men and women of all other racial and ethnic groups cannot be explained fully by training, education, work experience, or attachment to the labor force (Freeman, 1991). Discrimination alone accounts for a significant proportion of the wage gap between white women and men and women of color compared with white men (Freeman; National Committee on Pay Equity, 1995).

The wage gap is a statistical indicator often used as an index of the status of women's earnings relative to men's. It is also used to compare earnings of other races and ethnicities to those of white men, a group generally not subject to race or sex-based discrimination. The wage gap varies from 73 percent to 77 percent between men and women. These figures are based on the 2000 median annual earnings for year-round, full-time workers (see National Committee on Pay Equity, Q&A, (http://www.pay-equity.org/info.html). The wage gap exists, in part, because many women and people of color are still segregated into a few low-paying occupations. More than half of all women workers hold sales, clerical, nurses, teachers, and service jobs. Studies show that an occupation pays less when women or people of color dominate it (National Committee on Pay Equity, 1995).

Women still earn 73 cents to every dollar that men earned in 2000. African American women make only 63 cents and Latinas a mere 56 cents to every dollar earned by white men. Because of the lower earnings of women, families maintained solely by women are disadvantaged economically. Thus, the low earnings of white, African American, Latino, and Native American women have major effects on children; low wages for women are a major cause of child poverty. Even without children, being female and being a member of one of these racial and ethnic groups contributes to the chances of being poor: Poverty rates are approximately one in 10 for white men and women, one in three for white female heads of households, one in three for Hispanic men and women, one in two for Hispanic female heads of households, one in three for African American men and women, and one in two for African American female heads of households, demonstrating that race and gender each have a powerful influence on poverty in the United States (Mantsios, 1995). Pay equity by gender and by race and ethnicity is essential if the suffering of children in poverty is to be eliminated. If working women earned the same as men (those who work the same number of hours; have the same education, age, and union status; and live in the same region of the country), their annual family incomes would rise by $4,000 and poverty rates would be cut in half (National Women's Law Center, 2005).

Occupational segregation results in the "crowding" of women and people of color into a narrow range of professions and occupations. A relatively high percentage of white and Asian men are employed in managerial and professional occupations, whereas African American, Hispanic, and American Indian men tend to be concentrated in the "lower skilled," lower paid occupations of operators, fabricators, and laborers. Women of all groups are most likely to be employed in technical sales and administrative support occupations. A high percentage of white and Asian women are also employed in managerial and professional occupations, and a high percentage of African American, Hispanic, and American Indian women are also employed in service (Cotter, Hermsen, & Vanniman, 2003).

One characteristic of the occupational groups in which women who are employed are concentrated, and especially women from different racial and ethnic groups, is that many of them are involved with domestic work or service work that replaces the household work of others. Historically, social practice and social policy have rewarded and protected the unpaid family work of white middle- and upper-class women; programs such as Aid to Families with Dependent Children were originally started so that white widows would be able to rear their dependent children without having to resort to paid employment (Miller, 1992); however, the household and child-rearing work of women from different racial and ethnic groups in relation to their own dependent children has not been so protected (Abramovitz, 1988; Glenn, 1985). The ways in which this phenomenon has played out differed for each racial and ethnic group, depending on its immigration history. The forms of oppression the group as a whole has encountered in the United States, and the content of the dominant stereotypes of each group, has also varied (Amott & Matthei, 1991; Glenn). In fact, some groups of women, such as African American, some Asian and Pacific Islander, and some Hispanic women, have been employed to do the child-rearing and household work of affluent white women, and both men and women of color are often employed in the secondary labor market and the service sectors of the economy in devalued and poorly paid "dirty work" (Gilkes, 1990). Thus, what Abramovitz (1988) has termed "the family ethic" has been applied differently to rationalize the work of men and women and that of white Americans compared with people from different racial and ethnic groups.

African Americans, Hispanics, and American Indians are more likely than non-Hispanic white people or Asians to work in lower-paying, semi-skilled jobs as service workers. They are less likely to hold white-collar jobs, which range from managerial and professional to clerical positions. African Americans, Hispanics, and American Indians who hold these white-collar jobs are more likely than white people or Asians to work as typist, clerks, or salespeople rather than as higher-earning managers or professionals. Although the share of U.S. workers in farming, fishing, or forestry is small, it is greatest among Hispanics, reflecting the large number of Hispanics who work in agriculture (Population Reference Bureau, Racial Inequalities in Managerial & Professional Jobs, 2004).

An important consequence of the lower earnings and different jobs held by women and by men from different racial and ethnic groups is the effect of these patterns of employment on work-related benefits. The U.S. economy is organized in such a way that access to many economic resources in addition to income is determined by paid employment. Access to and levels of benefits from such publicly supported federal social insurance programs as unemployment insurance and Old Age and Survivors Disability Insurance for workers who are older and disabled and their dependents, as well as from state-controlled systems such as workers' compensation, are determined by a person's (or their spouse's) level of compensation and tenure on the job.

White American male workers have traditionally received higher levels of benefits from these programs than others because they are less likely to be underemployed or more likely to be employed in jobs with greater stability or with higher levels of compensation (Ozawa, 1989). The same is true of access to such privately funded job-related benefits as pension plans and affordable health insurance. The pattern of distribution of these noncash benefits mirrors and reinforces the pattern of earnings differences in which white American men tend to get more than women and more than men from other racial and ethnic groups. These differences in employment-related benefits affect these workers and their families not only during their years of employment, but also during retirement, because retirement income programs, both public and private, are involved. Thus, these employment-related differences contribute substantially to the higher rates of poverty that white women, especially those living alone, and men and women of color suffer in old age (Crawley, 1994). For example, the median income for all older African Americans was 59.6 percent of older white Americans, and the median income of older African American women was only 67.6 percent of that for older white women (Crawley).

Even in occupations and professions in which women predominate numerically, the glass ceiling has a major effect (Mason, 1992). This situation unfortunately pertains to the social work profession as well; recent studies have shown that women are paid less compared with men and are less likely than men to advance in the profession (Gibelman & Schervish, 1993, 1996). In the field of social work as a whole, women from different racial and ethnic groups are disproportionately found in the lowest level or paraprofessional positions (Martin & Chernesky, 1989). Although the earnings and advancement gaps in social work may be less than in other professions (Sokoloff, 1988), given the profession's commitment to ending discrimination in all forms and to developing diversity within the profession that will mirror the diversity in U.S. society, any gender-, ethnic-, or race-based discrimination in the profession is cause for concern.

ISSUES STATEMENT

NASW and the social work profession have long been concerned with working to eliminate discrimination in all forms. This commitment is embodied in the *Code of Ethics of the National Association of Social Workers* (NASW, 2000) and determines the major policies that NASW supports. Unfortunately, discrimination based on race, ethnicity, age, ability, sexual orientation,

and gender continues to be pervasive in modern American life. Discrimination has an enormous and pernicious impact on the lives of the diverse clients that the social work profession and NASW members serve. It also affects NASW members who are women (the majority of members), people of color, people with disabilities, sexual minorities, older people, and people of diverse religions. U.S. society and social policy are organized in such a way that employment is the major means for distributing income and most other essential material social benefits, such as health insurance, public and private retirement plans, and disability insurance, as well as many nonmaterial benefits, such as status and prestige. The 1993 Delegate Assembly voted to retain both a general statement on women's issues and a more specific statement on workplace discrimination. For these reasons, it is essential that NASW continue to have a strong and up-to-date policy statement addressing discrimination in the workplace to guide the association and its members in practice, advocacy, and policy development activities.

Discriminatory workplace policies and practices, such as those affecting advancement, training, and the working environment, limit opportunities for advancement and for participation in organizational decision making. These other forms of discrimination interact with wage discrimination to affect earnings, benefits, occupations, and personal and household income. Despite federal and state civil rights legislation, affirmative action programs, and other legislative and policy efforts to reduce these differences in the past several decades, workplace discrimination has not disappeared.

POLICY STATEMENT

Given the persistence and pervasiveness of workplace discrimination, pay and employment equity must remain a major policy issue for the social work profession and for the nation. The many aspects of the problem require that the solutions pursued also be multifaceted (Davis, 1994; Miller, 1992). NASW supports a number of principles and strategies for change in legislative, administrative, and educational areas.

There is evidence that men and women of all racial and ethnic groups benefit from unionization (Institute for Women's Policy Research, 1993). Unions with a high proportion of women in their membership have also broadened the scope of their negotiations to include such issues as affirmative action, family leave, and the elimination of sexual harassment on the job (Institute for Women's Policy Research). Therefore, worker's efforts to organize should be supported, including those that incorporate diverse membership, to promote progressive employment policies and address employment discrimination.

Affirmative action is another powerful tool that can be used to reduce inequities in the employment of all women and of men from different racial and ethnic groups. Affirmative action policies aim to open hiring systems and procedures and career development and advancement on the job to those who have historically been discriminated against. Affirmative action can be a powerful tool for helping men and women from different racial and ethnic groups gain access to higher paying jobs from which they have traditionally been excluded. It can also help eliminate the glass ceiling that prevents many white women and workers from different racial and ethnic groups from attaining the levels of advancement in their chosen fields that they are qualified to achieve. Affirmative action is one of the few methods identified for reducing the underrepresentation of white women and workers from different racial and ethnic groups in the highest levels of employment in America. NASW reaffirms its commitment to affirmative action in the public and private sectors and will publicize the nature and benefits of well-designed affirmative action programs. Affirmative action should also be a consideration as employers restructure and downsize.

NASW therefore reaffirms its commitment to its own program of affirmative action within the association, which has succeeded in identifying people from historically oppressed groups as leaders in the profession. All social work employers, associations of social workers, and social and human services agencies should develop and implement similar affirmative action programs.

Policies to end employment discrimination include the following:

■ federal and state legislative measures that aim to eliminate discrimination in employment, training, compensation, and job-related benefits

■ enforcement of all laws and regulations that forbid discrimination in the workplace, including adequate funding for the federal and state agencies charged with the enforcement of civil rights and antidiscrimination laws and regulations

■ public and private affirmative action programs that aim to ensure that people from historically oppressed populations have access to employment, opportunities for advancement, nondiscriminatory working conditions, and fair compensation

■ legislative, training, and educational programs that help people from historically oppressed populations qualify for and enter occupations and fields from which they have traditionally been excluded

■ adequate funding for social, health, and human services agencies and services so that inequities in employment and compensation that exist in social work and social work agencies can be eliminated

■ elimination of all federal and state measures that unfairly limit employment and otherwise have a negative impact on immigrants and undocumented workers

■ human and civil rights measures to protect all Americans, including lesbian, gay, bisexual transgender, and intersex

■ adoption of federal and state measures that prohibit discrimination based on sexual orientation and gender identity

■ promotion of quality child care to remove barriers to employment.

REFERENCES

Abramovitz, M. (1988). *Regulating the lives of women: Social welfare policy from colonial times to the present*. Boston: South End Press.

Age Discrimination in Employment Act of 1967 (ADEA). P.L. 90-202, 81 Stat. 602

Amott, T. L., & Matthei, J. A. (1991). Race, gender, and work: A multicultural economic history of women in the United States. Boston: South End Press.

Civil Rights Act of 1964, P.L. 88-352, 78 Stat. 241.

Cotter, D. A., Hermsen, J. A., & Vanniman, R. S. (2003). Segregation across race. *Sociological Quarterly, 44,* 1.

Crawley, B. (1994). Older women: Public policy issues for the twenty-first century. In L. V. Davis (Ed.), *Building on women's strengths: A social work agenda for the twenty-first century* (pp. 159–178). New York: Haworth Press.

Davis, L. V. (1994). Why we still need a women's agenda for social work. In L. V. Davis (Ed.), *Building on women's strengths: A social work agenda for the twenty-first century* (pp. 1–26). New York: Haworth Press.

Equal Pay Act of 1963, P.L. 88-38, 77 Stat. 56 (29 sect. 206).

Freeman, M. L. (1991). Pay equity and social work. *Affilia, 6,* 7–19.

Gibelman, M., & Schervish, P. H. (1993). The glass ceiling in social work: Is it shatterproof? *Affilia, 8,* 442–455.

Gibelman, M., & Schervish, P. H. (1996). *Who we are: A second look.* Washington, DC: NASW Press.

Gilkes, C. T. (1990). Liberated to work like dogs!: Labeling black women and their work. In H. Y. Grossman & N. L. Chester (Eds.), *The experience and meaning of work in women's lives* (pp. 165–188). Hillsdale, NJ: Lawrence Erlbaum.

Glenn, E. N. (1985). Racial ethnic women's labor: The intersection of race, gender and class oppression. *Review of Radical Political Economics, 17*(3), 86–108.

Mantsios, G. (1995). Class in America: Myths and realities. In P. S. Rothenberg (Ed.), *Race, class, and gender in the United States: An integrated study* (3rd ed., pp. 131–143). New York: St. Martin's Press.

Martin, P. Y., & Chernesky, R. H. (1989). Women's prospects for leadership in social welfare: A political economy perspective. *Administration in Social Work, 13*(3/4), 117–143.

Mason, M. A. (1992). Standing still in the workplace: Women in social work and other female-dominated occupations. *Affilia, 7,* 23–43.

Miller, D. C. (1992). *Women and social welfare: A feminist analysis.* New York: Praeger.

National Association of Social Workers. (2000). *Code of ethics of the National Association of Social Workers.* Washington, DC: Author.

National Committee on Pay Equity. (1995). In P. S. Rothenberg (Ed.), *Race, class, and gender in the United States: An integrated study* (3rd ed., pp. 144–151). New York: St. Martin's Press.

National Women's Law Center. (2005). *The wage gap.* Retrieved from http://www.inforplease.com/ipa/A0763170.html

Ozawa, M. N. (Ed.). (1989). *Women's life cycle and economic insecurity: Problems and proposals.* Westport, CT: Praeger.

Rothenberg, P. S. (1995). *Race, class, and gender in the United States: An integrated study* (3rd ed.). New York: St. Martin's Press.

Sokoloff, N. J. (1988). Evaluating gains and losses by black and white women and men in the professions, 1960–1980. *Social Problems, 35,* 336–340.

U.S. Equal Employment Opportunity Commission. (n.d.). *U. S. Equal Employment Opportunity Commission.* Retrieved on May 2, 2005, from http://www.eeoc.gov/

U.S. Equal Employment Opportunity Commission. (1964). *Furthering the protections against workplace discrimination and harassment.* Retrieved from www.eeoc.gov/about eeoc/35th/1990s/furthering.html

U.S. Equal Employment Opportunity Commission. (2003). *Pre 1965: Events leading to the creation of EEOC.* Retrieved from www.eeoc.gov/about eeoc/35th/pre1965/

SUGGESTED READINGS

American Association of University Women Educational Foundation. (1992). *How schools shortchange girls: A study of major findings on girls and education.* Washington, DC: Author.

American Civil Liberties Union. (1998) *Workplace rights: Lifestyle discrimination in the* workplace: Your right to privacy under attack. Retrieved from www.aclu.org/workplacerights/gen/13384res19981231.html

Furchtgott-Roth, D., Stolba, C. (1999). *Women's figures: An illustrated guide to the economic progress of women in America.* Washington, DC: American Enterprise Institute Press.

Hochschild, A. (1989). *The second shift: Working parents and the revolution at home.* New York: Viking Press.

Huffman, M. L., & Cohen, P. N. (2004). Occupational segregation and the gender gap in workplace authority: National versus local labor markets. *Sociological Focus, 19*(1), 121–147.

Immigration Reform and Control Act of 1986, P.L. 99-603, 100 Stat. 3359.

Institute for Women's Policy Research. (1993). *What do unions do for women?* Washington, DC: Author.

Lopez, J. A. (1995). Women face glass walls as well as glass ceilings. In P. S. Rothenberg (Ed.), *Race, class, and gender in the United States: An integrated study* (3rd ed., pp. 241–242). New York: St. Martin's Press.

McElroy, W., (2001). *Unlocking the potential of America's "pink collar" workers.* Retrieved July 24, 2001, from http://www.foxnews.com/story/0,2933,30307,00.html

Population Reference Bureau. (2001). *Record numbers of women in the U. S. labor force, and occupational segregation.* Retrieved from Template.cfm?Section=RaceandEthnicity&template=/Content

U.S. Department of Commerce. (1993). *Statistical abstract of the United States* (113th ed.). Lanham, MD: Bernan Press.

U.S. Department of Labor. (1991). *Report on the glass ceiling initiative.* Washington, DC: U.S. Government Printing Office.

Weinstein, D. (2003, Fall). Got religion? Accommodating America's diverse religious beliefs and practices in the workplace. *The Philadelphia Lawyer.*

Policy statement approved by the NASW Delegate Assembly, August 2005. This policy supersedes the policy statement on Gender, Ethnic-, and Race-Based Workplace Discrimination approved by the Delegate Assembly in 1996 and referred by the 2002 Delegate Assembly to the 2005 Delegate Assembly for revision. For further information, contact the National Association of Social Workers, 750 First Street, NE, Suite 700, Washington, DC 20002-4241. Telephone: 202-408-8600 or 800-638-8799; e-mail: press@naswdc.org

Genetics

BACKGROUND

With the completion of the human genome sequence in 2003, it is thought that all disease, with the possible exception of trauma, is a result of the interaction of one's genes and the environment. Emerging advances in the science of *genetics* (the study of single genes and their effects) and *genomics* (the study of the functions and interaction of all the genes in the human body) not only identify thousands of rare disorders, but also define genetic components of common diseases such as Alzheimer's, cancer, mental illness, diabetes, heart disease, and autism (Guttmacher & Collins, 2002). As predictive genetic testing becomes more available for some of these common diseases, it is imperative that social workers begin incorporating genetic thinking and genetic principles in their practices. Understanding the psychosocial and ethical implications of genetic testing is important for all social workers, no matter where they are practicing. Social workers can take an active part in ensuring that clients are protected against genetic discrimination by insurance companies, employers, schools, adoption agencies, and the government.

As social workers, we must respect genetic diversity and the uniqueness of the individual, regardless of his or her genetic makeup (Weiss, 2004), including the ability to recognize the difference between components of genetic makeup and learned traits. It is important that social workers recognize how vital their role is in helping clients come to terms with being at risk of a genetic condition or facing the uncertainty of a genetic diagnosis in the family.

Genetic research studies each individual's unique combination of approximately 30,000 genes located on the 23 pairs of chromosomes found in each human cell. Each gene or combination of genes in interaction with the environment is responsible for an individual's particular traits and disorders. For example, one's hair color, gender, and eye color are determined by genes. Genes also play an important role in health, mental health, and to a yet unknown degree, behavior. One interesting finding of the Human Genome Project was that all individuals are 99.9 percent the same with respect to their DNA sequence. Pharmacogenomics is a recent development of tailoring of drugs for patients on an individual basis. The National Human Genome Research Institute (1997) supports the dissemination of genome information to the public and health professionals.

Genetics is not a new science; Gregor Mendel discovered the laws of heredity in the 1800s (Bishop & Waldholz, 1990). Neither is genetics a new field for social workers; for the past 40 years, social workers have been providing genetic services and writing about the effect of genetic diagnoses on families (Schild, 1966; Schultz, 1966; Weiss, 1976). In recent years, the social work profession has taken a more active role in the arena of genetics and genomics. The Human Genome Education Model (HuGEM) project, funded by the National Institutes of Health and co-chaired by two social workers, offered workshops and training programs in genetics for social workers and other disciplines across the country from 1997 to 2001 (Lapham, Kozma, Weiss, Benkendorf, & Wilson, 2000). The National Coalition of Health Professional Education in Genetics (NCHPEG) was formed in 1996 and included two social workers representing both NASW and the Council on Social Work Education on its steering committee. NASW developed *Standards for Integrating Genetics in*

Social Work Practice in 2003 and an online continuing education course titled "Understanding Genetics: The Social Worker's Role" in 2007. What is new is the genetic information now available and its effect on both clients and practitioners. An array of issues related to genetics arises at all levels of social work practice—from clinical practice to family practice to policy making. Clients face both benefits and risks now and in the future as a result of genetic research.

Genetics is an expanding field of practice for social workers. Science and technology are quickly moving toward a time in which most human maladies can be identified and, once identified, treated, cured, or even prevented. Yet this seemingly liberating possibility for knowledge is fraught with potential for harm to the people social workers serve. Issues of informed consent and confidentiality arise, as do those of discrimination, self-determination, and the immediate benefits of genetic test results.

Unfortunately, in most cases, results of genetic tests are not clear-cut. One-to-one gene-disorder relationships are rare. In fact, most disorders are the combination of more than one gene and environmental factors. Predictive or presymptomatic tests can identify individuals at risk of getting a disease, such as certain types of cancer, before the onset of symptoms. However, although a particular gene combination may be identified with certainty, these tests cannot predict whether the disorder will ever be manifested, with the possible exception of identifying a late-onset condition, such as Huntington disease. For example, the genes linked to breast cancer, BRCA1 and BRCA2, can be identified by a predictive test. These genes are found in only 5 percent of the population, and even if the gene is found, 20 percent of individuals with a positive test will never get that type of breast cancer. On the other hand, even though the gene is not present, one in nine women (11 percent) will have breast cancer in their lifetime (Geller et al., 1997). Although genetic testing is becoming an integral part of health care, often the availability of the test is not followed by developed treatments. Advantages of genetic testing, such as facilitating choices about family planning, pre-

ventive lifestyle measures, or increased surveillance must be balanced against the risk of genetic discrimination. The advent of genetic testing, now available for about 1,000 diseases, raises many questions about how an individual's genetic information can be used, and the threat of discrimination hinders both genetic research and clinical practice (Williams, 2006). Direct-to-consumer marketing of genetic testing increases the risk that violations of genetic privacy will follow and eliminates face-to-face counseling (Roche & Annas, 2006).

To make an informed decision to have a genetic test, a client has to have access to current, accurate information regarding benefits and risks of genetic testing to the client and to family members. Information includes limits of protection of confidentiality under federal and state law; strengths and limitations of the test itself; availability of prevention, treatment, and cure; and potential risks of stigmatization, discrimination, and psychological distress, including risk to intrafamily relationships. Social workers may make referrals to other professionals, such as genetic counselors, to maximize the amount of knowledge available to the client for purposes of deciding whether to be tested.

People seek genetic testing usually for one of four reasons: (1) for diagnosis—to determine whether they currently have a particular disorder; (2) for asymptomatic testing—to determine whether they have a particular genetic disorder that will manifest itself in the future; (3) for prenatal planning—to determine whether they carry the gene or genes for a particular disorder that may affect future generations; or (4) for susceptibility testing—to determine whether they are susceptible to a particular disorder that could manifest itself in the future. The results of these tests carry unique psychological implications for individuals and their families (Fanos, 1997; Fanos & Johnson, 1995).

Once educated about whether treatment for a particular disease exists, each person must weigh the options on the basis of individual benefits and risks. In cases in which a treatment or cure is possible, the options seem clear. However, if the test can only establish susceptibility, if there is no treatment or cure, or both, then for some the risks of discrimination and psychological stress may outweigh the benefits. Social workers should ensure that the client has access to all of the information necessary to make the decision to be tested and that the decision reflects the self-determination of the client.

Minors often do not have the opportunity to make decisions for themselves about whether to be tested. The Task Force on Genetic Testing, the advisory committee of the National Human Genetic Research Institute (1997) stated the following: "Genetic testing of children for adult onset disease should not be undertaken unless direct medical benefit will accrue to the child and this benefit would be lost by waiting until the child has reached adulthood" (chapter 1). Many of the issues regarding children are still formative, including those relevant to testing minors for decisions to be made by adoptive parents, adopted children having the right to know their biological parents' genetic makeup, and children conceived by a gamete donor having a right to their donor's genetic test (Fanos, 1997; Wertz, Fanos, & Reilly, 1994). Research is continuing with regard to genetic determinants for psychiatric disorders, addictions, and social behavior, and some progress has been made. However, this raises the question of potential treatment when needed versus labeling and incarceration.

ISSUE STATEMENT

Fear of genetic discrimination could limit participation in research, willingness to have genetic testing, and genetic screening (Hall et al., 2005). At least three possibilities for discrimination arise regarding genetic testing. One is societal: People may be stigmatized or labeled if they are found to be susceptible, for example, to cancer or have a potential disability. Another is financial: An employer could turn down a person for employment because the person may cost the company too much money in insurance costs related to his or her genetic test results, or the person could be denied insurance coverage for the treatment of the disease. A third is access to potentially helpful genetic testing for members of minority groups and poor people (Hudson, Rothenberg, Andrews, Kahn, & Collins, 1995; Rothenberg et al., 1997, Wertz, 1998). Although many states have laws that provide protections from using genetic information in a discriminatory manner, the need for federal legislation has not been met (Smith, 2004).

Social work practice in the context of genetic testing is guided by the *NASW Code of Ethics* (2000) and the *NASW Standards for Integrating Genetics in Social Work Practice* (2003). Although several ethical standards apply to genetic practice, three are especially relevant: informed consent, confidentiality, and protection from discrimination. Ability to gain knowledge of one's genetic makeup or a family member's genetic makeup carries significant risks. A genetic test may alert people about the prevention, treatment, and cure of some disorders, but currently the ability to test for a genetic disorder often exceeds science's ability to prevent, treat, and cure genetic disease (Taylor-Brown & Johnson, 1998). In most cases, people are tested for diseases for which there is no known treatment or cure. Clients thus face significant psychological risks when learning of traits or disorders as a result of genetic testing (Lapham, Kozma, & Weiss, 1996). They also risk potential discrimination by insurance companies, employers, and society for traits or disorders. In addition, there are financial incentives for private companies to patent and sell genetic tests, even though their use is of limited benefit to some clients. Consequently, the requirement for comprehensive informed consent cannot be overstated.

To protect clients, social workers must know of the limitations of confidentiality to genetic test information. There are enormous financial incentives for insurance companies, employers, the criminal justice system, and other government agencies to have access to people's genetic information, and never before have these groups had the ability to know the potential for future health problems (Andrews, Fullarton, Holtzman, & Motulsky, 1994). Although most states have some protections against the discriminatory use of genetic information by health insurers and employers, the laws differ widely and there is no national standard at present. Current federal and state policies do not protect the use of genetic tests for purposes of discrimination in underwriting and employment (Hudson, 2007). Of particular concern to social workers is the potential for labeling individuals and withholding services for people with mental health, mental retardation, and behavioral disorders such as alcoholism, drug use, and even anger. Testing of minors is also a relevant issue here. The right to confidentiality extends to both the decision to be tested and the decision of who is allowed access to the test results. Ethical Standard 1.07(d), Privacy and Confidentiality, is applicable: "Social workers should inform clients, to the extent possible, about the disclosure of confidential information and the potential consequences, when feasible before the disclosure is made" (NASW, 2000, p. 10). Applied to genetic testing, this means that social workers should inform clients of the potential limitations to confidential test results and the consequences.

Two other significant issues involve competence in providing services alone and in teams and advocacy. If social workers are to provide services related to genetic testing, they must be competent in the content and services they provide, and they must remain competent as the field emerges (Ethical Standards 1.04, Competence, and 1.05, Cultural Competence). In light of the plethora of issues, the decision to be tested must be the client's, without coercion from insurance companies or family members and based on informed consent (Ethical Standard 1.02, Self-Determination). Because of the complexity of providing genetics services, social workers often practice with multidisciplinary teams. Ethical Standard 2.03, Interdisciplinary Collaboration, defines the social worker's role and ethical responsibilities to the client in relation to interdisciplinary collaboration. Finally, for social workers to help protect clients' and society's interest in the benefits of genetic testing, social workers' advocacy role in public policy is essential (Ethical Standard 6.04, Social and Political Action). The role of social workers as advocates in the field of genetics is defined in the *NASW Standards for Integrating Genetics in Social Work Practice*. Standard 9 discusses the need to advocate on behalf of clients to ensure fair social policies and access to quality genetic services (NASW,

2003). As more attention is paid to benefits and risks of stem cell research, reproductive technology, tissue cloning, and gene therapy, social workers will be called on to develop and confront emerging policies related to genetic testing and treatment.

POLICY STATEMENT

The Profession

■ NASW maintains a commitment to continue work to establish the social work profession as a leader in the field of genetics.

■ NASW encourages social workers to educate themselves through formal and informal educational opportunities as well as through reading professional journals and chapter materials regarding current issues in genetics.

■ NASW recommends that social workers become familiar with the *Standards of Integrating Genetics in Social Work Practice*.

■ NASW supports the development of programs, training, and information that provide social workers with current genetics information for use with clients.

State and Federal Policies

■ NASW opposes genetics policies that interfere with an individual's right to choose whether or not to be tested.

■ NASW opposes genetics testing policies that are discriminatory in terms of access to genetics services.

■ NASW opposes policies that coerce clients into reproductive decisions as a result of genetics test results that they would not otherwise make.

■ NASW opposes the use of genetic research to alter populations of people and to remove certain traits deemed by society as "unfit."

■ NASW opposes patenting naturally occurring human genetic structure.

- NASW supports policies that protect the client's ownership of his or her own genetic information and that protect the confidentiality of, access to, and use of an individual's genetic tests.

- NASW supports policies that provide protection for clients from discrimination in employment and by insurance companies or protection from efforts to limit freedom of education or other civil rights on the basis of a genetic test.

- NASW advocates for client-focused public policy for genetic testing, so that all clients may receive the benefits of genetic testing.

- NASW supports policies that protect the rights of minors to be tested only when there is a present and current benefit to the child that would be lost if the test is not done until the child becomes an adult.

- NASW supports responsible stem cell research.

Practice

- NASW encourages interdisciplinary research between social work and other disciplines to determine the effect of genetic testing on clients.

- NASW encourages ongoing collaborative research between social work practitioners and educators to determine the effect of genetic testing on clients.

- NASW supports the development of psychosocial support services for clients with genetic disorders.

- NASW encourages all social workers to take families histories that include medical intergenerational information whenever possible.

- NASW supports client self-determination regarding genetic testing decisions and encourages social workers to educate clients about the benefits and risks of genetic testing and to provide such education in a value-free, nondirective way.

REFERENCES

Andrews, L., Fullarton, J., Holtzman, N., & Motulsky, A. (Eds.). (1994). *Assessing genetic risks: Implications for health and social policy.* Washington, DC: National Academies Press.

Bishop, J., & Waldholz, M. (1990). *Genome.* New York: Simon & Schuster.

Fanos, J. (1997). Developmental tasks of childhood and adolescence: Implications for genetic testing. *American Journal of Medical Genetics, 71,* 22–28.

Fanos, J., & Johnson, J. (1995). Perception of carrier status by cystic fibrosis siblings. *American Journal of Human Genetics, 57,* 431–438.

Geller, G., Botkin, J., Green, M., Press, N., Biesecker, B., Wilfond, B., Grana, G., Daly, M., Schneider, K., & Kahn, M. (1997). Genetic testing for susceptibility to adult-onset cancer: The process and content of informed consent. *JAMA, 277,* 1467–1474.

Guttmacher, A., & Collins, F. S. (2002). Genomic medicine: A primer. *New England Journal of Medicine, 347,* 1512–1513.

Hall, M. A., McEwen, J. E., Barton, J. C., Walker, A. P., Howe, E. G.. Reiss, J. A., Power, T. E, Ellis, S. D., Tucker, D. C., Harrison, B. W., McLaren, G. D., Ruggiero, A., & Thomson, E. J. (2005). Concerns in a primary care population about genetic discrimination by insurers. *Genetics in Medicine, 7,* 311–316.

Hudson, K. (2007). Prohibiting genetic discrimination. *New England Journal of Medicine, 356,* 2021–2023.

Hudson, K., Rothenberg, K., Andrews, L., Kahn, M., & Collins, F. (1995, October 20). Genetic discrimination and health insurance: An urgent need for reform [Policy Forum]. *Science, 270,* 391.

Lapham, V., Kozma, C., & Weiss, J. (1996, October 25). Genetic discrimination perspectives of consumers. *Science, 274,* 621–624.

Lapham, E. V., Kozma, C., Weiss, J. O., Benkendorf, J. L., & Wilson, M. A. (2000). The gap between practice and genetics education of health professionals: HuGEM survey results. *Genetics in Medicine, 2,* 226–231.

National Association of Social Workers. (2000). *Code of ethics of the National Association of Social Workers*. Washington, DC: NASW Press.

National Association of Social Workers. (2003). *NASW standards for integrating genetics in social work practice*. Washington, DC: NASW Press.

National Human Genome Research Institute. (1997). *Promoting safe and effective genetic testing in the United States. Executive summary: Testing of children*. Retrieved April 6, 2006, from http://www.genome.gov/1000 2393

Roche, P. A., & Annas, G. J. (2006). DNA testing, banking, and genetic privacy. *New England Journal of Medicine, 355,* 545–546.

Rothenberg, K., Fuller, B. Rothstein, M., Duster, T., Kahn, M., Cunningham, R., Fine, B., Hudson, K., King, M., Murphy, P., Swergold, G., & Collins, F. (1997, March 21). Genetic information and the workplace. *Science, 275,* 1755–1757.

Schild, S. (1966). The challenging opportunity for social workers in genetics. *Social Work, 11*(2), 22–28.

Schultz, A. L. (1966). The impact of genetic disorders. *Social Work, 11*(2), 29–34.

Smith, M.J.W. (2004, October). Genetics and genetic testing: Policy implications. *Intersections in practice* (Vol. 3, pp. 11–13). (Available from NASW, Specialty Practice Section, 750 First Street, NE, Suite 700, Washington, DC 20002-4241)

Taylor-Brown, S., & Johnson, A. (1998). *Clinical practice update: Social workers' role in genetic services*. Retrieved June 1, 1998, from http://www.socialworkers.org/practice/health/genetics.asp

Weiss, J. O. (1976). Social work and genetic counseling. *Social Work in Health Care, 2,* 5–12.

Weiss, J. O. (2004, October). What social workers need to know about genetics. In *Intersections in practice* (Vol. 3, pp. 1, 17–20). (Available from NASW, Specialty Practice Section, 750 First Street, NE, Suite 700, Washington, DC 20002-4241)

Wertz, D. (1998). State laws on employer use of genetic information. *The gene letter* [Online Series]. Retrieved June 30, 1998, from http://www.geneletter.org/0398/state.htm

Wertz, D. C., Fanos, J. H., & Reilly, P. R. (1994). Genetic testing for children and adolescents: Who decides? *JAMA, 272,* 875–881.

Williams, S. (2006, October 24). The impact of genetic discrimination [Issue Briefs]. Available from http://www.dnapolicy.org/policy.issue.php?action=detail&issuebrief_id=37

Policy statement approved by the NASW Delegate Assembly, August 2008. This policy statement supersedes the policy statement on Genetics approved by the Delegate Assembly in 1999 and referred by the 2005 Delegate Assembly to the 2008 Delegate Assembly for revision. For further information, contact the National Association of Social Workers, 750 First Street, NE, Suite 700, Washington, DC 20002-4241. Telephone: 202-408-8600 or 800-638-8799; e-mail: press@naswdc.org

Health Care Policy

BACKGROUND

The past decade has seen an increasing awareness of the importance of promoting health throughout the U.S. population, as demonstrated in the goals and objectives set out in the Healthy People 2010 initiative (U.S. Department of Health and Human Services, 2000). Healthy People 2010 has two overarching goals: (1) to increase the quality and years of healthy life and (2) to eliminate health disparities within the U.S. population. Achieving these goals depends on both a health system that reaches all ages and all people in the United States and the integration of personal health care and population-based public health care. The vision of building healthy communities involves broad-based efforts to prevent common health problems by moving beyond health care settings such as hospitals, clinics, and physician's office into neighborhoods, schools, and workplaces within the community. Eliminating disparities in Healthy People 2010 focus areas such as prevention of health problems, tobacco and substance abuse, and injury and violence prevention requires coordination between clinical and public health disciplines, as well as strong community involvement.

Research on health care access has found that barriers to equitable health care for all segments of the population can arise at the public policy, community, organizational, and provider levels (Andersen, 1995; Institute of Medicine, 2002). A key barrier is lack of health care coverage. Individuals without health coverage use fewer health care services and are less healthy than those with coverage (Ayanian, Ginsburg, Schneider, Weismann, & Zaslavsky, 2000; Ku & Broaddus, 2006). The Institute of Medicine (2004) found that uninsured children and adults suffer worse health and die sooner than those with insurance. Delaying or not receiving treatment can lead to more serious illnesses and avoidable health problems. People without insurance are less likely to receive preventive care than those with insurance and more likely to be hospitalized for conditions that could have been avoided. Charitable care and the safety net of community clinics and public hospitals do not fully substitute for health insurance. State and local government ability to finance health care for uninsured people is most limited during economic downturns, when the need is the greatest.

Financing and Delivery of Health Care

Equitable access to health care services is complicated by the fragmented nature of health coverage in the United States. The two major methods of coverage are private insurance, whether employer-based or individually contracted, and public programs, such as Medicare, Medicaid, the State Children's Health Insurance Program, and military coverage. Individual states have provided coverage through Medicaid waiver programs for portions of their population not covered by basic Medicaid. However, these types of coverage leave substantial numbers of the population without health insurance coverage. In 2006, the Census Bureau reported that 59.7 percent of the U.S. population was covered by employment-based insurance, 9.1 percent was covered by directly purchased insurance, 13.6 percent was covered by Medicare, 12.9 percent was covered by Medicaid, and another 3.6 percent by military coverage (DeNavas-Walt, Proctor, & Smith, 2007).

Regardless of the financing, the delivery of health care has moved from fee for service to managed care such as health maintenance organizations and preferred provider organizations. A single payer system has been proposed as a way to provide universal health care in the U.S. However, the trend has been to revise the current multipayer system. The health care systems have become more complex and this causes barriers and challenges for individuals who need to access and navigate their own health care benefits.

ISSUE STATEMENT

In 2006, 47 million people were uninsured, an increase of 2.2 million from the previous year, largely because of a decline in employer-sponsored insurance. Since 2004, census data indicate that employer coverage has declined but public coverage has not increased, resulting in sharp increases in the number of uninsured adults and children. The increase in loss of insurance was highest among Hispanics compared with Asian, African American, and non-Hispanic white people. Uninsurance rates across states varied from 8.5 percent to 24.1 percent as a result of differences in state economies, patterns of employer coverage, the share of families with low incomes, and the scope of state Medicaid programs. Almost 80 percent of the uninsured are citizens (Kaiser Family Foundation, 2007).

Disparities in Health Care

Minority and poor populations are disproportionately uninsured. U.S. families with incomes below 200 percent of the federal poverty level run the highest risk of being uninsured. More than 80 percent of the uninsured people are in working families. Low-wage workers, those in small businesses, service workers, and part-time workers run a greater risk of being uninsured. African Amer-

icans and Hispanics are disproportionately likely to be uninsured compared with Asian and non-Hispanic white Americans (Kaiser Family Foundation, 2007). In addition, even among those with health coverage, racial and ethnic minority groups are more likely than are white people to be enrolled in "lower end" health plans characterized by lower reimbursement levels and stricter limits on covered services, leading to potential differences in provider behavior (Phillips, Mayer, & Aday, 2000).

The lack of insurance coverage for minority and poor populations exacerbates other barriers to access within the health care system that prevent vulnerable individuals from receiving appropriate health care. Stigmatizing practices in health care delivery, a lack of racial and ethnic diversity and cultural competence among health care providers, differences in health literacy between groups, and the failure to include minority populations in medical research produce a lower quality of health services for racial and ethnic minority groups even after adjustment for socioeconomic characteristics and other access-related factors (Institute of Medicine, 2002; Kressin & Petersen, 2001). This lower quality of care may be manifested through a failure to provide recommended care or the substitution of less desirable procedures. These disparities exist across a variety of conditions, including cancer, cardiovascular disease, HIV/AIDS, maternal and child health care, diabetes, and mental illness; they are found in treatment for serious disease and also in routine treatments for common health problems (Allison, Kiefe, Centor, Box, & Farmer, 1996; Barker-Cummings, McClellan, Soucie, & Kirshner, 1995; Cunningham, Mosen, & Morales, 2000; Johnson, Lee, Cook, Rouan, & Goldman, 1993). Preventive measures such as breast, cervical, and prostate cancer screenings are not always provided as recommended to minority individuals (Brownstein, 1992). More research is needed to fully understand how patient race or ethnicity, disease status, sexual orientation, and other characteristics may influence physician decision making and the experience of minority groups during health care encounters.

Trends in Health Care Social Work Services

Every state has deregulated their health care system and lifted regulated rate-setting mandates on hospitals. The subsequent restructuring resulted in a move away from professionally defined structures, such as departments of social work. Social work roles and responsibilities are changing to include case management, discharge planning, and working collaboratively on interdisciplinary teams. However, social workers are also experiencing an increase in workload and a decrease in the psychosocial or clinical component of social work practice (Mizrahi & Berger, 2001).

As part of deregulation, several proposals by the Centers for Medicare & Medicaid Services (which administers Medicaid and Medicare) have been made to lessen the regulations governing providers, including social workers who are reimbursed by Medicare and Medicaid (known as *conditions of participation*). These include actual downgrading or efforts to downgrade the definitions and qualifications for social workers who provide services through Medicare's home health, hospice, skilled nursing facilities, and end-stage renal disease programs. There is now a countervailing trend for increasing social work services in regulatory mandates that is still ahead of the reality of providing qualified health care social work services (Department of Health and Humans Services, 2007; Institute of Medicine, 2008).

POLICY STATEMENT

NASW supports

■ a national health care policy that ensures the right to universal access to a continuum of health and mental health care throughout all stages of the life cycle. The goal of such a policy is to promote wellness, maintain optimal health, prevent illness and disability, treat health conditions, ameliorate the effects of unavoidable incapacities, and provide supportive long-term and end-of-life care. This policy should result in the equitable delivery of services for all people in the United States, regardless of financial status, race, ethnicity, disability, religion, age, gender, sexual orientation, or geographic location.

■ efforts to increase health care coverage to uninsured and underinsured people until universal health and mental health coverage is achieved.

■ an equal right to continuous, high-quality care that is effective, efficient, safe, timely, and patient-centered.

■ ongoing dialogue and research about the best practices to finance health system.

■ efforts to eliminate racial, ethnic, and economic disparities in health service access, provision, utilization, and outcomes.

■ the coordination of NASW chapter efforts to influence state and federal health care policy.

■ policies and practices requiring that mandated medical social work services be provided by qualified social workers in all health care settings.

■ active participation of social workers on public and private health care policy and planning bodies.

■ efforts to provide comprehensive education in health care social work, working with the Council on Social Work Education.

■ policies and practices that promote and protect social work and social workers in all health and mental health settings.

■ improved access, choice, quality, and comprehensiveness of health and mental health services, including parity of mental health care with medical care.

■ policies and practices that ensure that patients receive necessary and appropriate care and guarantee patient rights protections.

■ workforce development to meet the needs of burgeoning and existing special populations (such as geriatrics, pediatrics, people with disabilities, and so forth).

■ active and organized consumer participation in the planning, implementation, evaluation, and maintenance and governance of health and mental health services.

REFERENCES

Allison, J. J., Kiefe, C. I., Centor, R. M., Box, J. B., & Farmer, R. M. (1996). Racial differences in the treatment of elderly Medicare patients with acute myocardial infarction. *Journal of General Internal Medicine, 11*, 736–743.

Andersen, A. M. (1995). Revisiting the behavioral model and access to health care: Does it matter? *Journal of Health and Social Behavior, 36*(1), 1–10.

Ayanian, J. Z., Ginsburg, J. A., Schneider, E. C., Weismann, J. S., & Zaslavsky, A. M. (2000). Unmet health needs of uninsured adults in the United States. *JAMA, 284*, 1260–1269.

Barker-Cummings, C., McClellan, W., Soucie, J. M., & Krishner, J. (1995). Ethnic differences in the use of peritoneal dialysis as initial treatment for end-stage renal disease. *JAMA, 279*, 1858–1862.

Brownstein, J. N. (1992). Breast and cervical cancer in minority populations: A model for using lay health educators. *Journal of Cancer Education, 7*, 321–326.

Cunningham, W. E., Mosen, D. M., & Morales, L. S. (2000). Ethnic and racial differences in long-term survival from hospitalization with HIV infection, *Journal of Health Care for the Poor and Underserved, 11*(2), 163–178.

DeNavas-Walt, C., Proctor, B. D., & Smith, J. (2007). *Income, poverty, and health insurance coverage in the United States: 2006* (Current Population Reports, P60-233). Washington, DC: U.S. Government Printing Office.

Department of Health and Humans Services. (March 2007). *Medicare program; hospital conditions of participation: requirements for approval and re-approval of transplant centers to perform organ transplants; final rule.* Retrieved March 11, 2008, from http://www.cms.hhs.gov/CFCsAndCoPs/downloads/trancenterreg2007.pdf

Institute of Medicine. (2002). *Unequal treatment: Confronting racial and ethnic disparities in health care.* Washington, DC: National Academies Press.

Institute of Medicine. (2004). *Insuring America's health: Principles and recommendations.* Washington, DC: National Academies Press.

Institute of Medicine. (2008). *Committee on Psychosocial Services to Cancer Patients/Families in a Community Setting. Cancer care for the whole patient: Meeting psychosocial health needs.* Washington, DC: National Academies Press.

Johnson, P. A., Lee, T. H., Cook, E. F., Rouan, G. W., & Goldman, L. (1993). Effects of race on the presentation and management of patients with acute chest pain. *Annals of Internal Medicine, 118*, 593–601.

Kaiser Family Foundation. (2007). *The uninsured: A primer.* Retrieved October 20, 2007, from http://www.kff.org/uninsured/upload/7451-03.pdf

Kressin, N. R., & Petersen, L. A. (2001). Racial differences in the use of invasive cardiovascular procedures: Review of the literature and prescription for future research. *Annals of Internal Medicine, 135*, 352–366.

Ku, L., & Broaddus, M. (2006). *Coverage of parents helps children, too.* Retrieved October 20, 2007, from http://www.cbpp.org/10-20-06health.htm

Mizrahi T., & Berger, C. S. (2001). Effect of a changing health care environment on social work leaders: Obstacles and opportunities in hospital social work. *Social Work, 46*, 170–182.

Phillips, K. A., Mayer, M. L., & Aday, L. A. (2000). Barriers to care of racial/ethnic groups under managed care. *Health Affairs, 19*(4), 65–75.

U.S. Department of Health and Human Services. (2000). *Healthy People 2010 midcourse review.* Retrieved October 20, 2007, from http://www.healthypeople.gov/data/midcourse/default.htm#pubs

Policy statement approved by the NASW Delegate Assembly, August 2008. This policy statement supersedes the policy statement on Health Care approved by the Delegate Assembly in August 1999 and referred by the 2005 Delegate Assembly to the 2008 Delegate Assembly for revision. The 1999 policy statement combined with and superseded the policy statement on Health Care Financing approved by the Assembly in 1990, the policy statement on the Role of Social Work in Health Maintenance Organizations approved by the Assembly in 1981 and reconfirmed by the Assembly in 1990, the policy statement on Social Work in Home Health Care approved by the Assembly in 1990 (that policy statement superseded the policy statement on Social Work in Home Health Care approved in 1981), and the policy statement on Social Work Practice in the Health Care Field approved by the Assembly in 1990 (that policy statement superseded the policy statement on Social Work Practice in the Health Care Field approved by the Assembly in 1984). For further information, contact the National Association of Social Workers, 750 First Street, NE, Suite 700, Washington, DC 20002-4241. Telephone: 202-408-8600 or 800-638-8799; e-mail: press@naswdc.org

HIV and AIDS

BACKGROUND

HIV and AIDS are serious global public health concerns with biological social and economic ramifications. Throughout the world, HIV and AIDS disproportionately affects marginalized and disempowered populations throughout the world. Today one in three people infected with HIV do not know they are living with HIV or AIDS (American Association for World Health [AAWH], 2001). The key areas of concern are prevention, testing, treatment, and the effect of HIV on individuals, families, and communities.

In the United States HIV and AIDS prevention and treatment services available today are the result of significant biomedical and social advocacy efforts by many groups over a long period of time (Wheeler, 2007). However, effectiveness of some prevention programs has been hindered by racism, sexism, heterosexism, and homophobia (Ferrales, 2003).

Limited government response resulted in the establishment of many community-based AIDS service organizations (ASO), and many are still in existence today. The design of AIDS prevention strategies largely occurred on a small scale because of limited funding options. Not only has there been a failure to develop effective programs, there has been a governmental and societal hindrance to the development of effective programs, such as needle exchange programs or sex education for young adults.

Testing

Testing is an important component of HIV prevention. Research has shown that people who are aware of being HIV-infected may be more likely to take steps to prevent transmitting the virus to others. In addition, when a positive test result is obtained, appropriate medical treatment can be initiated to slow the disease process (Zúñiga et al., 2007). The availability of testing on an anonymous or confidential basis is thought to maximize the number of people who choose to get tested. To protect confidentiality of HIV status, all states apply confidentiality laws to HIV test results. Throughout the pandemic, there have been many struggles over federal and state policies on imposing mandatory testing or mandatory reporting of test results for certain populations, including prisoners, pregnant women, and child care workers. In addition, a number of states have criminalized the potential transmission of HIV through sex, needle sharing, breast-feeding, or organ donation by a person who is HIV-positive or diagnosed with AIDS (American Civil Liberties Union, 2000). Unlike HIV serostatus, all diagnoses of AIDS must be reported to state public health departments.

The Centers for Disease Control and Prevention (CDC) Revised Recommendations for HIV Testing in Health Care Settings recommends that HIV testing be voluntary and recommended for patients in all health care settings after the patient is notified that testing will be performed unless the patient declines (or opts out of screening) (CDC, 2006). This recommendation replaces the practice of informed, written consent. These recommendations notwithstanding, many people obtain HIV tests without pre- or posttest counseling, especially when they test in a physician's office or in their own homes.

Treatment

The emergence of antiretroviral therapies (ART), and increased access through private insurance, Medicare, and AIDS Drug Assistance Programs (ADAPs), has resulted in a positive, dramatic change for many people living with HIV/AIDS (PLWH/As). For many, living with HIV or AIDS has transitioned to living with a lifelong, chronic illness, often with a renewed sense of hope and challenges (Tomaszewski, 2001). For others, however, the complexities of a strict medication regimen cannot be sustained over extended periods of time, because adherence is not as simple as taking medications. An increasing number of people living with AIDS are unable to tolerate the toxicity and severe side effects that are common with the medications (ART and prophylaxis treatments); others experience unexpected and unexplained health deterioration, or the drugs simply "fail the patient."

Economic issues continue to affect access to care. Few people can afford the drugs unless they are enrolled in a private health insurance plan with prescription drug benefits or state-administered Medicaid or ADAPs for those who are underinsured and uninsured. Although ADAP funding is available nationwide, some state ADAP programs limit coverage of certain medications, resulting in access and adherence problems, or have waitlisted or capped enrollment (National Alliance of State and Territorial AIDS Directors [NASTAD], 2007).

Effects of HIV/AIDS on Individuals, Families, and Communities

HIV/AIDS can have devastating consequences on affected individuals and members of their families and support systems. HIV and AIDS are highly stigmatized conditions (Fullilove & Fullilove, 1999), and people living with HIV/AIDS are likely to experience stigmatization and discrimination (Diaz & Ayala, 2001) in areas such as education, employment, housing, insurance, and health care. Although the Americans with Disabilities Act of 1990 (P.L. 101-336) has provided legal protection for such people, its scope has been reduced by subsequent court rulings. In addition, state laws regarding HIV/AIDS discrimination vary con-siderably, with some states allowing certain forms of discrimination (Gostin, Feldblum, & Webber, 1999). In too many cases, PLWH/As continue to be denied basic civil and human rights. They may face discrimination in employment, military service, housing, child care, access to health care services, and social and community support programs.

ISSUE STATEMENT

Social workers increasingly encounter HIV/AIDS, either directly or indirectly, regardless of their area of practice, geographic location, or practice setting. Because of its ecological perspective and commitment to social justice, social work is particularly well suited for addressing the complex problems associated with the epidemic, including those experienced by PLWH/As, their friends, and their families. Globally, HIV/AIDS continues to have catastrophic effects on communities, particularly those in resource poor countries where people cannot afford medications or access treatments.

Heterosexism and homophobia contribute to the spread of HIV in other populations as well. For example, HIV prevention and care programs for gay men that include explicit sexual information or language continue to be threatened periodically with loss of federal funding (Erickson, 2001). Also, the increase in HIV infection among African American men who have sex with men (MSM) may be due in part to these attitudes among African American communities and the continuing belief that AIDS is a "gay disease" (Fullilove & Fullilove, 1999). In addition, women may often contract HIV because their male sexual partners cannot admit that they also engage in high-risk sex with other men.

Racism contributes to the spread of HIV. For example, MSM of color might not benefit from prevention resources distributed within predominantly white gay and lesbian communities because of actual and perceived racism within them (Diaz & Ayala, 2001). Also, many of the strategies that have effectively prevented the spread of HIV in the white gay community are not effective among men of color because these programs lack in cultural context. In addition, racism is an important link to disempowerment and the lack of financial and other resources among communities of color, which prevents such communities from responding to the epidemic as effectively as the predominantly white gay community. Sexism contributes to the spread of HIV. For many years, virtually no attention was given to women's risks or needs with respect to prevention or treatment of HIV/AIDS. Consequently, knowledge about the specific ways in which HIV affected women, and the best ways to treat it, lagged far behind such knowledge in relation to men. Women may not feel empowered in relationships to insist that their sexual partners use condoms, or they may engage in sexual practices (such as anal sex) that are considered high-risk for HIV transmission in efforts to prevent pregnancy. Also, women who are impoverished are more likely to prioritize daily survival issues over safer sex (Kline, Kline, & Oken, 1992). Educational, occupational, and economic discrimination may lead some women into high-risk sex work and IV drug use. Finally, the lack of funding for female-specific microbicides is rooted in the historical lack of recognition for women's sexuality, reproductive health of women and girls, and the right to control one's body.

Discrimination against transgender people may lead to at-risk behaviors that increase risk for HIV and other STDs. Factors such as mental health concerns, physical abuse, social isolation, economic marginalization, and unmet transgender-specific healthcare needs can potentially lead to increased HIV risk (Herbst et al., 2008). In addition, the inability to obtain or pay for hormone therapy drives some transgender people to seek hormones illegally and to inject them with shared needles (Clements-Nolle, Marx, Guzman, & Katz, 2001).

Discrimination toward people who use street drugs also contributes to the spread of HIV. Federal policy continues to oppose clean needle exchanges (National Minority AIDS Council, 2002). Although research shows that needle exchange programs can reduce the transmission of HIV, federal policies and laws in many states and localities prevent the access of IV drug users to sterile syringes (Vertefeuille et al., 2000).

Prevention efforts continue to be underfunded and excessively influenced by moralistic politics instead of empirical research. Limitations created by federal and state policies, and funding levels and regulations, hamper the efforts of community-based organizations to reduce HIV/AIDS incidence in populations at high risk.

The CDC Revised Recommendations for HIV Testing in Health Care Settings (2006) recommends that HIV testing be voluntary and recommended for patients in all health care settings after the patient is notified that testing will be performed, unless the patient declines (opt-out screening). These recommendations remove the requirement for pretest and posttest counseling, a critical step in helping individuals prepare for a positive test result and providing the context for exploring behavioral risk regardless of test results. HIV antibody testing also provides an important opportunity for health professionals to elicit important information about partners of the person being tested. Such information can be used to help patients communicate to partners their risk for HIV infection. Partner notification laws, however, limit the confidentiality of testing results in some states.

HIV testing and counseling are important components of a comprehensive public health approach to reducing the devastation of HIV and AIDS, however, services for infected persons, and treatments for comorbidities (for example, other sexually transmitted diseases and substance abuse) must be available to persons after they receive their HIV testing results.

The advent of highly active antiretroviral therapy has greatly changed the quality of life for many people living with HIV/AIDS. Yet there is evidence that the effectiveness of HIV medications may cause some people to believe that HIV is no longer a threat, leading to an increase in risky sexual or drug-taking behaviors (Halkitis & Wilton, 1999). In addition to the high cost of medications, other medical care for people living with HIV/AIDS is exorbitant and unevenly available. Coverage for emergency room visits, hospital stays, diagnostic tests, physicians' fees, and nursing care may be inadequate for many people. Those enrolled in public health plans are unlikely to be able to obtain the same quality of care available to those with private insurance. The quality of HIV/AIDS-related medical care may depend on where people are living, given that specialized HIV/AIDS services are not universally available, especially in rural areas.

POLICY STATEMENT

Across fields of practice, social workers provide services to HIV-positive clients, their families, and clients who are at risk of becoming infected with HIV. Given the high incidence of HIV/AIDS and the rapid spread of the pandemic over the last two decades, the social work profession should take an active stand to mitigate the overwhelming psychological and social effects, including the inequality of access to health and mental health care and the lack of education and prevention in the United States and internationally.

NASW supports the following:

Prevention and Education

■ professional cooperation with existing HIV and AIDS educational, treatment, and research organizations to develop and implement programs that include educational and prevention strategies that meet the needs of all segments of our society.

■ prevention programs designed and implemented to ensure that they are tailored to the specific needs and risks of diverse populations. Programs must be culturally appropriate, taking into account the language, culture, ethnicity, sexual orientation, gender and gender identity, religion, and age of the target population.

■ the implementation of prevention strategies that focuses on harm reduction.

■ evidence-based prevention efforts that target children and adolescents in both public and private school systems and comprehensive sexuality education programs for youths and adults.

■ the establishment of both publicly and privately funded needle exchange programs and efforts to increase the quantity and quality of drug abuse treatment, to reduce HIV incidence among IV drug users.

Social Work Education

■ the education of all social workers so they are knowledgeable about behavioral strategies to prevent the transmission of HIV, including safer sex and harm reduction. Use of assessment tools that assess all clients for HIV risk and that educate clients about ways to reduce their risk.

■ social workers taking responsibility to continuously update their knowledge about all aspects of HIV disease, including new prevention strategies, treatment models, medication regimens, and policies.

■ social work education programs that include curriculums that examine the ramifications of HIV/AIDS from the perspective of the profession's core values. Content should cover the range of health and mental health issues of PLWH/As and their families, support systems, and communities and interventions at all levels of practice.

Testing

■ the education of all practitioners about both the availability and the accessibility aspects of HIV antibody testing and referrals related to living with HIV and AIDS.

■ voluntary and confidential testing which is available on an anonymous basis, and includes prior informed consent.

■ pre- and posttest counseling programs, provided by trained caregivers.

■ rapid testing conducted only by people trained and certified to do so and implemented only when consent is granted by the client or patient.

■ access to competent professional counseling by phone for people using home-testing kits at no additional charge and referral to a formal HIV testing site.

■ informed consent of pregnant and birthing mothers prior to mandatory HIV testing of themselves and their newborn child or children.

■ prior consent for release of clients' test results. Social workers with HIV-positive clients who have not informed sexual or needle-sharing partners about their sero status should use their clinical skills to encourage them to do so.

Service Delivery, Care, and Treatment

■ the right of people living with HIV/AIDS to receive the highest quality care, including those confined in correctional institutions.

■ a comprehensive services delivery system based on a quality case management model that includes access to suitable and affordable housing, mental and health care services, adult and child foster care, home health care, nursing home care, legal services, and transportation.

■ readily available comprehensive bio-psycho-social-spiritual support for people with HIV/AIDS and those affected. Service programs should be culturally competent, linguistically appropriate, and client and patient centered.

■ elimination of the inequities or obstacles in access to medication, clinical trials, and HIV care specialists; or services that ensure psychological, social, cultural, and economic well-being.

■ policies that facilitate access to affordable pharmaceuticals worldwide. Clients should have sufficient supports to help them maintain difficult medication regimens.

■ the right to confidentiality relating to HIV/AIDS status. Clients should be informed of the limits of confidentiality, including the existence of partner notification and record keeping. Social workers should be familiar with applicable state laws, regulations, and federal guidelines.

Political Action and Advocacy

■ continued public and private funding and advocacy for health and mental health care provider programs that address HIV/AIDS and related health and mental health issues, including state, local, national, and international HIV/AIDS prevention and treatment programs;

■ domestic and international initiatives that address structural factors such as poverty, community disinvestment, and interpersonal violence to curtail the HIV/AIDS epidemic;

■ leadership in advocacy efforts at the local, state, and federal levels to improve the quality of life of all PLWH/As and to protect their civil liberties, including maximum access to confidential testing, diagnosis, and treatment;

■ advocacy for adequate funding of research on all aspects of HIV/AIDS, including prevention, clinical interventions, and vaccine development.

Research

■ research, including epidemiological, clinical, and comprehensive, biopsychosocial–spiritual studies, funded at appropriate levels by the federal government.

■ research protocols that address the unique biomedical needs of women, children and adolescents, and the psycho–social–spiritual needs of all people affected by HIV/AIDS.

■ funding for research to accurately assess the effectiveness of primary and secondary prevention and educational strategies, service delivery models, and the effect of related policies. Research protocols must include the bio-psycho-social-spiritual issues of people living with and affected by HIV/AIDS; the unique needs of women, children, and adolescents; and the needs of all people affected by HIV/AIDS.

REFERENCES

American Association for World Health (AAWH). (2001). World AIDS Day resource booklet. *Factsheet on treatment information.* Washington, DC: Author.

American Civil Liberties Union. (2000). *State criminal statutes on HIV transmission.* Washington, DC: Author.

Americans with Disabilities Act of 1990, P.L. 101-336, 104 Stat. 327.

Centers for Disease Control and Prevention. (2006). *Revised recommendations for HIV testing of adults, adolescents, and pregnant women in health-care settings. Morbidity and Mortality Weekly Report, 55* (RR14), 1–17. Retrieved November 13, 2007, from http://www.cdc.gov/hiv/topics/testing/guideline.htm

Clements-Nolle, K., Marx, R., Guzman, R., & Katz, M. (2001). HIV prevalence, risk behaviors, health care use, and mental health status of transgender persons: Implications for public health intervention. *American Journal of Public Health, 91,* 915–921.

Diaz, R. M., & Ayala, G. (2001). *Social discrimination and health: The case of Latino gay men and HIV risk.* New York: Policy Institute of the National Gay and Lesbian Task Force.

Erickson, E. (2001, November 30). Audit calls into question funding for sexually explicit AIDS prevention programs for gays. *New York Blade News,* p. 7.

Ferrales, D. (2003). *The development of HIV/AIDS policy: An international policy analysis.* Austin: University of Texas at Austin, School of Social Work.

Fullilove, M. T., & Fullilove, R. E. (1999). Stigma as an obstacle to AIDS action: The case of the African American community. *American Behavioral Scientist, 42,* 1117–1129.

Gostin, L. O., Feldblum, C., & Webber, D. W. (1999). Disability discrimination in America: HIV/AIDS and other health conditions. *JAMA, 281,* 745–752.

Halkitis, P. N., & Wilton, L. (1999). Beyond complacency: The effects of treatment on HIV transmission. *Focus: A guide to AIDS research and counseling, 14*(5), 1–4.

Herbst, J., Jacobs, E., Finlayson, T., McKleroy,V., Neumann, M., & Crepaz, N. (2008). Estimating HIV prevalence and risk behaviors of transgender persons in the United States: A systematic review. Retrieved June 30, 2008, from http://www.medscape.com/viewarticle/571708

Kline, A., Kline, E., & Oken, E. (1992). Minority women and sexual choice in the age of AIDS. *Social Science and Medicine, 31,* 447–457.

National Alliance of State and Territorial AIDS Directors (NASTAD). (2007). *June 2007 ADAP watch.* Retrieved November 7, 2007, from http://www.nastad.org/Publications/adapwatch.aspx?Area=Publications

National Minority AIDS Council. (2002). *Bush administration HIV/AIDS report card.* Washington, DC: Author.

Tomaszewski, E. (Ed.). (2001). *Mental health and HIV/AIDS: Social work practice issues* [Trainer Manual]. Washington, DC: National Association of Social Workers.

Vertefeuille, J., Marx, M. A., Tun, W., Huettner, S., Strathdee, S. A., & Vlahov, D. (2000). Decline in self-reported high-risk injection-related behaviors among HIV-seropositive participants in the Baltimore needle exchange program. *AIDS and Behavior, 4,* 381–388.

Wheeler, D. P. (2007). HIV and AIDS today: Where is social work going? [National Health Line]. *Health & Social Work, 32,* 155–157.

Zúñiga, M. A., Baldwin, H., Uhler, D., Brennan, J., Olshefsky, A. M., Oliver, E., & Matthews, W. C. (2007). Supporting positive living and sexual health (SPLASH): A clinician and behavioral counselor risk-reduction intervention in a university-based HIV clinic. *AIDS Behavior, 11,* S58–S71.

Policy statement approved by the NASW Delegate Assembly, August 2008. This policy statement supersedes the policy statement on HIV and AIDS approved by the Delegate Assembly in August 2002 and the statement on AIDS/HIV approved by the Assembly in 1987 and reconfirmed by the Delegate Assembly in 1990, 1993, 1996, and 1999. For further information, contact the National Association of Social Workers, 750 First Street, NE, Suite 700, Washington, DC 20002-4241. Telephone: 202-408-8600 or 800-638-8799; e-mail: press@naswdc.org

Homelessness

BACKGROUND

The plight of children, women, men, and families who are without residence continues to befuddle social workers in their recent efforts, reaching back nearly three decades, to both serve people who are homeless and to find policy solutions. Indeed, scholars working in this area have suggested that the persistence of homelessness in the richest country in the world at the beginning of the 21st century is a consequence of massive policy failure (Stretch, 2004). Although sources disagree as to the exact strategies for determining the extent of the problem (Dworsky & Piliavin, 2002), on any given night, point prevalence estimates indicate that as many as 800,000 people are without shelter and are homeless in the United States. Furthermore, period prevalence estimates of the number of people who are homeless over a given year have been as high as 3.5 million (National Alliance to End Homelessness, 1999).

Considerable literature has accumulated in social work and related professions covering a myriad of strategies for both better understanding and better serving people who are homeless (First, Rife, & Toomey, 1999). Homelessness has been addressed broadly as a housing policy problem of largely political and economic origins, and more narrowly it has been discussed as a mental health issue often related to deinstitutionalization. It has been studied as a domestic violence concern, a veterans issue, a disability issue, a welfare reform dilemma, a teenage runway or "throwaway" problem, and a transitional or temporary housing situation. It has been investigated as a migrant and immigrant problem, and a concern for people with communicable diseases. The problem for the consumer of this literature has been to decide exactly how a particular contribution fits into this vast pool of data, dimensions of practice, and policy recommendations. Fortunately, a variety of summary resources has recently become available, both in the traditional published record (see for example, Levinson, 2004) and from more diffuse electronic sources (Table 1).

No matter what the practice, policy or theoretical orientation of practitioners, researchers, and policy advocates, it is routinely recognized that the persistence of homelessness is evidence that poverty and the lack of affordable housing in the United States still persist and are likely to remain critical policy issues for this next century. Homelessness is a complex problem that cannot be ameliorated until the shortcomings of past policies are recognized and the causes and consequences of persistent poverty combined with a lack of affordable housing are a matter of public record. The plight of people who are homeless must be better understood from the perspectives of those who suffer, and it can be seen in

1. people with psychiatric disorders who lack the social networks, health care, and other program supports to live independently in the community (North, Eyrich, Pollio, & Spitznagel, 2004; Wong, 2002);

2. individuals with physical disabilities, whose mobility limitations compound service inaccessibility (Pardeck & Rollinson, 2002);

3. women and children who are victims of domestic violence fleeing abusive domiciles (Bufkin & Bray, 1998; Danis, 2003);

4. asthmatic children in shelters who are not receiving adequate medical attention (Holden, Wade, Mitchell, Ewart, & Islam, 1998; McLean et al., 2004; Stretch & Kreuger, 1990);

Table 1. Sources of Information on Homelessness in the United States

Site	URL
National Coalition for the Homeless	www.nationalhomeless.org
National Alliance to End Homelessness	www.endhomelessness.org
National Law Center on Homelessness & Poverty	www.nlchp.org/
National Health Care for the Homeless Council	www.nhchc.org/
National Coalition for Homeless Veterans	www.nchv.org/
National Low Income Housing Coalition	www.nlihc.org
National Resource Center on Homelessness and Mental Illness	www.nrchmi.samhsa.gov/
HUD Homelessness Website	www.hud.gov/homeless/

5. individuals currently employed either full- or part-time, with too little income to afford adequate housing (Hutchison, Searight, & Stretch, 1986; Johnson, 1999), or food (Biggerstaff, Morris, & Nichols-Casebolt, 2002);

6. single mothers unable to work because of child care responsibilities or the lack of skills to meet the demands of a rapidly changing economy (Fogel, 1997; Johnson & Kreuger, 1989; North & Smith, 1993; Rivera, 2003);

7. runaway youths who are without access to adequate services (Baker, McKay, Lynn, Schlange, & Auville, 2003; Thompson, Safyer, & Pollio, 2001);

8. rural families who have been forced to abandon family farms or small towns due to economic crises in regional, national, and global markets (Goodfellow, 1999);

9. men, many of whom are veterans, who have only the life of the street for economic and social supports (Benda, 2002);

10. people with chemical dependencies, who are unable to maintain a stable residence (Bride & Real, 2003);

11. refugees, asylees, and migrants who have no place to turn to (Kohli, 2003);

12. individuals and families excluded because of their criminal history (Center for Law and Policy, 2003)

13. those displaced by disasters, whether natural, human-made or both (Zakour, 2000).

Past and Prologue

Throughout U.S. history policy on homelessness has tended to mirror societal responses to the conditions of the poorest of the poor population. At the beginning of the 20th century, policy focused on either homeless men or dependent children in need of care. Men were often immigrants and lived in boarding houses during the winter months until seasonal jobs resumed. Those who were classified as transients were given aid through such practices as "passing on," the forerunner to the "bus therapy" of today (Menzies & Webster, 1987). Interventions by the Charity Organization Society, the settlement house movement, and faith-based groups focused on encouraging moral treatment for worthy poor people and work for unworthy poor people.

During the Great Depression, policy focused on families with children standing in soup lines and newly caught in the web of abject poverty. These new poor populations joined together with the transients and older beggars of the 1930s. Policy efforts were numerous and focused on structural causes rather than the personal deficits of poor people.

In the 1950s the focus shifted to skid row, downtown areas populated by single adult men in cheap single room hotels. Policymaking focused on the housing crisis through new construction and loan programs; however, after urban renewal, residents were displaced and when they could no longer pay rent, they turned to the only available temporary services provided by organizations such as the Salvation Army.

From the mid-1960s to the early 1970s, the War on Poverty and the Great Society began to illuminate what had been a private problem and helped the nation to see that it required a public response. Welfare programs provided economic opportunity for poor people, but federal policy initiatives failed to give adequate attention to extreme poverty and the growing crisis in low-income housing (Blasi, 1994). The scope of the crisis in affordable housing was not well recognized or completely understood. It was generally assumed that homelessness had diminished or could be eliminated through other reform efforts.

The Past 25 Years

Beginning in the early 1980s, homelessness exploded as a social issue providing a sharp contrast to the values of opportunity for all. Before the public rediscovery of homelessness in the 1980s (Segal & Baumohl, 1980), it was widely assumed that homelessness was a social problem found either in Third World countries (now more accurately described as "dedeveloped nations," Crotty [2001]), or in an earlier and less enlightened era in the United States. However, by the mid-1980s, rising housing costs, changes in labor markets, deinstitutionalization of people with psychological or developmental disabilities (Bachrach, 1996; Fisk, Rowe, Laub, Calvocoressi, & DeMino, 2000; Segal & Baumhol, 1985), inadequate response to the needs of veterans, and related social forces cried out for greater response in the form of public policy. As this population grew, the estimated number of shelter accommodations rose from 275,000 beds in 1988 to almost 608,000 in 1996 (Blau & Abramovitz, 2004).

As U.S. communities began to face the challenge of increasing numbers of people who were homeless in shelters or living in public spaces in the 1980s, research efforts in social work and related disciplines began to better document the nature and scope of the problem. Charitable organizations such as the Robert Wood Johnson Foundation funded health care for the homeless coalitions around the nation. Fundraising for these new public–private part-

nerships and media focus increased national attention to homelessness as an ever-present problem. Debates about the numbers, characteristics, causes, and consequences revolved around the definition of the problem as a personal crisis in the lives of individuals and families who were unable to afford housing or to benefit from job opportunities in the emerging postindustrial economy. Media coverage focused on the plight of people who were homeless, and old myths about personal responsibility, worthy and unworthy poor people, and work continued to be perpetuated by conservative policy shapers and others as a part of the public debate. Advocacy groups were formed and focused on the need for affordable housing. Faith-based organizations set up community kitchens and other services; missions, public shelters, and local action groups grew in numbers and zeal.

After passage of the Stewart B. McKinney Homeless Assistance Act of 1987 (P.L. 100-77), initiatives and grant-in-aid structures began to emerge. In addition to emergency shelter care, local efforts in service delivery began to include transitional housing, outreach, and case management, particularly to people with mental disabilities who were homeless. However, the crisis of homelessness continued to grow, particularly among people of color (Kreuger & Stretch, 1987), women with children; people living in overcrowded and poorly maintained housing, people with psychiatric disabilities (Segal, Silverman, & Temkin, 1995), and other families who were unable to close the gap between affordable housing and total family income (Stretch & Kreuger, 1989).

Scholars such as Jahiel (1992) have identified a number of reasons for the growth of shelter-based services during the 1980s and 1990s, including their obvious preferable value to sleeping in harsh or dangerous conditions under bridges or in cardboard shacks. Shelters have been seen as providing emergency living quarters for low-income families who suffer from loss of residence as a result of random and unpredictable events such as fires and natural or human-made disasters. Critics have pointed out that shelters also developed partially in response to more predictable political or economic pressures (Kreuger & Stretch, 1995). For example, condemnations that arose from the demolition of low-cost housing because of gentrification also contributed to the growth of shelters. All too often, affordable housing was replaced by shopping malls and entertainment complexes. Shelters offer safe haven for victims of domestic and street violence, and they provide security as stopping off points for transients who otherwise would be stranded. Shelters have been seen as a mechanism for obtaining access to improved housing through residential placement networks and public subsidies such as vouchers for Section 8 assistance. Finally, shelters may provide alternative support for law enforcement officers who respond to requests from sometimes hostile city audiences to arrest people who are homeless. Shelters provide care for people who realistically need a place to live rather than more extreme alternatives such as hospitalization or punitive incarceration. Evaluation studies have assessed both shorter-term outcomes (Glisson, Thyer, & Fischer, 2001) and longer-term effectiveness (Stretch & Kreuger, 1993) of shelter services, with mixed conclusions.

In 1994 the federal government published the first federal plan to break the cycle of homelessness, entitled Priority: Home! (U.S. Department of Housing and Urban Development [HUD], 1994). The plan stated that "for the most part, homelessness relief efforts remain locked in an 'emergency register'" (p. 18). Homelessness is divided into two broad categories of problems: crisis poverty and chronic disability. The plan called for efforts to "reinvent the approach" because the "current approach is plainly not working and must be changed" (HUD, p. 4). A number of factors place people at risk of homelessness, including alcoholism; drug abuse; low education and illiteracy; sexual exploitation; chronic mental disability, developmental disabilities, or mild mental retardation; and HIV/AIDS. Our society systematically and traditionally viewed those labeled as "worthy" poor people in these situations as "unworthy" poor people.

On August 22, 1996, President Clinton ended "welfare as we know it" by signing the Personal Responsibility and Work Opportunity Reconciliation Act. This act ended the existing income maintenance system known as Aid to Families with Dependent Children, the Job Opportunities and Basic Skill Training Program, and Emergency Assistance. These programs were replaced by the new federal block grant program known as Temporary Assistance for Needy Families (TANF). Analysis by Sard (2001) of these changes in welfare spending indicates that some progress has been made in accommodating homelessness in TANF administration. However, consistent cuts in public expenditures for housing have been noted in the fact that HUD's budget has decreased from approximately $85 billion in 1978 to just $29.4 billion in 2002, in inflation-adjusted terms (Blau & Abramovitz, 2004).

Lessons from the Past

After a century of shifting definitions of the problem, political denial, and policy neglect, the core of the homelessness problem clearly is extreme poverty and lack of affordable housing. Policies on homelessness, with only a few exceptions, have emphasized the alleviation of individual need and have underestimated the influence of systemic factors that would be significant in reversing or preventing the underlying conditions of homelessness (Jones & Crook, 2001). Past policy failures (Johnson, Kreuger, & Stretch, 1989) together with reductions in public assistance, housing, health care, economic opportunity, education, nutrition, and affirmative action do not offer much hope that society is capable of learning from either past mistakes or accomplishments.

Too often policy-making processes at the federal, state, and local levels have been limited to local emergency measures, such as various health care for the homeless coalitions that began in the 1980s, rather than addressing the long-term structural and preventive dimensions of severe poverty and homelessness. Recurring themes of individual rather than communal responsibility and labels such as "bag ladies," "panhandlers," "handouts," "hobos," and "transients" have been the focus of public attention. Somewhat analogous to blaming each individual drop of rain for causing one to get wet, rather than responding to the larger weather system (structural foundations), policymakers have tended to rely on compartmentalized solutions. Critics have pointed out that too often people who are homeless are substance dependent, illegal immigrants, or psychiatric outpatients, whose conditions would seem to justify narrower problem-focused solutions. But according to Blau and Abramovitz (2004), when homelessness is seen through the lens of an inadequate supply of affordable housing, who other than people in extreme situations are likely to be left after competition for scarce low-cost housing has run its course?

However, valuable lessons are there to be learned. First, the scope of emergency measures during the Depression Era had a measurable effect in alleviating suffering and extreme poverty. Second, long-term structural measures such as social security and the indexing of these benefits, Medicare, and services to elderly citizens have been effective in protecting some low-income older Americans from the risks of homelessness. Third, the failure to adequately respond to the needs of individuals who were homeless in the 1980s and 1990s led to an even greater crisis in the 21st century. The new chronic homelessness is recognized as a more multifaceted and entrenched problem than in earlier decades, one exacerbated by new at-risk populations, including those with communicable diseases. And far too often, communities have responded with more punitive efforts to criminalize homelessness, rather than to work to prevent it ("Illegal to be homeless," 2003).

ISSUE STATEMENT

After three decades of disjointed efforts to address the crisis of homelessness in the United States, it remains a significant issue. The reasons for this are primarily systemic, and homelessness and poverty are inextricably linked. Being poor means living on the verge of being an accident, an illness, a paycheck, a violent event, or a condemnation away from living on the streets. Being poor means having limited resources to cover the necessities of housing, nutrition, child care, health care, and education. Affordable housing, which absorbs a large proportion of income for people who are poor, is too often abandoned when economic resources are insufficient to meet basic needs. The cost

and difficulty of trying to find low-income housing once a domicile has been lost can present tremendous obstacles, and cogent policies not supported by adequate resources exacerbate this problem. Studies indicate that whereas there were 6.5 million low-cost housing units for 6.2 million renters in 1970, by 1995 there were only 6.1 million low-cost units for 10.5 million renters (Blau & Abramovitz, 2004).

Policy making in relation to the problem of homelessness illustrates a drastic reshaping of the federal social welfare agenda in the United States during the past 25 years, but no single legislative answer has solved or significantly reduced homelessness (Burt, 2000). The dilemma of how to achieve this goal in a time of massive federal budget deficits, narrowly focused policy agendas, and the recent trend toward criminalization of people who are homeless, merits our attention. In keeping with an empowerment perspective, social workers can and must join with people who are homeless to make significant changes in their lives and in the social structures that surround them.

POLICY STATEMENT

To adequately address the problem of both shorter duration and chronic homelessness in the United States, policies should range from strengthening the capacities of the many people who are homeless who are system victims, to changing social and economic conditions that foster extreme poverty and increase the risk of homelessness. NASW advocates the following as supportive and long-term solutions to the problem of homelessness:

1. The goal of an affordable and adequate home and a suitable living environment for everyone in the United States (Housing Act of 1949) should be vigorously pursued (HUD, 2004).

2. Social workers need to be actively involved side by side with people who are homeless (see, for example, Busch-Geertsema, 2002) in national, state, and local coalitions to network with and create advocacy groups; to identify significant problems in localities and create linkages to address and alleviate these

problems; and to encourage state and local communities to use mainstream programs in building a continuum of care that integrates housing, income maintenance, and supportive services.

3. Federal, state, and local housing subsidies should be available as an entitlement for all households with new emphasis on advocacy for McKinney-Vento Homeless Assistance Programs; HOPWA (Housing Opportunities for Persons with AIDS); Section 811 for Persons with Disabilities; and programs for the Education for Homeless Children and Youth (EHCY).

4. The complex patchwork of housing assistance programs (Mulroy & Ewalt, 1996) for low-income families should be organized into a more efficient and coordinated system that targets very poor people and households at highest risk of homelessness.

5. Efforts to encourage state and local communities to use mainstream programs in building a continuum of care that integrates housing, income maintenance, and supportive services should be strengthened.

6. Education, job training, and related support services should be expanded to serve as key elements in the prevention of homelessness. Studies show that only 11 percent of people who are homeless receive SSI benefits, whereas almost 40 percent experience mental health problems, and 46 percent report having at least one chronic health condition (Interagency Council on Homelessness, 1999).

7. Homeless children need to be identified as a special population. They require proper nutrition, adequate clothing and hygiene, and continuous, appropriate education (including a space to study). Services to homeless children should be provided with an overall goal of stopping the cycle of homelessness.

8. Treatment and supportive services for special populations should be expanded and be focused on innovative approaches.

9. Federal, state, and local proposals to cut expenditures and restructure social welfare programs should be studied to determine their impact on homelessness.

10. The lack of bipartisan effort and consensus on policy goals to end mass homelessness continues and is a major stumbling block to federal leadership in agenda setting and appropriations. Political action strategies are needed to reverse this trend.

11. Support for a living wage to help prevent homelessness should be widespread.

Short-term program and policy changes are needed to cope with fiscal crises and the disjointed community system of emergency services for individuals and families who are homeless. Fiscal and programmatic recommendations contained in new ventures, including the development of a National Housing Trust Fund and the Bringing America Home Act (www. bringingamericahome.org), merit our attention. State and local communities as well as nonprofit and public agencies should rethink the place of shelter care within a larger continuum of services for special at-risk populations faced with crisis poverty and homelessness. Shelters have become an institutional response, but their presence should not be viewed as a policy solution (Kreuger, Stretch, Hodges, & Word, 2002). Social workers should be actively involved, in the company of people who are homeless, in the development of continuity of services for children and families. School social workers should work as advocates for the needs of children who are members of families who are homeless (Markward & Biros, 2001).

Excessive rent and other housing burdens on poor people in urban and rural communities must be alleviated. State and local resources, including voluntary efforts, must be mobilized to develop creative solutions and stopgap measures for protecting people who are precariously housed. Misconceptions about the causes of homelessness and severe poverty have contributed to the lack of public support for efforts to alleviate homelessness. Social workers in partnership with elected officials and others must lead the fight in the interests of people who are homeless. The impact of homelessness on women and people of color in U.S. society is an important national issue and for the social work profession that must be translated into more effective efforts at coalition building.

Although more demands are being placed on shelters and emergency services to help people who are homeless, mainstream programs for housing assistance, public assistance, and health care have been drastically cut to fund other political priorities. As programs are paralyzed by too many funding reductions, poverty becomes more severe and homelessness emerges as a growing and chronic reality for the poorest population.

After three decades of disjointed efforts to address the crisis of homelessness in the United States, gaps in federal and state policies and inadequate funding are producing more homeless individuals. The impact of homelessness necessitates immediate action on the part of the social work profession.

REFERENCES

Bachrach, L. (1996). Deinstitutionalization: Promises, problems and prospects. In J. Knudsen & G. Thornicrotf (Eds.), *Mental health service evaluation* (pp. 3–18). New York: Cambridge University Press.

Baker, A., McKay, M., Lynn, C., Schlange, H., & Auville, A. (2003). Recidivism at a shelter for adolescents: First-time versus repeat runaways. *Social Work Research, 27*, 84–93.

Benda, B. (2002). Test of a structural equation model of comorbidity among homeless and domiciled military veterans. *Journal of Social Service Research, 29*(1), 1–35.

Biggerstaff, M., Morris, P., & Nichols-Casebolt, A. (2002). Living on the edge: Examination of people attending food pantries and soup kitchens. *Social Work, 47*, 267–277.

Blasi, G. (1994). Ideological and political barriers to understanding homelessness. *American Behavioral Scientist, 37*, 563–586.

Blau, J., & Abramovitz, M. (2004). *The dynamics of social welfare policy.* New York: Oxford University Press.

Bride, B., & Real, E. (2003). Project Assist: A modified therapeutic community for homeless women living with HIV/AIDS and chemical dependency. *Health & Social Work, 28*, 166–168.

The Bringing America Home Act, H.R. 2897, 108 Cong., 1st Sess. (2004). Retrieved July 20, 2004, from www.bringingamericahome.org

Bufkin, J., & Bray, J. (1998). Domestic violence, criminal justice responses and homelessness: Finding the connection and addressing the problem. *Journal of Social Distress and the Homeless, 7*, 227–240.

Burt, M. (2000). *What will it take to end homelessness?* Retrieved April 11, 2004, from www.urban.org/url.cfm?ID=310305

Busch-Geertsema, V. (2002). When homeless people are allowed to decide by themselves. Rehousing homeless people in Germany. *European Journal of Social Work, 5*(1), 5–19.

Center for Law and Policy. (2003). *One strike and you're out: Low-income families barred from housing because of criminal records* (fact sheet). Washington, DC: Center for Law and Policy.

Crotty, R. (2001). *When histories collide: The development and impact of individualistic capitalism.* Walnut Creek, CA: AltaMira Press.

Danis, F. (2003). The criminalization of domestic violence: What social workers need to know. *Social Work, 48*, 237–246.

Dworsky, A., & Piliavin, I. (2002). Homeless spell exits and returns: Substantive and methodological elaborations on recent studies. *Social Service Review, 74*, 193–213.

First, R. J., Rife, J. C., & Toomey, B. G. (1999). Homeless families. In R. L. Edwards (Ed.-in-Chief), *Encyclopedia of social work* (19th ed., Vol. 2, pp. 1330–1337). Washington, DC: NASW Press.

Fisk, D., Rowe, M., Laub, D., Calvocoressi, L., & DeMino, K. (2000). Homeless persons with mental illness and their families: Emerging issues from clinical work. *Families in Society, 81*, 351–359.

Fogel, S. (1997). Moving along: An exploratory study of homeless women with children using a transitional housing program. *Journal of Sociology and Social Welfare, 24*(3), 113–133.

Glisson, G., Thyer, B., & Fischer, R. (2001). Serving the homeless: Evaluating the effectiveness of homeless shelter services. *Journal of Sociology and Social Welfare, 27*(4), 89–97.

Goodfellow, M. (1999). Rural homeless shelters: A comparative analysis. *Journal of Social Distress and the Homeless, 8*(1), 21–35.

Holden, B., Wade, S. L., Mitchell, H., Ewart, C., & Islam, S. (1998). Caretaker expectations and the management of pediatric asthma in the inner city: A scale development study. *Social Work Research, 22*, 51–59.

Hutchison, W. J., Searight, P., & Stretch, J. J. (1986). Multidimensional networking: A response to the needs of homeless families. *Social Work, 31*, 427–430.

Illegal to be homeless: The criminalization of homelessness in the United States. (2003, August). Washington, DC: National Coalition for the Homeless and the National Law Center for Homelessness and Poverty.

Interagency Council on Homelessness. (1999). *Homelessness: Programs and the people they serve—Findings from a National Survey of Homeless Providers and Clients.* Washington, DC: National Law Center for Homelessness and Poverty.

Jahiel, R. (Ed.). (1992). *Homelessness: A prevention-oriented approach.* Baltimore: Johns Hopkins University Press.

Johnson, A. (1999). Working and nonworking women: Onset of homelessness within the context of their lives. *Affilia, 14*, 42–77.

Johnson, A., & Kreuger, L. (1989). Toward a better understanding of homeless women [Briefly Stated]. *Social Work, 34*, 537–540.

Johnson, A., Kreuger, L., & Stretch. J. (1989). A court-ordered consent decree for the homeless: Process, conflict and control. *Journal of Sociology and Social Welfare, 16*(3), 29–42.

Jones, J., & Crook, W. (2001). Homelessness and the social welfare system: The Briar Patch revisited? *Journal of Family Social Work, 6*(3), 35–51.

Kohli, R. (2003). Child and family social work with asylum seekers and refugees. *Child and Family Social Work, 8*(3).

Kreuger, L., & Stretch, J. (1987, June 7). *Ethnic differentials among homeless families seeking shelter.* Paper presented at the Minority Issues Conference of the National Association of Social Workers, Washington, DC.

Kreuger, L., & Stretch, J. (1995, April). *Preventing homelessness: An empirical study of why shelter services don't work.* Paper presented at the annual meeting of the Society for Social Work and Research, Washington, DC.

Kreuger, L., Stretch, J., Hodges, J., & Word, D. (2002). Are governmental policies solving the problem of homelessness? In C. Breme, H. Karger, & J. Midgley (Eds.), *Controversial issues in social policy* (Vol. 2, pp. 57–64). Boston: Allyn & Bacon.

Levinson, D. (2004). *Encyclopedia of homelessness* (Vol. 2). Newbury Park, CA: Sage Publications.

Markward, M., & Biros, E. (2001). McKinney revisited: Implications for school social work. *Children & Schools, 23*, 182–187.

McLean, D., Bowen, S., Drezner, K., Rowe, R., Sherman, P., Schroeder, S., Redlener, K., & Redlener, I. (2004). Undercounting and undertreating the underserved. *Archives of Pediatric Adolescent Medicine, 158*, 244–249.

Menzies, R., & Webster, C. (1987). Where they go and what they do: The longitudinal careers of forensic patients in the medicolegal complex. *Canadian Journal of Criminology, 29*, 275–293.

Mulroy, E. A., & Ewalt, P. L. (1996). Affordable housing: A basic need and a social issue [Editorial]. *Social Work, 41*, 245–249.

National Alliance to End Homelessness. (1999). *Homelessness: Programs and the people they serve—Findings of the National Survey of Homeless Assistance Providers and Clients* [Highlights]. Washington, DC: Interagency Council on the Homeless.

North, C., Eyrich, K., Pollio, D., & Spitznagel, E. (2004). Are rates of psychiatric disorders in the homeless population changing? *American Journal of Public Health, 94*, 103–108.

North, C. S., & Smith, E. M. (1993). A comparison of homeless men and women: Different populations, different needs. *Community Mental Health Journal, 29*, 423–431.

Pardeck, J., & Rollinson, P. (2002). An exploration of violence among homeless women with emotional disabilities: Implications for practice and policy. *Journal of Social Work in Disability and Rehabilitation, 1*(4), 63–73.

Rivera, L. (2003). Changing women: An ethnographic study of homeless mothers and popular education. *Journal of Sociology and Social Welfare, 30*(2), 31–51.

Sard, B. (2001, April). *Using TANF funds for housing-related benefits to prevent homeless-*

ness. Center on Budget and Policy Priorities. Retrieved April 23, 2004, from http://www.cbpp.org/4-3-01TANF.htm

Segal, S. P., & Baumohl, J. (1980). Engaging the disengaged: Proposals on madness and vagrancy. *Social Work, 25,* 358–365.

Segal, S., & Baumohl, J. (1985). The community living room. *Social Casework, 66,* 111–116.

Segal, S., Silverman, C., & Temkin, T. (1995). Characteristics and service use of long-term members of self-help agencies for mental health clients. *Psychiatric Services, 46,* 269–274.

Stewart B. McKinley Homeless Assistance Act of 1987, P.L. 100-77, 101 Stat. 482.

Stretch, J. (2004, April). Opening plenary. Missouri Association for Social Welfare Conference on Homelessness, Jefferson City.

Stretch, J., & Kreuger, L. (1989, August). *Impact study on outcomes of services to homeless families: The results of a public-private partnership.* Paper presented to the National Association for Welfare Research and Statistics, Kalispell, MT.

Stretch, J., & Kreuger, L. (1990). The twig is bent: An empirical study of homeless children. *Health Progress, 1*(2), 14–19.

Stretch, J., & Kreuger, L. (1993). Five-year cohort study of homeless families: A joint policy research venture. *Journal of Sociology and Social Welfare, 19*(1), 73–88.

Thompson, S. J., Safyer, A. W., & Pollio., D. E. (2001). Differences and predictors of family reunification among subgroups of runaway youths using shelter services. *Social Work Research, 25,* 163–172.

U.S. Department of Housing and Urban Development. (1994). *Priority home!* (HUD-1454-CPD[1]). Washington, DC: Author.

Wong, Y. I. (2002). Tracking change in psychological distress among homeless adults: An examination of the effect of housing status. *Health & Social Work, 27,* 262–273.

Zakour, M. J. (Ed.). (2000). *Disaster and traumatic stress research and intervention: Tulane studies in social welfare.* New Orleans: Tulane University Press.

Policy statement approved by the NASW Delegate Assembly, August 2005. This policy supersedes the policy statement on Homelessness approved by the Delegate Assembly in 1996 and referred by the 2002 Delegate Assembly to the 2005 Delegate Assembly for revision. For further information, contact the National Association of Social Workers, 750 First Street, NE, Suite 700, Washington, DC 20002-4241. Telephone: 202-408-8600 or 800-638-8799; e-mail: press@naswdc.org

Hospice Care

BACKGROUND

The dramatic attention accorded to hospice care in the United States during the past two decades reflects the convergence of a variety of interests and needs (U.S. General Accounting Office, 1979). The issues of death and dying that have given impetus to the hospice movement include the effect on people with terminal illnesses and their families, medical advances that enable life to be prolonged in the face of degenerative diseases and impending death, renewed attention to home care and other alternatives to hospitalization, the scarcity of resources, the emphasis on holistic health, and recognition of the rights of people who are dying (Tannock & Boyer, 1990).

The 20th century was witness to changing attitudes toward people who are dying and to a self-determination focus for their care and treatment. In the early part of the 20th century, the family and physician provided care in the home as a matter of course. However, care gradually shifted to hospitals, where diagnosis, treatment, and cure were emphasized and the focus was on the physical condition of the dying person. Social and emotional needs were largely ignored. The trauma of dying and death for both the person and the family was inadequately understood and poorly handled. It was not until Dr. Cicely Saunders traveled to the United States in the early 1960s that people began to explore the idea of specialized care for people who were terminally ill. Recognition of the need for special knowledge, skills, and sensitivity grew. Gradually, the institutionally oriented, medically dominated health care system began to recognize and become responsive to these needs.

The term "hospice" is derived from the way station or inn, which was a place of succor and rest for weary travelers in the Middle Ages. Today, the National Hospice Foundation (NHF) defines *hospice* as "a team-oriented approach to expert medical care, pain management, and emotional and spiritual support expressly tailored to the patient's needs and wishes . . . extended to the patient's loved ones as well" (NHF, 2001). It is a philosophy of care, not a place. Hospice serves all people perceived to be terminally ill regardless of the etiology of their disease or their age, religion, race, or illness.

According to National Hospice and Palliative Care Organization (NHPCO) estimates,

> there are 3,139 operational or planned hospice programs in the U.S. today, including the District of Columbia, Puerto Rico and Guam. In 1999, 44% of hospices were independent, freestanding agencies, 33% were hospital based, 17% were home health agency based, and 4% were based in nursing homes or under other auspices. Seventy-six percent . . . were non-profit, 4% were government organizations, 18% were for-profit and 3% were not identified. (NHPCO, 2001)

NHPCO estimates that

> hospices admitted 700,000 patients in 1999, up from 540,000 in 1998. We further estimate that over 600,000 Americans died while receiving hospice care in 1999 (or 29% of all Americans who died that year).... Hospices now care for over half of all Americans who die from cancer, and a growing number of patients with other chronic, life-threatening illnesses, such as end-stage heart or lung disease. Hospices were leaders in caring for terminally ill patients with HIV/AIDS. (NHPCO, 2001)

When hospice care is compared with the cost of hospital and skilled nursing facilities, hospice is a cost-effective service, with lower per day costs than the others. In 1995 the National Hospice Organization (NHO)/Lewin–VHI study "found that the hospice beneficiaries who enrolled in the last month of life cost Medicare $2,884 less than the non-users" (NHO, 1995, p. 4).

More compelling than cost-effectiveness is the fact that hospice care delivers services in a humane and compassionate way. Family members, interviewed in a study of end-of-life experiences of 3,357 older and seriously ill patients who died, stated that "40% were in severe pain prior to their death and 25% experienced moderate to great anxiety or depression before they died" (Lynn et al., 1997, p. 100). It was reported that very few of these patients were in hospice care, which might have alleviated some of their distress. In addition, recent pilot studies reported effectiveness of postdeath support by 95.2 percent of family members using the service (Ryndes et al., 1998–2000).

ISSUE STATEMENT

Individual and societal attitudes toward death have historically affected how we treat those who are dying and their loved ones. Although death is certainly a part of our lives, "there is a tendency to view death as an event that can be deferred indefinitely rather than as a part of life" (Despelder & Strickland, 2001, p. 12). Furthermore, continued advancements in medical technologies have a major impact on how we die, and societal changes affect how we care for those who are dying. As a result people with life-threatening illnesses may have a limited understanding of available services directed toward end-of-life care that promote healing rather than curing.

Hospice services are a form of compassionate care for the dying in which the primary goal is to relieve pain and suffering so that the dying person can go on living as fully as possible until his or her death (Despelder & Strickland, 2001). It is a model of caring for terminally ill people that offers the dying person the right to make decisions about his or her care, the right to a pain-free death, the right to choose palliative care versus curative treatment, and the opportunity to die with dignity.

According to the NASW Code of Ethics (NASW, 1999), social workers are directed to recognize and promote the right of clients to self-determination. Hospice is a form of care that emphasizes this right to self-determination specifically for people with life-threatening illnesses and their families and support systems. For example, because hospice is usually a community-based service that can be provided in nursing homes, residential care facilities, senior housing, hospitals, or private homes, patients and families have a right to choose not just the kind of care, but also where to receive care. Hospice encourages the patient, family, and loved ones to participate in the caring process, with a special focus on individualizing care through a collaborative process with the hospice staff and volunteers.

Other vital concerns regarding the development of a policy statement on hospice care and services for people with life-threatening illnesses include reimbursement for hospice services, pharmaceutical costs, length of service, underserved populations, rationing of scarce resources, caregiver ability, and changes in illness trajectory.

Reimbursement for Hospice Services

Although Medicare, Medicaid, and private health insurance may cover much of the cost for hospice care, at least 15 percent of the U.S. population is without health care coverage. This situation leaves a portion of the population at risk of not receiving the care they may want or need at the final stage of their lives. There are also concerns that reimbursement rates for hospice care have not kept up with the increasing cost of providing care. Some hospice programs may be at risk of cutting costs or services due to increasing financial pressure, or they may have to rely more heavily on donations and fundraising to maintain a program of care (Cheung, Fitch, & Pyenson, 2001). Services at risk of being diminished due to cost include social work, pastoral counseling, and grief and bereavement services.

Pharmaceutical Costs

Although medications for terminally ill patients are frequently included in hospice care, these rapidly increasing costs put financial pressure on hospice programs. The 1983 Medicare Demonstration Project yielded that the per patient per day (PPPD) cost of pharmaceuticals accounted for 2 percent of the total PPPD costs to care for a hospice patient, whereas a recent hospice study commissioned by the NHPCO found that the 1999 PPPD costs of pharmaceuticals is now 13 percent of the total cost of care for a hospice patient (Cheung et al., 2001).

Length of Service

The number of individuals receiving hospice care is increasing, but the quantity of time these individuals are receiving care is decreasing. In the 1983 Medicare Demonstration Project, the mean length of hospice service was 70 days. The Milliman Study (Cheung et al., 2001) found that the mean length of hospice service had declined to 36 days. There are several plausible explanations for this trend, including an increase in use of newer, advanced medical technologies aimed at curing the illness, which might lead patients and physicians to wait longer before choosing hospice; an increased societal attitude toward denying death; lack of education regarding hospice services among health care providers, patients, and families; and concern about reimbursement if the patient lives longer than the original prognosis.

Underserved Populations

Only 8 percent of African Americans and 2 percent of Hispanic were identified as hospice patients in 2000. These numbers underestimate the proportion of these population groups within the United States. One recent study suggested several issues of concern regarding hospice access and use by African Americans, including lack of trust of African Americans in the health care system, a lack of knowledge of services, economic factors, lack of diversity among health care staff, and differ-

ences in values regarding medical care and spiritual beliefs between African Americans and European Americans (Reece, Ahern, Nair, O'Faire, & Warren, 1999). Members of racial and ethnic groups in general may be at risk of being underserved due to differences in cultural values versus hospice philosophy, mistrust of formalized health care systems, and lack of understanding regarding hospice care. People with HIV/AIDS may also constitute a population underserved by hospice. Although many hospice programs were pioneers in the provision of care for people with HIV/AIDS, it is unclear what percentage of people with end-stage HIV/AIDS are receiving hospice care. In 2000, 15,245 people died in the United States as a result of HIV/AIDS, compared with the 51,117 deaths that occurred in 1995. A decline in overall deaths due to HIV/AIDS is apparent, yet it is still a life-threatening condition with no known cure. Consequently, hospice is still a necessary and appropriate program of care for people at the end stages of HIV/AIDS.

Rationing of Scarce Resources

In the health care system, rationing resources occurs when limits exist to the amount of medical care or treatment a person can receive even though it may be considered beneficial to the patient. With the increasing cost of health care, the growth of the aging population, and people living longer with chronic illnesses, increasing concerns arise over how to determine appropriateness of health care choices and who should make those decisions. Choosing hospice means that patients have agreed to refrain from pursuing medical interventions intended to increase the longevity of life, thus the patient and family ration their health care treatment by choosing comfort care over curative care. The use of advance medical directives is another example of patients using their right to choose how they want to ration their health care treatment by documenting what they do or do not want during their last stages of terminal illness. Social workers play a key role in assisting communication among patients, families, and health care providers regarding the care of people with life-threatening illnesses.

Caregiver Availability

Most hospice programs require the existence of a full-time caregiver who is accessible at most times during the day. However, the geographic mobility of individuals in our society, as well as changes in the makeup of families, may result in fewer opportunities for family members and loved ones to assist with daily care in the home of a hospice patient. The issue of caregiver employment may also complicate hospice care at home. Flexibility in providing hospice to people who do not have a traditional caregiver available may be necessary to meet the changing needs of today's terminally ill patients.

Changes in Illness Trajectory

Advances in health care treatment also affect care for people with life-threatening illnesses. In the future hospice care may develop into several levels of care based on the expected prognosis of terminally ill people (for example, addressing differences in individuals in an acute stage of dying versus a chronic stage of dying or high-tech palliative care, such as radiation and chemotherapy [directed at symptom management], versus traditional palliative care, such as oral or intravenous pharmaceuticals [directed specifically at pain relief]).

The relationships that social workers facilitate within and among loved ones, health care professionals, and members of the community are vital to the process of achieving the goal of hospice, which is assisting dying people in living as full a life as possible until death. Social workers recognize that hospice is a model of care that emphasizes the patient as central to that care and that decisions made by or for the patient will inevitably affect the entire system surrounding that patient, including family, friends, and hospice staff. As a result of this awareness, social workers offer information and services that encourage communication within the patient's environment so that the process of death, dying, and bereavement may become physically, emotionally, socially, and spiritually less painful.

POLICY STATEMENT

Because death is a part of life, NASW supports hospice care as a way of helping people who are dying and their loved ones to maintain their dignity and humanity while receiving and participating in optimal physical, psychosocial, and spiritual care. It is an interdisciplinary approach, a philosophy, and an application of values, rather than a physical entity or program per se. The emphasis is on enabling people who are dying to live as fully as possible and to control their lives as much as possible. Hospice care seeks to eliminate the symptoms of illness through the control and palliation of the physical, emotional, spiritual, interpersonal, and financial aspects of disease. Hospice services should be available to people who are dying and their families and significant others, wherever they live and whatever their race, ethnicity, sexual preference, or socioeconomic status. Support services should continue beyond the death of the patient, for at least a year, for children and adolescent as well as adult survivors.

Hospice is a form of compassionate caring for dying people that is fully compatible with the values and ethics of the social work profession. NASW's position on hospice care is based on the following:

- that every dying person is of value and deserves individualized care while being served by hospice

- that social justice and a commitment to serve vulnerable and underserved populations is essential to ensuring that all people who are terminally ill have the opportunity to choose and receive hospice care

- that client self-determination is inherent in the provision of hospice care so that the dying can choose how they live until their death

- that the integrity of the hospice philosophy be pursued and maintained, that is, "the right to die pain-free and with dignity" and for loved ones to be supported (University of California San Francisco, 2001)

- that the quality of life, not merely its prolongation, should be of central concern

- that social workers must continue to demonstrate strong leadership within hospice by advocating for the needs of vulnerable populations who may benefit from hospice care but who historically have been less likely to receive services

■ that the social work profession must work to ensure that a "place at the table" remains for hospice social work services in this environment, directed at grasping cost-saving measures in health care to the detriment of society.

The health care system in the United States has been undergoing significant changes in recent years. Issues such as managed care, HIV/AIDS, the increase in the aging population, and the growth of the pharmaceutical industry are just a few examples of these changes. Any and all change in the health care system as a whole has an impact on hospice care. As a result it is the role of the social work profession to respond to these changes. "Social workers can serve a critical function within the hospice movement by calling attention to the ethical and systemic implications of growth and change . . . and by remaining flexible and responsive to these changes" (MacDonald, 1991, p. 279). In this process it is essential to recognize that social workers have an important role in helping to ensure that hospice care is available to dying people and their loved ones:

■ Social workers should advocate for new and flexible sources of private and public funding for hospice services. These activities can include marketing and development on a local level as well as political advocacy on a national level.

■ Social workers must work to ensure that hospice remains available in a variety of health care and home care settings, especially focused on the dying person's wishes or desires.

■ Social workers need to pursue changes in traditional hospice regulations concerning caregiver availability and respond to social changes in reference to today's definition of "family" or "caregivers." m

■ Social workers should be versed in understanding the symptoms and treatment of life-threatening conditions to assist with patient and family education and help access resources and services.

■ NASW social workers support efforts to influence the health care industry for improvements in symptom control measures for life-threatening conditions.

■ Social workers and other hospice professionals must be knowledgeable about ethnic, cultural, and spiritual beliefs, so that communication with clients and their families is carried out in a sensitive and meaningful manner.

■ Social workers should maintain an understanding of and sensitivity to the roles of the entire hospice team of professionals and volunteers. An environment of mutual respect among the interdisciplinary team will enhance the effectiveness of the care provided to patients and families, increase overall job satisfaction, and reduce staff burnout in this emotionally laden practice area.

■ Social workers should advocate within the structure of the hospice organization to build support systems with and among other disciplines.

■ New end-of-life issues should be incorporated into all levels of social work education.

The role of professional social workers is integral to hospice care. The hospice concept is the embodiment of social work values and principles. Themes central to social work education are self-determination and respect for individual worth and dignity; recognition of the interplay among the person who is dying, his or her family, his or her loved ones, and the community; the concepts of the team approach; and the use of natural helping networks and volunteers.

Social work intervention may include but need not be limited to

■ planning for adaptation to a life-threatening condition

■ ensuring adequate social support systems

- facilitating communication among family members and loved ones

- planning for minor children

- promoting collaborative care efforts with the interdisciplinary hospice team

- counseling

- discharge planning

- case management

- continuity of care during and after the patient's death

- referral to community resources

- crisis intervention

- advocacy

- patient and family education

- providing information and assistance regarding financial issues related to health care costs.

Using practice research data and practice experience, social workers have the expertise to engage in political activism and legislative change that may include issues regarding the role of social work in hospice care, hospice costs, reimbursement issues in hospice care, and potential changes in hospice services.

REFERENCES

Cheung, L., Fitch, K., & Pyenson, B. (2001, August). *The costs of hospice care—An actuarial evaluation of the Medicare hospice benefit.* Milliman USA, commissioned by the National Hospice and Palliative Care Organization.

Despelder, L. A., & Strickland, A. E. (2001). *The last dance: Encountering death and dying* (6th ed.). Columbus, OH: McGraw-Hill.

Lynn, J., Teno, J., Phillips, R., Wu, A., Desbiens, N., Harrold, J., et al. (1997). Perceptions by family members of the dying experience of older and seriously ill patients. *Annals of Internal Medicine, 126,* 97–106.

MacDonald, D. (1991). Hospice social work: A search for identity. *Health & Social Work, 16,* 274–281.

National Association of Social Workers. (1999). *NASW code of ethics.* Washington, DC: Author.

National Hospice and Palliative Care Organization (2002). *NHPCO facts and figures.* [Online]. Available: http://www.nhpco.org

National Hospice Foundation. (2001). *What is hospice care?* [Online]. Available: http://hospiceinfo.org

Reece, D. J., Ahern, R. E., Nair, S., O'Faire, J. D., & Warren, C. (1999). Hospice access and use by African Americans: Addressing cultural and institutional barriers through participatory action research. *Social Work, 44,* 549-559.

Ryndes, T., Connor, S., Cody, C., Merriman, M., Bruno, S., Fine, P., & Dennis, J. (1998–2000). *Report on the alpha and beta pilots of end result outcomes measures constructed by the Outcomes Forum: A joint effort of the National Hospice and Palliative Care Association and the National Hospice Work Group* [Online]. Available: http://www.nhpco.org

Tannock, I. F., & Boyer, M. B. (1990). When is cancer treatment worthwhile? *New England Journal of Medicine, 323,* 989–990.

University of California San Francisco (UCSF) Medical Center, Cancer Resource Center. (2001). *Peaceful dying—Hospice* [Online]. Available: http://cc.ucsf.edu

U.S. General Accounting Office. (1979, March). *Hospice care: A growing concept in the United States* (Report to the U.S. Congress by the Comptroller General). Washington, DC: U.S. Government Printing Office.

Policy statement approved by the NASW Delegate Assembly, August 2002. This statement supersedes the policy statement on Hospice Care approved by the Delegate Assembly in 1981 and reconfirmed by the Delegate Assembly in 1993. For further information, contact the National Association of Social Workers, 750 First Street, NE, Suite 700, Washington, DC 20002-4241. Telephone: 202-408-8600; e-mail: press@naswdc.org

Housing

BACKGROUND

Housing and community environments that meet the universal need for shelter, privacy, and positive social relationships are essential for stable family life, personal development, and health and safety. Deteriorating housing results in a four-way loss to (1) the health and welfare of the population, (2) property values and economic vitality, (3) community morale, and (4) housing stock. Thus, decisions regarding housing cannot be left wholly to the interplay of the supply and demand of the marketplace. The private real estate market cannot be expected to meet the needs of many groups adequately, particularly those with low incomes. Policy choices, along with market forces, drive housing and community development, and it is up to public policy, primarily at the federal level, to take the lead in developing affordable housing within livable communities (Dreier, Mollenkopf, & Swanstrom, 2001). Historically, federal housing policy development has occurred within the context of varying political agendas and reflects wide differences in ideology that shift with political forces. These philosophical variations have resulted in waves of disconnected housing policies at best (Marcuse & Keating, 2006). National policy has evolved slowly, in a patchwork manner, leaving many gaps and discrepancies that often work to the disadvantage of those who most need assistance and protection. In 1949, Congress set forth a national housing goal—not a policy—of "a decent home and suitable living environment for every American family." For 30 years, progress toward this goal was measured in the statistics of dollars allocated, units planned, and housing starts rather than in the quality of housing or improvements in communities. Still missing is a national policy on housing that ensures equity within regional, economic, and racial differences and that emanates not from concepts of property values but from concepts of human need and healthy communities (Dreier et al., 2001).

National policy has eroded financing and the efficacy of the housing programs that emerged as well as related fair housing and financial enforcement (for example, anti-redlining) (Bryson, 2006). Housing should be a national priority and a right as a basic human need. Housing affects other services and clearly illustrates the concept of mutuality. Foster care, shelters, mental and physical health, and education are affected by housing programs. When decent housing is available, the benefit in financial and human terms is well documented.

The foremost federal policy, the Fair Housing Act (P.L. 90-284), was passed by Congress in 1968 (Title VIII of the Civil Rights Act of 1968). The U.S. Department of Housing and Urban Development (HUD) is the agency with statutory authority to administer and enforce the act, through HUD's Office of Fair Housing and Equal Opportunity (FHEO). FHEO administers federal laws and establishes national policies that ensure all Americans have equal access to the housing of their choice and prohibits discrimination in housing on the basis of race, color, religion, sex, national origin, age, disability, and familial status.

ISSUE STATEMENT

Adequate, affordable housing is a basic right that is critical for the flourishing of individuals and families (Keyes, 2007).

Housing Supply and Affordability

In the 1949 Housing Act, Congress declared "a decent home and a suitable living environment for every American family" to be our national housing goal. Today, little more than half a century later, upwards of 100 million people in the United States live in housing that is physically inadequate, unsafe, overcrowded, or unaffordable (Bratt, Stone, & Hartman, 2006). The supply of suitable and affordable housing to meet the diverse needs of individuals and families in the United States continues to be inadequate (Atlas & Drier, 2007). Housing has become more expensive and has not kept up with wages, and the key to housing affordability is that it must meet the needs of the people who provide the services everyone depends on—teachers, police officers, nurses, firefighters, and other public servants, as well as millions of Americans in the services and retail industries (National Association of Home Builders, 2008).

The real cause of affordable housing shortages is a shortage of overall housing caused by government restriction on supply (Powell & Stringham, 2004). Inclusionary zoning has two major effects on local economies; The costs in the housing market drain wealth out of the local economy and the zoning leads to losses in state and local government revenue (Powell & Stringham, 2004).

Populations with Special Needs

For those who are poor, there are few housing options that meet their needs. With the expansion of community-based support services, many older adults and people with disabilities remain in their communities and are able to live reasonably independently. Many youths whose needs are not met by the child welfare system, and an increasing number of individuals who are returning to the community from institutions, have few or no suitable housing options. These groups, along with others with special housing needs—immigrants, people in "isolated and depressed communities," and large families who have lost their homes and are deprived socially and economically—now are swelling the ranks of the homeless population. A greater awareness of populations with special needs and the crisis of homelessness are forcing new approaches to housing (Segal, 1995).

Relationship of Housing and Social Services

The interface of housing and supportive services has received increased attention, which is in part due to federal emphasis on the Housing First model and is beginning to be understood by planners and policymakers (U.S. Department of Housing and Urban Development 2008). However, the allocation of resources that could tie together the delivery of housing with the delivery of services remains minimal and haphazard. Supportive services must be an integral part of a housing program (Cohen, Phillips, Mendez, & Ordonez, 2000).

Housing and the Community Infrastructure

In the past there was little integrated planning for housing and the community infrastructure of facilities and services, such as transportation, schools, public services, and civic and neighborhood organizations. Such planning must be encouraged now and in the future. The current cost of energy, which circumscribes the area within which families can live suitably and meet their economic and social needs, demands the integrated planning of housing and urban or rural development (Naparstek & Dooley, 1997).

Housing and Employment

The cause-and-effect relationship between housing and jobs has been acknowledged belatedly in the aftermath of the suburban expansion of the past three decades, resulting in urban sprawl and economic segregation. Lack of federal policy and conservative market forces have caused distinct disparities in job opportunities and income levels (Dreier et al., 2001); low- and moderate-income families have been unable to take advantage of employment opportunities because without an adequate income they are unable to meet the cost of housing in areas where new job opportunities have become available. Unemployed people, particularly, are locked in, unable to meet their housing costs and unable to relocate.

POLICY STATEMENT

NASW supports

■ the right of all individuals and families to have affordable housing that meets their basic needs for shelter and provides for a rewarding community life.

■ a national housing policy that views housing as a social utility and a basic human need for all income groups that includes programs of government-sponsored or nonprofit rental housing, cooperative housing, the rehabilitation of housing, and homeownership.

■ housing policies that ensure the availability of accessible housing that meets diverse needs and that are distributed geographically.

■ the adoption of policies at all levels of government that stimulate and support the rehabilitation, construction, and maintenance of rented and owned dwellings to meet the needs of all populations.

■ programs to revitalize deteriorated public housing structured in such a manner as to ensure that there is no reduction in the number of affordable housing units in the community and that maximum possible efforts are undertaken to preserve existing neighborhoods and communities.

■ federal, state, and local government programs, including housing trust funds and land trusts, which provide the maximum possible funding to assist with the production, operation, and maintenance of affordable housing, through both homeownership and rental assistance programs. Such funding should be available to both public and private, including commercial and nonprofit, organizations.

■ varied public and private sector efforts to meet the housing needs of Americans with low incomes. These options should include shared or accessory housing, single-room occupancy housing and congregate-living arrangements.

■ citizen participation and community involvement in development of housing policy.

■ inclusive decision making about housing planning and operation by consumers, tenants, landlords, real estate and building interests, and community groups.

■ new housing development or existing housing rehabilitation linked to employment opportunities and community services.

■ enforcement of fair housing and financing laws.

■ enforcement and expansion of the Community Reinforcement Act of 1977.

■ the recognition of housing programs as integral to national economic growth and stability.

■ income tax codes, property assessments, and monetary policies that address the needs of low-income people.

■ further research to determine the most effective types of housing assistance programs and best practices in housing policy and program implementation.

REFERENCES

Atlas, J., & Drier, P. (2007). *The conservative origins of the sub-prime mortgage crisis.* Retrieved April 4, 2008, from http://www .prospect.org/cs/articles?article=the_ conservative_origins_of_the_subprime_ mortgage_crisis

Bratt, R. G., Stone, M. E., & Hartman, C. (Eds.). (2006). *A right to housing: Foundation for a new social agenda.* Philadelphia: Temple University Press.

Bryson, D. (2006). *The role of the courts and a right to housing.* In M. E. Stone & C. Hartman (Eds.), *A right to housing: Foundation for a new social agenda* (pp. 193–212). Philadelphia: Temple University Press.

Burt, M., Aron, L. Y., Lee, E., & Valente, J. (2001). *Helping America's homeless: Emergency shelter or affordable housing.* Washington, DC: Urban Institute Press.

Cohen, C. S., Phillips, M. H., Mendez, M. A., & Ordonez, R. (2000). Sustaining strong communities in a world of devolution: Empowerment-based social services in housing settings. In R. Perez-Koenig & B. D. Rock (Eds.), *Social work in the era of devolution: Toward a just practice.* New York: Fordham University Press.

Community Reinvestment Act of 1977, P.L. 95-128, Title VIII, Oct. 12, 1977, 91 Stat. 1147.

Dreier, P., Mollenkopf, J., & Swanstrom. T. (2001). *Place matters: Metropolitics for the twenty-first century.* Lawrence: University Press of Kansas.

Fair Housing Act, P.L. 90-284, Title VIII, Apr. 11, 1968, 82 Stat. 81.

Housing Act of 1949, 63 Stat. 413.

Keyes, C. (2007). Towards a mentally flourishing society: mental health promotion, not cure [Guest Editorial]. *Journal of Public Mental Health.* Available at http://www.pavpub.com/pavpub/journals/JPMH/showjournal.asp?Title=Journal+of+Public+Mental+Health

Marcuse, P., & Keating, W. D. (2006). The permanent housing crisis: The failures of conservatism and the limitations of liberalism. In M. E. Stone & C. Hartman (Eds.), *A right to housing: Foundation for a new social agenda* (pp. 139–162). Philadelphia: Temple University Press.

Naparstek, A. J., & Dooley, D. (1997). Community building. In R. L. Edwards (Ed.-in-Chief), *Encyclopedia of social work* (19th ed., 1997 Suppl., pp. 77–89). Washington, DC: NASW Press.

National Association of Home Builders. (2008). *Regulatory barriers to housing affordability.* Retrieved from http://www.nahb.org/page.aspx/category/sectionID=1016

Powell, B., & Stringham, E. (2004). *Housing supply and affordability: Do affordable housing mandates work?* Retrieved from http://www.reasons.org/ps318polsum.pdf

Segal, S. P. (1995). Deinstitutionalization. In R. L. Edwards (Ed.-in-Chief), *Encyclopedia of social work* (19th ed., Vol. 1, pp. 704–712). Washington, DC: NASW Press.

U.S. Department of Housing and Urban Development. (2008). Washington, DC: Author.

Policy statement approved by the NASW Delegate Assembly, August 2008. This policy statement supersedes the policy statement on Housing approved by the Delegate Assembly in 1999 and referred by the 2005 Delegate Assembly to the 2008 Delegate Assembly for revision. The 1999 Assembly also voted to not combine this policy statement with the policy statement on Homelessness. This policy statement also supersedes the policy statement on Housing approved by the Delegate Assembly in 1984 and reconfirmed by the Assembly in 1990. For further information, contact the National Association of Social Workers, 750 First Street, NE, Suite 700, Washington, DC 20002-4241. Telephone: 202-408-8600 or 800-638-8799; e-mail: press@naswdc.org

Immigrants and Refugees

BACKGROUND

International migration is substantially changing the demographic profile of many communities across the United States. Immigration increased rapidly in the 1990s, when more than 13 million people moved to the United States. Throughout our national history, policies on immigrants and refugees have been influenced by the competing values and themes of humanitarian response, human rights, national security, and economics. At different points, one or more of these themes have gained ascendancy and brought about changes in immigration laws, affecting the lives of those within and outside U.S. borders.

Current Migration Statistics

As of 2006, approximately 31 million residents in the United States were foreign-born. Of these, most were either lawful permanent residents or naturalized citizens (60 percent); refugees and asylees made up another 7 percent; however, an estimated 29 percent were undocumented (U.S. Census Bureau, 2006). Representation by foreign-born individuals in the U.S. population—11 percent in 2006—is expected to increase.

The demographic picture shows that noncitizen households are far more likely to contain children (55 percent compared with 35 percent) and that 85 percent of immigrant families with children are so-called "mixed-status" families—a situation whereby members of the same family may include various combinations of citizens and noncitizens; for example, undocumented parents, citizen children, and undocumented siblings (Fix & Zimmerman, 1999). These families present distinct challenges for

human services providers in the face of recent federal, state, and local legislation that has sought to restrict substantially the legal and social rights of immigrants ("Problems facing immigrant families," 2002). Many immigrant populations remain invisible or marginally recognized.

History of Immigration Policy in the United States

In 1965 the Immigration and Nationality Act Amendments (P.L. 89-236) provided a sweeping change in immigration law. The national origins system was abolished and a new set of priorities for admitting immigrants was adopted. Priority was given to family members of U.S. citizens and permanent residents and to those with skills needed by the U.S. labor market (Drachman, 1995). Race and country of origin were removed as criteria for admission, which provided the foundation for an increase in immigration. Laws passed in the 1980s and 1990s largely reflected concern with the economic impact of immigration and led to the Immigrant Reform and Control Act of 1986 (P.L. 99-603), that introduced employer sanctions for hiring undocumented individuals. However, the act also provided for legalization of several million undocumented immigrants.

Of special concern to social workers in the child welfare system and those who work with victims of family violence, the Immigration Act of 1990 (P.L. 101-649) allowed eligible immigrant children and youths in long-term foster care to adjust their immigration status and become permanent residents. This immigration relief process is known as Special Immigrant

Juvenile Status and must be undertaken before the child turns 21 or ages out of care. Likewise, the Violence Against Women Act of 1990 allows certain eligible immigrant spouses and their children who are victims of domestic violence to apply for legal permanent residency.

Although legislative changes at the federal level in 1996 instituted immigration status as a category determining eligibility for certain types of benefits and services, the Illegal Immigration Reform and Immigrant Responsibility Act of 1996 (P.L. 104-208) and the Antiterrorism and Effective Death Penalty Act of 1996 (P.L. 104-132) both contain deportation provisions that can have devastating effects nationally and internationally at both the family and societal levels. These laws redefined deportable offenses and retroactively reclassified minor offenses as felonies. Deportable offenses include convictions for domestic violence and child abuse or neglect (Medina, 1997). The laws also removed the right to judicial review in many deportation cases and authorized "expedited removal" of people who arrive at the U.S. border without proper documents.

The terrorist attacks of September 11, 2001, ignited national security concerns, and the Uniting and Strengthening America by Providing Appropriate Tools Required to Intercept and Obstruct Terrorism Act of 2001 (USA PATRIOT ACT) (P.L. 107-56) allowed the government to "impose guilt by association on immigrants; authorize the indefinite lock up of aliens on mere suspicion . . . and the use of secret evidence in immigration proceedings that aliens cannot confront or rebut" (p. 620). Young Muslim men and those who appeared to be of Middle Eastern origin were particularly targeted with special registration requirements. The Immigration and Naturalization Service was reorganized as the U.S. Citizenship and Immigration Services under the newly created Department of Homeland Security (Snyder, May, Zulcic, & Gabbard, 2005).

Admissions of Refugees and Asylum Seekers

A *refugee* is defined as a person with a "well-founded fear of persecution on the basis of race, religion, nationality, membership in a particular social group or political opinion" (Capps, 2006). Historically, U.S. policy has favored involvement in conflicts in Europe over those in Africa and other developing parts of the world. Refugee policy reflects both important humanitarian efforts and foreign policy priorities. This has been particularly played out in the contrast between treatment of Cubans and Haitians; whereas the former have been welcomed as refugees, Haitians, labeled "economic refugees," are not official refugees under U.S. law, are interdicted at sea, and quickly returned to Haiti (Newland & Grieco, 2004).

In March 2002 the Division of Unaccompanied Children's Services (DUCS) program was brought under the auspices of the Office of Refugee Resettlement. The Unaccompanied Refugee Minors Program provides specialized resettlement and foster care services for refugee minors who either have no living relative overseas or whose family situation breaks down soon after arrival. The DUCS program may also receive minors under the age of 18 who enter the United States alone and are undocumented, are victims of trafficking, or fit some other categories of eligibility for reclassification as refugee minors.

Immigrant Policy

Immigrant policy consists of laws, regulations, and programs that affect immigrants' access to health and human services (Siegel & Kappaz, 2002). Since the passage of the Personal Responsibility and Work Opportunity Reconciliation Act of 1996 (P.L. 104-193), only a categorical group of qualified immigrants has been entitled to receive assistance from federal benefits programs. Furthermore, all new legal immigrants were barred, for a period of five years, from accessing federal means-tested benefits, including TANF, Medicaid, and the Child Health Insurance Program, while states were given the option to define to what extent they wished to pursue these categorical distinctions for immigrants to access state aid programs. The unintended consequence of this policy is that many immigrant families have not accessed services to which they are legally entitled (Fix & Zimmerman, 1999). As a result, immigrant families and their children are disproportionately poor and lack adequate health care, food, and shelter (Capps et al., 2002).

ISSUE STATEMENT

"Migration is an important, complex and multi-dimensional issue" (Global Migration Group, 2006). The Universal Declaration of Human Rights (United Nations, 1948) and subsequent treaties recognize the right to leave one's country as a basic human right when stating, "Everyone has the right to leave any country, including his own, and to return to his country." However, there is no corresponding principle of a right to enter. Isbister (1996) referred to immigration policies as "inherently immoral" because they require choices between competing goods or competing evils and often involve the protection of privilege. Deciding whether priority should be given to refugees fleeing oppression, reuniting a long-separated immigrant family, or whether amnesty should be granted to undocumented people rather than increasing entry for those who obey the laws are moral and ethical policy dilemmas.

Often, social workers' capacity to assist clients is constrained by immigration policies, especially policies that limit family visitation and family reunification. Immigration policies intervene in social work practice when family offenses become grounds for deportation and thereby impede willingness to report. The impact on families can be devastating; marital partners have been separated and parents have been deported, leaving their U.S.-born citizen children without support or parental supervision (Segal & Mayadas, 2005). Furthermore, although security concerns dictate restrictive procedures for entry into this country, the challenge is to determine the reasonable balance between security and human rights. The United Nations Declaration on the Human Rights of Individuals Who Are Not Nationals of the Country in which They Live (Office of the United Nations High Commissioner for Human Rights, 1985), specifically

states that aliens shall enjoy "the right to life and security of person; no alien shall be subjected to arbitrary arrest or detention" (Article 5:1). Procedures to protect security should be within the guidelines of basic human rights protections.

Throughout U.S. history, conflicting views about the economic effects of immigration have shaped immigration policies. One view defines immigrants as a drain on the economy and users of public benefits who take needed jobs away from Americans; the opposing view sees immigrants as enhancing the economy through payment of taxes, investment in small businesses, and reinvigoration of the rapidly aging U.S. native-born population (Capps, Passel, Perez-Lopez, & Fix, 2003). Although studies show a positive economic effect, and some credit relatively high immigration with strengthening the U.S. economic position vis-à-vis western Europe and Japan ("U.S. Immigration," 2001), Isbister (1996) cautioned that high rates of immigration may harm low-income Americans.

Current debates about possible guest worker programs or provisions to legalize segments of the undocumented population raise additional policy questions. Policies must be developed that address the situation of long-term resident undocumented families, many of whom have U.S. citizen children. At the same time precautions must be taken to address the fairness implications for those who "played by the rules" and entered the United States through legal channels. Special care must be taken in the design of guest worker programs not to tie immigrants to potentially abusive or exploitative employers.

Social workers will undoubtedly encounter immigrants and their children in schools, health and mental health care, child welfare, and other human service-related settings (Earner & Rivera, 2005; Matthews & Ewen, 2006; Reardon-Anderson, Capps, & Fix, 2002). Social workers not only need to be aware of the special needs of this population, but also need to understand the dynamics of migration and the interface between immigration and immigrant policies (Drachman, 1995; Padilla, 1997).

POLICY STATEMENT

NASW supports federal, state, and local policies and procedures that

■ provide support for victims of the African slave trade, internally displaced people, and victims of trafficking.

■ expand research on the dynamics of migration, especially as it relates to social work practice.

■ fairly and equally apply the definition of migration to all populations, including those caught up by armed conflict.

■ uphold and support equity and human rights for immigrants and refugees, while at the same time protecting national security.

■ promote social justice and avoid racism and discrimination or profiling on the basis of race, religion, country of origin, gender, sexual orientation, or other grounds.

■ ensure due process for all individuals, including immigrants.

■ guarantee the human service and education needs of all children are met regardless of their or their parent's legal status.

■ promote training of social workers and other human services providers on the effect of immigration status on access to human services.

■ ensure access to language-appropriate services in the form of interpreters, translated documents, and other resources as needed.

■ provide for the alleviation of economic and political conditions that force people to flee their homes and ensure that victims of human conflict in the poorest, least strategically important countries of the world do not continue to be ignored.

■ replace the current patchwork of immigration laws and procedures with a fair, equitable, and comprehensive national plan.

■ support restoration of federal and state entitlements for legal immigrants.

■ ensure access to emergency health and mental health care for all immigrants.

■ ensure appropriate immigration-related services to undocumented minors in foster care and, if they are eligible, adjustment of their status before they leave foster care.

■ ensure access to higher education for the children of immigrants.

■ provide for efforts to remove penalties on the children of undocumented immigrants for their parents' actions.

■ promote knowledge of immigration and immigrant issues as a factor in culturally competent service provision.

■ protect all immigrants from family violence, including the undocumented, with provisions to protect women from gender-specific forms of violence.

■ ensure fair treatment and due process in accordance with international human rights for all asylum seekers.

■ remove offenses of domestic violence, child abuse and neglect, and child abandonment from the category of automatically deportable offenses, to ensure reporting, protection, and safeguarding the long-term family preservation rights of children.

■ continue guarantee of citizenship for those born in the United States.

■ ensure and affirm English-access legislation.

■ oppose mandatory reporting of immigration status by health, mental health, social service, education, police, and other public service providers.

■ ensure procedures and policies do not target immigrants solely on the basis of country of origin, religion, or race.

■ support the human rights of day laborers.

■ support immunity from deportation for those who report substantiated incidents of severe employment abuses or criminal activities.

■ support humanitarian measures to protect victims of and enforcement to prevent human trafficking.

■ eliminate backlogs and lengthy delays in processing of immigration status and related applications.

• provide reasonable student, temporary, and transit visa regulations and processes that welcome and encourage international intellectual exchange.

• provide adequate U.S. contributions to refugee assistance globally through support of the UNHCR budget and other aid programs.

• provide fair refugee admissions policies and priorities that respond to human emergencies, including review of policies such as interdiction at sea that violate international human rights law.

• provide refugee resettlement programs adequate in length and substance to include English language training, trauma and mental health counseling, and job readiness and placement.

• restore the right to judicial review and modification of expedited removal provisions, especially for those claiming the right to asylum.

Although daunting, the challenges of working toward fair and just immigration and refugee policies are appropriate for the profession of social work. Social workers must promote greater education and awareness of the dynamics of global migration and of the impact of U.S. and other countries' immigration and foreign policies on human well-being and world peace and stability.

REFERENCES

Antiterrorism and Effective Death Penalty Act of 1996, P.L. 104-132, 110 Stat. 1214.

Capps, R. (2006, July 24–26). *The demography of U.S. children of immigrants.* Presentation at Migration and Child Welfare Roundtable, American Humane Association; Loyola University, Chicago.

Capps, R., Ku, L., Fix, M. E., Furgiuele, C., Passel, J. S., Ramchand, R., McNiven, S., & Perez-Lopez, D. (2002). *How are immigrants faring after welfare reform? Preliminary evidence from Los Angeles and New York City—Final report.* Washington, DC: Urban Institute.

Capps, R., Passel, J. S., Perez-Lopez, D., & Fix, M. (2003). *The new neighbors: A user's guide to data on immigrants in U.S. communities.* Washington, DC: Urban Institute.

Drachman, D. (1995). Immigration statuses and their influence on service provision, access, and use. *Social Work, 40,* 188–197.

Earner, I., & Rivera, H. (2005). Special edition: Immigrants and refugees in child welfare. *Journal of Child Welfare, 84,* 531–536.

Fix, M. E., & Zimmerman, W. (1999). *All under one roof: Mixed-status families in an era of reform.* Washington, DC: Urban Institute.

Global Migration Group. (2006). *Global migration group.* Retrieved September 18, 2007, from http://www.un.int/iom/GMGFlyer.pdf

Illegal Immigration Reform and Immigrant Responsibility Act of 1996, P.L. 104-208, 110 Stat. 3009-546.

Immigration Act of 1990, P.L. 101-649, 104 Stat. 4978.

Immigration and Nationality Act Amendments, P.L. 89-236, 79 Stat. 911 to 920 (1965).

Immigration Reform and Control Act of 1986, P.L. 99-603, 100 Stat. 3359.

Isbister, J. (1996). *The immigration debate: Remaking America.* West Hartford, CT: Kumarian Press.

Matthews, H., & Ewen, D. (2006). *Reaching all children? Understanding early care and education participation among immigrant families.* Washington, DC: Center for Law and Social Policy.

Medina, I. (1997). Judicial review—A nice thing? Article III, separation of powers and the Illegal Immigration Reform and Immigrant Responsibility Act of 1996. *Connecticut Law Review, 29,* 1525–1563.

Newland, K., & Grieco, E. (2004). *Haiti and the United States: Connected by crisis. A migration information source spotlight.* Retrieved September 18, 2007, from http://www.migrationpolicy.org/news/2004_04_05.php

Office of the United Nations High Commissioner for Human Rights. (1985). *Declaration on the human rights of individuals who are not nationals of the country in which they live.* Retrieved September 18, 2007, from http://www.ohchr.org/english/law/individual.htm

Padilla, Y. C. (1997). Immigrant policy: Issues for social work practice. *Social Work, 42,* 595–606.

Personal Responsibility and Work Opportunity Reconciliation Act of 1996, P.L. 104-193, 110 Stat. 2105.

Problems facing immigrant families in the child welfare system: Hearing before the New York State Assembly Standing Committee on Children and Families and New York State Assembly Legislative Task Force on New Americans (2002, July 11). (Testimony of Jennifer Baum and Barrie L. Goldstein, The Legal Aid Society).

Reardon-Anderson, J., Capps, R., & Fix, M. E. (2002). *The health and well-being of children in immigrant families.* Washington, DC: Urban Institute.

Segal, U. A., & Mayadas, N. S. (2005). Assessment of issues facing immigrant and refugee families. *Journal of Child Welfare, 84,* 563–583.

Siegel, W. L., & Kappaz, C. M. (2002). *Strengthening Illinois' immigrant policy: Improving health and human services for immigrants and refugees* [Project report of the Health and Human Services Immigrant Policy Working Group]. Chicago: Illinois Immigrant Policy.

Snyder, C. S., May, J. D., Zulcic, N. H., & Gabbard, W. J. (2005). Social work with Bosnian Muslim refugee children and families: A review of the literature. *Child Welfare, 74,* 607–630.

United Nations. (1948). *Universal declaration of human rights.* Retrieved September 18, 2007, from http://www.un.org/Overview/rights.html

Uniting and Strengthening America by Providing Appropriate Tools Required to Intercept and Obstruct Terrorism Act of 2001 (USA PATRIOT Act), P.L. 107-56, 115 Stat. 272.

U.S. Census Bureau. (2006). *The foreign-born population in 2004.* Retrieved September 18, 2007, from http://www.census.gov/population/pop-profile/dynamic/ForeignBorn.pdf

U.S. immigration at the beginning of the 21st century: Testimony before the Subcommittee on Immigration of the U.S. House of Representatives and Claims Hearing on "The U.S. Population and Immigration" Committee on the Judiciary U.S. House of Representatives (2001, August 2) (testimony of Michael E. Fix and Jeffrey S. Passel, the Urban Institute). Retrieved November 19, 2007, from http://www.urban.org/publications/900417.html

Policy statement approved by the NASW Delegate Assembly, August 2008. This policy statement supersedes the policy statement on Immigrants and Refugees approved by the Delegate Assembly in 2005 and 1996 and referred by the 2002 Delegate Assembly to the 2005 Delegate Assembly for revision. For further information, contact the National Association of Social Workers, 750 First Street, NE, Suite 700, Washington, DC 20002-4241. Telephone: 202-408-8600 or 800-638-8799; e-mail: press@naswdc.org

International Policy on Human Rights

BACKGROUND

History of Human Rights

From the Babylonian *Code of Hammurabi* (1750 B.C.E.) to the present, there is written evidence of humanity's struggle to protect the rights of vulnerable people from exploitation by more powerful individuals, groups, or the state itself. Social justice concepts appeared in the writings of Confucius (551–479 B.C.E.) and the ancient Greeks (4th century B.C.E.). The Romans recognized the need to protect individuals from the potential abuses of political authority; from its origins in the 7th century, Islam valued the sanctity of human life and the right to seek justice. Closer to our roots in the Western world, the Hebrew and Christian scriptures spoke of the inherent dignity and worth of the person and equality under the law. Great Britain's *Magna Carta* (1215) referred to the values of human dignity and justice, while affirming the notion that a ruler has an obligation to serve society. The 17th and 18th centuries gave birth to notions of natural rights, the social contract, the limitations of state powers, and the rights of people to rebel if their rights were trampled (Falk, 2005; Laqueur & Rubin, 1979; Lauren, 1998; McKinney & Park-Cunningham, 1997; Wronka, 1995, 1998).

The U.S. *Declaration of Independence* [1776], and *Bill of Rights* [1791], and the French *Declaration of the Rights of Man and the Citizen* [1936] clearly articulated a set of political rights, including the rights to life, liberty, and the pursuit of happiness; freedom of speech, the press, and religion; property rights; and the right to a trial by jury. During the 19th century, women's rights and the rights of ethnic and cultural minority groups were developed (Laqueur &

Rubin, 1979). The human rights perspective thus has roots in the religious, political, and intellectual traditions of many cultures. Crossing cultural boundaries, human rights identify the essential qualities of life for all people everywhere that must be valued and protected.

In response to the horrors of the Holocaust, under the leadership of Eleanor Roosevelt, representatives of the nations of the world came together to find a way to prevent such an event from ever happening again. The first step was the *Universal Declaration of Human Rights*, which was presented in 1948 to the U.N. General Assembly and the world as a foundation document upon which an edifice of protections for human rights could be built. This document has become the standard reference for all subsequent United Nations human rights efforts. It has heralded the inherent dignity and equal and inalienable rights of both male and female adults and children as members of the human family. Human rights were defined from the start to include the universal right to a standard of living that is adequate for the health and well-being of individuals and their families. The document spells out the essential resources to meet such a standard—food, clothing, housing, and medical care. It calls for the right to security in the event of unemployment, sickness, disability, widowhood, old age, or other circumstances beyond one's control. And it calls for "necessary social services" (United Nations, 1948, Article 25, 1).

The *Declaration* is distinctive in that it gave the world, for the first time in history, the right to ask of sovereign nations questions that were previously considered to be their internal affairs. By 1990 the document had become customary international law. Now even nonmember nations, however reluctantly, recognize that the world should not turn its back on social and humanitarian concerns within their borders (Wetzel, 1993, 1998).

Since the Universal Declaration of Human Rights was developed in 1948, more than 100 U.N. human rights instruments have been ratified, providing an even stronger legal mandate to protect human rights and fulfill human needs (Office of the United Nations High Commissioner for Human Rights, 2007). The most fundamental and general U.N. human rights instruments include the following:

■ the Charter of the United Nations (1945)

■ the Universal Declaration of Human Rights (1948)

■ the two Covenants on Human Rights (1966)

   1. International Covenant on Civil and Political Rights (the right to life, liberty, and security; the right not to be subjected to cruel, inhuman, or degrading treatment, or punishment; prohibition of slavery; and the right not to be detained arbitrarily)

   2. International Covenant on Economic, Social and Cultural Rights (the right to work, right to social security, right to protection of the family, and the right to an adequate standard of living).

■ There are also a number of U.N. human rights instruments (United Nations, 1994) that address the needs of specific groups, among them: the International Convention on the Elimination of All Forms of Racial Discrimination (1965); the Convention on the Elimination of All Forms of Discrimination against Women (1981); the Convention against Torture and Other Cruel, Inhuman and Degrading Treatment or Punishment (1984); the Convention on the Rights of the Child (1996); and the International Convention on the Protection of the Rights of All Migrant Workers and Members of Their Families (1990).

The United States ratified the Covenant on Civil and Political Rights in 1966, but it has never ratified the Covenant on Economic, Social and Cultural Rights, a fact that explains much about the absence of support for social legislation in this country. For example, education, housing, health care, income maintenance, and child care are not considered human rights in the United States. Neither has the United States ratified the Convention on the Elimination of All Forms of Discrimination against Women or the Convention on the Rights of the Child, two documents that call into question the most recent erosion of economic support and social services. These documents are essential to the human development and quality of life of people in the United States, as well as in other nations.

Link with Social Work

When the Universal Declaration of Human Rights was ratified, human rights concerns had been the bedrock of the social work profession in the United States for more than 50 years. Discrimination and social exclusion based on racial and religious intolerance; gender inequality and violence; denial of the rights of women and children, refugees, and older people—all are social justice issues that long have concerned social work (Wetzel, 1993, 1998; Wronka, 1995, 1998). Social workers know that civil and political rights must be supplemented by economic, social, and cultural rights. Social work, with its person-in-environment perspective, is vividly aware of the deleterious effects of human rights violations on the development of individuals, families, and communities. Social workers, on whatever level they practice, advocate for people's rights to have paid employment, adequate food, education, shelter, health care, as well as the right to freedom from violence and freedom to pursue their dreams (Hokenstad & Midgley, 1997; United Nations, 1995; Wetzel, 1993).

But the realization of social work's professional social justice goals and aspirations, like the United Nation's, is in evolution. NASW (1981), the Council on Social Work Education (2002), the International Federation of Social Workers (IFSW, 1996), the International Association of Schools of Social Work (1996), and United Nations (1993), have all acknowledged the importance of a global human rights perspective, the fact is, the profession does not fully use human rights as a criterion with which to evaluate social work policies, practice, research, and program priorities (Ife, 2001).

According to the Preamble to the NASW *Code of Ethics* (NASW, 2000), "the primary mission of the social work profession is to enhance human well-being and help meet the basic human needs of all people, with particular attention to the needs and empowerment of people who are vulnerable, oppressed, and living in poverty" (p. 1).

ISSUE STATEMENT

Human rights violations are prevalent throughout the world, including the United States. Civilians are injured, maimed, and killed in times of conflict, far outnumbering military personnel. Refugees and immigrants are fleeing their countries in record numbers. Women everywhere continue to be treated as second-class citizens and subjected to violence in epidemic proportions. The social situation of children and elderly people alike is of grave concern the world over and appears to be deteriorating. There has been a resurgence of violence and oppression against ethnic and racial minority groups, and against lesbian, gay, bisexual, and transgender people in many regions of our globe, and poverty is endemic, fueling the fires of unrest and making a sham of the very concept of human rights. The U.S. government's repeated insistence from 2001 through 2008 (Amnesty USA AI Index: AMR 2008) on redefining torture to allow practices disallowed by the Geneva Convention is an example of eroding human rights values (U.S. Department of Justice, 2002). Because the United States is the most powerful nation on earth, our policies and practices influence and affect not only our own people, but also those in developed and developing countries. The National Association of Social Workers is the most influential professional social work body in the world. Its effectiveness in the 21st century will depend on the extension of its social justice values within the context of global human rights.

The events of the 20th and 21st centuries demonstrate that the struggle for human rights goes on. For example,

■ events such as wars, genocide, and ethnic cleansing; discrimination and social exclusion based on race, ethnicity, caste, or religious identity; gender inequality, battering, rape, and the sale of women; child abuse; sweatshops, child labor, and slavery

■ suppression of the rights of ethnic and cultural minority groups, migrants, refugees, asylum seekers, indigenous peoples, older people, and people with mental and physical disabilities; and terrorism

■ denial of access to clean water, adequate nutrition, shelter, and health care; and environmental degradation

■ recognizing that the death penalty has not been found to be a deterrent to violent crime and that it provides inhumane and degrading punishment, as well as an irreversible act regardless of proven innocence at a later date.

Common Values and Mission

"Human rights condenses into two words the struggle for dignity and fundamental freedoms which allow the full development of human potential" (IFSW, 1996). The human rights value base, which has been articulated throughout history in religious texts and legal documents, in political writings and those of philosophers and social activists, parallels the values put forth in NASW's *Code of Ethics* (NASW, 2000) (especially, social justice and dignity and worth of the person) and the ethical principles that flow from those values. The *Code's* Ethical Standard 6.01 states that "social workers should promote the general welfare of society, from local to global levels, and the development of people, their communities, and their environments" (p. 26). Furthermore, social workers are urged to act to prevent and eliminate domination, exploitation, and discrimination.

The aim of the human rights edifice created during the past half century, which includes United Nations' declarations and treaties; UN administrative bodies; and regional, governmental, and nongovernmental organizations, is to root out oppression and to establish conditions in which human beings can meet their needs, develop their humanity, and flourish. This aim is closely akin to social work's mission.

Social work can be proud of its heritage. It is the only profession imbued with social justice as its fundamental value and concern. But social justice is a fairness doctrine that provides civil and political leeway in deciding what is just and unjust. Human rights, on the other hand, encompasses social justice, but transcends civil and political customs. It takes into consideration the basic life-sustaining needs of all human beings, without distinction.

Common Roles in Society

The human rights movement was formally recognized by the global community to identify barriers to the protection of human rights and to set up policies and procedures to abolish such barriers and thereby guarantee that human dignity and essential freedoms are protected for every person. Similarly, social work is expected by society to address the needs of people who are vulnerable to the vicissitudes of social life, while working toward establishing a more just society. The United Nations declarations, conventions, and treaties provide a human rights template. Social work can provide a biopsychosocial, body of knowledge gleaned from more than 100 years of experience to bring life to such a plan, grounding human rights in the everyday lives of the people (Wetzel, 1998).

POLICY STATEMENT

As social work practitioners and advocates of human rights, NASW's position is

■ to endorse the principle that the rights of people take precedence over social customs when those customs infringe on human rights. Ritual female genital mutilation, a practice that persists internationally despite governmental sanctions, is a case in point.

■ to promote U.S. ratification of the Universal Declaration of Human Rights; critical UN treaties, such as the Covenant on Economic, Social and Cultural Rights (1966); the Convention on the Elimination of All Forms of Discrimination Against Women (1981); and the Convention on the Rights of the Child (1996).

■ to be especially vigilant about human rights violations related to children's rights and exploitation such as child labor, child prostitution, and other crimes of abuse and to take leadership in developing public and professional awareness regarding the issues.

■ to endorse the UN resolution that women's rights are human rights, no longer simply to be considered civil and political rights.

■ to advocate for the rights of vulnerable people and to condemn policies, practices, and attitudes of bigotry, intolerance, and hate that put any person's human rights in grave jeopardy. The violation of human rights on the basis of race, ethnicity, gender, gender identity or expression, sexual orientation, age, disability, immigration status, or religion are examples.

■ the support of the right to a standard of living that is adequate for the health and well-being of all people and their families, without exception, and the essential resources to meet such a standard; adequate housing; basic health care; education; security in the event of unemployment, sickness, disability, widowhood, old age, or other lack of livelihood beyond one's control; and necessary social services.

■ to support the right not to be subjected to dehumanizing treatment and punishment.

■ to advocate the elimination of the death penalty.

■ to work in collaboration with nongovernmental organizations and community groups when entitlements are nonexistent or inadequately implemented and to become a leading force for the health and welfare of all people, including the world's most vulnerable.

■ to continue our work with the United Nations in advancing human development and human rights, including economic human rights and closing the economic gap.

- to work for the eradication of modern-day slavery and growing incidence of human trafficking.

- to advocate for the elimination of the practice of torture.

- to advocate for policies within the U.S. government in its methods of providing homeland security and combating terrorism that are consistent with human rights values and ethics.

The struggle for human rights remains a vital priority for the social work profession in the 21st century.

REFERENCES

Amnesty USA. (2008, June 13). *USA: Time for real change as Supreme Court rules on Guantanamo detentions.* Retrieved from www.amnestyusa.org/document.php?id=ENGAMR510612008&lang=e

Council on Social Work Education. (2002). *Educational policy and accreditation standards.* Alexandria, VA: Author.

Falk, D. S. (2005). *Human rights in global perspective.* Course outline and website. In R. J. Link, and L. M. Healy (Eds.), *Teaching international content: Curriculum resources for social work education* (pp. 103–109). Alexandria, VA: Council on Social Work Education.

Hokenstad, M. C., & Midgley, J. (Eds.). (1997). *Issues in international social work: Global challenges for a new century.* Washington, DC: NASW Press.

Ife, J. (2001). *Human rights and social work: Towards rights-based practice.* Cambridge, England: Cambridge University Press.

International Association of Schools of Social Work & International Federation of Social Workers. (1994). *Human rights and social work: A manual for schools of social work and the social work professions.* Professional training series. United Nations Centre for Human Rights: Geneva and New York.

International Federation of Social Workers. (1996). *International policy on human rights.* Retrieved October 20, 2007, from http://www.ifsw.org/en/p38000212.html

Laqueur, W., & Rubin, B. (Eds.). (1979). *The human rights reader.* Philadelphia: Temple University Press.

Lauren, P. G. (1998). *The evolution of international human rights: Visions seen.* Philadelphia: University of Pennsylvania Press.

McKinney, C. M., & Park-Cunningham, R. (1997, Spring). Evolution of the social work profession: An historical review of the U.S. and selected countries, 1995. In *Proceedings: 28th Annual Conference, New York State Social Work Education Association* (pp. 3–9). Syracuse: New York State Social Work Education Association.

National Association of Social Workers. (1981). *International policy on human rights.* [NASW Delegate Assembly Proceedings]. Washington, DC: Author.

National Association of Social Workers. (2000). *Code of ethics of the National Association of Social Workers.* Washington, DC: NASW Press.

Office of the United Nations High Commissioner for Human Rights. (2007). *International law.* Retrieved June 22, 2007, from http://www.ohchr.org/english/law/

United Nations. (1948). *Universal declaration of human rights.* New York: Author.

United Nations. (1993). *Declaration on the elimination of violence against women.* New York: Author.

United Nations. (1994). *Human rights and social work: A manual for schools of social work and the social work profession* (Professional Training Series No. 4). New York and Geneva: Author.

United Nations. (1995). *The United Nations and human rights: 1945–1995.* New York: U.N. Department of Public Information.

U.S. Department of Justice, Office of Legal Counsel. (2002). Memorandum for Alberto R. Gonzales Counsel to the President Re: Standards of conduct for interrogation under 18 U.S.C. 2340-2340A. Retrieved June 22, 2007, from http://www.washingtonpost.com/wp-srv/nation/documents/dojinterrogationmemo20020801.pdf

Wetzel, J. W. (1993). *The world of women: In pursuit of human rights.* London: Macmillan.

Wetzel, J. W. (1998). *Human rights values: An international challenge to social work.* Paper presented at the 15th Annual Social Work Day at the United Nations, New York, March 25; at the International Association of Schools of Social Work symposium, Council of Social Work Education Annual Program Meeting, Orlando, FL, March 8; at the University of Texas "Celebrate International Social Work," Austin, March 27.

Wronka, J. (1995). Human rights. In R. L. Edwards (Ed.-in-Chief), *Encyclopedia of social work* (19th ed., Vol. 1, pp. 1405–1418). Washington, DC: NASW Press.

Wronka, J. (1998). *Human rights and social policy in the 21st century: A history of the idea of human rights and comparison of the United Nations Universal Declaration of Human Rights with United States federal and state constitutions* (rev. ed.). Lanham, MD: University Press of America.

SUGGESTED READINGS

Reichert, E. (2003). *Social work and human rights: A foundation for policy and practice.* New York: Columbia University Press.

Reichert, E. (2006). *Understanding human rights: An exercise book.* Thousand Oaks, CA: Sage Publications.

Reichert, E. (Ed.). (2007). *Challenges in human rights: A social work perspective.* New York: Columbia University Press.

Tessitore, J., & Woolfson, S. (Eds.). (1997). *A global agenda: Issues before the 52nd General Assembly of the United Nations.* New York: Rowman & Littlefield.

Wetzel, J. W. (2001). Human rights in the 20th century: Weren't gays and lesbians human? In M. E. Swigonski & R. Mama (Eds.), *From hate crimes to human rights: Resources for lesbian, gay & bisexual empowerment & social action—A tribute to Matthew Shepard* (pp. 15–31). Binghamton, NY: Haworth Press.

Policy statement approved by the NASW Delegate Assembly, August 2008. This policy statement supersedes the policy statement on International Policy on Human Rights approved by the Delegate Assembly in 1999 and referred by the 2005 Delegate Assembly to the 2008 Delegate Assembly for revision. For further information, contact the National Association of Social Workers, 750 First Street, NE, Suite 700, Washington, DC 20002-4241. Telephone: 202-408-8600 or 800-638-8799; e-mail: press@naswdc.org

Juvenile Justice and Delinquency Prevention

BACKGROUND

The plight of children and youths has been a major concern to people in social work, from the earliest social reformers to the current professional organization. When the British settled the United States, children were subject to the same rules as adults concerning criminal responsibility. It did not take long for early reformers to realize it was neither humane nor effective to treat children and youths in the same manner as adults.

The treatment of children and adults became separate with the opening of the first juvenile court in Cook County, Illinois, in 1899. The philosophy of differentiating children and adult justice system treatment rapidly spread throughout the country. The first juvenile court judge in Denver, Judge Benjamin Lindsay, described the new role of the courts as follows: "The purpose of this institution . . . was not to punish people, but to save them. If they could only be saved by punishment, it would punish, but not otherwise. . . . Revenge would be no part of the program. Its work would be medicinal, restorative" (National Council of Juvenile and Family Court Judges [NCJFCJ], 1998, p. 6).

Slightly more than 100 years later, the juvenile court function has been challenged, and the juvenile justice system is in complete disarray. Criticism of the juvenile justice system actually began as early as the 1930s and 1940s because of the failure of the courts to rehabilitate youths (NCJFCJ, 1998).

The Juvenile Justice and Delinquency Prevention Act (P.L. 93-415) was passed in 1974, but the legislation did not include a commitment of the resources and protections necessary to support the type of system needed in the United States. By the end of the 1970s, any type of progressive philosophy toward the

treatment of troubled children and youths was no longer evident.

States slowly began reducing the age of criminal responsibility for certain crimes. Diversion and treatment decreased as sentences became lengthier. As crime increased in New York and Florida, these states led the nation into a punitive response to delinquent behavior. New York used legislative exclusion from the jurisdiction of the juvenile court to treat juveniles more harshly, whereas Florida developed the mandatory waiver and prosecutorial discretion to direct file juveniles into adult criminal court.

When juvenile crime reportedly increased from 1982 to 1991, the states responded with increasingly punitive action. The statistical picture played a major role in the punitive response of the nation. Recent studies show, in fact, that

> trends in juvenile crime provide no evidence that young people have become more crime prone or dangerous in past years. The juvenile proportion of all arrests for serious, violent crime in 1998 was about average for the preceding 25 years, while the percentage of property crime arrests involving juveniles actually declined. The one category that has diverged significantly is murder. (*The Sentencing Project*, 2001, p. 2)

The result of the changes in the juvenile justice system over the past years has significantly affected the plight of troubled children and youths and the ability of the helping professions to respond in an effective manner. Hurst (as cited in NCJFCJ, 1998) argued that "the death of an individualized justice system for children turns the clock back an entire century" (p. 44).

Now, the United States prosecutes 200,000 youths a year in adult criminal court. Of these youths 180,000 are prosecuted in the 13 states that have established an age of 15 for adult court prosecution. In 1996 more than half of the cases transferred to adult criminal court were nonviolent drug or property offenses (*The Sentencing Project*, 2001).

The effect on the processing of African American youths has been tremendous. The result is that 67 percent of juveniles in adult court are African American. In addition, 77 percent of the juveniles who are sent to adult prison are African American. Despite the fact that African Americans use drugs at a lower rate than other groups, 75 percent of juveniles charged with drug offenses in adult court are African American and 95 percent of the juveniles sentenced to adult prisons for drug offenses are African American (*The Sentencing Project*, 2001). Considering that these youths who are sent to adult prisons are treated as adults, it is no wonder that youths in adult prisons fare much worse than their adult counterparts. Youths are 7.7 times more likely to commit suicide, five times more likely to be sexually assaulted, 50 percent more likely to be physically assaulted by guards, and twice as likely to be attacked with a weapon (*The Sentencing Project*, 2001).

The outcome of the current juvenile justice policies is devastating. The Coalition for Juvenile Justice (2000) reported that 50 percent to 70 percent of the juvenile offenders incarcerated as adults are rearrested one to two years after release. Another outcome is that African American youths are transferred to adult courts at twice the rate as white youths (Office of Juvenile Justice and Delinquency Prevention [OJJDP], 1999). In summary, youths treated as adult criminals are rearrested more often, sooner, and for more serious crimes later on than their youthful counterparts who are treated in a juvenile court setting (National Conference of State Legislatures, 1999).

Children and youths have been treated in an increasingly shameful manner through the decline of our justice system. The outcomes have been alarming enough to warrant a new emphasis on the needed changes in policy and practice within the juvenile justice system.

ISSUE STATEMENT

A review of juvenile justice literature (see Suggested Readings) demonstrates that there are some prominent issues that stand out as a result of trends over the past 10 years. Unfortunately, there has been no national agenda to address these controversial and costly issues. The underlying problem is that the response to a public demand for "tough on crime" policies has been the undermining of the key concept behind the establishment of the juvenile court system. The concept is that children are developmentally different from adults and therefore more amenable to treatment and rehabilitation. The U.S. public policy response to the perceived or real increase in juvenile crime has been on punishment, as opposed to prevention, treatment, and rehabilitation.

The most critical specific issues facing all professionals that deal with children, youths, and their families are as follows:

■ inequitable processing of African American youths through the system, resulting in the overrepresentation of African American youths in the justice system

■ the criminalization of children and youths with special needs

■ inadequate cross-disciplinary system of services

■ the treatment of children and youths in the juvenile justice system as if they were in the adult criminal justice system

■ insufficient early intervention services

■ the use of the death penalty for juveniles

■ inadequate substance abuse and mental health treatment services that are culturally competent.

As social workers, the ability to work effectively with children, youths, families, and communities is seriously affected by these particular issues. Without a system set up to be culturally appropriate and to that effectively assesses and treats youths with disabilities, social workers cannot provide the needed services for troubled children, youths, and families. Furthermore, the profession will continue to come into conflict with the justice system as long as the developmental theory that has traditionally differentiated juvenile and adult treatment needs is undermined.

Notwithstanding the issues identified, the fact that U.S. public policy and practice stands alone in the world in the execution of juveniles continues to place a burden on the work of professional social workers because of their historical belief that juveniles are different from adults and should be treated as such. The lack of priority placed on children and youths in this country, as exemplified by the policy of subjecting people under the age of 18 years to capital punishment, places the United States in a particularly bad light internationally. Social workers are in a unique position, given their training, skills, and ethics, to advocate for more humane and developmentally appropriate responses to juveniles who commit serious crimes including murder (Guin & Merrill, 2002). These issues are the most obvious and alarming trends that demonstrate the ineffectiveness of current juvenile justice policy across the nation.

POLICY STATEMENT

NASW recommends that the processing and treatment of children and youths who enter the juvenile justice system be differentiated from the treatment of adults through every phase of contact, including prevention, early intervention, formal diversion, detention, probation, residential care, incarceration, and postrelease care. NASW supports the fact that children and youths are developmentally different from adults and must be treated appropriately. This overall policy can be programmatically supported through the following priority actions:

■ *Overall system improvement.* There is support for the theory that the treatment of juveniles as adults has increasingly occurred because there are few viable systems of care or a continuum of care that can address the problems of troubled children, predelinquent youths, and delinquent youths. Without an effective and responsive screening, assessment, treatment, and aftercare protocol, children pro-

gressively move through the stages of delinquency development and ongoing adult criminality. This type of failure results in the public perception that a separate juvenile system cannot work. A true system of care would provide for local coordination and oversight to ensure that children and youths do not fall through the cracks. An effective system also would ensure accountability in transfer policies and a more equitable system of processing and treating of African American youths.

■ *Establishment of accountable oversight measures.* Very early in elementary schools or on initial involvement with the juvenile system, accountable oversight measures should be established to prevent the cumulative effect of inequitable treatment of African American youths. Local systems of care must adjust policies and practices within local communities to address systemic causes of bias that propel African American youths into the justice system. Three related problems in the inequitable treatment of African American youths are (1) inadequate defense for indigent juveniles, (2) lack of culturally competent screening and treatment, and (3) lack of family services.

■ *Responsiveness to identified problem.* When a youth enters any phase of the justice system, especially in prevention and diversion programs, assessment, screening, and treatment must be responsive to the problems. Years of research have clearly demonstrated that treatment works, but the treatment has to be appropriate for the diagnosed problem. Program evaluation and accountability are a critical piece to this policy-recommended action.

■ *Hiring of social workers.* NASW advocates, supports, and requires the hiring of professional social work practitioners who have skills in case management, counseling, intake, interviewing, and cross-cultural competency to the needs of youths and families engaged in the juvenile justice system.

■ *Cross-disciplinary services.* Cross-disciplinary services exemplify social work practice and values and provide effective and efficient services to youths and their families. These services include:

- early sustained prevention efforts

- advocacy

- assessment of the person-in-environment and development stages

- communication at all levels (youth, family, and systems)

- knowledge of children's developmental issues

- awareness of the decision-making limitations of children and youths

- access to resources for children and youths

- follow-up services with a continuum of care.

- *Release of information.* Juvenile services systems need to supply the public and policymakers with information on racial disparity and other issues of concern (for example, a youth being tried as an adult and the requirements for optimal professional services; Young, 2000).

- *Replacement of state correctional systems by local systems of community-based care.* Juvenile incarceration should always be the very last resort for dealing with juvenile delinquency. When it has been determined that a youth must enter a correctional facility, there must be an accountable way to measure treatment effectiveness, including the involvement of the family in treatment. In addition NASW promotes tailoring work done with youths according to the individual youth's problems or issues (for example, if they are learning disabled; are substance dependent; have a mental illness; or struggle with gay, lesbian, bisexual, and transgender issues). There is no place in the current climate for the large correctional institutions for youths. These institutions must be replaced with small correctional facilities, located around the state so that no youths are ever more than one hour away from their family. There is little doubt that incarceration of juveniles does very little good without an effective postrelease plan and extensive aftercare programming.

Inasmuch as issues related to poverty are likely to prevent communities from developing these protective factors, NASW encourages the allocation of state and federal funding in partnership with strong community-building efforts to address the housing, living wage employment, and child care issues that have a documented effect on the social organization of disadvantaged neighborhoods. NASW suggests that these community-building bodies be headed and staffed primarily by children, adolescents, parents, citizens, and other lay leaders within those zip codes particularly afflicted by child delinquency (that is, stakeholders, rather than solely administrators). In addition, juvenile system workers need to

- support systematic initiatives in communities across the nation to increase the protective factors that reduce the likelihood of delinquency. Protective factors most closely related to the prevention of juvenile delinquency include strong commitment to school; appropriate levels of parental supervision; association by youths with prosocial peers; and positive bonding with parents, peers, and the community (OJJDP, 2001).

- promote the dissemination of outcomes related to effective juvenile delinquency prevention and diversion initiatives. Promising approaches and best practices that have undergone rigorous evaluation and multiple site replication are published by OJJDP as "Blueprints for Violence Prevention" (Michigan Council on Crime and Delinquency, 2002).

- advocate for fully funded juvenile delinquency prevention, early intervention, and diversion programs throughout the nation.

- include Balanced and Restorative Justice (BARJ) as a critical principle in the application of juvenile justice initiatives. BARJ "promotes increased use of restitution, community service, victim–offender mediation, and other innovative programs designed to hold juvenile offenders accountable and protect the community while, at the same time, developing the competency of juveniles" (OJJDP, 2001, p. 15). When a crime is committed, the parties affected include the victim, the community, and the offender. BARJ requires that offenders take personal responsibility for their actions and then actively work to repair the harm they have caused the community and the victim. It involves the victim, offender, and community in the search for solutions that promote reparation, reconciliation, reassurance, and restoration. BARJ also uses tools of accountability, restitution, mediation, advocacy, support, penitence, and forgiveness to blind bind parties together in a justice process that closes the wounds of crime. Other examples of BARJ include educational programs for offenders and community sentencing.

■ provide age-appropriate treatment when a juvenile is transferred to the adult system. For the youths who are waived to an adult court system and sent to an adult correctional facility, it is highly recommend that treatment continue to be delivered from the perspective of the child. Juveniles need special care and protection in the adult court and prison system, even if their chronological age is legislated to be adult.

The National Association of Social Workers

■ opposes the death penalty for juveniles and the incarceration of all youths younger than age 18 in the adult criminal justice system. The execution of youths under the age of 18 is a violation of many international standards for humane and ethical treatment of children, including the United Nations Convention and Amnesty International. It is important for NASW members to promote the value of children in the United States, even the most troubled children, and to educate the public continuously against executing children younger than 18

■ supports due process and proper representation for all juveniles

■ supports engaging in research that produces effective evidence-based practices.

REFERENCES

Coalition for Juvenile Justice. (2000). *Handle with care: Serving the mental health needs of young offenders, 2000 annual report.* Washington, DC: Author.

Guin, C. C., & Merrill, T. S. (2002). Life or death: Using multidisciplinary life history research in forensic social work. In I. A. Neighbors, A. Chambers, E. Levin, G. Nordman, & C. Tutrone (Eds.), *Social work and the law: Proceedings of the National Organization of Forensic Social Work, 2000* (pp. 78–89). New York: Haworth Press.

Juvenile Justice and Delinquency Prevention Act of 1974, P.L. 93–415, U.S.C. 5601 et seq.

Michigan Council on Crime and Delinquency. (2002, Summer). Best practices. *Council Bulletin,* p. 5.

National Conference of State Legislatures. (1999). *Comprehensive juvenile justice: A legislator's guide, treating juveniles like adult criminals.* Washington, DC: Author.

National Council of Juvenile and Family Court Judges. (1998). *Juvenile and family court journal: A centennial celebration of the juvenile court, 1899–1999* (Vol. 49, No. 4). Reno, NV: Author.

Office of Juvenile Justice and Delinquency Prevention. (1999). *National report series: Minorities in the juvenile justice system.* Washington, DC: U.S. Department of Justice.

Office of Juvenile Justice and Delinquency Prevention. (2001, June). *OJJDP annual report 2000.* Washington, DC: U.S. Department of Justice.

The Sentencing Project: Prosecuting Juveniles in Adult Court [Online]. (2001). Available: www.sentencingproject.org/brief/juveniles.html

Young, M. (2000, August). Providing effective representation for youth prosecuted as adults. *Bureau of Justice Assistance Bulletin.*

SUGGESTED READINGS

American Bar Association. (2001). *Youth in the criminal justice system: Guidelines for policymakers and practitioners.* Washington, DC: ABA Criminal Justice Section & Task Force on Youth in the Criminal Justice System.

Austin, J., Dedel Johnson, K., & Gregoriou, M. (2000, October). Juveniles in adult prisons and jails. *Bureau of Justice Assistance Monograph* (NCJ 182503). Washington, DC: Office of Juvenile Justice and Delinquency Prevention.

Bernard, T. J. (1992). *The cycle of juvenile justice.* New York: Oxford University Press.

Bilchik, S. (1997, July). *Mobilizing communities to prevent juvenile crime.* Washington, DC: U.S. Department of Justice, Office of Juvenile Justice and Delinquency Prevention.

Black youths treated more harshly by juvenile justice system than whites. (2000). *Jet, 97*(23), 37.

Brown, M. P. (1998, January 1). Juvenile offenders: Should they be tried in adult courts? *USA Today Magazine,* 52–55.

Celeste, G., & Puritz, P. (2001). *The children left behind: An assessment of access to counsel and quality of representation in delinquency proceedings in Louisiana.* Washington, DC: American Bar Association.

Cocozza, J. J., & Skowyna, K. R. (2000). Youth with mental health disorders: Issues and emerging responses. *Juvenile Justice, 7*(1), 3–13.

DeFrances, C. J., & Strom, K. J. (1997). *Juveniles prosecuted in state criminal courts.* Washington, DC: U.S. Department of Justice, Office of Juvenile Justice and Delinquency Prevention.

Hatchett, G. (1998). Why we can't wait: The juvenile court in the new millennium. *Crime and Delinquency, 44*(1), 83–88.

Hayes, L. M. (2000). Suicide prevention in juvenile facilities. *Juvenile Justice, 7*(1), 25–34.

Males, M., & Macallair, D. (1999). *Building blocks for youth: The color of justice: An analysis of juvenile adult court transfers in California* [Online]. Available: http://www.cjcj.org/colorofjustice

Maryland Juvenile Justice Coalition. (2001). *Principles of a model juvenile justice system.* Baltimore: Author.

McCord, J., Widom, C. S., & Crowell, N. A. (2001). *Juvenile crime, juvenile justice—Panel on juvenile crime: Prevention, treatment, and control.* Washington, DC: National Academy Press.

Office of Juvenile Justice and Delinquency Prevention. (1999). *National report series: Juveniles, offenders and victims.* Washington, DC: U.S. Department of Justice.

Schmaller, F. (2001). *Criminal justice today* (6th ed.). Englewood Cliffs, NJ: Prentice Hall.

Streib, V. L. (2001). *The juvenile death penalty today: Death sentences and executions for juvenile crimes, January 1, 1973–December 31, 2000.* Ada: Ohio Northern University.

U.S. Public Health Service. (2000). *Report of the Surgeon General's conference on children's mental health: A national action agenda.* Washington, DC: U.S. Department of Health and Human Services.

Wolford, B. I. (2000). *Juvenile justice education: "Who is educating the youth?"* Richmond, KY: Council for Educators of At-Risk and Delinquent Youth.

Policy statement approved by the NASW Delegate Assembly, August 2002. This statement supersedes the policy statement on Juvenile Justice and Adult Crime approved by the Delegate Assembly in 1977, which incorporated portions of the policy statements on Juvenile Delinquency and Adult Crime (approved in 1969) and Prisons and Jails (approved in 1971) and reconfirmed in 1993. For further information, contact the National Association of Social Workers, 750 First Street, NE, Suite 700, Washington, DC 20002-4241. Telephone: 202-408-8600; e-mail: press@naswdc.org

Language and Cultural Diversity in the United States

BACKGROUND

Cultural diversity encompasses the cultural differences that exist between people, such as language, dress and traditions, and the way societies organize themselves, their conception of morality and religion, and the way they interact with the environment (Wikipedia, 2008).

"[E]very human language is an exquisitely complex intellectual masterpiece" (Wilkinson, 2005, p. 361) that expresses the culture that created it. Culture can often influence language, identity, dress, music, and food, as well as problem solving and coping with various life circumstances, and goes far beyond race and ethnicity. Culture can be applied to geographic areas of the country, professions, developmental stages of life, socioeconomic status, sexual orientation, religion and spirituality, and institutions and can even be issue oriented, such as drug or gang cultures (Lopez, 2007).

Different languages represent different ways of thinking about our surroundings and ourselves. "Every language offers a unique insight into the nature of speech and thought" (Vaux, cited in Lewis, 1998, p. A14). As a result of past government policy, many American Indian languages and Alaskan Native languages have become extinct (Native American Languages Act Amendments, 2000). Linguists report that the extinction of a language is a significant loss of knowledge about human achievement and thought (Lewis, 1998). The history of the United States has shown the significant contributions to the development of this country by the African Americans, American Indians, Asian Americans and Pacific Islanders, and Hispanic/Latino peoples. One example of this was the use of Navajo and other tribal code talkers in World War II. They were greatly responsible for shortening the war and for winning the Pacific by using a language code that could not be broken. There are more than 6,900 languages spoken in the world today, but 90 percent of them are spoken by fewer than 100,000 people, and some languages are even rarer—46 are known to have just one native speaker. "There are 357 languages with under 50 speakers," said Professor Bill Sutherland, a population biologist at the University of East Anglia in Norwich (Connor, 2003). Indigenous cultures and immigration have deeply transformed the racial and ethnic composition of the United States. Ethnic minorities currently compose approximately one-third of the population of the United States (Russell Searight & Gafford, 2005).

The growth of the Latino population has been the fastest rate of any major racial category, and in 2006 the Latino population made up nearly 4 percent of the U.S. population (U.S. Census Bureau, 2006). In 2006, the total population of the United States surpassed the 300 million mark (Lelchuck, 2006) and the percentage of people who speak a language other than English at home has increased to 17.9 percent (U.S. Census Bureau, 2000). Similarly, in 2003 the percentage of people five years and older who speak English less than very well was 8.4 percent of the total census population (U.S. Census Bureau, 2003).These demographic shifts have affected the care and services provided by health and human services providers.

The past several years have been rife with proposed English-only legislation—especially after the events of September 11, 2001. The ultimate goal of the English-only movement, which emerged in the 1980s was to amend the U.S. Constitution to declare English the official language of this nation. This also occurred in the early part of the 20th century in reaction against speakers of the German language. It is a resurgence reflecting economic and political tensions. The decade of the 1990s and the first years of the 21st century have brought continuing hostility and violence toward populations of ethnic minority groups, racism, and xenophobia, of which the attack on bilingual education is but one example (Edwards & Curiel, 1989; Macedo, 2000). Supporters of the movement have worked energetically and have succeeded in obtaining passage of legislation. To date, 30 states have made English the official language of the state. In 2007–2008, bills were introduced in 20 states that would make English the official language or strengthen existing official English laws (U.S. English, 2008). In practice, implementation has meant that government institutions only provide services and information in English. Use of other languages has been prohibited. Some of the states that have enacted English-only legislation are among the largest and most populous in the country with extremely diverse cultural populations (Crawford, 2000).

In terms of social work and mental health services, according to national data on Latino and Asian American cultures (Alegria, Mulvaney-Day, Torres, Gao, & Oddo, 2006), cultural factors such as nativity, language, age at immigration, year of residence in the United States, and generational status affect the use of mental health services. English proficiency not only affects treatment for adults, but also can affect the care of children. Yu and colleagues (2006) compared children in English-speaking households and non-English-speaking households and found that children in non-English-speaking households are less likely to have access to health insurance and physician care and are more likely to go to other countries for their health care.

Recent developments in the immigration debate have sparked interest in the issues of diversity in the United States. The systematic issues of discrimination and social justice should be addressed to develop a system that is equitable to the growing immigrant population in the United States. "As society evolves, we encounter more diversity in our workplaces, in our neighborhoods, and in every other facet of our lives. Our entire country depends on individuals obtaining a greater understanding of the similarities and differences among ethnic, racial, and cultural groups" (Daniel K. Inouye, U.S. Senator, Hawaii, January 1996).

ISSUE STATEMENT

The essence of the social work profession is to promote social justice and eliminate discrimination. Language and cultural diversity are recognized as issues that are intrinsic to the profession's mission and commitment to advocacy of access to services, to quality of care, and ultimately to outcomes. According to Title VI of the Civil Rights Act of 1964, no persons on the grounds of race, color, or national origin should be denied services (U.S. Department of Health and Human Services, 2000). Agencies and service providers receiving federal financial assistance are obligated to not discriminate or have methods of administering services that may subject an individual to discrimination. The ramifications of discrimination are far reaching and affect clients in all fields and settings in which social workers practice.

In 2001, the NASW Standards for Cultural Competence in Social Work Practice affirmed the importance of cultural diversity and linguistic access in Standard 9, Language Diversity: "Social workers shall seek to provide and advocate for the provision of information, referrals, and services in the language appropriate to the client, which may include the use of interpreters" (p. 27) and translators.

NASW past—President Craig de Silva pointed out that "immigration weaves the frayed threads of poverty and racism with strings of fear." She also credited social workers as being "instrumental in helping newcomers make the transition into American society and helping communities embrace increased diversity" (Craig de Silva, 2006, p. 3). The social work literature on cultural competency helps shape our profession to improve the quality of social work services and work toward eliminating racial and ethnic disparities in services (Garcia & Van Soest, 2006; National Association of Social Workers, 2001).

Assessing a client's cultural background and values may be challenging for the social worker because individuals might belong to several cultures (Lopez, 2007).

POLICY STATEMENT

As social workers, we understand that language is a source and extension of personal identity and culture, and, therefore, is one way individuals interact with others in their families and communities and across different cultural groups. To limit or deny language as an extension of culture is to reject that aspect of human beings that helps to define them. NASW embraces the view that language access to services is a right and people's native language should be celebrated and encouraged as an example of diversity. NASW considers the use of various languages as a right and a resource that is closely aligned with the ethical principles of service and social justice.

Therefore, NASW

■ supports the continuity and preservation of native indigenous languages such as the languages of Native Alaskan, American Indian, and Native Hawaiian peoples. NASW rejects any hostility toward foreign-born or foreign-language-speaking individuals. NASW rejects such racially and culturally biased xenophobia.

■ believes that human service programs should have written limited-English-proficiency policies that include the following elements: assessment of language needs and capabilities, recruitment and hiring of bilingual and bicultural staff of major groups in the program's service area, training on how best to meet language needs of clients, use of interpreters and translators, and translation of documents (Barnett, 2004).

■ advocates for the provision of information, referrals, and services in the language and culture appropriate to the client.

■ supports research on culture and linguistic diversity that enhances the lives of all people.

■ supports educational programs that accept the importance of other languages within the mainstream culture, such as bilingual education and multicultural programs.

■ encourages schools of social work to recruit culturally and linguistically diverse students and faculty. The curriculum should also teach the skills necessary for culturally competent practice, which might include use of interpreters.

■ opposes any legislation that promotes English-only agendas.

REFERENCES

Alegria, M., Mulvaney-Day, N., Torres, M., Gao, S., & Oddo, V. (2006). Correlates of past-year mental health services among Latinos: Results from the national Latino and Asian American study. *American Journal of Public Health, 97,* 76–83.

Barnett, H. (2004). *Services to clients with limited English proficiency* (Program letter 04-2). Retrieved June 8, 2007, from www.lri.lsc .gov

Connor, S. (2003, May 13). Alarm raised on world's disappearing languages. *The Independent/UK.* Retrieved May 30, 2008, from http://www.commondreams.org/head lines03/0515-05.htm

Craig de Silva, E. (2006, August). Weaving the fabrics of diversity. *NASW News, 51,* p. 3.

Crawford, J. (2000). *Anatomy of the English-only movement.* Retrieved May 30, 2008, from http://ourworld.compuserve.com/home-pages/jWCRAWFORD/anatomy.htm

Edwards, R. L., & Curiel, H. (1989). Effects of the English-only movement on bilingual education. *Social Work in Education, 12,* 53–66. Retrieved May 30, 2008, from socialwork.rut-gers.edu/oldssw/documents/cvedwards 106.doc

Garcia, B., & Van Soest, D. (2006). *Social work practice for social justice: Cultural competence in action.* Alexandria, VA: Council on Social Work Education.

Native American Languages Act Amendments Act of 2000: Hearing before the Senate Committee on Indian Affairs, 106th Cong., 648 (2000) (statement of Michael E. Krauss). Retrieved May 20, 2008, from http://indian .senate.gov/2000hrgs/nala_0720/krauss.pdf

Lelchuck, I. (2006). *The changing face of America.* Retrieved June 8, 2007, from http://www .sfgate.com/cgi-bin/article.cgi?fil.../a/ 2006/10/15/MNGA4LPT7H1.DTL& type=printable

Lewis, P. (1998, August 15). Too late to say 'extinct' in Ubykh, Eyak or Ona; Thousands of languages are endangered. *New York Times,* p. A14. Retrieved May 30, 2008, from http://www.uwm.edu/~vaux/ubykh.htm

Lopez, S. (2007, November/December). *Honoring cultural diversity at the end of life. Social Work Today, 7*(6), 36. Retrieved May 30, 2008, from http://www.socialworktoday.com/ archive/novdec2007p36.shtml

Macedo, S. (2000). *Diversity and distrust: Civic education in a multicultural democracy.* Cambridge, MA: Harvard University Press. Retrieved May 30, 2008, from http://edrev .asu.edu/reviews/rev171.htm

National Association of Social Workers. (2001). *NASW standards for cultural competence in social work practice.* Washington, DC: NASW Press.

Russell Searight, H., & Gafford, J. (2005). *Cultural diversity at the end of life: Issues and guidelines for family physicians.* Retrieved May 30, 2008, from http://www.aafp.org/ afp/20050201/515.html

U.S. Census Bureau. (2000). *Quickfacts: Current population reports.* Washington, DC: U.S. Government Printing Office. Retrieved June 8, 2007, from http://quickfacts.census.gov

U.S. Census Bureau. (2003). *Factfinder: Current population reports.* Washington, DC: U.S. Government Printing Office. Retrieved June 8, 2007, from http://www.factfinder.census .gov

U.S. Census Bureau. (2006). *Quickfacts: Current population reports.* Washington, DC: U.S. Government Printing Office. Retrieved June 8, 2007, from http://quickfacts.census.gov

U.S. Department of Health and Human Services. (2000). *HHS guidelines on Title V of the Civil Rights Act of 1964.* Retrieved June 8, 2007, from www.hhs.gov/ocr/lep

U.S. English. (2008). *Legislation introduced to make English the official language of Texas.* Retrieved November 17, 2008, from http://www .usenglish.org/view/518

Wikipedia. (2008). Cultural diversity. Retrieved May 30, 2008, from http://en.wikipedia .org/wiki/Cultural_diversity

Wilkinson, C. (2005). *Blood struggle. The rise of modern Indian nations.* Retrieved May 30, 2008, from http://books.google.com/books ?id=moDHKMJXfKwC&pg=PA361&dq= %22Every+human+language+is+an+exq uisitely+complex+intellectual+master piece%22&sig=ACfU3U1c94i_sgE9WJzOm H3c2xT0KtzeSA

Yu, S., Huang, J., Schwalberg, R., & Nyman, R. (2006). Parenting English proficiency and children's health service access. *American Journal of Public Health, 96,* 1449–1455.

Policy statement approved by the NASW Delegate Assembly, August 2008. This policy statement supersedes the policy statement on Linguistic/Cultural Diversity in the United States approved by the Delegate Assembly in 1999. The 1999 Delegate Assembly also voted to not combine this statement with the policy statements on Affirmative Action or Immigrants and Refugees. This policy statement also supersedes the policy statement on Cultural and Linguistic Diversity in the United States approved by the Assembly in 1990. For further information, contact the National Association of Social Workers, 750 First Street, NE, Suite 700, Washington, DC 20002-4241. Telephone: 202-408-8600; e-mail: press@naswdc.org

Lesbian, Gay, and Bisexual Issues

BACKGROUND

In U.S. society, lesbian, gay, bisexual, transgender, and intersex people are still considered by some to be immoral, unnatural, and/or dysfunctional. Until 1973, homosexuality was defined as a mental illness by the American Psychiatric Association's (APA) Diagnostic and Statistical Manual (DSM) (APA, 1952). Lesbian, gay, bisexual, transgender, and intersex (LGBTI) people do not have civil and statutory protection under the law (Title VII of the Civil Rights Act) (Herek & Berrill, 1992). In fact, the government takes a leading role in the subjugation of lesbians and gay men by denying legal recognition of same-sex marriage. There is much violence and social injustice that must be overcome before sexual minority people are able to enjoy the full benefits of our society (Sloan & Gustavsson, 1998). It is important that NASW take a strong stance on behalf of LGBTI people and work to end the prejudice, oppression, and discrimination that confront LGBTI people on a daily basis. Although LGBTI people share many of the same discrimination and concerns, NASW has a separate policy statement on transgender and gender identity issues, therefore, this policy primarily addresses lesbian, gay, and bisexual people (LGB).

Discrimination against LGB people has a long history in the United States. Following World War II, President Eisenhower banned gay men and lesbians from all federal jobs; many state and local governments and private companies followed suit (Garraty & Foner, 1991). Until 1961, sodomy and homosexuality were illegal in all 50 states. Sodomy laws were used in many states to deny lesbians and gay men custody of their children, employment, and the opportunity to foster or adopt children in state care (National Gay and Lesbian Task Force [NGLTF], 2004c). Throughout the 1950s and 1960s, police frequently raided gay bars, arresting employees and patrons.

By the late 1950s, the gay rights movement was beginning to grow and reject the discrimination faced by LGB people. On June 27, 1969, when New York City police raided a Greenwich Village gay bar, the LGB community was ready to fight back. As police arrested employees and patrons of the Stonewall Inn, a fight ensued and soon hundreds of people were protesting and rioting. Over the next three days, the crowd of protesters grew to over 1,000. Although not the beginning of the gay rights movement, the Stonewall riots were an important milestone in the gay rights movement. Over the next decades, changes would spread across the country. In 1973, APA removed homosexuality from its list of mental disorders. By 1975, the federal government had lifted the employment ban on lesbians and gay men (in most jobs) (Garraty & Foner, 1991). On June 26, 2003, the Supreme Court ruled sodomy laws unconstitutional (*Lawrence v. State of Texas*, 2003). Later in 2003, the Massachusetts Supreme Court ruled that banning lesbians and gay men from marrying was a violation of the state's constitution, opening the way for same-sex couples to legally marry in the state.

Internationally, other countries were also beginning to fight against discrimination of LGB people. In 1994, the United Nations ruled that discrimination based on sexual orientation violates the International Covenant on Civil and Political Rights. In 1996, post-apartheid South Africa became the first country to include nondiscrimination based on sexual orientation in its constitution (Human Rights Watch [HRW], 2004). From 1981 to 2003, the European Court of Human Rights overturned sodomy, recognized gay and lesbian partnerships, condemned discriminatory age-of-consent laws (that is, differing age of consent to engage in sex for heterosexual versus LGB youths), and gave transgender people the right to legally change their identity and to marry (HRW). In 1998, Denmark legalized same-sex partnerships; within two years, Norway, Sweden, Iceland, and France followed. In 2001, the Netherlands legalized same-sex marriages, followed in 2003 by Belgium and the Canadian provinces of Ontario and British Columbia. In 2004, Quebec, the Yukon, Manitoba, Nova Scotia, and Saskatchewan legalized same-sex marriage.

ISSUE STATEMENT

Despite the successes of the gay rights movement, there continues to be discrimination against LGB people. Thirty-five states do not protect LGB people from discrimination in employment, education, credit, housing, and other public accommodation. Six states do not allow lesbians or gay men to adopt (Florida and Mississippi), or foster children (North Dakota, Utah, Arkansas, and Oklahoma) (NGLTF, 2004a). Thirteen states passed state constitutional amendments that prohibit same-sex marriage (although the courts in Louisiana struck down their amendment). Alabama, Arizona, Mississippi, South Carolina, and Texas prohibit any discussion of homosexuality in school or "mandate that any references to homosexuality be exclusively negative" (NGLTF, 2004b, p. 1).

The federal government has also failed to support nondiscrimination against LGB people. The 1994 Employment Non-Discrimination Act (ENDA), which would protect LGB people from workplace discrimination, has failed to pass Congress. In 1996, the federal government passed the Defense of Marriage Act (DOMA), allowing states to not recognize gay marriages sanctioned in other states or countries. Currently, President Bush proposed a constitutional amendment to define marriage as between one man and one woman.

The impact of discrimination, homophobia, heterosexism, and biphobia have a serious impact on LGB people. Homophobia and heterosexism inhibit effective and appropriate service delivery for sexual minority people. Hate crimes based on sexual orientation account for 16 percent of all hate crimes reported to law enforcement (FBI, 2004). Research suggests that harassment and hatred of LGB people is related to higher rates of depression, suicide, high school drop out, and teen homelessness (HRW, 2001). Gay men earn 20 percent less than heterosexual men, and due to the inequity in women's salaries compared with men, lesbian couples earn less than heterosexual couples (Badgett, 1998).

Discrimination within the LGB community must be acknowledged. LGB people represent all of the diversity of our society—people of color, people who are disabled, people who are elderly, people who are immigrants and refugees, and people of all religious and political beliefs. LGB people facing multiple forms of oppression also face discrimination from LGB people. In addition, bisexual identity is often dismissed by lesbians and gay men as a means to avoid the full brunt of homophobia, and not a true sexual orientation. Bisexuals are frequently told that bisexuality is just a phase, and they will either eventually identify as heterosexual or homosexual. The complexities of multiple forms of oppression cannot be ignored.

Homophobic or heterosexist views also reduce the effectiveness of support services and treatment social workers offer to gay and lesbian clients. Homophobia and/or heterosexism may cause social workers to minimize or exaggerate the importance of sexual orientation in the gay, lesbian, or bisexual individual's life, perpetuating self-hatred experienced by some gay and lesbian clients (Brown, 1996; McHenry & Johnson, 1993; Peterson, 1996). Taken to the extreme, homophobia in social workers and other practitioners can lead to the use of conversion or reparative therapies, which are explicitly condemned by NASW, the American Psychological Association, the American Counseling Association, and the American Psychiatric Association (American Academy of Pediatrics et al., n.d.; American Psychiatric Association, 1998; NASW, 2000).

POLICY STATEMENT

It is the position of the NASW that same-gender sexual orientation should be afforded the same respect and rights as other-gender orientation. Discrimination and prejudice directed against any group is damaging to the social, emotional, and economic well-being of the affected group and of society as a whole. NASW is committed to advancing policies and practices that will improve the status and well-being of all lesbian, gay, and bisexual people. NASW reaffirms its support of the Transgender and Gender Identity Issues policy statement, recognizing the intersection of oppression among lesbian, gay, bisexual, transgender, and intersex people.

Nondiscrimination

■ NASW supports all social agencies, universities, professional associations, and funding organizations in their efforts to broaden statements of nondiscrimination to include sexual orientation.

■ NASW supports the adoption of local, state, federal, and international policies/legislation that ban all forms of discrimination based on sexual orientation. LGB people must be granted all rights, privileges, and responsibilities that are granted to heterosexual people, including but not limited to inheritance rights, insurance, marriage, child custody, employment, credit, and immigration.

■ NASW supports the adoption of local, state, federal, and international policies/legislation that protect the rights and well-being of the children of lesbian, gay, and bisexual people.

■ NASW supports efforts to end discrimination and harassment of lesbian, gay, and bisexual youths in public schools. NASW also supports the rights of LGB youths and allies to organize and operate in schools.

■ NASW is committed to working toward the elimination of prejudice, social injustice, violence, and discrimination of LGB people in all aspects of society.

Social Work Profession and Education

■ NASW encourages curriculum policies in schools of social work that eliminate discrimination against lesbian, gay, and bisexual people. Schools of social work are expected to articulate the NASW position in curriculum policy and standards; to require content on lesbian, gay, and bisexual people throughout the curriculum, in field instruction, and in continuing education programs and through the selection of textbooks; and to provide training for classroom instructors, field supervisors, and field advisers regarding lesbian, gay, and bisexual issues.

■ NASW encourages social workers to increase their awareness of oppression, heterosexism, homophobia, and the intersection of multiple forms of oppression.

■ NASW encourages all social work organizations and associations to use inclusive, gender-neutral language, non-homophobic, non-heterosexist language in all materials.

■ NASW encourages licensing bodies to include questions specific to lesbian, gay, and bisexual sex issues.

■ NASW strives for full representation and establishment of means to affirm the presence of lesbian, gay, and bisexual people at all levels of leadership and employment in social work and in NASW and its chapters.

Education and Public Awareness

■ NASW encourages the development of programs, training, and information regarding the specific health, mental health, and development needs of lesbian, gay, and bisexual youths and their families.

■ NASW encourages the development of programs to increase public awareness of the violence and social injustice experienced by lesbian, gay, and bisexual people. Public awareness and education in schools should include information on the contributions made to society by lesbian, gay, and bisexual people.

- NASW encourages the development of programs, training, and information that promote proactive efforts to end the violence and stereotypes perpetrated against lesbian, gay, and bisexual people.

- NASW applauds organizations that fund, develop, and provide programming that portrays the lesbian, gay, and bisexual communities compassionately and accurately.

Health and Mental Health Services

- NASW supports the right of the individual to self-disclose, or to not disclose, sexual orientation and encourages the development of supportive practice environments for lesbian, gay, and bisexual clients and colleagues.

- NASW reaffirms its stance against reparative therapies and treatments designed to change sexual orientation or to refer clients to practitioners or programs that claim to do so (NASW, 2000).

- NASW strongly advocates for the availability of culturally appropriate comprehensive health and mental health services for LGB people across the life span, including HIV prevention and treatment; substance abuse treatment; psychological stress and dysfunction prevention and treatment; and suicide prevention.

- NASW recognizes the increasing number of lesbian, gay, and bisexual people who are making reproductive choices and encourages the establishment of legal, medical, and psychological supports for these families.

Political Action

It is important for NASW and its chapters to develop and participate in coalition with other human rights, social action, and professional associations to lobby for the rights of lesbian, gay, and bisexual people; to defeat efforts to limit the rights of lesbian, gay, and bisexual people; to advocate for increased funding for programs designed to eliminate hate crimes and antigay violence; to advocate for increased funding for programs designed to provide education, health and mental health services; and to advocate for increased funding for research

that increases our understanding of issues affecting lesbian, gay, and bisexual people.

REFERENCES

American Academy of Pediatrics. (n.d.). *Just the facts about sexual orientation and youth: A primer for principals, educators, and school personnel.* Retrieved January 26, 2004, from http://www.apa.org/pi/lgbc/facts.pdf

American Psychiatric Association. (1952). *Diagnostic and statistical manual: Mental disorders.* Washington, DC: Author.

American Psychiatric Association. (1998). *Lesbian, gay and bisexual issues fact sheet: APA fact sheet pertinent to gay and lesbian issues.* Retrieved January 26, 2004, from http://www.psych.org/public_info/gaylesbianbisexualissues22701.pdf

Badgett, M. V. (1998). *Income inflation: The myth of affluence among gay men, lesbians, and bisexuals.* New York: Policy Institute of the National Gay and Lesbian Task Force and Institute for Gay and Lesbian Strategic Studies.

Brown, L. S. (1996). Preventing heterosexism and bias in psychotherapy and counseling. In E. Rothblum & L. Bond (Eds.), *Preventing heterosexism and homophobia* (pp. 36–58). Thousand Oaks, CA: Sage Publications.

Defense of Marriage Act, P.L. 104-199, 110 Stat, 2419.

Federal Bureau of Investigation. (2004). *Hate crimes 2003.* Washington, DC: Author [Available from author, U. S. Department of Justice, Washington, DC 20535].

Garraty, J., & Foner, E. (Eds.). (1991). *A reader's companion to American history.* New York: Houghton Mifflin.

Herek, G. M., & Berrill, K. T. (1992). *Hate crimes: Confronting violence against lesbians and gay men.* Newbury Park, CA: Sage Publications.

Human Rights Watch. (2001). *Hatred in the hallways: Violence and discrimination against lesbian, gay, bisexual and transgender students in U.S. schools.* New York: Author.

Human Rights Watch. (2004). *Lesbian and gay rights: Resource library for international jurisprudence on sexual orientation and gender identity*. Retrieved March 25, 2005, from http://hrw.org/lgbt/jurisprudence.htm

Lawrence v. State of Texas, 123 S.Ct. 2472 (2003).

McHenry, S. S., & Johnson, J. W. (1993). Homophobia in the therapist and gay or lesbian client: Conscious and unconscious collusions in self-hate. *Psychotherapy, 30,* 141–151.

National Association of Social Workers. (2000). *Position statement: "Reparative" and "conversion" therapies for lesbians and gay men.* Retrieved April 18, 2004, from http://www.naswdc.org/diversity/lgb/reparative.asp

National Gay and Lesbian Task Force. (2004a). *Anti-gay parenting laws in the U.S.* Retrieved March 24, 2005, from http://www.thetask-force.org/downloads/adoptionmap.pdf

National Gay and Lesbian Task Force. (2004b). *Youth.* Retrieved March 24, 2005, from http://www.thetaskforce.org/theissues/issue.cfm?issueID=13

National Gay and Lesbian Task Force. (2004c). *Sodomy.* Retrieved March 24, 2005, from http://www.thetaskforce.org/theissues/issue.cfm?issueID=11

Peterson, K. J. (1996). Preface: Developing the context: The impact of homophobia and heterosexism on the health care of gay and lesbian people. In K. J. Peterson (Ed.), *Health care for lesbians and gay men: Con-fronting homophobia and sexism* (pp. xx). Binghamton, NY: Harrington Park Press.

Sloan, L. M., & Gustavsson, N. (1998). *Violence and social injustice against lesbian, gay and bisexual people.* New York: Haworth Press.

United Nations. (1994). Toonen v Australia. *Human Rights Committee Communication No. 488/1992.* Retrieved March 25, 2005, from http://www.hrw.org/lgbt/pdf/toonen.pdf

SUGGESTED READINGS

Davies, D. (1996). Towards a model of gay affirmative therapy. In D. Davies & C. Neal (Eds.), *Pink therapy: A guide for counselors and therapists working with lesbian, gay and bisexual clients* (pp. 24–40). Philadelphia: Open University.

National Gay and Lesbian Task Force. (2003). *National Gay and Lesbian Task Force welcomes Supreme Court sodomy decision—Calls opinion a major advance for individual liberty.* Retrieved April 17, 2004, from http://www.thetaskforce.org/news/release.cfm?releaseID=551

National Gay and Lesbian Task Force. (2005). *Second parent adoption in the U.S.* Retrieved March 24, 2005, from http://www.thetask-force.org/downloads/secondparentadoptionmap.pdf

Policy statement approved by the NASW Delegate Assembly, August 2005. This policy supersedes the policy statement on Lesbian, Gay, and Bisexual Issues approved by the Delegate Assembly in 1996 and referred by the 2002 Delegate Assembly to the 2005 Delegate Assembly for revision. For further information, contact the National Association of Social Workers, 750 First Street, NE, Suite 700, Washington, DC 20002-4241. Telephone: 202-408-8600 or 800-638-8799; e-mail: press@naswdc.org

Long-Term Care

BACKGROUND

According to Barker (2003), *long-term care* (LTC) is "a system of providing social, personal, and health care services over a sustained period to people who in some way suffer from functional impairment, including a limited ability to perform activities of daily living. LTC services are required mostly by older people, adults with developmental disabilities, people who are mentally ill, and people with disabling and prolonged chronic illness. It is provided by professionals, family members, and volunteers under public or private auspices in nursing homes, boarding houses, assisted-living facilities, adult day care centers and home community-based facilities. In addition to health care and case management services, LTC services can include transportation, escort, homemaker services, night sitting, recreation, home health services, home meals, and ombudsperson services" (p. 253).

The U.S. Senate Special Committee on Aging (2000) stated that the goal of LTC is to allow an individual to attain and maintain an optimal level of functioning. This makes LTC distinct from acute health care, which is primarily designed to cure illness. LTC includes diagnostic, preventive, supportive, rehabilitative, maintenance, and personal care services provided by informal caregivers, such as family or friends, or formal caregivers, such as specially trained or licensed professionals. Care may be provided in a nursing facility or in a less restrictive environment, such as a person's home, or assisted-living facilities. Support for living in a less restrictive environment is complemented by community-based programs, such as home health care, respite care, and adult day care.

There has been substantial growth in the numbers of people needing LTC as a result of a growing aging population, a higher prevalence of chronic illness and disability, and an increasing number of people with chronic, infectious diseases such as HIV, and dementias such as Alzheimer's disease. In 2001 about 7 million men and women over age 65 needed LTC. The number is projected to increase to 12 million people by the year 2020. Family and friends provide care for 70 percent of the older adults (American Association of Retired Persons, 2004). The demand for formal LTC will continue to grow as a result of changes in family dynamics—that is, the stress of the psychosocial aspect of LTC on family caregivers, spousal impoverishment, and the changing role of women who have provided the majority of informal LTC services.

Consumers are demanding more home- and community-based services, a movement that gained support from the Olmstead decision (Centers for Medicare and Medicaid Services, 2004), which indicated support for encouraging aging and disabled populations to live in the least restrictive settings as long as possible. The ideal formal LTC system would offer a full continuum of care, including acute medical services (for example, rehabilitative care, skilled care at home), LTC services (for example, nursing home care, adult day care, home-delivered meals, personal care attendants), social services (for example, assistance with Medicare and Medicaid forms, socialization opportunities), and housing services (for example, assisted living, subsidized housing) (Branch, 2001). Such a system also needs to include client choice, and financial and emotional support to clients and caregivers, especially in home-based situations. As a result of the Olmstead decision, new providers and new services have developed, often in an uncoordinated manner. The present system of LTC is characterized as fragmented, inappropriate, and inadequate. Home- and community-based services (for example, mental health, transportation, and adult day care) have various, fragmented funding sources and auspices. Service availability differs from state to state; even in communities there are gaps in the continuum of care (Branch, 2001). There is tremendous need for reform to create an integrated, cohesive, and comprehensive system of services and better funding (U.S. Senate Special Committee on Aging, 2002).

Currently, services are funded primarily by state and federal programs with Medicaid as the primary payer of LTC. During fiscal year 2000, Medicaid paid for 45 percent of the $137 billion that the United States spent on LTC. Despite the allocation of state and federal monies to long-term care, older adults and their families either pay out-of-pocket for much of the LTC services rendered or receive care provided by informal (unpaid) support systems such as family, neighbors, and friends (Branch, 2001; U.S. Senate Special Committee on Aging, 2002). Clearly, caregiving of this type needs to be supported, especially financially, or replaced.

Medicaid has allowed for great variability in benefits for optional services such as case management, psychosocial rehabilitation, and clinical services entailing outpatient therapy, partial hospitalization, and home-based personal care by nonphysician providers. Availability of these services is limited, inequitable, and in some states, unavailable. There has been great variability in Medicaid services for older people with chronic, severe physical disabilities, mental illness, or dementia, and it had provided few additional services. Lack of services or overuse of physical restraints and psychotropic drugs has been the response of many nursing homes to people with chronic mental illness, mental retardation or developmental disabilities, and those who exhibit behavioral symptoms of dementia. Legislation has sought to eliminate this ineffective, custodial-oriented response ("Medicare and Medicaid: Requirements," 1989). Nursing home regulations have sought to correct abusive situations by providing adequate safeguards for promoting maximization of independence, discharge planning,

and resident rights through ombudsman programs and efforts to enhance the quality of life of residents.

There is a lack of services available to older adults who are developmentally disabled and are either residents in nursing homes or being cared for at home by their families. Nursing home employees are not adequately trained to meet the specialized mental and emotional needs of this population. In addition, most professionals working in LTC, including social workers, have a lack of educational opportunities and lack of continuing education in gerontology (Council on Social Work Education, 2001; Health Resources & Services Administration, 1995). There is a continued need for increased field practicum opportunities in home- and community-based LTC services and a continued need to integrate aging and LTC content into the curriculum of all bachelor's and master's degree programs in social work (Scharlach, Damron-Rodriguez, Robinson, & Feldman, 2000). This should also include attitude changes and reduction of ageism.

Financial pressures on the health care system have resulted in the promotion of managed care programs for health services. The growth of managed care has had an effect on older people and others with chronic mental and physical illnesses who are eligible for Medicare and Medicaid. A growing number of retirees are enrolled in Medicare managed care plans. In addition, many states have opted to seek Medicaid waivers of federal regulatory requirements to experiment with providing cost-effective services to recipients, including managed care models (Cauchi, 1999).

Although managed care organizations have made respectable attempts to provide cost-effective, quality services for people with chronic illnesses (Cauchi, 1999), the philosophy of managed care is not easily adapted to optimum delivery of LTC services. Managed care methods of intervention, although effective for many patients, are not the most effective for providing services to isolated, frail people (Knight & Kaskie, 1995). Also, the managed care approach generally has not promoted outreach services to vulnerable clients, LTC research, and training, including field instruction. Managed care has tended to exacerbate the fragmentation problem of LTC services delivery and has not promoted the development of a continuum of care approach (Greene, 1995).

As a result of the development of managed care and the increased growth in the numbers of vulnerable, frail, and disabled people, there is a need for heightened attention to ethical and legal considerations in LTC. Some of the areas that warrant attention are

■ fairness and adequacy of care

■ client and professional input in decision making and rationing of care decisions

■ supportive, client-oriented services in making end-of-life decisions

■ flexible and humane policies related to guardianship

■ accountability and protection regarding use of client and client records

■ government responsibility for protecting vulnerable people and providing services to the economically poor people (Fahey, 1995; Kane, 1996).

The involvement of the National Association of Social Workers (NASW) in LTC includes both advocacy efforts and the development of standards for the field. NASW supports national health care reform and has taken the position that there is a need to regulate the managed care industry (NASW, 1998). NASW was instrumental in recommending revisions to the Omnibus Reconciliation Act (OBRA) nursing home regulations and actively participated in the 1995 White House Conference on Aging. The development of professional standards includes participation in the formation of LTC accreditation standards for the Joint Commission on Accreditation of Healthcare Organizations. In addition, NASW is a participating member of the Quality Improvement Organization's Public Advisory Panel, which is composed of allied health and mental health organizations and advocates who are interested in discussing ways to improve the quality of care in skilled-nursing facilities (Yagoda, 2004). NASW has created *Standards for Social Work Services in Long-Term Care Facilities* (NASW,

2003), *Clinical Indicators for Social Work and Psychosocial Services in Nursing Homes* (NASW, 1993), and *Standards for Social Work Practice in Palliative and End-of-Life Care* (NASW, 2004).

ISSUE STATEMENT

Long-term care services are characterized by deficit focus, stereotypical medical models on aging, an inadequate funding system, and a lack of continuity and coordination between insufficient use of a continuum of acute and chronic care to promote maximum self-determination of clients in the least restrictive setting. The government at all levels and the private sector have had little success in integrating or coordinating the growing array of available services into a viable system to meet individual and functional needs of clients, caregivers, and families. There is no comprehensive policy that includes guiding principles as a focus for ongoing planning, policy development, and change. The increasing societal need for LTC must be a catalyst for the health care system to re-examine and improve its low emphasis on prevention and client satisfaction and high emphasis on cost-effectiveness of services. Major problem areas within the LTC system include access to care (that is, urban versus rural), eligibility for and availability of services, the provision of quality care, the need for guiding principles for policy development, definition of ethical underpinnings, and the financing of LTC services.

In response to the changes occurring in LTC, the social work profession must examine its role and function throughout the continuum of care. Social work practice approaches, such as strength-based case management, family intervention, psychosocial assessment, interdisciplinary teamwork, and practice-based evaluation, can provide effective and efficient integration of services in LTC. Social workers also need to be active and take a leadership role in advocacy and policy making related to LTC.

The important social work role of advocacy for appropriate, culturally competent quality care and quality of life for clients and caregivers is critical in meeting the needs for consumer protection and consumer involvement. Careful consideration must be given to an ethical review that includes redefinition of roles, changes in legal perspective, and much more emphasis on self-determination and autonomy. The changing LTC environment presents both a challenge and an opportunity for the profession.

POLICY STATEMENT

NASW advocates for the continued reform of the LTC system with emphasis on strengthening the social work role in a continuum of care services delivery model. NASW supports inclusion of the following principles in LTC reform:

Access, Eligibility, and Availability of Services

■ access to a variety of physical and mental health and support services, based on individual needs to enable individuals to attain and maintain their optimal level of functioning in the least restrictive environment

■ access to LTC services for all who need them, regardless of age, income, disability, race, national origin, gender, sexual orientation, ethnicity, or geographic location

■ access to qualified, professional social work services at all levels of care to facilitate the integration of services in LTC to meet individual needs

■ promotion of the integration of competency-based gerontological content in BSW and MSW curriculum

■ eligibility for LTC services based on individual, functional need and economic and social support not solely on medical necessity

■ inclusion of social workers in managed care planning teams to ensure equitable use of resources in care and treatment

■ availability of services on a continuum that links all levels of LTC and addresses the physical, social, mental, cultural, and spiritual needs of the individual, family, and caregivers

■ availability of social work services based on individual functional need that is not solely related to medical diagnosis or dependent on the involvement of another health or mental health discipline

■ availability of specialized care for individuals with cognitive and functional impairments

■ social work services that address the needs of informal caregivers for people who are chronically ill, so that both the caregiver and the receiver of care enjoy a good quality of life.

Quality of Life and Quality of Care

■ emphasis on the quality of life for each client and quality care in services across the continuum of LTC

■ promotion and support of client self-determination in making choices and client participation in decisions that affect the delivery and provision of LTC services, including initiatives that encourage people to use advance directives in planning health care

■ participation of client-designated family members, and other client-designated caregivers, to ensure choice and quality at all levels of care

■ assurance of confidentiality and ethical considerations in all areas of decision making

■ ongoing expansion of education, staff development, training, and continuing education programs, including learning and understanding about the impact of the societal ageism and ableism on LTC policies for all levels of social workers employed along the LTC continuum

■ use of standards for gerontological social work that enhances the proficiency of social work practitioners in our aging society

■ adherence to regulatory requirements that recognize both quality-of-care and quality-of-life issues

■ dignified, humane, effective, and client-based services that are consistent with professional social work values

■ promotion of practice-based research on social, mental health, and substance abuse issues in LTC, with a focus on racial, cultural, ethnic, ability, and gender perspectives

■ program evaluation, including client satisfaction surveys, focus groups, professional performance appraisals, evaluation and assessment of client goals, and service/treatment plans with full participation of clients and their families.

Financing

■ development of an adequate financing system for LTC that preserves, increases, and redistributes revenue to increase access and provide coverage based on the client's need

■ solvency of social security, Medicare, and Medicaid programs as well as the pursuit of alternative sources for LTC funding

■ federal and state funding for cost-effective community-based alternatives to nursing home care, including assisted living, adult day care, shared housing, home health care, home-delivered meals, transportation, and hospice care

■ initiatives that encourage all people to plan for health care needs and retirement

■ continuation of the provision of consumer protection guidelines for LTC insurance, even for those who have established chronic disabilities, so cost of coverage is reasonable.

REFERENCES

American Association of Retired Persons. (2004). *Home and community-based long-term care.* Retrieved May 31, 2004, from http://research.aarp.org/health/hcb_ltc.html

Barker, R. L. (2003). *The social work dictionary* (5th ed.). Washington, DC: NASW Press.

Branch, L. G. (2001). Community long-term care services: What works and what doesn't? *Gerontologist, 41,* 307–308.

Cauchi, R. (1999, March). Managed care: Where do we go from here? In *State legislatures.* Retrieved May 31, 2004, from http://www.ncsl.org/programs/pubs/399mancare.htm#facts

Centers for Medicare and Medicaid Services. (2004, September). Americans with Disabilities Act/Olmstead Decision. Retrieved December 13, 2004, from http://www.cms.hhs.gov/olmstead

Council on Social Work Education. (March 2001). *A blueprint for the new millennium.* Alexandria, VA: Author.

Fahey, C. (1995). The ethical underpinnings of long-term care reform. *Care Lines, 2*(4), 1.

Greene, R. (1995). Family involvement in mental health care for older adults: From caregiving to advocacy and empowerment. In M. Gatz (Ed.), *Emerging issues in mental health and aging* (pp. 210–230). Washington, DC: American Psychological Association.

Health Resources and Services Administration, Bureau of Health Professions. (1995). *A national agenda for geriatric education: White papers.* Washington, DC: Author.

Kane, R. (1996). The ethics of health care delivery to elders in a managed care environment. *Managed Care & Aging, 3*(1), 1.

Knight, B., & Kaskie, B. (1995). Models for mental health service delivery to older adults: Implications for reform. In M. Gatz (Ed.), *Emerging issues in mental health and aging* (pp. 231–255). Washington, DC: American Psychological Association.

Medicare and Medicaid: Requirements for Long Term Care Facilities. (1989, February 2). *Federal Register, 54,* 5333, 5335.

National Association of Social Workers. (1993). *NASW clinical indicators for social work and psychosocial services in nursing homes.* Washington, DC: Author.

National Association of Social Workers. (1998). NASW position paper on managed care. Retrieved May 31, 2004, from http://www.socialworkers.org/archives/advocacy/positions/mngdcare.asp

National Association of Social Workers. (2003). *NASW standards for social work services in long-term care facilities.* Washington, DC: Author.

National Association of Social Workers. (2004). *NASW standards for social work practice in palliative and end-of-life care.* Washington, DC: Author.

Scharlach, A., Damron-Rodriguez, J., Robinson, B., & Feldman, R. (2000). Educating social workers for an aging society: A vision for the 21st century. *Journal of Social Work Education, 36,* 521–538.

U.S. Senate Special Committee on Aging. (2000). *Developments in aging: 1997 and 1998* (Report 106-229). Washington, DC: U.S. Government Printing Office.

U.S. Senate Special Committee on Aging. (2002). *Long-term care report* (Report 107-74). Washington, DC: U.S. Government Printing Office.

Yagoda, L. (2004). *Aging highlights*. Retrieved May 31, 2004, from http://www.social-workers.org/practice/aging/021304notes.asp

Policy statement approved by the NASW Delegate Assembly, August 2005. This policy supersedes the policy statement on Long-Term Care approved by the Delegate Assembly in 1996, 1993, and 1979 and referred by the 2002 Delegate Assembly to the 2005 Delegate Assembly for revision. For further information, contact the National Association of Social Workers, 750 First Street, NE, Suite 700, Washington, DC 20002-4241. Telephone: 202-408-8600 or 800-638-8799; e-mail: press@naswdc.org

Mental Health

BACKGROUND

The field of mental health, or mental illness, as some prefer to call it (Torrey, 1989), is characterized by many controversies, and social workers as core mental health professionals have taken part in these debates. Some of these debates center on the fundamental issues of how mental health and illness should be defined (Mechanic, 1989) and the basis on which diagnoses and assessments should be made (Kirk & Kutchins, 1992).

Many mental health professionals, including social workers, view mental health and mental illness in biopsychosocial terms, and social workers have been educated to conduct client assessments and provide treatment using an ecological perspective (Germain & Gitterman, 1995). Severe mental illness is thought to consist of neurobiological disorders, primarily schizophrenia, schizoaffective disorder, bipolar disorder, autism, major depression, panic disorder, and obsessive–compulsive disorder (Torrey, 1997).

The *Diagnostic and Statistical Manual of Mental Disorders, Fourth Edition* (DSM-IV; American Psychiatric Association, 1994) and the *Diagnostic and Statistical Manual of Mental Disorders, Fourth Edition, Text Revision* (DSM-IV-TR; American Psychiatric Association, 2000) are widely used in the United States as a classification system for mental disorders, although they have been challenged on methodological as well as political grounds (Kirk & Kutchins, 1992). In most other countries the *International Classification of Diseases, 10th Revision* (ICD-10) classification system is used. Third-party reimbursement generally requires the use of a classification system. Mechanic (1989) characterized the history of treatment for mental illness in the United States as one of "advances and setbacks." In the mid-1800s Dorothea Dix worked to separate people with mental disorders from those incarcerated for criminal activity, and she and other reformers sought to develop more humane institutions for those with severe mental illness. Reformers who followed early in the 20th century, such as Clifford Beers, Albert Meyer, and others involved in the mental hygiene movement, pressed for community-based hospital care as well as clinic treatment, but the institutional philosophy prevailed. State mental hospitals have improved in many respects, partly in response to concerned journalists (for example, Deutsch's *The Shame of the States* [1948]) but in some states improvement has come primarily as the result of major court decisions and legislation (see, for example, *Wyatt v. Stickney*, 1972) rather than public concern.

World War II had an important effect on mental health policy. Many potential recruits were rejected for military service and others were later discharged for psychiatric reasons (Mechanic, 1989). The accuracy of these screenings was highly suspect; nonetheless, the exercise served to focus attention on mental health concerns and provided impetus for passage of the Mental Health Act of 1946 (P.L. 79-487) (Mechanic, 1989). The act established the National Institute of Mental Health (NIMH). The creation of this institute, along with the introduction of psychotropic drugs in the 1950s, spurred the community mental health movement. The Mental Health Study Act of 1955 (P.L. 84-182) provided funds for the Joint Commission on Mental Illness and Health to produce a report, *Action for Mental Health*, published in 1961. This report contributed to the development and passage of the Mental Retardation Facilities and Community Mental Health Centers Construction Act of 1963 (P.L. 88-164). In 1965 amendments to P.L. 88-164 (P.L. 89-105) authorized initial funding for professional and technical personnel for community mental health centers (CMHCs) and provided for the establishment of CMHCs throughout the United States. CMHCs were to provide at least five essential services—inpatient, outpatient, partial hospitalization, 24-hour emergency, and education and consultation to community caretakers. Services were to be provided with continuity and to catchment areas of 200,000. The federal government expected the states and localities to match funding in annually increasing amounts for "maintenance of effort."

The idea of community-based treatment was consistent with the emphasis on civil rights of the 1960s. However, by the 1970s, as federal contributions decreased, a number of programs could not obtain matching funds. As a result, the movement toward deinstitutionalization came to be viewed as a way for states to avoid responsibility for the care of individuals with severe mental illness by returning them to the communities (Mechanic, 1989; Scull, 1977). The principles of normalization and inclusion were neglected because of a lack of resources to provide the range and depth of community services that individuals with severe mental disorders need.

In the late 1960s most states revised their mental health codes to protect consumers' civil rights and to standardize criteria for involuntary hospitalization. In most cases involuntary hospitalization can only take place if a person must be found to be a current danger to self or others or gravely disabled and incapable of self-care by reason of mental illness.

Over the past 30 years, there has been movement from the use of institutional treatment to community-based programs. Wisconsin's Program for Assertive Community Treatment (PACT) has served as a model across the nation. Progress toward independence and improvement in areas of functioning as a result of this program is well documented.

Efforts during the Carter administration to substantially improve and expand community mental health care were dashed with the ad-

vent of the Reagan presidency and its preference for block grants, reduced funding, and state responsibility for determination and delivery of services. Mental health care is generally considered a state responsibility (Torrey, 1997), but federal assistance can play an important role in bolstering mental health services. Much of the federal–state relationship in community mental health services comes as a result of the State Comprehensive Mental Health Services Plan Act of 1986 (P.L. 99-660), with its focus on people with severe mental illness, especially those who are homeless. The failures of deinstitutionalization to provide less-restrictive housing alternatives also has prompted legislation that has established housing options for people with mental illnesses who are homeless. The Stewart B. McKinney Homeless Assistance Act of 1987 (P.L. 100-77) also offers assistance to this population through Projects for Assistance in Transition from Homelessness and Access to Community Care and Effective Services and Support, now administered through the Center for Mental Health Services of the Substance Abuse and Mental Health Services Administration (SAMHSA, the successor to NIMH).

Several pieces of legislation have focused on the needs of other subgroups. The 1975 Education for All Handicapped Children Act (P.L. 94-142), now called the Individuals with Disabilities Education Act (IDEA), guarantees all children with disabilities a free public school education and encourages mainstreaming or inclusion whenever possible. In 1984 NIMH awarded the first grants under the Child and Adolescent Service System Program. In 1992 with the establishment of SAMHSA came the community mental health services block grant, which included a focus on children and adolescents who have "serious emotional disturbance" (Kessler et al., 1996). SAMHSA includes an Office for Women, an Associate Administrator for Minority Concerns, and an Office on AIDS. The nursing home reform amendment in the 1987 Omnibus Budget Reconciliation Act (P.L. 100-203) helps to ensure that individuals with mental illness are treated in the least restrictive environments (Fellin, 1996).

Many other policies also influence the treatment of people with mental illness. Cash assistance is provided through the Social Security Disability Insurance (SSDI) program for former workers and through the Supplemental Security Income (SSI) program for people with disabilities who have very limited financial resources. Both programs use stringent criteria for determination of mental disorders. There has been a good deal of controversy over the federal system of disability determination. More stringent criteria have been imposed for determining mental disorders in children. Individuals with only a substance use disorder no longer qualify for SSDI or SSI.

The Medicare program is an important source of physical and mental health care for people who are elderly, regardless of income, and for former workers who have been disabled at least two years. The Medicaid program is equally important for those with mental illness who are poor and meet other program criteria.

The Americans with Disabilities Act of 1990 (P.L. 101-336) covers people with mental and physical disabilities and provides protections to job applicants, employees, and individuals wishing to use public and private accommodations. It does not, however, grant all the same employment protections to those with substance use disorders that it does to individuals with other mental disorders.

In 1993 President Clinton proposed the Health Security Act, which would have entitled all Americans to a basic package of physical health care services and which would have eventually done the same for mental health services. The act also would have integrated the public and private tiers of the health and mental health systems. The proposal failed because of resistance from health insurance and managed care agencies as well as partisan conflicts. Among the arguments against the proposal was the further intrusion of government into health care. NASW had its own bill in Congress at that time promoting the right to universal health care under a single-payer system. What has occurred instead is a sweeping change in health and behavioral health (mental health and chemical dependency) care from a fee-for-service system to a variety of managed care arrangements, with large variances and inconsistencies in the coverage of mental health and substance abuse treatment.

Some of the impetus for these changes came in the Health Maintenance Organization Act of 1973 (P.L. 93-222). In the 1990s managed care arrangements grew rapidly as a cost-saving mechanism. Managed care has the potential to provide health and mental health coverage to more Americans, but its use in the behavioral health care arena has been met with at least as much skepticism as it has in the physical health care arena.

Despite the many attempts to provide mental health services for everybody in need of these services, there is inadequate systematic or comprehensive coverage or follow-up after discharge from hospitals or correctional facilities. (In 2001 *Brad H. v. City of New York* challenged the lack of availability of follow-up mental health services for inmates discharged from jail.) Continuity of service in community mental health care also is lacking for many patients. The shortage of mental health resources has caused some state mental health systems to limit their services to individuals who meet the criteria for involuntary treatment. As a result people who request mental health services because they feel the need for them may be rejected.

Recently, a number of instances of violent behavior on the part of individuals with mental disorders—random shootings, hate crimes, and "suicide by cop" (see, for example, Winerip, 1999)—have evoked knee-jerk reactions and pressure for the increased use of mental health services as social control, just as occurred in the 1960s. The laws specifying criteria for involuntary treatment were considered too limiting, and legislatures were urged to facilitate and extend involuntary or court-ordered treatment; to make criteria for inpatient treatment more permissive; to extend the periods of commitment; and to simplify procedures, including involuntary administration of medication. Lately, states have added legislation for "assisted" or court-ordered outpatient treatment with an emphasis on medication compliance. In 1999 New York State passed "Kendra's Law," named after Kendra Webdale, who was pushed off a subway platform by a man who had been known to a number of mental health programs and had requested care several times but had not received continuing care.

In 2000 the California Senate Committee on Rules commissioned the Rand Institute for Civil Justice to study the effectiveness of involuntary outpatient treatment. The study of involuntary outpatient treatment in eight states (Ridgely, Borum, & Petrila, 2001) found that whereas "community-based care by multidisciplinary teams of highly trained mental health professionals with high staff to client ratios" (p. 99) produces good outcomes, the question of whether court orders improve outcomes was left unanswered. At a time when there are few adequate services and fiscal restraints limit funding for any mental health services, the costs of bureaucratic aspects of involuntary care may use up resources needed for outreach, follow-up care, and other services that people request.

Like each of the professions serving clients with mental illness, social workers bring a unique perspective to their work. Social workers are adept at conducting multidimensional, biopsychosocial assessments of clients and at developing interventions that target individual, family, community, and larger social systems. Social workers have led the way in working directly with patients, including families and using community resources in the treatment of people with mental disorders. Assessing the client's competence requires the social worker to balance the limitations inherent in the DSM classification system, consider the profession's historic person-in-environment focus, understand the cultural meanings ascribed to mental illness, and pay attention to potential social and economic injustices (Zide & Gray, 2001).

In addition to their clinical functions, social workers play an important role in primary prevention, early diagnosis, treatment, habilitation, and rehabilitation of emotional problems and mental illness. They can play a significant part in preventing developmental lags in preschool, nursery school, and day care. They can help youths with traumatic or problem situations that interfere with personal and social development. They can help people be better

partners and parents. The importance of their role in personal and developmental aspects of group and recreational programs or the preventive and corrective aspects of programs to reduce isolation among elderly people must not be underestimated.

Social workers also can play an important supportive and preventive role through education and consultation to community caretakers, ranging from primary physicians to child care workers and educators to police officers and other personnel in the criminal justice system. Prepared correctional personnel are more likely to avoid the give and take that results in mistreatment of individuals with mental illnesses or even suicide by cop.

NASW continues to emphasize its commitment to seeking social and economic justice for all groups and its special mission to serve those who are vulnerable, oppressed, and poor (Goldstein & Beebe, 1995). This group includes people with mental illness, especially those who are misunderstood or have difficulty in obtaining needed services.

ISSUE STATEMENT

Data collected from 1990 to 1992 for the congressionally mandated National Comorbidity Survey indicate that nearly 50 percent of a representative sample of Americans ages 15 to 54 years reported having at least one psychiatric disorder (including substance use) during their lifetime (Blazer, Kessler, McGonagle, & Swartz, 1994). The 12-month prevalence of serious mental illness is estimated at 6 percent (Kessler et al., 1996). Data on children and adolescents are less comprehensive, but the prevalence of serious emotional disturbances among those ages nine to 17 is estimated between 9 percent and 13 percent (Friedman, Katz-Leavy, Manderscheid, & Sondheimer, 1996). Indications are that emotional disturbances among young people are increasing (Cohen, Provet, & Jones, 1996). As the population ages it is expected that depression, suicide (which is already at an alarming rate among elderly people), and dementia will continue to increase.

Both severe and persistent mental disorders as well as acute mental disorders can have profound consequences for individuals, their families, and society, affecting their ability to learn, to grow into healthy adults, to nurture children, to work, to secure housing, and to engage in other routines of living. In 1990 the monetary costs of alcohol, drug, and mental disorders were $314 billion. Of this, $148 billion was attributed to mental disorders exclusive of alcohol and other drug disorders. Of this $148 billion, $67 billion was attributed to health care costs (including the direct costs of treatment for mental illness); $63 billion to loss of productivity as a result of illness; $12 billion to loss of productivity because of premature death; and $6 billion to crime, criminal justice costs, and property losses (Rouse, 1995).

NIMH (1995) provided considerable evidence of the effectiveness of treatments for many mental illnesses, but most people with mental disorders do not receive treatment for their condition from the specialty mental health or general health sector. Some people are unaware that their conditions (or those of a loved one) are treatable mental disorders. Many people who have serious medical conditions or terminal illnesses also experience undiagnosed and untreated mental disorders. Others may not perceive the need for treatment of their condition or avoid treatment because of the stigma of mental illness or because of unacceptable side effects of medication. In some cases individuals seek help for symptom relief but encounter professionals who fail to identify their condition. Still others may want treatment for themselves or a loved one but are unable to obtain it because of a lack of available or accessible resources or a lack of knowledge about the means of securing care.

An ever-increasing percentage of Americans have neither private nor public health insurance. Despite efforts to increase insurance parity for mental and substance use disorders, most people who do have insurance do not enjoy the same access to care for these problems that they do for physical illness (Rouse, 1995). Most insurance contracts tend to limit numbers of sessions or days of treatment or set lifetime "caps," making effective treatment for chronic or cyclical conditions unrealistic. After a June 1999 mental health summit led by Tipper Gore, President Clinton granted parity

to federal employees, ensuring that serious mental illnesses would be treated the same way as other medical conditions. Attempts at instituting a national health insurance program, including mental health care, have failed thus far. Americans now find themselves in an era of managed health and behavioral health care that raises new concerns about access to mental health services. Moreover, even very comprehensive insurance-based services would need to be supplemented by special outreach mental health services for those who do not recognize their difficulties or do not seek help on their own.

Along with psychiatry, psychology, marriage and family therapy, and nursing, social work is one of the five core mental health disciplines. Among NASW members, 33 percent identify mental health as their primary practice area (Ginsberg, 1995). If one considers the preventive role played by child welfare agencies, school social workers, family services, and services to elderly people, almost each of the 150,000 members of NASW makes an important contribution to the mental health field.

Recognizing the prevalence of mental disorders and the costs they exact, social workers want to see that mental illness is prevented whenever possible. When mental illness is manifested, social workers want to ensure that clients receive the most effective and least restrictive treatment available that is acceptable. In addition to inadequate access to mental health services for financial reasons, social workers are aware of other problems that stand in the way of effective prevention, assessment, and treatment. Among these problems are lack of public and private investment in a continuum of care that provides for adequate transition among institutional, residential, partial hospitalization, and outpatient services that an individual may need. An example of a program that provides for adequate transition is a community support program, especially one that adheres to a PACT (programs for assertive community treatment) model (Test, 1998). Problems in obtaining services, especially for those with severe mental illness, are further exacerbated by the fragmented nature of the services delivery system, in which one agency provides mental health treatment, another social insurance and public assistance payments for people with disabilities, another housing, and still others vocational rehabilitation and other rehabilitation or habilitation services (Torrey, 1989). Often mental health policy works at cross-purposes, for example, by providing benefits only if an individual's condition does not improve rather than supporting the individual to achieve the greatest degree of independence possible or by requiring services in a more restrictive and more costly setting than the individual requires.

Historically, some subgroups of the population have been underserved or poorly served. They generally include groups with little power, specifically, women, children, members of racial and ethnic groups, and those of the lowest socioeconomic status. There is a lack of culturally competent service providers, including bilingual and bicultural practitioners, to serve members of the various ethnic groups represented in the United States (McNeil & Kennedy, 1997). Because of gender biases women may be diagnosed with mental disorders (Walker, 1994) and prescribed medication too frequently (Fellin, 1996). Racism, classism, and ageism result in biased diagnoses and treatment. Many incarcerated individuals suffer from mental disorders (Rouse, 1995) but receive inadequate mental health care, and many people are being incarcerated as an alternative to receiving treatment for mental disorders (Torrey, 1997).

Shortages of resources and personnel lead to various economy measures and shortcuts: Medication may be prescribed without sufficient follow-up or exploration about its effectiveness or side effects. Medical problems, living situation, interpersonal relationships, recurring or obsessive thoughts, or hallucinations may not be heard by mental health workers because there has not been sufficient continuity of contact for the development of a trusting relationship that would permit the patient to share these. Some individuals in involuntary outpatient treatment are reluctant to complain about medication side effects because they fear their challenge of the medical regimen may result in rehospitalization. A lack of preventive services and missed opportunities for treatment referrals from existing preventive services lead to delays in needed intervention, exacerbation of conditions, and increased chronicity.

NASW believes that social workers should work to improve education, research, and services provision. As part of the social work profession's goal of achieving social and economic justice for all those residing in the United States, and because social workers are key providers of mental health services, NASW is concerned about ensuring a mentally healthy United States of America.

POLICY STATEMENT

To further improvements that have been made in the prevention, diagnosis, assessment, and treatment of mental illness, it is the position of NASW that

■ all people in the United States, including immigrants and refugees, be entitled to a comprehensive system of person-centered mental health care, both for severe and persistent mental illness and for acute and episodic mental health problems that impair the individual's functioning

■ mental health treatment be provided in parity with treatment for other types of illness in all health care plans

■ social workers should advocate for the elimination of stigma associated with mental illness

■ social workers should recognize outreach services as an important part of mental health services

■ managed health care and other health care plans should rely on the best judgment of mental health clinicians in conjunction with consumers' judgment about the type and duration of services needed. Mechanisms for appeal of treatment decisions are needed to ensure protection of both the consumer and the provider.

■ the preventive functions of social work practice, including education, consultation, and early intervention, should be recognized and fully funded, with the goal of maximizing individual and family wellness and fostering resilience

- social workers should be knowledgeable about and involved in emergency preparedness planning and policy development as well as direct intervention with affected individuals, families, and communities

- social workers, in collaboration with the consumer, should involve family members and significant others in assessment and treatment planning. Consumers should be given choices among service options that meet their needs and individual preferences.

- social workers should seek to maximize family wellness, with an emphasis on all levels of prevention

- family members should have access to supportive services to help them cope with the problems posed by the mental illness of a loved one

- the correctional system should not be used as a de facto mental health system. In addition, incarcerated individuals should have access to mental health services, including assessment, screening, medication, counseling, discharge planning, and referral

- a more integrated system of care should be developed, with an emphasis on empowerment and recovery

- social workers should support a broader range of housing and vocational services to improve the quality of life, enhance independent community living, and build effective and stable interpersonal relationships

- services should be fully integrated for consumers with severe mental illness and co-occurring disorders such as substance abuse and mental retardation

- people with substance abuse disorders and mental illness should be treated fairly in assessing functional capacity and in rendering social insurance, public assistance, and social services

- social insurance and public assistance payments should be increased to a level equal to or above the federal poverty standard

- the efforts of people with mental illness to work should be encouraged and should not result in negative sanctions from social insurance, public assistance, or other programs

- the Omnibus Budget Reconciliation Act, the Americans with Disabilities Act of 1990, and related legislation should be fully enforced so that people with mental disorders can achieve full inclusion in all aspects of life in the least restrictive environment

- social workers have a vital role to play in mental health research and should be encouraged to seek research funding to test their treatment methodologies and outcomes. In addition, social workers should engage in research or advocate for further research on mental health issues, with particular emphasis on traditionally underrepresented populations, including, but not limited to, children and adolescents, women, members of racial and ethnic groups, elderly people, and people with disabilities.

- in light of the trend toward involuntary outpatient commitment, careful evaluation must be done to ensure protection of consumers' right to self-determination and safety of family members in the community

- culturally responsive treatment in the most therapeutic and least restrictive environment, including use of the consumer's native language, should guide the practice of social work

- social workers should take the lead in advocating for viable, comprehensive, community-based mental health services

- social workers specializing in mental health should be accorded the same status as other core mental health professionals

- social workers play a key role in educating the public about mental illness as a means of fostering prevention, encouraging early identification and intervention, promoting treatment, and reducing the stigma associated with mental illness. This responsibility includes efforts to influence public policy in ways that will foster improved prevention and diagnosis and promote comprehensive, continuous treatment of mental illness for all individuals who need these services and not only those who might be considered a threat to society.

REFERENCES

American Psychiatric Association. (1994). *Diagnostic and statistical manual of mental disorders* (4th ed.). Washington, DC: Author.

American Psychiatric Association. (2000). *Diagnostic and statistical manual of mental disorders* (4th ed., Text Revision). Washington, DC: Author.

Americans with Disabilities Act of 1990, P.L. 101-336, 104 Stat. 327.

Blazer, D. G., Kessler, R. C., McGonagle, K. A., & Swartz, M. S. (1994). The prevalence and distribution of major depression in a national community sample: The National Comorbidity Survey. *American Journal of Psychiatry, 151,* 979–986.

Brad H. v. City of New York, 185 Misc. 2d 420. (2001).

Cohen, P., Provet, A. G., & Jones, M. (1996). Prevalence of emotional and behavioral disorders during childhood and adolescence. In B. L. Levin & J. Petrila (Eds.), *Mental health services: A public health perspective* (pp. 193–209). New York: Oxford University Press.

Deutsch, A. (1948). *The shame of the states.* New York: Harcourt, Brace, and Co.

Education for All Handicapped Children Act of 1975, P.L. 94-142, 89 Stat. 773.

Fellin, P. (1996). *Mental health and mental illness: Policies, programs, and services.* Itasca, IL: F. E. Peacock.

Friedman, R. M., Katz-Leavy, J., Manderscheid, R. W., & Sondheimer, D. L. (1996). Prevalence of serious emotional disturbance in children and adolescents. In R. W. Manderscheid & M. A. Sonnenschein (Eds.), *Mental health, United States, 1996* (pp. 71–89). Washington, DC: U.S. Government Printing Office.

Germain, C. B., & Gitterman, A. (1995). Ecological perspective. In R. L. Edwards (Ed.-in-Chief), *Encyclopedia of social work* (19th ed., Vol. 1., pp. 815–824). Washington, DC: NASW Press.

Ginsberg, L. (1995). *Social work almanac* (2nd ed.). Washington, DC: NASW Press.

Goldstein, S. R., & Beebe, L. (1995). National Association of Social Workers. In R. L. Edwards (Ed.-in-Chief), *Encyclopedia of social work* (19th ed., Vol. 2, pp. 1747–1764). Washington, DC: NASW Press.

Health Maintenance Organization Act of 1973, P.L. 93-222, 87 Stat. 914.

Joint Commission on Mental Illness and Health. (1961). *Action for mental health.* New York: Basic Books.

Kessler, R. C., Berglund, P. A., Zhao, S., Leaf, P. J., Kouzis, A. C., Bruce, M. L., et al. (1996). The 12-month prevalence and correlates of serious mental illness (SMI). In R. W. Manderscheid & M. A. Sonnenschein (Eds.), *Mental health, United States, 1996* (pp. 59–70). Washington, DC: U.S. Government Printing Office.

Kirk, S. A., & Kutchins, H. (1992). *The selling of DSM: The rhetoric of science in psychiatry.* New York: Aldine de Gruyter.

McNeil, J. S., & Kennedy, R. (1997). Mental health services in minority groups of color. In T. R. Watking & J. W. Calicutt (Eds.), *Mental health policy and practice today* (pp. 235–257). Thousand Oaks, CA: Sage Publications.

Mechanic, D. (1989). *Mental health and social policy* (3rd ed.). Englewood Cliffs, NJ: Prentice Hall.

Mental Health Act of 1946, P.L. 79-487, 60 Stat. 421.

Mental Health Centers Act Amendments of 1965, P.L. 89-105.

Mental Health Study Act of 1955, P.L. 84-182, 69 Stat. 381.

Mental Retardation Facilities and Community Mental Health Centers Construction Act of 1963, P.L. 88-164, 77 Stat. 282.

National Institute of Mental Health. (1995). *Mental illness in America: The National Institute of Mental Health agenda* [Online]. Available: http://www.nimh.gov/research/amer.html

Omnibus Budget Reconciliation Act of 1987, P.L. 100-203, 101 Stat. 1330.

Ridgely, M. S., Borum, R., & Petrila, J. (2001). *The effectiveness of involuntary outpatient treatment: Empirical evidence and the experience of eight states.* Santa Monica, CA: RAND Health, RAND Institute for Civil Justice.

Rouse, B. A. (Ed.). (1995). *Substance abuse and mental illness sourcebook* (DHHS Publication No. SMA 95-3064). Washington, DC: U.S. Government Printing Office.

Scull, A. T. (1977). *Decarceration, community treatment and the deviant: A radical view.* Englewood Cliffs, NJ: Prentice Hall.

State Comprehensive Mental Health Services Plan Act of 1986, P.L. 99-660, 100 Stat. 482.

Stewart B. McKinney Homeless Assistance Act of 1987, P.L. 100-77, 101 Stat. 482.

Test, M. A. (1998). Community-based treatment models for adults with severe and persistent mental illness. In J. W. B. Williams & K. Ell (Eds.), *Mental health research: Implications for practice.* Washington, DC: NASW Press.

Torrey, E. F. (1989). Thirty years of shame: The scandalous neglect of the mentally ill homeless. *Policy Review, 48,* 10–15.

Torrey, E. F. (1997). *Out of the shadows: Confronting America's mental illness crisis.* New York: John Wiley & Sons.

Walker, L. E. A. (1994). Are personality disorders gender biased? Yes. In S. A. Kirk & S. D. Einbinder (Eds.), *Controversial issues in mental health* (pp. 21–30). Boston: Allyn & Bacon.

Winerip, M. (1999, May 23). Bedlam on the streets. *New York Times Magazine.*

Wyatt v. Stickney, 344 F. Supp. 373 (M.D. Ala. 1972).

Zide, M. R., & Gray, S. W. (2001). *Psychopathology: A competency-based assessment model for social workers.* Pacific Grove, CA: Brooks/Cole.

Policy statement approved by the NASW Delegate Assembly, August 2002. This policy statement supersedes the policy statement on Mental Health approved by the Delegate Assembly in 1990 and reconfirmed by the Delegate Assembly in 1999. For further information, contact the National Association of Social Workers, 750 First Street, NE, Suite 700, Washington, DC 20002-4241. Telephone: 202-408-8600; e-mail: press@naswdc.org

Parental Kidnapping

BACKGROUND

Parental abduction of children is integrally linked with major social changes that have affected U.S. families during the past 20 years and with single parenthood and shifting roles within families that affect child care and custody (Finkelhor, Hotaling, & Sedlak, 1991; Greif & Hegar, 1993). The number of children affected by divorce in the United States has exceeded 1 million per year since 1975, and by 1990 more than 6 million children lived with a divorced parent (U.S. Bureau of the Census, 1991). In addition to children of divorce, children whose parents have separated are also potential victims of parental abduction.

A study sponsored by the Justice Department estimated that there are as many as 350,000 cases of parental abduction annually, when "abduction" is defined broadly using the broadest definition (Finkelhor et al., 1991). The issue of definition is important in parental kidnapping, with legal definitions varying among states and national and international jurisdictions. Some legal definitions include any parent whose actions deprive the other parent of custody or access to the child, whether the couple is married, separated, or divorced. At the other end of the continuum, some states have laws that define abduction only in terms of violating a custody order.

Studies that have defined parental abduction broadly identify men as the abductors in 42 percent to 55 percent of the cases (Hegar & Greif, 1991a; Janvier, McCormick, & Donaldson, 1990; Sagatun & Barrett, 1990). Older studies that considered only abductions by noncustodial parents reported a much higher proportion of male perpetrators (Agopian, 1984). Boys and girls were abducted in almost equal numbers in all of the studies reviewed, and the

studies indicated that toddlers and preschoolers may be at greatest risk. Children who have been abducted encounter a range of experiences, from dislocation and confusion to child abuse and the trauma of repeated snatchings. The effect of parental abduction is often devastating for the parents left behind (Greif & Hegar, 1993; Sagatun & Barrett, 1990).

Although public awareness of parental kidnapping has grown recently because of coverage in the print and broadcast media, it is a long-standing problem that has been recognized, at least implicitly, in federal and state policies for decades. For almost 50 years parents who kidnapped their children were specifically exempt from criminal prosecution under the federal Kidnapping Act. Because of the uneven nature of state laws and practices regarding child custody during this period, some parents who failed to receive custody in one state kidnapped their children and sought custody in another state (Sagatun & Barrett, 1990).

The problem of finding abducted children who were taken out of the country was particularly acute because, until the 1980s, there was no major treaty that addressed return of internationally abducted children. In two studies abducted children were known or believed to have been taken out of the country in 20 percent and 40 percent of the situations, respectively (Hegar & Greif, 1991b; Janvier et al., 1990), and approximately 4,000 cases of internationally abducted U.S. children had been reported to the U.S. Department of State (Hegar & Greif, 1991a, 1991b).

Significant policy developments at the state, federal, and international levels have been initiated in the past two decades. To date, most efforts to combat parental kidnapping have emphasized primarily one approach: to prevent abducting parents from going to another jurisdiction to obtain a custody order in their favor (Hegar, 1990). To that end, all states have adopted some version of the model Uniform Child Custody Jurisdiction Act and have passed additional legislation aimed at reducing parental kidnapping.

At the federal level, in 1980 the National Center for Missing and Exploited Children was founded and the Parental Kidnapping Prevention Act was enacted. However, enforcement of the act depends in part on state criminal law, because its "UFAP" (unlawful flight to avoid prosecution) provisions apply only if a state felony has been committed. The act encourages cooperation among the states and provides for Federal Bureau of Investigation (FBI) assistance in locating and returning kidnapped children (Coombs, 1990).

One Supreme Court case has interpreted parts of the Parental Kidnapping Prevention Act. In *Thompson v. Thompson* (1988), the Supreme Court established that parents generally are unable to resort to the federal courts to resolve conflicting awards of custody in state courts as a result of noncompliance with the Parental Kidnapping Prevention Act.

Civil suits (torts) arising out of loss of physical custody also are possible in many states. Some states have made or have proposed statutory provisions for civil suits in parental kidnapping cases (Oberdorfer, 1991).

In 1980 participants from 29 countries, including the United States, drafted the Hague Convention on the Civil Aspects of International Child Abduction. The Hague Convention provides for children under age 16 years to be returned to the country in which they were habitually resident immediately before a breach of custody or access rights.

Enforcement of the convention has been hampered by a number of factors. The United States signed the convention in 1981 and ratified it in 1986, but its provisions were not implemented until July 1988, when the International Child Abduction Remedies Act (P.L. 100-300) took effect. That act provides specific mechanisms for the United States to comply with the convention and makes the U.S. State Department the agency in charge of enforcement (Pfund, 1990). By 1999 there were 54 subscribing nations; however, some nations were demonstrating patterns of noncompliance with the provisions of the convention.

Despite these policy developments on state, national, and international levels, there is evidence that U.S. state laws remain uneven in their provisions and judicial interpretations (Greif & Hegar, 1993; Sagatun & Barrett, 1990). With increasing numbers of children joining the groups at highest risk—those with separating, separated, or divorced parents—it is critical that the social work profession work with the other disciplines involved with the problem to curb and resolve parental abductions of children.

ISSUE STATEMENT

Abduction of children by their parents is a complex social and legal problem that is receiving increased public and professional attention. Many of the issues have only begun to be recognized and must be addressed in multiple arenas. Among the problems interwoven with parental abduction are the acrimony of many child custody disputes (Bautz & Hill, 1991; Bentch, 1986), dissatisfaction with custody and visitation rights within many separated and divorced families, high rates of domestic violence and the special difficulties of parents who take their children and flee abuse (Berliner, 1990), and the need for specialized services of all types to prevent and resolve abductions and to help the families who experience them (Greif & Hegar, 1991; Long, Forehand, & Zogg, 1991).

It is incumbent on social workers to become more knowledgeable about the problem of parental kidnapping and its causes and to participate actively in shaping policies at all levels that will prevent or reduce its occurrence. Furthermore, social workers should incorporate knowledge about parental kidnapping and its consequences for family members into their practice so they can render more effective services to the family members who have experienced such an event or who may be susceptible to its occurrence. Social workers may encounter families who are at risk of or who have experienced abduction in their roles in couples and families; in school social work; in child protection and foster care agencies; in battered women's programs and shelters; and in forensic settings, such as police departments, prosecutors' and public defenders' offices, and prisons.

POLICY STATEMENT

In regard to the problem of parental kidnapping, NASW strongly supports the following:

■ developing social services, such as supervised visitation, to prevent the abduction of children by their parents and the developing of postkidnapping counseling and mediation services to ameliorate the effects of the kidnapping and diminish the likelihood of its recurrence.

■ developing and using of consensual modes, such as divorce mediation and negotiation, to work out divorce and postdivorce conflicts regarding child custody, except in cases in which domestic violence, the threat of violence, child abuse and neglect, or sexual exploitation is an issue in the family.

■ adopting statutes in each state that include custody arrangements, such as joint custody, that reinforce the continued involvement of both parents in the important decisions about their children's welfare and upbringing, except in potentially dangerous situations.

■ establishing public education programs about the problems associated with parental kidnapping and the use of print and broadcast media to educate the public and to locate abducted children.

■ establishing professional education programs to inform practitioners about the causes, dynamics, and laws regarding parental kidnapping and abduction.

■ alerting child care providers to the potential for parental kidnapping and analyzing and strengthening policies of agencies in which children usually are present, particularly schools and child care facilities, to reduce the likelihood that those agencies will become sites of parental kidnapping.

■ reviewing, analyzing, and strengthening of state and federal laws concerning parental kidnapping, particularly toward achieving uniform definitions of abduction, and uniform compliance of child custody and enforcement laws across state borders.

■ examining, with other concerned professionals and citizens' groups, services that are available to victims and perpetrators of parental kidnapping and encouraging interdisciplinary cooperation to ensure the availability of comprehensive services.

■ recognizing the potential danger to an abducted child; being mindful of the need to work toward a coordinated national network for the reunion of abducted children and their families; and encouraging the full and active assistance of law enforcement agencies, particularly the FBI, in locating abducted children, with increased efforts on eliminating all discriminatroory barriers that affect the definition of parental kidnapping and the efforts to locate children of color.

■ working through international professional organizations to encourage adoption by more countries of the Hague Convention on the Civil Aspects of International Child Abduction and to strongly advocate for compliance with the convention by existing signatory countries.

■ advocacyting for state criminal statutes that allow distinction among abductions on the basis of circumstances, such as the use of force, harm done to the child, length of absence, or whether the child was concealed from the searching parent. Statutes should include a defense against the charge of parental abduction if the abductor acted to prevent or avoid harm to the child.

REFERENCES

Agopian, M. W. (1984). The impact on children of abduction by parents. *Child Welfare, 63*, 511–519.

Bautz, B. J., & Hill, R. M. (1991). Mediating the breakup: Do children win? *Mediation Quarterly, 8*, 199–210.

Bentch, S. T. (1986). Court-sponsored custody mediation to prevent parental kidnapping: A disarmament proposal. *St. Mary's Law Journal, 18*, 361–393.

Berliner, L. (1990). Protecting or harming: Parents who flee with their children. *Journal of Interpersonal Violence, 5,* 119–120.

Coombs, R. M. (1990). Progress under the PKPA. *Journal of the American Academy of Matrimonial Lawyers, 6,* 59–102.

Finkelhor, D., Hotaling, G., & Sedlak, A. (1991). Children abducted by family members: A national household survey of incidence and episode characteristics. *Journal of Marriage & the Family, 53,* 805–817.

Greif, G. L., & Hegar, R. L. (1991). Parents whose children are abducted by the other parent: Implications for treatment. *American Journal of Family Therapy, 19,* 215–225.

Greif, G. L., & Hegar, R. L. (1993). *When parents kidnap: The families behind the headlines.* New York: Free Press.

Hegar, R. L. (1990). Parental kidnapping and U.S. social policy. *Social Service Review, 64,* 407–421.

Hegar, R. L., & Greif, G. L. (1991a). Abduction of children by parents: A survey of the problem. *Social Work, 36,* 421–426.

Hegar, R. L., & Greif, G. L. (1991b). Parental kidnapping across international borders. *International Social Work, 34,* 353–363.

International Child Abduction Remedies Act (ICARA), P.L. 100-300, 102 Stat. 437 (1988).

Janvier, R. F., McCormick, K., & Donaldson, R. (1990). Parental kidnapping: A survey of left-behind parents. *Juvenile & Family Court Journal, 41,* 1–8.

Long, N., Forehand, R., & Zogg, C. (1991). Preventing parental child abduction: Analysis of a national project. *Clinical Pediatrics, 30,* 549–554.

Oberdorfer, D. (1991). Larson v. Dunn: Toward a reasoned response to parental kidnapping. *Minnesota Law Review, 75,* 1701–1730.

Parental Kidnapping Prevention Act of 1980, P.L. 96-611, §§ 6–10, 94 Stat. 3568, 3569.

Pfund, P. H. (1990). The Hague Convention on International Child Abduction, the International Child Abduction Remedies Act, and the need for availability of counsel for all petitioners. *Family Law Quarterly, 24,* 35–51.

Sagatun, I. J., & Barrett, L. (1990). Parental child abduction: The law, family dynamics, and legal system responses. *Journal of Criminal Justice, 18,* 433–442.

Thompson v. Thompson, 108 S.Ct. 513 (1988).

U.S. Bureau of the Census. (1991). *Marital status and living arrangements: March 1990* (Series P-20, No. 450). Washington, DC: U.S. Government Printing Office.

Policy statement approved by the NASW Delegate Assembly, August 2002. The 2002 Delegate Assembly also voted not to combine this policy statement with the policy statement on Child Abuse and Neglect as recommended by the 1999 Delegate Assembly. This policy statement supersedes the policy statement on Parental Kidnapping approved by the Delegate Assembly in 1984 and 1993. For further information, contact the National Association of Social Workers, 750 First Street, NE, Suite 700, Washington, DC 20002-4241. Telephone: 202-408-8600; e-mail: press@naswdc.org

Peace and Social Justice

BACKGROUND

The terrorist events on U.S. soil on September 11, 2001, have led to a multidimensional paradigm shift in public thinking, which relates in important ways to any policy about peace and social justice. Although the version of this policy approved by the NASW Delegate Assembly in August 1993 focused on the end of the cold war, consideration must now be given to a new type of war on U.S. soil, fought by the United States and others around the world.

The Role of the Military and a "New Kind of War"

Between 1989 and 2001 the U.S. government cut defense spending by closing bases; cutting troop strength; and eliminating numbers of planes, missiles, and ships (Cooper, 2001). Even so, in 1995 military expenses continued to represent 35 percent of this country's total expenditures (U.S. Bureau of the Census, 2000) during the same year that social welfare expenditures under public programs accounted for only 20.9 percent of the gross domestic product (U.S. Bureau of the Census, 2000). Furthermore, in 2001, before the September terrorist attacks, President Bush was focusing future military spending on his request for $8.3 billion in 2002 alone to fund a missile defense program (Cooper, 2001). After September 11 the military budget obviously soared in new ways not experienced since the Gulf War of 1991.

Economic Struggles and Justice

The United States plays a huge part in economic policy around the world. As the major player in global capitalism—through our dom-

inant role in the World Bank, the International Monetary Fund, and the World Trade Organization—we must bear responsibility for the social justice travesties that our policies create. Our corporate practices clearly disrupt rather than support justice in some emerging economies, and "there's no point denying that multinationals have contributed to labor, environmental, and human-rights abuses" (Danaher, 2001, p. 14). Many countries spend more on repaying foreign debt than on health care and other basic needs. For example, social services represent only 34.5 percent of Brazil's government expenditures in contrast to debt repayments that consumed 75.6 percent of the government's revenue. In India social services are only 11.9 percent of government expenditures, but India pays 33.6 percent of revenues in debt repayment (CQ Researcher, 2001).

Other countries with different types of government and economies need to be supported to find their own ways rather than necessarily conforming to ours. This can be encouraged by equitable negotiations about debt relief and programs that support appropriate, more localized responses to economic problems. "Foreign countries with entirely different legal, economic, and political systems do not need the International Monetary Fund to forcibly impose on them what is a dubious form of capitalism even in the United States" (Johnson, 2000, p. 225).

The Use of Violence

The United States continues to be one of the most violent nations in the world. We have much disagreement about the role of guns in our society, with the percentage of people feeling it is more important to control gun ownership growing from 57 percent in 1993 to 65 percent in 1999. At the same time among others in the same study, those feeling it is most important, instead, to protect the rights of gun owners decreased from 34 percent in 1993 to 30 percent in 1999 (Bureau of Justice Statistics, 1999). When participants were asked about the primary causes of gun violence in the United States in a 2000 study, there was a distinct gender difference. Only 18 percent of men laid blame on the availability of guns compared with 24 percent of women. The way that parents raise children was seen as the cause of gun violence by 51 percent of the men but only 38 percent of the women, and the influence of popular culture was identified as the reason for gun violence by 23 percent of men and 29 percent of women.

In contrast with much of the rest of the world, a majority of Americans (71 percent) in 1999 believed in the death penalty. Again this varies by gender and race: 66 percent of women favor this punishment compared with 75 percent of men, whereas a more dramatic 39 percent of black people were in agreement compared with 77 percent of white people (Bureau of Justice Statistics, 1999). A more even split exists between those who feel that using the death penalty for those who have committed murder will deter others from the same crime: 47 percent opt for deterring and 49 percent feel that it does not have much effect (Bureau of Justice Statistics, 1999).

The number of prisoners executed in the United States grew steadily from 23 in 1990 to 56 in 1995; there was a large jump in 1999 to 98 individuals (U.S. Bureau of the Census, 2000). Some of our violence is explicitly directed toward children, women, immigrants, and, after September 11, Muslims and people from the Middle East. Clearly, both terrorism and state-supported violence affect people worldwide in negative ways that perpetuate the opposite of peace and social justice.

International Cooperation

Although the terrorist attacks of September 11 have led to unprecedented outreach for international cooperation, this has not been done primarily through the United Nations, which represents the most appropriate format.

Poverty, violence, racism, sexism, homophobia, and environmental degradation are problems throughout the world. Patterns of consumption in the United States directly relate to many of these problems, and, as a country, we need to take responsibility for the results of our lifestyle. We must accept "the fact that the economic situation we enjoy and the privileges it gives us are at the expense of two-thirds of the people of the world. Our world has finite resources, and what we have is related to the fact that the majority of people do not have enough" (Isasi-Diaz, 1999, p. 220).

ISSUE STATEMENT

Beyond the destruction and trauma of war is the continual drain on human and material resources—the diversion of energies and goods and services to meet military needs while the social welfare of millions of people in the United States and abroad goes unmet. Wars also sap the nation's resources, resulting in the pollution of the earth and the atmosphere and posing a threat to the world's public health. Already we are faced with epidemic-scale international health threats associated with AIDS and starvation. Groups at high risk of threats to health and survival, such as children, elderly people, people with disabilities, and women, inevitably suffer most from war and violence. In addition to the physical, social, and economic consequences, the arms race, the introduction of chemical and biological warfare, and the threat of nuclear war pose unique psychological consequences worldwide.

In a world economy with a single nation more powerful than all the others, military approaches predictably run the risk of increasing violence rather than paving the way for peace. Although the strengths and weaknesses of U.S. culture are highly visible and broadcast around the world, resentments inevitably are created by the wide discrepancies in basic needs such as food, shelter, and a livable wage. This, in turn, creates a dramatic risk for all of us, regardless of ideology or politics. "Given its wealth and power, the United States will be a prime recipient in the foreseeable future of all of the more expectable forms of blowback, particularly terrorist attacks against Americans in and out of the armed forces anywhere on earth, including within the United States" (Johnson, 2000, p. 223). Of course responding to terrorism, especially against civilians and on our own shores, in ways that do not maim and kill is a tremendous challenge, but it appears to be a vital step for establishing and maintaining peace.

Issues of social justice have special meaning for women, particularly in a world in which education, the vote, work outside the home, and rights within marriage and the family are not assured for significant numbers of women. Women in many countries, though, including those countries in which the roles of women are strictly limited, tend to have a strong interest in working for peace, especially through nonviolent strategies, because of their "concern for human life, especially for children, but also for themselves and other women" (Brock-Utne, 1985, p. 37). It is imperative that the United States ratify the Convention to End Discrimination of All Women (CEDAW). Because social work historically has been a female-dominated profession, in terms of the majority of both workers and clients, it is not surprising that members of this profession feel passionately about peace and social justice.

Racism, negative attitudes toward immigrants, and generalizations about members of certain ethnic and religious groups are not new to the United States. Indigenous people within the United States and Africans who were brought here under slavery also suffered immensely. Violence, persecution, and discrimination, both historic and present, are realities experienced by gay, lesbian, bisexual, and transgender populations, as well as by women, children, and other disenfranchised populations. Chinese people were excluded from our shores for many years, people of Japanese descent were put in internment camps at the beginning of World War II, European Jews were denied entry as refugees from fascism, and Haitian refugees were accepted and then sent back during the 1970s and 1980s. The events of September 11 have opened up a new and similarly intolerable series of acts against Muslims and people of Middle Eastern descent that require diligence and determination to bring to an end. True peace and social justice can never be attained for one group without applying it to everyone.

POLICY STATEMENT

In spite of the challenges of terrorism, we need to reduce the use of violence in our language and as a solution to domestic and international problems. Waging "drug wars" that do not include real treatment and carrying out the "war on crime" with its increased and inequitable use of lengthy incarceration and increased capital punishment—which have not been shown to reduce crime and are meted out disproportionately against certain racial and ethnic groups—are both counterproductive to peace and social justice.

Economic and Military Issues

Although we have recently gone through a new military buildup and actions against terrorist groups and the countries that harbor them, the United States needs to emphasize economic support rather than Western dominance in its foreign policy language and actions. The welfare of all people and the balanced economic and social development of nations should be the goals of U.S. foreign policy.

Whenever possible, the United States must foster cooperation in its foreign policy rather than unilateral military action. A long-range goal should be reduction of military spending and diversion of the subsequent savings to social needs. At such a time, it will be important that the government support economic conversion from war production to peaceful pursuits, with special assistance for personnel moving from military to civilian life.

In addition, the United States should work through peaceful efforts for the abolition of nuclear testing by all nations and the eventual elimination of nuclear weapons worldwide. Similarly, this country needs to support the abolition of all chemical and biological warfare, urge all countries to cease production of such compounds and to destroy any existing stockpiles, and support a U.N.-sponsored multinational treaty calling for strong sanctions against any countries that possess biochemical weapons.

International Cooperation

Even in the face of overt terrorist attacks on the United States, it is still vital that we work in creative ways with other nations and international organizations to reduce violence against innocent civilians. Indeed, finding constructive and nonviolent means to deal with international conflicts must be a priority.

Full participation with such organizations as the United Nations, the World Health Organization, and the World Court are critical first steps in such an effort. In addition, the United States should endeavor to decrease the numbers of refugees by providing economic and social assistance rather than military shipments to other nations. Refugees must be granted asylum if they are faced with violence and death.

By recognizing the equal worth of all humans and the equal loss in terms of the death of any innocent person, concepts such as asylum should not be based on race, ethnicity, or country of origin. The United States should ratify and support implementation of the 1948 Universal Declaration of Human Rights and related U.N. treaties. This declaration states that each person has the right to a standard of living that is adequate for his or her health and well-being. "Human rights principles hold up the vision of a free, just, and peaceful world and set minimum standards for how individuals and institutions everywhere should treat people" (Mittal & Rosset, 1999, p. 164).

The United States should support each country's right to political and economic self-determination, in compliance with international law and U.N. conventions on human rights; to nonintervention; and to control over its own natural resources. In considering the tragic and growing phenomena of world poverty and hunger, internationally coordinated efforts must include redistribution of global resources (such as technology transfer, reduction of Third World debt burden, and reduction of overconsumption patterns of the West), improvement of women's status, and population stabilization.

The United States needs to stimulate and support the use of government funds, free of military or political purposes, to promote social and economic development and protection of the environment and to meet basic human needs in education, housing, health, and welfare services. Whenever possible such programs should be funded and coordinated through the United Nations and emphasize human values and their contribution to human welfare.

Social Work's Role

Social workers have consistently advocated for a just and peaceful world. Social justice is central to the profession's values and specifically emphasized in its *Code of Ethics* as social work professionals are instructed to "promote policies that safeguard the rights of and confirm equity and social justice for all people" (NASW, 1999, p. 7). Social workers similarly are encouraged to learn other languages, become informed about all aspects of other cultures, and apply the profession's values to work with clients of all races, ethnicities, and sexual orientations.

On more macro levels, social workers frequently work with existing organizations with a world focus, such as the United Nations, as well as participate in grassroots organizations that address peace, human rights, freedom, environmental issues, participation, human diversity, and the special needs of children and women. Furthermore, as a global profession, social work promotes internships, travel, and international work opportunities that allow practitioners to join with others in the struggle for a more peaceful and equitable world. It is critical for social workers to hold social welfare positions in multilateral and bilateral programs of technical assistance such as community development. Additional training needs to be provided to prepare qualified social workers for international service. NASW's International Committee should be strong and active, and NASW should build strong connections with the International Federation of Social Workers.

The United States needs to continue using qualified professional social workers to serve the armed forces and military dependents to ensure that a high priority is given to human values and social welfare needs in those settings. The profession's domestic peace and justice agenda needs to include gun control legislation and the stopping of illegal weapons trade. To prevent violence that turns U.S. communities into war zones, social workers must promote early and ongoing intervention through economic revitalization and educational and employment opportunities to give young people hope and direction. In addition, social workers need to address the role of the media and other institutions in the glorification of violence and the use of weapons.

Finally, it is appropriate for the issue of peace and world justice to permeate social work education on all levels. Teaching the connections between direct client services and the larger sociopolitical context and providing avenues for students to learn and practice social action skills will bring social work back to its roots. Building on the profession's activist tradition is one of the most powerful ways to carry the message of peace and social justice and help make it a reality.

REFERENCES

Brock-Utne, B. (1985). *Education for peace: A feminist perspective.* New York: Pergamon Press.

Bureau of Justice Statistics. (1999). *Sourcebook of criminal justice statistics.* Washington, DC: U.S. Department of Justice.

Cooper, M. H. (2001, September 7). Bush's defense strategy [CQ Researcher]. *Congressional Quarterly,* pp. 691–695.

CQ Researcher. (2001, September 28). *Congressional Quarterly,* p. 764.

Danaher, K. (Ed.). (2001). *Democratizing the global economy: The battle against the World Bank and the IMF.* Monroe, ME: Common Courage Press.

Isasi-Diaz, A. M. (1999). Economics, ethics, and the everyday: Reflections from another shore. In P. K. Brubaker & M. E. Hobgood (Eds.), *Welfare policy: Feminist critiques* (pp. 215–224). Cleveland: Pilgrim Press.

Johnson, C. (2000). *Blowback: The costs and consequences of American empire.* New York: Owl Company.

Mittal, A., & Rosset, P. (1999). *America needs human rights.* Oakland, CA: Food First Books.

National Association of Social Workers. (1999). *NASW code of ethics.* Washington, DC: Author.

U.S. Bureau of the Census. (2000). *Statistical abstract of the United States: The national data book* (120th ed.). Washington, DC: U.S. Government Printing Office.

Policy statement approved by the NASW Delegate Assembly, August 2002. This statement supersedes the policy statement on Peace and Social Justice approved by the Delegate Assembly in 1990 and reconfirmed by the Delegate Assembly in 1993. For further information, contact the National Association of Social Workers, 750 First Street, NE, Suite 700, Washington, DC 20002-4241. Telephone: 202-408-8600; e-mail: press@naswdc.org

People with Disabilities

BACKGROUND

In 2001, the U.S. Census Bureau reported that 52.6 million (nearly 20 percent of the population) people have some level of disability and 33 million (nearly 4 percent of the population) have severe disability. With medical advances and an aging population, that number grows daily. A study by the Population Reference Bureau states that "due to better trauma care . . . severe brain injuries and spinal cord injuries account for an estimated 80,000 new disabilities a year" (Fujiura, 2001). The disability community consists of a wide array of individuals from all races, ages, and genders with a tremendous variety of backgrounds and life experiences. The term "disability" itself is difficult to define; people with disabilities vary widely and experience physical, sensory, and cognitive impairments, as well as mental, physical, and chronic illness. Disabilities can be acquired, congenital, physical, cognitive, or a combination of multiple conditions. The experience of disability may be different for each person. Disabilities may be visible; in some instances disabilities are invisible and are not readily apparent to others. Functional limitations from disabilities range from none to profound. Many disabilities are temporary; however, once acquired, most are lifelong. Numerous polls and studies have documented that people with disabilities, as a group, are relegated to an inferior status in our society and are severely disadvantaged socially, vocationally, economically, and educationally (Americans with Disabilities Act of 1990 [ADA] [P.L. 101-336]). What is considered a disability at a certain point in time derives from informal and formal societal processes whereby subjective definitions of disability become objective and socially accepted. For example, much of the general public think of disability as the person's type of physical impairment or functional limitation before the reference to the person, such as a "blind man," "paralyzed woman," or "mental patient," all of which are derogatory. In the past socially acceptable labels used to describe people with disabilities were even more demeaning, with terms like "invalid," "cripple," "moron," or "crazy."

During the past 40 years, social attitudes and policies in the United States have slowly begun to recognize the civil rights of people with disabilities. Since the late 1960s, Congress has passed more than a dozen laws addressing issues related to people with disabilities. These laws include the Architectural Barriers Act of 1968 as amended (P.L. 42 U.S.C. §§ 4151 *et seq.*) Title VII of the Civil Rights Act of 1968 (P.L. 90-284) and the Fair Housing Amendment Act of 1988 (P.L. 42 U.S.C. §§ 4151 *et seq.*) which addressed fair housing issues, and the Mental Health Bill of Rights Act of 1985, which expanded state protection and advocacy systems to cover mental illness, and the Americans with Disabilities Act of 1992. Yet these laws continue to afford only limited protection to people with disabilities. For example, the Rehabilitation Act of 1973 (P.L. 93-112) prohibited discrimination and mandated affirmative action in employment and education for people with disabilities in the federal government and with any organizations or entities receiving federal assistance or contracts. In 1975 the Education for All Handicapped Children Act (P.L. 94-142) provided federal funds to states that provided appropriate and free public education to children with disabilities. In 1986 amendments to the Education for All Handicapped Children Act expanded educational services, from birth, to all children with disabilities. Numerous reauthorizations have expanded this law, such as the Individuals with Disabilities Education Act (IDEA) (P.L. 90-247). The Developmentally Disabled Assistance and Bill of Rights Act (P.L. 94-103) further enhanced treatment and care for people with developmental disabilities.

Although these laws worked to address the inequities affecting people with disabilities, a common limitation was that they offered protection only in activities and programs involving the government. In recent decades, people with disabilities have become an active political force in the United States (De Jong, 1979). Simultaneously, direct consumer involvement saw the disability rights movement grow with the development of the independent living (IL) movement in the early 1970s. IL applied this model to the political process of gaining civil rights for people with disabilities (Berkowitz, 1987). Whereas traditional culture and traditional models of professional treatment focused on individual pathology of people with disabilities, IL focused on discrimination of an oppressed minority group and societal responses as the root of their problems. The disability rights movement and the IL movement, specifically, were founded on the belief that people with disabilities have the right to participate fully both in society and in the development and implementation of social policies affecting people with disabilities. The advocacy efforts of people with disabilities, joined by people without disabilities, created a sociopolitical force that resulted in the passage of the ADA (P.L. 101-336). With enactment of the ADA, people with disabilities for the first time were afforded rights in all segments of society. The content of the legislation is clearly addressed in the purpose of the act:

■ to provide a clear and comprehensive national mandate for the elimination of discrimination against individuals with disabilities

■ to provide clear, strong, consistent, enforceable standards addressing discrimination against individual disability

■ to ensure that the federal government plays a central role in enforcing the standards established in the act on behalf of individuals with disabilities

■ to invoke the sweep of congressional authority, including the power to enforce the fourteenth amendment and to regulate commerce, in order to address the major areas of discrimination faced day-to-day by people with disabilities. (ADA, 2, 204)

The evolution of the disability rights movement continues today. The Rehabilitation Act Amendments of 1992 established the purpose of Title VII (P.L. 94-1442) as mandating the "creation of statewide networks of Centers for Independent Living," with the goal of ensuring greater involvement and authority of people with disabilities in services delivery and program management. The New Freedom Initiative is a comprehensive program to promote the full participation of people with disabilities in all areas of society. The aim of the initiative is to increase access to assistive and universal design technology, expand educational and employment opportunities, promote home ownership, integrate Americans with disabilities into the workforce, expand transportation options, and promote increased access into daily community life (http://www.whitehouse.gov/infocus/newfreedom/).

ISSUE STATEMENT

A common experience that the vast majority of people with disabilities share is that of social and economic injustice. People with disabilities often have difficulty with social and economic issues, including employment, income, health care, housing, and full participation in their communities. Although there are tens of millions of people with disabilities—actually having a disability can be a very solitary experience. Negative attitudes regarding people with disabilities (for example, that they are needy, less productive, dangerous, frightening, or distasteful to others), continue to facilitate discrimination and segregation. Other challenges may be created by the devaluation and discrimination of people who are perceived to have a disability, such as people who are HIV-positive, people who have a mental illness, or people who have survived cancer. Services are often interrupted and do not comprehensively continue throughout their lifetime. Many people with psychiatric diagnoses are inappropriately or forcibly treated (National Council on Disability, 2000).

Although it is certainly true that social and economic justice issues are intrinsically connected to race and gender, those same issues are just as relevant to disability. Many adults and children with disabilities are denied or cut off from benefits and live in serious income inadequacy and poverty (Axin & Levin, 1992) with inadequate health care, food, and shelter. The U.S. Census Bureau 2001 noted that the presence of a disability lowers income and increases the likelihood of poverty. The poverty rate for people with disabilities is 28 percent compared with 8.3 percent of the general population. According to the National Organization on Disability, 2002, people with disabilities are more likely to put off or postpone medical care because of cost (28 percent compared with 12 percent) even though they may be insured; since 1994 this differential has increased 13 percent.

Social workers have worked with the disability rights movement throughout their struggle in a variety of roles, including self-advocacy. Historically, however, professionals and helpers have abrogated decision making by people with disabilities and denied them self-determination (Salsgiver & Mackelprang, 1993). The traditional model emphasizes pathology, deficit, and malfunctioning and relies on the medical model, according to which disability is a chronic disease requiring various forms of treatment (Roth, 1987). Although this definition no longer is used exclusively, it still has an overwhelming effect on disability issues and on people with disabilities by inappropriately viewing them as passive, dependent, and deficient. More progressive models used to identify and work with people with disabilities view the person as participating in and contributing to society ("Communication," 1991).

A core social work value is that of self-determination. Accordingly, this principle is a model in which social workers work with clients,

rather than providing services for them. This approach encompasses a continuum that ranges from involving the client in the decision making about the treatment plan to having people with disabilities define the goals of such a plan. People with disabilities may define program objectives in organizations where they are themselves employed as decision makers, only using professionals for their specialized expertise and for access to resources. People with disabilities may become these experts, assisting others as well.

Contemporary views of disability have moved beyond focusing on the disability to focusing first on the person. One example is the use of people first language—placing the individual first rather than the disability (for example, people who have a mental illness rather than the mentally ill). By identifying people with disabilities as "people first," we make the presence of a disability a characteristic, not the individual's sole identity while honoring their right to self-determination. Social workers, along with people with disabilities, must affirm the practice of self-determination and use of appropriate language that places people first in all areas of social work practice and the community at large. Although people with disabilities may be handicapped by environmental or individual or societal attitudes, they are not "disabled" or "handicapped" people.

POLICY STATEMENT

NASW supports

■ a national policy that ensures the right of people with disabilities to participate fully and equitably in society. This participation includes the freedom, to the fullest extent possible, to live independently, to exercise self-determination, to make decisions about their living conditions and treatment plans, to obtain an education, to be employed, and to participate as citizens.

■ state and federal funding to allow people with disabilities to participate fully and equitably in society with appropriate supports to meet individual needs.

- the right of people with disabilities to have public access to goods and services available to others, including transportation and reasonable accommodations to provide ready access to buildings throughout the community. Physical access includes internal and external building access (for example, ramps, doors, rest rooms, drinking fountains, and elevators), telecommunications, and alternate means of communication (for example, Braille, sign-language interpreters).

- the right of people with disabilities to a basic level of income that allows all people with disabilities to have the necessities of life and to participate in the community.

- the right of people with disabilities to pursue vocational and occupational opportunities in accessible environments with reasonable accommodations, in accordance with laws that ensure nondiscriminatory access to employment.

- the right of individuals with disabilities to affordable, accessible, and comprehensive health care.

- the right of individuals with disabilities to have early and continued access to individualized appropriate education and vocational opportunities that are accessible in the least restrictive environment possible.

- the development of social workers' expertise in partnering with people with disabilities, by the study of disability history, culture, research, best practices, and civil rights in the curriculums of schools of social work and in continuing education.

- the inclusion of social workers with disabilities in all areas of the professional organization, including policy-making boards, staff and administrative positions, and the board of directors.

- advocacy in collaboration with people with disabilities and their families to reduce discrimination, stigma, and restriction of rights based on inaccurate perceptions of individuals with disabilities in their communities and in society.

REFERENCES

Americans with Disabilities Act of 1990, P.L. 101-336, 104 Stat. 327.

Architectural Barriers Act of 1968, P.L. 90-480, 82 Stat. 718 (Aug. 12, 1968), codified at 42 U.S.C. § 4151 et seq.

Axin, J., & Levin, H. (1992). Social welfare: A history of the American response to need (3rd ed.). New York: Longman.

Berkowitz, E. D. (1987). Disabled policy: America's programs for the handicapped. London: Cambridge University Press.

Civil Rights Act of 1968, P.L. 90-284, 82 Stat. 73 (Apr. 11, 1968).

Communication about disability. (1991). RehabBrief, 13(12), 2.

De Jong, G. (1979). The movement for independent living: Origins, ideology, and implications for disability research. East Lansing: Michigan State University, University Center for International Rehabilitation.

Developmentally Disabled Assistance and Bill of Rights Act, P.L. 94-103, 89 Stat. 486 to 506 (Oct. 4, 1975).

Developmental Disabilities Assistance and Bill of Rights Act of 2000, P.L. 106-402, 104 Stat. 1191 (Oct. 31, 1990).

Education for All Handicapped Children Act of 1975, P.L. 94-142, 89 Stat. 773 (Nov. 29, 1975).

Fair Housing Amendment Act of 1988, P.L. 42 U.S.C. 3601 (1988) seq.

Fujiura, G. (2001). Emerging trends in disability. Retrieved November 12, 2004, from Population Today Web site: http://www.prb.org

Freire, P. (2004). Pedagogy of the oppressed. New York: Continuum.

Halantic, F., & Berg, G. (1995). Perceptions of disabilities among Kel Tamasheq of Northern Mali. In B. Ingstad & S. R. Whyte (Eds.), Disability in a cross-cultural perspective (Working Paper No. 4). Oslo: University of Oslo, Department of Social Anthropology.

Individuals with Disabilities Education Act (IDEA), P.L. 90-247, Title 1, § 154, 81 Stat. 804 (Jan. 2, 1968).

Longmore, P. K. (1987). Elizabeth Bovia, assisted suicide and social prejudice. Issues in Law and Medicine, 3, 141–168.

National Association of Social Workers. (2000). *Code of ethics of the National Association of Social Workers*. Washington, DC: NASW Press.

National Council on Disability. (2000). *From privileges to rights: People labled with psychiatric disabilities speak for themselves*. Washington, DC: Author.

Nerney, T., & Shumway, D. (1998, July). *The importance of income* [Monograph sponsored by the Robert Wood Johnson Foundation]. Durham: University of New Hampshire, Institute of Disability Research.

Rehabilitation Act of 1973, P.L. 93-112, 87 Stat. 355 (Sept. 26, 1974).

Rehabilitation Act Amendments of 1992, P.L. 94-1442 (1977).

Roth, W. (1987). Disabilities: Physical. In A. Minahan (Ed.-in-Chief), *Encyclopedia of social work* (18th ed., Vol. 1, pp. 434–438).

Silver Spring, MD: National Association of Social Workers.

Salsgiver, R., & Mackelprang, R. (1993, February). *Persons with disabilities and social work practice: Historical and contemporary issues*. Paper presented at the Annual Program Meeting of the Council on Social Work Education, New York.

Sargent, C. F. (1982). *The cultural context of therapeutic choice: Obstetrical care decisions among the Bariba of Benin*. Boston: D. Reidel.

Tuvim, M. B. (1991). *Reasonable accommodation v. undue hardship: The ADA on trial*. Unpublished law review article, University of California, Los Angeles.

Vachon, R. A. (1989–1990). Employing the disabled. *Issues in Science and Technology, 6*(2), 44–50. Retrieved from http://cdrc.ohsu.edu/oodh/publications/DisabilityandPublicHealthCurriculumOutline.htm

Policy statement approved by the NASW Delegate Assembly, August 2008. This policy statement supersedes the policy statement on People with Disabilities approved by the Delegate Assembly in 1999 and 1993, the policy statement on Handicapped Persons: Rehabilitation approved in 1967, and the policy statement on Handicapped Persons: Rights and Needs approved in 1977. For further information, contact the National Association of Social Workers, 750 First Street, NE, Suite 700, Washington, DC 20002-4241. Telephone: 202-408-8600 or 800-638-8799; e-mail: press@naswdc.org

Physical Punishment of Children

BACKGROUND

Discipline of children has always been a controversial issue. "Not only in the home but in the classroom, corporal punishment was a means to mold children into moral, God-fearing, respectful human beings" (Crosson-Tower, 1999, p. 3). *Physical punishment* and *corporal punishment* are interchangeable terms; both mean the intentional infliction of physical pain or discomfort on the body of a child as a penalty for behavior disapproved of by the punisher or as a method of modifying negative behavior. When punishment occurs in the home with the parent or caregiver as punisher, it is often described as physical punishment. This policy statement pertains to punishment in the home, schools, and custodial settings. The term *physical punishment* is used in this policy statement because of the commonality of issues in any setting. Physical punishment does not include physical restraint to prevent a child from harming himself or herself or others or to protect property, nor does it include self-defense by an adult.

Several countries have policies or laws that prohibit parents from using corporal punishment as a means of discipline (Austria, Croatia, Cyprus, Denmark, Finland, Germany, Israel, Italy, Latvia, Norway, and Sweden) (Bitensky, 1998, EPOCH-USA, 2000), yet, corporal punishment is strongly supported and used in the United States. According to Straus and Stewart (1999), 94 percent of American parents spank their children by the time they are three or four years old. There is much controversy regarding the benefits and harm of corporal punishment. Some studies have revealed that corporal punishment is effective and desirable (Baumrind, 1996a, 1996b, 1997; Larzelere, 1996, 2000). Other studies, however, have demonstrated

that corporal punishment is related to short- and long-term negative effects on children: increased antisocial behavior (Giles-Sims, Straus, & Sugarman, 1995); higher levels of psychological distress and depression (Straus, 1994; Turner & Finkelhor, 1996); lower IQ scores (Smith & Brooks-Gunn, 1997); and increased likelihood of suicidal ideation, physically abusing one's children, alcohol abuse, engaging in masochistic sex, and lower income (Straus, 1994).

According to Davidson (1997), legal statutes in 48 states and the District of Columbia specify what constitutes corporal punishment in their definition of child abuse. Corporal punishment encompasses the use of "reasonable" force in 29 states; some states add that corporal punishment must be "appropriate" (Alabama, Arkansas, Arizona, California, Colorado), "moderate" (Arkansas, Delaware, South Carolina, South Dakota), or "necessary" (Montana, New Hampshire, New York, Oregon, Texas, Wisconsin); and corporal punishment is limited to "nondeadly force" in Arkansas, New York, and Texas. Corporal punishment has been investigated as a form of abuse. Some states include the term "excessive corporal punishment" in their definitions of child maltreatment (Davidson, 1997). Corporal punishment also is included in some state laws as physical abuse.

It is important to consider social and cultural systems when examining physical punishment of children. Customs and practices in some cultures would be considered abusive by child protective services. For example, some Vietnamese families engage in the ritual of *cao gio* (rubbing their children with a very hot coin that leaves burn marks); the purpose of this ritual is to cure several ills. Child-rearing patterns are determined by parenting beliefs, goals, and expectations inherent in the culture's model of parent–child relations (Greenfield & Suzuki, 1998); this is often referred to as cultural capital (Xu, Tung, & Dunaway, 2000). When physical punishment is the accepted and expected norm in a culture, some parents may feel justified in using it as a means of discipline. The acceptance of physical punishment as normative and beneficial by children largely depends on whether this disciplinary measure is acceptable or unacceptable in the larger cultural context (Deater-Decker & Dodge, 1997).

Studies of physical punishment and parents' ethnicity have been inconclusive. Some studies found that African American parents used corporal punishment more often than did European American parents (Day, Peterson, & McCracken, 1998; Giles-Sims et al., 1995; Loeber et al., 2000; Pinderhughes, Dodge, Bates, Pettit, & Zelli, 2000; Straus & Stewart, 1999). Other studies have shown that European Americans spank their children the most (Escovar & Escovar, 1985; Straus, 1994), and that Latino/a Americans or Asian Americans were least likely to spank their children (Hashima & Amato, 1994; Wissow, 2001). Findings from other studies have shown no differences in frequency between ethnic groups (Ellison, Thompson, & Segal, 1995; Hemenway, Solnick, & Carter, 1994).

Social workers in the field of child abuse observe that, in some instances, what starts out as physical punishment may become abuse when the adult goes too far and injures the child or places the child at risk of injury. Children age three and younger are most often the victims of child fatalities; this population is the most vulnerable because of their dependency, small size, and inability to defend themselves. According to the U.S. Administration for Children and Families (ACF), 30 percent of the reported child fatalities were the result of physical abuse; the rate of child abuse and neglect fatalities increased from 1.84 per 100,000 children in 2000 to 1.96 in 2001 and 1.98 in 2002 (U.S. Department of Health and Human Services, 2004). In 2003, a Child Abuse Prevention Initiative was launched by the ACF, Children's Bureau, Office of Child Abuse and Neglect. The purpose of this initiative was to raise awareness of the issue in communities throughout the United States as a way to keep children safe and provide support for families to stay together and raise children and youths to be happy, secure, and stable adults.

ISSUE STATEMENT

Physical punishment in institutions, foster care (including kinship care, residential settings, and institutions), and day care settings is no longer tolerated by most licensing authorities. Having a humane, effective, and consistent philosophy of discipline in schools, custodial settings, and homes is thought to be highly desirable by adults who are responsible for the care of children in these settings and by society in general. It is not congruent to oppose physical punishment in schools and custodial settings as being inhumane and ineffective without recognizing that the same concerns exist when physical punishment is inflicted on children by their parents. Many parents who use physical punishment are adamantly opposed to and do not engage in abusive physical punishment. Conversely, punishment that does not involve physical contact, such as denigrating statements and excessive timeouts, can also be abusive.

It is important to support actions and conditions that facilitate the healthy emotional, physical, and mental development of children. Discipline is necessary for children to become social, productive, and responsible adults. Physical punishment is one form of discipline. The weight of the evidence has repeatedly shown that physical punishment of children is not as effective as other means of behavior management. There are many effective types of discipline that promote socially acceptable behavior in constructive, nonphysical ways. Physical punishment has been banned in several states and school districts. Legislation is pending in other states and school districts. The National Mental Health Association, a leader in advocacy and social action on behalf of the mental health of children and adolescents, supports the elimination of corporal punishment from all schools in our nation. The National Parent Teachers Association, American Academy of Pediatrics, American Academy of Child and Adolescent Psychiatry, National Congress of Parents and Teachers, National Education Association, and American Bar Association also support the abolishment of corporal punishment in schools in this country.

In 2001, the Global Initiative to End All Corporal Punishment of Children (2001) was launched to

■ form a strong alliance of human rights agencies, key individuals, and nongovernmental organizations against corporal punishment

■ make corporal punishment of children visible by building a global map of its prevalence and legality, ensuring that children's views are heard, and charting progress to end it

■ lobby state governments to ban all forms of corporal punishment and develop public education programs

■ provide detailed technical assistance to support states with these reforms.

The Committee on the Rights of the Child, which monitors implementation of the Convention on the Rights of the Child, has always maintained that legal and social acceptance of physical punishment of children in the home and in institutions is not compatible with the Convention. Since 1993 the Committee has recommended prohibition of physical punishment in the family and institutions. It has also recommended campaigns to encourage positive, nonviolent child rearing and education. In September 2000 the Committee on the Rights of the Child held the first of two General Discussion days on violence against children and recommended

that States parties review all relevant legislation to ensure that all forms of violence against children, however light, are prohibited, including the use of torture, or cruel, inhuman or degrading treatment (such as flogging, corporal punishment or other violent measures) for punishment or disciplining within the child justice system, or any other context. The Committee recommends that such legislation incorporate appropriate

sanctions for violations and the provision of rehabilitation for victims. The committee urges the launching of public information campaigns to raise awareness and sensitize the public about the severity of human rights violations in this domain and their harmful impact on children, and to address cultural acceptance of violence against children promoting instead "zero-tolerance" of violence. (Committee on the Rights of the Child, 2004, p. 4)

Social workers encourage parents and caregivers to use other discipline methods, such as time-out and negative reinforcement when disciplining their children. Social workers and much of the general public increasingly advocate nonviolence and peace in the family as well as in the social, political, educational, and economic environments.

POLICY STATEMENT

The National Association of Social Workers (NASW) believes in the right of every child to have a safe and nurturing environment, including home and educational experiences that promote every child's optimal growth and development. The use of physical force against people, especially children, is antithetical to the best values of a democratic society and of the social work profession. Thus, NASW opposes the use of physical punishment in homes, schools, and all other institutions, both public and private, where children are cared for and educated.

NASW affirms that all children need parental guidance and discipline and that most parents want to be able to discipline in a way that works and is helpful to children. Therefore, NASW will support

■ parenting programs and evidence-based practices that provide parents with access to training and support for learning and using nonviolent disciplinary techniques, such as positive reinforcement, time-out, and verbal problem solving

- professional social work practice, social programs, and social policies that allow children to have their basic needs met so that parents have the energy and emotional resources to use nonviolent disciplinary procedures with their children

- a media-supported public and professional education campaign to abolish physical punishment

- legislation that prohibits the use of physical punishment in schools, other child-care facilities, and institutions

- programs to help prepare administrators, teachers, school personnel, child care workers, and parents to use nonviolent forms of discipline

- research about alternative forms of discipline that are effective in changing behavior.

In adopting this policy, NASW is proud to support the movement to promote the nonviolent discipline and care of children in the United States.

REFERENCES

Baumrind, D. (1996a). A blanket injunction against disciplinary use of spanking is not warranted by the data. *Pediatrics*, *98*, 828–831.

Baumrind, D. (1996b). The discipline controversy revisited. *Family Relations*, *45*, 405–415.

Baumrind, D. (1997). Necessary distinctions. *Psychological Inquiry*, *8*, 176–182.

Bitensky, S. H. (1998). Spare the rod, embrace our humanity: Toward a new legal regime prohibiting corporal punishment of children. *University of Michigan Journal of Law Reform*, *31*, 353–474.

Committee on the Rights of the Child. (2004). The committee's general discussion days on violence against children. Retrieved June 1, 2004, from http://www.endcorpalpunishment.org/pages/hrlaw/crc_session.html

Crosson-Tower, C. (1999). The maltreatment of children from a historical perspective. In C. Crosson-Tower (Ed.), *Understanding child abuse and neglect* (4th ed., pp. 1–20). Boston: Allyn & Bacon.

Davidson, H. (1997). The legal aspects of corporal punishment in the home: When does physical discipline cross the line to become child abuse? *Children's Legal Rights Journal*, *17*, 18–29.

Day, R. D., Peterson, G. W., & McCraken, C. (1998). Predicting spanking of younger and older children by their mothers and fathers. *Journal of Marriage and the Family*, *60*, 79–94.

Deater-Deckard, K., & Dodge, K. A. (1997). Externalizing behavior problems and discipline revisited: Nonlinear effects and variation by culture, context, and gender. *Psychological Inquiry*, *8*, 161–175.

Ellison, C. G., Thompson, T. E., & Segal, M. L. (1995). *Race differences in the parental use of corporal punishment*. Unpublished manuscript, University of Texas at Austin.

EPOCH-USA. (2000). *Legal reforms: Corporal punishment of children in the family*. Retrieved June 2, 2004, from http://www.stophitting.com/legalReform.php

Escovar, L. A., & Escovar, P. L. (1985). Retrospective parental child-rearing practices in three culturally different college groups. *International Journal of Intercultural Relations*, *9*, 31–49.

Giles-Sims, J., Straus, M. A., & Sugarman, D. B. (1995). Child, maternal, and family characteristics associated with spanking. *Family Relations*, *44*, 170–176.

Global Initiative to End All Corporal Punishment of Children. (2001). *End all corporal punishment of children*. Retrieved June 1, 2004, from http://www.endcorporalpunishment.org/

Greenfield, P. M., & Suzuki, L. K. (1998). Culture and human development: Implications for parenting, education, pediatrics, and mental health. In W. Damon, I. E. Siegel, & K. A. Renninger (Eds.), *Handbook of child psychology: Vol 4. Child psychology in practice* (5th ed., pp. 1059–1109). New York: John G. Wiley & Sons.

Hashima, P. Y., & Amato, P. R. (1994). Poverty, social support, and parental behavior. *Child Development*, *65*, 394–403.

Hemenway, D., Solnick, S., & Carter, J. (1994). Child-rearing violence. *Child Abuse & Neglect, 18*, 1011–1020.

Larzelere, R. E. (1996). A review of the outcomes of parental use of nonabusive or customary physical punishment. *Pediatrics, 98*(4, Pt. 2), 824–828.

Larzelere, R. E. (2000). *Child outcomes of nonabusive and customary physical punishment by parents: An updated literature review.* Unpublished manuscript, University of Nebraska Medical Center, Omaha, and Father Flanagan's Boys Home, Boys Town, NE.

Loeber, R., Drinkwater, M., Yin, Y., Anderson, S. J., Schmidt, L. C., & Crawford, A. (2000). Stability of family interaction from ages 6 to 18. *Journal of Abnormal Child Psychology, 28*, 353–369.

Pinderhighes, E. E., Dodge, K. A., Bates, J. E., Pettit, G. S., & Zelli, A. (2000). Discipline responses: Influences of parents socioeconomic status, ethnicity, beliefs about parenting, stress, and cognitive–emotional processes. *Journal of Family Psychology, 14*, 380–400.

Smith, J. R., & Brooks-Gunn, J. (1997). Correlates and consequences of harsh discipline for young children. *Archives of Pediatric and Adolescent Medicine, 151*, 777–786.

Straus, M. A. (1994). *Beating the devil out of them: Corporal punishment in American families.* New York: Lexington Books.

Straus, M. A., & Stewart, J. H. (1999). Corporal punishment by American parents: National data on prevalence, chronicity, severity, and duration, in relation to child and family characteristics. *Clinical Child and Family Psychology Review, 2*, 55–70.

Turner, H. A., & Finkelhor, D. (1996). Corporal punishment as a stressor among youth. *Journal of Marriage and the Family, 58*, 155–166.

U.S. Department of Health and Human Services. (2004). *Child abuse and neglect fatalities: Statistics and interventions.* Retrieved June 6, 2004, from http://nccanch.acf.hhs.gov/pubs/factsheets/fatility.cfm

Wissow, L. S. (2001). Ethnicity, income, and parenting contexts of physical punishment in a national sample of families with young children. *Child Maltreatment, 6*, 118–129.

Xu, X., Tung, Y., & Dunaway, R. G. (2000). Cultural, human, and social capital as determinants of corporal punishment: Toward an integrated theoretical model. *Journal of Interpersonal Violence, 15*, 603–630.

SUGGESTED READINGS

Ashton, V. (2001). The relationship between attitudes toward corporal punishment and the perception and reporting of child maltreatment. *Child Abuse & Neglect, 25*, 389–399.

Kanoy, K., Ulku-Steiner, B., Cox, B., & Burchinal, M. (2003). Marital relationship and individual psychological characteristics that predict physical punishment of children. *Journal of Family Psychology, 17*(1), 20–28.

Mahoney, A., Donnelly, W. O., Lewis, T., & Maynard, C. (2000). Mother and father self-reports of corporal punishment and severe physical aggression toward clinic-referred youth. *Journal of Clinical Child Psychology, 29*, 266–281.

National Maternal and Child Health Center for Child Death Review: Web site: www.childdeathreview.org

O'Neil, C. (2001). Avoiding saying too much: The complexity of relationships between permanent parents and social workers. *Children Australia, 26*(2), 19–25.

Thompson, J. (2000). Smacking children: Attitudes and alternatives. *Social Work Now, 15*, 39–44.

Trocme, N., & Durant, J. (2003). Physical punishment and the response of the Canadian child welfare system: Implications for legislative reform. *Journal of Social Welfare and Family Law, 25*(1), 39–56.

U.S. Department of Health and Human Services. (2001). *Child maltreatment 1999: Reports from the states to the national child abuse and neglect data system.* Washington, DC: U.S. Government Printing Office.

U.S. Department of Health and Human Services. (2004). *Child maltreatment 2002: Reports from the states to the national child abuse and neglect data system*. Washington, DC: U.S. Government Printing Office.

Whaley, A. L. (2000). Sociocultural differences in the developmental differences in the developmental consequences of the use of physical discipline during childhood for African Americans. *Cultural Diversity and Ethnic Minority Psychology, 6*, 5–12.

Policy statement approved by the NASW Delegate Assembly, August 2005. This policy supersedes the policy statement on Physical Punishment of Children approved by the Delegate Assembly in 1990 and referred by the 2002 Delegate Assembly to the 2005 Delegate Assembly for revision and the statement on Corporal Punishment of Children in Schools and Custodial Settings approved by the Delegate Assembly in 1984. The 1999 Delegate Assembly voted not to combine this policy statement with Child Abuse and Neglect. For further information, contact the National Association of Social Workers, 750 First Street, NE, Suite 700, Washington, DC 20002-4241. Telephone: 202-408-8600 or 800-638-8799; e-mail: press@naswdc.org

Poverty and Economic Justice

BACKGROUND

A just society not only ensures that basic human needs are met, but also invests in the social well-being of all of its members, especially those who are unable to provide for themselves. Historically, the social work profession has advocated for socially just income and employment policies. The profession has fought to protect the most vulnerable and the most oppressed: children, single parents, older adults, and, in particular individuals, families, and communities who are in economic distress.

A just society not only ensures that basic human needs are met, but also invests in the social well-being of all of its members, especially those who are unable to provide for themselves.

As the social work profession moves into in the 21st century, iteration of critical economic policy priorities is essential. These priorities include promoting just policies that build a universal system of support, promote financial security, and provide an adequate safety net for those in need.

Moreover, economic systems, institutions, and practices influence how well individuals and groups fulfill their needs and achieve optimum development. People's health and general well-being depend on how well their intrinsic needs are fulfilled. Consistent frustration of these needs tends to cause physical, emotional, and social problems, and correcting these problems at their root is critical.

In 2006, the Census Bureau estimated that 36.5 million Americans or 12.3 percent of the population, lived in poverty, and over 15.4 million of the poor population lived in severe poverty, defined as annual income below 50 percent of the poverty threshold (DeNavas-Walt, Proctor, & Smith, 2007). Over 5.5 million children under 18 years of age lived in severe poverty in 2006.

America's "new economy" is a tale of skewed wealth and income (Ozawa, Kim, & Joo, 2006). The new economy generates extraordinary riches for the few, but creates declining wages, rising debt, and the risk of deep and persistent poverty for many.

In the State of Working America 2006/2007, researchers at the Economic Policy Institute examined America's new economy and the relationship of poverty and the job market (Mishel, Bernstein, & Allegretto, 2007). In 2004, the top 1 percent of wealthy families received almost 17 percent of all income, and more than 42 percent of net assets. Wealth in the United States (defined as net worth, which is the value of assets minus debts) is concentrated at the very top of the economic ladder. One-one-hundredth percent of U.S. families, or about 15,000 families, control 5 percent of the nation's income (Uchitelle, 2007).

U.S. workers are dividing a shrinking share of the economic pie (Aron-Dine & Shapiro, 2007). Danziger (2005) analyzed trend from 1964 to 2004, affecting weekly earnings of U.S. private sector, nonfarm, and nonsupervisory production workers. Danziger concluded that, by 2004, when adjusted for inflation, weekly earnings averaged $529 per week, and "were still about 19 percent below the 1973 level" (p. 4). Furthermore, a large part of the U.S. workforce, approximately one-fourth of the U.S. labor force, works at "poverty-level" wages (Mishel et al., 2007).

Another residual problem is the manner in which the U.S. Census Bureau determines income thresholds for establishing who is in poverty. Administratively, the U.S. Census Bureau continues to use a set of income thresholds, which vary by the number of adults or children in a family, to ascertain poverty levels. Indeed, selected government assistance programs are not required to use the official poverty thresholds as eligibility criteria, and many programs use different measures. Mollie Orshansky, an analyst at the Social Security Administration, developed the formula for calculating the poverty thresholds in 1964. The thresholds do not vary geographically or include actual living expenses or noncash benefits such as food stamps. The Census Bureau updates the thresholds annually and makes adjustments for inflation; however, Orshansky's basic formula for calculating who is poor is unchanged. Other industrialized countries use "relative measures" of poverty, typically set at about 50 percent of the nation's median income. The median household income in the United States in 2006 was $48,200 (DeNavas-Walt et al., 2007).

To calculate who is poor in the United States, the Census Bureau compares a family's annual, pretax, income to their poverty threshold. If the income falls below the threshold, the family is considered poor. In 2006, the weighted average poverty threshold for four people was set at $20,614; for three people, $16,079; for two people, $13,167; and for one person, $10,294 (U.S. Census Bureau, 2007).

Following the passage of welfare reform legislation in 1996, welfare caseloads plunged, by about half, between 1996 and 2000 (Urban Institute, 2006). In 1997, the portion of welfare recipients working in the prior 12 months was 31 percent; by 1999 this portion rose to 44 percent, and by 2002 it began to drop to 39 percent. Many parents who left welfare, especially single mothers, found low-wage jobs and their annual wages, according to the calculations of Urban Institute, left them at a poverty level income—a poverty-level wage. Although many of these families continue to need some level of support, researchers have identified the components of welfare reform programs that are successful in moving families from welfare to work.

ISSUE STATEMENT

Each day, in their work with individuals, families, and communities, social workers see firsthand the devastating costs and consequences of poverty and unemployment. Joblessness and economic insecurity contribute to the incidence of mental illness, family violence, suicide, substance abuse, crime, and diminished capacity for healthy family and community functioning. Effective provision of traditional social work services, including individual and family therapy, group work, vocational counseling, or community organization is compromised when provided in the context of economic insecurity. It is this knowledge and experience that gives the social work profession a special responsibility to advocate for income, employment, and social support policies that promote the economic justice and social well-being of all members of society.

Disparities in Wealth

Analysts found "vast" differences between the economic status of black families and white families when examining their respective median and average financial wealth (Mishel et al., 2007). The data on median wealth indicated that the disparities were extreme; in 2004, the median wealth of black families was $300 and the median wealth for white families was more than $36,000, a black–white ratio of less than 1 percent. The data on average wealth was no less extreme, in 2004; black families had an average wealth of $61,500 and white families had an average wealth of $402,500, a black–white ratio of 15 percent. A full 17 percent of all U.S. households had zero or negative net worth in 2004 (Mishel et al., 2007).

A Rise in Debt

To make ends meet, Americans have taken on large amounts of debt and report that their prime concern is not enough money for life's basics (Gallup Poll, 2007). Household debt in the United States "has consistently trended upward," and by 2005 "it was over 130 percent of disposable personal income." About 25 percent of low-income households, and close to

14 percent of middle-income families, had "debt-service obligations that exceeded 40 percent of their income" (Mishel et al., 2007). The deregulation of credit card interest, fees, and aggressive marketing tactics has exposed low- and middle-income consumers to predatory lending practices, which jeopardize their economic future and increasingly lead to bankruptcies (Warren, 2007).

Counting the Poor

Poverty reaches deeply across the United States and is concentrated among the young. Children under 18 years of age represent 24.9 percent of the total population, but account for 35.2 percent of people in poverty. The number of people 65 years and older living in poverty declined from 3.6 million in 2005 to 3.4 million in 2006. (Danziger, 2005). Poverty among America's 100 million people in ethnic minority groups is widespread, and skewed, in ratio to their representation in the population (U.S. Census Bureau, 2007).

Concentrated Poverty

The geographic isolation and concentration of the urban poor population are key determinants of the complexity and persistence of poverty in the United States. Hurricane Katrina exposed the geographic concentration of poverty in what Wilson (2007) called the new urban poverty. "Poor, segregated neighborhoods in which substantial percentages of individual adults are either unemployed or have dropped out or never been a part of the labor force" (Wilson, 2007, p. 93).

The Effects of Welfare Reform

The combination of wages, tax credits, cash assistance, and other benefits such as food stamps, Medicaid, and subsidies for child care and transportation led to a sustainable success in the transition to work for many families. However, some families continued to face barriers to stable employment because they are challenged by a lack of skills or education, or disabling medical, physical, or emotional con-

ditions (Joyce Foundation, 2002). Therefore, a higher level of support is needed to secure stable employment for these families.

Employment Measures

All employment and unemployment measures should be carefully analyzed to obtain a clear understanding of what is being measured. For example, in September 2007, the Labor Department reported that 7.2 million people were unemployed and that an additional 1.3 million people were "marginally attached to the labor force (without jobs, interested in working)." According to the Bureau of Labor Statistics (2007) "marginally attached workers" are considered unemployed, even though they are defined as without jobs. Another confounding measure used by the Labor Department is a subgroup of marginally attached workers known as "discouraged workers": those who want a job, but who are without hope of finding work. In September 2007, discouraged workers accounted for 276,000 of the 1.3 million people reported as marginally attached to the labor force by the Department of Labor. The highest rate of unemployment reported by the Labor Department in September 2007 was 16 percent for teenagers; that number excluded discouraged workers and marginally attached workers (Bureau of Labor Statistics, 2007).

POLICY STATEMENT

NASW supports a national economic policy that invests in "human capital" and recognizes that a nation's well-being derives not only from an economic balance sheet, but also from the well-being of its members. Specifically, NASW supports

■ an economic policy that includes the elimination of poverty and race-based barriers to opportunity, reducing the dynamics of individual and intergroup competition and thus reducing economic sources of discrimination by race, gender, age, and other factors.

■ broad social, economic, and political actions to end poverty and the vast inequalities in wealth and income.

- the full use and development of available, productive, and creative human resources and capacities, and the rejection of the notion that the United States cannot afford economic reform.

- efforts to educate social workers and the public about the unequal distribution of income and wealth, with particular attention to its effects on communities, women, people of color, and those living in poverty.

- efforts to engage the public in understanding that it is in everyone's interest to reduce economic inequalities.

- proposals to protect the long-term viability of economic security programs for all Americans.

- proposals to improve economic programs for low-wage workers, women, children, people of color, people living in poverty, and people with disabilities.

- federal tax, budget, and spending mechanisms that help to narrow gaps in the resources available to people at different levels, as well as an adequate safety net for those unable to provide for themselves.

- economic policies that either avoid recession and inflation or mitigate their impact.

- a policy of full employment at all levels for all those able to work, with a range of alternative work patterns and strategies to address conditions if the economy is unable to sustain full employment.

- income levels that meet or exceed the federal poverty guidelines for anyone who works full-time.

- a federal minimum wage indexed to cost-of-living increases and is a living wage.

- fair labor practices for all workers, including children, youths, and those on public employment programs; equity and enforcement of equal opportunity, and affirmative action legislation.

- national policy that creates a seamless support system for intergenerational well-being, including stable and viable economic and employment policies, and care provisions for dependent family members.

- policies that support compensation for individuals engaged in the care of dependent family members.

- quality, accessible, and affordable child care for those working outside the home

- unstigmatized financial support at a level that enables those who are unable to work to live in dignity.

- federal programs that invest in education and retraining, particularly addressing the need for competence in the global economy, especially for low-income workers, displaced workers, current public assistance recipients, and former public assistance recipients. Such programs should include financial support and tuition subsidies, and opportunities to obtain higher education available to all who can benefit from it, without regard to ability to pay.

- equitable community development and revitalization, including the strengthening of communities through job creation; affordable, accessible, and quality housing; quality public education; affordable and accessible public transportation; safe work sites, neighborhoods, and homes; high-quality and affordable health care, including comprehensive mental health services, and accessible opportunities for training and employment, which lead to better jobs at living wages.

- expanded efforts by the United States at international economic cooperation and development of a comprehensive international industrial policy, including trade agreements that protect the environment, ensure the right to organize and bargain collectively, and provide a living wage.

REFERENCES

Aron-Dine, A., & Shapiro, I. (2007, March 29). *Share of national income going to wages and salaries at record low in 2006: Share of income going to corporate profits at record high.* Retrieved October 9, 2007, from http://www.cbpp.org/8-31-06inc.html

Bureau of Labor Statistics. (2007, September). The employment situation: September 2007. *Employment Situation Summary, NEWS Bureau of Labor Statistics*. Retrieved October 7, 2007, from http://www.bls.gov/news.release/empsit.nr0.html

Danziger, S. (2005). Poverty and low-wage work 40 years after the declaration of the war on poverty. *Poverty Research Insights*, pp. 3–6. Retrieved October 7, 2007, from http://www.npc.umich.edu/publications/newsletter/fall05/

DeNavas-Walt, C., Proctor, B. D., & Smith, J. (2007). *Income, poverty, and health insurance coverage in the United States: 2006* (U.S. Census Bureau, Current Population Reports, P60-233). Retrieved September 27, 2007 from http://www.census.gov/prod/2007pubs/p60-233.pdf

Gallup Poll. (2007, June 19). Seventy percent of Americans say that the economy is getting worse. Retrieved October 9, 2007, from http://www.galluppoll.com/content/?ci=27922

Joyce Foundation. (2002). *Welfare to work: What have we learned?* Chicago: Author. Retrieved October 9, 2007, from http://www.joycefdn.org/pdf/welrept/welfarereport.pdf

Mishel, L., Bernstein, J., & Allegretto, S. (2007). *The state of working America 2006/2007*. Ithaca, NY: Cornell University Press. Data available at http://epi.org

Ozawa, M. N., Kim, J., & Joo, M. (2006). Income class and the accumulation of net worth in the United States. *Social Work Research, 30*, 211–222.

Urban Institute. (2006, July 26). *A decade of welfare reform: Facts and figures: Assessing the new federalism*. Retrieved October 9, 2007, from http://www.urban.org/UploadedPDF/900980_welfarereform.pdf

U.S. Census Bureau. (2007, May 17). *Minority population tops 100 million*. Retrieved October 9, 2007, from http://www.census.gov/Press-Release/www/releases/archives/population

Warren, E. (2007). The vanishing middle class. In J. Edwards, M. Crain, & A. L. Kalleberg (Eds.), *Ending poverty in America: How to restore the American dream* (pp. 38–52). New York: New Press.

Wilson, J. W. (2007). A new agenda for America's ghetto poor. In J. Edwards, M. Crain, & A. L. Kalleberg (Eds.), *Ending poverty in America: How to restore the American dream* (pp. 88–98). New York: New Press.

Policy statement approved by the NASW Delegate Assembly, August 2008. This policy statement supersedes the policy statement on Economic Policy approved by the Assembly in 1999 and referred by the 2005 Delegate Assembly to the 2008 Delegate Assembly for revision., and the policy statement approved by the Assembly in 1993 and 1990. For further information, contact the National Association of Social Workers, 750 First Street, NE, Suite 700, Washington, DC 20002-4241. Telephone: 202-408-8600 or 800-638-8799; e-mail: press@naswdc.org

Professional Impairment

BACKGROUND

Professional impairment among social workers is a significant and growing concern in the profession. Professional impairment has been defined in many ways.

One of the earliest and most widely used definitions cites interference with professional functioning that is reflected in one or more of the following: an inability or unwillingness to acquire and integrate professional standards into one's repertoire of professional behavior; an inability to acquire professional skills to reach an acceptable level of competency; and an inability to control personal stress, psychological dysfunction, or excessive emotional reactions that interfere with professional functioning (Lamb et al., 1987). The *Social Work Dictionary* defines an *impaired social worker* as "one who is unable to function adequately as a professional social worker and provide competent care to clients as a result of a physical or mental disorder or personal problems, or the ability or desire to adhere to the *code of ethics* of the profession. These problems most commonly include alcoholism, substance abuse, mental illness, burnout, stress, and relationship problems" (Barker, 2003, p. 210).

Impaired functioning should be distinguished from incompetence or inexperience by evidence that the social worker has previously functioned acceptably according to standards of social work practice.

Professional impairment can manifest in different ways. The most frequently discussed form of impairment is that of alcohol and other drug (AOD) use (Bissell, Fewell, & Jones, 1980; Fewell, King, & Weinstein, 1993; Siebert, 2003, 2005). One earlier study of alcohol abuse among colleagues and families, using samples of NASW members, confirmed the existence of significant alcohol and drug abuse problems within the social work profession (Fewell et al., 1993). A more recent study, also using a sample of NASW members in a chapter, indicated troubling levels of AOD use among social workers. Twelve percent of the sample was at serious risk of AOD abuse. Of those considered high risk, 53 percent reported some type of impairment and 20 percent reported three or more impairment incidents (Siebert, 2003). Effects of professional impairment reported by respondents included the following: providing inadequate or substandard client care, being late or missing appointments, engaging in inappropriate relationships, missing days from work, being confronted by a coworker, being disciplined by an employer, or being forced to change jobs (Siebert, 2003).

Concern for professional impairment in the field of social work education was highlighted in an article examining commonly occurring ethical dilemmas faced by social work educators in their roles of teaching, scholarship, and service (Strom-Gottfried & D'Aprix, 2006). Alcohol use in master's-level social work students has been explored in one comparison study of graduate MSW students and undergraduate students. Findings indicated that the MSW sample of three universities in the northeastern United States did not drink as aggressively as the undergraduate students. One explanation for the lower rate was that MSW students may enter the social work profession seeking to better understand drinking problems of their own or the problems of members of their families, and to help others with their drinking problems (Gassman, Demone, & Wechsler, 2002).

Mental health conditions may significantly affect a social worker's performance. Depression, as a form of professional impairment, has received little attention in the field of social work. One significant study of depression among social workers, using a sample of NASW members, found that 19 percent reported current symptoms of depression, 16 percent had seriously considered suicide at some time, 20 percent were currently taking medication for depression, and 60 percent self-evaluated as either currently depressed or depressed at some time in the past. However, it was also found that respondents with more years of experience, professional designations, and higher degrees were less likely to report depressive symptoms. But the most alarming finding from the study was that the percentage of respondents self-assessed as depressed represented three times the lifetime depression rate in the general population (Siebert, 2004).

Burnout, compassion fatigue, secondary traumatic stress, and vicarious traumatization are also conditions that may contribute to a form of professional impairment (Bride, 2007; Figley, 1995; Jayaratne & Chess, 1984; Soderfeldt, Soderfeldt, & Warg, 1995). These conditions are often considered to be related to the organizational climate, work stressors, and negative psychological effects of helping.

Impairment often leads to professional mistakes, failure in providing competent care to clients, and violation of the ethical standards of the profession (Berliner, 1989; Houston-Vega & Nuehring, 1997; Lowenberg, Dolgoff, & Harrington, 2000; Reamer, 1992, 1994, 1998). The inability or unwillingness to identify impairment in a colleague's performance and lack of knowledge and guidance on how to respond effectively are stumbling blocks for social work professionals in encouraging their colleagues to seek help. Denial of one's own professional impairment has been documented as a serious concern, especially related to AOD abuse (Siebert, 2003).

Through the efforts of three chapters, New York City, New York State and New Jersey, NASW formally acknowledged the problems of impaired social workers in 1979 in the release of a public policy on alcoholism and alcohol-related problems (NASW, 2006; Reamer, 1992).

In 1980, Social Workers Helping Social Workers was formed to provide mutual support and assistance to social work professionals with impairment issues.

In 1994, NASW formally addressed professional impairment in the *Code of Ethics,* with further revisions in 1996 and 1999 (NASW, 2000, 2006). The *Code of Ethics* addresses impairment issues through four specific standards, which basically mandate action in two significant areas—when social workers suspect impairment in colleagues or when social workers are impaired (NASW, 2000).

Despite the recent increase in attention and organized efforts directed toward the problem of professional impairment, there is still significant work to be undertaken to effectively create awareness about different forms of impairment and to address a serious and growing concern in the profession of social work.

ISSUE STATEMENT

Professional impairment among social workers is a critically important issue to address for a variety of reasons. The ability of social workers to perceive situations clearly and objectively is pivotal to their work. Social workers suffering from AOD abuse disorders, psychiatric stressors and disorders, secondary traumatic stress, and other causal factors of impairment may compromise performance, jeopardizing the rights of their clients and the effectiveness of the treatment provided. Although research on the impairment of social workers is limited, findings suggest that services to clients are affected by the degree of impairment (Siebert, 2003, 2004, 2005). Social workers practicing while impaired are at greater risk of unethical conduct and malpractice (Houston-Vega & Nuehring, 1997; Lowenberg et al., 2000; Reamer, 1998). Impaired social workers may pay inconsistent attention to work requirements, fail to complete assignments, engage in excessive absenteeism, or commit treatment errors that may lead to serious ethical violations.

Professional impairment in social work is also important because of its impact on the profession in general. Although all misconduct is not the result of impairment, highly publicized cases of unethical actions caused by impairment portray social workers in an embarrassing light, damaging the reputation of the profession and causing questions to be raised about the competence of the profession overall.

The issue of impaired practice presents real dilemmas and challenges for the profession that are compounded by little guidance on the issue from regulatory boards and professional organizations. Clients who are affected most by impaired performance generally do not recognize it. Unfortunately, many social workers avoid "interfering" in the lives of their troubled colleagues, despite the ethical mandates to intervene (NASW, 2000). A 1992 study of NASW members indicated that the majority—41 percent were uncertain about reporting, 36 percent favored reporting, and 23 percent were against reporting (Elpers, 1992). Social workers are often fearful about colleagues' reactions to their confrontation and its effect on their future working relationships, making practitioners reluctant to intervene even when they suspect impairment of their colleagues (Reamer, 1992). Finally, a lack of recognition of their problems makes it unlikely that professionals who are impaired will self-initiate appropriate actions such as seeking treatment, making adjustments in workload, terminating services or practices, or taking other steps necessary to protect clients. Data from one study of NASW members suggested that social workers do not frequently seek help, even when they are considered to be at high risk of AOD use (Siebert, 2005). Reasons for not seeking help included concern about confidentiality and professional consequences, the belief that treatment provider options were unacceptable, feeling uncomfortable because they knew the providers personally or professionally, believing that they could not take time from work to obtain assistance, and viewing counseling as ineffective.

The social work profession must address the needs of its members and protect the welfare of its clients. Addressing the issues that arise from the identification and treatment of professional impairment will continue to present a challenge for those social work professionals who have denied their vulnerability.

POLICY STATEMENT

NASW recognizes that the prevention, identification, and treatment of professional impairment is vital to protect the welfare of clients, practicing social workers, the work environment, and the integrity of the profession. A multisystemic approach, focusing on prevention, identification, and treatment, must be used to address professional impairment among social workers.

Prevention

Recognizing that preventive education is critical, NASW supports social work education programs that enhance awareness through incorporating material about student and professional impairment, and ethical responsibilities related to impairment, into their recruitment, screening, and curriculum.

This material may include evidence-based research on the identification of risk factors associated with professional impairment, the characteristics of impaired functioning, the strategies available for approaching and assisting social work colleagues believed to be impaired, treatment and other options available for professionals with impairments, and the ethical obligations of social workers with regard to professional impairment.

NASW supports

■ mandatory continuing education addressing professional impairment as part of the ethics requirement of each state's regulatory boards.

■ ongoing individual and group services for both social work students and practitioners as a means to discuss workplace stressors and the physical and psychological effect of working within social work settings.

■ advocacy efforts directed toward ensuring that social workers operate in a safe work environment with adequate resources that maximize the efficacy and efficiency of the social worker and that minimize environmental stressors and the resultant negative psychological impact that increase the risk of impairment.

Identification and Treatment

It is imperative that confidential and non-punitive treatment options aimed at identifying and assisting social workers in returning to competent functioning be available to social workers who are impaired. NASW encourages the establishment of colleague-assistance programs that confidentially help to identify colleagues with impairments, encourage them to obtain treatment, identify appropriate treatment options available, and facilitate integration back into the workplace upon recovery.

NASW supports

■ insurance benefits that provide access to comprehensive preventive and treatment services addressing professional impairment issues.

■ programs for at-risk and recovering social workers that offer the opportunity for additional supervision and consultation.

■ fair, nondiscriminatory, and accessible rehabilitative practices, addressing professional impairment, which are enforced by employers, regulatory boards, schools of social work, and other professional organizations.

■ the education of clients on procedures for reporting their concerns regarding potential violations of their rights, resulting from professional impairment.

Macro Level Initiatives

On a macro level, NASW supports

■ additional research on professional impairment, including prevention, assessment, treatment, and help-seeking behaviors among impaired social workers and social work students.

■ updating and dissemination of practical guidelines for social workers to identify colleagues at risk and practical strategies for approaching impaired colleagues.

■ civil immunity laws that protect those who report colleagues believed to be impaired.

REFERENCES

Barker, R. L. (2003). *The social work dictionary* (5th ed.). Washington, DC: NASW Press.

Berliner, A. K. (1989). Misconduct in social work practice. *Social Work, 34,* 69–72.

Bissell, L., Fewell, C. H., & Jones, R. W. (1980). The alcoholic social worker: A survey. *Social Work in Health Care, 5,* 421–433.

Bride, B. E. (2007). Prevalence of secondary traumatic stress among social workers. *Social Work, 52,* 63–70.

Elpers, K. (1992). *Social work impairment: A statewide survey of the National Association of Social Workers.* Evansville, IN: Author.

Fewell, C. H., King, B. L., & Weinstein, D. L. (1993). Alcohol and other drug abuse among social work colleagues and their families: Impact on practice. *Social Work, 38,* 565–570.

Figley, C. R. (Ed.). (1995). *Compassion fatigue: Coping with secondary traumatic stress disorder in those who treat the traumatized.* New York: Brunner-Mazel.

Gassman, R. A., Demone, H. W., & Wechsler, H. (2002). College student's drinking: Master's in social work compared with undergraduate students. *Health & Social Work, 27,* 184–193.

Houston-Vega, M. K., & Nuehring, E. M. (with Daguio, E. R.). (1997). *Prudent practice: A guide for managing malpractice risk.* Washington, DC: NASW Press.

Jayaratne, S., & Chess, W. A. (1984). Job satisfaction, burnout and turnover: A national study. *Social Work, 29,* 448–453.

Lamb, D. H., Presser, N. R., Pfost, K. S., Baum, M. C., Jackson, V. R., & Jarvis, P. A. (1987). Confronting professional impairment during the internship: Identification, due process, and remediation. *Professional Psychology: Research and Practice, 18,* 597–603.

Loewenberg, F. M., Dolgoff, R., & Harrington, D. (2000). *Ethical decisions for social work practice* (6th ed.). Itasca, IL: F. E. Peacock.

National Association of Social Workers. (2000). *Code of ethics of the National Association of Social Workers.* Washington, DC: NASW Press.

National Association of Social Workers. (2006). Professional impairment. In *Social Work* speaks: *National Association of Social Workers policy statements* (7th ed., pp. 296–300). Washington, DC: NASW Press.

Reamer, F. G. (1992). The impaired social worker. *Social Work, 37,* 165–170.

Reamer, F. G. (1994). *Social work malpractice and liability: Strategies for prevention.* New York: Columbia University Press.

Reamer, F. G. (1998). *Ethical standards in social work: A critical review of the NASW code of ethics.* Washington, DC: NASW Press.

Siebert, D. C. (2003). Denial of AOD use: An issue for social workers and the profession. *Health & Social Work, 28,* 89–97.

Siebert, D. C. (2004). Depression in North Carolina social workers: Implications for practice and research. *Social Work Research, 28,* 30–40.

Siebert, D. C. (2005). Help seeking for AOD misuse among social workers: Patterns, barriers, and implications. *Social Work, 50,* 65–75.

Soderfeldt, M., Soderfeldt, B., & Warg, L. E. (1995). Burnout in social work. *Social Work, 40,* 638–646.

Strom-Gottfried, K., & D'Aprix, A. (2006). Ethics for academics. *Social Work Education, 25,* 225–244.

Policy statement approved by the NASW Delegate Assembly, August 2008. This policy statement supersedes the policy statement on Professional Impairment approved by the Assembly in August 1999 and referred by the 2005 Delegate Assembly to the 2008 Delegate Assembly for revision, and the policy statement on The Impaired Professional approved by the Delegate Assembly in 1987 and reconfirmed by the Delegate Assembly in 1993. This policy statement was previously titled A Colleague-Assistance Program. For further information, contact the National Association of Social Workers, 750 First Street, NE, Suite 700, Washington, DC 20002-4241. Telephone: 202-408-8600 or 800-638-8799; e-mail: press@naswdc.org

Professional Self-Care
and Social Work

BACKGROUND

Professional self-care is an essential underpinning to best practice in the profession of social work. The need for professional self-care has relevance to all social workers in the setting within which they practice. The practice of self-care is critical to the survival and growth of the profession. Yet professional self-care has not been fully examined or addressed within the profession.

The profession of social work offers unique challenges that are both rewarding and potentially overwhelming for the professional social worker. Authors such as Munson (2002) and Shulman (1993) discussed the importance of understanding the stress reactions of social workers and the role that supervisors may play in helping social workers to prevent or overcome stress. Some authors specifically emphasize an ongoing self-awareness and urge preparation for our work by seeking and creating supportive networks (Murphy & Dillon, 2003).

It is not often that social workers engage in thoughtful discourse of the unique challenges of our profession and ways of addressing and managing the effect. Numerous stressors are prevalent in the social work arena such as long hours, time constraints and deadlines, large and professionally challenging client caseloads, limited or inadequate resources, crises and emergencies, low pay, safety concerns (Whitaker, Weismiller, & Clark, 2006), and lack of recognition and autonomy. These stressors tend to be related to the organizational structure and operations of agencies, as well as the cultural, community, and political context affecting clients and practice.

The earliest explorations of the effect of helping in social work practice recognized the risk of stress and burnout (Arches, 1991; Edelwich, & Brodsky, 1980; Gillespie, 1987; Powell, 1994; Söderfeldt, Söderfeldt, & Warg, 1995; Um & Harrison, 1998). Many early authors connected with the work of Maslach (1993, 2003) who defined *burnout* as "a syndrome of emotional exhaustion, depersonalization, and reduced personal accomplishment that can occur among individuals who do 'people-work' of some kind." Later definitions included a loss of enthusiasm for the work, a loss of a sense of commitment to the profession, and a disengagement and distancing from clients (Conrad & Joseph, 2003; Joseph, 1988).

Later research helped to enlighten social workers and other helping professionals about conditions that could result from the process of listening to the clients' stories and the therapeutic conversations, with themes of helplessness and hopelessness. Frameworks have been developed for understanding specific experiences such as compassion fatigue (Figley, 1995, 2002), secondary traumatic stress (Figley, 2002; Stamm, 1999), and vicarious traumatization (McCann & Pearlman, 1990; Pearlman, 1995; Pearlman & Saakvitne, 1995). *Compassion fatigue,* or secondary traumatic stress, is defined "as the natural, predictable, treatable, and preventable unwanted consequence of working with suffering people, that is, the cost of caring" (Figley, 1995; Stamm, 1999). *Vicarious traumatization* refers to a cumulative transformative effect or condition experienced by trauma therapists as they work with specific populations of survivors of traumatic life events (McCann & Pearlman, 1990; Pearlman & Saakvitne, 1995). The common characteristic is that they represent the negative, unwanted, psychological effects of the experience of helping and therefore, uniquely affect the helping professional.

Particular focus of the literature has been on the effect of trauma work on social workers in settings dealing with family violence (Bell, 2003; Bell, Kulkami, & Dalton, 2003), child protective service (Cornille & Meyers, 1999; Dane, 2000; Pryce, Shackelford, & Pryce, 2007; Regehr, Hemsworth, Leslie, Howe, & Chau, 2004), sexual abuse (Couper, 2000; Cunningham, 1999), and grief and loss (Walsh-Burke, 2006). Cunningham (2003) described two types of trauma: human induced trauma, such as sexual abuse, and naturally caused trauma such as cancer. Some studies have examined the effect of disasters on social workers (Adams, Boscarino, & Figley, 2006; Boscarino, Figley, & Adams, 2004) and the incidence of secondary traumatic stress in child welfare (Pryce et al., 2007). Greene (2007) and others have expanded resilience to the workplace, and the risks for those professionals involved with the "occupational hazards that presents for Social Work professionals time and again . . . of taking care of others, both before and more than ourselves" (Fink-Samnick, 2007).

Some attention has been focused on educating social work students about these conditions through classroom experiences where stress management techniques are taught (Dziegielewski, Tumage, & Roest-Marti, 2004) and through lectures exploring vicarious trauma as one of the psychological effects of helping (Cunningham, 2004).

Throughout the explorations and discussions of these stress factors, most authors emphasize the need for social workers and other helping professionals. Some recommend specific strategies that are self-affirming, self-protecting, and self-nurturing (Pearlman & Saakvitne, 1995). Others discuss survival strategies and tools that address the physical, psychological, professional, interpersonal, and spiritual aspects of the practitioner (Figley, 1995). One study, using the strengths perspective in family violence work, identified five distinct characteristics of the more resilient workers as having a sense of competence about coping, maintaining an objective motivation, resolving personal traumas, drawing on positive role models of coping, and having buffering personal beliefs (Bell, 2003).

ISSUE STATEMENT

In light of recent and significant research indicating that social workers engaged in direct practice are likely to develop symptoms of secondary traumatic stress, it is imperative that the social work profession devotes greater attention to and creates greater awareness of these issues.

The critical key to prevention and management of adverse conditions such as stress, burnout, compassion fatigue, and secondary traumatic stress or vicarious trauma is the practice of self-care. Baker (2003) conceptualized self-care as the combination of three processes: self-awareness, self-regulation, and balancing connections between self, others, and the larger community. *Professional self-care* in social work can be defined as a core essential component to social work practice and reflects a choice and commitment to become actively involved in maintaining one's effectiveness as a social worker. Furthermore, in promoting the practice of professional self-care, a repertoire of self-care strategies is essential to support the social worker in preventing, addressing, and coping with the natural, yet unwanted, consequences of helping (Lopez, 2007).

Professional self-care is vital to the profession of social work for several reasons:

■ Professional self-care is an essential component in competent, compassionate, and ethical social work practice, requiring time, energy, and commitment.

■ Promoting the practice of professional self-care in social work explicitly acknowledges the challenging and often overwhelming nature of our work.

■ Professional self-care places emphasis on primary prevention of these unwanted conditions and implies that tools and strategies should be part of one's overall professional self-care plan. Actively preparing social workers with knowledge and skill for overcoming these experiences is key.

■ Professional self-care in social work is critical to maintaining ethical and professional behavior and providing competent services to clients across diverse settings.

■ Although the practice of professional self-care applies to all social workers, it is especially critical for social workers providing care to traumatized populations

■ Acknowledging professional self-care in social work is an important first step in preserving the integrity of social workers and in retaining valued professionals in the profession. Actively preparing social workers to effectively face these conditions will support social workers in maintaining their commitment to the profession.

POLICY STATEMENT

NASW recognizes and acknowledges the unique and valuable contributions of the professional social worker. NASW supports the practice of professional self-care for social workers as a means of maintaining their competence, strengthening the profession, and preserving the integrity of their work with clients. Education, self-awareness, and commitment are considered key to promoting the practice of professional self-care. In recognition of social workers as valued professional resources across diverse practice settings, NASW supports

■ the establishment and implementation of organizational policies that promote participatory decision making, interactive coping styles, and environments in which organizational values and conflict can be openly discussed and negotiated.

■ the establishment and enforcement of organizational policies and practices that address and enhance safety in the workplace. Organizations may be supportive by examining the organizational culture, redefining workload, providing essential supervision, encouraging self-care practices, allowing for group support, and creating a supportive work environment.

■ the promotion, support, and modeling of the practice of professional self-care by social work supervisors with social work supervisees.

■ the promotion and support of the practice of professional self-care by social work administrators. Social work administrators can demonstrate support for self-care by reflecting

self-care in policies and in the process of evaluation; offering supportive supervision, ongoing processing and debriefing after traumatic or stressful occurrences, staff retreats, team building with a focus on rejuvenating social work staff; and actively sponsoring healthy lifestyle activities within the work environment, such as walking, running, aerobics, healthy eating, encouraging time off, taking breaks and mental health days, and providing relaxing and nurturing environments for meditating.

■ the development of individual professional self-care plans by all social workers that includes a repertoire of personalized strategies for maintaining health, preventing burnout and compassion fatigue, and addressing secondary traumatic stress or vicarious trauma. The plan should also include the development or enhancement of interactive coping styles that deal directly with the management of organizational conflict and differences with colleagues. Social workers should cultivate and maintain self-awareness of their personal and professional limitations and monitor their efforts to promote the practice of professional self-care and to support social work colleagues in these processes as well.

■ the development of continuing education programs on professional self-care and conditions such as stress, burnout, compassion fatigue, secondary traumatic stress, and vicarious trauma.

■ the development of creative and innovative support services for social workers, which may include support groups, professional retreats, Web site resources, online support, and chat groups.

■ the recognition by social work education programs of their critically important roles in educating social work students about the practice of professional self-care by integrating such content into existing student standards, policies, foundation and advanced curriculums, field practicum, and assignments and projects.

■ the training of social work students about professional self-care in their field experiences and the modeling of these behaviors by field instructors.

- further research to continue the exploration of the prevalence of secondary traumatic stress and vicarious trauma among social workers in a variety of settings and to examine resiliency factors and self-care practices among social workers.

- further development of publications that address the issue of professional self-care and social work and that offer tools and strategies for thriving in social work practice.

REFERENCES

Adams, R. E., Boscarino, J. A., & Figley, C. R. (2006). Compassion fatigue and psychological distress among social workers: A validation study. *American Journal of Orthopsychiatry, 76*, 103–108.

Arches, J. (1991). Social structure, burnout, and job satisfaction. *Social Work, 36*, 202–206.

Baker, E. (2003). *Caring for ourselves as psychologists*. Retrieved May 30, 2008, from http://www.google.com/search?hl=en&as_q=Baker+and+2003&as_epq=professional+self-care&as_oq=&as_eq=&num=10&lr=lang_en&as_filetype=&ft=i&as_sitesearch=&as_qdr=all&as_rights=&as_occt=any&cr=&as_nlo=&as_nhi=&safe=images

Bell, H. (2003). Strengths and secondary trauma in family violence work. *Social Work, 48*, 513–522.

Bell, H., Kulkarni, S., & Dalton, L. (2003). Organizational prevention of vicarious trauma. *Families in Society, 84*, 463–470.

Boscarino, J. A., Figley, C. R., & Adams, R. E. (2004). Compassion fatigue following the September 11 terrorist attacks: A study of secondary trauma among New York city social workers. *International Journal of Emergency Mental Health, 6*(2), 57–66.

Conrad, A. P., & Joseph, M. V. (2003). Spirituality and burnout prevention. In *Solid Practice III* (pp. 18–42). Hong Kong: Cosmos Books.

Cornille, T. A., & Meyers, T. W. (1999). Secondary traumatic stress among child protective service workers: Prevalence, severity and predictive factors. *Traumatology, 5*, 15–31.

Couper, D. (2000). The impact of the sexually abused child's pain on the worker and the team. *Journal of Social Work Practice, 14*(1), 9–16.

Cunningham, M. (1999). The impact of sexual abuse treatment on the social work clinician. *Child and Adolescent Social Work Journal, 16*, 277–290.

Cunningham, M. (2003). Impact of trauma on social work clinicians: Empirical findings. *Social Work, 48*, 451–459.

Cunningham, M. (2004). Teaching social workers about trauma: Reducing the risks of vicarious traumatization in the classroom. *Journal of Social Work Education, 40*, 305–317.

Dane, B. (2000). Child welfare workers: An innovative approach for interacting with secondary trauma. *Journal of Social Work Education, 36*, 27–38.

Dziegielewski, S. F., Turnage, B., & Roest-Marti, S. (2004). Addressing stress with social work students: A controlled evaluation. *Journal of Social Work Education, 40*, 105–119.

Edelwich, J., & Brodsky, A. (1980). *Burn-out*. New York: Human Sciences Press.

Figley, C. R. (Ed.). (1995). *Compassion fatigue: Coping with secondary traumatic stress disorder in those who treat the traumatized*. New York: Brunner/Mazel.

Figley, C. R. (Ed.). (2002). *Treating compassion fatigue*. New York: Brunner-Routledge.

Fink-Samnick, E. (2007). Fostering a sense of professional resilience. *The New Social Worker, 14*(3), 24–27.

Gillespie, D. F. (Ed.). (1987). *Burnout among social workers*. New York: Haworth Press.

Greene, R. R. (2007). *Social work practice: A risk and resilience perspective*. Belmont, CA: Brooks/Cole.

Joseph, M. V. (1988, January). The roots of burnout: Implications of church ministries. *Church Personnel Issues*, pp. 1–6.

Lopez, S. A. (2007, July 20). *Professional self-care & social work*. Opening keynote Address—NASW Texas Chapter Sandra A. Lopez Leadership Institute, Austin.

Maslach, C. (1993). Burnout: A multidimensional perspective. In W. B. Schaufeli, C. Maslach, & T. Marek (Eds.), *Professional burnout: Recent developments in theory and research* (pp. 19–32). Washington, DC: Taylor & Francis.

Maslach, C. (2003). *The burnout: The cost of caring.* Cambridge, MA: Malor Book.

McCann, L. L., & Pearlman, L. A. (1990). Vicarious traumatization: A contextual model for understanding the effects of trauma on helpers. *Journal of Traumatic Stress, 3,* 131–149.

Munson, C. E. (2002). *Handbook of clinical social work supervision* (3rd ed.). New York: Haworth Press.

Murphy, B. C., & Dillon, C. (2003). *Interviewing in action: Relationship, process, and change.* Pacific Grove, CA: Brooks/Cole.

Pearlman, L. A. (1995). Self-care for trauma therapists: Ameliorating vicarious traumatization. In B. H. Stamm (Ed.), *Secondary traumatic stress: Self-care issues for clinicians, researchers, and educators* (pp. 51–64). Lutherville, MD: Sidran Press.

Pearlman, L. A., & Saakvitne, K. W. (1995). *Trauma and the therapist: Countertransference and vicarious traumatization in psychotherapy with incest survivors.* New York: W. W. Norton.

Powell, W. E. (1994). The relationship between feelings of alienation and burnout in social work. *Families in Society, 75,* 229–235.

Pryce, J., Shackelford, K., & Pryce, D. (2007). *Secondary traumatic stress and the child welfare professional.* Chicago: Lyceum Books.

Regehr, C., Hemsworth, D., Leslie, B., Howe, P., & Chau, S. (2004). Predictors of posttraumatic distress in child welfare workers: A linear structural equation model. *Ontario Association of Children's Aid Societies Journal, 48*(4), 25–30.

Shulman, L. (1993). *Interactional supervision.* Washington, DC: NASW Press.

Söderfeldt, M., Söderfeldt, B., & Warg, L.-E. (1995). Burnout in social work. *Social Work, 40,* 638–646.

Stamm, B. H. (Ed.). (1999). *Secondary traumatic stress: Self-care issues for clinicians, researchers and educators* (2nd ed.). Baltimore: Sidran Press.

Um, M-Y., & Harrison, D. F. (1998). Role stressors, burnout, mediators, and job satisfaction: A stress–strain–outcome model and an empirical test. *Social Work Research, 22,* 100–115.

Walsh-Burke, K. (2006). *Grief and loss: Theories and skills for helping professionals.* Boston: Pearson Education, Inc.

Whitaker, T., Weismiller, T., & Clark, E. (2006). *Assuring the sufficiency of a frontline workforce: A national study of licensed social workers* [Executive Summary]. Washington, DC: National Association of Social Workers.

Policy statement approved by the NASW Delegate Assembly, August 2008. For further information, contact the National Association of Social Workers, 750 First Street, NE, Suite 700, Washington, DC 20002-4241. Telephone: 202-408-8600 or 800-638-8799; e-mail: press@naswdc.org

Prostituted People, Commercial Sex Workers, and Social Work Practice

BACKGROUND

Since the beginnings of the social work profession, social workers have worked with prostituted people and individuals engaged in commercial sex work. During the 1920s, social workers tried to rehabilitate "fallen women" by changing their personalities through casework and therapy. Social workers used interventions that focused on the individual. The thinking was that as long as the causes of prostitution lay with the individual, then it could be eliminated if only all of the fallen women could be redeemed. For 40 years after World War I, the discourse on prostitution was largely shaped by psychiatrists who theorized that the causes of prostitution could be traced back to the individual neurotic, frigid, or masochistic female (Hobson, 1987). Not until the cultural and social protests of the 1960s and 1970s did prostitution again become an issue of sexual politics or social justice. Ever mired in controversy, however, discourse on prostitution and commercial sex work would continue to stagnate and be dogged by conflicts in class and gender politics (Hobson, 1987).

For the sake of this policy, NASW recognizes a difference between prostitution which is involuntary, and commercial sex work which is voluntary. *Prostitution* is defined as involuntary or forced sexual activity in exchange for remuneration. *Commercial sex work* is a term coined within the past two decades that is inclusive of many activities in which resources are voluntarily exchanged for sexual stimulation, gratification, or other sex acts (World Health Organization [WHO], 1994). *Trafficking* is another term often used interchangeably with prostitution, although trafficking is much broader than sexual trafficking and is defined by the United Nations (2000) as the illegal or illicit movement of people through force or coercion. Trafficking is a separate issue that will not be addressed in this policy.

In the 1970s, commercial sex workers around the world began organizing for safety and respect. Many commercial sex workers argued that their undocumented status increased their vulnerability to violence, exploitation, and disease.

With the rise of the HIV/AIDS epidemic in the 1980s, commercial sex workers again became scapegoats for the spread of sexually transmitted infections (STIs) (Sacks, 1996). However, many prostituted people and commercial sex workers are unable to enforce the use of condoms and therefore are at greater risk of HIV/AIDS and other STIs (WHO, Regional Office for the Western Pacific [ROWP], 2001). Social workers in almost any setting may encounter commercial sex workers, but those active in needle exchange programs, substance abuse treatment programs, HIV/AIDS outreach programs, safer sex education and public health programs for people with HIV/AIDS have the most frequent contact. Although several of the prostitution and sex worker-focused HIV/AIDS education programs and "John Schools" (diversion programs that educate men who are arrested for soliciting a prostitute) in the 1990s were organized and run by current and former prostituted people and commercial sex workers, some employ the services of social workers.

The average age of recruitment into prostitution is between 13 and 16 years; however, nationally, direct care service providers say that the victims they have encountered in the past five years are even younger (Lloyd, 2005; Silbert & Pines, 1981; Spangenberg, 2001). Girls who are exposed to "the life" are put in violent and dangerous situations. Girls are beaten, raped, and threatened by their pimps, clients, or even other prostituted women. One study of 800 prostituted women found that 85 percent had experienced rapes; 95 percent, assaults; and 77 percent, kidnapping by pimps (Council for Prostitution Alternatives [CPA], 1991). Another study found that almost 20 percent of the women interviewed had been assaulted, sexually assaulted, or propositioned by law enforcement personnel (Nixon, Tutty, Downe, Gorkoff, & Ursel, 2002).

Boys and girls are drawn into prostitution; the trauma to them is the same, and the social causes are similar. Both boys and girls who run away from home are at risk of turning to survival sex (exchange of sex for resources): at least 10 percent of shelter youths and 28 percent of street youths reported engaging in survival sex (Greene, Ennett, & Ringwalt, 1999). However, the causes of running away are somewhat different for boys and girls. Girls (20 percent to 40 percent) are more likely than boys (10 percent to 30 percent) to run away because of abuse (Estes & Weiner, 2001), and it is thought that boys are more likely than girls to be "thrown away" or to run away because of negative parental reaction to their sexual orientation (Savin-Williams, 1998). Approximately 25 percent to 35 percent of prostituted boys self-identify as gay, bisexual, or transgender transsexual (Estes & Weiner, 2001). Children with histories of family abuse, drug use, and STIs were more likely to engage in survival sex than those without these histories (Greene et al., 1999). Boys experience health concerns similar to those of girls: drug use, violence, rape, and risk of HIV/AIDS and STIs because of high rates of unprotected sex. Although boys are to be included in this policy statement, it is important to note that the vast majority of studies and research focus on girls, who, more often than boys, are victims of pimps and other traffickers (Estes & Weiner, 2001).

ISSUE STATEMENT

The pressing concerns about prostitution and commercial sex work are nested within a broader cultural context of economic injustice and social inequality. Research indicates that 75 percent to 85 percent of women would leave prostitution if they had secure housing. Although sexual exploitation can affect youths from all backgrounds, it is the "youth from low-socioeconomic backgrounds who are at high risk for recruitment and often find it harder to leave" (Lloyd, 2005, p. 16). The undocumented status of many prostituted people and commercial sex workers increases their vulnerability to violence, exploitation, and disease. Prostituted people and commercial sex workers, who are predominately female, are arrested 10 times more often than their customers, who are predominately male (WHO, ROWP, 2001). Female prostitutes and commercial sex workers of color are disproportionately targeted by law enforcement for prostitution regulation.

Violence is just one of the major problems for prostituted people and commercial sex workers. Although figures vary, an early study of violence against prostituted people and commercial sex workers indicated that 60 percent of the abuse against street prostitutes is perpetrated by clients, 20 percent by police, and 20 percent by domestic partners (Jaget, 1980). A more recent study of 130 street workers (most homeless) who engaged in prostitution or survival sex found that 80 percent had been physically assaulted (Farley & Barkan, 1998). Among prostituted people and commercial sex workers seeking services to leave prostitution at the CPA, a Portland, Oregon, organization, 85 percent of prostitutes and clients reported a history of childhood sexual abuse; 70 percent reported incest (CPA, 1991).

Substance abuse is another oft-cited concern for prostituted people and commercial sex workers. Studies in the United States have found prevalence rates of substance use and addiction up to 84 percent, depending on the exact population being studied (Alexander, 1987; Sloan, 1997; Weiner, 1996). In the United States and Canada, substance addiction is relatively common among street prostitutes who may engage in prostitution or commercial sex work to support their drug habits (Cepeda & Valdez, 2003; Monroe & Sloan, 2004). In addition, some prostitution or commercial sex work venues provide ready access to alcohol and other substances. Substance abuse is less common, however, among "off-street" and legal commercial sex workers in parts of Nevada and much of Canada.

The rate of HIV/AIDS and STIs among prostituted people and commercial sex workers varies on the basis of the rate of infection in the general population, venue, and, the type of sexual behavior in which the prostituted person or commercial sex worker engages. Prostituted people and commercial sex workers who are not able to enforce the use of condoms when engaged in high-risk behavior are placed at increased risk of HIV/AIDS and other STIs (WHO, ROWP, 2001). The experience in many Asian countries suggests that strong antiprostitution laws create barriers for prostituted people and commercial sex workers enforcing 100 percent condom usage programs (WHO, ROWP, 2001). In Thailand, for example, 80 percent of men infected with HIV/AIDS are reported to have contracted the disease from prostituted people or commercial sex workers (WHO, ROWP, 2001). By contrast, in New South Wales, Australia, where condom use is strongly enforced and the rate of HIV/AIDS is low in the general population, prostituted people and commercial sex workers have low rates of HIV/AIDS and other STIs.

One of the most common characteristics of prostituted people is their history of childhood abuse, especially sexual abuse. In 20 recent studies of adult women who were involved in prostitution or commercial sex work, the percentage of those who had been sexually abused as children ranged from 33 percent to 84 percent (Raphael, 2004). These children quickly learn that they and their bodies are only valued for sex. Therefore, they are likely to equate sex with love, and degradation with caring. A profound sense of shame and guilt develops, and often leads to depression and hopelessness. Children who encounter this type of abuse without any protective supports from family or community services will more than likely end up battered and scorned, and are searching for a way to escape their pain (Salvatore, 2002). These individuals become easy targets for sex predators, most notably pimps, who may lure them with romantic promises of a better life. A 1994 National Institute of Justice report stated that children who were sexually abused are 28 times more likely to be arrested for prostitution at some point in their lives than children who were not sexually abused (as reported in Spangenberg, 2001). The earlier-identified risk factors make traumatized children more vulnerable to prostitution and commercial sex work.

Given all of these factors prostitution like ". . . No other 'employment' has comparable rates of physical assault, rape, and homicide, except for war combat. The symptoms of profound emotional distress that result from prostitution . . . are: depression, suicidality, anxiety, posttraumatic stress disorder, dissociation, and substance abuse, and they cannot be ignored" (Farley, 2005, p. 2).

POLICY STATEMENT

NASW supports

■ the right of commercial sex workers and prostituted people to be treated with dignity and respect.

■ vigorous enforcement of laws protecting prostituted people and commercial sex workers from violence, including from partners, customers, or police.

■ policies and services that promote access and remove barriers (like criminal records) to education, housing, health care services (including mental health and substance abuse treatment), and ability to secure employment.

■ access for prostituted people and commercial sex workers to appropriate victim services and criminal justice response to criminal offenses committed against them.

■ the United Nations Convention on the Elimination of all Forms of Discrimination against Women in 1979, and the United Nations Declaration on the Elimination of Violence against Women in 1993. Both of these documents condemn prostitution and support the elimination of sexual exploitation.

■ advocacy for laws which decriminalize prostitution so prostituted people and commercial sex workers are not jailed and can still access services.

- intervention services such as housing, job training, and supports that would enable people to leave a life of prostitution or commercial sex work if they choose.

- services for male and female youths who are at risk of involvement in prostitution.

REFERENCES

Alexander, A. (1987). Prostitution: A difficult issue for feminists. In F. Delacoste & P. Alexander (Eds.), Sex work: Writings by women in the sex industry (pp. 184–214). San Francisco: Cleis Press.

Cepeda, A., & Valdez, A. (2003). Female sex workers and injecting drug use on the U.S.–Mexico border: Nuevo Laredo, Tamaulipas. Journal of Border Health, 7(1), 84–93.

Council for Prostitution Alternatives. (1991). Annual report. Portland, OR: Author.

Estes, R., & Weiner, N. (2001). The commercial sexual exploitation of children in the U.S., Canada, and Mexico. Philadelphia: University of Pennsylvania.

Farley, M. (2005, August). Unequal. Nation Magazine, pp. 1–5. Retrieved November 3, 2007, from www.prostitutionresearch.com

Farley, M., & Barkan, H. (1998). Prostitution, violence, and posttraumatic stress disorder. Women & Health, 27(3), 37–49.

Greene, J. M., Ennett, S. T., & Ringwalt, C. (1999). Prevalence and correlates of survival sex among runaway and homeless youth. American Journal of Public Health, 89, 1406–1409.

Hobson, B. M. (1987). Uneasy virtue: The politics of prostitution and the American reform tradition. Chicago: University of Chicago Press.

Jaget, C. (Ed.). (1980). Prostitutes, our life. Bristol, England: Falling Wall Press.

Lloyd, R. (2005). Acceptable victims? Sexually exploited youth in the U.S. Encounter: Education for Meaning and Social Justice, 18(3), 16–18.

Monroe, J., & Sloan, L. M. (2004, September). The truth about sex work. Paper presentation at the 1st National Conference on Prostitution, Sex Work, and the Commercial Sex Industry: The State of Women's Health. Toledo, OH: University of Toledo.

Nixon, K., Tutty, L., Downe, P., Gorkoff, K., & Ursel, J. (2002, September). The everyday occurrence: Violence in the lives of girls exploited through prostitution. Violence Against Women, 8, 1016–1043.

Raphael, J. (2004). Listening to Olivia: Violence, poverty, and prostitution. Boston: Northeastern University Press.

Sacks, V. (1996). Women and AIDS: An analysis of media misrepresentations. Social Science & Medicine, 42, 59–73.

Salvatore, J. (2002). The prostituted child. Franklin, MA: NESPIN.

Savin-Williams, R. C. (1998). The disclosure to families of same-sex attractions by lesbian, gay, and bisexual youths. Journal of Research on Adolescence, 8, 49–68.

Silbert, M., & Pines, A. (1981). Occupational hazards of street prostitutes. Criminal Justice and Behavior, 8, 395–399.

Sloan, L. M. (1997). A qualitative study of women who work as topless dancers. Unpublished doctoral dissertation, University of Texas at Austin.

Spangenberg, M. (2001). Prostituted youth in New York City: An overview. New York City: ECPAT-USA.

United Nations. (2000). United Nations Convention Against Transnational Organized Crime. Vienna, Austria: Author.

Weiner, A. (1996). Understanding the social needs of streetwalking prostitutes. Social Work, 41, 97–105.

World Health Organization. (1994). HIV/AIDS and sex workers. Retrieved June 2004, from http://www.who.org

World Health Organization, Regional Office for the Western Pacific. (2001). Sex work in Asia. Manila, Philippines: Author.

Policy statement approved by the NASW Delegate Assembly, August 2008. This policy statement supersedes the policy statement on Commercial Sex Workers and Social Work Practice approved by the Delegate Assembly in 2005. For further information, contact the National Association of Social Workers, 750 First Street, NE, Suite 700, Washington, DC 20002-4241. Telephone: 202-408-8600 or 800-638-8799; e-mail: press@naswdc.org

Public Child Welfare

BACKGROUND

Public child welfare services are child centered and family focused and include an array of preventive and support services, as well as protective services out-of-home care, and other permanency options such as placement with relatives/kinship care, and adoption. The public child welfare agencies fulfill society's mandated commitment to help families or family substitutes provide safe, stable, and permanent homes for their children. Decision making about the most appropriate environment for children and youths not only calls for an extensive knowledge of child development and an understanding of where a particular youth may be in the course of development, but also requires an ability to bring together different groups who have interests in the outcome that can be competing and conflictual. The rights of biological parents, the demands of juvenile courts, the requirements of federal and state rules and procedures, and the assessments of other professionals, all must be synthesized into a coherent, consistent, comprehensive plan that will achieve safety, stability, and permanency for each child and youth.

Although professional social work practice in public child welfare exemplifies the profession's values and mission to serve the most vulnerable, high turnover rates, with significant delays in replacement, among professional social workers have increased over the past two decades (Barnes, 2000; Kraus, 2000). Social work students continue to be more interested in social work practice in private clinically oriented settings, health care, education, aged, or employee assistance programs (Barnes). Poor working environments, high rates of ex-

posure to critical events, high levels of accountability to multiple and conflicting stakeholders, poor or inadequate supervision, the widespread practice of splitting clinical intervention from case management work, noncompetitive salaries, few promotional opportunities, and intrusiveness into their personal lives discourage new graduate social workers from entering public child welfare and influence qualified experienced staff to leave the child welfare field (Barak, Nissly, & Levin, 2001; Bednar, 2003; Cyphers, 2001, 2005; Ellett, Ellett, & Rugutt, 2003; GAO, 2003, 2004; Regehr, Chau, Leslie, & Howe, 2002; Rycraft, 1994; Samantrai, 1992). This inability to attract and retain social workers causes concern because the tasks to be accomplished and the critical decisions to be made demand a high degree of professional expertise that is applied consistently over extended periods.

ISSUE STATEMENT

The lifelong effects of child welfare decisions demand highly qualified personnel in public child welfare administration and services who have a thorough knowledge of child and youth developmental needs, comprehensive knowledge of the resources needed to meet those needs, ability to find and develop the necessary resources, and commitment to serving children and youths from impoverished environments (Cyphers, 2001, 2005; Ellett et al.; GAO, 2003, 2004). Decisions made by public child welfare staff are critical; they can alter the future course of a child's life and that of his or her family. Decisions such as whether a child was abused, should be removed from the home, should be placed in a particular type of treatment setting, should be returned home or whether to petition a court for termination of parental rights are typical of those made daily by child welfare workers. In addition, child welfare workers must work with public child welfare agencies, government rules and regulations, private child welfare agencies, courts, and parents and family members, all of whom frequently have competing and conflicting interests in the decisions and who hold the child welfare worker accountable for the decision that is made (Barak et al., 2001; Ellett et al., 2003). Only individuals who have had professional training should be given the responsibility for such important decision making.

The social work profession needs to assert its role in public child welfare by supporting three principles:

1. An undergraduate social work degree should be required for the delivery, and a graduate social work degree should be required for the supervision and administration, of social services in public child welfare to ensure that workers have the necessary skills, knowledge, and values to provide high-quality services.

2. The development of an educational curriculum and professional training is vital to the recruitment and retention of professional social workers in public child welfare.

3. The profession must organize at the local, state, and national levels to promote public understanding of and financial support for the public child welfare system, its services to clients, including equal access of resources to guardians and kinship providers, and its workers.

POLICY STATEMENT

The National Association of Social Workers (NASW) recognizes that effective services to the children and families in public child welfare demand the values, knowledge, and skills that are intrinsic to social work education.

Therefore, undergraduate social work education should be required for the delivery of social services in public child welfare, and graduate social work education should be required for the supervision and administration of social services in public child welfare. NASW supports the initiatives that encourage recruitment, education, and retention of professional social workers (BSWs or MSWs) in the public child welfare system, such as loan forgiveness programs, payment of licensure fees, financial incentives for rural practice, and statewide access to social work education programs.

NASW believes that children and families who are served through the public child welfare system have a right to the same level and quality of services delivered by professional social workers in other fields of practice. Furthermore, because the philosophical base of public child welfare requires both rehabilitative and preventive services, social workers need skill and professionalism to provide these services under the legally mandated authority of the public agency.

The same elements that undergird all professional social work practice should guide social work practice in public child welfare. Nonjudgmental respect for the dignity of the individual child and family, the use of a helping relationship, support for family self-determination, confidentiality, the right to culturally and ethnically sensitive service, and advocacy with meso and macro systems are among the essential elements in social work practice. Social workers also must address the vulnerability of women, people of color, and people with a non-heterosexual orientation in the delivery and receipt of public child welfare services and attempt to resolve their disempowerment.

NASW advocates high standards of professional ethics and practice in child protection, intact family services, kinship care, foster care, group care, and adoption, with an emphasis on keeping children connected to families of origin.

NASW supports increased activities for the recruitment, education, training, and retention of professional social workers in public child welfare. NASW also supports federal funding for education and training programs to prepare social workers for practice in child welfare.

National and local units of NASW will work together to support and promote the use of professional social workers in state and local child welfare agencies.

Public child welfare agencies and workers face unique demands and stresses. Social workers must work with other groups and professional organizations to succeed in the following activities:

- promoting public understanding of and financial support for public child welfare services to clients, the public child welfare system, including research of that system and services, and public child welfare workers

- supporting efforts to reform the public child welfare system to keep families strong, increase the safety of children, and ensure quality service delivery

- creating greater opportunities for the professional development of public child welfare workers

- securing adequate salary levels for public child welfare workers

- advocating for loan forgiveness programs for professional social workers in the child welfare system

- establishing a maximum caseload standard nationwide

- promoting job flexibility

- providing supervision that is consultative and supportive

- promoting evidence-based practice

- ensuring working conditions that are suitable and professional

- supporting title protection, which allows only workers with a social work degree to use that title.

Social workers should be allied with leaders in the public child welfare field to develop appropriate public policy in this arena. NASW reaffirms that professional social work practice in public child welfare exemplifies the profession's values and mission to serve the most vulnerable.

REFERENCES

Barak, M.E.M., Nissly, J. A., & Levin, A. (2001). Antecedents to retention and turnover among child welfare, social work, and other human service employees: What can we learn from past research? A review and met-analysis. *Social Service Review, 75,* 625–661.

Barnes, S. W. (2000). Inside story. *Policy and Practice of Public Human Services, 58*(2), 4–5.

Bednar, S. G. (2003). Elements of satisfying organizational climates in child welfare agencies. *Families in Society, 84,* 7–12.

Cyphers, G. (2001). Report from the child welfare workforce survey: State and county data and findings. Washington, DC: American Public Human Services Association.

Cyphers, G. (2005). Report from the 2004 child welfare workforce survey: State agency findings. Washington, DC: American Public Human Services Association.

Ellett, A. J., Ellett, C. D., & Rugutt, J. K. (2003, March). A study of personal and organizational factors contributing to employee retention and turnover in child welfare in Georgia, Athens: School of Social Work, University of Georgia.

General Accounting Office. (2003). *Child welfare: HHS could play a greater role in helping child welfare agencies recruit and retain staff.* Washington, DC: Author.

General Accounting Office. (2004). *D.C. Child and Family Services Agency: More focus needed on human capital management issues for caseworkers and foster parent recruitment and retention.* Washington, DC: Author.

General Accounting Office Report to Congressional Requestors. (2004, April). *Child and family services reviews: Better use of data and improved guidance could enhance HHS's oversight of state performance.* Retrieved from http://www.gao.gov/highlights/d04333high.pdf

Kraus, A. (2000). Changing personnel practices to support health and human service reform. *Policy and Practice of Public Human Services, 58*(2), 19–26.

Regehr, C., Chau, S., Leslie, B., & Howe, P. (2002). An exploration of supervisor's and manager's responses to child welfare reform. *Administration in Social Work, 26*(3), 17–36.

Rycraft, J. R. (1994). The party isn't over: The agency role in the retention of public child welfare caseworkers. *Social Work, 39,* 75–80.

Samantrai, K. (1992). Factors in the decision to leave: Retaining social workers with MSWs in public child welfare. *Social Work, 37,* 454–458.

Policy statement approved by the NASW Delegate Assembly, August 2005. This statement supersedes the statement approved by the Delegate Assembly in November 1987 and reconfirmed in 1993 and referred by the 1999 Delegate Assembly to the 2002 Delegate Assembly to be combined with policy statements on Foster Care and Adoptions and Child Abuse and Neglect, which was not completed for the 2002 Delegate Assembly but was submitted to the 2005 Delegate Assembly for review. For further information, contact the National Association of Social Workers, 750 First Street, NE, Suite 700, Washington, DC 20002-4241. Telephone: 202-408-8600 or 800-638-8799; e-mail: press@naswdc.org

Racism

BACKGROUND

Racism is pervasive in U.S. society and remains a silent code that systematically closes the doors of opportunity to many individuals. Contextually, *racism* is the belief or practice through demonstrated power of perceived superiority of one group over others by reason of race, color, ethnicity, or cultural heritage. This perceived power or right is part of the cultural inheritance of the United States. At the birth of the nation, racism was particularly demonstrated in the intent to conquer Indian nations and the perpetuation of black slavery (Perea, Delgado, Harris, & Wildman, n.d.). "The unresolved legacy of those early racial dilemmas . . . as well as additional, complex issues that we confront today as a result of our demographics" (Perea et al., n.d.) are intertwined with social and economic interests that make it difficult to safeguard contemporary policy based on law. It has been scientifically documented that races are not biological groupings but rather are social constructions (Petit, 1998). Racism is indefensible. Race and ethnicity intersect with a multitude of coexisting cultural identities, including class, religion, gender, sexual orientation, and age, that illuminate and shape the meaning given to racial, social, and economic status. These coexisting identifiers classify, categorize, and construct the social value that is assigned to individuals; position them within society; and legitimize either indignities or privilege (Harley, Jolivette, McCormick, & Tice, 2002). Contexts specific to time, place, and situation also shape racial or ethnic meaning and contribute to the placement of individuals in superior or inferior positions. For example, in the United States, whiteness conveys an ideology of privilege and power. Research has suggested the phenomenon of *white transparency*, which is the tendency among white people to not see themselves in racial terms and their lack of awareness, as an "invisible knapsack of privilege" (McIntosh, 2004). The denial of the effect of whiteness on interactions between individuals and groups contributes to the problem of racism.

Awareness of the changing demographics of racial and ethnic minority groups is important as these numbers have grown dramatically in the United States. In some areas they no longer constitute a numeric minority; yet, they are disadvantaged. Since 1980, the populations of Asian Americans have tripled, Hispanics have doubled, Native Americans have increased by 62 percent, and African Americans have increased by 31 percent; the white population remains almost the same (Ethnic Majority, 2004). By the year 2050 it has been predicted that what are often now referred to as minority populations will comprise half of the U.S. population (Day, 1996). The change in the 2000 Census to capture people of mixed racial and ethnic background has added another factor to the equation. The 2000 census categorized eight mutually exclusive and exhaustive racial and ethnic groups: American Indian/Alaskan Native only, Asian only, black or African American only, Hispanic American, Native Hawaiian/other Pacific Islander only, white only, some other race only, and two or more races. The expanded options allow for 63 confusing categories. For example, the most common multiracial combinations in 2000 were white and American Indian/Alaskan Native (1 million), white and Asian (868,000), white and black (785,000), and black and American Indian/Alaskan Native (182,000) (U.S. Census Bureau, 2001).

To establish consistency in this paper, heuristic reference is made to "oppressed racial and ethnic groups." The terms "oppressed" and "oppression" are used to clarify reference to those who are discriminated against because of their race or ethnicity. Many members of oppressed racial and ethnic groups continue to struggle for equal access and opportunity, particularly during times of slow economic growth, strident calls for tax cuts, dwindling natural resources, inflation, widespread unemployment and underemployment, and conservative judicial opinions within hegemonic structural and institutional systems that are precursors to greater racial oppression and deprivation. Unless curbed, these conditions will lead to greater ethnic and racial disputes and to greater cultural, political, social, and economic discrimination.

NASW has assumed increasing leadership in developing policies and programs to eliminate racism in society and in the social work profession. According to the NASW *Code of Ethics*, "Social workers . . . should advocate for changes in policy and legislation to improve social conditions in order to meet basic human needs and promote social justice. . . . Social workers should act to prevent and eliminate domination of, exploitation of, and discrimination against any person, group, or class" (NASW, 2000, p. 27). NASW will continue to assume a leadership role in developing practice strategies and programs that are culturally proficient.

The major demographic changes for the United States, in the number of individuals from oppressed racial and ethnic groups, "alter and increase the diversity confronting social workers daily in their agencies . . . and the complexities associated with cultural diversity" (NASW, 2001, p. 7). Cultural competence standards have been developed to enhance cultural appropriateness in service delivery to diverse client groups. The *NASW Standards for Cultural Competence in Social Work Practice* (NASW, 2001) encourage "the development of a high level of social work practice that encourages cultural competence among all social workers so that they can respond effectively, knowledgeably, sensitively, and skillfully to the diversity inherent in the agencies in which they work and with the clients and communities they serve" (p. 14).

Education

The educational system in the United States systematically denies equal access and opportunity to racially and ethnically diverse children and adults, especially those who are poor. Inadequate attention is paid to the impact of the societal forces of racism, segregation, language, and racial discrimination (for example, limited English proficiency students, poverty, and urbanization) on educational achievement. Individuals from oppressed racial and ethnic communities, including African Americans, American Indians and Alaskan Natives, Asian Americans and Pacific Islanders, and Latino or Hispanic Americans, are disproportionately represented among the impoverished segments of the population.

More astute attention is needed to address the impact of racial and ethnic discrimination in our education systems. The necessity for comprehensive multilingual and multicultural curriculums is not sufficiently recognized in national policy or local practice. In higher education, racial and ethnic groups are not proportionately represented at staff, student, faculty, or administrative levels. Insufficient financial resources exacerbate these and other problems related to education disparities.

Employment

For many members of oppressed racial and ethnic groups, there is always an economic depression. Often, individuals from these marginalized groups are the last hired and the first fired. As a result, budget cuts, downsizing, outsourcing, and privatization may disproportionately hurt these groups. Furthermore, there is a growing shortage of manufacturing and other jobs that they have historically held. In January 2004 the unemployment rate for African Americans was 10.5 percent; for Hispanics or Latinos it was 7.3 percent, below overall rates of 5.6 percent. Data was not available for American Indians; other groups had rates better than the overall rate (U.S. Bureau of Labor Statistics

[BLS], 2004). A record 120,000 African Americans dropped out of the labor market in February 2004.

The unemployment rate for adolescents from oppressed racial and ethnic groups is approximately four times that of white adolescents (BLS, 2004); it is not surprising that women and men in these groups continue to be underrepresented in decision-making and administrative positions. Affirmative action programs are not sufficiently enforced and supported and in some cases have produced conflict and polarity among employees.

Housing

Many members of marginalized racial and ethnic groups have little choice as to where they live, and they pay higher rents for less adequate housing. Mortgage and lending institutions continue the illegal practice of redlining. An $11 million settlement regarding red lining mortgages in marginalized neighborhoods was agreed to in the metropolitan Washington, DC, area. Studies conducted by the Federal Reserve, the U.S. Department of Housing and Urban Development (HUD), and the Urban Institute have found persistent discrimination against African Americans and Hispanic Americans and other ethnically diverse groups by financial institutions, landlords, and real estate agencies (Congressional Black Caucus Foundation, 1995). A more recent study conducted in 2000 by HUD to measure the extent of housing discrimination in metropolitan areas against people of color found that although generally down, housing discrimination still exists at unacceptable levels (HUD, 2004). The greatest share of discrimination for Hispanic and African American home seekers can still be attributed to being told rental units are unavailable when compared with non-Hispanic white home seekers. Although discrimination is down on most measures for African American and Hispanic homebuyers, "there are worrisome upward trends of discrimination in the areas of geographic steering for African Americans and, relative to non-Hispanic whites, the amount of help agents provide to Hispanics with obtaining financing" (HUD, 2004). The same study found consistent adverse treatment and systematic discrimination against Native Americans and Asian and Pacific Islanders in both the rental and homebuyer fields.

The maintenance of public housing continues to be a serious problem. In the new millennium, homeless shelters too often become the solution for housing millions of men, women, and children. The fact that African Americans and other oppressed groups are disproportionately affected by homelessness further aggravates the reality of the differential treatment of oppressed minority groups.

Health Care and Mental Health Services

Striking disparities exist for Americans of oppressed racial and ethnic groups in access, quality, and availability of health care and mental health services. For example, in the United States life expectancy for these groups is significantly less than it is for white people (Arias, 2004). The infant mortality rate of African Americans is more than twice that of white people (Matthews, Menacker, & MacDorman, 2002). Death from asthma is two to six times more likely to occur among African Americans and Hispanics than among white people (Health Resources and Services Administration, 2000). Suicide rates for American Indians/Alaskan Natives are 50 percent higher than the national rate, and as many as 40 percent of Hispanic Americans report limited English-language proficiency (U.S. Surgeon General, 2001), a factor that has a major impact on both access to and quality of health services.

Discrimination has had a direct impact on the health of minority populations. "Racism in the health care delivery system has a long history. Its impact is felt today in both the experiences individuals have in entering the system and the quality of care they receive" (Grant Makers in Health, 2000).

The dual health care systems of fee-for-service and public care are not meeting the needs of many members of marginalized racial and ethnic groups. Most health care costs continue to increase in the private and public sectors, and for many the quality and accessibility of services decline. "Especially disturbing is that racial and ethnic minorities comprised a disproportionate burden of the uninsured population. Though African Americans are only 12 percent of the population, 20.2 percent of African Americans were uninsured in 2002. Twenty-six percent of blacks in poverty were without health insurance year-round" (Congressional Black Caucus Foundation, 2003). For Hispanics, more than one-third (33.3 percent) under age 65 are uninsured, the poorest rate of any group (National Alliance for Hispanic Health, 2004). African Americans, Hispanics, and Asian/Pacific Islanders comprise 29 percent of the U.S. population and 52.3 percent of the nation's year-round uninsured population (Congressional Black Caucus Foundation, 2003). A majority of the nation's uninsured suffer the highest rates of chronic diseases that could have been prevented with access to quality health care.

Many health care facilities, mental health services, and health care providers tend to be located in areas that are inaccessible to low-income urban neighborhoods and rural districts, where many members of marginalized racial and ethnic groups reside. For example, older African Americans tend to reside in geographical clusters corresponding to racially stratified residential patterns. As a result racial discrimination can occur through a process of "medical redlining" (Rockeymoore & Hawkinson, 2004). With the decline of free public hospitals and of public or low-cost mental health care, the residents of racially stratified residential areas go without care. Public services, such as sanitation, are more likely to be neglected in low-income areas, thus creating additional health hazards. Use of folk wisdom and traditional healing, common practices in diverse racial and ethnic communities, are beginning to be recognized and integrated into the health care arena, yet, they are limited in many communities, and the quality of culturally proficient health care interventions is often considered a low priority or simply neglected.

Public Welfare

Oppressed racial and ethnic groups are overrepresented in the public welfare system because of their overrepresentation in the ranks of poor people. As a result they have received the brunt of the effects of the dismantling of the federal government's commitment to a philosophy of providing support for families impoverished because of unemployment and/or ill health. Stereotypes about poor people negate the reality that the U.S. economy and the job market cannot provide sufficient employment to produce the necessary income for all those who are now dependent on welfare benefits. Although acknowledged to be necessary concomitants to successful reduction of dependence on public welfare, limited services for job training, education, child care, family planning, and health care or unemployment insurance are limited or unavailable. Disregard for personal rights and human dignity, inconsistent policies, and violation of regulations have often characterized the administration and delivery of public assistance and keep people of racial and ethnic backgrounds who apply for assistance at a disadvantage.

Social Services

Social services programs are not staffed to respond to the needs of racial and ethnic oppressed populations. Often, the result is nonuse or underutilization of services by people who confront racial, cultural, and linguistic barriers. Although generally responsive to immediate basic needs, the services provided by social services agencies often dilute the intensity and negative impact of the larger structural problems such as racism, unemployment, illiteracy, and poverty. Too often society "blames the victim" and focuses on adjusting the individual to existing societal conditions, disregarding the need for structural, environmental, and institutional change and responsiveness. Social services workers who do not fully inform their clients of available entitlements or, when appropriate, do not encourage their clients to use those entitlements are an intrinsic element of the system that fails members of racial and ethnic groups.

Criminal Justice

Incarceration rates of individuals from oppressed racial and ethnic populations are so high that criminal justice has become the civil rights movement of this generation (Center on Juvenile and Criminal Justice [CJCJ], 2004). Overrepresentation of oppressed racial and ethnic groups in the justice system exists in every state in the country and at every stage of the process. Racial and ethnic disparities are more pronounced at intake, but they are compounded at each decision point. The CJCJ report indicated that nationwide African Americans are 26 percent of juvenile arrests, 44 percent of those detained, 46 percent of youths who are judicially waived to criminal court, and 58 percent of youths admitted to state prison. Hispanic American and Asian American youths with felony arrests are 3.8 times more likely than white youths with felony arrests to be sentenced to the California Youth Authority. The Juvenile Justice and Delinquency Prevention Act of 2002 (P.L. 107-273) identified disproportionate confinement of individuals of racial and ethnic groups as a condition that continues to exist.

Political Activity

Members of marginalized racial and ethnic groups are grossly underrepresented in federal and local elective and appointed positions. Thus, legislation affecting all people is produced by nonrepresentative legislative bodies. A study found an apparent pattern of harassment against African American elected officials in the United States using tactics of Internal Revenue Service audits, surveillance, phone taps, recall movements, and so forth (Congressional Black Caucus Foundation, 1995).

Hate crimes are violent acts against people, property, or organizations because of the group to which they belong or identify with. The largest determinant of hate crimes is race or ethnicity. Hate crimes are not necessarily random, uncontrollable, or inevitable occurrences, according to current research. There is overwhelming evidence that society can intervene to reduce or prevent violence that threatens whole categories or groups of people. The Violent Crime Control and Law Enforcement Act of 1994 (P.L. 103-322) provides for longer sentences if the offense is determined to be a hate crime and proven to be motivated by race, color, religion, national origin, ethnicity, gender, disability, or sexual orientation. Law enforcement officials, community leaders, educators, researchers, and policymakers need to continue to work together against hate crimes.

Research

Culturally proficient indicators are a major priority for those interested in measuring systems, performance, and outcomes. NASW's (2001) cultural competence standards address ethical responsibilities of the social work profession. Further research to enhance and enrich culturally proficient practice and policy can be an effective way to address social justice, equality, and empowerment.

Social Work Profession

NASW supports and encourages the use of its standards for culturally competent social work practice, and the advancement of practice models that have relevance for the range of needs and services represented by diverse client populations (NASW, 2003).

ISSUE STATEMENT

Racism is the ideology or practice through demonstrated power of perceived superiority of one group over others by reason of race, color, ethnicity, or cultural heritage. In the United States and elsewhere, racism is manifested at the individual, group, and institutional levels. It has been institutionalized and maintained in educational, economic, political, religious, social, and cultural policies and activities. It is observable in the prejudiced attitudes, values, myths, beliefs, and discriminatory practices of many people and institutions in positions of power. Racism is functional—that is, it serves a purpose. In U.S. society, racism functions to maintain structural inequities that are to the disadvantage of individuals in certain racial and ethnic groups.

Organized discrimination against members of certain racial and ethnic groups has permeated every aspect of their lives, including education, employment, contacts with the legal system, economics, housing, politics, religion, and social relationships. It has become institutionalized through folklore, legal restrictions, values, myths, the media, and social mores that are openly supported by a substantial number of people, including those who maintain control of the major institutions of U.S. society.

The history of racism in this country began with the genocide of American Indians and Alaskan Natives and includes the atrocities of slavery, colonialism. The subjugation of individuals of Spanish, Mexican, and American Indian descent in the southwest and along the southern border of the United States, the victimization of Chinese and Asian immigrants during the construction of the U.S. railway system, and the more recent internment of Japanese Americans during Work War II are also a part of that history. This same history has been used to justify the conquering of American Indians and Alaskan Natives, African Americans, Puerto Ricans and other Latinas, and Native Hawaiians and Pacific Islanders to obtain land, promote slavery, and perpetuate exploitation through labor and control over the distribution of resources. These conquered population groups became involuntary U.S. citizens.

Newer immigrants face many of the same stereotypes, myths, and prejudices that the conquered populations had faced. Historically, all immigrants entering the country experience racism and discrimination. The effects of racism are documented in a variety of ways: inadequate physical and mental health care services, low wages, high unemployment and underemployment, racial profiling, overrepresentation in the criminal justice systems, substandard housing, higher rates of school dropout, increased suicide, less access to higher education, and other institutional maladies.

Racism negatively affects both the oppressed and the oppressor. Institutional racism has historical roots in injustices perpetrated by our ancestors on indigenous and other populations in conquering and populating this country. Recognition of historical injustices is the first step in combating racism. It should be acknowledged that the sons and daughters are not responsible for the sins of their parents, but the sons and daughters must analyze the present reality to ascertain the antecedents that have resulted in one group in society being in a more advantageous and favorable position at the expense of other groups. It is incumbent in solidarity and in alliance with groups who are inappropriately considered subordinate to join forces with the social work profession to bring about a more just and equitable society in which power, status, wealth, services, and opportunities, are enjoyed by all. Most common to racism is the unconscious behavior associated with white privilege and the benefits of discrimination against others. Racism limits and minimizes the contributions of many, as well as the contributions that will be made.

Social workers often hold jobs in which they confront the damaging effects of racism at conscious and unconscious levels and at individual and institutional levels. As professional administrators, educators, organizers, planners, case managers, clinicians, supervisors, consultants, caseworkers, and researchers, today's social workers have firsthand knowledge of the difficulties that many encounter in their efforts to combat white privilege, gain access to resources, and obtain a professional education.

Most social workers also witness the scarcity of professional peers from oppressed racial and ethnic groups to act as role models and to provide services to diverse client populations. Furthermore, employment opportunities in the upper echelons of the social work delivery systems and academia historically have been elusive to social workers of oppressed racial and ethnic groups.

POLICY STATEMENT

NASW supports an inclusive, multicultural society in which racial, ethnic, class, sexual orientation, age, physical and mental ability, religion and spirituality, gender and other cultural and social identities are valued and respected. Racism will not be tolerated at any level. Emphasis must be placed on self-examination, learning, and change that encompass an ability to deconstruct racist beliefs and practices to become culturally proficient and to ally with others in the full appreciation of diversity.

NASW (2001) charges social workers with the ethical responsibility to be culturally competent.

The association seeks the enactment of public social policies that will protect the rights of and ensure equity and social justice for all members of diverse racial and ethnic groups. It is the ethical responsibility of NASW members to assess their own practices and the agencies in which they work for specific ways to end racism.

The basic goal should be to involve social workers in education programs designed to bring about measurable changes in provider agencies and in NASW national units, chapters, and local units. This is based on the premise that to engage in constructive intraprofessional relationships and to effectively serve clients, social workers must engage in deconstruction of their own biases and stereotypes and work in concerted alliance with others to enhance social justice and equity for all. Racism is embedded in our society and unless we identify specific instances and work together to remove them, we are part of the problem rather than a mechanism for the solution.

Education

NASW advocates the following:

■ supporting the development and implementation of comprehensive multilingual and multicultural curricula—such curricula must call attention to white privilege, the pain of oppression, the legacy of racism, and the contributions of racially and ethnically oppressed groups

■ implementing programs and policies designed to produce high-quality education through a range of effective approaches

■ addressing and seeking censure against educators and educational systems that practice discrimination against students, faculty, staff, and their families because of their race or ethnicity

■ creating educational systems in which faculties, staff, students, administrators, and boards of education reflect the cultural diversity of neighborhoods and the larger society

■ supporting the highest standard of all educational systems to ensure that fair and adequate treatment of, and funding for, diverse racial and ethnic communities is upheld.

Employment

NASW advocates the following:

■ implementation of a national policy of full and fair employment insurance in times of economic downtimes

■ development of comprehensive job training programs

■ maintenance and strengthening of affirmative action plans so that they have the necessary authority and resources to be implemented successfully as demonstrated by measurable outcomes

■ genuine compliance, rather than tokenism, with affirmative action and equal employment opportunity requirements

■ implementation of an adequate minimum wage that reflects the realities of the cost of living and minimum standards of subsistence

■ providing effective, affordable, comprehensive, multicultural, multilingual, and accessible child care

■ supporting workforce policies that prohibit the negative impact on employees of marginalized racial and ethnic groups.

Housing and Community

NASW advocates the following:

■ enactment and practice of an open housing policy designed to eliminate externally imposed segregation in housing resulting from concentrated public housing, redlining, renovation, and conversion of apartment houses to condominiums

■ establishment of government and support programs that promote revitalization in marginalized racial and ethnic communities.

Health Care and Mental Health Services

NASW advocates the following:

■ empowerment of health and mental health practitioners to learn and use culturally relevant healing practices

■ self-study by health and mental health providers to identify oppressive policies, practices, and strategies and target dates for change

■ accessible, affordable, and culturally proficient health care, mental health services, and private practitioners in all neighborhoods

■ enhanced recruitment and training of marginalized racial and ethnic groups and individuals as health and mental health providers, particularly social workers.

Public Welfare Services

NASW advocates the following:

■ positive regard and respect for each individual's personal rights and human dignity

■ elimination of violations of regulations and inconsistent policies in public welfare that place some members of racial and ethnic groups at a disadvantage

■ use of racial, ethnic, and cultural expertise in the development and delivery of public welfare services

■ elimination of broader problems such as unemployment, illiteracy, and poverty that create the need for public welfare.

Social Services

NASW advocates the following:

■ development of social services that target needs articulated by the community to be served

■ development of model social programs that emphasize empowerment of the community and stress economic independence

■ addressing the underrepresentation of marginalized racial and ethnic groups in the social services professions and policy-making boards of social services agencies.

Criminal Justice System

NASW advocates the following:

■ fair and equitable treatment of individuals from oppressed racial and ethnic groups involved in the criminal justice system

■ monitoring and promoting criminal justice policies, statutes, and laws that do not discriminate against individuals on the basis of race, ethnicity, class, political affiliation, sexual orientation, nationality, ability, age, or place of residence

■ addressing the problem of overrepresentation of marginalized racial and ethnic groups within the criminal justice system

■ striving to end racism and discrimination in recruitment, hiring, retention, and promotion in employment of members of racial and ethnic groups in all levels of the criminal justice system

■ availability and accessibility to professionally trained and culturally proficient interpreters in situations where language differences may inhibit communication

■ developing initiatives to examine and correct policies and regulations of hate crimes.

Civil Rights

NASW advocates the following:

■ developing initiatives to examine and correct the discriminating and inhumane detention and deportation policies and regulations of the U.S. Immigration and Naturalization Service (INS).

■ developing initiatives to rectify the discrimination provisions and civil rights violations of the Patriot Act

■ holding law enforcement agencies accountable when they use racial profiling

■ providing education and training to law enforcement agencies on how to discontinue the use of racial profiling.

Political Activity

NASW advocates the following:

- passage of legislation that acknowledges, maintains, or enhances the sovereign rights and religious freedom of indigenous populations

- election and appointment of legislators from underrepresented racial and ethnic groups

- passage of federal antidiscrimination laws, statutes, and regulations to ensure full legal protection against discrimination and hate crimes

- programs that offer training for police and victim-assistance professionals in early interventions to help hate crime victims better cope with trauma

- increase in public interest groups that are racially and ethnically diverse

- passage of legislation that will have a favorable impact on people of diverse racial and ethnic backgrounds

- massive voter registration and education

- campaigns against legislators who sponsor or support bills that are racist in intent or implementation

- cultural proficiency training for public officials

- proactive involvement in regional processes that actively promote participation of diverse racial and ethnic communities

- initiatives that support policies and procedures to sustain affirmative action and equal employment opportunity.

Research

NASW advocates the following:

- promotion and support of social work research about culturally proficient practice strategies

- encouragement of representation of and participation by underrepresented racial and ethnic groups in research

- funding that will enhance research to promote social justice in marginalized racial and ethnic communities.

Social Work Profession

NASW advocates the following:

- continuously acknowledging, recognizing, confronting, and addressing all forms of racism within social work practice at the individual, agency, and institutional levels and within the broader community

- full representation of groups oppressed because of race, color, ethnicity, or national origin at all levels of leadership and employment, policy formulation, research, administration, supervision, and direct services in social work agencies and professional organizations and associations.

- implementation of the concepts of affirmative action in all facets of the profession at both the voluntary and the paid levels of service, especially in practice, education, research, and professional development

- development of guidelines for multicultural social work curricula that emphasize social work as a profession that strives to empower those with less power because of racial or ethnic identification.

REFERENCES

Arias, E. (2004). *United States life tables 2001* (National Vital Statistics Reports, Vol. 52, No. 14, Table 12). Hyattsville, MD: National Center for Health Statistics.

Center on Juvenile and Criminal Justice. (2004). *Myths and facts about youth and crime.* Retrieved September 10, 2004, from http://cjcj.org/jjic/myths_facts.php

Congressional Black Caucus Foundation. (1995). *The mean season for African Americans.* Washington, DC: Author.

Congressional Black Caucus Foundation. (2003, September 29). *Congressional Black Caucus Foundation denounces rise in the number of uninsured: Census figures reveal minorities hardest hit* [Press Release]. Retrieved September 29, 2004, from http://www.cbcfonline.org/Uninsured.html

Day, J. C. (1996). *Population projections of the Unites States by age, sex, race, and Hispanic origin: 1995 to 2050* (Current Population

Reports, Series p. 25-1130). Washington, DC: U.S. Census Bureau.

Ethnic Majority. (2004). "African, Hispanic and Asian American demographics" [Homepage]. Retrieved October 18, 2004, from http://www.ethnicmajority.com/demographics_home.htm

Grant Makers in Health. (2000). *Strategies for reducing racial and ethnic disparities in health* (Issue Brief No. 5). Washington, DC: Author.

Harley, D. A., Jolivette, K., McCormick, K., & Tice, K. (2002). Race, class, and gender: A constellation of positionalities with implications for counseling. *Journal of Multicultural Counseling and Development, 30*, 216–236.

Health Resources and Services Administration. (2000). *Eliminating health disparities in the United States.* Washington, DC: U.S. Department of Health and Human Resources.

Institute on Race and Poverty. (2002). *Racism and metropolitan dynamics: The civil rights challenge of the 21st century.* Minneapolis: Author.

Juvenile Justice and Delinquency Prevention Act of 2002, P.L. 107-273, 116 Stat. 1869.

Matthews, T. J., Menacker, F., & MacDorman, M. F. (2002). *Infant mortality statistics from the 2000 period linked birth/infant death data set* (National Vital Statistics Reports, Vol. 50, No. 12, Table 1). Hyattsville, MD: National Center for Health Statistics.

McIntosh, P. (2004). White privilege. Unpacking the invisible knapsack. In M. L. Anderson & P. H. Collins (Eds.), *Race, class and gender* (5th ed., pp. 103–108). Belmont, CA: Wadsworth/Thomson.

National Alliance for Hispanic Health. (2004). *Delivering health care to Hispanics* (3rd ed., p. 128). Washington, DC: Estrella Press.

National Association of Social Workers. (2000). *Code of ethics of the National Association of Social Workers.* Washington, DC: Author.

National Association of Social Workers. (2001). *NASW standards for cultural competence in social work practice.* Washington, DC: Author.

National Association of Social Workers. (2003). Cultural competence in the social work profession. In *Social work speaks: National Association of Social Workers policy statements* (6th ed., pp. 71–74). Washington, DC: NASW Press.

Perea, J. F., Delgado, R., Harris, A., & Wildman, S. M. (n.d.). *Race and racism in American law.* Retrieved November 8, 2004, from http://academic.udayton.edu/race/syllabi/race/index.htm

Petit, C. (1998, February 23). No biological basis for race scientists say. *San Francisco Chronicle.* Retrieved February 1, 2005, from http://www.geocities.com/CapitolHill/Lobby/2788/race2.html

Rockeymoore, M., & Hawkinson, L. (2004). *Structured inefficiency: The impact of Medicare reform on African Americans* (Policy Report No. 1, pp. 3–20). Washington, DC: Congressional Black Caucus Foundation, Center for Policy Analysis and Research.

U.S. Bureau of Labor Statistics. (2004). *Labor force statistics from the Current Population Survey: Black or African American, Hispanic or Latino.* Retrieved October 10, 2004, from http://data.bls.gov/cgi-bin/surveymost

U.S. Census Bureau. (2001). *United States Census 2000.* Washington, DC: Author.

U.S. Surgeon General. (2001). *Culture counts in mental health services and research finds new surgeon general report* [Press release]. Retrieved April 4, 2004, from http:www.surgeongeneral.gov/library/mentalhealth

Violent Crime Control and Law Enforcement Act of 1994, P.L. 103-322, 108 Stat. 1796.

SUGGESTED READINGS

Banton, M. (1988). *Racial consciousness.* London: Longman.

Bowser, B. P., Jones, T., & Young, G. A. (Eds.). (1995). *Toward the multicultural university.* Westport, CT: Praeger.

Federico, C., & Sidanius, J. (2001). *Racism, ideology, and affirmative action revisited: The antecedents and consequences of "principled objections" to affirmative action* (Working Paper #183). Retrieved March 1, 2004, from www:russellsage.org

Freire, P. (1998). *Pedagogy of freedom: Ethics, democracy, and civic courage.* Lanham, MD: Rowman & Littlefield.

Gray, W. (1996, May). *Speech for the 100th anniversary of Plessy vs. Ferguson.* Cambridge: Harvard University, W.E.B. Du Bois Institute. (C-Span, August 13, 1996).

Jackson, S., & Solis, J. (1995). *Beyond comfort zones in multiculturalism: Confronting the politics of privilege.* Westport, CT: Bergin & Garvey.

Kivel, P. (2002). *Uprooting racism: How white people can work for racial justice.* Philadelphia: Ingram.

Mahalingam, R., & McCarthy, C. (2000). *Multicultural curriculum. New directions for social theory, practice and policy.* New York: Routledge.

Reeves, T., & Bennette, C. (2003). The Asian and Pacific Islander population in the US: March 2002. In *Current Population Reports* (P20-540). Washington, DC: U.S. Census Bureau.

Policy statement approved by the NASW Delegate Assembly, August 2005. This policy supersedes the policy statement on Racism approved by the Delegate Assembly in 1996 and the policy statement on Racism approved by the NASW national Board of Directors in October 1993 following recommendations by the Delegate Assembly in August 1993, and referred by the 2002 Delegate Assembly to the 2005 Delegate Assembly for revision. For further information, contact the National Association of Social Workers, 750 First Street, NE, Suite 700, Washington, DC 20002-4241. Telephone: 202-408-8600 or 800-638-8799; e-mail: press@naswdc.org

Role of Government, Social Policy, and Social Work

BACKGROUND

Since the colonial beginnings of this country, government has been involved in addressing social problems. As a reaction to the strong central authority of European monarchies from which the founders fled or rebelled, they favored a theory of negative government, meaning the less government, the better. This preference for limited government responsibility for social services led Jansson (2001) to label the United States a "reluctant welfare state" as a way of distinguishing it from the traditional European welfare states. Despite this obvious and strong preference for private and individual solutions, government has mitigated the fallout from an unregulated economy and protected disadvantaged populations. As far back as the early 1700s, Massachusetts's colonists received aid from the general treasury to care for sick and displaced people (Trattner, 1999). Although government assistance goes back to our earliest beginnings, there has always been a struggle over how much government should be involved in helping cure the social ills of the nation.

An infamous instance of the hands-off approach is found in the "Pierce Veto." In the 1850s, Franklin Pierce vetoed legislation that would have designated federal lands to be used to establish psychiatric hospitals. Pierce vetoed the legislation because he feared that the federal government would become the "great almoner" to poor people (Pumphrey & Pumphrey, 1967). He did not want to set an "untenable precedent and draw the federal government into an inappropriate and unconstitutional relationship with the nation's needy" (Hall, 2004, p. 1).

Trends and countertrends addressed the most extreme dimensions of poverty, inequal-ity, and oppression. In the early years of the 20th century, the Progressive Era tempered the harshness of the free market economy and protected the most vulnerable people. The Roaring Twenties returned the country to a time of limited government involvement. This was exemplified by the Hoover administration, which refused to support government intervention into the serious hardship experienced by people at the beginning of the Great Depression.

Ultimately, the Great Depression and response of Franklin Delano Roosevelt's New Deal administration in the 1930s firmly established the responsibility of the federal government to ameliorate a capitalistic system. During the subsequent 40 years, the presidential leadership of both parties further established and expanded at the federal level rights of citizenship that included new social, political, and economic benefits.

Leadership by the federal government in promoting an equality-of-opportunity social agenda peaked in the Kennedy–Johnson era of the 1960s. More socially progressive legislation was passed in the 1960s than at any time in U.S. history, and even continued under the Nixon administration. President Nixon instituted block grants to the states, as part of a "new federalism" without abdicating federal leadership, and instituted Title XX support for a range of social programs. Nixon supported the "federalization" of categorical welfare entitlements eventually enacted as Supplemental Security Income, or SSI, benefits. Finally, he proposed the federal takeover of Aid to Families with Dependent Children and introduced national health insurance legislation that would have extended Medicare- and Medicaid-like health coverage to new categories of citizens.

Although the administrations of Presidents Ford and Carter tampered little with social programs and priorities, the "stagflation" during the 1970s led to increasing calls for limits on taxes and on social spending at both the federal and state levels and a shift from universal to selective approaches to services. Concurrently, public hostility toward poor people and other marginalized groups was captured by the republican party's appeals to the "silent majority" or those who were unwilling participants in government intervention on behalf of these groups.

The Reagan and Bush administrations in the 1980s even more vigorously promoted an ideology of individualism and privatization, challenged many established entitlements, and scaled down the government role in "interfering" with the marketplace and corporate profits. Supply-side economics and tax policies forced real cuts in social program spending, a reversal of social program priorities, and efforts to deregulate businesses. The gap between rich and poor increased dramatically. Both administrations continued the concept of a "safety net" supplemented by private charity for meeting the needs of the "truly needy." Although this safety net was selective, the administrations still considered government as the provider of last resort, and there was no attempt to remove federal protection for special groups, such as abused and neglected children.

President Bill Clinton's victory in 1992 did not lead to a return to the philosophy on which the New Deal was based. Instead, Clinton, a neo-liberal Democrat, announced that the "era of big government is over." Consequently, he signed the 1996 Personal Responsibility and Work Opportunity Reconciliation Act (P.L. 104-193), which limited entitlement to public assistance for children and their families that the Roosevelt administration had established in 1935 with the passage of the Social Security Act. The Clinton administration restricted government provision and reduced record-setting deficits that had deepened during the Reagan–Bush years.

Both parties concurred that government should be reduced in size and scope. In the 1994 national elections, candidates supporting further limitations on government won the majority of congressional seats for the first time in 40 years. A majority of state governors was also elected on a platform of less government and lower taxes. These newly elected leaders sought to curtail the federal government in social program guarantees and funding, in protecting vulnerable populations, in restricting monitoring of business and investments, and in promoting affirmative action and other equity programs. At the same time they sought a greater social control role for government in shaping how families, and women in particular, may behave and in restricting who may come to this country and the rights they could exercise while in residence.

In the 2000 election, George W. Bush described himself as a "compassionate conservative." His social welfare policies were similar to those of his father's and Reagan's with the further elaboration of privatizating social services programs, an emphasis on faith-based initiatives, and profit-making social services programs.

In the early years of the 21st century attacks on the role of the federal government have grown from a preference for limited federal involvement to view recipients of services in ways that are antithetical to social work values in several ways: There is a shift from blaming victims to punishing them. The category of "undeserving poor" has expanded to include almost everyone, even those formerly protected, such as children, veterans, elderly people, and people with mental and physical illnesses. Users of public resources are subject to greater social control measures. Consumers of both market and social services are granted fewer real protections and are simply admonished to "let the buyer beware." Stereotypical views of personal characteristics or behaviors of certain groups by virtue of their racial, ethnic, or citizenship status (in the form of acts of racism, ageism, sexism, homophobia, and xenophobia) are justified under the guise of returning to "a supposed" normalcy or "survival of the fittest."

Consistent with this social agenda are economic tenets that include spending cuts and tax breaks for upper-income groups coupled with balanced budget legislation, shifts of minimum programs back to the states without any entitlement provisions, heavy deregulation of industry, the lifting of consumer and environmental protections, and mandates for personal responsibility legislation.

Results of national elections in the first decade of the 21st century reflect seriously divided public opinion over the role of government. Public policy is the dominant variable in determining the nature of social work practice, and it is profoundly affected by government policy. Although social agencies and social work professionals can help shape policies and practices, the nature of the services delivery system and the legitimacy of social work as a profession is established by public social policy. Changes in government policies affect clients, their eligibility, and their ability to obtain benefits and services. In conclusion, restructuring and limiting government responsibility has profoundly altered the availability and the delivery of social work services and the role and status of social work as a profession.

ISSUE STATEMENT

Advances in science and technology, food production, public health, worker safety, and the environment have resulted in improvements in the quality of life undreamed of in the past. At the same time, dislocations and problems that have accompanied many of these changes have caused considerable misery and inequities for many people and communities. From Franklin D. Roosevelt to Jimmy Carter, the electorate chose representatives who viewed government as a mediating structure that modified the vagaries and inequities found in the marketplace. This view was accompanied by ideologies to create equality of opportunity to fulfill the vision of the United States of America as an open, pluralistic, caring, and inclusive society.

From 1935 to the late 1970s, federal government efforts moved in the direction of sharing the benefits of economic growth among its citizens, moderating the harshness of an unregulated economy, and protecting vulnerable people. During this period, government has fulfilled this by

- regulation and oversight

- designing and funding programs created specifically to meet its policy goals

- stimulating the economy through industrial, taxation, and other fiscal policies

- redistributing the wealth of the society through the tax system.

However, regressive "Reaganomics" interrupted the progressive ideals of the government. Recent administrations have replaced fundamental values of the New Deal with their own agendas of privatization, personal responsibility, corporate welfare, and faith-based and profit-making social services.

The combination of severe cuts in funding of social programs to provide tax cuts for the wealthiest citizens, deregulation of legal rights and protections, and devolution of programs to states or private corporations with less funding and little or no regulation and standards with very short notice can cause great harm to our society and especially to its most vulnerable populations.

Since the beginning of social work as a profession and the inception of NASW, two basic assumptions have been made: The social ills of the nation and its citizens need public attention, resources, and solutions, and government has a major role and responsibility to meet human needs. Moreover, there has been increasing recognition that major shifts in the structure and functions of society, including demographic, economic, health, and family factors require universal social welfare benefits and services.

The George W. Bush administration saw problems as being individual in origin rather than social or environmental in nature, and too often the etiology of problems in society is being characterized in moral, racial and cultural, or intellectual terms. The influence of social, economic, or political factors on community and family life has been minimized or ignored. At the beginning of the 21st century, government is no longer regarded as an instrument of problem solution; instead, in some quarters, by some factions, it is portrayed as the problem or an exacerbating factor of the problem. Although state governments have been given more responsibility and opportunities to address these issues with fewer resources, there are yet more requirements that states meet the needs of vulnerable and oppressed populations.

POLICY STATEMENT

It is the position of NASW that federal, state, and local governments must have a role in developing policies and programs that expand opportunities, address social and economic justice, improve the quality of life of all people in this country, with special emphasis on oppressed groups, and enhance the social conditions of the nation's communities. NASW reaffirms its commitment to the promotion of the positive role of federal, state, and local governments as guarantors of the social safety net and as the mechanisms by which people through their elected representatives can ensure equitable and accountable policies to address

■ curbing the excesses of a free market economy

■ entitlements to assist in the elimination of poverty

■ access to universal comprehensive health care

■ standards for public services

■ enabling citizen participation in the development and implementation of social programs

■ taxation that is progressive and fair and promotes a reduction of poverty

■ an income floor for working poor people through earned income tax credits and other mechanisms

■ adequate federal minimum wage laws indexed to annual cost-of-living increases

■ standards and laws for the protection of workers in the workplace

■ standards and laws for the protection of vulnerable populations

■ product safety standards

■ access to legal services

■ commitment to full employment

■ adequate and affordable housing

■ assurance of adequate public education and educational standards for all schools

■ a justice system rooted in law and administered impartially

■ laws that protect and maintain the fragile, natural environment

■ ensuring the civil rights of citizens and noncitizen residents, and the right of all to marry

■ nondiscrimination and affirmative action

■ international initiatives based on collaborative and cooperative relationships with other nations.

The key to accomplishing these policy goals is a view of government as an embodiment of and by the people, rather than an entity above and apart from its citizens. This policy calls for a renewed commitment to civic responsibility by an informed community through participation in democratic forums. This policy can be achieved with civic and political participation by all, and with campaign finance reform that levels the political playing field. It demands open debate on a wide variety of policies and programs while maintaining the basic functions listed. As necessary, such a process would support the reform of government when it is consistent with the social work value base.

NASW reaffirms the essential role of government. The role of the federal government is to ensure uniform standards, adequate resources, equal protection under the law, monitoring and evaluating of outcomes, and provision of technical assistance to state and local governments. NASW also recognizes the role of state and local governments in social programs. State governments are often in better positions to understand the needs of the people in those states. As a part of a national community, states must work together to implement a federal policy that supports the well-being of the people of this nation. Thus, social programs are most effective when there is consistency in federal standards and guidelines with adequate funding and accountability mechanisms for states and localities to administer programs in ways that are best adapted to meet the needs of people, examining the effectiveness, efficiency, and accountability of programs necessary to ensure the success of that role. Laws, regulations, and program guidelines need constant and thorough review. NASW can provide significant leadership in evaluating existing programs and in designing and recommending new ones that advance the goals of the social policy it has reaffirmed.

NASW believes that social workers can be effective at all levels of and in many roles in government. Social workers can fulfill roles as elected officials and leaders in government and as administrators in agencies. The recent reintroduction of block grants is an opportunity for social workers to support the collaborative efforts of government and the people. This policy asserts that government should actively and creatively guide, negotiate, and participate in cooperative efforts with nongovernmental organizations to provide programs that expand and support opportunities, address social and economic justice, and improve the quality of life for all people.

REFERENCES

Hall, P. (2004). *Beyond affliction: Dorothea Dix and Franklin Pierce highlight page.* Retrieved June 21, 2004, from www.npr.org/programs/disability/project.dir/project.html

Jansson, B. (2001). *The reluctant welfare state with infotrac: American social welfare policies—Past, present and future.* Belmont, CA: Wadsworth.

Personal Responsibility and Work Opportunity Reconciliation Act, P.L. 104-193, 110 Stat. 2105.

Pumphrey, R., & Pumphrey, M. (1967). *The heritage of American social work.* New York: Columbia University Press.

Trattner, W. (1999). *From poor law to welfare state.* New York: Free Press.

Policy statement approved by the NASW Delegate Assembly, August 2005. This policy supersedes the policy statement on Role of Government approved by the Delegate Assembly in August 1996. For further information, contact the National Association of Social Workers, 750 First Street, NE, Suite 700, Washington, DC 20002-4241. Telephone: 202-408-8600 or 800-638-8799; e-mail: press@ naswdc.org

Rural Social Work

BACKGROUND

Social Work Values and Ethics

Rural social work practice contributes to the social work mission of advocating for social justice and extending access to services for underserved populations. Rural practice requires a sophisticated level of understanding of values and ethics and highly developed skills in applying them. Small communities pose challenges to confidentiality, particularly when relatively few professional social workers interact with providers and community members who may have limited understanding of professional ethics. Effective rural practice involves locality-based community development. It is frequently inappropriate to maintain "professional distance" from the community. Instead, it is essential to participate in community activities and establish trust among the residents.

Rural social workers interact with clients and their families in a variety of ways, such as at schools, churches, sports events, or fundraisers. Protecting clients from any negative consequences of dual relationships in rural settings has less to do with limiting social relationships and more to do with setting clear boundaries. Discussing possible conflicts and apprising clients of options is essential. However, the general lack of resources limits referral alternatives.

Residents of rural areas can be judgmental toward clients and services that reflect cultures and lifestyles different from community norms. Education of community members requires a sustained effort based on trust. Empowering clients who have limited opportunities can be challenging, but some rural communities provide examples of support and commitment that enhance the services social workers can provide. The professional litera-ture deals so little with aspects of rural practice that the preparation that all social workers should receive to work in rural communities or with clients from rural cultures is limited.

Professional Services and Education

Rural areas face a shortage of social welfare services to meet their needs. Those services that do exist are further diminished by issues related to professional training among staff (Daley & Avant, 1999; Ginsberg, 1993; NASW, 1994). Agencies often are forced to use high proportions of bachelor's-level social workers who provide needed frontline services but are assisted by large percentages of nonprofessional staff. This practice is less common in nonrural areas (Johnson, 1980). It is common for workers to be isolated from direct professional supervision.

Recruitment and retention issues are, in part, by-products of a social work educational system that developed largely from urban roots and pays relatively little attention to rural populations (NASW, 1994). Most social workers receive little content on rural social work in their professional training. This general lack of preparation creates a major barrier to developing the professional social work labor force needed to address the needs of rural clients and the unique social problems of rural communities.

Most authors agree that generalist preparation is the best approach for rural practice (Daley & Avant, 1999; Davenport & Davenport, 1995; Ginsberg, 1976), yet graduate education tends to force students away from this approach. The appearance of new social work programs in rural areas, some with advanced generalist concentrations, is encouraging. They create an opportunity to address the shortage of professional social workers in rural areas. The educational challenge that remains is to continue to strengthen the content in rural social work and integrate it in the overall curriculum.

Rural Poverty

Great wealth has been extracted from rural America; yet, it remains the site of some of the nation's most intense and persistent poverty (Rural Policy Research Institute, 1995). People in rural areas experience lower income levels, higher unemployment, and higher poverty rates than people in urban areas. However, public assistance utilization rates are lower because rural residents lack access to program information and because of the stigma attached to public assistance in rural areas (Rank & Hirschl, 1993).

In 1997 the poverty rate in nonmetropolitan counties was 15.9 percent compared with 12.6 percent in metropolitan counties (U.S. Bureau of the Census, 1998). Poverty levels in metropolitan areas have slowly decreased but have not gone down in rural areas (U.S. Bureau of the Census, 1998). Nonmetropolitan counties have a higher percentage of children in poverty, and more rural children live in female-headed households (U.S. Bureau of the Census, 1998). Of the 200 consistently poorest U.S. counties, 195 are rural. Twenty-three percent of people in nonmetropolitan counties are considered persistently poor. Studies indicate that the duration of poverty is a strong predictor of school attainment and early patterns of employment (Caspi, Wright, Moffitt, & Silva, 1998; Duncan, Young, Brooks-Gunn, & Smith, 1998). Children in nonmetropolitan areas who become poor or are born poor are more likely than urban children to stay in poverty; non-metropolitan children in female-headed households are at even greater risk of persistent poverty (Sherman, 1992).

The increasingly global economy and the proliferation of international corporate conglomerates have further transformed the political, social, and economic landscape of rural areas. Rural manufacturing operations relocate to places with cheap labor. Without the training to move to a technology-based economy and with underfunded school systems and limited taxation capacity, even more rural people are left out of the economic mainstream and remain in or near poverty (Dilger et al., 1999).

Some rural communities experience an "inmigration" of population, often made up of midcareer baby boomers seeking a more peaceful way of life. Ironically, the resulting increase in property values forces long-term rural residents out because they cannot afford the higher property taxes, nor can they afford to turn down the money offered for their land. Rural newcomers press and vote for citylike services—such as libraries, recreation centers, and road maintenance—that again raise taxes. Because they commute to urban jobs or keep only weekend homes in rural settings, they do not tend to make major purchases locally, participate in local events, become invested in the rural culture, or have true concern for the success or failure of neighbors. The new job opportunities they create tend to be low-wage service jobs. Rural service sector wage earners drive long distances to work because increased property values and taxes make it impossible to live where they work (Dilger et al., 2001).

Rural Communities

Rural communities often retain traditional structures and faith-based service delivery systems that can be assets as well as challenges. They provide self-monitoring and vigilance, making rural communities safer than urban areas, and have a strong informal helping system. However, the same structures may be less hospitable to individuals perceived as outside the mainstream, such as people of color; women; or gay, lesbian, bisexual, and transgender populations.

The "strip and leave" practices of extractive industries and the crisis of urban and industrial waste have left rural areas with real potential ecological disasters and few resources to deal with them.

Service Delivery Systems

Many rural areas are part of larger geographic service areas. Multicounty social and health services programs based in population centers are designated to serve rural areas. Rural communities are generally offered fewer services than their numbers in the service area justify. Services may be offered primarily at a central location. All social workers should develop knowledge and skills for effective rural social work. Regional agencies must ensure that rural communities receive accessible and appropriate services and include rural residents in planning processes. Regional agencies should train staff to provide rural services in effective ways, such as assigning responsibility for particular rural sections and making efforts to build trust with residents of rural communities.

ISSUE STATEMENT

Social work practice in rural areas historically has sought to resolve issues of equity, service availability, and isolation that adversely affect rural populations and to support and advocate for vulnerable and at-risk people living in rural communities. Practitioners of rural social work are confronted with rural poverty that is more pervasive and hidden than urban poverty. Rural communities tend to be closed to outsiders. The dominant rural culture may harshly judge those who are perceived to be different. Rural communities are experiencing diminishing infrastructure systems and resources. Social workers in rural practice face professional and personal challenges that urban social workers may never face. The relative closeness of rural cultures, communities, and people greatly magnifies these concerns. Confidentiality can be an especially difficult practice issue in rural areas, where professional distance is difficult to maintain.

Effective rural social work practice demands that the social worker have command of impressive levels of expertise, subtlety, and sophistication and practice skill sets to match. The lack of professional preparation for rural social work practice is a concern that must be addressed. The recruitment and retention of social workers for rural practice is a major problem for the profession, leading to declassification, resistance to legal regulation, and the siphoning of social work jobs to those with little professional training.

Throughout history rural people have migrated to urban centers seeking economic security in the face of joblessness, disaster, conflict, or war, sometimes creating rural ghettos in the city. Urban social workers should develop and maintain a proficiency in practice skills effective with rural individuals, families, and communities.

Rural areas are challenged by a lack of economic opportunities, resources, and influence of the popular culture. Worldwide, young rural residents turn away from their cultures, families, and traditions after exposure to television images and media presentations of "the good life."

Rural social workers deal with challenging issues of poverty, at-risk populations, and service delivery at the community, family, and individual intervention levels that are unique and different from urban practice. These and other factors raise crucial issues for social work practice and educational preparation for social work practice in rural areas.

POLICY STATEMENT

The understanding of rural people and cultures is a pressing issue of cultural competence in professional social work. Rural people, with their diverse cultural backgrounds, occupy and influence the majority of the earth's landmass. Unfortunately, the strengths of this influence are being rapidly lost in the cultural mainstream. The following information describes the factors necessary to an understanding of rural social work:

■ Twenty-five percent of the population resides in rural areas that comprise 83 percent of the landmass of the United States (Davenport & Davenport, 1995).

■ Rural areas are characterized by a sense of community, individual character, an awareness of place, and a sense of family and tradition.

■ When rural people relocate, by necessity or choice, to take advantage of urban and suburban economic opportunity, their unique cultural values, norms, and conventions go with them. Special skills are needed to work effectively with displaced rural people.

■ Social work practice in rural communities challenges the social worker to embrace and effectively use an impressive range of professional intervention and community skills. NASW encourages practice expertise at the micro, mezzo, and macro levels.

NASW should:

■ recognize the existence of rural populations and encourage research and education to practice in a culturally competent manner

■ support the application of professional ethical constructs to analyze relationship issues and otherwise behave in the best interest of clients. NASW must support research efforts that address crucial areas of social work practice such as the dilemmas of dual relationships, confidentiality, recruitment and retention of indigenous practitioners, and the presence of persistent poverty.

Rural areas suffer disproportionately when urban-based policies are forced on them. Corporate mergers, centralization, managed care, globalization, and similar cost-saving strategies solely based on urban models are disadvantageous to rural areas, where distance and time are barriers to efficiency of and access to social services, health care delivery, and health maintenance.

It is known that many rural people experience economic poverty but not well understood that they experience persistent poverty. Such lack of infrastructure, development, housing, education, and adequate health care is usually associated with blighted urban areas. The factors that foster despair, hopelessness, substance abuse, and domestic violence in the inner cities exist among rural poor populations.

Ethical practice in rural areas requires special attention to dual relationship issues. Few other settings expose social workers more to the risk of violating the *NASW Code of Ethics'* admonition that social workers are to "take steps to protect clients and are responsible for setting clear, appropriate, and culturally sensitive boundaries" (NASW, 1999, section 1.06[c]). Social workers practicing in rural areas must have advanced understanding of ethical responsibilities, not only because dual or multiple relationships are unavoidable, but also because the setting may require that dual or multiple relationships be used and managed as an appropriate method of social work practice. Public and social policy must take into account the unique nature of rural areas and residents. NASW should lead efforts of social workers in forming equitable policies so that urban and rural populations and jurisdictions are not pitted against each other over issues of livelihood, lifestyle, economy, or ecology.

■ NASW must continue to support the development of social work practice in rural areas by maintaining a presence that creates networking of current social workers and role modeling for future social workers who live in and need encouragement to remain in rural communities. Isolation and geographic distance are persistent challenges to rural social work practice that NASW must help to overcome.

■ Through continuing education opportunities and support of distance education, NASW supports the need for social workers to provide a broad range of services, including clinical and health practice, community organization, administration and management, public welfare, and community-based services.

■ NASW must work to develop social work that addresses the needs of clients across all age groups, particularly elderly people, who are the largest-growing group in rural communities.

■ NASW must assist educational programs in teaching cultural competency in social work, to expand and include the understanding of rural cultures, diversity issues, and people in a contextual practice skills framework. Specialized coursework and advanced practice concentrations could be offered to prepare and encourage bachelor's as well as master's-level social work practice in rural areas.

■ The eclectic skills of professional social workers are uniquely suited to helping rural people organize their lives; maintain families, communities, and organizations; and capitalize on their strengths to overcome adversity, identify and develop resources, and change their lives for the better.

- NASW must promote advocacy, legislation, and policy development that improve rural infrastructure, economic development, and availability and access to needed health care, reliable transportation, service delivery, public services, and education.

REFERENCES

Caspi, A., Wright, B., Moffitt, T., & Silva, P. (1998). Early failure in the labor market: Childhood and adolescent predictors of unemployment in the transition to adulthood. *American Sociological Review, 63,* 424–451.

Daley, M., & Avant, F. (1999). Attracting and retaining professionals for social work practice in rural areas: An example from East Texas. In I. B. Carlton-Laney, R. L. Edwards, & P. N. Reid (Eds.), *Preserving and strengthening small towns and rural communities* (pp. 335–345). Washington, DC: NASW Press.

Davenport, J. A., & Davenport, J., III (1995). Rural social work overview. In R. L. Edwards (Ed.-in-Chief), *Encyclopedia of social work* (19th ed., Vol. 3, pp. 2076–2085). Washington, DC: NASW Press.

Dilger, R. J., Blakely, E., Dorton, K. V. H., Latimer, M., Locke, B., Mencken, C., Plein, C., Potter, L., Williams, D., & Yoon, D. P. (1999). *West Virginia WORKS case closure study* [Online]. Morgantown: West Virginia University Institute for Public Affairs. Available: http://www.polsci.wvu.edu/ipa/par/Report17_1.pdf

Dilger, R. J., Blakely, E., Latimer, M., Locke, B., Mencken, C., Plein, C., Potter, L., & Williams, D. (2001). *West Virginia WORKS 2000: The recipients' perspective* [Online]. Morgantown: West Virginia University Institute for Public Affairs. Available: http://www.polsci.wvu.edu/ipa/par/Report18_3.pdf

Duncan, G., Young, W., Brooks-Gunn, J., & Smith, J. (1998). How much does childhood poverty affect the life chances of children? *American Sociological Review, 63,* 406–423.

Ginsberg, L. H. (1976). An overview of social work education for rural areas. In L. H. Ginsberg (Ed.), *Social work in rural communities: A book of readings* (pp. 1–12). Alexandria, VA: Council on Social Work Education.

Ginsberg, L. H. (1993). An overview of social work education for rural areas. In L. H. Ginsberg (Ed.), *Social work in rural communities: A book of readings* (2nd ed., pp. 1–17). Alexandria, VA: Council on Social Work Education.

Johnson, L. C. (1980). Human service delivery patterns in non-metropolitan communities. In H. W. Johnson (Ed.), *Rural human services* (pp. 69–81). Itasca, IL: F. E. Peacock.

National Association of Social Workers. (1994). Social work in rural areas. In *Social work speaks* (3rd ed., pp. 244–248). Washington, DC: NASW Press.

National Association of Social Workers. (1999). *NASW code of ethics.* Washington, DC: Author.

Rank, M., & Hirschl, T. (1993). The link between population density and welfare populations. *Demography, 30,* 607–623.

Rural Policy Research Institute. (1995). *Opportunities for rural policy reform: Lessons learned from recent farm bills* [Online]. Columbia, MO: Author. Available: http://www.rupri.org/archive/old/rupolicyP95-2.html

Sherman, A. (1992). *Falling by the wayside: Children in rural America.* Washington, DC: Children's Defense Fund.

U.S. Bureau of the Census. (1998, September). *Poverty in the United States: 1997* (Current Population Reports, No. P60-201). Washington, DC: U.S. Government Printing Office.

SUGGESTED READINGS

Barker, R. L. (1995). *Social work dictionary* (3rd ed.). Washington, DC: NASW Press.

Carlton-LaNey, I., Edwards, R., & Reid, N. (2000). *Preserving and strengthening small towns and rural communities.* Washington, DC: NASW Press.

Congress, E. P. (2000). What social workers should know about ethics: Understanding and resolving practice dilemmas. *Advances in Social Work, 1*(1), 1–25.

Conklin, J. J. (1995). Distance learning in continuing social work education: Promise of the year 2000. *Journal of Continuing Social Work Education, 6*(3), 15–17.

Farley, O. W., Griffiths, K. A., Skidmore, R. A., & Thackeray, M. G. (1982). *Rural social work practice.* New York: Free Press.

Hardcastle, D. A., Wenocur, S., & Powers, P. R. (1997). *Community practice: Theories and skills for social workers.* New York: Oxford University Press.

Hargrove, D. S. (1982). An overview of professional considerations in the rural community. In P. A. Keller & J. D. Murray (Eds.), *Handbook of rural community mental health* (pp. 169–182). New York: Human Sciences Press.

Horner, B., & O'Neil, J. F. (1981). *Child welfare practice in rural areas and small communities.* Washington, DC: U.S. Department of Education. (ERIC Document Reproduction Service No. ED239783).

Jayaratne, S., Croxton, T., & Mattison, D. (1997). Social work professional standards: An exploratory study. *Social Work, 42,* 187–199.

Lennox, N. D., & Murty, S. A. (1994). Choice, change, and challenge: Managing regional services. In B. Locke & M. Egan (Eds.), *Fulfilling our mission: Rural social work in the 1990s* (pp. 150–159). Morgantown: West Virginia University Press.

Martinez-Brawley, E. E. (1980). *Pioneer efforts in rural social welfare.* University Park: Pennsylvania State University Press.

Martinez-Brawley, E. E. (1990). *Perspectives on the small community.* Silver Spring, MD: NASW Press.

Merrell, I. E., Pratt, S., Forbush, D., Jentzsch, C., Nelson, S., Odell, C., & Smith, M. (1994). Special education, school psychology, and community mental health practice in rural settings: Common problems and overlapping solutions for training. *Rural Special Education Quarterly, 13,* 28–36.

Miller, P. (1998). Dual relationships in rural practice: A dilemma of ethics and culture. In L. H. Ginsberg (Ed.), *Social work in rural communities* (pp. 55–62). Alexandria, VA: Council on Social Work Education.

Murty, S. (2001). Regionalization and rural service delivery. In R. Moore (Ed.), *The hidden America: Social problems in rural America in the 21st century* (pp. 199–216). Cranbury, NJ: Associated University Presses.

Oliver, S., & Haulotte, S. M. (2001, June). *A strategy for uncovering, accessing, and maximizing social services in rural areas.* Paper presented at the 26th National Institute on Social Work and Human Services in Rural Areas, Austin, TX.

Rural Policy Research Institute. Various publications and resources [Online]. Columbia, MO: Author. Available: http://www.rupri.org

Ryder, R., & Hepworth, J. (1990). AAMFT ethical code: Dual relationships. *Journal of Marital and Family Therapy, 16,* 127–132.

Southern Regional Education Board Rural Task Force Manpower Education and Training Project. (1993). Education assumptions for rural social work. In L. H. Ginsberg (Ed.), *Social work in rural communities: A book of readings* (2nd ed., pp. 18–21). Alexandria, VA: Council on Social Work Education.

Weber, G. K. (1980). Preparing social workers for practice in rural social systems. In H. W. Johnson (Ed.), *Rural human services* (pp. 209–210). Itasca, IL: F. E. Peacock.

Weil, M. O. (1996). Community building: Building community practice. *Social Work, 41,* 481–497.

Policy statement approved by the NASW Delegate Assembly, August 2002. For further information, contact the National Association of Social Workers, 750 First Street, NE, Suite 700, Washington, DC 20002-4241. Telephone: 202-408-8600; e-mail: press@naswdc.org

School Truancy and Dropout Prevention

BACKGROUND

The outcomes and consequences of school dropout are dramatic and compelling. Each year's class of dropouts costs the country more than $200 billion during their lifetimes in lost earnings and unrealized tax revenue. Students from low-income families have a dropout rate of 10 percent; students from middle-income families have a dropout rate of 5.2 percent, and 1.6 percent of students from high-income families dropout (National Center for Educational Statistics, 2001).

High school graduates, on the average, earn $9,245 more per year than high school dropouts (Employment Policy Foundation, 2002). The unemployment rate for this group was 29.8 percent—almost 12 percentage points higher than the unemployment rate for recent high school graduates who were not enrolled in college (U.S. Department of Labor, 2003). The cost to taxpayers of adult illiteracy is $224 billion per year (National Reading Panel, 1999). U.S. companies lose nearly $40 billion annually because of illiteracy (National Reading Panel, 1999). If literacy levels in the United States were the same as those in Sweden, the U.S. GDP would rise by approximately $463 billion, and tax revenues would increase by approximately $162 billion (Alliance for Excellent Education, 2003a, b, c, d, e). For juvenile offenders involved in quality reading instruction programs while incarcerated, recidivism was reduced by 20 percent or more (Alliance for Excellent Education, 2003a, b, c, d, e).

High school dropouts are 3.5 times more likely than high school graduates to be arrested in their lifetime (Alliance for Excellent Education, 2003a); 75 percent of state prison inmates are high school dropouts (Harlow, 2003). A 1 percent increase in high school graduation rates would save approximately $1.4 billion in incarceration costs, or about $2,100 per year for each male high school graduate (Alliance for Excellent Education, 2003a, b, c, d, e). A one-year increase in average education levels would reduce arrest rates by 11 percent (Alliance for Excellent Education, 2003a, b, c, c, e).

Male and female students with low academic achievement are twice as likely to become parents by their senior year of high school compared with students with high academic achievement (Alliance for Excellent Education, 2003a, b, c, d, e). The U.S. death rate for people with fewer than 12 years of education is 2.5 times higher than the rate of those with 13 or more years of education (Alliance for Excellent Education, 2003a, b, c, d, e).

The U.S. Department of Justice, Office of Juvenile Justice and Delinquency Prevention summarizes the causes and correlates of truancy into the following broad categories (Baker, 2000): family factors, school factors, economic influences, and student variables. Family factors include lack of guidance or parental supervision, domestic violence, poverty, drug or alcohol abuse in the home, lack of awareness of attendance laws, and differing attitudes toward education. School factors include school climate issues, such as school size and attitudes of teachers, other students, and administrators and inflexibility in meeting the diverse cultural and learning styles of the students. Schools often have inconsistent procedures for dealing with chronic absenteeism and may not have meaningful consequences available for truant youths (for example, out-of-school suspension). Economic influences include employed students, single-parent homes, high mobility rates, parents who hold multiple jobs, and a lack of affordable transportation and child care. Student variables include drug and alcohol abuse, lack of understanding of attendance laws, lack of social competence, mental health difficulties, and poor physical health.

Although not mentioned specifically, the community significantly influences the occurrence of truancy as well. Community factors are folded into the four areas mentioned. For example, economic conditions and differing culturally based attitudes toward education are also important factors in the community.

Truancy and dropout constitute a school, family, community, and juvenile justice system problem. Therefore, all segments of the community need to be involved and work collaboratively to have a positive effect on reducing truancy and dropout in that community. Early intervention at the first sign of truancy is essential. Prevention, early and consistent intervention, and individualized flexible and creative educational and youth and family services are all keys to success.

ISSUE STATEMENT

Since 1996 school truancy and dropout have stayed the same or worsened. On average, school truancy and dropout have worsened in urban areas and with special populations (for example, special education students and juvenile delinquents). Preventing school truancy and dropout must become a priority social policy issue. The public and private sectors share equally in providing leadership, resources, and solutions to this important problem. Dropping out is the "quiet killer of the American dream" (National Foundation for the Improvement of Education, 1986). Students are at educational and dropout risk because of limited English proficiency, poverty, race, geographic location, or economic disadvantage. Children living in poverty enter school with health and learning difficulties that may result from inadequate prenatal care or the effects of substance abuse. These conditions correlate to dropping out of school before completion of secondary education. School dropout can pose lifelong challenges for the individual student and concomitant costs for society. Consequently, effective

action in the area of school truancy and dropout prevention has never been greater.

To support student learning and success, NASW's policy on school truancy and dropout prevention is consistent with its mission of enhancing the functioning of individuals, families, and society at large, particularly in light of current social and funding trends: schools' diminished ability to provide for students who require educational services beyond the conventional; a competitive labor market that requires entry-level employees to have not only basic skills, but also advanced technical abilities; increasing political pressure for decreasing and redirecting funding for government educational and social welfare assistance; and imposing financial penalties on those who are poor.

Truancy and dropout prevention programs assist individuals in obtaining self-sufficiency and dignity. These programs help individuals to compete in the global marketplace and therefore are cost-effective and humane. The projected loss in human capital of youths' not completing high school is staggering. Dropouts are more likely than high school graduates to be unemployed and are more likely to be incarcerated.

The social work profession has a special responsibility and possesses the skills to address school truancy and dropout, including expertise in parental involvement, community collaboration, early prevention through strength-based life skills building; enhancing individual, family, and community protective factors; and reducing risk factors.

The Office of Juvenile Justice offers the following promising prevention, reduction, and intervention efforts:

■ consistent attendance policy and practice, known to all students, parents, staff, and community agencies

■ early intervention especially with elementary students after three to five absences; swift, appropriate consequences for students and parents; accountability monitoring of schools and related systems

■ a continuum of prevention and intervention services, along with incentives and graduated sanctions for students and parents

- meaningful parental involvement—the most significant area for success, fun, prevention, and intervention

- special attention to health (for example, providing onsite responses for asthmatic children, meeting special education needs)

- data-driven decision making

- student attendance review boards of all involved systems in collaboration

- quasi-judicial proceedings (for example, truancy "court" or review boards)

- business involvement

- focus on school transition years

- public education and awareness campaigns.

Some flexible, individualized empirical validated interventions include truancy mediation for elementary students and their parents and teachers, twilight or evening school for high school-age youths, the choice of quality community and charter schools, and home-based family services for severe multi-need cases.

POLICY STATEMENT

It is the policy of NASW to promote comprehensive and individualized services to enhance each student's opportunity to successfully complete school and to have the opportunities of a full and productive adult life. Regarding school truancy and dropout prevention, NASW supports the following:

- implement prevention programs, fully funded and staffed student service teams for each school that include school social workers and essential school–community collaborations with parent groups, law enforcement, child protective services, juvenile justice, business and so forth, and adequate school social work resources to meet the needs of the student body.

- student assistance programs to systematically identify and support students with risk factors for truancy and dropout as early as possible in their school experience. Supportive services provided in a way that avoids stigmatization.

- access to alternative education programs for at-risk students, with an adequate number of school social workers to address the myriad problems that this population presents. Appropriate ratios for school social work staff to students depending on the characteristics of the student population to be served. NASW believes that alternative education programs within schools, or separate alternative programs, are to be regarded as a student's right and not a punishment for unproductive and disruptive behaviors. A full continuum of creative programming should be available. Programs should be flexible and address the individual student's social, academic, and future world of work needs.

- recruitment of adults as role model mentors, advocates, and tutors for potential dropouts. It is particularly important that men of African American, Latino/Hispanic and other diverse cultures be recruited as such mentors.

- a substantial role for school social workers in promoting family engagement and empowering parents of at-risk multi-need students to participate more fully in decision making about school programs and services.

- increased public school responsiveness to the needs of at-risk and multi-need students, and incorporation of policies and practices that are respectful of differences among people, including race, gender, cultural heritage, language, sexual orientation, socioeconomic status, and behavior issues.

- inclusion of bilingual education or dual language programs in all schools where there is an identified need.

- taking steps to make schools safe learning environments, particularly those schools located in violent communities.

- collaborative, integrated, holistic, individualized services for at-risk and multi-need students and their families, because the needs of potential dropouts and their families cannot be addressed by the public schools alone. The multiple and interconnected needs of at-risk children and their families demand that health, social, justice, and economic services be delivered in a "timely, coordinated, and comprehensive fashion" (Behrman, 1992).

- school-linked, integrated service programs to meet the varied needs of at-risk and multi-need students and their families. These integrated and coordinated health and social services should be offered in the school and in the child's community and family and should involve school social workers in coordination and delivery of services. Constructive and engaging after-school opportunities on the school campus are essential enhancements.

- early childhood education and elementary school early screening and assessment procedures that identify risk and protective factors, to provide prevention and life skills building services to students, families, and schools, including early literacy development.

- opportunities for at-risk and multi-need students to increase their attachment to and connectedness with their school, while simultaneously working to decrease their alienation and disengagement from school. This can be accomplished by systemic renewal, professional and teacher development, student active learning, educational technology, individualized instruction, and career and technical education.

- implementation of proven transition programs for students as they move into the junior and senior high school grades, with individualized support for students who have struggled academically, emotionally, or socially during earlier grades.

- educational curriculum that specifically helps students to understand, in their own terms, the relationship among the education they receive, their understanding of meaningful adult roles, and the world of work. Students at risk of school dropout often display a "disconnect" between the above factors.

- flexible scheduling, school-based mental health and child care services, and vocational internships for all students.

- social worker support, consultation, and education, when needed, to assist educators with the complexities of meeting the social and emotional needs of students.

- social worker advocacy with local, state and national policymakers to increase educa-

tional resources, including, but not limited to, reduced school and class sizes, more school social workers, and increased salaries.

- education of the public and the media about the reasons for school dropouts and needs of at-risk students.

- development of relevant data systems and evaluation of the effectiveness of truancy and dropout prevention programs. Findings should be reported to policymakers so that the most successful truancy and dropout prevention programs can be replicated.

REFERENCES

Alliance for Excellent Education. (2003a, November). *FactSheet: The impact of education on: Crime*. Washington, DC: Author.

Alliance for Excellent Education. (2003b, November). *FactSheet: The impact of education on: Health and well being*. Washington, DC: Author.

Alliance for Excellent Education. (2003c, November). *FactSheet: The impact of education on: Personal income and employment*. Washington, DC: Author.

Alliance for Excellent Education. (2003d, November). *FactSheet: The impact of education on: Poverty and homelessness*. Washington, DC: Author.

Alliance for Excellent Education (2003e, November). *FactSheet: The impact of education on: The economy*: Washington, DC: Author.

Baker, M. L. (2000). *Evaluation of the Truancy Reduction Demonstration Program: Interim report*. Denver: Colorado Foundation for Families and Children.

Behrman, R. E. (1992). Introduction. *Future of Children, 2*(1), 4–5.

Bell, A. J., Rosen, L. A., & Dynlacht, D. (1994). *Truancy intervention. Journal of Research and Development in Education, 57*, 203–211.

Dryfoos, J. G. (1990). *Adolescents at risk: Prevalence and prevention*. New York: Oxford University Press.

Employment Policy Foundation 2002 Report from National Dropout Prevention Center. (2003, October 3), Retrieved from http://www.dropoutprevention.org.

Garry, E. M. (1996). *Truancy: First step to a lifetime of problems* [Bulletin]. Washington, DC: U.S. Department of Justice, Office of Justice Programs, Office of Juvenile Justice and Delinquency Prevention.

Harlow, C. W. (2003, January). *Education and correctional populations* [Bureau of Justice Statistics Special Report]. Washington, DC: U. S. Department of Justice.

Hawkins, J. D., & Catalano, R. (1995). *Risk focused prevention: Using the social development strategy*. Seattle. WrapAround Developmental Research and Programs, Inc.

Huizinga, D., Loeber, R., & Thronberry, T. (1995). *Urban delinquency and substance abuse: Initial findings*. Washington, DC: U.S. Department of Justice, Office of Justice Programs, Office of Juvenile Justice and Delinquency Prevention.

Ingersoll, S., & LeBoeuf, D. (1997). *Reaching out to youth out of the education mainstream*. Washington, DC: U.S. Department of Justice, Office of Justice Programs, Office of Juvenile Justice and Delinquency Prevention.

Kelley, B. T., Loeber, R., Keenan, K., & DeLamarte, M. (1997). *Developmental pathways in boys' disruptive and delinquent behavior*. Washington, DC: U.S. Department of Justice, Office of Justice Programs, Office of Juvenile Justice and Delinquency Prevention.

Mone, M. (2002). *Big reductions in truancy/tardiness prompt state to expand parent/school mediation program*. Columbus: Ohio Commission on Dispute Resolution and Conflict Management.

National Center for Educational Statistics. (2001). *Dropout rates in the United States: 2000*. Retrieved November 28, 2001, from http://nces.ed.gov/pubsearch/pubsinfo.asp?pubid=2002114

National Dropout Prevention Center. (2003, October 3). *Effective strategies*. Retrieved from http://www.dropoutprevention.org/effstrat/family_inv/family_over.htm

National Foundation for the Improvement of Education. (1986). *A blueprint for success*. Washington, DC: Author.

National Reading Panel. (1999). *1999 NRP progress report*. Retrieved January 8, 2004, from http://www.nationalreadingpanel.org

Office of Juvenile Justice and Delinquency Prevention. (2004, January/February). *Truancy reduction: Keeping youth in school and out of trouble* (News @ a Glance, Vol. 3, no. 1). Washington, DC; U.S. Department of Justice.

Rohrman, D. (1993). *Combating truancy in our schools—A community effort*. Bulletin, 76(549), 40–51.

U.S. Department of Education. (1993). *Conditions of education: 199 indicators 32 and 32*. Washington, DC: Author.

U.S. Department of Labor. (2003, June). *College enrollment and work activity of 2002 high school graduates*. Retrieved August 2004, from http://www.bls.gov/news.release/hsgec.toc.htm

SUGGESTED READINGS

Baker, M. L., Nady Sigmon, J., & Nugent, M. E. (2001). *Truancy reduction: Keeping students in school*. Washington, DC: U.S. Department of Justice.

Bernat, F. P. (1996). *Survey evaluation for the Governor's Division for Children: State truancies and unexcused absences* (Final Report). Phoenix, AZ: Governor's Division for Children.

Bureau of Labor Statistics. (2001). *A profile of the working poor, 1999* (Report 947). Washington, DC: U. S. Department of Labor.

Catalano, F. R., Arthur, M. W., Hawkins, J. D., Berglund, L., & Olson, J. J. (1998). In R. Loeber & D. Farrington (Eds.), *Comprehensive community and school based interventions to prevent antisocial behavior in serious and violent juvenile offenders: Risk factors and successful interventions*. Thousand Oaks, CA: Sage Publications.

Catterall, J. S. (1985, September). *On the social costs of dropping out of schools* (Report No. 86). Stanford, CA: Stanford University, Center for Educational Research.

Doland, E. (2001). *Give yourself the gift of a degree*. Retrieved May 2002, from http://www.epf.org/media/newsreleases/2001/nr20011219.htm

Dynarski, M., & Gleason, P. (1999). *How can we help? Lessons from federal dropout prevention programs*: Princeton, NJ: Mathematica Policy Research, Inc.

Heaviside, S., Rowand, C., Williams, C., & Farris, E. (1998). *Violence and discipline problems in U. S. public schools 1996–1997*. Washington, DC: U.S. Department of Education, Office of Educational Research and Improvement, National Center for Education Statistics.

Henderson, A. T., & Mapp, K. L. (2002). *A new wave of evidence: The impact of school, family, and community connections on student achievement*. Austin, TX: Southwest Educational Development Laboratory and the National Center for Family and Community Connections with Schools.

Hennepin County Attorney. (2004). *What's your excuse? Truancy intervention*. Minneapolis: Author.

Howell, J. C. (1995). *Guide for implementing the comprehensive strategy for serious, violence and chronic juvenile offenders*. Washington, DC: U.S. Department of Justice, Office of Justice Programs, Office of Juvenile Justice and Delinquency Prevention.

Loeber, R., & Farrington, D. (2000). *Young children who commit crime: Epidemiology, developmental origins, risk factors, early interventions, and policy implications*.

Loeber, R., & Farrington, D. P. (Eds.). (2001a). *Child delinquents: Development, intervention, and service needs*. Thousand Oaks, CA: Sage Publications.

Loeber, R., & Farrington, D. P. (2001b). *The significance of child delinquency*. Thousand Oaks, CA: Sage Publications.

Minneapolis Public Schools. (2004). *School attendance review board*. Minneapolis: Author.

Morley, E., & Rossman, S. B. (1997). *Helping at-risk youth: Lessons from community-based initiatives*. Washington, DC: Urban Institute.

National Center for Juvenile Justice. (1996). *Easy access to FBI arrest statistics, 1990–1999*. Pittsburgh: Author.

Omni Institute. (1992). *Working together: A profile of collaboration*. Denver: Author.

Reimer, S., & Cash, T. (2003). *Alternative schools: Best practices for development and evaluation*. Clemson, SC: National Dropout Prevention Center Network.

Robins, L. N., & Ratcliff, K. S. (1978). *Long-range outcomes associated with school truancy*. Washington, DC: U.S. Public Health Service.

Roderick, M, Chiong, J., Arney, M., DaCosta, K., Stone, M., Villarreal-Sosa, L., & Waxman, E. (1997). *Habits hard to break: A new look at truancy in Chicago's public high schools* [Research in Brief]. Chicago: University of Chicago, School of Social Service Administration.

Schargel, F. P., & Smink, J. (2001). *Strategies to help solve our school dropout problem*. Larchmont, NY: Eye on Education.

Schorr, L. B. (1997). *Common purpose: Strengthening families and neighborhoods to rebuild America*. New York: Doubleday.

Seoane, M., & Smink, J. (1991, June). *Incentives and education: A series of solutions and strategies*. Clemson, SC: National Dropout Prevention Center.

Sigmon, J. N., Neguen, M. E., & Engelhardt-Greer, S. (1999). *Abolish Chronic Truancy now diversion program: Evaluation report*. Alexandria, VA: American Prosecutors Research Institute.

Snyder, H. N., & Sickmund, M. (1995). *Juvenile offenders and victims: A national report*. Washington, DC: U.S. Department of Justice, Office of Justice Programs, Office of Juvenile Justice and Delinquency Prevention.

Stegelin, D. A. (2003). *Literacy education: First steps toward dropout prevention*. Clemson, SC: National Dropout Prevention Center Network.

Thorstensen, B. I. (2004). *If you build it, they will come: Investing in public education*. Retrieved January 13, 2004, from http://abec.unm.edu/resources/gallery/present/invest_in_ed.pdf

Policy statement approved by the NASW Delegate Assembly, August 2005. This policy supersedes the policy statement on School Dropout Prevention approved by the Delegate Assembly in 1996 and in 1987, and referred by the 2002 Delegate Assembly to the 2005 Delegate Assembly. For further information, contact the National Association of Social Workers, 750 First Street, NE, Suite 700, Washington, DC 20002-4241. Telephone: 202-408-8600 or 800-638-8799; e-mail: press@naswdc.org

School Violence

BACKGROUND

School violence is a complicated societal problem. To understand the scope of the problems schools are facing in violence prevention, one must understand the effect violence is having on children and youths in the United States. Violence is a public health issue, and there is much research that illuminates its harmful effects on children (Office of the Surgeon General, 2001). Millions of children are exposed to violence every year. According to the U.S. Department of Justice (2000) report *Safe from the Start: Taking Action on Children Exposed to Violence,*

■ national estimates based on a 1993 survey indicate that of 22.3 million children between the ages of 12 and 17, approximately 1.8 million have been the victims of serious sexual assault, 3.9 million have been victims of serious physical assault, and almost 9 million have witnessed serious incidents of violence

■ in 1997 young people represented about 18 percent of all arrests but made up 25 percent of all crime victims

■ estimates based on data from 44 states indicate that in 1997 approximately 984,000 children were victims of child abuse and neglect nationwide and that approximately 1,000 children die yearly as a result of abuse and neglect

■ data from a survey in 1992 estimate that before a child turns 18, he or she will witness more than 200,000 acts of violence on television, including 16,000 murders

■ approximately 2 million adolescents ages 12 to 17 appear to have suffered from posttraumatic stress disorder (PTSD), presumably stemming from violent incidents in their past.

Also, "there is an increasing body of research that 'explain how exposure to media violence would activate aggressive behaviors in some children (and youths)' " (U.S. Department of Health and Human Services [p. 3], as cited in NASW *Practice Update*, 2002).

Although gang activity is considered an urban problem, it exists in almost every community, large and small, among all socioeconomic and ethnic groups, and negatively affects learning and school safety.

Every day nearly 10 U.S. children are murdered, 16 die from gunshot wounds, 316 are arrested for crimes of violence, and 8,042 are reported to be abused and neglected (Children's Defense Fund, 1997).

Despite the highly publicized homicides in schools, recent research on school violence indicates that most schools are comparatively safe and secure. In fact students ages 12 to 17 were more likely to be injured or a victim of serious violence in their own home or community than in their school (Dwyer, Osher, & Warger, 1998a). In 1996 thefts accounted for about 62 percent of all serious crimes against students in schools. Since 1993 the actual overall school crime rate has declined slightly, as did crime victimization against youths outside the school. What has increased, however, is the number of homicides in schools and the number of multiple-victim homicides. Although the number of homicides has increased, there is a less than one-in-a-million chance of suffering a school-associated violent death (Dwyer et al., 1998a).

Contrary to popular perception the number of students bringing weapons to school has decreased in recent years. Between 1993 and 1997 there was an overall decline in the percentage (from 8 percent to 6 percent) of students who reported carrying a weapon to school at least once in the past 30 days (Dwyer et al., 1998a). The presence of deadly weapons in schools creates an intimidating and threatening atmosphere, making both teaching and learning difficult. Students and staff reported feeling less safe than 10 years ago. In 1989, 6 percent of students ages 12 to 19 feared they were going to be attacked or harmed at school. In 1995 the figure had grown to 9 percent, and it is projected to be higher since that time. The percentage of students fearing they would be attacked going to and from school also increased from 4 percent to 7 percent during the same period (Dwyer et al., 1998a).

The following risk factors are commonly accepted as factors to consider when evaluating a student's capacity to commit a violent act:

- history of violent or aggressive behaviors

- frequent disciplinary infractions in school

- bringing a weapon to school

- a pattern of violent threats when angry

- threats to hurt others or self

- access to weapons or possession of weapons

- history of abuse, neglect, or violence in family

- social withdrawal, isolation, or poor peer relationships

- history of depression or mental illness

- academic failure or poor attachment to school

- history of alcohol or substance abuse

- history of cruelty to animals

- involvement in a street gang

- fire setting.

None of these factors alone are sufficient for predicting aggressive actions, so a host of variables should be considered when evaluating a child's risk.

School violence is strongly influenced by the community in which the school is located and by the size of the school. Teachers of urban schools were twice as likely to report serious violent crimes as those in suburban towns and in rural locations, and the larger the school, the more likely that incidents of violent crimes have occurred. The presence of street gangs in the community also influences violence trends. Between 1989 and 1995 the percentage of students who reported the presence of street gangs in their community increased from 15 percent to 28 percent. Urban students were more likely to report that there were street gangs in their schools (41 percent) than were suburban students (26 percent) or rural students (20 percent). Research also supports that involvement in a street gang is a strong risk factor for future violent behavior (Office of the Surgeon General, 2001).

School Response to Violence Prevention: A Historical Perspective

Before the multiple school shootings in the late 1990s, many schools were somewhat complacent about violence prevention. Many districts had disaster plans in place that only addressed natural disasters such as tornadoes or hurricanes. Few faculty ever saw the plans. With the new research on critical incident stress management and its effectiveness in preventing PTSD after a traumatic event in the early 1990s, some schools adopted crisis plans and crisis teams that could be used postcrisis in the unlikely event that there was a suicide or death of a student or faculty member (American Academy of Experts in Traumatic Stress, 1999).

Schools, by nature of their mission, have always been more focused on academics than on addressing social and emotional learning. Social workers and psychologists often are employed to serve the needs of special education students rather than the entire school population. Most school districts still tend to deal with students who commit violent acts as "bad kids" likely coming from "bad families" who have chosen to defy the rules. Interventions with these students are often very limited and rigidly proscribed in the district school discipline code, with the emphasis on managing and eliminating the maladaptive behavior (usually by suspension or expulsion from school) versus teaching students prosocial, adaptive skills to replace the maladaptive, counterproductive behaviors. This "one-size-fits-all" approach to discipline for acts of school violence fails to address the variables of the school environment or the often complex interactions of the students with the environment (Klein, 1998).

Some schools and communities have focused their energies and resources on increased security measures such as hiring school security officers, installing metal detectors, or both. Although evaluating the school's overall security plan and working closely with the community police is an important part of any school violence prevention plan, the experience learned from the school shootings in Columbine is that increased security without addressing the climate and culture of the school and intervening effectively with students at risk is not enough to prevent tragedies from occurring.

Recent Developments in Social Policy and Practice

In 1993 the National Education Goals 2000 listed the goal that "every school in the United States will be free of drugs, violence, and the unauthorized presence of firearms and alcohol and will offer a disciplined environment conducive to learning" (Goals 2000: Educate America Act, P.L. 103-227, 1 U.S.C., §102, pt. 7A). That same year federal legislation created the Safe Schools Act (P.L. 103-227, 7 U.S.C., §702) to establish grants to support local school efforts to reduce school violence, promote safety, and assist schools in achieving the aforementioned goal. The Gun-Free Schools Act (P.L. 103-882) was created the next year, in October 1994, and requires schools that receive federal funds to adopt a gun-free school policy and to expel, for one year, students who carry a gun to school (zero tolerance).

After a high number of fatal school shootings in the 1996 to 1997 school year, President Clinton directed the U.S. Departments of Education and Justice to prepare the first Annual Report on School Safety (Dwyer et al., 1998a). This was the first serious attempt to gather accurate data on violence in schools and to start developing a strategy to address the

growing problem in the United States. Before this report there was great inconsistency in the kind of information available on crime in schools. Many school districts did not regularly report incidents of crime to their local law enforcement agency for fear of community or school board reaction. Some districts reported only the more serious crimes, but not theft or vandalism.

In 1998 NASW participated in the White House Conference on School Violence. Information from that conference, along with information in the Annual Report on School Safety, was used to generate Early Warning, Timely Response: A Guide to Safe Schools (Dwyer, Osher, & Warger, 1998b). NASW participated in the work group that developed the government document Safeguarding Our Children: An Action Guide (Dwyer & Osher, 2000). This guide identifies early warning signs of which all school personnel should be aware and discusses recommended intervention steps for students, parents, school personnel, and community members.

Attention must be paid to the school's culture. Harassment of girls; gay, lesbian, bisexual, and transgender students; immigrant children; children of various racial and ethnic backgrounds; and others who are different must be addressed in the earliest stages. Social workers play an important role in raising the consciousness of teachers, administrators, and other staff as risk behaviors gone unchecked can escalate into physical violence. Even if these behaviors do not escalate into physical violence, they still create an atmosphere of intimidation and are a form of psychological violence.

ISSUE STATEMENT

Social workers rely on best practice models to guide practice. By having a written, publicly accessible school violence policy, social workers have a framework within which to develop and refine policies that are productive and have a research base.

Prevention of school violence has taken on a new urgency in U.S. schools. The highly publicized school shootings in recent years have shocked the nation. The Columbine High

School shooting in the spring of 1999, the worst of the tragedies in terms of number of deaths, was a dramatic wake-up call to government, school officials, and the mental health community that somehow society and schools were not doing enough to prevent these types of tragic events and not doing enough, early enough, to reach out to youths at risk. After the tragic losses at Columbine, President Clinton and Congress requested a report summarizing what research has revealed about youth violence, its causes and prevention. "The world remains a threatening, often dangerous place for children and youths. And in our country today, the greatest threat to the lives of children and adolescents is not disease or starvation or abandonment, but the terrible reality of violence," reported then–Secretary of Health and Human Services Donna Shalala in the foreword of *Youth Violence: A Report of the Surgeon General* (Office of the Surgeon General, 2001, p. 1).

Although the media have highlighted the most horrific violent acts that occurred in schools, violence in schools can encompass a broad continuum of behaviors, including name calling, bullying, racial comments, gang activity, theft, vandalism, sexual harassment, threats, assaults, and the most severe, homicide. School violence, on any level, threatens the physical, psychological, and emotional well-being of students and staff.

There is no easy answer to why one young person will become violent and another will not, but research scientists have identified a number of variables that put youths at risk of violent behaviors as well as variables that will protect them (Office of the Surgeon General, 2001). A *risk factor* is generally seen as any factor that increases the probability that a person will suffer from harm, and a *protective factor* is something that decreases the potential harmful effect of a risk factor. To effectively develop intervention programs, schools and communities need to consider both variables.

Violence is a public health issue and not one that schools alone can combat. Every day 10 American children are murdered, 16 die from gunshot wounds, 316 are arrested for violent acts, and 8,042 are reported to be abused and neglected (Children's Defense Fund, 1997). Former Surgeon General Dr. David Satcher's

Report on Youth Violence (Office of the Surgeon General, 2001) noted that the most effective violence prevention programs combine both individual risk factors and environmental conditions, particularly building individual skills and competencies, providing parent effectiveness training, improving the climate of the schools, and making changes in the type and level of involvement in peer groups. Dr. Satcher's report further suggested that violence prevention initiatives that target change in the social context appear to be more effective than those that attempt to change individual attitudes, skills, and risk behaviors.

The surgeon general's *Report on Youth Violence* supports what social workers have long maintained—that violence prevention starts in the family and the community. To combat the problem, one must provide services to families and communities in crisis. And, there are effective, proven prevention programs such as the Families and Schools Together Program (FAST), developed by social worker Dr. Lynn McDonald. Others are being developed but are too new to have the history needed to prove successful (Dwyer et al., 1998a).

Children who witness violence and abuse—even if they themselves have not been the victim of the abuse—can suffer psychological trauma, including PTSD. These children also can display an array of emotional and behavioral disturbances, including low self-esteem; withdrawal; nightmares; self-blame; and aggression against peers, family members, and property (Peled, Jaffee, & Edelson, 1995).

Several research studies have shown that chronic exposure to violence can adversely affect a child's ability to learn (Barton, Coley, & Wenglinsky, 1998). Children who achieve in school and who develop adequate critical thinking, problem-solving, and communication skills are better able to cope with stressful situations. Academic achievement enhances the development of positive self-esteem and self-efficacy, both of which are necessary for experiencing emotional well-being and achieving success in life (Prothrow-Stith & Quaday, 1995). Children who have a positive relationship with their school are also seen as being at reduced risk of school violence. School social workers can play a crucial role in providing counseling and other support services to the victims of violence so that healthy coping strategies and healthy self-esteem can be developed and school can return to being a place for positive growth, learning, and a sense of belonging.

Given that depression, feelings of isolation, and worthlessness were issues for many assailants of the recent school shootings, providing more school social work services along with other support services in school is one way to prevent further tragedies (Office of Juvenile Justice and Delinquency Prevention, 1999). School social workers are uniquely trained to identify students and families at risk, to provide diagnostic assessments, to understand the risk factors for individuals and families, to counsel students and families, and to arrange for referrals to appropriate community resources.

POLICY STATEMENT

NASW believes that all children have the right to attend a physically and emotionally safe school where they can maximize their academic potential. Although most schools are safe, violence occurring in the community has found its way inside many schools. All schools have the responsibility to develop comprehensive violence prevention plans so that every child in school is both emotionally and physically safe.

NASW's position is that school violence reflects the social, economic, moral, and ethical problems of the larger society. Given this systems perspective, any approach to school violence prevention must be comprehensive in nature and seek the participation of students; parents; school staff; and community resources, including the police, to be effective.

NASW supports the comprehensive approach to school violence prevention outlined in *Safeguarding Our Children: An Action Guide* (Dwyer & Osher, 2000). This approach identifies three levels for intervention: (1) schoolwide foundation and primary prevention, (2) early intervention, and (3) urgent response and crisis intervention.

NASW strongly supports the position that prevention initiatives are the most desirable for

controlling and positively redirecting these behaviors and that they have the greatest long-term effect. Early intervention plans must be in place if violence does erupt. These plans must include the evaluation of the situation and each of the students involved, with the guidance of the school discipline code, and any laws pertaining to the infractions. Crisis plans should focus on schoolwide, and even school–community, interventions to minimize the impact of crises of greater proportions.

Schoolwide Foundation and Primary Prevention

A school environment in which all students and staff are respected, nurtured, safe, and supported helps students feel attached to their school and reduces student conflicts. All teachers and school staff need to be culturally aware and competent and participate in ongoing training. Activities such as conflict resolution training in grades kindergarten through high school, character education programs, antibullying and peacemaking programs, and bias awareness activities all can positively affect the school climate and culture. Programs that can teach children tolerance, civility, and how to deal with prejudice and differences should be included in the curriculum in every school and at every grade level. All of these programs are most effective if implemented in grades kindergarten through high school and if the material offered is developmentally appropriate to each grade level. Clearly, this creates the need for more social work service. NASW advocates for funding of social workers in all schools.

Crucial to building a schoolwide initiative is developing an effective schoolwide behavior management system and code of conduct. There must be clear guidelines for student behavior that are enforced consistently by school staff. These rules should be reviewed regularly by students, staff, and parents. Consequences for failure to follow the codes of conduct must be appropriate to the offense and should, whenever possible, offer the opportunity for restitution and reflection on the social impact of the misconduct by the student(s) involved. Schools also should take opportunities to recognize students who make positive choices and positive contributions to the school climate and culture.

School pupil services teams should be used in every school to address overall school performance on school safety issues as well as to address individual student performance and problems. NASW supports school social workers serving on schoolwide and individual student support teams. School social workers play a major role on such teams by using their unique knowledge of mental health; their knowledge of community resources; and their ability to work with students, families, and other school personnel.

Early Intervention

All staff in schools should become familiar with behavior that can be considered "red flags" or risk factors for violent behavior. School administrators have a responsibility to provide in-service programs to all professional and support staff on early and immediate warning signs. There must also be clear procedures and referral mechanisms in the school for referring and evaluating students at risk for emotional difficulties, including violent behavior. Troubled children typically exhibit multiple warning signs repeatedly, which increase over time. All schools should have in place a confidential and reliable referral process so that students who exhibit warning signs can get the intervention they need to evaluate the seriousness of their risk to harm themselves or others. School social workers and other qualified mental health professionals should be used to assess students at risk; to provide a clinical assessment; to provide individual, group, and family counseling; and to identify community resources that are necessary to help the student and his or her family.

Other important components of early intervention programs to reduce violence in schools are social skills training, peer support groups, peer mediation programs, anger management programs, mentoring programs, sexual harassment programs (important for both victims and perpetrators), before- and after-school programs, and parent education classes. Social work counseling for students at risk and their families at risk creates supports for school suc-

cess. Such supports can also stimulate effective parenting and discipline practices and provide referrals to community resources for additional or more intensive help for the family.

Crisis Intervention: Providing Intensive Interventions to Troubled Students

When children experience significant emotional or behavioral problems that interfere with the learning process or endanger the health and welfare of others, then more intensive interventions are needed. All school staff must be familiar with their school safety–crisis plan so that in case of an acute emergency they can take steps to ensure the immediate safety of all children and staff. This plan must be reviewed regularly with staff so that all are familiar with the appropriate procedures to follow in a variety of different situations (that is, hostage situation, school shooting, student or staff suicide, bomb threat, natural disaster, and so forth).

Some intervention approaches that have been successful in meeting the needs of severely troubled students are comprehensive, school-based mental health services; special education and related services; alternative education programs, including separate alternative schools; and individualized mental health services and supports. NASW supports developmentally appropriate interventions that increase prosocial competence and better protective factors. NASW also supports models of intervention that are more therapeutic in nature (that is, referrals to a day treatment program with intensive counseling and clinical interventions) rather than punitive in nature and lacking clinical services (that is, out-of-school suspension or expulsion with no services). Students in need of alternative education due to violent or aggressive behavior should be offered, whenever possible, alternatives that include individual behavior therapy focused on skill building in problem solving; empathy training; and nonaggressive, more effective methods of dealing with their feelings. Families of such students may benefit from parent management training, with an emphasis on effective supervision of their child and the use of encouragement, discipline, and problem solving.

Role of School Social Workers

School social workers, given their unique training, offer schools a way to link student, family, community, and the school. School social workers play a major role in the development of their schools' comprehensive violence prevention plans. NASW believes school social work services should be available to every student in the United States, meaning both special education students and all regular education students who may need their services. NASW believes that school social workers belong on districtwide and individual student support teams. School social workers are knowledgeable about the theory and practice of critical incident stress management so that they can work to reduce the harm to children who may have witnessed a tragic event in school or the community and are knowledgeable about children who display signs of distress.

School social workers are trained to identify and counsel students at risk of violence, students who are victims of violence, and students at risk of school failure. School social workers can assume a leadership role in creating or implementing school violence prevention efforts such as character education programs, social skills training, conflict resolution programs, and peer mediation programs, all of which have proven to help improve school climate and reduce violence in schools. Programs on dating violence should be introduced into school curricula at the middle school or junior high school level and reinforced every grade thereafter. Dating violence is ubiquitous, starts early, and is a precursor to family violence.

School social workers should seek to create opportunities in their schools that strengthen family and parent relationships with the school and that improve parenting skills and communication. They should work in coalition with other community agencies and resources that service children and youths and look for opportunities to partner with such agencies and programs, with the goal of improved mental health services in schools. Social workers must collaborate with school administrators in developing and revising codes of conduct and consequences for improper student behavior.

School social workers also can provide a valuable service to their schools by providing in-service and staff development programs and consultation on the risk factors for school violence. They can teach methods of behavior management in the classroom, ways to avoid conflicts, and alternative ways to manage defiant behavior.

All of the above initiatives for prevention and early intervention with children who display violent or unsettled behavior require long-term as well as shorter, more intensive interventions of immediate crisis response. Continued input about the need for such long-term and intensive services may need to be repeatedly and skillfully relayed to the school administration and staff so that there is agreement that the whole school will benefit from additional availability of services to prevent violence.

REFERENCES

American Academy of Experts in Traumatic Stress. (1999). *A practical response to a crisis in our schools* (3rd ed.). Commack, NY: Author.

Barton, P. E., Coley, R., & Wenglinsky, H. (1998). *Order in the classroom: Violence, discipline and student achievement* [Online]. Available: www.ets.org/research/pic

Children's Defense Fund. (1997). Everyday in America. *Children's Defense Fund Reports, 18*(2), 15.

Dwyer, K., & Osher, D. (2000). *Safeguarding our children: An action guide*. Washington, DC: U.S. Departments of Education and Justice, American Institutes for Research.

Dwyer, K., Osher, D., & Warger, C. (1998a). *Annual report on school safety* [Online]. Available: www.ed.gov/pubs/AnnSchoolRept98

Dwyer, K., Osher, D., & Warger, C. (1998b). *Early warning, timely response: A guide to safe schools* [Online]. Available: www.ed.gov/pubs/AnnSchoolRept98

Goals 2000: Educate America Act, P.L. 103-227, 108 Stat. 125–191 (1993).

Gun-Free Schools Act of 1994, P.L. 103-882, 108 Stat. 270.

Klein, J. R. (1998, August). Violence in our schools: The school social work response. *The Section Connection, 4*(2), 8–9.

NASW Practice Update. (2002). The influence and role of the media in the entertainment industry. *Children, Families and Schools, 2*(3), 4.

Office of Juvenile Justice and Delinquency Prevention and the Communities in Schools. (1999, Fall). *Facts you can use: Recognizing and preventing school violence* (Vol. 3, No. 3). Washington, DC: U.S. Government Printing Office.

Office of the Surgeon General. (2001). *Youth violence: A report of the surgeon general* [Online]. Available: www.surgeongeneral.gov/library/youthviolence

Peled, E., Jaffee, P. G., & Edelson, J. L. (Eds.). (1995). *Ending the cycle of violence: Community responses to children of battered women.* Thousand Oaks, CA: Sage Publications.

Prothrow-Stith, D., & Quaday, S. (1995). *Hidden casualties: The relationship between violence and learning.* Washington, DC: National Health and Education Consortium for African-American Children. (ERIC Document Reproduction Service No. ED390552)

Safe Schools Act of 1994, P.L. 103-227, 108 Stat. 204.

U.S. Department of Justice. (2000, November). *Safe from the start: Taking action on children exposed to violence.* Washington, DC: U.S. Government Printing Office.

Policy statement approved by the NASW Delegate Assembly, August 2002. For further information, contact the National Association of Social Workers, 750 First Street, NE, Suite 700, Washington, DC 20002-4241. Telephone: 202-408-8600; e-mail: press@naswdc.org

Slavery and Human Trafficking

BACKGROUND

Today, between 12.3 million (International Labor Organization, 2005) and 27 million people (Free the Slaves, 2007) are held against their will in violent conditions and forced to work without pay. The U.S. government believes that the majority are women and children (U.S. Department of State, 2007). The phenomenon has grown dramatically over the past several decades, fueled primarily by the large increase in worldwide population and poverty, the economic devastation that globalization has brought to many global communities, and widespread government corruption that turns a blind eye to and even profits directly from slavery (Bales, 1999).

Modern slavery and trafficking represent the commodification of human beings—objects or "goods" to be bought, sold, used, shipped, and traded for money in response to the growing demands for sexual and labor exploitation of children and adults. Slavery exists in every country in the world—including the United States (U.S. Department of State, 2004).

Human trafficking is a component of modern slavery. Although not all slaves are transported from one location to another, criminals take advantage of the ease of modern transport and the growth in global communications and technology to use abduction, violence, threats against family, or the false promise of gainful work to move annually about 800,000 people illegally across borders worldwide. It is estimated that between 14,500 and 17,500 of these victims are trafficked into the United States (U.S. Department of State, 2007).

The United States is both a source and a destination country for thousands of victims of slavery. The precise number of U.S. citizens and legal residents who are enslaved in the United States is unknown, but what is known is that the vast majority are trafficked into the country from East Asia, Eastern Europe, Mexico, and Central America for domestic work, migrant farm labor, or work in the sex industry (U.S. Department of State, 2007).

In terms of prevalence, the largest group works in agriculture. But slaves are used in many other kinds of labor: brick making, mining or quarrying, prostitution, gem working and jewelry making, cloth and carpet making, and domestic service (Bales, 1999). Modern-day slavery also encompasses individuals or families in indentured servitude, including debt bondage and victims captured and used by marauders or in armed conflicts.

The human costs (physical, emotional, and spiritual) to victims of slavery are among the most severe and lasting of any prolonged trauma. The economic costs are equally staggering. According to Interpol, human trafficking is a $44.5 billion business and now ranks among the three largest criminal enterprises, along with the sale of guns and drugs (Interpol, 2007). Without the demand for illegal commodities (including human beings) and associated profit such enterprises would not thrive.

Globalization and the promise of good jobs, economic opportunity, and personal freedom also serve to lure women and men to what they believe will bring them a better life. Determining whether a person has been trafficked or is an illegal migrant is often a complicated process that is based on the presence of three factors: the use or threat of force, fraud, or coercion. Although many people migrate freely and are able to maintain their freedom while being smuggled across borders and after arriving at their destination, trafficking victims may be abducted and are always deceived by false promises of a better existence. Only after trafficking victims arrive at their destination do they realize that the person who transported them will use whatever force or coercion necessary to keep them under his or her control. It is also common practice to sell trafficking victims to someone else who will use the same terror tactics to keep them enslaved.

People are recruited in several different ways, such as through fake employment agencies, acquaintances, newspaper ads, front businesses, word of mouth, or abduction (Freedom Network, 2003). Traffickers, for example, may be neighbors, friends, family members who sell their own children (Harrison, 2007), agricultural operators, owners of small businesses, diplomats, and other people of privilege (Lewis, 2007). Increasingly, however, traffickers are organized crime syndicates, often operating in collaboration with corrupt law enforcement entities, government officials or employers, who may use several intermediaries from the first point of contact to the final destination of the victim. Slaveholders and traffickers are willing to do whatever it takes to maintain their total domination over their victims, isolating them from the public, including family members or support networks. They often confiscate their passports or identification documents and use the threat of violence against family, induce shame, prey on their fear of imprisonment or deportation, and control their money.

Human trafficking has grown in part as a result of the advances in Internet and communication technology, which make information fast, anonymous, and easily accessible to predators and traffickers worldwide. According to Naim (2005) the modern-day slave auction is electronic, wherein local pimps can examine and purchase via e-mail women and girls from wholesalers in other countries and where retail customers can order up the prostitute of their choice. In fact, sex tourism is one of the world's largest industries and has become integrated into the economy of many countries.

Given the many forms that trafficking and modern-day slavery take both worldwide and in the United States, the solutions to this phenomenon need be multipronged, including an educated profession and public, legislative protections for individuals at risk, and, to decrease one's vulnerability to slavery, opportunities for education, sustainable livelihoods, and politically and psychologically empowered local communities.

ISSUE STATEMENT

If social workers are to assume a leadership role in ensuring and promoting human rights, they need to be knowledgeable about human trafficking and modern-day slavery and apply their tools and skills broadly and creatively, taking into account issues of culture, power, privilege, and oppression. This effort includes collaborating across professions; intervening in local, state, and national policy arenas as advocates and thought leaders; recognizing, assisting, and supporting victims and survivors; and galvanizing others to do so as well.

The NASW *Code of Ethics* (NASW, 2000) and existing policy statements provide ample justification for the association to take a position in strong opposition to modern slavery and human trafficking and to propose a series of solutions to eradicate both. The core values enumerated in the code's Preamble emphasize the profession's commitments to social justice and the dignity and worth of each person. It encourages social workers to pursue social change, particularly with and on behalf of vulnerable and oppressed individuals and groups, and specifically targets poverty, unemployment, and discrimination—all of which increase an individual's vulnerability to slavery and trafficking—as worthy targets for intervention.

In the same spirit, standard 6.01 of the code challenges NASW members to exercise their ethical responsibilities to promote the general welfare of society, locally and globally, and to advocate for living conditions conducive to the fulfillment of basic human needs. Standard 6.04(d) is particularly applicable to the eradication of slavery and human trafficking, calling on social workers to "act to prevent and eliminate domination of, exploitation of, and discrimination against any person, group, or class on the basis of race, ethnicity, national origin, color, sex, sexual orientation, age, marital status, political belief, religion, or mental or physical disability" (NASW, 2000, p. 27).

Standard 6.04(a) calls on NASW members to "engage in social and political action that seeks to ensure that all people have equal access to the resources, employment, services, and opportunities they require . . . to develop fully" (NASW, 2000, p. 27), and exhorts social workers to "advocate for changes in policy and legislation to improve social conditions in order to meet basic human needs and promote social justice" (NASW, 2000, p. 27).

Combating slavery and human trafficking is also a logical application of NASW's International Policy on Human Rights, which promotes U.S. ratification of the Universal Declaration of Human Rights (UDHR). The policy exhorts social workers to be especially vigilant about human rights violations related to children's rights and exploitation such as child labor and child prostitution (NASW, 2006). Twenty-four of the UDHR's 30 articles are applicable to eradicating slavery. Article 4 states the following: "No one shall be held in slavery or servitude; slavery and the slave trade shall be prohibited in all their forms," (United Nations, 1948) and article 5 declares that "No one shall be subjected to torture or to cruel, inhuman or degrading treatment or punishment" (United Nations, 1948). In addition, the existence today of human trafficking and slavery runs directly counter to NASW's strong support for human rights as the foundational principle for social work theory and practice (Asamoah, Healy, & Mayadas, 1997; Wetzel, 1993, 1998).

POLICY STATEMENT

NASW supports public awareness and advocacy for legislative and administrative change to end human trafficking and slavery in the United States and around the world, and supports public education efforts that ensure that this perspective has a strong presence in the media and legislatures.

Public Awareness and Advocacy

■ NASW supports public education campaigns that teach communities to recognize the warning signs of all aspects of human trafficking and slavery and to report suspicious behavior to the appropriate social services or law enforcement agency.

■ NASW supports efforts to identify successful initiatives and best practices for freeing slaves, and to help freed individuals to engage in rehabilitation, community reintegration, and the development of sustainable livelihoods.

■ NASW supports the enforcement and strengthening of the Trafficking Victims Protection Reauthorization Act of 2003.

Services to Victims and Survivors

■ NASW promotes social workers taking leadership in compiling and further developing and applying sound clinical practices and in formulating appropriate public policy for helping people emerging from slavery.

■ NASW encourages social workers to help government and community-based organizations to address short-term needs of survivors, including developing mechanisms to protect victims who come forward, and families vulnerable to retaliation and threats by traffickers in their home country or community.

Professional Development and Continuing Education

■ NASW supports the development and implementation of culturally competent social work curriculums that prepare students to meet the psychosocial and empowerment needs of survivors of slavery.

- NASW supports cross-sector training and collaboration among social workers, law enforcement, and community workers and other gatekeepers to freedom in the identification of potential victims and consumers of slavery, helping survivors to safety, protecting them from further harm, and successfully prosecuting slaveholders.

Legal and Political Action/Mobilizing Civil Society/Public Policy

- NASW encourages local, state and national governments to construct, implement, and enforce effective and well-resourced plans to prevent and end slavery within their borders.

- NASW encourages the U.S. government to use diplomacy, trade policy, and foreign aid as leverage in fighting slavery internationally.

- NASW supports the development and implementation of legislation and policies that enforce the prosecution of consumers.

- NASW condemns practices that enable investment in and production of goods and services that use slave labor, in recognition of the rights of people who are enslaved.

- NASW supports greater legal protections and monitoring of workers in sectors particularly vulnerable to slavery.

- NASW advocates for the elimination of incentives in immigration policy for unscrupulous employers to use forced labor.

REFERENCES

Asamoah, Y., Healy, L., & Mayadas, N. (1997). Ending the international–domestic dichotomy: New approaches to a global curriculum for the millennium. *Journal of Social Work Education, 33*, 389–401.

Bales, K. (1999). *Disposable people: New slavery in the global economy.* Berkeley: University of California Press.

Freedom Network. (2003). *Institute on Human Trafficking and Slavery: Tools for an effective response participant tool kit.* Retrieved November 26, 2007, from http://www.castla.org

Free the Slaves. (2007). *Ending slavery.* Retrieved November 26, 2007, from http://www.freetheslaves.net/NETCOMMUNITY/Page.aspx?pid=183&srcid=-2)face

Harrison, D. (2007). *Children for sale: UK's new slave trade.* Retrieved April 24, 2008, from http://www.telegraph.co.uk/news/main.jhtml?xml=/news/2008/01/27/nslave127.xml

International Labor Organization. (2005). *A global alliance against forced labour—Executive summary.* Retrieved November 24, 2007, from http://www.ilo.ru/news/200505/FLGR_ExSum.pdf

Interpol. (2007). *Trafficking in human beings.* Retrieved November 25, 2007, from http://www.Interpol.int/Public/THB/Default.asp

Lewis, L. (2007). *Diplomatic abuse of servants hard to prosecute.* Retrieved April 24, 2008, from http://www.npr.org/templates/story/story.php?storyId=7672967

Naim, M. (2005). *Illicit: How smugglers, traffickers and copycats are hijacking the global economy.* New York: Doubleday.

National Association of Social Workers. (2000). *Code of ethics of the National Association of Social Workers.* Washington, DC: NASW Press.

National Association of Social Workers. (2006). *International policy on human rights* [Abstract]. Retrieved November 26, 2007, from http://www.socialworkers.org/resources/abstracts/abstracts/international.asp

United Nations. (1948). *Universal declaration of human rights.* New York: Author.

U.S. Department of State. (2004). *Victims of Trafficking and Violence Protection Act of 2000: Trafficking in persons report.* Retrieved March 21, 2008, from http://www.state.gov/g/tip/rls/tiprpt/2004/

U.S. Department of State. (2007). *Trafficking in persons report.* Retrieved May 30, 2008, from http://www.state.gov/g/tip/rls/tiprpt/2007/

Wetzel, J. W. (1993). *The world of women: In pursuit of human rights.* London: Macmillan.

Wetzel, J. W. (1998). *Human rights values: An international challenge to social work.* Paper presented at the 15th Annual Social Work Day at the United Nations, New York, March 25; at the International Association of Schools of Social Work symposium, Council of Social Work Education Annual Program Meeting, Orlando, FL, March 8; at the University of Texas "Celebrate International Social Work," Austin, March 27.

Policy statement approved by the NASW Delegate Assembly, August 2008. For further information, contact the National Association of Social Workers, 750 First Street, NE, Suite 700, Washington, DC 20002-4241. Telephone: 202-408-8600 or 800-638-8799; e-mail: press@naswdc.org

Social Services

BACKGROUND

Before the 1900s social services were provided by family members, neighbors, church groups, private charitable organizations, and local governments in the form of indoor and outdoor relief. In fact, the Charity Organization Societies of the late 1800s, which helped poor people, preferred to provide social services rather than financial aid. During the first half of the 20th century, the federal and state governments largely provided cash and in-kind assistance to destitute people. Although child welfare services were part of the original Social Security Act of 1935, most social services remained outside federal purview until 1956, when Congress amended the Social Security Act to provide social services to families on relief (DiNitto, 2000).

Social services has its roots in the charitable–voluntary agencies and limited government institutions that were created to fill perceived societal needs and reduce problems. The charitable–voluntary institutions have largely evolved into the private nonprofit agencies of today and continue to be reflected in community fundraising and allocation entities, such as the United Way. Once limited government influence has evolved into a pervasive government involvement because of greater societal needs and the necessity of a broader economic base to meet those needs. A system of laws also has evolved to ensure equal opportunity and access to and availability of services, as well as mandates for the operation of certain services (Brieland, 1987; Leiby, 1987).

A complementary relationship between private and public resources is necessary to sustain the web of services that are essential to maintain, encourage, develop, and promote family and individual well-being (Kahn, 1987; Maroney, 1987; Wenocur, 1987).

Social services is defined in the *Social Work Dictionary* (Barker, 1999) as

> the activities of social workers and others in promoting the health and well-being of people and in helping people to become more self-sufficient; preventing dependency; strengthening family relationships; and restoring individuals, families, groups, or communities to successful *social functioning*. Specific kinds of social services include helping people obtain adequate financial resources for their needs, evaluating the capabilities of people to care for children or other dependents, counseling and psychotherapy, referral and channeling, mediation, advocating for social causes, informing organizations of their obligations to individuals, facilitating health care provisions, and linking clients to resources. (pp. 453–454, italics in original)

An assessment of current patterns of providing social services indicates a wide disparity between the needs of people and the services provided to meet those needs, among the public bureaucracies and the private nonprofit agencies created to provide those services, and between the available funding base and the need for services. The public agencies are funded by fluctuating tax dollars, and the private nonprofits depend on ephemeral government contracts, private fundraising efforts, and community resources. Program development becomes focused on those areas that currently are in vogue, that is, fundable. The competition for available financial resources, particularly in recessionary times, becomes a struggle for the survival and maintenance of existing programs that do not fit the current focus. Furthermore, the lack of direction and the confusion in planning and service provision stem from a fundamental ambivalence resulting from the need to provide services and the need to control and account for the allocation of financial resources (Loarenbrack & Keys, 1987).

The heightened demand for accountability and program evaluation has provided the impetus for more social work research and for refinements in evaluation measures and design. It has focused attention on discovering what works and how to generalize that information. It also has focused attention on cost-effectiveness as related to program outcome (Holland & Petschers, 1987; Tripodi, 1987).

Results can be immediately demonstrated in short-term programs with limited goals and objectives. It is more difficult and more complex to demonstrate any immediate results in long-term programs designed to affect multiple problems within individuals and families. Community organization projects have a similar difficulty. A variety of environmental factors further complicate cause and effect (Austin, 1987; Coulton, 1987; Tropman, 1987).

The public–private partnership of service provision and resource allocation is unresponsive to the needs of the individual, the family, or the community. The lack of direction, comprehensiveness, and continuity in service provision and planning creates an environment in which the needs of the bureaucracy seem to supersede the needs of the individuals and communities it is meant to serve (Morris, 1987; Yankey, 1987).

Social policy is defined in the *Social Work Dictionary* (Barker, 1999) as

> the activities and principles of a society that guide the way it intervenes in and regulates relationships between individuals, groups, communities, and social institutions. These principles and activities are the result of the society's values and customs and largely determine the distribution of resources and level of well-being of its people. (p. 452)

In a democratic society, the social services system exists to assist families and individuals in making optimal use of existing resources and opportunities to sustain and enhance their social functioning in a highly complex social and physical environment. Historically, social work has developed from a social reform orientation and individual-oriented change. This has given the profession its unique perception of the individual in the context of family and environment. The traditional base of social work practice—casework, group work, and community organization—reflects those interrelationships (Gilbert & Specht, 1987; Maroney, 1987).

Social work education and training have expanded to include other theoretical models and methods in response to family and individual needs and societal change. Social work should play a paramount role in the provision and planning of social services (Austin, 1987; Yankey, 1987).

ISSUE STATEMENT

There is a glaring absence of a national policy defining the need, significance, and role of social services in the United States. These activities form a complex system that is continuously influenced and bound by social, economic, and political forces on the national, state, and local levels. The social services system is in a chronically reactive position to these forces.

Services are established and provided in an unsystematic, fragmented manner; individuals and families become compartmentalized by problems; and resources are allocated by categories. Implicit decisions are made as to who is eligible for service, under what circumstances services are to be offered, and how long services will last without consideration of the social work value of self-determination. Services are not uniformly available or accessible on the basis of eligibility criteria, including income. This issue is central to any policy and planning (Kahn, 1987; Morris, 1987).

Core services that provide the foundation for a comprehensive system are seriously impaired by funding cuts and inconsistent policy decisions that are sometimes at cross-purposes (Kahn, 1987; Yankey, 1987). The objective, then, is the development of a new, comprehensive social services system in the United States that helps families and individuals to sustain and enhance efficiently their social functioning in a given community.

POLICY STATEMENT

The social worker of today is both liberated and burdened by the opportunity to face a future that will be quite different from social work's formative years. Social workers are challenged to increase their visibility as leaders in policy making and service provision. NASW advocates the following principles:

Universal Access

All people shall have access to services. Services must be accessible, attainable, and offered in a way that encourages voluntary use. No arbitrary criteria, including gender, marital status, sexual orientation, disability, religion, political views, race, and ethnic and national origin, shall be exercised to limit services access. Eligibility for social services is present when a reasonable request is made to a practitioner who, or social services agency that, possesses the required skills to meet the request, subject to the willingness of the recipient to make a reasonable investment in the service. Availability of services may be subject to community priorities when the community has identified them as recommended or discretionary. However, when services are imposed by courts, considered mandatory, or based on needs that may result in significant life changes for an individual or family, such services shall be available in a timely manner and according to best practice standards. Appropriate private administrative review and reasonable subsidy shall be available in instances in which the service is imposed by court action or mandated by public law.

Comprehensive Services

The social services system must develop a broad spectrum of public and private services to meet the short- and long-term service requests and needs of individuals, groups, and families. No single service or continuum of services shall be prescribed or mandated as the sole option when services are imposed. Alternatives for consumers, access and movement from one service to another, and specific competence to fulfill defined purposes should be included in services systems that are supported by public funds to any degree. The social services system must include multiple types and levels of providers, as well as prominent roles for federal, state, and local governments, to meet various needs. The professional expertise of social workers must be integrated into the decision-making process at all levels.

Informed Consent

The use of social services presumes some appropriate dependency by the consumer. Mechanisms must ensure that each consumer has informed self-determination regarding choice of services, protection of individuality, and ability to participate in policy matters, if not directly, then through selected or assigned advocates. Confidentiality is not absolute but dictates that sharing of information is done at all times in the best interest of those served.

Simplicity and Efficiency

At no other time since the early years following World War II has the social work profession been so intertwined with a culture deeply engaged in macro and micro level technological, social, political, and global change. This often turbulent and ever-changing environment reinforces the need for the social work professional to be a stabilizing force advocating for policies and regulations that foster social services.

Systems to establish accountability for social services must be designed to ensure simplicity of procedures and administration. Required documentation should be limited to what is essential. Systems for accountability should not become ends in themselves.

Establishment of Policies and Priorities

Establishment of policies and priorities for the social services system must include active participation of social work professionals. Policy design and standard setting must include consumers and the community at large, in addition to organizational representatives. Social workers should take the initiative in facilitating broad participation in the design of policy, and priority setting in the social services should reflect the principle of full participation.

Planning and Evaluation

The social services system must contain the mechanisms to provide maximum accountability. Funding sources, policy-making bodies, administrators, service personnel, and consumers should obtain regular and precise information about the operations, trends, problems, and results of the services delivered. Provisions for the rapid retrieval of data to monitor the quality, quantity, and impact of services are necessary to achieve accountability. However, they should not be used at the expense of the consumer's right to service. Social workers must take a more active leadership role in developing accountability systems.

To ensure competent and responsible delivery of social services, guarantee accountability, and meet developing needs, the planning and evaluation processes must involve social work professionals, agency managers, the community, and the consumer.

Advocacy

Advocacy has always been the cornerstone of the social work profession. All social workers in their specialized fields of practice must commit to advocacy. The social worker is a key part of the advocacy process that will shape the social and economic conditions of the years ahead. To be an effective part of the process, the time is now to take seriously the role of multiple advocates; being a change agent remolds the draconian to the inclusive and the humane. Barker (1999) defined advocacy as "1. the act of directly representing or defending others. 2. In social work, championing the rights of individuals or communities through direct intervention or through *empowerment*" (p. 11, italics in original). The social worker is called on to be involved at the micro, mezzo,

and macro levels of practice. Social workers advocate for social justice, alleviating social ills and oppression at all levels of society.

Particularly important for the social worker advocate is the need to compel policymakers to revamp the funding mechanisms that provide financial assistance for formal education and training for welfare recipients.

Finance and the Education of the Funding Community

Financing of the social services system is the joint responsibility of all citizens and all levels of government. Public–private partnerships should be facilitated to enhance these services. The role of social workers is to take the lead in educating the funding community about the nature and necessity of social services.

REFERENCES

Austin, D. M. (1987). Social planning in the public sector. In A. Minahan (Ed.-in-Chief), *Encyclopedia of social work* (18th ed., Vol. 2, pp. 620–625). Silver Spring, MD: National Association of Social Workers.

Barker, R. L. (1999). *The social work dictionary* (4th ed.). Washington, DC: NASW Press.

Brieland, D. (1987). History and evolution of social work practice. In A. Minahan (Ed.-in-Chief), *Encyclopedia of social work* (18th ed., Vol. 1, pp. 739–754). Silver Spring, MD: National Association of Social Workers.

Coulton, C. J. (1987). Quality assurance. In A. Minahan (Ed.-in-Chief), *Encyclopedia of social work* (18th ed., Vol. 2, pp. 443–445). Silver Spring, MD: National Association of Social Workers.

DiNitto, D. M. (2000). *Social welfare politics and public policy* (5th ed.). Needham Heights, MA: Allyn & Bacon.

Gilbert, N., & Specht, H. (1987). Social planning and community organization. In A. Minahan (Ed.-in-Chief), *Encyclopedia of social work* (18th ed., Vol. 2, pp. 602–619). Silver Spring, MD: National Association of Social Workers.

Holland, T. P., & Petschers, M. K. (1987). Organizations: Context for social service delivery.

In A. Minahan (Ed.-in-Chief), *Encyclopedia of social work* (18th ed., Vol. 2, pp. 204–214). Silver Spring, MD: National Association of Social Workers.

Kahn, A. J. (1987). Social problems and issues: Theories and definitions. In A. Minahan (Ed.-in-Chief), *Encyclopedia of social work* (18th ed., Vol. 2, pp. 632–644). Silver Spring, MD: National Association of Social Workers.

Leiby, J. (1987). History of social welfare. In A. Minahan (Ed.-in-Chief), *Encyclopedia of social work* (18th ed., Vol. 1, pp. 755–777). Silver Spring, MD: National Association of Social Workers.

Loarenbrack, G., & Keys, P. (1987). Settlements and neighborhood centers. In A. Minahan (Ed.-in-Chief), *Encyclopedia of social work* (18th ed., Vol. 2, pp. 556–561). Silver Spring, MD: National Association of Social Workers.

Maroney, R. M. (1987). Social planning. In A. Minahan (Ed.-in-Chief), *Encyclopedia of social work* (18th ed., Vol. 2, pp. 593–602). Silver Spring, MD: National Association of Social Workers.

Morris, R. (1987). Social welfare policy: Trends and issues. In A. Minahan (Ed.-in-Chief), *Encyclopedia of social work* (18th ed., Vol. 2, pp. 664–681). Silver Spring, MD: National Association of Social Workers.

Tripodi, T. (1987). Program evaluation. In A. Minahan (Ed.-in-Chief), *Encyclopedia of social work* (18th ed., Vol. 2, pp. 366–379). Silver Spring, MD: National Association of Social Workers.

Tropman, J. E. (1987). Policy analysis: Methods and techniques. In A. Minahan (Ed.-in-Chief), *Encyclopedia of social work* (18th ed., Vol. 2, pp. 268–283). Silver Spring, MD: National Association of Social Workers.

Wenocur, S. (1987). Social planning in the voluntary sector. In A. Minahan (Ed.-in-Chief), *Encyclopedia of social work* (18th ed., Vol. 2, pp. 625–632). Silver Spring, MD: National Association of Social Workers.

Yankey, J. (1987). Public social services. In A. Minahan (Ed.-in-Chief), *Encyclopedia of social work* (18th ed., Vol. 2, pp. 417–426). Silver Spring, MD: National Association of Social Workers.

Policy statement approved by the NASW Delegate Assembly, August 2002. This statement supersedes the policy statement on Social Services approved by the Delegate Assembly in 1975 and reconfirmed by the Delegate Assembly in 1993. For further information, contact the National Association of Social Workers, 750 First Street, NE, Suite 700, Washington, DC 20002-4241. Telephone: 202-408-8600; e-mail: press@naswdc.org

Social Work in the Criminal Justice System

BACKGROUND

In 2006, there were 2,245,189 individuals incarcerated in local, state, and federal correctional facilities in the United States (Sabol, Minton, & Harrison, 2007). The United States has the highest incarceration rate in the world, and the rate increased 700 percent between 1970 and 2005 (Public Safety Performance Project, 2007). In addition, up to 60 percent of incarcerated individuals who are released will be reincarcerated within two years (Langan & Levin, 2002). Professionals anticipate that incarceration rates in this country will continue to increase, and this projected increase creates concerns about the social and economic effects of incarceration. Social workers have a unique set of professional skills to assist in addressing both the policy and practice issues surrounding incarceration in the United States.

Statistics clearly indicate that a disproportionate number of individuals of a racial or ethnic minority are incarcerated. Disproportionate arrest rates, racial profiling, discrimination, and denial of vital resources continue to exacerbate this problem. In 2005, 3,145 out of every 100,000 black men, 1,244 out of every 100,000 Hispanic men, and 471 out of every 100,000 white men in the population were incarcerated (Sabol et al., 2007). Although women have lower incarceration rates than do men, women who are racial or ethnic minorities are more likely to be incarcerated. In 2004, black women had incarceration rates two and one-half times higher than did Hispanic women and nearly four times higher than white women. These differences were consistent across all age groups. Among people convicted of drug felonies, white people were less likely than were black people to be incarcerated (33 percent versus 51 percent) (Durose & Lanagan, 2001). In addition to traditionally defined "women" and "men," there is a growing body of evidence documenting the disproportionate effect that criminal justice policies and laws have on transgender communities in the United States. Although studies have been scarce, advocates for the transgendered conservatively estimate that one in three transgender people have been imprisoned, with advocates pointing to systemic discrimination leading to pervasive poverty as the main cause for such high rates of imprisonment (TGI Justice Project [TGIJP], 2007; Sylvia Riveria Law Project, 2007).

Homeland Security and Immigration

An emphasis on homeland security and immigration regulations has affected incarceration rates and trends. Between 1995 and 2003 the number of incarcerated individuals in federal institutions for public offenses increased by 170 percent, and this increase primarily was due to an increase in the number of individuals incarcerated for immigration-related offenses. In 1995, 3,420 individuals were incarcerated because of an immigration-related offense compared with 16,903 individuals in 2003 (Beck & Harrison, 2005).

Substance Use

The number of incarcerated individuals in state correctional facilities for drug-related offenses was 19,000 in 1980 compared with 250,900 in 2003 (Sabol et al., 2007). Mandatory sentencing laws have increased incarceration rates, leading to a correctional system clogged with incarcerated individuals who have a substance dependence disorder. Involvement in a criminal episode frequently occurs following the use of drugs and alcohol (McNeece & Roberts, 1996). The U.S. Department of Justice (Mumola & Karberg, 2006) reported that 32 percent of state prisoners and 26 percent of federal prisoners reported using substances at the time of their offense, with 53 percent of state prisoners and 45 percent of federal prisoners reporting a history of substance abuse and dependence.

Mental Health

Correctional facilities have become the treatment facility of last resort for individuals who have been failed by other systems. The dismantling of the psychiatric hospital system and the fragmentation of community mental health systems has shifted the care of those with chronic mental health issues to the correctional system. Substantial numbers of offenders have mental health disorders that have not been diagnosed or treated. Many of these individuals have comorbid substance abuse issues. Weedon (2005) reported there are five times more persons with mental illnesses in jails than in state psychiatric hospitals. Conservative estimates propose that 10 percent of offenders have a mental illness (Norton, 2005), with rates of mental health problems in incarcerated individuals reported as high as 64 percent (James & Glaze, 2006).

Health Care Needs

Increasing numbers of incarcerated individuals have special health needs, including those who have been exposed to hepatitis, tuberculosis, HIV, and other infectious diseases. The special health care needs of female incarcerated individuals, including care for those who are pregnant, must be considered. The health care needs of aging incarcerated individuals are increasingly important as this population continues to grow in the correctional system. The special needs of those incarcerated individuals with impairments in mobility, vision, hearing, or speech must be considered in correctional facilities, including the health needs of incar-

cerated transgender people (Rosenblum, 2000; Thaler, 2007; Women in Prison Project, 2007).

Family Impact

Incarcerated individuals describe their inability to be involved in the daily lives of their children and other loved ones as a source of great psychological stress (Lanier, 1993). Approximately 70 percent of female incarcerated individuals lived with their minor children before incarceration. In about one-third of such cases, child protective services and other agencies were involved in out-of-home placement of the children (Versay, 1998). In almost all cases, lesbian, gay, bisexual, and transgender prisoners are not allowed conjugal visits from same-sex partners. Studies show that incarcerated individuals who maintain strong family and friendship ties during incarceration and who assume responsible marital and parental roles upon their release have lower recidivism rates (Hairston, 1988).

Privatization

A private correctional facility houses incarcerated individuals for a profit. The operation of private correctional facilities is a point of controversy. The U.S. Bureau of Justice reported that approximately 7 percent of state and federal incarcerated individuals were held in private correctional facilities (Blakely & Bumphus, 2004). Advocates of privatization posit that private facilities operate more efficiently, thereby reducing costs to the public. Opponents argue that the government must retain responsibility for the direct provision of programs for the incarceration and rehabilitation of offenders to safeguard the interests of society and the rights of individuals. Development of standards and continued research are necessary to ensure that the interests of society are protected and that responsible care and rehabilitation occur.

Incarcerated Women

Sabol et al. (2007) reported that there were 111,403 female individuals incarcerated in state and federal correctional facilities and that the population had increased at approximately twice the rate of male incarcerated individuals during the study period. Because correctional facilities tend to be designed for men, the differences in the sexes are ignored, causing increased stress for female incarcerated individuals (Versay, 1998). Transgender women are usually housed in men's facilities and are at risk of sexual propositions, harassment, assault, and infection with HIV.

Female incarcerated individuals frequently have experienced past trauma and abuse. In one study, 48 percent of female incarcerated individuals met diagnostic criteria for posttraumatic stress disorder. Zlotnik (1997) reported that 87 percent of the women experienced at least one assault in their lifetime, with 55 percent experiencing childhood physical abuse, 53 percent experiencing rape in adulthood, and 63 percent experiencing physical assault in adulthood. According to advocates for the transgender community in San Francisco, at least 75 percent of transgender women facing criminal charges in county jail also reported surviving physical or sexual abuse, frequently as children (TGJIP, 2007). Furthermore, transgender women prisoners in California are 13 times more likely to be sexually assaulted than are those in the non-transgender prison population (Jenness et al., 2007).

Juvenile Justice

A dramatic rise in juvenile violence, particularly homicides, which began in the mid to late 1980s and peaked in the early 1990s, generated concern among the public and led to policy changes by federal, state, and local governments. Most states stiffened their laws relating to juvenile justice, including measures that allow, or in many cases mandate, youngsters to be transferred to the adult system at younger ages and for a greater variety of offenses. Sabol and colleagues (2007) reported that there were 2,364 juveniles in state prisons in June 2006. Juveniles are also housed in adult federal correctional facilities. The practice of incarcerating juveniles with adult offenders is especially problematic. Vulnerability to exploitation and abuse is high for these youth. Exposure to offenders with extensive criminal backgrounds may foster a pattern of incarceration rather than successful reentry for this population.

ISSUE STATEMENT

The current incarcerated population has surpassed 2 million individuals. This population is expected to increase by 192,000 by the end of 2011 (Public Safety Performance Project, 2007). The incarcerated population suffers from myriad social, economic, health, mental health, and addiction issues. The provision of services to this population has created an ever expanding need for social work services.

As Showalter and Hunsinger (2007) stated, "in essence our prisons are full of people extremely short on resources and long on problems" (p. 366). Social workers trained in the corrections field are uniquely qualified to provide services addressing all the problem areas. Yet little has been written about delivery of services in this field, and schools of social work rarely address correctional social work and criminal justice. Incarceration needs to be closely analyzed by the profession as the "increasing incidence of severe and terminal physical illness, mental disorder, developmental delays and severe substance abuse problems among these individuals make this need even more pressing" (Ivanhoff, Smyth, & Dulmus, 2007, p. 349). The functioning of the incarcerated person's family is affected as well, resulting in economic burdens, stigma, emotional distress, and an increased risk of children to commit crimes (Rowe & Farrington, 1997), which also cause difficulties for incarcerated individuals, their families, and their communities. Social workers must become involved in corrections and rehabilitation as advocates and treatment providers for this vulnerable population.

Several specific areas are pertinent to the profession of social work. Our mission of promoting social functioning requires us to examine the following:

■ safe and humane environments that protect the public, provide cost-effective services, and are responsive to the needs of the community.

■ the role of social work within the criminal justice system.

- the role of social work in transition planning for successful reentry of incarcerated individuals into their communities.

- ongoing advocacy for the creation and enforcement of policies to protect the basic human rights, safety, and fair treatment of all incarcerated people is essential. Transgender people are at greater risk of physical and sexual abuse by incarcerated individuals, guards, and others in positions of authority. Human rights and safety for transgender people may include the continuation of ongoing hormone treatments first instituted prior to their incarceration.

- the role of social work in advocacy for policies that improve access to services and resources for formerly incarcerated individuals, with special attention to the needs of racial, sexual, and gender minorities, juveniles, elderly persons, and women.

- integrations of social work services within the framework of the criminal justice system.

- prevalence of substance abuse and mental health issues within the correctional system.

- the special issues of sexual offenders within the criminal justice system.

- trends toward incarceration and mandatory sentencing instead of the provision of community-based treatment, particularly their impact on people of color and other vulnerable populations.

- the biopsychosocial needs of all incarcerated individuals, with special attention to the needs of racial, sexual, and gender minorities, juveniles, elderly, and female offenders.

POLICY STATEMENT

NASW recognizes the importance of providing quality social work interventions to the incarcerated population. The provision of an adequate level of professional social work services could reduce the rates of recidivism, reentry, and incarceration for the betterment of the individual as well as society. Thus, NASW supports

- ongoing advocacy to address issues surrounding and leading to disproportionate rates of incarceration for individuals of racial or ethnic minorities, juveniles, women, and undocumented individuals;

- increased use of professional forensic social workers to provide culturally competent treatment and intervention for the growing population of incarcerated individuals, including mental health and substance abuse services;

- safe, humane, and equitable treatment for all incarcerated individuals, including cessation of sexual abuse, sexual harassment, and differential sentencing and treatment;

- access to quality health care, medications, nutrition, treatment, rehabilitation programs and support for incarcerated individuals including resisting all forms of discrimination based on diagnosis in delivery of medical care;

- appropriate educational and vocational opportunities to assist incarcerated individuals with transitioning back into their communities;

- access to affordable and adequate housing to assist incarcerated individuals with transitioning back into their communities;

- establishment of best practice standards for professional social work in criminal justice settings;

- specialized training on the unique application of social work skills and values in a correctional environment for social workers practicing in criminal justice settings;

- research to identify effective alternatives to incarceration, such as diversion programs.

- expansion of prevention, screening, and treatment efforts, including issues such as substance abuse and dependence, mental illness, sexually transmitted disease, blood and airborne pathogens, confidential testing, and domestic violence;

- increased funding for community-based options, especially for those individuals with substance dependence or serious mental illness who may be better rehabilitated by these services;

- identification of and response to the special needs of any individual under the supervision of the criminal justice system, including, but not limited to, racial, sexual, and gender minorities; juveniles; women (including pregnant women); the elderly; and those with impairments;

■ advocacy and social work leadership to establish national policy on criminal justice, issues in collaboration with other organizations.

REFERENCES

Bachrach, L. (1980). Overview: Model programs for chronic mental patients. *American Journal of Psychiatry, 137,* 1023–1031.

Blakely, C., & Bumphus, V. (2004). Private and public sector prisons: A comparison of select characteristics. *Federal Probation, 68,* 27–31.

Ditton, P. (1999). *Mental health treatment of incarcerated individuals and probationers.* Washington, DC: U.S. Department of Justice, Bureau of Justice Statistics.

Hairston, C. (1988). Family ties during imprisonment: Do they influence future criminal activity? *Federal Probation, 52,* 48–52.

Ivanhoff, A., Smyth, N., & Dulmus, C. (2007). Preparing social workers for practice in correctional institutions. In A. R. Roberts & D. W. Springer (Eds.), *Social work in juvenile and criminal justice settings* (pp. 341–350). Springfield, IL: Charles C Thomas.

James, D., & Glaze, L. (2006). *Mental health problems of prison and jail incarcerated individuals.* Washington, DC: U.S. Department of Justice, Bureau of Justice Statistics.

Jenness, V., Maxson, C. L., Matsuda, K. N., & Sumner, J. M. (2007). *Violence in California correctional facilities: An empirical examination of sexual assault. A report submitted to the California Department of Corrections & Rehabilitation, Center for Evidence-Based Corrections.* Irvine, CA: University of California.

Juvenile Justice and Delinquency Prevention Act of 1974, P.L. 93-415, 88 Stat. 1109.

Langan, P., & Levin, D. (2002). Recidivism of incarcerated individuals released in 1994. *Federal Sentencing Reporter, 15*(1), 58–65.

Lanier, C. (1993). Affective states of fathers in prison. *Justice Quarterly, 10,* 49–65.

McNeece, C. A., & Roberts, A. (1996). *Policy and practice in the justice system.* Chicago: Nelson-Hall.

Mumola, C. J., & Karberg, J. C. (2006). *Drug use and dependence, state and federal incarcerated individuals, 2004* (NCJ 213530). Washington, DC: U.S. Department of Justice, Bureau of Justice Statistics.

Norton, S. (2005, February). Successfully managing mentally ill offenders: Thoughts and recommendations. *Corrections Today, 67,* 28–33.

Public Safety Performance Project. (2007). *Public safety, public spending: Forecasting America's prison population 2007–2011.* Retrieved July 1, 2007, from www.pewpublicsafety.org

Rosenblum, D. (2000). 'Trapped' in Sing Sing: Transgendered prisoners caught in the gender binarism. *Michigan Journal of Gender & Law, 6,* 522–526.

Rowe, D., & Farrington, D. (1997). The familial transmission of criminal convictions. *Criminology, 35,* 177–183.

Sabol, W. J., Minton, T. D., & Harrison, P. M. (2007). *Prison and jail incarcerated individuals at midyear 2006* (NCJ 217675). Washington, DC: U.S. Department of Justice, Bureau of Justice Statistics.

Showalter, D., & Hunsinger, D. (2007). Social work within a maximum security setting. In A. R. Roberts & D. W. Springer (Eds.), *Social work in juvenile and criminal justice settings* (pp. 366–375). Springfield, IL: Charles C Thomas.

Sylvia Riveria Law Project. (2007). *It's war in here; A report on the treatment of transgender and intersex people in New York State men's prison.* Retrieved March 19, 2008, from http://www.srlp.org/index.php?sec=03N&page=warinhere

Texeira, M. (2007). Review of 'Women behind bars: Gender and race in U.S. prisons.' *Gender and Society, 21,* 304–307.

Thaler, C. (2007). *Putting transgender health care myths on trial.* Retrieved July 14, 2007, from http://www.lambdalegal.org/our-work/publications/page.jsp?itemID=32007335

TGI Justice Project. (2007). Overview of issues facing transgender, gender variant, & intersex prisoners. Retrieved March 19, 2008, from http://www.tgijp.org/giraldo/protest.html

Versay, B. (1998). Specific needs of women diagnosed with mental illness in U.S. jails. In B. L. Levin, A. K. Blanch, & A. Jennings (Eds.),

Women's mental health services (pp. 368–389). Thousand Oaks, CA: Sage Publications.

Weedon, J. (2005, February). The incarceration of the mentally ill. *Corrections Today, 67,* 16–20.

Women in Prison Project. (2007). *Transgender issues and the criminal justice system.* Retrieved April 24, 2007, from http://www.correctional association.org/WIPP/publications/Trans gender_Issues_2007.pdf

Zlotnick, C. (1997). Posttraumatic stress disorder (PTSD), PTSD comorbidity, and childhood abuse among incarcerated women. *Journal of Nervous and Mental Disorders, 185,* 761–763.

Policy statement approved by the NASW Delegate Assembly, August 2008. This policy statement supersedes the policy statement on Correctional Social Work approved by the Delegate Assembly in 1999 and referred by the 2005 Delegate Assembly to the 2008 Delegate Assembly for revision. For further information, contact the National Association of Social Workers, 750 First Street, NE, Suite 700, Washington, DC 20002-4241. Telephone: 202-408-8600 or 800-638-8799; e-mail: press@naswdc.org

Sovereignty and the Health of Indigenous Peoples

BACKGROUND

This policy statement refers to the following population groups: Native Americans within the geographical boundaries of the continental United States (or First Nations Peoples), *Kanaka Maoli* (Native Hawaiians), Alaska Natives, Chamorus of Guam and the Northern Mariana Islands, Taino Indians of Puerto Rico, and American Samoans. These groups all share in common the fact that they have been colonized by the United States and as a result their sovereignty has been seriously suppressed.

Because of space limitations, background and historical information on the indigenous groups included in this policy statement are by necessity abbreviated. The authors acknowledge the inherent limitations in describing the complex and rich cultures of our brother and sister nations in this document and refer readers to the references section for more literature about all the indigenous groups discussed herein.

Native Americans (First Nations Peoples)

■ The Articles of Confederation of 1781 gave the federal government sole and exclusive authority over Native American people. This authority was later solidified in the U.S. Constitution, which granted Congress power over Native Americans and established laws that regulated their affairs.

■ The 1790 and 1834 Trade and Intercourse Acts separated Native Americans and non–Native Americans and subjected all interaction between the two groups to federal control with the underlying belief that the "Indians were culturally inferior and that the American Government had a responsibility to raise them to the level of the rest of society, which meant to 'Christianize and Civilize'" (Lewis, 1995, p. 218).

■ The Indian Removal Act of 1830 arranged the forced transfer of indigenous tribes from the eastern United States to the western United States.

■ The Indian General Allotment Act of 1887 (The Dawes Act) "allocated" 160 acres of land to be held in trust for 25 years for native peoples by the government. On expiration of the trust the native peoples would receive title to their allotment and would have U.S. citizenship; surplus lands would revert to the government. As a result the amount of Native American–held land declined from 138 million acres in 1887 to 48 million acres in 1934.

Kanaka Maoli (Native Hawaiians)

■ The first foreigners to become involved with the Hawaiian rulers were sea traders seeking commercial advantages and Christian missionaries seeking mass religious conversion of Hawaiians. These foreigners would play a major role in the disenfranchisement of *Kanaka Maoli* and their *aina* (land). As Blaisdell (1996) wrote, "It was the missionary who drafted our first constitution of 1840, which was modeled after the American Constitution. And it was the missionaries who drafted our *mahele* land laws, which set up a legal system to steal our lands."

■ On January 16, 1893, American annexationists, with the assistance of the U.S. Marines, overthrew the lawful Hawaiian government and gave all remaining crown and government lands to the United States without compensation. Subsequently, Queen Lili'uokalani, the last ruling monarch of the Republic of Hawai'i, was unlawfully imprisoned in her own home and eventually dethroned by American industrialists (Kamauu, 1989).

Alaska Natives

■ From 1750 to 1800 the Russians colonized the Aleuts and coastal Indians to exploit the sea otter trade. In the 1850s the Eskimos made contact with American whalers.

■ The discovery of oil in the 1960s and the Alaska Native Claims Settlement Act of 1971 established a capitalistic, industrial structure through which U.S. and international corporations established access to abundant oil deposits in the northern region. The Claims Act provided $962.5 million and the title to 44 million acres to state-charted native corporations. It required native people to set up village and regional corporations. The land that the Claims Act transferred ownership of did not belong to individual Alaska Natives or tribes but to corporations (Lally & Haynes, 1995).

■ This single set of events has been responsible for both positive and negative consequences for Alaskan Natives related to rapid changes in access to resources and technology, without requisite attention to aboriginal land rights, the retention of hunting and gathering practices, or strategic cultural and economic self-determination (Berger, 1985).

Chamorus

■ The Chamorus first made contact with the Western world in 1521, when Ferdinand Magellan, sailing under Spanish authority, arrived on Guam. After decades of Spanish–Chamoru wars, the Chamoru population was decimated from approximately 100,000 to less than 4,000 in 1710. Guam remained a colony of Spain until the signing of the Treaty of Paris in 1898, at which time the island became a possession of the United States. At that time Guam was politically separated from the rest of the Mariana Islands, hence dividing the Chamoru people. Chamorus became colonial subjects who reported to a governing body determined by which island they were living on. This created a significant barrier in maintaining the identity of the Chamoru people as a collective unit.

■ During World War II Japan invaded Guam and occupied the island for nearly three years. Japanese cultural practices were forced upon the Chamoru, who were forbidden to speak their native tongue. This period of warfare resulted in the death of many Chamorus. After World War II traditional villages were levied off as land was redistributed. In addition, the U.S. federal government seized approximately 42 percent of land for its own use.

■ Under the continuous control of the U.S. Navy and the Department of Interior, the people of Guam have been repeatedly frustrated by the U.S. federal government's failure to address Guam's quest to establish a participatory plan for decolonization.

Taino Indians

■ In the early 1800s the King of Spain granted a *Cedula de Bracia* (The Document of Bracia) to increase the European population of Puerto Rico by awarding land grants to immigrants from South American colonies, Spain, and other European countries.

■ The Taino Indians disappeared very early after the Spanish colonization. The main influence in Puerto Rican culture, values, and lifestyles has been the Spanish colonization; they have been under their dominion for almost 500 years.

■ During the Spanish–American War, U.S. troops invaded Puerto Rico at Guanica on July 25, 1898.

■ At the end of the Spanish–American War, the United States demanded Puerto Rico as "war payment" from Spain in the Treaty of Paris. In 1917, all Puerto Ricans were granted U.S. citizenship.

American Samoans

■ The Dutch explorer Jacob Roggoveen was the first European to "discover" Samoa in 1722. Subsequent European expansion into the islands led to disorder and violence, which were compounded by tribal warfare.

■ A tripartite treaty in 1899 among Great Britain, the United States, and Germany reorganized U.S. interest east of longitude 171° W; Germany was granted the western islands (which later went to New Zealand), and Great Britain withdrew in consideration of rights in Tonga and the Solomon Islands.

■ In 1962 the independent nation of Western Samoa was created from the New Zealand territory; the eastern islands remained under U.S. control as American Samoa.

Social workers must recognize that the effects of colonization on indigenous peoples have resulted in not only the loss of ancestral lands, the violation of the right to self-governance, and the violation of self-determination, but also extreme violation of the basic human right to health in mind, body, and spirit. Within two centuries after first contact with foreigners, the First Nations Peoples experienced a decline of almost 75 percent due to disease and the systematic decimation of tribes and families.

Similar to the First Nations Peoples, Alaska Natives are burdened by high rates of unemployment, poverty, crime, and incarceration. Alaska's teenage pregnancy rate, 45 percent among Alaska Native young women, is the highest in the United States. The suicide rate of Alaska Natives ages 10 to 24 years is three times that of white Alaskans. The majority of these suicides are linked to alcohol abuse, as are child and intimate partner violence and various other types of crimes (Lally & Haynes, 1995).

According to the Office of Technology Assessment (1988, cited in U.S. Senate, 2001), which compared Native Hawaiian health with that of other ethnic groups residing within U.S. boundaries,

> there is little doubt that the health status of Native Hawaiians is far below that of other U.S. population groups and that in a number of areas, the evidence is compelling that

Native Hawaiians constitute a population group for whom the mortality rate associated with certain [chronic] diseases exceeds that for other U.S. populations in alarming proportions. (p. 53)

Look and Braun (1995) reported mortality from chronic illnesses over the past 80 years as two to five times greater for Native Hawaiians than for other ethnic populations living in Hawaii.

Chamorus on Guam represent the largest ethnic group on the island, at only 38 percent. Nonetheless, their rates for numerous social conditions are significantly higher than their percentage, with an oppressive history in their homelands. For example, the percentage of total Chamorus deaths from heart disease is 61.4 percent; from cancer, 59.3 percent; from diabetes mellitus, 77.6 percent; from chronic liver disease, 66.7 percent; and from HIV/AIDS, 61.5 percent (Workman, 1999).

For the Taino Indians, within one generation of that first contact by Columbus, virtually the entire race of Taino were dead from foreign diseases, starvation, massacres, and abusive enslavement by white colonists.

ISSUE STATEMENT

As a result of cultural loss due to colonization and the resulting overwhelming sense of despair, indigenous peoples historically experience the effect of becoming strangers in their own lands. Sovereignty requires, as a precondition, the right to spiritual, emotional, and physical health. When the body, mind, or spirit of an indigenous person is affected, the spiritual, physical, and emotional health of indigenous peoples diminish.

Due to the extensive colonization of indigenous peoples by the United States and the resultant violation of cultural practices, lifestyles, and the violation of the right to self-determination, the indigenous peoples of the United States and its territories and commonwealths have suffered extreme loss of their right to self-governance and land access and extraordinary violation of physical, emotional, and spiritual health and well-being. When indigenous peoples are oppressed in their own lands, it causes their mind, body, and spirit to become unhealthy with physical ailments, mental illnesses, aimlessness, and other spiritual and health problems.

The ability to have some control over one's environment is basic to emotional, spiritual, and physical health. Within this context indigenous peoples could make choices in accordance with their own values. For example, the best use of land might not be for the money it brings in, but rather for the amount of food, shelter, and spiritual sustenance it can provide.

POLICY STATEMENT

■ NASW advocates for concrete sovereignty issues (for example, self-government, self-determination, native languages, tradition, and health practices).

■ NASW should identify policies or practices adverse to the health of indigenous peoples.

■ NASW should continue dialogue with indigenous peoples regarding sovereignty and self-determination because these issues affect their spiritual, emotional, and physical well-being.

■ NASW supports policy changes at the local, state, and federal levels that acknowledge the right of a tribe to determine its own membership.

■ Social workers are expected to be educated and aware of sovereignty and self-determination as these issues relate to indigenous peoples.

■ NASW acknowledges that all people are necessary to one another to survive and to thrive on this planet and in so doing joins in the efforts of all indigenous peoples colonized by the United States, including its states, territories, and commonwealths, toward sovereignty as uniquely defined by the indigenous peoples themselves.

■ Social workers need to understand the core value differences between the dominant culture and the culture of indigenous peoples (that is, the role within the family, the commu-

nity, and the land and ultimately with Mother Earth).

■ NASW recognizes that the overall well-being of indigenous peoples is tied to their economy.

■ NASW recognizes that the struggle of indigenous peoples for sovereignty reflects genocidal practices and ethnic cleansing, which have led to their historic violation and the compromise of self-determination; their profound disenfranchisement as a group; and their concomitant violation of physical, mental, and spiritual health.

■ NASW recognizes and acknowledges that health is an important goal of the sovereignty movement; therefore, NASW members support indigenous peoples' efforts to regain their physical, mental, and spiritual health.

■ Social workers support the incorporation and use of traditional medicines and healing practices within their employing agencies and advocate for funding parity with payers. The incorporation of effective traditional health practices and healing methods into health care will accord it the same legitimacy as effective Western practices.

■ Social workers recognize and acknowledge the culture, heritage, and environmental and economic well-being of indigenous peoples that have been grievously endangered and in so doing support and honor the preservation of the traditional spiritual, health, and cultural practices of indigenous peoples.

■ NASW advocates and supports the rights of indigenous peoples in their efforts to gain health and self-determination and sustain the physical, emotional, and spiritual health of these people that are consistent with the principles, values, and roles of social work.

■ NASW supports all efforts to educate and train indigenous peoples in the profession of social work as practitioners, educators, and policymakers.

■ NASW advocates and supports the integration of cultural content related to patients' rights and in the treatment of disease.

REFERENCES

Berger, T. (1985). *Village journey: The report of the Alaska native review commission.* New York: Hill and Wang.

Blaisdell, K. (1996). *Autobiography of protest in Hawaii.* In R. H. Mast & A. B. Mast (Eds.) Honolulu: University of Hawaii Press.

Kamauu, M. (1989/1992). The historical precedence for sovereignty. In *He Alo A He Alo: Hawaiian voices on sovereignty.* Honolulu: American Friends Service Committee.

Lally, E. M., & Haynes, H. A. (1995). Alaska natives. In R. L. Edwards (Ed.-in-Chief), *Encyclopedia of social work* (19th ed., Vol. 1, pp. 194–203). Washington, DC: NASW Press.

Lewis, R. G. (1995). American Indians. In R. L. Edwards (Ed.-in-Chief), *Encyclopedia of social work* (19th ed., Vol. 1, pp. 216–225). Washington, DC: NASW Press.

Look, M., & Braun, K. (1995). *A mortality study of the Hawaiian people 1910–1990.* Honolulu: Queen's Health System.

U.S. Senate. (2001). Committee on Indian Affairs. *Expressing the policy of the United States regarding the United States relationship with Native Hawaiians.* Prepared by Daniel K. Inouye. 107th Cong., 1st sess., Report 107-66, Calendar No. 165. Available: www.nativehawaiians.com/pdf/crn107.66.pdf

Workman, R. (1999). *Safe and drug free schools and communities study of youth risk behaviors community development report, 1999.* Mangilao: University of Guam, Guam Cooperative Extension.

Policy statement approved by the NASW Delegate Assembly, August 2002. For further information, contact the National Association of Social Workers, 750 First Street, NE, Suite 700, Washington, DC 20002-4241. Telephone: 202-408-8600; e-mail: press@naswdc.org

Technology and Social Work

BACKGROUND

The seminal contribution of Mary Richmond offers the first mention of technology and social work. Richmond (1917) noted the importance of using the telephone in social work practice. At the turn of the 20th century social workers were somewhat uncertain of telephone technology. However, they eventually accepted the telephone as an important practice tool. More recently, social work has been challenged by the reconciliation of social work values and ethics with the utilization of technology as evidenced by the introduction of the telephone in the 19th century up through our current digital age.

Three unlikely technological streams of historical connections led to useful computer applications for social work practice. First, military applications were the impetus for computers (Burks & Burks, 1988) and the Internet (Marson, 1997). Although these applications were clear improvements for war and defense goals, they were neither user friendly or affordable. Highly specialized university professors produced much of the advances in technological war and defense applications. Because of the second connection, academic freedom, the advances in military technology were spread throughout the academic community—including schools of social work. Although academic social workers were employing computer-related technologies to social service research, these technological advances were not user friendly and could not be efficiently applied to social work practice. Here enters the third connection—commercialization of technology. Starting in the early 1960s (Redin, 2007), technology entrepreneurs were motivated by profit to reduce costs and to make technology user friendly. Even with such rapid advances in reducing cost and increasing user friendliness, resistance among social workers to use computer technology as a tool for daily practice is well documented (Huff & Edwards, 1998; Lamb, 1990). With his 1981 inaugural issue of a newsletter titled *Computer Use in Social Services Network Newsletter*, Dick Schoech advocated for the integration of technology in social work practice. In 1985, Schoech's newsletter evolved into a practice journal, the *Journal of Technology in Human Services*, and thus had a greater impact. However, unlike military and business uses of technology, social worker applications demanded understanding more than merely when it can be used and how it works.

"Technology has changed the educational landscape in terms of how information is delivered and to whom, the speed of access to information, and in terms of choice of options for courses, programs, and colleges and universities" (Truluck, 2007). Social work education is part of that landscape.

ISSUE STATEMENT

The evolution and proliferation of information technologies has expanded the ways in which social workers provide services to clients, administer agencies, educate practitioners, and conduct research and evaluation. Accompanying these dramatic developments are a number of compelling issues for social workers that include direct practice, management, education, and research.

Direct Practice

Electronically mediated communication technologies make practice possible on a global scale and with all sizes of systems. With improving interactive technology, both direct practice and consultation can take place between people who are separated in space and time. This use of technology poses new challenges for social workers in establishing therapeutic relationships, making appropriate assessments and referrals, monitoring and evaluating interventions, and providing emergency assistance. Information technology use is becoming increasingly frequent for practitioners, which raises ethical issues surrounding their use, such as document loss or interception and lack of privacy, "Confidentiality in an electronic medium can quickly evaporate; jurisdiction, liability, and malpractice issues blur when state lines and national boundaries are crossed electronically" (NASW, 2005).

Management

Managerial uses of various technologies for administrative work, including fiscal planning, scheduling, billing, and human resources have long been a part of agency practice. Such information is valuable for designing agency systems and program planning. Social workers are also challenged to manage information systems related to client data. However, information about client systems and employees must be protected from access and use without the person's knowledge or permission, and in ways that may not be in the best interests of consumers or the profession. Ethical and pragmatic decisions must be made about the collection, storage, retrieval, and protection of client and employee information.

Education

The advances in educational technology systems have now become an alternative to traditional instruction. This has led to significant changes in how social work curriculums are constructed and delivered. Students can now access educational learning in many different environments, for example, interactive television (ITV), Blackboard, interactive bulletin boards, e-mail, software-based program instruction, net meetings, chat rooms, pod-casts and the World Wide Web (East et al., 2006).

Classes that lend themselves to these various instruction modalities are necessary. Miller and King (2003) stated the selection of technologies should be based on appropriateness for the learner and the curriculum. Consideration should be given to student learning styles and to cultural and individual differences.

Faculty development and continued technological skill training benefit not only students but also the faculty member. According to Regan (2005), curriculum committees must provide guidance and supportive processes for faculty who are interested in teaching distance education courses.

Distance education has been an asset to rural communities where technology is promoting new and innovative partnerships. Collaborative higher education programs provide students in rural areas access to online masters' programs with accredited social work programs in other states. Heitkamp (2007) noted low wages and out migration from rural areas have resulted in a workforce shortage in mental health, addiction, and child welfare practitioners, particularly in rural and reservation communities. This technology could allow rural students to remain in their home communities and ultimately practice in rural or underserved areas.

In addition, Web-based continuing education programs are now being offered by many social work professional organizations and universities. "The proliferation of distance learning programs, coursework, and new technologies allows the lifelong learner the ability to continually advance his/her skills in a changing knowledge and digital economy, anywhere, and at any time" (Portugal, 2006).

The use of information technology must also be addressed when designing professional development and in-service trainings. Education and training should include legal, ethical, and competency-based standards.

Research Issues

The social work profession is strengthened when practitioners use the evidence from social work research to guide their choice of practice interventions and to evaluate their effectiveness. Social work researchers contribute to the knowledge base of the social work profession by developing, organizing, and implementing research founded on sound, ethical principles. Although technology has enabled faster access to and use of data, social work researchers continue to safeguard the confidentiality of client records, follow human subjects' protection guidelines, and understand the importance of gathering valid and reliable data. It is also important for social work researchers to disseminate their findings widely and advocate for the advancement of ethical human subjects research in general, and for practitioners to use these findings to help guide their work to improve the quality of life for individuals, families, groups, organizations, and the communities in which all function.

Ethical Issues

Although the last two decades have revolutionized technology in all aspects of social work practice, "social workers should ensure that the use of technology conforms to all practice and regulatory standards addressing ethical conduct and protection of the public" (NASW, 2005).

The NASW *Code of Ethics* (NASW, 2000) also recommends that social workers take precautions to ensure and maintain the confidentiality of information transmitted to other parties through the use of computers, electronic mail, facsimile machines, telephone and telephone answering machines, and other electronic or computer technology.

As technology continues to influence social work knowledge and practice, ethical issues will continue to be monitored and revised.

POLICY STATEMENT

It is important that the use of technology in social work be directed by the social work values and ethics that are the essential principles of the profession. With this in mind, NASW supports

■ the maintenance, review, and revision of competencies for the use of technology in social work practice. These competencies are based in the areas of direct and indirect prac-

tice, management, social work education, and research.

■ a continuing leadership role in using technology to improve service to NASW members and to further the goal and mission of the association.

■ advocacy efforts for the efficiency and efficacy of technology on the profession and its clients.

■ policies that promote informing clients about the process, associated benefits and risks, and their rights and responsibilities when technology is used in practice.

■ adequate resources to ensure the availability and accessibility of basic technology to all members of society, especially in rural and underserved areas.

■ public funding for the advancement of technology.

■ policies that ensure that technology does no harm to people, in particular support of the Internal Review Board process.

REFERENCES

Burks, A. R., & Burks, A. W. (1988). *The first electronic computer: The Atanasoff story.* Ann Arbor: University of Michigan Press.

East, J., Alter, C., Haddow, J., La Mendola, W., Molidor, C., Petrila, A., & Walls, N. G. (2006). *Distance education for social work education: models, technologies, and best practices.* Proposal submitted to the Council on Social Work Education Commission of Reaccreditation.

Heitkamp, T. (2007). *Twenty years later: Lessons learned in administering distance education programs: Preparing the next generation of educators.* Paper presented at the 53rd Annual Program Meeting, Council of Social Work Education: San Francisco.

Huff, M. T., & Edwards, S. L. (1998, March 6). *Using electronic journals in social work education.* Paper presented at the 44th Annual Program Meeting of the Council on Social Work Education, Orlando, FL.

Lamb, J. A. (1990). Teaching computer literacy to human service students. In R. L. Reinoehl & B. J. Mueller (Eds.), *Computer literacy in human service* (pp. 31–43). Binghamton, NY: Haworth Press.

Marson, S. M. (1997). A selective history of the Internet technology and social work. *Computers in Human Services, 14*, 35–49.

Miller, T. W., & King F. B. (2003). Distance education: Pedagogy and best practices in the new millennium. *International Journal of Leadership in Education, 6*, 283–297.

National Association of Social Workers. (2000). *Code of ethics of the National Association of Social Workers.* Washington, DC: NASW Press.

National Association of Social Workers. (2005). *NASW & ASWB Standards for Technology and Social Work Practice.* Washington, DC: Author.

Portugal, L. M. (2006). Emerging leadership roles in distance education: Current state of affairs and forecasting future trends. *Online Journal of Distance Learning Administration, 9*(3). Retrieved February 19, 2008, from http://westga.edu/~distance/ojdla/fall93/portugal93.htm

Redin, J. (2007). *The calculator wars.* Retrieved November 16, 2007, from http://www.xnumber.com/history_pages/history6.htm

Regan, J. R. C. (2005). Faculty issues in distance education. In P. Abel (Ed.), *Distance education in social work* (pp. 119–139). New York: Springer.

Richmond, M. E. (1917). *Social diagnosis.* New York: Russell Sage Foundation.

Truluck, J. (2007, Spring). Establishing a mentoring plan for improving retention in online graduate degree programs. *Online Journal of Distance Learning Administration, 10*(1). Retrieved February 19, 2008, from http://westga.edu/~distance/ojdla/spring101/truluck101.htm

Policy statement approved by the NASW Delegate Assembly, August 2008. This policy statement supersedes the policy statement on Technology and Social Work approved by the Delegate Assembly in 1999 and referred by the 2005 Delegate Assembly to the 2008 Delegate Assembly. For further information, contact the National Association of Social Workers, 750 First Street, NE, Suite 700, Washington, DC 20002-4241. Telephone: 202-408-8600 or 800-638-8799; e-mail: press@naswdc.org

Transgender and Gender Identity Issues

BACKGROUND

Gender is a human social system of differentiation by sex for roles, behaviors, characteristics, appearances, and identities (for example, "man" or "woman"), which maps cultural meanings and norms about both sex and gender onto human bodies. Everyone has an internal sense of his or her "gender," and this sense is called "gender identity" (Stone, 2004). "Most people's gender identity is congruent with their assigned sex, but many people experience their gender identity to be discordant with their natal sex" (Lev, 2004, p. 397).

"Transgender" is a broad term used to describe those whose gender, gender identity, or gender expression is in some sense different from, or transgresses social norms for, their assigned birth sex. Transgender may include those who identify as being transsexual, cross-dressers, androgynous, bi-gender, no-gender, multi-gender, genderqueer, and a growing number of people who do not identify as belonging to any gender category at all. For some transgender individuals the discomfort with social gender role is accompanied by a profound sense of mismatch of the physical body to their internal bodily experience. This body dysphoria (known as "gender dysphoria") causes significant distress, negatively affects daily functioning and well-being, and requires medical services to realign the body with the self. Although there are many transgender people with medically diagnosed intersex conditions (Xavier, Honnold, & Bradford, 2007) most people with intersex conditions are not transgender (Intersex Society of North America, n.d.; Koyama, n.d.).

In the absence of systematic data collection, estimates vary widely as to the number of transgender individuals in the United States, ranging from 3 million to as many as 9 million individuals (Bushong, 1995; Olyslager & Conway, 2007). Prevalence of transgender identities is "likely to be on the order of at least 1:100 (i.e., 1%)" (Olyslager & Conway, 2007, p. 23), and transsexualism is also not rare, with prevalence now being estimated at between 1:2000 and 1:500 (Olyslager & Conway, 2007). Reports now indicate there may be roughly equal numbers of male-to-female and female-to-male transsexual people (Bullough, Bullough, & Elias, 1997; MacKenzie, 1994).

Transgender people encounter difficulties in virtually every aspect of their lives, both in facing the substantial hostility that society associates with those who do not conform to gender norms and in coping with their own feelings of difference. Considerable verbal harassment and physical violence accompany the powerful social stigma faced by transgender people (Clements-Nolles, Marx, & Katz, 2006; Lombardi, Wilchins, Priesing, & Malouf, 2001; Wyss, 2004) and may be accompanied by racial and ethnic discrimination (Juang, 2006). Transgender people also experience dismissal from jobs, eviction from housing, and denial of services, even by police officers and medical emergency professionals (Xavier, 2000; Xavier, Honnold, & Bradford, 2007). Restrooms, the most mundane of public and workplace amenities, often become sites of harassment and confrontation, with access often denied (Transgender Law Center, 2005).

Transgender and transsexual people are often denied appropriate medical and mental health care and are uniquely at risk of adverse health outcomes (Dean et al., 2000; Xavier et al., 2004). Basic services may be denied because of ignorance about or discomfort with a transgender client. To align the physical body with the experienced sense of self, usually as an integral part of social transition away from the sex assigned at birth, transsexuals and some other individuals require medical services (for example, hormone replacement, facial electrolysis, or surgical and other procedures, as appropriate to the individual). Despite ongoing evidence that the vast majority who access such services achieve congruence and well-being (De Cuypere et al., 2005; Newfield, Hart, Dibble, & Kohler, 2006; Pfafflin & Junge, 1998; Rehman, Lazer, Benet, Schaefer, & Melman, 1999; Ross & Need, 1989), medical and mental health providers routinely refuse to provide such services, and health insurance carriers and governmental payers (for example, Medicare, Medicaid, VA, and Tri-Care) routinely deny coverage for them, sometimes under the belief that such care is "experimental" or "cosmetic" (Dean et al., 2000; JSI Research and Training Institute, Inc., 2000; Middleton, 1997; Spack, 2005; Spade, 2006; Thaler, 2007). Access to medically necessary transition-related services is thus largely limited to a privileged few who can pay out-of-pocket for services. Continued barriers to health care may have been shown to contribute to lowered self-esteem and well being, or may be experienced as posttraumatic stress, and may lead some to self-medicate through street hormones or over-the-counter treatments or to resort to high-risk injection silicone use—all without medical supervision (Risser & Shelton, 2002; Xavier, 2000). It is important to underscore the denial of basic health care, and also the extreme race and socioeconomic status disparities: Needs assessments in major cities show that severe marginalization and barriers to transition contribute to high rates of joblessness and disproportionately affect people of color. Lack of employment leaves many without health insurance, and because insurance carriers often deny coverage for transgender individuals' other nontransition-related services, transgender individuals often lack access to all ongoing basic health services, even when employed (Xavier et al., 2004).

Gender identity disorder, or GID (American Psychiatric Association, 2000), a diagnosis often required by providers as a prerequisite to transgender transition-related health services, is also seen as a barrier to health care. GID has been criticized for further stigmatizing nontypical gender expression and reinforcing gender stereotypes, for pathologizing transgender realities as mental illness, and for failing to accurately describe the "symptoms" experienced by transsexual people. The diagnosis is vague regarding the medical necessity for and demonstrated success of treatment, particularly medically assisted transsexual transition, which prevents insurance reimbursements for care and leaves transgender youths and adults vulnerable to so-called "reparative" treatment (Bockting & Ehrbar, 2005; Hill, Rozanski, Carfagnini, & Willoughby, 2005; Lev, 2005; Spack, 2005; Winters, 2005). Although some individuals experience the current diagnosis as a good fit, many transgender health advocates seek either greatly revised language or a medical (physical, nonpsychiatric) diagnosis to replace it (Green, 2004; Lev, 2004; Stone, 2004).

Mental health providers, including social workers, are often positioned as "gatekeepers" in the medical process (for example, as providers of referrals for hormonal therapy and surgery), which may hamper the therapeutic alliance between them and their transgender clients. More recently, many community-based urban clinics and individual providers have developed protocols and practices that do not require a GID diagnosis (Lev, 2004; Tom Waddell Health Center, 2001). Clients benefit from treatment with therapists who have expertise in transgender issues (Lurie, 2005; Rachlin, 2002). Those therapists with little training or familiarity in this arena often require that a diagnosis be assigned, and apply its criteria narrowly, denying access to nontranssexual transgender people or forcing clients to wait months or years before they can obtain medicalized transition services (Califia, 1997; Lev, 2004; Meyerowitz, 2002).

Many transgender children and youths face harassment and violence in school environments, and those who do not feel safe or valued at school cannot reach their potential and may drop out (D'Augelli, Grossman, & Starks, 2006; Gay, Lesbian and Straight Education Network, 2004; Grossman, D'Augelli, & Slater, 2006; Wyss, 2004). Although medical protocols exist for children whose body dysphoria may lead to severe depression and suicidality, including endocrinologic intervention to prevent or delay unwanted puberty (Cohen-Kettenis & van Goozen, 1997; Smith, van Goozen, & Cohen-Kettenis, 2001; Spack, 2005), there are still few support resources for transgender children, their parents, or surrounding social institutions, leaving transgender youths particularly vulnerable to so-called "reparative" treatments. (Menvielle, Tuerk, & Perrin, 2005; PFLAG, 2004).

Although there is no federal law protecting individuals from discrimination on the basis of gender identity or gender expression, a handful of states and a growing number of local jurisdictions, as well as employers, are beginning to extend such protections (Lambda Legal Defense Fund, n.d.). Federal administrations and most states require proof of genital or other surgery before altering the sex marker on passports, birth certificates, or other documents. Such policies reinforce the myth that all transgender people undergo a single "sex change operation," regardless of an individual's need or ability to undergo, or afford, transition procedures (Thaler, 2007). Inaccurate identity documentation is a common barrier to employment, housing, and appropriate services from gender-segregated facilities. The increased vulnerability—to violence and harassment, to loss of social support and mounting despair—suggests that policies that prevent changing documentation to align with gender identity represent serious barriers to health and well-being. Transsexual individuals and their partners may also be denied access to civil marriage on the basis that they are in a same-sex relationship (Minter, 2003) or be denied access to same-sex domestic partnerships or to same-sex domestic partnerships on the basis that they are in an opposite-sex relationship, and thus are denied access to the social status, rights, and privileges of civil marriage or domestic partnerships.

A host of institutional settings in the United States are hostile to transgender people, especially those that are segregated by sex, many of which require transgender individuals to have undergone genital surgery to be placed according to their gender identity. Homeless shelters and other facilities that refuse to house clients with the appropriate gender place individuals at risk of sexual propositions, harassment, and assault. Sex-based dress codes affect youths in particular, who are often disciplined and ejected from the facilities for violating such policies (Mottet & Ohle, 2003; Ray, 2006). Those incarcerated in jails and prisons face similar barriers to accessing gender-appropriate facilities, and in many jurisdictions, transgender people in state custody are also denied access to ongoing hormone therapy and other transgender transition-related procedures, including surgery (Jenness et al., 2007; Rosenblum, 2000; Sylvia Rivera Law Project, 2007; Thaler, 2007; Women in Prison Project, 2007). Although few resources exist regarding aging and the transgender population, residential and care facilities may pose familiar barriers such as sex segregation and lack of culturally competent caregivers at a time of life when transgender individuals may be unable to advocate for themselves; many older transgender people may also fear abuse and neglect (Cook-Daniels, 1997, 2002; Gapka & Raj, 2003).

Lack of appropriately trained service providers, including mental health providers, makes it hard to obtain culturally competent legal, medical, and advocacy services (Lurie, 2005; Xavier et al., 2004). Although social workers are frontline providers of mental health and other services for many transgender individuals, most schools of social work have little in their curriculums on transgender issues.

Transgender individuals and communities are increasingly impatient with a backseat role in shaping policies that affect their lives. In the face of stigma, increasing numbers of transgender individuals are becoming powerful community advocates and are encouraging others to join with them.

ISSUE STATEMENT

Transgender people experience the stigma, prejudice, discrimination, and extreme hostility known as transphobia on a daily basis. Although gender nonconforming experience can be traced across history and the successful social and medical transition of transsexuals is well documented since the middle of the 20th century, only in recent years has this emerged in the public discourse. Unfortunately, most in our society have little or no understanding of the profound discomfort some may feel in trying to conform to rigid gender roles assigned to them by virtue of their physiology. Similarly, ignorance and insensitivity prevail regarding the debilitating distress that accompanies body dysphoria, and the damage done to those left without access to medical and social transition.

Social workers have the responsibility to understand and appreciate the full range of differences that exist among human beings and to explore any and all prejudices that result in oppressive and unjust treatment. It is incumbent upon the social work profession to embrace and explore this domain of human variation and help educate the public in a manner that mitigates stigma and supports the rights of transgender, transsexual, and gender nonconforming individuals, consistent with NASW's *Code of Ethics* (2000) which states the following:

■ "Social workers should not practice, condone, facilitate, or collaborate with any form of discrimination on the basis of race, ethnicity, national origin, color, sex, sexual orientation, age, marital status, political belief, religion, or mental or physical disability." (pp. 22–23)

■ "Social workers should act to expand choice and opportunity for all people, with special regard for vulnerable, disadvantaged, oppressed, and exploited people and groups." (p. 27)

■ "Social workers should promote conditions that encourage respect for cultural and social diversity within the United States and globally. Social workers should promote policies and practices that demonstrate respect for difference, support the expansion of cultural knowledge and resources, advocate for programs and institutions that demonstrate cultural competence, and promote policies that safeguard the rights of and confirm equity and social justice for all people." (p. 27)

Social workers are trained to work with clients who are different along many dimensions of diversity. Gender-diverse individuals should be included among this constituency. As clinicians, social workers must be equipped to provide their clients with education and re-sources on gender experience, gender expression and sexuality, including specific examples of successful role models in society. Social workers must also be prepared to provide services and referrals for those clients who may require social or medical transition to a sex different from that assigned at birth. All legal impediments to the full equality of rights and opportunities for anyone, regardless of that person's gender identity or expression must be eliminated. Individuals, families, schools, and communities should have the resources to welcome and support gender-diverse people. At the community and policy-making levels, inclusive environments and provision for access to services should all be respected, valued, and empowered. Social workers should be partnered with the transgender community to modify laws, medical protocols, research, and policies in ways that preserve and protect the quality of life for transgender, transsexual, and gender nonconforming citizens. In the domain of gender diversity, prejudice and oppression should be replaced with compassion, support, and celebration of difference.

POLICY STATEMENT

NASW recognizes the considerable diversity in gender expression and identity among our population. NASW believes that people of diverse gender—including all those who are included under the transgender umbrella—should be afforded the same respect and rights as that for any other people. NASW asserts that discrimination and prejudice directed against any individuals on the basis of gender identity or gender expression, whether real or perceived, are damaging to the social, emotional, psychological, physical, and economic well-being of the affected individuals, as well as society as a whole, and NASW seeks the elimination of the same both inside and outside the profession, in public and private sectors.

NASW believes that a nonjudgmental and affirming attitude toward gender diversity enables social workers to provide maximum support and services to those whose gender departs from the expected norm. Social workers and the social work profession can support and empower such people in all aspects of their development, helping them to lead fully actualized and engaged lives on the basis of their genuine gender identities. NASW supports the development of supportive and knowledgeable practice environments for those struggling with gender expression and identity issues (both clients and colleagues) and for those who are struggling with prejudices, biases, and transphobia.

Professional and Continuing Education

■ NASW supports curriculum policies in schools of social work that eliminate discrimination against those who are transgender, transsexual, genderqueer, cross-dressers, and of other minority gender identities; provide equal opportunities to all students for investigating issues of relevance to these populations; develop and provide training for classroom instructors, field supervisors, and field advisors regarding gender diversity issues; and seek field opportunities for students interested in working with transgender people.

■ NASW encourages the implementation of continuing education programs on practice and policy issues relevant to gender diversity, to include the distinctive, complex biopsychosocial needs of transgender individuals and their families, legal and employment issues, ethical dilemmas and responsibilities, and effective interventions and community resources.

Antidiscrimination

■ NASW reaffirms a commitment to human rights and freedom and opposes all public and private discrimination on the basis of gender identity and of gender expression, whether actual or perceived, and regardless of assigned sex at birth, including denial of access to employment, housing, education, appropriate treatment in gender segregated facilities, appropriate medical care and health care coverage, appropriate identity documents, and civil marriage and all its attendant benefits, rights, and privileges.

■ NASW encourages the repeal of discriminatory legislation and the passage of legislation protecting the rights, legal benefits, and privileges of people of all gender identities and expressions.

■ NASW encourages all institutions that train or employ social workers to broaden any nondiscriminatory statement made to students, faculty, staff, or clients, to include "gender identity or expression" in all nondiscrimination statements.

Public Awareness and Advocacy

■ NASW supports efforts to provide safe and secure educational environments, at all levels of education, that promote an understanding and acceptance of self and in which all youths, including youths of all gender identities and expressions, may be free to express their genuine gender identity and obtain an education free from discrimination, harassment, violence, and abuse.

■ NASW supports the development of, and participation in, coalitions with other professional associations and progressive organizations to lobby on behalf of the civil rights for all people of diverse gender expression and identity.

■ NASW supports collaboration with organizations and groups supportive of the transgender community to develop programs to increase public awareness of the mistreatment and discrimination experienced by transgender people and of the contributions they make to society.

■ NASW encourages the development of programs, training, and information that promote proactive efforts to eliminate psychological, social, and physical harm directed toward transgender people and to portray them accurately and compassionately.

■ NASW supports the development of programs within schools and other child and youth services agencies that educate students, faculty, and staff about the range of gender diversity and the needs of transgender children and youths.

■ NASW supports the creation of scientific and educational resources that inform public discussion about gender identity and gender diversity, to promote public policy development and to strengthen societal and familial attitudes and behaviors that affirm the dignity and rights of all individuals, regardless of gender identity or gender expression.

Health and Mental Health Services

■ NASW endorses policies in the public and private sectors that ensure nondiscrimination, that are sensitive to the health and mental health needs of transgender people, and that promote an understanding of gender expression and gender identity issues.

■ NASW advocates for the availability of comprehensive psychological and social support services for transgender people and their families that are respectful and sensitive to individual concerns.

■ NASW supports the rights of all individuals to receive health insurance and other health coverage without discrimination on the basis of gender identity, and specifically without exclusion of services related to transgender or transsexual transition (or sex change), to receive medical and mental health services through their primary care physician and the appropriate referrals to medical specialists, which may include hormone replacement therapy, surgical interventions, prosthetic devices, and other medical procedures.

■ NASW encourages the development of an appropriate, non-stigmatizing medical diagnosis for transgender individuals whose self-experienced gender does not match the sex assigned at birth and who require medical services to align the body with the experienced self.

■ NASW supports the collaboration of organizations with the U.S. surgeon general to implement data collection and production of comprehensive reports on prevention of hate crimes against adults and youth violence prevention, including such issues as bullying, prejudice, and discrimination, including violence and discrimination that are based on gender identity, gender expression, or both.

■ NASW advocates for the implementation of programs to address the education, housing, employment, health, and mental health needs of adults and youths who are struggling with gender issues and who are thus at high risk of suicide, vulnerable to violence or assault, at increased risk of HIV/AIDS, or otherwise at risk.

■ NASW supports the creation of a national health survey that incorporates a representative sample of the U.S. population of all ages (including adolescents); that includes questions on gender identity, gender expression, and sexual orientation; and that explores the barriers to health care experienced by transgender people. NASW also supports inclusion of transgender individuals in existing national and state health surveys and data collection, by inclusion of questions on gender identity, to enable research on health and other disparities in the transgender population.

Legal and Political Action

■ NASW advocates for increased funding for education, treatment services, and research on behalf of people of diverse gender expression and gender identity.

■ NASW supports the legal recognition of transgender individuals as members of the gender with which they identify, regardless of assigned sex at birth or subsequent surgical or other medical interventions.

■ NASW supports the legal recognition of marriage, domestic partnership, and civil unions, regardless of either the sex or gender status of the betrothed or partnered individuals.

■ NASW encourages the repeal of laws and discriminatory practices that impede individuals in their identification with, and their expression of, the gender that matches their sense of themselves, in all areas of the public arena, especially employment, health care, education, and housing, including in custodial settings.

■ NASW encourages the adoption of laws that will prohibit discrimination against, protect the civil rights of, and preserve the access to health care and well-being of, individuals who identify with and express their gender identities, in education, housing, inheritance, health and other types of insurance, child custody, property, and other areas. NASW particularly encourages such protections in education; housing, including custodial settings; inheritance and pensions; health coverage and all other types of insurance; provision of health care and medical services; child custody; property; as well as other areas.

■ NASW acknowledges the importance of social group work and community organizing to support transgender community development and help the larger community to overcome ignorance and fear of transgender people, and to move toward inclusion, equality, and justice.

REFERENCES

American Psychiatric Association. (2000). *Diagnostic and statistical manual of mental disorders* (4th ed., text rev.). Washington, DC: Author.

Bockting, W. O., & Ehrbar, R. D. (2005). Commentary: Gender variance, dissonance, or identity disorder? *Journal of Human Sexuality, 17*(3/4), 125–134.

Bullough, V. L., Bullough, B., & Elias, J. (1997). *Gender blending.* New York: Prometheus Books.

Bushong, C. W. (1995). The multi-dimensionality of gender. *Transgender Tapestry, 72,* 33–37.

Califia, P. (1997). *Sex changes: The politics of transgenderism.* San Francisco: Cleis Press.

Clements-Nolles, K., Marx, R., & Katz, M. (2006). Attempted suicide among transgender persons: The influence of gender-based discrimination and victimization. *Journal of Homosexuality, 51*(3), 53–69.

Cohen-Kettenis, P. T., & van Goozen, S. H. M. (1997). Sex reassignment of adolescent transsexuals: A follow-up study. *Journal of the American Academy of Child and Adolescent Psychiatry, 36*(2), 263–271.

Cook-Daniels, L. (1997). Lesbian, gay male, bisexual and transgendered elders: Elder abuse and neglect issues. *Journal of Elder Abuse & Neglect, 9*(2), 35–49.

Cook-Daniels, L. (2002). *Transgender elders and SOFFAS: A primer.* Paper presented at the 110th Convention of the American Psychological Association. Retrieved August 13, 2004, from http://www.forge-forward.org/handouts/TransEldersSOFFAs-web.pdf

D'Augelli, A. R., Grossman, A. H., & Starks, M. T. (2006). Childhood gender atypicality, victimization, and PTSD among lesbian, gay, and bisexual youth. *Journal of Interpersonal Violence, 21,* 1462–1482.

Dean, L., Meyer, I. H., Robinson, K., Sell, R. L., Sember, R., Silenzio, V. M. B., Bowen, D. J., Bradford, J., Rothblum, E., White, J., Dunn, P., Lawrence, A., Wolfe, D., & Xavier, J. (2000). Lesbian, gay, bisexual, and transgender health: Findings and concerns. *Journal of the Gay and Lesbian Medical Association, 4*(3), 102–151.

De Cuypere, G., T'Sjoen, G., Beerten, R., Selvaggi, G., De Sutter, P., Hoebeke, P., Monstrey, S., Vansteenwegen, A., & Rubens, R. (2005). Sexual and physical health after sex reassignment surgery. *Archives of Sexual Behavior, 34,* 679–690.

Gapka, S., & Raj, R. (2003). *Trans Health Project: A position paper and resolution.* Retrieved July 14, 2007, from: http://www.opha.on.ca/ppres/2003-06_pp.pdf

Gay, Lesbian and Straight Education Network. (2004). *2003 National School Climate Survey: The school-related experiences of our nation's lesbian, gay, bisexual and transgender youth.* New York: Author.

Green, J. (2004). *Becoming a visible man.* Nashville, TN: Vanderbilt University Press.

Grossman, A. H., D'Augelli, A. R., & Slater, N. P. (2006). Male-to-female transgender youth: Gender expression milestones, gender atypicality, victimization, and parents' responses. *Journal of GLBT Family Studies, 2*(1), 71–92.

Hill, D. B., Rozanski, C., Carfagnini, J., & Willoughby, B. (2005). Gender identity disorders in childhood and adolescence: A critical inquiry. *Journal of Human Sexuality, 17*(3/4), 7–34.

Intersex Society of North America. (n.d.). *What's the difference between being transgender or transsexual and having an intersex condition?* Retrieved July 15, 2007, from http://www .isna.org/faq/transgender

Jenness, V., Maxson, C. L., Matsuda, K. N., & Sumner, J. M. (2007, April). *Violence in California correctional facilities: An empirical examination of sexual assault.* Report submitted to the California Department of Corrections & Rehabilitation, Center for Evidence-Based Corrections, University of California, Irvine.

JSI Research and Training Institute, Inc. (2000). *Access to health care for transgendered persons in greater Boston.* Boston: Author.

Juang, R. M. (2006). Transgendering the politics of recognition. In S. Stryker & S. Whittle (Eds.), *The transgender studies reader* (pp. 706–717). New York: Routledge.

Koyama, E. (n.d.). *Is gender identity disorder an intersex condition?* Retrieved July 12, 2007, from http://www.intersexinitiative.org/ articles/gid.html

Lambda Legal Defense Fund. (n.d.). *The rights of transgender people.* Retrieved May 7, 2007, from http://www.lambdalegal.org/our-work/issues/rights-of-transgender-people/

Lev, A. I. (2004). *Transgender emergence: Therapeutic guidelines for working with gender-variant people and their families.* Binghamton, NY: Haworth Clinical Practice Press.

Lev, A. I. (2005). Disordering gender identity: Gender identity in the DSM-IV-TR. *Journal of Human Sexuality, 17*(3/4), 35–69.

Lombardi, E. L., Wilchins, R. A., Priesing, D., & Malouf, D. (2001). Gender violence: Transgender experiences with violence and discrimination. *Journal of Homosexuality, 42*(1), 89–101.

Lurie, S. (2005). Identifying training needs of health-care providers related to treatment and care of transgendered patients: A qualitative needs assessment conducted in New England. *International Journal of Transgenderism, 3*(2/3), 93–112.

MacKenzie, G. O. (1994). *Transgender nation.* Bowling Green, OH: Bowling Green State University, Popular Press.

Menvielle, E. J., Tuerk, C., & Perrin, E. C. (2005). To the beat of a different drummer: The gender-variant child. *Contemporary Pediatrics, 22*(2), 38–46.

Meyerowitz, J. (2002). *How sex changed: A history of transsexuality in the United States.* Cambridge, MA: Harvard University Press.

Middleton L. (1997). Insurance and the reimbursement of transgender health care. In G. Israel & D. Tarver (Eds.), *Transgender care: Recommended guidelines, practical information & personal accounts* (pp. 215–224). Philadelphia: Temple University Press.

Minter, S. (2003). *Representing transsexual clients: Selected legal issues.* Retrieved August 3, 2004, from: http://www.transgenderlaw.org/ resources/translaw.htm

Mottet, L., & Ohle, J. (2003). *Transitioning our shelters: A guide to making homeless shelters safe for transgender people.* Retrieved September 9, 2005, from http://www.thetaskforce .org/reports_and_research/trans_homeless

National Association of Social Workers. (2000). *Code of ethics of the National Association of Social Workers.* Washington, DC: Author.

Newfield, E., Hart, S., Dibble, S., & Kohler, L. (2006). Female-to-male transgender quality of life. *Quality of Life Research, 15,* 1447–1457.

Olyslager, F., & Conway, L. (2007, September). *On the calculation of the prevalence of transsexualism.* Paper presented at the WPATH 20th International Symposium, Chicago.

Pfafflin, F., & Junge, A. (1998). *Sex reassignment. Thirty years of international follow-up studies after sex reassignment surgery: A comprehensive review, 1961–1991.* Retrieved November 22, 2007, from http://www.symposion.com/ijt/ pfaefflin/1000.htm

PFLAG North Bay Chapter. (2004). *The transgender umbrella: Parents, Families and Friends of Lesbians and Gays North Bay Chapter.* San Francisco: Author.

Rachlin, K. (2002). Transgendered individuals' experiences of psychotherapy. *International Journal of Transgenderism, 6*(1). Retrieved November 22, 2007, from http://www.sym posion.com/ijt/ijtvo06no01_03.htm

Ray, N. (2006). *Lesbian, gay, bisexual, and transgender youth: An epidemic of homelessness.* Washington, DC: National Gay and Lesbian Task Force Policy Institute and the National Coalition for the Homeless. Retrieved July 14, 2007, from http://www.thetaskforce .org/downloads/HomelessYouth.pdf

Rehman, J., Lazer, S., Benet, A. E., Schaefer, L. C., & Melman, A. (1999). The reported sex and surgery satisfactions of 28 postoperative male-to-female transsexual patients. *Archives of Sexual Behavior, 28*(1), 71–89.

Risser, J., & Shelton, A. (2002). *Behavioral assessment of the transgender population, Houston, Texas.* Galveston: University of Texas School of Public Health.

Rosenblum, D. (2000). 'Trapped' in Sing Sing: Transgendered prisoners caught in the gender binarism. *Michigan Journal of Gender & Law, 6,* 522–526.

Ross, M. W., & Need, J. A. (1989). Effects of adequacy of gender reassignment surgery on psychological adjustment: A follow-up of fourteen male-to-female patients. *Archives of Sexual Behavior, 18*(2), 145–153.

Smith, Y. L. S., van Goozen, S. H. M., & Cohen-Kettenis, P. T. (2001). Adolescents with gender identity disorder who were accepted or rejected for sex reassignment surgery: A prospective follow-up study. *Journal of American Academy of Child and Adolescent Psychiatry, 40,* 472–481.

Spack, N. (2005, Fall). Transgenderism. *Lahey Clinic Journal of Medical Ethics.* Retrieved February 13, 2007, from http://www.lahey.org/NewsPubs/Publications/Ethics/JournalFall2005/Journal_Fall2005_Feature.asp

Spade, D. (2006). Compliance is gendered: Struggling for self-determination in a hostile economy. In P. Currah, R. M. Juang, & S. M. Minter (Eds.), *Transgender rights* (pp. 217–241). Minneapolis: University of Minnesota Press.

Stone, M. R. (2004, September 10). *Gender identity is for everyone: Creating a paradigm of change.* Paper presented at the 6th International Congress on Sex and Gender Diversity, Manchester, England.

Sylvia Rivera Law Project. (2007). *It's war in here: A report on the treatment of transgender and intersex people in New York State men's prisons.* Retrieved March 19, 2008, from http://www.srlp.org/index.php?sec=03N&page=warinhere

Thaler, C. (2007). *Putting transgender health care myths on trial.* Retrieved July 14, 2007, from http://www.lambdalegal.org/our-work/publications/page.jsp?itemID=32007335

Tom Waddell Health Center. (2001). *Protocols for hormonal reassignment of gender.* Retrieved July 15, 2007, from http://www.dph.sf.ca.us/chn/HlthCtrs/HlthCtrDocs/TransGendprotocols.pdf

Transgender Law Center. (2005). *Peeing in peace: A resource guide for transgender activists and allies.* San Francisco: Author.

Winters, K. W. (2005). Gender dissonance: Diagnostic reform of gender identity for adults. *Journal of Human Sexuality, 17*(3/4), 71–89.

Women in Prison Project (WIPP). (2007). *Transgender issues and the criminal justice system.* Retrieved April 24, 2007, from http://www.correctionalassociation.org/publications/factsheets.htm

Wyss, S. E. (2004). 'This was my hell': The violence experienced by gender non-conforming youth in US high schools. *International Journal of Qualitative Studies in Education, 17,* 709–730.

Xavier, J. (2000). *Final report of the Washington Transgender Needs Assessment Survey.* Retrieved June 18, 2004, from http://www.gender.org/resources/dge/gea01011.pdf

Xavier, J., Hitchcock, D., Hollinshead, S., Keisling, M., Lewis, Y., Lombardi, E., Lurie, S., Sanchez, D., Singer, B., Stone, M. R., & Williams, B. (2004). *An overview of U.S. trans health priorities: A report by the Eliminating Disparities Working Group.* Retrieved March 26, 2006, from http://www.nctequality.org/HealthPriorities.pdf

Xavier, J., Honnold, J. A., & Bradford, J. (2007). *The health, health-related needs, and lifecourse experiences of transgender Virginians.* Richmond: Virginia Department of Health.

Policy statement approved by the NASW Delegate Assembly, August 2008. This policy statement supersedes the policy statement on Transgender and Gender Identity Issues approved by the Delegate Assembly in 1999 and referred by the 2005 Delegate Assembly to the 2008 Delegate Assembly for revision. For further information, contact the National Association of Social Workers, 750 First Street, NE, Suite 700, Washington, DC 20002-4241. Telephone: 202-408-8600 or 800-638-8799; e-mail: press@naswdc.org

Voter Participation

BACKGROUND

The concept of voter apathy can now be seen as a misplaced explanation for low voter participation in the United States. Although voter apathy is the most discussed and accepted reason for the lack of voter participation, events in the 2000 general elections revealed that many citizens encountered obstacles in casting their votes. Numerous reports of systemic failures throughout the country prompted many calls for electoral reform. Which citizens are eligible to vote, which citizens do vote, how efficiently they can vote, and how effectively their votes are counted, both numerically and collectively, are a more dramatic story than many citizens realized before the fall of 2000.

The 2000 general election highlighted several irregularities in U.S. electoral systems that usually go unnoticed by citizens, public officials, political parties, and commentators. In particular, the Florida election illuminated old and enduring problems in the harsh light of a closely contested presidential race. None of these problems are new. All are fundamental to current voting systems throughout the United States. The anomalies require close scrutiny and strong corrective action. Although the exceptions center on voting problems, they are symptomatic of larger flaws in the U.S. political system, including how to finance campaigns and elections, media reporting and operations, how ex-felons are treated as voters compared with military absentee voters, and the differences in election administration between richer and poorer areas.

The U.S. Supreme Court ultimately resolved the Florida vote count. Nationally, one major candidate received 500,000 more popular votes than the other major candidate, but the candidate who failed to receive the popular vote became the nation's 43rd president because he won more electoral votes.

The areas highlighted in the 2000 election included voting rights, voting mechanics, voting systems, and voter participation. *Voting rights* refers to issues such as which citizens are eligible to register to vote, how a citizen registers to vote, how a voter's registration is processed within particular voting jurisdictions, and how a voter exercises his or her right to vote in elections without intimidation, interference, or confusion. *Voting mechanics* refers to matters such as voting in a precinct or polling place; early voting; absentee ballot programs; and the location, staffing, and equipping of polling places. *Voting systems* refers to how votes are counted and tallied for candidates—winner take all, proportional representation, instant run-off voting, and fusion (a candidate can be the nominee of more than one party). *Voter participation* refers to which citizens in the electorate vote and which do not vote.

Apathy may be a problem for some citizens, but it may not be the biggest problem depressing voter participation. Information, political party outreach and mobilization, and opportunities to register and vote easily and efficiently may be more important factors. Although "voter apathy" leads people to believe that voter participation is the individual voter's problem, our government and elected officials, through their control over voting rights, voting mechanics, and voting systems, have a much greater impact over the participation of all voters. These four areas—voting rights, mechanics, systems, and voter participation—interact with each other in powerful ways to influence the outcome of elections and who will control the various offices of government throughout the U.S. political system. For example, less than 52 percent of eligible voters voted in the 2000 general elections. There were numerous stories from Florida about voters unable to vote at polling places, although properly registered, because their names had not been transferred from central registration files to their neighborhood precincts. Others did not get to vote because lines were too long and understaffed polling stations could not accommodate them. Other citizens reported being harassed or intimidated by authorities when they attempted to go to the polls. In one county the design of the ballot confused some voters, causing them to cast faulty votes.

The structural problems and difficulties in these four areas add new dimensions and insights to perceived problems of voter apathy. Two commentators have ascribed low voter turnout to other factors, such as lack of specific voter mobilization programs by political parties and technical barriers to participation (Piven & Cloward, 2000; Rakove, 2001).

A historian on voting in the United States noted that "the two major political parties are in the business of winning elections rather than promoting democracy, and elections can be won by disenfranchising opponents, making it procedurally difficult to vote or not counting their votes at all. As political professionals learned long ago, an electorate that is predictable in size and composition is generally far preferable to large turnouts and mass participation" (Keyssar, 2001, sec. 4, p. 13).

In fact in the 1996 elections, 17 percent of nonvoting registered people reported that they did not vote in 1996 because of apathy (U.S. Bureau of the Census, 1998). However, voter apathy alone does not fully explain this problem. According to the U.S. Bureau of the Census (1998), nearly 5 million registered voters said they did not vote because they could not take off from work or school or were otherwise too busy.

In surveying 601 voters and 602 nonvoters, the League of Women Voters (1998a) found that voters were more likely than nonvoters to recognize the effect of elections on issues of direct and personal concern. Voters were much more likely than nonvoters to perceive major differences between the parties on issues such

as jobs and economic security, social security, Medicare, taxes, and the deficit. And voters were much more likely than nonvoters to see a positive role for government in their lives.

The survey also found that nonvoters were less likely than voters to believe that they had access to accurate information about the candidates and their positions on issues; in other words, information that would help them understand the importance of an election and compel them to vote. One-third of the nonvoters said that they had very little or almost no accurate information when they were thinking about candidates they would vote for, compared with 13 percent of the voters (League of Women Voters, 1998a).

The National Voter Registration Act of 1993 (Motor–Voter Law) was passed to simplify the process of voter registration for all citizens, with the hope of removing one of the major procedural barriers to voter participation. This federal law requires states to register voters in three specific ways:

1. simultaneous application for driver's license and voter registration
2. mail application for voter registration
3. application in person at designated government agencies, including public assistance agencies and agencies that provide services to people with disabilities (League of Women Voters, 1998b).

Many states fought implementation of the Motor-Voter Law by using old "state's rights" arguments to inhibit temporarily increased voter registration throughout the country (Piven & Cloward, 2000). Only 66 percent of the voting-age population reported that they were registered in 1996, the lowest rate for any presidential election since 1968 (U.S. Bureau of the Census, 1998).

Because several states resisted full implementation of the Motor-Voter Law, numerous people in those states encountered difficulties on Election Day 2000 with casting ballots in their local precinct. Often precinct records were inaccurate, and the process for checking central registration files was inadequate and became a barrier to voting for many citizens. Other problems at local polling places included understaffing, unclear instructions on how to correct a voting mistake, faulty voting equipment, and poorly designed ballots that confused some voters. The widespread manifestation of so many voting problems prompted urgent calls for electoral reform across the political spectrum. Efforts to make voter registration simple and easy need to be supplemented by other reforms that help get all citizens to the polls and all votes counted accurately.

It is important for social workers to reorient themselves from the perspective of voter apathy to an understanding that voter participation should be a central goal in a democratic society. A perspective focused on voter participation provides a way for virtually every social worker in the United States to contribute to the goal of better voter turnout. Many laws are passed that adversely affect those who do not exercise their right to vote.

ISSUE STATEMENT

The low level of voter registration and participation in the United States represents a serious challenge to the values and ethical principles that guide the social work profession—democracy, self-determination, informed decision making, social justice, inclusion, diversity, empowerment, and participation. Many citizens who are not participating by voting complain that their votes do not count. Yet many laws are passed that adversely affect them.

The electoral process itself often discourages voters. Months before an election voters are bombarded by negative campaigning and special-interest advertising that prevent them from making an informed vote. Antiquated voting laws and individual states' indifference impede voters from obtaining equal access and opportunity to vote.

NASW has worked to expand social workers' involvement in the electoral process. Many social workers also have been leaders in local community activities to register voters and make all government more accessible and responsive to the average citizen. Given this tradition of commitment and involvement and the deepening crisis over low American voter participation among U.S. residents, it is imperative that NASW address voter reform issues.

POLICY STATEMENT

Low voter registration in the United States is a threat to the democratic process and to the U.S. political system. Voting is a basic right, and citizens should be assisted in all possible ways to exercise that right; any action that denies access or discourages any citizen from voting should be prohibited. Access to voter registration and polling places should be improved for all citizens, with special consideration for people with disabilities, homeless people, people of color, and elderly individuals.

Social workers are encouraged to work with and support established organizations and entities to increase voter registration and participation in all elections. Registration is a beginning step in the political empowerment of clients. Social workers are encouraged to help educate clients to be informed voters and to mobilize them to vote in elections. Social workers have a responsibility to model informed voter participation and to be involved in all levels and aspects of the political process. Social workers have a responsibility to advocate in the local, state, and federal legislatures for voting rights and increased voter access for their clients.

In support of voter registration reform laws and voter practices:

■ NASW supports full implementation of the National Voter Registration Act in all states, including voter registration activities by public and private social services agencies.

■ NASW supports continued efforts to reform and liberalize registration election laws.

■ NASW supports research into nontraditional methods of casting ballots to increase voter participation.

■ NASW supports efforts to make Election Day a national holiday for federal elections.

■ NASW supports the use of machinery and technology to assist individuals with disabilities in exercising their right to vote.

■ NASW supports the use of ballots in other languages.

■ NASW supports uniform national rules for all absentee ballots in federal elections.

- NASW supports a federal constitutional amendment establishing and protecting the right to vote.

- NASW supports the full restoration of voting rights for all ex-felons who have completed their sentences.

- NASW supports responsible and accurate media coverage to promote informed voter participation.

- NASW supports social workers who work to increase voter registration and to secure the electoral reforms outlined in this policy statement.

- NASW supports efforts to explore other voting systems such as proportional representation, instant run-off, and fusion (a candidate can be the nominee of more than one party).

- NASW supports federal and state campaign finance reform.

- NASW supports social workers working in polls and encourages active involvement in the administration of the electoral process.

- NASW supports the involvement of social work professionals and students in activities during the election process that work against the intimidation of voters, in particular in localities represented by historically oppressed populations.

- NASW supports the education of citizens on the importance of voting.

- NASW supports the extension of the Voting Rights Act of 1965.

REFERENCES

Keyssar, A. (2001, August 5). Reform and an evolving electorate. *New York Times*, sec. 4, p. 13, col. 2.

League of Women Voters. (1998a). *Alienation not a factor in nonvoting.* Available: http://www.lwv.org/elibrary/pub/mellman.htm

League of Women Voters. (1998b). *Citizen's guide to the National Voter Registration Act of 1993.* Available: http://www.nmia.com/lwvabc/TOC.html

National Voter Registration Act of 1993 (Motor–Voter Law), P.L. 103-31, 107 Stat. 77.

Piven, F. R., & Cloward, R. A. (2000). *Why Americans still don't vote: And why politicians want it that way.* Boston: Beacon Press.

Rakove, J. (Ed.). (2001). *The unfinished election of 2000.* New York: Basic Books.

U.S. Bureau of the Census. (1998, August 17). *Hectic lifestyles make for record low election turnout* (Census Bureau reports) [Online]. Available: http://www.census .gov/Press-Release/cb98-146.html

Voting Rights Act of 1965, 42 U.S.C.A., § 1973 et seq.

SUGGESTED READINGS

Election Reform Information Project [Online]. (2001). Available: http://www.electionline .org

Keyssar, A. (2000). *The right to vote: The contested history of democracy in the United States.* New York: Basic Books.

Policy statement approved by the NASW Delegate Assembly, August 2002. This statement supersedes the policy statement on Voter Participation approved by the Delegate Assembly in 1990 and reconfirmed in 1999. For further information, contact the National Association of Social Workers, 750 First Street, NE, Suite 700, Washington, DC 20002-4241. Telephone: 202-408-8600; e-mail: press@naswdc.org

Welfare Reform

BACKGROUND

Enacted in 1996, the Personality Responsibility and Work Opportunity Reconciliation Act dramatically changed the way the federal government provides financial assistance to needy families. This act created Temporary Assistance for Needy Families (TANF), which limited assistance to 60 months and required recipients to work. However, TANF failed to contain appropriate provisions for education and job training. There were strong work requirements, a performance bonus to reward states for moving welfare recipients into jobs, state maintenance of effort requirements, comprehensive child support enforcement, and some supports for families in moving them from welfare to work, including increased funding for child care and guaranteed medical coverage (U.S. Department of Health and Human Services, 2005). Major provisions of the act include the following:

■ Welfare recipients will be required to work after two years.

■ Cash payments will be provided for no more than five years during recipients' lives.

■ Unwed mothers under 18 years of age are ineligible for assistance unless they live in the home of an adult relative or in another adult-supervised arrangement.

■ States will be allowed to deny cash payments to children born into families already receiving assistance.

■ State must comply with mandated work participation rates to maintain block grants (Ozawa & Kirk, 1996).

Although welfare rolls declined by 60 percent between August 1996 and September 2006, from 4.41 million to 1.76 million families, the cycle of poverty and permanent self-sufficiency were not outcomes for the many single mothers and poor families. According to the U.S. Department of Health and Human Services (2007), "Only 32 percent of TANF families with an adult participated for enough hours to count and almost three-fifths of TANF adults had no reported hours in work activities, nevertheless using up their time-limited benefits" (p. 2).

Changes in the law that mandated states to engage TANF families in productive work activities that would facilitate self-sufficiency included the following:

■ First, the law changed the base year of the calculation of the caseload reduction credit from FY 1995 to FY 2005. The caseload reduction credit had inadvertently undermined TANF work requirements.

■ The law included in the work participation rates families in separate state programs, which were previously excluded from the rates. Under prior law and rules, some states moved families to programs essentially identical to their TANF programs but funded with state money used toward the maintenance-of-effort (MOE) requirement.

■ The law eliminated provisions for the High Performance Bonus and the Illegitimacy Reduction Bonus and replaced them with a $150 million-a-year research, demonstration, and technical assistance fund. This fund is for competitive grants to strengthen family formation, promote healthy marriages, support responsible fatherhood, and improve coordination between tribal TANF and child welfare services.

- The DRA expanded a state's ability to meet its MOE requirement. States may now count expenditures that provide pro-family benefits and services to anyone, without regard to financial need or family composition, if the expenditure is to prevent and reduce the incidence of out-of-wedlock births (TANF purpose 3), or encourage the formation and maintenance of two-parent married families (TANF purpose 4).

- It increased federal child care funding by $200 million per year, $1 billion over five years. With the inclusion of state matching funds required to draw down these additional dollars, new funding for child care totals $1.8 billion over five years (U.S. Department of Health and Human Services, 2007).

Because of the drastic increase in families working without a significant increase in earnings, working poverty has replaced welfare. According to Carnevale and Reich (2000), although the overall rate of poverty has declined, poor people are poorer and more working families are living in poverty. Because educational access is inextricably linked to economic security, poor single women and families must have access to education and job training to achieve permanent self-sufficiency and economic security. Education and training programs must not be seen as separate entities from work but as part of a continuum of activities that result in work.

A major facet of welfare reform is supporting healthy marriages and responsible fatherhood. Congress stipulated in the Welfare Reform Law of 1996 that three of the four purposes of the block grant to states should be related to promoting healthy marriages; when the Deficit Reduction Act of 2005 was signed in 2006 to reauthorize welfare reform, $150 million was included for support of programs designed to help couples form and sustain healthy marriages (Dion, 2006).

ISSUE STATEMENT

The social work profession is keenly aware that poverty serves as an impediment to promoting the general welfare of society from the local and global levels. It is an impediment to the development of people, their communities, and their social environments. Recent policy efforts directed at offering a political decision to address a complex issue has not been effective at moving individuals from living in poverty to self-sufficiency. *Self-sufficiency* can be defined as able to provide for your own needs without help from others. It is an ideal. Social workers realize that for some, true self-sufficiency is not attainable to all members of society. There are members of our communities who because of disabilities and limitations cannot achieve this ideal.

The work requirements of TANF and other barriers forced many single-parent recipients to leave school to maintain their welfare payments (Price, 2005). During 1995–1996, more than 650,000 welfare recipients were enrolled in education beyond high school. By 1999 this number decreased by almost one half (U.S. Department of Education, 1999). Many jobs in today's job market require credentials, skills, and cognitive tasks. Welfare recipients with low skills and educational levels are faring poorly in the labor market. The most successful welfare programs use more than one approach, only job search for some and for others, career development, short-term training, and education that are focused on obtaining specific jobs. Even though earnings have been shown to increase with these mixed strategies, recipients still remain in poverty (Gueron & Hamilton, 2002). More attention needs to be placed on poverty reduction strategies that lead to career development. Research demonstrates that mothers' successful educational outcomes significantly affect their children's cognitive abilities and educational achievements (Kates, 2001).

In addressing the effects of poverty, social workers need to acknowledge that poverty imposes an enormous cost on society at large. The lost potential of children reared in poor households, the lower productivity and earnings of poor adults, the poor health, increased crime, and broken neighborhoods all serve as counterproductive to moving individuals, families, and communities toward self-sufficiency.

It is now the responsibility of organizations such as NASW to engage in this policy-making process by campaigning to change voters' stereotypes about poor people, offering a humane and efficacious approach to income assistance programs, and working to modify the impact of the 1996 legislation on poor people and families. As stated earlier, this legislation rests on the assumption that the economy and the job market can provide sufficient employment to produce the necessary income for those who are now receiving welfare benefits.

POLICY STATEMENT

NASW affirms the value and importance of work in a free market economy. We acknowledge the importance of wealth building for all citizens, while being clear that our economic system has structural inequities that keep some individuals and families poor. We reject the perspective that views failure to develop wealth as a personal failure without reference to these structural inequities. As Ozawa and Kirk (1996) noted, "the economic system and the wage structure are . . . changing rapidly. Under these circumstances of social change, it is inevitable that some mothers and their children will be economically dependent. Blaming them for their economic predicament and for other social problems is not only simplistic, it is a cruel hoax." (p. 195)

Key principles include the following:

■ the restoration of a safety net that protects the most vulnerable individuals while supporting their efforts to become economically self-sufficient.

■ universal social welfare system that does not stigmatize, categorize, or pathologize people.

■ entitlement of all people to be treated with dignity, respect, and well-being regardless of their economic status.

NASW supports

■ comprehensive child support for all single custodial parents.

■ universal health care.

■ meaningful employment training (both postsecondary education and skill building) for available employment opportunities.

■ higher education for people on welfare that will provide opportunities for economic security.

■ assistance in obtaining employment at a living wage, including partnerships with the private sector; healthy, safe working conditions; child care; and unemployment insurance.

■ increase in EITC (earned income tax credit) participation in all states.

■ adequate services to address domestic violence, sexual abuse, mental health needs, substance abuse, and literacy problems.

■ the need to address problems that contribute to poverty, such as substance abuse, domestic violence, mental illness, illiteracy, and others.

■ policies to encourage job creation and campaigns to expand definitions of job training and efforts to unionize low-wage jobs.

■ social work redefining itself regarding income maintenance services.

■ an economic system that ensures every person has a job at a livable wage and safe and humane working conditions.

■ the recognition of the economic value of child rearing and caregiving.

■ policies on the administration of welfare benefits and programs that promote national standards and policies for the delivery of benefits and programs that serve as a safety net for all people.

■ advocacy at the state level for the development and improvement of state welfare policies in the various state legislatures and with local officials.

■ collaborative public–private efforts to move welfare recipients into work experiences that offer a living wage, appropriate levels of training, adequate health benefits, and an intentional effort to provide opportunities for economic advancement.

■ policies that protect the entitlement status of Medicaid and food stamps for all who meet eligibility criteria, including immigrants, refugees, and noncitizens.

■ the integration and expansion of professional social work personnel into the delivery of public and private social services for welfare recipients.

■ advocacy efforts for legislation and funding for research activities that track recipients who are dropped from welfare programs. Data collection also is essential to document the subsequent policy impact on child development, employment, and increases in child abuse and termination of parental rights. In addition, research must investigate the long-term effects of welfare reform on poverty.

■ the integration of welfare policies with housing, child welfare, economic, and mental health policies so there is a holistic approach to reducing and eliminating poverty.

■ policies that allow people to receive benefits for as long as they need them and eliminate punitive measures such as full family sanctions and family caps, including sanctions imposed during the time period that health, domestic violence, family, and addiction problems are being addressed.

■ the promotion of strategies that enable welfare recipients to build personal and financial assets, such as individual development accounts.

■ promotion of intensive work supports for low-income families with children, including child care subsidies, Medicaid and expansion of SCHIP, food stamp program promotion, and EITC availability.

■ the promotion and support of intensive case management services to welfare teenagers, elimination of the living-arrangement rule, and relaxation of school attendance requirements as per individual circumstances.

REFERENCES

Carnevale, A. P., & Reich, K. (2000). *A piece of the puzzle: How states can use education to make work pay for welfare recipients.* Princeton, NJ: Education Testing Services.

Dion, M. R. (2006, December). *The Oklahoma Marriage Initiative: An overview of the longest-running statewide marriage initiative in the U.S.* [ASPE Research Brief]. Washington, DC: U.S. Department of Health and Human Services, Office of the Assistant Secretary for Planning and Evaluation, Office of Human Services Policy.

Gueron, J. M., & Hamilton, G. (2002). *The role of education and training in welfare reform.* Brookings Institution.

Kates, E. (2001, Summer). Welfare reform and access to education: Penalizing mothers and children. *CYD Journal, 2*(3).

Ozawa, M. N., & Kirk, S. A. (1996). Welfare reform [Editorial]. *Social Work Research, 20,* 194–195.

Personal Responsibility and Work Opportunity Reconciliation Act of 1996, P.L. 104-193, 110 Stat. 2105.

Price, C. (2005, September). Reforming welfare reform postsecondary education policy: Two state case studies in political culture, organizing, and advocacy. *Journal of Sociology and Social Welfare, 32*(3).

U.S. Department of Health and Human Services. (2005). *1996 Personal Responsibility and Work Opportunity Reconciliation Act.* Washington, DC: Author.

U.S. Department of Health and Human Services. (2007). *The next phase of welfare reform* (pp. 1–7). Washington, DC: Author.

Policy statement approved by the NASW Delegate Assembly, August 2008. This policy statement supersedes the policy statement on Temporary Assistance for Needy Families: Welfare Reform approved by the Delegate Assembly in 1999 and referred by the 2005 Delegate Assembly to the 2008 Delegate Assembly for revision, the policy statement on Aid to Families with Dependent Children Reform approved by the Delegate Assembly in 1990, and the policy statement on Welfare Reform approved by the Delegate Assembly in 1987. For further information, contact the National Association of Social Workers, 750 First Street, NE, Suite 700, Washington, DC 20002-4241. Telephone: 202-408-8600 or 800-638-8799; e-mail: press@naswdc.org

Women in the Social Work Profession

BACKGROUND

The history of social work is a "herstory" of female reformers, suffragists, and charity workers (Vandiver, 1980). A partial list of social work pioneers includes such prestigious names as Grace Abbott, Jane Addams, Sophonisba Breckenridge, Florence Kelly, Julia Lathrop, Lillian Ward, Mary Richmond, Bertha Reynolds, and Francis Perkins. African American reformers were prominent as well and included such luminaries as Mary Church Terrell, Ida B. Wells-Barnett (Peebles-Wilkins & Francis (1990), and Nannie Helen Burroughs (Perkins, 1997).

Although women were prominent in the newly developing profession of social work, men often held managerial positions and directed the frontline, and predominantly female, workforce. As early as 1880 women noted and protested this uneven representation (Vandiver, 1980). Social work frequently has been referred to as a "female-dominated profession," although that supposition has been challenged over the years (Giovannoni & Purvine, 1974; Meyer, 1982). McPhail (2004) contends that a more accurate characterization of social work is a "female majority, male-dominated" profession.

Today women continue to make important contributions to the social work profession while comprising the numerical majority of social workers. For instance, 87.8 percent of students awarded baccalaureate (BSW) degrees and 84.6 percent awarded master's (MSW) degrees in 1999 and 2000 were women (Lennon, 2002). Women represent approximately 73 percent of all social work doctoral degrees (Di Palma, 2005). A recent representative sample of NASW members found that 80 percent were female (NASW, 2005a). In a book celebrating the faces and voices of social work exemplars (Dumez, 2003), 43 percent of the social workers featured are women.

Women in social work, like their male counterparts, demonstrate a range of professional skills; assist people in overcoming some of life's most difficult challenges, such as poverty, discrimination, abuse, and addiction (NASW, n.d.); act in a variety of roles such as academics, clinical practitioners, activists, educators, legislators, and policy analysts; bring knowledge, training, determination, professionalism, energy, and enthusiasm to the complex profession of social work; and epitomize social work values as they work for social and economic justice. The strengths of female social workers are a wonder to behold as they make a difference in the lives of people every day.

However, women in social work face challenges inside the profession. Social workers operate in a world that continues to reflect traditional male bias and power in its institutions, structures, and theoretical models. Dressel (1987) argued that "the numerical dominance of women in social work has not translated into authority, power, and pay equity or equality" (p. 297). Female social workers are not immune from the problems women in many other professions confront in the workplace, including pay inequities, the glass ceiling, sexual harassment, and a problem that has only recently received increased attention, the maternal wall. As a result, female social workers face an ironic situation: working in a profession largely comprised of women, primarily serving women and their children, they are often second-class citizens in the profession they are said to dominate. Although women in the social work profession have made much progress, inequities continue to exist.

Pay Inequities

Gender-based wage disparities in the social work profession have been documented since 1961, when the first labor force study was conducted by NASW (Becker, 1961) and have been reaffirmed in subsequent investigations (Gibelman & Schervish, 1997; Huber & Orlando, 1995). In an analysis of the *Current Population Survey*, a U.S. Census-administered monthly survey of the labor market that allows respondents to make their own determination of whether they are a social worker, the average hourly wage in 1999 for social workers was $15.56 per hour for female respondents and $17.90 per hour for male respondents (Barth, 2003). Surveying a random sample of Pennsylvania social workers in 1994, Koeske and Krowinski (2004) found male social workers' salaries significantly higher than female social workers' salaries, even after controlling for years of experience in social work, job role, and status; female social workers received about 90 cents to the dollar made by male social workers, a difference of more than $3,500 over the course of a year. Among NASW members in 1995, the median income of female respondents was $34,135 compared with $37,503 for male respondents (Gibelman & Schervish, 1997), a difference of $3,368. A random sample of regular NASW members conducted in 2000 revealed that men earned about $10,780 more than women, with a median income for men reported at $54,290 and for women, $43,510 (NASW, 2002).

Comparing salaries by industry and the proportion of women in the industry, Gibelman (2003) found that "the proportion of women in an occupational group has an inverse relationship to weekly salary levels; that is, as the proportion goes up, salaries go down" (p. 25). Although minor exceptions exist, Gibelman noted that the pattern is consistent and strong.

Pay inequities in social work reflect pay inequities across the board in women's employment. For example, the U.S. Census Bureau

(2000) reported that the median annual earnings of year-round, full-time women in the paid labor force were 73 percent of the median annual earnings of year-round, full-time men in the labor force. The numbers show racial as well as gender disparities: African American women earned 65 percent and Latinas earned 52 percent of their male counterparts' earnings.

Glass Ceilings and Escalators

The U.S. Department of Labor defined the *glass ceiling* as "those artificial barriers based on attitudinal or organizational bias that prevent qualified individuals from advancing upward into management-level positions" (cited in Gibelman & Schervish, 1993, p. 443). In a study of NASW members, Gibelman & Schervish (1997) found evidence of a glass ceiling in social work; after accumulating 10 or more years of experience, 32.5 percent of men compared with 22.7 percent of women held management positions. Zunz (1991) found that although female social workers seem to have equal access to education, training, and mentors, they move into management positions at a slower pace than men, often lacking self-confidence and finding it a riskier proposition than do men. Another study, based on interviews with female leaders in human services organizations, identified respondents' greatest barriers to professional advancement as prejudice and discrimination based on race, ethnicity, gender, and heterosexism (Gardella & Haynes, 2004).

In a study of undergraduate directors at accredited BSW programs and deans or chairs of accredited MSW programs from 1985 to 1996, DiPalma and Topper (2001) found that the percentage of women directors of BSW programs increased significantly over the years, from 43.4 percent in 1985 to 57.2 percent in 1996. The number of women deans or chairs of MSW programs also increased during this same time period, from 29.3 percent in 1985 to 44.7 percent in 1996. The researchers attributed the gains to two factors: (1) concerted efforts of the Council on Social Work Education's (CSWE) Commission on the Role and Status of Women, and (2) an increase in the number of women in social work academia. This study is encouraging and, as the title of the article suggests, could mean the glass ceiling is beginning to crack.

In social work academia Petchers (1996) found that although there was an increase in the number of women faculty in graduate social work programs from 1972 to 1993, many of these women were clustered in nontenure-track positions. For instance, from 1983 to 1993 the most common rank for male faculty in graduate programs was full professor, whereas female faculty members were more likely to hold a nonprofessorial rank, such as instructor or lecturer. Petchers noted that "as the status level increased, the percentage of female faculty decreased" (pp. 25–26). Di Palma (2005) found that although women continue to be underrepresented on faculties of colleges and universities across disciplines, in contrast women social work faculty have made greater progress: by the year 2000 in graduate social work education 43 percent of full professors were women, 62 percent of associate professors, and 67 percent of assistant professors. Di Palmer also noted the dramatic increase in the number of positions for both men and women in nontenure-track positions, in a similar gender ratio as the assistant professor position.

In a study women faculty were asked about their perceptions of obtaining tenure, and they noted the following obstacles: Most tenured faculty are men and thereby dominate the tenure review process; female faculty were perceived to be held to a higher standard of work and effort than male faculty; women felt responsible for more of the "organizational housework" or administrative tasks than male faculty; and in the tenure process more emphasis was placed on scholarship (especially quantitative research methods) than teaching and service, which ran counter to the preferences of many respondents (DiNitto, Aguilar, Franklin, & Jordan, 1995). In an informal survey of CSWE women board members, concerns for women in social work education included gender disparities in salaries, conservative backlash and a drift away from affirmative action, the glass ceiling, lack of real power, and rising expectations for promotion, tenure, and assuming administrative tasks (Bentley, Valentine, & Haskett, 1999).

Researchers also have found that men in the profession take on administrative tasks and move into administrative positions more often and at a much faster rate than women, with significant differences appearing three to 10 years after receiving an MSW degree (Gibelman & Schervish, 1993; Lambert, 1994; Zunz, 1991). Koeske and Krowinski (2004) found that men were more likely to occupy administrative roles, whereas women were more likely to be in direct practice positions. In a study that examined the status of men in predominantly female professions (social work, library science, and teaching), Williams (1995) found that men in these professions often received preference in hiring, were closely mentored by other men in the profession, and were actively encouraged to move into leadership positions. In contrast to the glass ceiling facing women moving into traditionally "male professions," Williams described the opposite phenomenon, men moving quickly up the management ladder in the so-called "women's professions," as analogous to riding a "glass escalator."

Maternal Wall

The glass ceiling phenomenon has received increased attention over the past couple of decades, but less attention has been given to the maternal wall, which refers to the problems women face in juggling their roles as employed workers with that of mother and caregiver. In a survey of university faculty in California, Mason and Goulden (2004) found that tenure-track faculty differ from their male counterparts in that they are less likely to marry and have children and more likely to divorce. The authors conclude that, "rather than blatant discrimination against women, it is the long work hours and the required travel, precisely at the time when most women with advanced degrees have children and begin families, that force women to leave the fast-track professions" (p. 90).

This problem has largely been invisible, often seen as a personal rather than political struggle for women based on their "choice" to have children or care for aging parents. This attitude is changing. As Crittenden (2001) said, "What is needed is across-the-board recognition—in the workplace, in the family, in the law, and in social policy—that someone has to do the necessary work of raising children and sustaining families, and that the reward for such vital work should not be professional marginalization, a loss of status, and an increased risk of poverty" (p. 10). This unequal distribution of caregiving between women and men affects women in the social work profession as well as the largely female clientele they serve.

Because most female social work researchers are academicians, not surprising, research on the status of women in social work has primarily focused on women in the academy. Less is known about how female social workers fare outside of the academy. A random sample of 10,000 social workers drawn from social work licensure lists in 48 states and the District of Colombia shed some light on social workers outside academic settings (NASW, 2005b). Female social workers were found in many practice settings with women comprising 90 percent of social workers in the field of aging, 79 percent in behavioral health, 83 percent in children and families, and 87 percent in health care venues. Although other results were not reported by gender, the study found serious challenges facing social workers today. For instance, the social work labor force is older than most professions, the current labor force is expected to decrease significantly over the next two years, the profession is not keeping pace with population trends in its ability to attract social workers of color, and social workers have experienced increased demands in their work in recent years, but decreased resources and supports. How these challenges affect women similarly or differently than their male counterparts is unknown.

Other Inequities

Sexual harassment has been documented in social work at agencies and educational institutions (Risley-Curtiss & Hudson, 1998; Singer, 1989). Across the board men have been the most frequent perpetrators of sexual harassment, and women have been the most common victims. Sexual harassment has been categorized as violence against women and as a form of economic coercion (Hill, 2003). Another serious issue for women in social work is client violence perpetrated against social workers. Newhill (1996) found gender to be a risk factor in client violence, and other studies have documented client threats or physical violence directed toward social workers (Spencer & Munch, 2003).

Publication rates have traditionally been higher among male than female faculty, including among African American scholars (Bentley, Hutchison, & Green, 1994; Rosenblatt, Turner, Patterson, & Rollosson, 1970; Schiele, 1992). In addition, although the majority of social workers and social work clients are female, traditional male-model theories continue to be taught (that is, Freud, Erickson, and Piaget) instead of newer theories that take into account female growth and development and the structural issues that negatively affect women.

Curricular content on women had to be mandated for inclusion in social work education in 1977 (Bentley et al., 1999), and evidence suggests that it still is not fully integrated in the social work curriculum (Figueira-McDonough, Netting, & Nichols-Casebolt, 1998). To more fully integrate gender in the curriculum, Nichols-Casebolt, Figueira-McDonough, and Netting (2000) suggested assessing both the school's resources and culture to plan an effective change strategy that matches appropriate tactics with the school's culture.

ISSUE STATEMENT

Although it may seem ironic that a profession often termed "female-dominated" would need a policy statement on the status of women in the profession, such a statement is necessary. Although some of the greatest social reformers have been women, Jane Addams, Mary Richmond, Ida Wells-Barnett, and Mary Church Terrell to name a few, the personal and structural sexism and discrimination that women face in the larger society exists in the profession as well. Rather than being an exception to the systemic discrimination women face in the world, the social work profession is a microcosm of that world.

This state of affairs may be invisible to many within and outside the social work profession for several reasons (McPhail, 2004). First, the fact that historically women have played an important role in the profession and are frequently (and naively) credited with founding the profession may cause some to overlook the subordinate status of women within the profession. The fact that women comprise the numerical majority of social workers often conceals the power imbalance in the profession. But, as observed in other professions and societies, having the numerical majority may not translate into wielding the majority of the power. In addition, the semantics of calling a profession female-dominated or a "women's profession" can distract or disguise the second-class status of women within the profession.

The background provided in this policy statement systematically makes the case that women do not dominate the profession, and in fact, are often subordinate in terms of salary, prestige, position, and the curriculum. Although the profession has taken helpful and effective steps to document and address some of these inequities, such as NASW's affirmative action stance that places women in leadership positions in proportion to their numbers among the membership, much work needs to be done.

Some might describe the present time period "post-patriarchal" or "post-feminist," however, the research findings presented here challenge such a characterization. Although gains have been made and can be celebrated, social workers must continue to examine and document the status of women in the profession and seek new, innovative ways to support women. Such a stance is necessary, fair, and can be accomplished without blaming or denigrating men.

Some social workers might believe that the focus on women in the profession is misplaced and constitutes a distraction from work with clients. A helpful metaphor to address this potential concern is the preflight emergency instructions given by flight attendants to passengers who are traveling with small children or those needing additional assistance. Passengers are advised to first put on their own oxygen mask before assisting others. Similarly, if female social workers do not advocate for and empower themselves by confronting sexism

and discrimination in their professional lives, it is hard (and hypocritical) to teach those skills and strategies to female clients operating in the larger world. The health and well-being of social work clients should not come at the expense of female social workers.

Although women have made great strides, the successes have been uneven. For instance, although some structural barriers have fallen in the public realm, women struggle with inequality in the home, which affects their lives at work. In addition, although some institutions have changed to accommodate women in the workforce, the underlying institutional structures, theoretical models, and work requirements continue to be imbued with a subtle, and not so subtle, bias that privileges men. The mixed messages women receive and the multiple roles they are expected to play have profound consequences for both female social workers and their clients. In addition, the gains that have been achieved often benefit women differently based on their race, ethnicity, sexual identity, socioeconomic status, caregiving roles, and level of ability.

POLICY STATEMENT

NASW has actively responded to the issues that negatively affect women in the social work profession—in the workplace, in social work education, and in program development and design. According to the *Code of Ethics of the National Association of Social Workers* (NASW, 2000), social workers should act to prevent and eliminate discrimination in organizations and in society. In 1973 NASW adopted a policy to address sexism and sex discrimination in the profession and in society. An affirmative action plan was initiated to ensure that NASW leadership would reflect the racial and gender composition of the membership and that women and people of color would have equal employment opportunities in NASW.

The National Committee on Women's Issues became a standing committee of NASW in 1975 to encourage and monitor activities aimed at the elimination of sexism in the association, the profession, and society. In 1976 NASW's journal *Social Work* published a special issue on women; in 1977 the NASW Delegate Assembly adopted a policy statement on women's issues; in 1980 the first NASW Conference on Social Work Practice with Women was held. In 1987 the Delegate Assembly revised the policy statement on women's issues to express a commitment to increase women's leadership in professional organizations and social services agencies and to ensure equal pay for men and women with similar qualifications and responsibilities. The 1993 Delegate Assembly approved a resolution titled "NASW Personnel Policies on Sexual Harassment" that addressed the need for educational materials, personnel policies, and procedures to protect NASW employees and social workers from sexual harassment. The NASW *Standards for Social Work Personnel Practices* (NASW, 2003) addresses discriminatory hiring and personnel actions, comparable worth, and employer's support of the family responsibilities of caregivers. NASW has made progress in addressing these issues within the organization and the larger society; however, much remains to be done.

Therefore, NASW supports the following:

■ continued attention to and documentation of the status of women in the social work profession, both within and outside of social work academia, including disparities faced by subpopulations of women due to race, ethnicity, disability, and sexual identity, focusing on, but not limited to, pay inequities, leadership and tenure-track positions, sexual harassment, gender inclusion in the curriculum, publication rates in professional journals, disparities in receipt of research funding, and the work–family conflict.

■ identifying and overcoming barriers to the advancement of women in social work, including internal and external obstacles, by teaching female social work students job negotiation, confidence-building, and assertiveness skills; establishing support and networking groups for women planning a managerial career; challenging internalized restrictive gender-role stereotypes; increasing management training for women including financial statement analysis and budget development; educating social workers about pay inequities in the profession; teaching women about legal remedies such as

filing a claim with the Equal Employment Opportunity Commission; using the accreditation process to hold schools accountable for attention to women's issues; continuing to develop mentoring programs for women starting early in their careers; and increasing union membership and the use of comparable worth policies as a way to increase women's salaries.

■ adopting and teaching non-oppressive leadership styles to male and female social work administrators that more congruently fit both social work values and women's preferred style of interactional leadership.

■ continued use of affirmative action programs inside and outside NASW as an effective tool for the advancement of women and other marginalized groups, while countering the current backlash and premature curtailing of such programs across the nation.

■ initiatives that maximize the flexibility of working conditions to support the caregiving roles of both female and male social workers, including tenure-track flexibility, better and less-expensive child care, and improved maternity and paternity leaves.

■ policies and procedures designed to eliminate violence and sexual harassment in social work agencies and educational institutions and research to document the extent of these problems and the outcomes of educational and intervention efforts.

■ working for the advancement of women in academia. Petchers (1996) recommended setting goals and strategies and specific, objective, and quantifiable targets for the proportional representation of women at each academic rank, and strengthening the function of accreditation review to enforce remedial measures. DiNitto and colleagues (1995) recommended greater value placed on qualitative research, teaching, and service; adequate representation of women on promotion and tenure committees; and male faculty taking greater responsibility for organizational tasks.

■ conducting research that more fully examines the reasons for pay and position inequities in social work. For instance, are the barriers internal and external? Are women choosing less well paid and lower status positions to better juggle work and family? And if so, why must women choose between family and work while men are less likely to have to choose between the two? Are the barriers the result of institutionalized sexism and discrimination? How are the barriers similar and different for women of color, lesbian women, and women with disabilities? Research must take the profession beyond documenting the disparities to understanding them more fully and addressing them with change at structural levels.

REFERENCES

Barth, M. C. (2003). Social work labor market: A first look. *Social Work, 48,* 9–19.

Becker, R. (1961). *Study of salaries of NASW members.* New York: National Association of Social Workers.

Bentley, K. J., Hutchison, E. D., & Green, R. G. (1994). Women as social work scholars: An empirical analysis. *Affilia, 9,* 171–189.

Bentley, K. J., Valentine, D., & Haskett, G. (1999). Women's issues and social work accreditation: A status report. *Affilia, 14,* 344–363.

Crittenden, A. (2001). *The price of motherhood: Why the most important job in the world is still the least valued.* New York: Henry Holt.

DiNitto, D., Aguilar, M. A., Franklin, C., & Jordan, C. (1995). Over the edge? Women and tenure in today's academic environment. *Affilia, 10,* 255–279.

Di Palma, S. (2005). Progress for women faculty in social work academia. *Affilia, 20,* 71–86.

Di Palma, S. L., & Topper, G. G. (2001). Social work academia: Is the glass ceiling beginning to crack? *Affilia, 16,* 31–45.

Dressel, P. (1987). Patriarchy and social welfare work. *Social Problems, 34,* 294–309.

Dumez, E. W. (Ed.). (2003). *Celebrating social work: Faces and voices of the formative years.* Alexandria, VA: Council on Social Work Education.

Figueira-McDonough, J., Netting, F. E., & Nichols-Casebolt, A. (Eds.). (1998). *The role of gender in practice knowledge: Claiming half of the human experience.* New York: Garland.

Gardella, L. G., & Haynes, K. S. (2004). *A dream and a plan: A woman's path to leadership in human services.* Washington, DC: NASW Press.

Gibelman, M. (2003). So how far have we come?: Pestilent and persistent gender gap in pay. *Social Work, 48,* 22–32.

Gibelman, M., & Schervish, P. H. (1993). The glass ceiling in social work: Is it shatterproof? *Affilia, 8,* 442–455.

Gibelman, M., & Schervish, P. H. (1997). *Who we are: A second look.* Washington, DC: NASW Press.

Giovannoni, J. M., & Purvine, M. E. (1974). The myth of the social work matriarchy. In *Official Proceedings 100th Annual Forum of the National Conference on Social Welfare* (pp. 166–195). New York: Columbia University Press.

Hill, A. (2003). The nature of the beast: Sexual harassment. In R. Morgan (Ed.), *Sisterhood is forever* (pp. 296–305). New York: Washington Square Press.

Huber, R., & Orlando, B. P. (1995). Persisting gender differences in social workers' incomes: Does the profession really care? *Social Work, 40,* 585–591.

Koeske, G. F., & Krowinski, W. J. (2004). Gender-based salary inequity in social work: Mediators of gender's effect on salary. *Social Work, 49,* 309–317.

Lambert, S. J. (1994). A day late and a dollar short: Persistent gender differences amid changing requirements for organizational advancement. *Journal of Applied Social Sciences, 18(1),* 89–108.

Lennon, T. (2002). *Statistics on social work education in the United States: 2000.* Alexandria, VA: Council on Social Work Education.

Mason, M. A., & Goulden, M. (2004). Marriage and baby blues: Redefining gender equity in the academy. *Annals of the American Academy, 596,* 86–103.

McPhail, B. A. (2004). Setting the record straight: Social work is not a female-dominated profession. *Social Work, 49,* 323–326.

Meyer, C. H. (1982). Issues for women in a 'woman's profession.' In A. Weick & S. T. Vandiver (Eds.), *Women, power, and change* (pp. 197–205). Washington, DC: NASW Press.

National Association of Social Workers. (2000). *Code of ethics of the National Association of Social Workers.* Washington, DC: Author.

National Association of Social Workers. (2002). *Social work income 2*, PRN 1(6). Retrieved October 14, 2005, from http://www.naswdc.org/naswprn

National Association of Social Workers. (2003). *Standards for social work personnel practices.* Washington, DC: NASW Press.

National Association of Social Workers. (n.d.). General fact sheets: Social work profession. Retrieved October 14, 2005, from http://naswdc.org/pressroom/features/general/profession.asp

National Association of Social Workers. (2005a). *Practice Research Network III* (Final Report). Washington, DC: Author.

National Association of Social Workers. (2005b). *Assuring the sufficiency of a front-line workforce: A national study of licensed social workers* (Preliminary Report). Washington, DC: NASW Center for Workforce Studies.

Newhill, C. E. (1996). Prevalence and risk factors for client violence toward social workers. *Families in Society, 77,* 488–495.

Nichols-Casebolt, A., Figueira-McDonough, J., & Netting, F. E. (2000). Change strategies for integrating women's knowledge into social work curricula. *Journal of Social Work Education, 36,* 65–78.

Peebles-Wilkins, W., & Francis, E. A. (1990). Two outstanding black women in social welfare history: Mary Church Terrell and Ida B. Wells-Barnett. *Affilia, 5,* 87–100.

Perkins, L. C. (1997). Nannie Helen Burroughs: A progressive example for modern times. *Affilia, 12,* 229–239.

Petchers, M. S. (1996). Debunking the myth of progress for women social work educators. *Affilia, 11,* 11–38.

Risley-Curtiss, C., & Hudson, W. W. (1998). Sexual harassment of social work students. *Affilia, 13,* 190–210.

Rosenblatt, A., Turner, E. M., Patterson, A. R., & Rollosson, C. K. (1970). Predominance of male authors in social work publications. *Social Casework, 51,* 421–430.

Schiele, J. H. (1992). Disparities between African-American women and men on social work faculty. *Affilia, 7,* 44–56.

Singer, T. (1989). Sexual harassment in graduate schools of social work: Provocative dilemmas. *Journal of Social Work Education, 25,* 68–76.

Spencer, P. C., & Munch, S. (2003). Client violence toward social workers: The role of management in community mental health programs. *Social Work, 48,* 532–544.

U.S. Census Bureau. (2000). *Median earnings in 1999 (dollars) by work experience by sex for the population 16 years and older with earnings by race.* Washington, DC: U.S. Department of Commerce.

Vandiver, S. T. (1980). A herstory of women in social work. In E. Norman & A. Mancuso (Eds.), *Women's issues and social work practice* (pp. 21–38). Itasca, IL: F. E. Peacock.

Williams, C. L. (1995). *Still a man's world: Men who do women's work.* Berkeley: University of California Press.

Zunz, S. J. (1991). Gender-related issues in the career development of social work managers. *Affilia, 6,* 39–52.

Policy statement approved by the NASW Delegate Assembly, August 2005. This policy supersedes the policy statement on Women in the Social Work Profession approved by the Delegate Assembly in 1996. For further information, contact the National Association of Social Workers, 750 First Street, NE, Suite 700, Washington, DC 20002-4241. Telephone: 202-408-8600 or 800-638-8799; e-mail: press@naswdc.org

Women's Issues

BACKGROUND

Throughout history, with rare exceptions, women have been relegated to second-class status, their lives controlled, regulated, and limited. In the United States, women were denied the right to vote, attend school, own property, keep their wages, or obtain custody of their children. Although gains have been realized, largely because of the first and second waves of the women's movement, much remains to be done. There is a measure of water in the glass, although some might view it as half empty and others as half full. Documentation of the current status of women and girls through numerical evidence builds a case for the social work profession to continue to monitor women's issues and progress (or lack thereof), with a special focus on unique populations of women who are disparately affected by discrimination as a result of the intersecting oppressions of race or ethnicity, sexual orientation and gender identity, citizenship status, disability, socioeconomic status, or religious affiliation. The following statistics indicate the continued disparity between men and women:

■ In 2002 there were 144 million females in the United States, 51 percent of the population (U.S. Census Bureau, 2003).

■ In 2002, 60 percent of women were in the labor force compared with 74 percent of men (U.S. Census Bureau, 2003). The majority of women were in occupations traditionally identified as "female." For instance, women held 79 percent of administrative support positions, whereas men held 91 percent of the jobs in precision production, craft, and repair occupations (U.S. Census Bureau, 2003).

■ There continued to be a gender gap in earnings between men and women. Median weekly earnings for women employed in full-time work were $530 in 2002, or 78 percent of the $680 median for their male counterparts (U.S. Department of Labor, Bureau of Labor Statistics, 2003). Also, earnings differed according to race. For instance, the median weekly earnings for white women were $549 compared with $702 for white men; $474 for black women compared with $523 for black men, and $396 for Latinas compared with $449 for Latinos (U.S. Department of Labor, Bureau of Labor Statistics, 2003).

■ Household income varied dramatically by type of family. For instance, in 2001 among married heterosexual-couple families only 2 percent had an income below $10,000 compared with 17 percent for female-headed households with no spouse present, and 8 percent for male-headed households with no spouse present (U.S. Census Bureau, 2003).

■ Women are more likely to live in poverty than men. For ages 18 to 64, the poverty rate for women was 11.6 percent compared with 8.5 percent for men (U.S. Census Bureau, 2003). The differences in rates are more pronounced for older women. For those 65 years and older, the poverty rate for women was 12.4 percent compared with 7.0 percent for men. Poverty, like income, varied by household type. Of families living in poverty in 2001, 50.9 percent were female-headed households with no spouse present, 40.5 percent were married-couple families, and 8.5 percent were male-headed households with no spouse present (U.S. Census Bureau, 2003). Poverty also varies by race. In 2002, 24.0 percent of African Americans lived in poverty compared with 21.8 percent of Hispanics, 10.2 percent of Asian Americans, and 8.0 percent of European Americans.

■ Women are still not represented in government in proportion to their representation in the population. As noted, women are 51 percent of the population, but make up only 14.3 percent of the president's cabinet, 14 percent of the U.S. Senate, 13.6 percent of the U.S. House of Representatives, 22 percent of the U.S. Supreme Court, 20.6 percent of federal judges, 16.0 percent of state governors, 20.8 percent of state senators, 23.0 percent of state representatives, 9.0 percent of state judges, and 20.8 percent of big-city mayors (GenderGap, 2004).

■ The status of women in the area of educational attainment shows substantial progress over the years. In 1978, for the first time, more women were enrolled in undergraduate education in both two- and four-year degree-granting institutions than men. That trend continues today with women's undergraduate enrollment increasing at a faster pace than men's (National Center for Education Statistics, 2004). Since 1976, female enrollment in graduate programs has increased by 73 percent, while male enrollment has increased by only 9 percent. High school completion rates for men and women over age 24 were both 84 percent; men were more likely to have a bachelor's degree or more and women were more likely than men to have some college or have completed an associate's degree (U.S. Census Bureau, 2003).

■ Although more low-income single parents are working after the institution of welfare "reform," more than three-fourths of those workers are concentrated in typically low-wage occupations (Institute for Women's Policy Research [IWPR], 2003b). Low-income single-mother families experienced a decrease in their incomes following welfare reform (from $664 to $647 per month) and a decrease in participation in Temporary Assistance for Needy Families (TANF) (from 27.8 percent to 14.6 percent). As a result, these families slid deeper into poverty.

■ Violence against women remains a continuing problem that affects all women, regardless of race, sexual identity, socioeconomic status, or any other identifying characteristic. One study found that almost 3 percent of college women experienced a completed or attempted rape (Fisher, Cullen, & Turner, 2000). Of the 691,710 nonfatal violent victimizations committed by intimate partners, 85 percent of the incidents were committed against women (Rennison, 2003). In 2000, 1,247 women were killed by an intimate partner in the United States. Between 1992 and 2000, on average for each year, 131,950 females were the victims of completed rapes, 98,970 females were the victims of attempted rapes, and 135,550 females were the victims of completed and attempted sexual assault (Rennison, 2002). Female victims accounted for 94 percent of all completed rapes, 91 percent of attempted rapes, and 89 percent of all completed and attempted sexual assaults.

■ Women face unique health risks, and women's health issues have received increased attention in the past decades. Heart disease kills more women than men each year, although on average women develop the disease 10 years later than men (Society for Women's Health Research [SWHR], 2004). Women are two to three times more likely than men to suffer from depression. Female smokers are more likely to develop lung cancer than male smokers, at the same level of exposure (SWHR). In fact, lung cancer kills more women than breast cancer. Women are two times more likely than men to contract a sexually transmitted disease, and 10 times more likely to contract HIV during unprotected sex with an infected partner (SWHR). Women are 18 percent of the cumulative AIDS cases in the United States with the most common exposure due to heterosexual sex, followed by injection drug use (Centers for Disease Control and Prevention [CDC], Division of HIV/AIDS Prevention, 2003). An estimated 14 percent of the population was without health insurance in 2000, which included more than 18 million girls and women (U.S. Census Bureau, 2001).

■ Almost half (49 percent) of all pregnancies among U.S. women are unintended, and almost half of these end in abortion (Alan Guttmacher Institute, 2002). In 2000, 1.31 million abortions took place, with the rate of abortions slowly decreasing each year since a record high in 1980. At the state and federal levels there are concerted efforts to regulate and restrict legal abortion, including no federal funding of abortion unless the mother's life is in danger; the reinstatement of the global gag rule, which bans federal aid to family planning clinics overseas that counsel on or provide abortions; expanding definitions of children and people that include fetal life; and numerous state regulations such as mandated waiting periods, restriction of minor's access, and restriction of the inclusion of abortion and family planning coverage in insurance plans (IWPR, 2003a). Many women consider the right to control their bodies as fundamental to their rights as free citizens in a democratic nation. The issue is also about health and safety, as risks to women are significantly reduced when abortion remains legal and accessible (IWPR, 2003a). This highlights the necessity to view women's rights as human rights (Jansen, 2000).

ISSUE STATEMENT

Women make up a majority of the U.S. population and clients that social workers serve. Attention to women's issues is essential because of the disadvantages and discrimination women continue to face in many aspects of their lives. Women perform the majority of the world's work but control a disproportionately small share of its resources. Although women in the more prosperous Western nations often fare better in life circumstances than women in many of the less wealthy nations of the world, economic, political, social, and cultural forces in most societies operate to the disadvantage of women and girls. These disadvantages affect education; health care, including reproductive and mental health; crime, especially as victims of violence; employment; and social welfare, especially income maintenance programs. These disadvantages affect the well-being of women and their families at all stages of the life cycle, from girlhood through old age.

The social work profession has a long-standing commitment to the elimination of all forms of discrimination against women. Many efforts have been made to address the disadvantages and discrimination women face. However, continuing efforts to develop social work practices, policies, and services that better meet the needs of women are essential for enhancing the health, development, and well-being of all

U.S. women, especially our clients and others at great risk.

The social work profession's continued leadership in the struggle for women's increased opportunities is essential. Although social work is often mischaracterized as a "female-dominated profession," the profession is more appropriately described as a "female majority, male-dominated profession" (McPhail, 2004). Although the majority of both social workers and social work clients are female, the underlying structures and functions of the profession are often based on male models and theories. Therefore, achieving gender equity is paramount for both the profession and the clients served. The social work profession commits itself to social justice and ending the oppression of all people (NASW, 2000). This statement of belief exemplifies the perspective of women's rights as human rights (Jansen, 2000). In addition, the National Association of Social Workers' *Code of Ethics* incorporates an antidiscrimination clause, which includes the category of sex (NASW, 2000). Also, the Code states, "Social workers should act to expand choice and opportunity for all people, with special regard for vulnerable, disadvantaged, oppressed, and exploited people and groups" (NASW, 2000, 6.04b). In the history of our nation, women as a group are characterized by those adjectives, essentially second-class citizens in a country that holds out the promise of equality and justice. Part of operationalizing this mandate is continuing to monitor and document the status of women while seeking to make and influence policy and practices that improve the status of women and girls in this society.

Because different groups of women experience their gender differently and often in interaction with other oppressions, termed intersectionality (Collins, 2000), special attention must be devoted to women of color, lesbians, women with disabilities, older women, immigrant women, and poor women.

Although women are gaining parity with men in selected areas, often achieving liberal feminist goals, the goal of changing structures and institutions to make them more equitable for both women and men, rather than merely having women join fundamentally flawed institutions in equal numbers as men, has not been realized (Saulnier, 1996). Although women have gained some measure of equity in the public spheres, the private spheres remain largely unchanged. Therefore, social work needs to continue to monitor, assess, and advocate for women's issues in policy and practice.

POLICY STATEMENT

NASW recognizes the wide range of issues that affect women and is committed to advancing policies and practices to improve the status and well-being of all women. Although every issue is a "woman's issue," only a select number of policies and practices are highlighted in this document. More important than a focus on specific issues, it is vital for social workers to develop a critical consciousness about gender (Brown, 2004) or use a feminist policy analysis (McPhail, 2003) that enables the ramifications of gender to be made visible in every issue, in every policy and every practice, at all three levels—micro, meso, and macro.

EMPLOYMENT

NASW supports the following:

■ legislative and administrative strategies that address pay equity and comparable worth initiatives for increasing women's wages in both the public and private sectors, including addressing the pay inequities within the profession of social work (Koeske & Krowinski, 2004)

■ breaking the "glass ceiling," the "Lucite ceiling" for women of color, and the "maternal wall" that affects mothers in the paid labor force, while addressing the "glass escalator" phenomenon for men in social work (Williams, 1995)

■ ending sexual harassment and occupational segregation, which clusters women in low-paying, "pink-collar" occupations

■ initiatives that conceptualize caring as work, to value it socially, legally, and economically, which might include reducing the paid work week, creating more part-time jobs with benefits, equalizing social security for spouses, offer-

ing work-related social insurance programs to all workers (including unwaged caregivers), universal preschool for all three- and four-year-olds, subsidized child care, child allowances, free health care coverage to all children and their primary caregivers, and including unpaid caregiving labor into the calculations of the nation's gross domestic product (Crittenden, 2001).

PUBLIC ASSISTANCE PROGRAMS

NASW supports the following:

■ comprehensive funding of TANF that would address structural causes of poverty as well as provide temporary assistance, which would include creating stable jobs with living wages, with special attention to the inner cities; allowing education (including college) and training as alternatives to work requirements; subsidized child care and health insurance coverage while on TANF and continuing after leaving the program; transportation assistance; and addressing the multiple problems that often affect women and their children who receive assistance, such as mental and physical health issues, learning disabilities, domestic violence, and drug and alcohol abuse (Anderson, Halter, & Gryzlak, 2004; Taylor & Barush, 2004)

■ programs for the enforcement, collection, and distribution of child support

■ initiatives for social security and Medicare reform to provide increased retirement security for women who are disproportionately poor as they age

■ viewing housing as a women's issue and increasing funding to programs that provide affordable housing.

Education

NASW supports the following:

■ adequate and equitable funding for non-sexist public education for all students, including vocational education, special education, and higher education for all women

- curricula that include women's issues, history, and experiences, including social work education, especially theories developed by and about women such as the relational-cultural theory or the "tend-and-befriend" model of stress response (Jordan & Hartling, 2002; Taylor et al., 2000)

- vigorous enforcement of Title IX and other civil rights laws, including affirmative action initiatives that address sexual discrimination in education.

Health and Mental Health

NASW supports the following:

- initiatives to reduce teenage pregnancy, as it has been demonstrated that, intended or unintended, adolescent motherhood truncates the educational, vocational, and economic lives of young women

- adequate funding and increased research on health and mental health services and issues that address the special needs of women, including adolescent women, poor women, women of color, lesbians, older women, and women with disabilities

- access to adequate health and mental health services regardless of financial status, race and ethnicity, age, or employment status, which would require universal health care coverage, although incremental expansions of coverage for low-income women and their children are a first step

- developing practices and programs that empower women and girls, enabling them to resist gender stereotypes; become resilient to shame; critique sexist and misogynist media representations of females; develop positive self-esteem and body image; confront internal and external sexism, racism, and homophobia; and challenge sexual double standards, so girls and women might develop the power and sense of entitlement that fuels self-advocacy

- reproductive freedom and safe access to the full range of reproductive health services for all women, including access to abortion; over-the-counter emergency contraception; comprehensive sexual education; family planning services; education and screening for a variety of sexually transmitted diseases, including HIV, with special attention to groups of women at increased risk, such as African American women

- gender-sensitive and culturally competent substance abuse programs that provide child care and other child services along with integrated substance abuse and mental health services for dually diagnosed women (DiNitto & Crisp, 2002).

- participation in both prevention and intervention efforts that address all forms of violence against women across the life span, including adequate health and mental health services, crime victim assistance, and other social services while educating all social workers about violence, including screening for past and current violence in all psychosocial assessments (Danis & Lockhart, 2004)

- efforts to seek out, study, develop, and disseminate theories of psychosocial development and models of services delivery in the social work curriculum that recognize, and do not pathologize, the unique developmental patterns of women, recognizing the diversity of women's experiences, situations, cultural and ethnic identifications, and sexual orientation and gender identities, including critiques of the gender bias in the *Diagnostic and Statistical Manual of Mental Disorders* (Caplan, 1995).

Global Women's Issues

NASW supports the following:

- ratification by the United States of the Convention to Eliminate All Forms of Discrimination against Women (CEAFDW)

- international programs that address women's rights as human rights, including having women in each country involved in defining their needs, identifying their oppressions, and developing programs that meet their needs

- increased attention by social work education to problems facing women internationally, often due to the effects of globalization and colonization, as well as traditional patriarchal structures.

REFERENCES

Alan Guttmacher Institute. (2002). *Induced abortion: Facts in brief.* New York: Author.

Anderson, S. G., Halter, A. P., & Gryzlak, B. M. (2004). Difficulties after leaving TANF: Inner-city women talk about reasons for returning to welfare. *Social Work, 49,* 185–194.

Brown, B. (2004). *Women & shame: Reaching out, speaking truths, & building connection.* Austin, TX: 3C Press.

Caplan, P. J. (1995). *They say you're crazy: How the world's most powerful psychiatrists decide who's normal.* Reading, MA: Addison-Wesley.

Centers for Disease Control and Prevention, Division of HIV/AIDS Prevention. (2003). *HIV/AIDS Surveillance report.* Atlanta: Author.

Collins, P. H. (2000). *Black feminist thought* (2nd ed.). New York: Routledge.

Crittenden, A. (2001). *The price of motherhood.* New York: Holt, Rinehart & Winston.

Danis, F. S., & Lockhart, L. L. (Eds.). (2004). *Breaking the silence in social work education: Domestic violence modules for foundation courses.* Alexandria, VA: Council on Social Work Education.

DiNitto, D. M., & Crisp, C. (2002). Addictions and women with major psychiatric disorders. In S.L.A. Straussner & S. Brown (Eds.), *The handbook of addiction treatment for women* (pp. 423–450). San Francisco: Jossey-Bass.

Fisher, B. S., Cullen, F. T., & Turner, M. G. (2000). *Sexual victimization of college women* (NCJ 182369). Washington, DC: U.S. Department of Justice, National Criminal Justice Reference Service.

GenderGap. (2004). *Gender gap in government.* Retrieved May 13, 2004, from http://gendergap.com/goverme.htm

Institute for Women's Policy Research. (2003a). *Policy update on safe and legal abortion 30 years after Roe v. Wade* (No. B241). Washington, DC: Author.

Institute for Women's Policy Research. (2003b). *Before and after welfare reform.* Washington, DC: Author.

Jansen, G. G. (2000, Feb.). *Women's rights are human rights: Violence against women redefined.* Paper presented at CSWE 46th APM, New York. (The phrase is part of the Vienna Declaration from the UN sponsored Human Rights Conference in Vienna, 1993.)

Jordan, J. V., & Hartling, L. M. (2002). New developments in relational-cultural theory. In M. Ballou & L. S. Brown (Eds.), *Rethinking mental health & disorder: Feminist perspectives* (pp. 48–70). New York: Guilford Press.

Koeske, G. F., & Krowinski, W. J. (2004). Gender-based salary inequity in social work. *Social Work, 49,* 309–317.

McPhail, B. A. (2003). Feminist policy analysis framework: Through a gendered lens. *Social Policy Journal, 2*(2/3), 39–61.

McPhail, B. A. (2004). Setting the record straight: Social work is not a female-dominated profession [Commentary]. *Social Work, 49,* 323–326.

National Association of Social Workers. (2000). *Code of ethics of the National Association of Social Workers.* Washington, DC: Author.

National Center for Education Statistics. (2004). *The condition of education 2003* (NCES 2003-067). Washington, DC: U.S. Department of Education, Institute of Education Sciences.

National Council for Research on Women. (2004). *Missing: Information about women's lives.* Washington, DC: Author.

National Women's Law Center. (2004). *Slip sliding away: The erosion of hard-won gains for women under the Bush administration and an agenda for moving forward.* Washington, DC: Author.

Rennison, C. M. (2002). *Rape and sexual assault* [Crime Data Brief] (Publication No. NCJ 194530). Washington, DC: U.S. Department of Justice, Office of Justice Programs.

Rennison, C. M. (2003). *Intimate partner violence, 1993–2001* [Crime Data Brief.] (Publication No. NCJ 197838). Washington, DC: U.S. Department of Justice, Office of Justice Programs, Bureau of Justice Statistics.

Saulnier, C. F. (1996). *Feminist theories and social work.* New York: Haworth Press.

Society for Women's Health Research. (2004). *Women and men: 10 differences that make a difference.* Retrieved from http://www.womens-health.org/sbb/10diff.htm

Taylor, M. J., & Barusch, A. S. (2004). Personal, family, and multiple barriers of long-term welfare recipients. *Social Work, 49,* 175–183.

Taylor, S. E., Klein, L. C., Lewis, B. P., Gruenewald, T. L., Gurung, R.A.R., & Updegraff, J. A. (2000). Biobehavorial responses to stress in females: Tend-and-befriend, not fight-or-flight. *Psychological Review, 107,* 411–429.

U.S. Census Bureau. (2001). *Health insurance coverage: 2000.* Washington, DC: U.S. Department of Commerce, Economics and Statistics Administration.

U.S. Census Bureau. (2003). *Women and men in the United States: March 2002.* Washington, DC: U.S. Department of Commerce, Economics and Statistics Administration.

U.S. Department of Labor, Bureau of Labor Statistics. (2003). *Highlights of women's earnings in 2002.* Washington, DC: Author.

Williams, C. L. (1995). *Still a man's world: Men who do women's work.* Berkeley: University of California Press.

Policy statement approved by the NASW Delegate Assembly, August 2005. This policy supersedes the policy statement on Women's Issues approved by the Delegate Assembly in 1996, in 1987, in 1977, and referred by the 2002 Delegate Assembly to the 2005 Delegate Assembly for revision. For further information, contact the National Association of Social Workers, 750 First Street, NE, Suite 700, Washington, DC 20002-4241. Telephone: 202-408-8600 or 800-638-8799; e-mail: press@naswdc.org

Youth Suicide

BACKGROUND

In 1999 former Surgeon General David Satcher, MD, PhD, released "The National Strategy for Suicide Prevention: Goals and Objectives for Action." This document, which reflected national awareness of suicide as a serious public health problem, was also designed to be "a catalyst for social change" by offering a comprehensive and integrated approach to suicide awareness and prevention. (U.S. Public Health Service [PHS], 1999). This approach was based on the growing body of knowledge about the biological and psychological factors that contribute to suicidal behaviors as well as recognition of the critical importance of trained, coordinated interdisciplinary resources for suicide prevention and intervention.

In 2002 the President's New Freedom Commission on Mental Health specifically recognized youth suicide early intervention and prevention as urgent public health priorities. Although suicides account for 1.2 percent of deaths in the United States annually, they comprise 12.8 percent of all deaths among 15- to 24-year-olds. In that age group, suicide ranks as the third leading cause of death, although in several states, particularly in western regions of the nation, suicide is the second leading cause of death in this age group (Centers for Disease Control and Prevention [CDC], 1999). Suicide also ranks as the third cause of death in 10- to 14-year-olds, which reflects a 99 percent increase between 1980 and 1997 (American Association of Suicidology, 2001; Children's Safety Network National Injury and Violence Prevention Resource Center, 2004). Although the suicide rate in this youth cohort remains highest for white males, the rate for African American males ages 15 to 19 is increasing rapidly and has more than doubled from 2.9

per 100,000 to 6.1 per 100,000 from 1981 to 1998. (CDC, 2000). The suicide rate for Native American youths is also exceedingly high compared with the overall rate for males ages 10 to 19 (19.3 per 100,000 versus 8.5 per 100,000) (CDC, 2000).

The rate for youth suicide attempts is difficult to estimate because many attempters may not be treated in a hospital or recorded as self-injury (Miller, Covington, & Jensen, 1998). The potential relationship among homicide, "suicide by cop" (youth intentionally escalates law enforcement into lethal use of force), excessive speed, and driving under the influence to suicide rates for youths warrants further research (Lindsay & Lester, 2004). Self-report data from 1999, however, indicate that 19.3 percent of high school students seriously considered attempting suicide, 14.5 percent made plans to attempt suicide, and 8.3 percent made an attempt in the year preceding the survey (CDC, 2000). This survey's data also indicated that Latino students, both male and female, were significantly more likely than white students to have reported a suicide attempt (12.8 percent versus 6.7 percent), with Latino females almost three times more likely than males (18.9 percent versus 6.6 percent) to have reported a suicide attempt. The most likely explanation for ethnic rate differences is variations in cultural norms related to suicide, including cultural views on adolescence and communication expectation among family members.

Firearms are the most common method for suicide completion by youths across sex, race, and age. More than 60 percent of suicides among youths between ages 10 and 19 in 1998 were firearm-related. The rate of youth suicides involving firearms increased 38 percent between 1981 and 1994, and although there has been a slight decrease since 1994, these numbers remain critically high (CDC, 2000).

Just as in adult suicide, the causation of youth suicide is complex, multidetermined, and reflects an interaction of risk and protective factors (Berman, Jobes, & Silverman, 2005). Risk factors for completion include previous suicide attempts, a family history of suicide, childhood trauma, and a mental health or substance abuse disorder. Studies show that 90 percent of youths who completed suicide were suffering from a diagnosable mental illness at the time of their death (American Foundation for Suicide Prevention, http://www.afsp.org). Other risk factors include exposure to domestic violence, sexual abuse, impulsive and aggressive behavior, family instability, and a recent severe stressor. This stressor is rarely the cause of suicide, but often acts as a precipitating event or trigger for high-risk youths (Gould, Fisher, Parides, Flory, & Shaffer, 1996). A particularly significant trigger is incarceration. One study found that suicide in juvenile detention facilities was more than four times greater than the overall rate for youths in general (Hayes, 2000).

Exposure to the suicidal behavior of others, whether through personal experience or through real or fictionalized accounts in the media, has been shown to increase the suicide risk in vulnerable teenagers. There is also evidence that local epidemics of suicides, known as clusters, can have a contagious effect on youths who were only marginally connected to the suicide completer (Velting & Gould, 1997).

Although there is growing concern that gay and lesbian youths are at an elevated risk of suicide because of sexual orientation, no national statistics exist for completion rates in this group. Part of the challenge in assessing the implications of sexual orientation on suicide risk is that experts disagree about the best ways to measure sexual orientation; in addition, many adolescents may be reluctant to report issues related to sexual identity (National Institute of Mental Health, 1999). Clearly, this area requires further investigation.

Research indicates a positive association between the accessibility and availability of firearms in the home and the risk of youth suicide (Brent et al., 1993). The risk presented by guns is proportional to their accessibility and their number in the home (Kellerman et al., 1992).

In addition to the assessment of suicide risk factors, it is critical to recognize the protective factors that mitigate risk. Protective factors for youths include learned skills in problem solving, impulse control, skills in conflict resolution, family and community support, access to appropriate mental health care and support for help seeking, restricted access to lethal methods of suicide, and life-affirming cultural and religious beliefs that discourage suicide (PHS, 1999).

Despite national recognition of youth suicide as a major public health problem, there has been little systematic evidence on what is effective in regard to prevention (Briss et al., 2000). There has been, however, increasing awareness of the complexity of the problem as well as the implementation of scientific approaches to describing and monitoring youth suicide; understanding risk and protective factors; developing, implementing, and evaluating prevention strategies; and disseminating information about effective strategies (PHS, 1999).

The research on risk and protective factors suggests that a promising prevention strategy among school-age children is to reduce early risk factors for depression, substance abuse, and aggressive behaviors and to implement programs that enhance resilience. A confidential screening instrument has been developed to identify depression, substance abuse, and suicidal ideation among high school youths; subsequent evaluation by mental health professionals can then facilitate referral for appropriate treatment (Shaffer & Craft, 1999).

Other school-based interventions, such as general awareness programs, and dissemination of lists of "warning signs," have been less promising. These programs have sometimes had the unintended effect of suggesting that suicide is an option for many young people (PHS, 1999). Obviously, the need for carefully evaluated program development that is informed by existing research is essential.

ISSUE STATEMENT

The suicide rate has long been understood to correlate with cultural, social, political, and economic forces (Goldsmith, Pellmar, Kleinman, & Bunney, 2002). Because social work values are so intrinsically related to supporting the individual's right to self-determination in a societal context, it has both the responsibility and the opportunity to apply its expertise to the multifaceted, systemic challenges presented by youth suicide. Few professions have as ubiquitous a presence in systems that involve children, from the family and the school to child protective agencies and the juvenile justice system.

Unfortunately, social work education has been slow to include suicide assessment and prevention in graduate coursework or continuing education requirements. Feldman and Freedenthal (2003), in a recent national survey of social workers, reported that 78 percent of respondents felt that they were inadequately trained in suicide prevention in their MSW program. Only 55 percent had some classroom instruction in suicide intervention and of those, 78 percent reported they had received two hours or less of instruction. At the same time, 86 percent recommended required continuing education in suicide management.

The profession of social work is not alone in this oversight. Goal 6 in the National Strategy for Suicide Prevention states that "many mental health professionals are not adequately trained to provide proper assessment, treatment, and management of suicidal patients, nor do they know how to refer clients for specialized assessment and treatment" (PHS, 1999, p. 79). It also indicates that there is lack of awareness of the mental health issues faced by family members of loved ones who have died by suicide. The National Strategy for Suicide Prevention, therefore, recognizes that the training of community gatekeepers, including social workers, must be improved to provide proper assessment, treatment, and management of suicidal people (PHS). The accessibility of current epidemiological data and research information on nationally recognized Internet sites enhances this learning process and is a valuable educational resource.

Given that many social workers serve as community gatekeepers, social workers are in a unique position to address the stigma associated with mental illness, substance abuse, and suicide. Not only does this stigma inhibit help seeking, but it also has contributed to inadequate funding for preventive services and to low reimbursements for treatment (PHS, 1999). Transforming public attitudes requires broad-based support, and the systemic approach of social work can bring community linkage skills to this critical public education need. In fact, because the community is truly at the core of many youth suicide prevention and intervention initiatives, social work networking and community organization techniques can facilitate the coordination of interorganizational communication and service delivery related to youth suicide awareness and prevention.

Social work is also in a position to contribute to the increasing body of knowledge about prevention strategies, treatment interventions, and the enhancement of protective factors that mitigate risk, especially in school and community settings. As in all social problems, the profession plays a vital role in the development of public policy that is theoretically grounded in evidence-based research and is directed toward the development of comprehensive youth suicide prevention plans.

POLICY STATEMENT

NASW is in agreement with the surgeon general's recognition of youth suicide as a major public health problem. It is the position of NASW to address the social and mental health issues related to youth suicide, by supporting the following:

■ undergraduate, graduate, and continuing professional education about the scope of youth suicide and the current evidence-based prevention and intervention strategies.

■ provision of a range of prevention, intervention, and postvention services at the community level for families and others affected by the suicide of children and youths.

- evidence-based research into the unique risk factors of ethnically, sexually, and gender diverse youths.

- involvement of social workers in the development and implementation of youth suicide awareness and prevention (including continuing education programs for and consultation services to non–mental health staff) in schools, child welfare agencies (child protection teams), juvenile detention facilities, courts, and other settings where youths may be at elevated risk.

- media education for the general public and community gatekeepers (including clergy, police, hospital personnel, emergency personnel, and recreation staff) to minimize the risk of suicide contagion and encourage the dissemination of information on mental health resources for youth suicide prevention at the community level.

- interdisciplinary strategies developed in collaboration with professional associations and community agencies to decrease the stigma associated with mental illness, substance abuse, and suicide.

- research concerning posttraumatic stress syndrome and its impact on youth suicide.

- educational and legislative measures that restrict access of youths to firearms

- family, school, and community-based programs that enhance protective factors for families and youths.

- school-based, evidence-based, multifactored screening as an important tool in the identification of at-risk youths. Training on the use of this tool provided to the gatekeepers (including administrators, counselors, coaches, teachers, school social workers). NASW supports the administration of such tools only by qualified mental health personnel.

- development and funding of multidisciplinary research projects aimed at extending the knowledge base about youth suicide and demonstrating which interventions have proven efficacy.

- legislative efforts to provide grants to state and local governments and nonprofit organizations to help develop, coordinate, and expand early intervention and prevention strategies and community mental health services for at-risk youths.

- evaluation of the effectiveness and efficacy of youth suicide prevention and early intervention activities.

- social work involvement in the development of policies, procedures, and protocols that facilitate interdisciplinary collaboration with professional associations and community agencies in the provision of early identification, intervention, and postvention services.

- advocacy on state and local levels, to ensure an appropriate continuum of care, from least restrictive to most restrictive, is available for youths at risk of suicide.

REFERENCES

American Association of Suicidology. (2001). *Youth suicide fact sheet.* Retrieved May 24, 2004, from http://www.suicidology.org

Berman, A. L., Jobes, D. A., & Silverman, M. M. (2005). *Adolescent suicide: Assessment and intervention* (2nd ed.). Washington, DC: American Psychological Association.

Brent, D., Perper, J., Moritz, G., Baugher, M., Schweers, J., & Roth, C. (1993). Firearms and adolescent suicide: A community case-control study. *American Journal of Disease of Children, 147,* 1066–1071.

Briss, P., Zasa, S., Pappaioanou, S., Fielding, J., Wright-de Aguero, L., Truman, B. L., Hopkins, D. P., Mullen, P. D., & Thompson, R. S. (2000). Developing an evidence-based guide to community prevention services-method. *American Journal of Preventive Medicine, 18*(1S).

Centers for Disease Control and Prevention. (1999). *10 leading causes of injury deaths, United States, 1997, all races, both sexes.* Atlanta: CDC, NCIPC.

Centers for Disease Control and Prevention. (2000). Youth risk behavior surveillance—United States, 1999. In *CDC surveillance summaries, June 9, 2000. Morbidity and Mortality Weekly Report, 49* (No. SS-5).

Children's Safety Network National Injury and Violence Prevention Resource Center. (2004). *Youth suicide statistics.* Retrieved May 24, 2004, from http://www.edc.org/HHD/csn

Feldman, B., & Freedenthal, S. (2003). *Social work education in suicide assessment and intervention: An unmet need?* Unpublished manuscript, University of New Hampshire School of Social Work.

Goldsmith, S. K., Pellmar, T. C., Kleinman, W. E., & Bunney, W. E. (Eds.). (2002). *Reducing suicide: A national imperative.* Washington, DC: National Academies Press.

Gould, M., Fisher, P., Parides, M., Flory, M., & Shaffer, D. (1996). Psychosocial risk factors of child and adolescent completed suicide. *Archives of General Psychiatry, 53,* 1155–1162.

Hayes, L. (2000). Suicide prevention in juvenile facilities. *Juvenile Justice, 7*(1), 24–32.

Kellerman, A. L., Rivara, F. P., Rushford, N., Somes, G., Reay, D. T., Francisco, J., Barton, J. G., Podzinski, J., Fligner, C. L., & Hackman, B. B. (1992). Suicide in the home in relationship to gun ownership. *New England Journal of Medicine, 327,* 467–472.

Lindsay, M., & Lester, D. (2004). *Suicide by cop: Committing suicide by provoking police to shoot you.* Amityville, NY: Baywood.

Miller, T. R., Covington, K. L., & Jensen, A. F. (1998). Costs of injury by major cause, United States, 1995: Cobbling together estimates. In S. Mulder (Ed.), *Measuring the burden of injuries: Proceedings of a conference in Noordwijkerhout, Netherlands: May 13–15, 1998.* Unpublished manuscript.

National Institute of Mental Health. (1999). *Frequently asked questions about suicide.* Retrieved May 24, 2004, from http://www.nimh.nih.gov/suicideprevention/index.cfm

Shaffer, D., & Craft, L. (1999). Methods of adolescent suicide prevention. *Journal of Clinical Psychiatry, 60*(Suppl. 2), 70–74.

U.S. Public Health Service. (1999). *National strategy for suicide prevention: Goals and objectives for action.* Rockville, MD: Public Health Service (Document No. SMA 3517). Retrieved May 24, 2004, from http://www.mentalhealth.org/suicideprevention

Velting, D., & Gould, M. (1997). Suicide contagion. In R. Maris & M. Silverman (Eds.), *Review of suicidology* (pp. 96–137). New York: Guilford Press.

SUGGESTED READING

Centers for Disease Control. (1992). *Youth suicide prevention programs: A resource guide.* Atlanta: Author. (Updated 1998).

Policy statement approved by the NASW Delegate Assembly, August 2005. This policy statement supersedes the policy statement on Youth Suicide approved by the Delegate Assembly in 1996 and referred by the 2005 Delegate Assembly to the 2005 Delegate Assembly, and the statement approved in 1987. For further information, contact the National Association of Social Workers, 750 First Street, NE, Suite 700, Washington, DC 20002-4241. Telephone: 2002-408-8600 or 800-638-8799; e-mail: press@naswdc.org.

NASW
CODE OF ETHICS

NASW Code of Ethics

PREAMBLE

The primary mission of the social work profession is to enhance human well-being and help meet the basic human needs of all people, with particular attention to the needs and empowerment of people who are vulnerable, oppressed, and living in poverty. A historic and defining feature of social work is the profession's focus on individual well-being in a social context and the well-being of society. Fundamental to social work is attention to the environmental forces that create, contribute to, and address problems in living.

Social workers promote social justice and social change with and on behalf of clients. "Clients" is used inclusively to refer to individuals, families, groups, organizations, and communities. Social workers are sensitive to cultural and ethnic diversity and strive to end discrimination, oppression, poverty, and other forms of social injustice. These activities may be in the form of direct practice, community organizing, supervision, consultation, administration, advocacy, social and political action, policy development and implementation, education, and research and evaluation. Social workers seek to enhance the capacity of people to address their own needs. Social workers also seek to promote the responsiveness of organizations, communities, and other social institutions to individuals' needs and social problems.

The mission of the social work profession is rooted in a set of core values. These core values, embraced by social workers throughout the profession's history, are the foundation of social work's unique purpose and perspective:

- service
- social justice
- dignity and worth of the person

- importance of human relationships
- integrity
- competence.

This constellation of core values reflects what is unique to the social work profession. Core values, and the principles that flow from them, must be balanced within the context and complexity of the human experience.

PURPOSE OF THE NASW CODE OF ETHICS

Professional ethics are at the core of social work. The profession has an obligation to articulate its basic values, ethical principles, and ethical standards. The *NASW Code of Ethics* sets forth these values, principles, and standards to guide social workers' conduct. The *Code* is relevant to all social workers and social work students, regardless of their professional functions, the settings in which they work, or the populations they serve.

The *NASW Code of Ethics* serves six purposes:

1. The *Code* identifies core values on which social work's mission is based.
2. The *Code* summarizes broad ethical principles that reflect the profession's core values and establishes a set of specific ethical standards that should be used to guide social work practice.
3. The *Code* is designed to help social workers identify relevant considerations when professional obligations conflict or ethical uncertainties arise.
4. The *Code* provides ethical standards to which the general public can hold the social work profession accountable.

5. The *Code* socializes practitioners new to the field to social work's mission, values, ethical principles, and ethical standards.
6. The *Code* articulates standards that the social work profession itself can use to assess whether social workers have engaged in unethical conduct. NASW has formal procedures to adjudicate ethics complaints filed against its members.[1] In subscribing to this *Code,* social workers are required to cooperate in its implementation, participate in NASW adjudication proceedings, and abide by any NASW disciplinary rulings or sanctions based on it.

The *Code* offers a set of values, principles, and standards to guide decision making and conduct when ethical issues arise. It does not provide a set of rules that prescribe how social workers should act in all situations. Specific applications of the *Code* must take into account the context in which it is being considered and the possibility of conflicts among the *Code*'s values, principles, and standards. Ethical responsibilities flow from all human relationships, from the personal and familial to the social and professional.

Further, the *NASW Code of Ethics* does not specify which values, principles, and standards are most important and ought to outweigh others in instances when they conflict. Reasonable differences of opinion can and do exist among social workers with respect to the ways in which values, ethical principles, and ethical standards should be rank ordered when they conflict. Ethical decision making in a given situation must apply the informed judgment of the individual social worker and should also consider how the issues would be judged in a peer review process where the ethical standards of the profession would be applied.

Ethical decision making is a process. There are many instances in social work where simple answers are not available to resolve complex ethical issues. Social workers should take into consideration all the values, principles,

and standards in this *Code* that are relevant to any situation in which ethical judgment is warranted. Social workers' decisions and actions should be consistent with the spirit as well as the letter of this *Code.*

In addition to this *Code,* there are many other sources of information about ethical thinking that may be useful. Social workers should consider ethical theory and principles generally, social work theory and research, laws, regulations, agency policies, and other relevant codes of ethics, recognizing that among codes of ethics social workers should consider the *NASW Code of Ethics* as their primary source. Social workers also should be aware of the impact on ethical decision making of their clients' and their own personal values and cultural and religious beliefs and practices. They should be aware of any conflicts between personal and professional values and deal with them responsibly. For additional guidance social workers should consult the relevant literature on professional ethics and ethical decision making and seek appropriate consultation when faced with ethical dilemmas. This may involve consultation with an agency-based or social work organization's ethics committee, a regulatory body, knowledgeable colleagues, supervisors, or legal counsel.

Instances may arise when social workers' ethical obligations conflict with agency policies or relevant laws or regulations. When such con-flicts occur, social workers must make a responsible effort to resolve the conflict in a manner that is consistent with the values, principles, and standards expressed in this *Code.* If a reasonable resolution of the conflict does not appear possible, social workers should seek proper consultation before making a decision.

The *NASW Code of Ethics* is to be used by NASW and by individuals, agencies, organizations, and bodies (such as licensing and regulatory boards, professional liability insurance providers, courts of law, agency boards of directors, government agencies, and other professional groups) that choose to adopt it or use it as a frame of reference. Violation of standards in this *Code* does not automatically imply legal liability or violation of the law. Such

---

[1] *For information on NASW adjudication procedures, see* NASW Procedures for the Adjudication of Grievances.

determination can only be made in the context of legal and judicial proceedings. Alleged violations of the *Code* would be subject to a peer review process. Such processes are generally separate from legal or administrative procedures and insulated from legal review or proceedings to allow the profession to counsel and discipline its own members.

A code of ethics cannot guarantee ethical behavior. Moreover, a code of ethics cannot resolve all ethical issues or disputes or capture the richness and complexity involved in striving to make responsible choices within a moral community. Rather, a code of ethics sets forth values, ethical principles, and ethical standards to which professionals aspire and by which their actions can be judged. Social workers' ethical behavior should result from their personal commitment to engage in ethical practice. The *NASW Code of Ethics* reflects the commitment of all social workers to uphold the profession's values and to act ethically. Principles and standards must be applied by individuals of good character who discern moral questions and, in good faith, seek to make reliable ethical judgments.

ETHICAL PRINCIPLES

The following broad ethical principles are based on social work's core values of service, social justice, dignity and worth of the person, importance of human relationships, integrity, and competence. These principles set forth ideals to which all social workers should aspire.

Value: *Service*

Ethical Principle: *Social workers' primary goal is to help people in need and to address social problems.*

Social workers elevate service to others above self-interest. Social workers draw on their knowledge, values, and skills to help people in need and to address social problems. Social workers are encouraged to volunteer some portion of their professional skills with no expectation of significant financial return (pro bono service).

Value: *Social Justice*

Ethical Principle: *Social workers challenge social injustice.*

Social workers pursue social change, particularly with and on behalf of vulnerable and oppressed individuals and groups of people. Social workers' social change efforts are focused primarily on issues of poverty, unemployment, discrimination, and other forms of social injustice. These activities seek to promote sensitivity to and knowledge about oppression and cultural and ethnic diversity. Social workers strive to ensure access to needed information, services, and resources; equality of opportunity; and meaningful participation in decision making for all people.

Value: *Dignity and Worth of the Person*

Ethical Principle: *Social workers respect the inherent dignity and worth of the person.*

Social workers treat each person in a caring and respectful fashion, mindful of individual differences and cultural and ethnic diversity. Social workers promote clients' socially responsible self-determination. Social workers seek to enhance clients' capacity and opportunity to change and to address their own needs. Social workers are cognizant of their dual responsibility to clients and to the broader society. They seek to resolve conflicts between clients' interests and the broader society's interests in a socially responsible manner consistent with the values, ethical principles, and ethical standards of the profession.

Value: *Importance of Human Relationships*

Ethical Principle: *Social workers recognize the central importance of human relationships.*

Social workers understand that relationships between and among people are an important vehicle for change. Social workers engage people as partners in the helping process. Social workers seek to strengthen relationships among people in a purposeful effort to promote, restore, maintain, and enhance the well-being of individuals, families, social groups, organizations, and communities.

Value: *Integrity*

Ethical Principle: *Social workers behave in a trustworthy manner.*

Social workers are continually aware of the profession's mission, values, ethical principles, and ethical standards and practice in a manner consistent with them. Social workers act honestly and responsibly and promote ethical practices on the part of the organizations with which they are affiliated.

Value: *Competence*

Ethical Principle: *Social workers practice within their areas of competence and develop and enhance their professional expertise.*

Social workers continually strive to increase their professional knowledge and skills and to apply them in practice. Social workers should aspire to contribute to the knowledge base of the profession.

ETHICAL STANDARDS

The following ethical standards are relevant to the professional activities of all social workers. These standards concern (1) social workers' ethical responsibilities to clients, (2) social workers' ethical responsibilities to colleagues, (3) social workers' ethical responsibilities in practice settings, (4) social workers' ethical responsibilities as professionals, (5) social workers' ethical responsibilities to the social work profession, and (6) social workers' ethical responsibilities to the broader society.

Some of the standards that follow are enforceable guidelines for professional conduct, and some are aspirational. The extent to which each standard is enforceable is a matter of professional judgment to be exercised by those responsible for reviewing alleged violations of ethical standards.

1. SOCIAL WORKERS' ETHICAL RESPONSIBILITIES TO CLIENTS

1.01 Commitment to Clients

Social workers' primary responsibility is to promote the well-being of clients. In general, clients' interests are primary. However, social workers' responsibility to the larger society or specific legal obligations may on limited occasions supersede the loyalty owed clients, and clients should be so advised. (Examples include when a social worker is required by law to report that a client has abused a child or has threatened to harm self or others.)

1.02 Self-Determination

Social workers respect and promote the right of clients to self-determination and assist clients in their efforts to identify and clarify their goals. Social workers may limit clients' right to self-determination when, in the social workers' professional judgment, clients' actions or potential actions pose a serious, foreseeable, and imminent risk to themselves or others.

1.03 Informed Consent

(a) Social workers should provide services to clients only in the context of a professional relationship based, when appropriate, on valid informed consent. Social workers should use clear and understandable language to inform clients of the purpose of the services, risks related to the services, limits to services because of the requirements of a third-party payer, relevant costs, reasonable alternatives, clients' right to refuse or withdraw consent, and the time frame covered by the consent. Social workers should provide clients with an opportunity to ask questions.

(b) In instances when clients are not literate or have difficulty understanding the primary language used in the practice setting, social workers should take steps to ensure clients' comprehension. This may include providing clients with a detailed verbal explanation or arranging for a qualified interpreter or translator whenever possible.

(c) In instances when clients lack the capacity to provide informed consent, social workers should protect clients' interests by seeking permission from an appropriate third party, informing clients consistent with the clients' level of understanding. In such instances social workers should seek to ensure that the third party acts in a manner consistent with clients' wishes and interests. Social workers should take reasonable steps to enhance such clients' ability to give informed consent.

(d) In instances when clients are receiving services involuntarily, social workers should provide information about the nature and extent of services and about the extent of clients' right to refuse service.

(e) Social workers who provide services via electronic media (such as computer, telephone, radio, and television) should inform recipients of the limitations and risks associated with such services.

(f) Social workers should obtain clients' informed consent before audiotaping or videotaping clients or permitting observation of services to clients by a third party.

1.04   Competence

(a) Social workers should provide services and represent themselves as competent only within the boundaries of their education, training, license, certification, consultation received, supervised experience, or other relevant professional experience.

(b) Social workers should provide services in substantive areas or use intervention techniques or approaches that are new to them only after engaging in appropriate study, training, consultation, and supervision from people who are competent in those interventions or techniques.

(c) When generally recognized standards do not exist with respect to an emerging area of practice, social workers should exercise careful judgment and take responsible steps (including appropriate education, research, training, consultation, and supervision) to ensure the competence of their work and to protect clients from harm.

1.05   Cultural Competence and Social Diversity

(a) Social workers should understand culture and its function in human behavior and society, recognizing the strengths that exist in all cultures.

(b) Social workers should have a knowledge base of their clients' cultures and be able to demonstrate competence in the provision of services that are sensitive to clients' cultures and to differences among people and cultural groups.

(c) Social workers should obtain education about and seek to understand the nature of so-cial diversity and oppression with respect to race, ethnicity, national origin, color, sex, sexual orientation, gender identity or expression, age, marital status, political belief, religion, immigration status, and mental or physical disability.

1.06   Conflicts of Interest

(a) Social workers should be alert to and avoid conflicts of interest that interfere with the exercise of professional discretion and impartial judgment. Social workers should inform clients when a real or potential conflict of interest arises and take reasonable steps to resolve the issue in a manner that makes the clients' interests primary and protects clients' interests to the greatest extent possible. In some cases, protecting clients' interests may require termination of the professional relationship with proper referral of the client.

(b) Social workers should not take unfair advantage of any professional relationship or exploit others to further their personal, religious, political, or business interests.

(c) Social workers should not engage in dual or multiple relationships with clients or former clients in which there is a risk of exploitation or potential harm to the client. In instances when dual or multiple relationships are unavoidable, social workers should take steps to protect clients and are responsible for setting clear, appropriate, and culturally sensitive boundaries. (Dual or multiple relationships occur when social workers relate to clients in more than one relationship, whether professional, social, or business. Dual or multiple relationships can occur simultaneously or consecutively.)

(d) When social workers provide services to two or more people who have a relationship with each other (for example, couples, family members), social workers should clarify with all parties which individuals will be considered clients and the nature of social workers' professional obligations to the various individuals who are receiving services. Social workers who anticipate a conflict of interest among the individuals receiving services or who anticipate having to perform in potentially conflicting roles (for example, when a social worker is asked to testify in a child custody dispute or divorce proceedings involving clients) should clarify their role with the parties involved and take appropriate action to minimize any conflict of interest.

1.07 Privacy and Confidentiality

(a) Social workers should respect clients' right to privacy. Social workers should not solicit private information from clients unless it is essential to providing services or conducting social work evaluation or research. Once private information is shared, standards of confidentiality apply.

(b) Social workers may disclose confidential information when appropriate with valid consent from a client or a person legally authorized to consent on behalf of a client.

(c) Social workers should protect the confidentiality of all information obtained in the course of professional service, except for compelling professional reasons. The general expectation that social workers will keep information confidential does not apply when disclosure is necessary to prevent serious, foreseeable, and imminent harm to a client or other identifiable person. In all instances, social workers should disclose the least amount of confidential information necessary to achieve the desired purpose; only information that is directly relevant to the purpose for which the disclosure is made should be revealed.

(d) Social workers should inform clients, to the extent possible, about the disclosure of confidential information and the potential consequences, when feasible before the disclosure is made. This applies whether social workers disclose confidential information on the basis of a legal requirement or client consent.

(e) Social workers should discuss with clients and other interested parties the nature of confidentiality and limitations of clients' right to confidentiality. Social workers should review with clients circumstances where confidential information may be requested and where disclosure of confidential information may be legally required. This discussion should occur as soon as possible in the social worker–client relationship and as needed throughout the course of the relationship.

(f) When social workers provide counseling services to families, couples, or groups, social workers should seek agreement among the parties involved concerning each individual's right to confidentiality and obligation to preserve the confidentiality of information shared by others. Social workers should inform participants in family, couples, or group counseling that social workers cannot guarantee that all participants will honor such agreements.

(g) Social workers should inform clients involved in family, couples, marital, or group counseling of the social worker's, employer's, and agency's policy concerning the social worker's disclosure of confidential information among the parties involved in the counseling.

(h) Social workers should not disclose confidential information to third-party payers unless clients have authorized such disclosure.

(i) Social workers should not discuss confidential information in any setting unless privacy can be ensured. Social workers should not discuss confidential information in public or semipublic areas such as hallways, waiting rooms, elevators, and restaurants.

(j) Social workers should protect the confidentiality of clients during legal proceedings to the extent permitted by law. When a court of law or other legally authorized body orders social workers to disclose confidential or privileged information without a client's consent and such disclosure could cause harm to the client, social workers should request that the court withdraw the order or limit the order as narrowly as possible or maintain the records under seal, unavailable for public inspection.

(k) Social workers should protect the confidentiality of clients when responding to requests from members of the media.

(l) Social workers should protect the confidentiality of clients' written and electronic records and other sensitive information. Social workers should take reasonable steps to ensure that clients' records are stored in a secure location and that clients' records are not available to others who are not authorized to have access.

(m) Social workers should take precautions to ensure and maintain the confidentiality of information transmitted to other parties through the use of computers, electronic mail, facsimile machines, telephones and telephone answering machines, and other electronic or computer technology. Disclosure of identifying information should be avoided whenever possible.

(n) Social workers should transfer or dispose of clients' records in a manner that protects clients' confidentiality and is consistent with state statutes governing records and social work licensure.

(o) Social workers should take reasonable precautions to protect client confidentiality in the event of the social worker's termination of practice, incapacitation, or death.

(p) Social workers should not disclose identifying information when discussing clients for teaching or training purposes unless the client has consented to disclosure of confidential information.

(q) Social workers should not disclose identifying information when discussing clients with consultants unless the client has consented to disclosure of confidential information or there is a compelling need for such disclosure.

(r) Social workers should protect the confidentiality of deceased clients consistent with the preceding standards.

1.08   Access to Records

(a) Social workers should provide clients with reasonable access to records concerning the clients. Social workers who are concerned that clients' access to their records could cause serious misunderstanding or harm to the client should provide assistance in interpreting the records and consultation with the client regarding the records. Social workers should limit clients' access to their records, or portions of their records, only in exceptional circumstances when there is compelling evidence that such access would cause serious harm to the client. Both clients' requests and the rationale for withholding some or all of the record should be documented in clients' files.

(b) When providing clients with access to their records, social workers should take steps to protect the confidentiality of other individuals identified or discussed in such records.

1.09   Sexual Relationships

(a) Social workers should under no circumstances engage in sexual activities or sexual contact with current clients, whether such contact is consensual or forced.

(b) Social workers should not engage in sexual activities or sexual contact with clients' relatives or other individuals with whom clients maintain a close personal relationship when there is a risk of exploitation or potential harm to the client. Sexual activity or sexual contact with clients' relatives or other individuals with whom clients maintain a personal relationship has the potential to be harmful to the client and may make it difficult for the social worker and client to maintain appropriate professional boundaries. Social workers—not their clients, their clients' relatives, or other individuals with whom the client maintains a personal relationship—assume the full burden for setting clear, appropriate, and culturally sensitive boundaries.

(c) Social workers should not engage in sexual activities or sexual contact with former clients because of the potential for harm to the client. If social workers engage in conduct contrary to this prohibition or claim that an exception to this prohibition is warranted because of extraordinary circumstances, it is social workers—not their clients—who assume the full burden of demonstrating that the former client has not been exploited, coerced, or manipulated, intentionally or unintentionally.

(d) Social workers should not provide clinical services to individuals with whom they have had a prior sexual relationship. Providing clinical services to a former sexual partner has the potential to be harmful to the individual and is likely to make it difficult for the social worker and individual to maintain appropriate professional boundaries.

1.10   Physical Contact

Social workers should not engage in physical contact with clients when there is a possibility of psychological harm to the client as a result of the contact (such as cradling or caressing clients). Social workers who engage in appropriate physical contact with clients are responsible for setting clear, appropriate, and culturally sensitive boundaries that govern such physical contact.

1.11   Sexual Harassment

Social workers should not sexually harass clients. Sexual harassment includes sexual advances, sexual solicitation, requests for sexual favors, and other verbal or physical conduct of a sexual nature.

1.12 Derogatory Language

Social workers should not use derogatory language in their written or verbal communications to or about clients. Social workers should use accurate and respectful language in all communications to and about clients.

1.13 Payment for Services

(a) When setting fees, social workers should ensure that the fees are fair, reasonable, and commensurate with the services performed. Consideration should be given to clients' ability to pay.

(b) Social workers should avoid accepting goods or services from clients as payment for professional services. Bartering arrangements, particularly involving services, create the potential for conflicts of interest, exploitation, and inappropriate boundaries in social workers' relationships with clients. Social workers should explore and may participate in bartering only in very limited circumstances when it can be demonstrated that such arrangements are an accepted practice among professionals in the local community, considered to be essential for the provision of services, negotiated without coercion, and entered into at the client's initiative and with the client's informed consent. Social workers who accept goods or services from clients as payment for professional services assume the full burden of demonstrating that this arrangement will not be detrimental to the client or the professional relationship.

(c) Social workers should not solicit a private fee or other remuneration for providing services to clients who are entitled to such available services through the social workers' employer or agency.

1.14 Clients Who Lack Decision-Making Capacity

When social workers act on behalf of clients who lack the capacity to make informed decisions, social workers should take reasonable

steps to safeguard the interests and rights of those clients.

1.15 Interruption of Services

Social workers should make reasonable efforts to ensure continuity of services in the event that services are interrupted by factors such as unavailability, relocation, illness, disability, or death.

1.16 Termination of Services

(a) Social workers should terminate services to clients and professional relationships with them when such services and relationships are no longer required or no longer serve the clients' needs or interests.

(b) Social workers should take reasonable steps to avoid abandoning clients who are still in need of services. Social workers should withdraw services precipitously only under unusual circumstances, giving careful consideration to all factors in the situation and taking care to minimize possible adverse effects. Social workers should assist in making appropriate arrangements for continuation of services when necessary.

(c) Social workers in fee-for-service settings may terminate services to clients who are not paying an overdue balance if the financial contractual arrangements have been made clear to the client, if the client does not pose an imminent danger to self or others, and if the clinical and other consequences of the current nonpayment have been addressed and discussed with the client.

(d) Social workers should not terminate services to pursue a social, financial, or sexual relationship with a client.

(e) Social workers who anticipate the termination or interruption of services to clients should notify clients promptly and seek the transfer, referral, or continuation of services in relation to the clients' needs and preferences.

(f) Social workers who are leaving an employment setting should inform clients of appropriate options for the continuation of services and of the benefits and risks of the options.

2. SOCIAL WORKERS' ETHICAL RESPONSIBILITIES TO COLLEAGUES

2.01 Respect

(a) Social workers should treat colleagues with respect and should represent accurately and fairly the qualifications, views, and obligations of colleagues.

(b) Social workers should avoid unwarranted negative criticism of colleagues in communications with clients or with other professionals. Unwarranted negative criticism may include demeaning comments that refer to colleagues' level of competence or to individuals' attributes such as race, ethnicity, national origin, color, sex, sexual orientation, gender identity or expression, age, marital status, political belief, religion, immigration status, and mental or physical disability.

(c) Social workers should cooperate with social work colleagues and with colleagues of other professions when such cooperation serves the well-being of clients.

2.02 Confidentiality

Social workers should respect confidential information shared by colleagues in the course of their professional relationships and transactions. Social workers should ensure that such colleagues understand social workers' obligation to respect confidentiality and any exceptions related to it.

2.03 Interdisciplinary Collaboration

(a) Social workers who are members of an interdisciplinary team should participate in and contribute to decisions that affect the well-being of clients by drawing on the perspectives, values, and experiences of the social work profession. Professional and ethical obligations of the interdisciplinary team as a whole and of its individual members should be clearly established.

(b) Social workers for whom a team decision raises ethical concerns should attempt to resolve the disagreement through appropriate channels. If the disagreement cannot be resolved, social workers should pursue other avenues to address their concerns consistent with client well-being.

2.04 Disputes Involving Colleagues

(a) Social workers should not take advantage of a dispute between a colleague and an employer to obtain a position or otherwise advance the social workers' own interests.

(b) Social workers should not exploit clients in disputes with colleagues or engage clients in any inappropriate discussion of conflicts between social workers and their colleagues.

2.05 Consultation

(a) Social workers should seek the advice and counsel of colleagues whenever such consultation is in the best interests of clients.

(b) Social workers should keep themselves informed about colleagues' areas of expertise and competencies. Social workers should seek consultation only from colleagues who have demonstrated knowledge, expertise, and competence related to the subject of the consultation.

(c) When consulting with colleagues about clients, social workers should disclose the least amount of information necessary to achieve the purposes of the consultation.

2.06 Referral for Services

(a) Social workers should refer clients to other professionals when the other professionals' specialized knowledge or expertise is needed to serve clients fully or when social workers believe that they are not being effective or making reasonable progress with clients and that additional service is required.

(b) Social workers who refer clients to other professionals should take appropriate steps to facilitate an orderly transfer of responsibility. Social workers who refer clients to other professionals should disclose, with clients' consent, all pertinent information to the new service providers.

(c) Social workers are prohibited from giving or receiving payment for a referral when no professional service is provided by the referring social worker.

2.07 Sexual Relationships

(a) Social workers who function as supervisors or educators should not engage in sexual activities or contact with supervisees, students, trainees, or other colleagues over whom they exercise professional authority.

(b) Social workers should avoid engaging in sexual relationships with colleagues when there is potential for a conflict of interest. Social workers who become involved in, or anticipate becoming involved in, a sexual relationship with a colleague have a duty to transfer professional responsibilities, when necessary, to avoid a conflict of interest.

2.08 Sexual Harassment

Social workers should not sexually harass supervisees, students, trainees, or colleagues. Sexual harassment includes sexual advances, sexual solicitation, requests for sexual favors, and other verbal or physical conduct of a sexual nature.

2.09 Impairment of Colleagues

(a) Social workers who have direct knowledge of a social work colleague's impairment that is due to personal problems, psychosocial distress, substance abuse, or mental health difficulties and that interferes with practice effectiveness should consult with that colleague when feasible and assist the colleague in taking remedial action.

(b) Social workers who believe that a social work colleague's impairment interferes with practice effectiveness and that the colleague has not taken adequate steps to address the impairment should take action through appropriate channels established by employers, agencies, NASW, licensing and regulatory bodies, and other professional organizations.

2.10 Incompetence of Colleagues

(a) Social workers who have direct knowledge of a social work colleague's incompetence should consult with that colleague when feasible and assist the colleague in taking remedial action.

(b) Social workers who believe that a social work colleague is incompetent and has not taken adequate steps to address the incompetence should take action through appropriate channels established by employers, agencies, NASW, licensing and regulatory bodies, and other professional organizations.

2.11 Unethical Conduct of Colleagues

(a) Social workers should take adequate measures to discourage, prevent, expose, and correct the unethical conduct of colleagues.

(b) Social workers should be knowledgeable about established policies and procedures for handling concerns about colleagues' unethical behavior. Social workers should be familiar with national, state, and local procedures for handling ethics complaints. These include policies and procedures created by NASW, licensing and regulatory bodies, employers, agencies, and other professional organizations.

(c) Social workers who believe that a colleague has acted unethically should seek resolution by discussing their concerns with the colleague when feasible and when such discussion is likely to be productive.

(d) When necessary, social workers who believe that a colleague has acted unethically should take action through appropriate formal channels (such as contacting a state licensing board or regulatory body, an NASW committee on inquiry, or other professional ethics committees).

(e) Social workers should defend and assist colleagues who are unjustly charged with unethical conduct.

3. SOCIAL WORKERS' ETHICAL RESPONSIBILITIES IN PRACTICE SETTINGS

3.01 Supervision and Consultation

(a) Social workers who provide supervision or consultation should have the necessary knowledge and skill to supervise or consult appropriately and should do so only within their areas of knowledge and competence.

(b) Social workers who provide supervision or consultation are responsible for setting clear, appropriate, and culturally sensitive boundaries.

(c) Social workers should not engage in any dual or multiple relationships with supervisees in which there is a risk of exploitation of or potential harm to the supervisee.

(d) Social workers who provide supervision should evaluate supervisees' performance in a manner that is fair and respectful.

3.02 Education and Training

(a) Social workers who function as educators, field instructors for students, or trainers should provide instruction only within their areas of knowledge and competence and should provide instruction based on the most current information and knowledge available in the profession.

(b) Social workers who function as educators or field instructors for students should evaluate students' performance in a manner that is fair and respectful.

(c) Social workers who function as educators or field instructors for students should take reasonable steps to ensure that clients are routinely informed when services are being provided by students.

(d) Social workers who function as educators or field instructors for students should not engage in any dual or multiple relationships with students in which there is a risk of exploitation or potential harm to the student. Social work educators and field instructors are responsible for setting clear, appropriate, and culturally sensitive boundaries.

3.03 Performance Evaluation

Social workers who have responsibility for evaluating the performance of others should fulfill such responsibility in a fair and considerate manner and on the basis of clearly stated criteria.

3.04 Client Records

(a) Social workers should take reasonable steps to ensure that documentation in records is accurate and reflects the services provided.

(b) Social workers should include sufficient and timely documentation in records to facilitate the delivery of services and to ensure continuity of services provided to clients in the future.

(c) Social workers' documentation should protect clients' privacy to the extent that is possible and appropriate and should include only information that is directly relevant to the delivery of services.

(d) Social workers should store records following the termination of services to ensure reasonable future access. Records should be maintained for the number of years required by state statutes or relevant contracts.

3.05 Billing

Social workers should establish and maintain billing practices that accurately reflect the nature and extent of services provided and that identify who provided the service in the practice setting.

3.06 Client Transfer

(a) When an individual who is receiving services from another agency or colleague contacts a social worker for services, the social worker should carefully consider the client's needs before agreeing to provide services. To minimize possible confusion and conflict, social workers should discuss with potential clients the nature of the clients' current relationship with other service providers and the implications, including possible benefits or risks, of entering into a relationship with a new service provider.

(b) If a new client has been served by another agency or colleague, social workers should discuss with the client whether consultation with the previous service provider is in the client's best interest.

3.07 Administration

(a) Social work administrators should advocate within and outside their agencies for adequate resources to meet clients' needs.

(b) Social workers should advocate for resource allocation procedures that are open and fair. When not all clients' needs can be met, an allocation procedure should be developed that is nondiscriminatory and based on appropriate and consistently applied principles.

(c) Social workers who are administrators should take reasonable steps to ensure that adequate agency or organizational resources are available to provide appropriate staff supervision.

(d) Social work administrators should take reasonable steps to ensure that the working environment for which they are responsible is consistent with and encourages compliance with the *NASW Code of Ethics*. Social work administrators should take reasonable steps to eliminate any conditions in their organizations that violate, interfere with, or discourage compliance with the *Code*.

3.08 Continuing Education and Staff Development

Social work administrators and supervisors should take reasonable steps to provide or arrange for continuing education and staff development for all staff for whom they are responsible. Continuing education and staff development should address current knowledge and emerging developments related to social work practice and ethics.

3.09 Commitments to Employers

(a) Social workers generally should adhere to commitments made to employers and employing organizations.

(b) Social workers should work to improve employing agencies' policies and procedures and the efficiency and effectiveness of their services.

(c) Social workers should take reasonable steps to ensure that employers are aware of social workers' ethical obligations as set forth in the *NASW Code of Ethics* and of the implications of those obligations for social work practice.

(d) Social workers should not allow an employing organization's policies, procedures, regulations, or administrative orders to interfere with their ethical practice of social work. Social workers should take reasonable steps to ensure that their employing organizations' practices are consistent with the *NASW Code of Ethics*.

(e) Social workers should act to prevent and eliminate discrimination in the employing organization's work assignments and in its employment policies and practices.

(f) Social workers should accept employment or arrange student field placements only in organizations that exercise fair personnel practices.

(g) Social workers should be diligent stewards of the resources of their employing organizations, wisely conserving funds where appropriate and never misappropriating funds or using them for unintended purposes.

3.10 Labor–Management Disputes

(a) Social workers may engage in organized action, including the formation of and participation in labor unions, to improve services to clients and working conditions.

(b) The actions of social workers who are involved in labor–management disputes, job actions, or labor strikes should be guided by the profession's values, ethical principles, and ethical standards. Reasonable differences of opinion exist among social workers concerning their primary obligation as professionals during an actual or threatened labor strike or job action. Social workers should carefully examine relevant issues and their possible impact on clients before deciding on a course of action.

4. SOCIAL WORKERS' ETHICAL RESPONSIBILITIES AS PROFESSIONALS

4.01 Competence

(a) Social workers should accept responsibility or employment only on the basis of existing competence or the intention to acquire the necessary competence.

(b) Social workers should strive to become and remain proficient in professional practice and the performance of professional functions. Social workers should critically examine and keep current with emerging knowledge relevant to social work. Social workers should routinely review the professional literature and participate in continuing education relevant to social work practice and social work ethics.

(c) Social workers should base practice on recognized knowledge, including empirically based knowledge, relevant to social work and social work ethics.

4.02 Discrimination

Social workers should not practice, condone, facilitate, or collaborate with any form of discrimination on the basis of race, ethnicity, national origin, color, sex, sexual orientation, gender identity or expression, age, marital status, political belief, religion, immigration status, or mental or physical disability.

4.03 Private Conduct

Social workers should not permit their private conduct to interfere with their ability to fulfill their professional responsibilities.

4.04 Dishonesty, Fraud, and Deception

Social workers should not participate in, condone, or be associated with dishonesty, fraud, or deception.

4.05 Impairment

(a) Social workers should not allow their own personal problems, psychosocial distress, legal problems, substance abuse, or mental health difficulties to interfere with their professional judgment and performance or to jeopardize the best interests of people for whom they have a professional responsibility.

(b) Social workers whose personal problems, psychosocial distress, legal problems, substance abuse, or mental health difficulties interfere with their professional judgment and performance should immediately seek consultation and take appropriate remedial action by seeking professional help, making adjustments in workload, terminating practice, or taking any other steps necessary to protect clients and others.

4.06 Misrepresentation

(a) Social workers should make clear distinctions between statements made and actions engaged in as a private individual and as a representative of the social work profession, a professional social work organization, or the social worker's employing agency.

(b) Social workers who speak on behalf of professional social work organizations should accurately represent the official and authorized positions of the organizations.

(c) Social workers should ensure that their representations to clients, agencies, and the public of professional qualifications, credentials, education, competence, affiliations, services provided, or results to be achieved are accurate. Social workers should claim only those relevant professional credentials they actually possess and take steps to correct any inaccuracies or misrepresentations of their credentials by others.

4.07 Solicitations

(a) Social workers should not engage in uninvited solicitation of potential clients who, because of their circumstances, are vulnerable to undue influence, manipulation, or coercion.

(b) Social workers should not engage in solicitation of testimonial endorsements (including solicitation of consent to use a client's prior statement as a testimonial endorsement) from current clients or from other people who, because of their particular circumstances, are vulnerable to undue influence.

4.08 Acknowledging Credit

(a) Social workers should take responsibility and credit, including authorship credit, only for work they have actually performed and to which they have contributed.

(b) Social workers should honestly acknowledge the work of and the contributions made by others.

5. SOCIAL WORKERS' ETHICAL RESPONSIBILITIES TO THE SOCIAL WORK PROFESSION

5.01 Integrity of the Profession

(a) Social workers should work toward the maintenance and promotion of high standards of practice.

(b) Social workers should uphold and advance the values, ethics, knowledge, and mission of the profession. Social workers should protect, enhance, and improve the integrity of the profession through appropriate study and research, active discussion, and responsible criticism of the profession.

(c) Social workers should contribute time and professional expertise to activities that promote respect for the value, integrity, and competence of the social work profession. These activities may include teaching, research, consultation, service, legislative testimony, presentations in the community, and participation in their professional organizations.

(d) Social workers should contribute to the knowledge base of social work and share with colleagues their knowledge related to practice, research, and ethics. Social workers should seek to contribute to the profession's literature and to share their knowledge at professional meetings and conferences.

(e) Social workers should act to prevent the unauthorized and unqualified practice of social work.

5.02 Evaluation and Research

(a) Social workers should monitor and evaluate policies, the implementation of programs, and practice interventions.

(b) Social workers should promote and facilitate evaluation and research to contribute to the development of knowledge.

(c) Social workers should critically examine and keep current with emerging knowledge relevant to social work and fully use evaluation and research evidence in their professional practice.

(d) Social workers engaged in evaluation or research should carefully consider possible consequences and should follow guidelines developed for the protection of evaluation and research participants. Appropriate institutional review boards should be consulted.

(e) Social workers engaged in evaluation or research should obtain voluntary and written informed consent from participants, when appropriate, without any implied or actual deprivation or penalty for refusal to participate; without undue inducement to participate; and with due regard for participants' well-being, privacy, and dignity. Informed consent should include information about the nature, extent, and duration of the participation requested and disclosure of the risks and benefits of participation in the research.

(f) When evaluation or research participants are incapable of giving informed consent, social workers should provide an appropriate explanation to the participants, obtain the participants' assent to the extent they are able, and obtain written consent from an appropriate proxy.

(g) Social workers should never design or conduct evaluation or research that does not use consent procedures, such as certain forms of naturalistic observation and archival research, unless rigorous and responsible review of the research has found it to be justified because of its prospective scientific, educational, or applied value and unless equally effective alternative procedures that do not involve waiver of consent are not feasible.

(h) Social workers should inform participants of their right to withdraw from evaluation and research at any time without penalty.

(i) Social workers should take appropriate steps to ensure that participants in evaluation and research have access to appropriate supportive services.

(j) Social workers engaged in evaluation or research should protect participants from unwarranted physical or mental distress, harm, danger, or deprivation.

(k) Social workers engaged in the evaluation of services should discuss collected information only for professional purposes and only with people professionally concerned with this information.

(l) Social workers engaged in evaluation or research should ensure the anonymity or confidentiality of participants and of the data obtained from them. Social workers should inform participants of any limits of confidentiality, the measures that will be taken to ensure confidentiality, and when any records containing research data will be destroyed.

(m) Social workers who report evaluation and research results should protect participants' confidentiality by omitting identifying information unless proper consent has been obtained authorizing disclosure.

(n) Social workers should report evaluation and research findings accurately. They should not fabricate or falsify results and should take steps to correct any errors later found in published data using standard publication methods.

(o) Social workers engaged in evaluation or research should be alert to and avoid conflicts of interest and dual relationships with participants, should inform participants when a real or potential conflict of interest arises, and should take steps to resolve the issue in a manner that makes participants' interests primary.

(p) Social workers should educate themselves, their students, and their colleagues about responsible research practices.

6. SOCIAL WORKERS' ETHICAL RESPONSIBILITIES TO THE BROADER SOCIETY

6.01 Social Welfare

Social workers should promote the general welfare of society, from local to global levels, and the development of people, their communities, and their environments. Social workers should advocate for living conditions conducive to the fulfillment of basic human needs and should promote social, economic, political, and cultural values and institutions that are compatible with the realization of social justice.

6.02 Public Participation

Social workers should facilitate informed participation by the public in shaping social policies and institutions.

6.03 Public Emergencies

Social workers should provide appropriate professional services in public emergencies to the greatest extent possible.

6.04 Social and Political Action

(a) Social workers should engage in social and political action that seeks to ensure that all people have equal access to the resources, employment, services, and opportunities they require to meet their basic human needs and to develop fully. Social workers should be aware of the impact of the political arena on practice and should advocate for changes in policy and legislation to improve social conditions in order to meet basic human needs and promote social justice.

(b) Social workers should act to expand choice and opportunity for all people, with special regard for vulnerable, disadvantaged, oppressed, and exploited people and groups.

(c) Social workers should promote conditions that encourage respect for cultural and social diversity within the United States and globally. Social workers should promote policies and practices that demonstrate respect for difference, support the expansion of cultural knowledge and resources, advocate for programs and institutions that demonstrate cultural competence, and promote policies that safeguard the rights of and confirm equity and social justice for all people.

(d) Social workers should act to prevent and eliminate domination of, exploitation of, and discrimination against any person, group, or class on the basis of race, ethnicity, national origin, color, sex, sexual orientation, gender identity or expression, age, marital status, political belief, religion, immigration status, or mental or physical disability.

Index

American Indians/Alaska Natives (*continued*)
    language use and, 214, 216
    poverty and, 335
    racism and, 286
    substance abuse and, 33, 335
    workplace discrimination and, 154–156
American Red Cross, 82, 111
American Samoans, 335
Americans with Disabilities Act of 1990 (ADA), 64, 154, 172, 231, 247
Annual Report on School Safety (Dwyer), 311
Anti-Drug Abuse Act of 1986, 112
Antiretroviral therapy (ART), 172, 173
Antiterrorism and Effective Death Penalty Act of 1996, 197
Architectural Barriers Act of 1968, 247
Articles of Confederation of 1781, 333
Ashcroft, John, 117
Asian Americans, 168
ATOD. *See* Substance abuse

Baby boomers, 134–135
Balanced and Restorative Justice (BARJ), 211–212
"Battered-Child Syndrome" (Kempe et al.), 43
Bergh, Henry, 43
Bilingual education, 305
Bipartisan, 106
Birth control. *See* Reproductive choice
Bisexuals. *See* Gays; Lesbian, gay, transgender and bisexual issues; Lesbians; Sexual orientation
Brad H. v. City of New York (2001), 231
Bringing America Home Act, 182
Burnout, 268. *See also* Professional self-care
Bush, George H. W., 293
Bush, George W., 50, 293, 294

California Master plan, 80
Capital punishment
    background on, 38–39
    crime and, 38–41, 49–50
    issue statement on, 40
    juveniles and, 38–39
    policy statement on, 40–41
Career education, 101
Caregivers
    for elderly individuals, 16
    in families, 135–136
    hospice, 189
    parents as, 93
Carson, Rachel, 121
Carter, Jimmy, 22, 293
Catholic Charities, 82
Censorship, civil liberties and, 50
Center for Restorative Justice and Peacemaking (University of Minnesota), 66
Center for Workforce Study, 78
Center for World of Work (Columbia University), 111
Centers for Disease Control and Prevention (CDC), 3, 171, 173
Centers for Medicare & Medicaid Services, 169
Chafee Foster Care Independent Living Act, 146, 151
Chamorus, 334, 335
Charity Organization Societies, 322
Child abuse and neglect. *See also* Family violence; Physical punishment of children
    background on, 42–44
    child welfare workers and, 278

family violence and, 44, 140–142
issue statement on, 44–45
physical punishment as, 253
policy statement on, 45–46
substance abuse and, 44, 140
Child Abuse Prevention and Treatment Act (CAPTA), 43
Child Abuse Prevention Initiative, 253
Child and Adolescent Service System Program, 230
Child care
    background on, 91–92
    issue statement on, 92–93
    physical punishment in, 253
    policy statement on, 93–94
    substance abuse programs and, 371
Child custody, 238–240
Children. *See also* Adolescents; Early childhood care; Juvenile justice
    environmental degradation and, 122
    exposed to violence, 309
    high-risk, 97–98
    homeless, 182
    legislative efforts to protect, 43–44
    mental health issues in, 232
    parental abduction of, 238–240
    with parental substance abuse problems, 30
    physical punishment of, 252–255
    poverty among, 147, 155, 260
    sexual exploitation of, 45
    who witness domestic violence, 141–142
Children of alcoholics (COAs), 30
Children's Bureau (Department of Health and Human Services), 42, 43
Children's Defense Fund, 91
Children's Health Insurance Plan (CHIP), 5–6
Child welfare
    background on, 277
    current status of, 44
    education and retention of social workers in, 153
    issue statement on, 277–278
    lesbian, gay, transgender and bisexual adolescents and, 146–147
    policies regarding, 43–44
    policy statement on, 278–279
Child Welfare League of America (CWLA), 43, 146
Christian Reformed World Belief, 82
Civil liberties
    background on, 49–50
    issue statement on, 50
    policy statement on, 50–53
Civil rights, 288
Civil Rights Act of 1964, Title VII, 22, 154, 215
Civil Rights Act of 1968, 247
Clients
    crime victims or, 67
    informed consent and, 324
    privacy and confidentiality for, 63 (*See also* Confidentiality; Privacy)
    rural, 297
Clinical Indicators for Social Work and Psychosocial Services in Nursing Homes (National Association of Social Workers), 225
Clinical Trials Network (National Institute on Drug Abuse), 33
Clinton, Bill, 49, 105, 180, 231, 233, 293, 311, 312
Code of Ethics. *See NASW Code of Ethics*
Columbine High School shooting, 311–312

Disaster Relief Act of 1970, 82
Disasters
    background on, 82–84
    explanation of, 82
    issue statement on, 84
    policy statement on, 84–85
Disaster Services Human Resources System, 82
Discipline, 102. *See also* Physical punishment of children
Discrimination. *See also* Affirmative action; Racism
    in American history, 24
    explanation of, 154
    gender identity and, 342, 344
    genetic testing and, 163, 164
    HIV/AIDS and, 172
    lesbians, gays, and bisexuals and, 136, 218–220
    workplace, 154–158 (*See also* Workplace discrimination)
Disease. *See* Illness
Distance education, 339
Diversity. *See* Cultural diversity; People of color; *specific groups*
Division of Unaccompanied Children's Services (DUCS), 197
Dix, Dorothea, 229
Domestic violence. *See* Family violence
Do not attempt resuscitation (DNAR), 115
Do not resuscitate (DNR), 115
Double effect, 115
Drug abuse. *See* Substance abuse
Drug-Free Workplace Act of 1986, 88, 89
Drug tests. *See also* Substance abuse
    background on, 88
    issue statement on, 88–89
    policy statement on, 89–90
Due process, access to, 51
Durable Power of Attorney for Health Care, 114
Durable Power of Attorney for Medical Decision Making, 115

Early childhood care. *See also* Children
    background on, 91–92
    issue statement on, 92–93
    policy statement on, 93–94
Early Warning, Timely Response: A Guide to Safe Schools
        (Dwyer et al.), 311
Economic Opportunity Act of 1964, 54
Education. *See also* Schools; Social work education
    adolescent pregnancy and, 11
    alternative, 98
    bilingual, 305
    career and vocational, 101
    components of, 100–103
    early childhood, 101
    families and communities and, 98, 101
    federal and state funding for, 97
    federal legislation on, 96–97
    females and, 368, 370–371
    funding for, 102
    health and mental health, 101–102
    high-risk students and, 97–98
    issue statement on, 99–100
    on lesbian, gay, transgender and bisexual issues, 220–221
    nondiscriminatory and integrated, 102
    policy statement on, 100–103
    political, 106–107
    racism and, 282, 287
    school safety and security and, 98
    school truancy and dropout rate and, 303–306
    sex, 99, 174
    social workers and, 99

Education for All Handicapped Children Act Amendments
        of 1986, 247–248
Education for All Handicapped Children Act of 1975, 96,
        230, 247
Eisenhower, Dwight, 218
Elderly individuals. *See also* Aging; End-of-life care
    abuse of, 16–17, 134, 140, 141
    background on, 14–15
    caregiving for, 16
    diversity among, 14, 17
    economic security for, 16
    ethical issues related to, 17
    family structure and, 134
    health care for, 15–16
    housing for, 16
    issue statement on, 15–17
    policy statement on, 17–18
    poverty among, 15, 260
    training to work with, 14, 17
Electoral politics. *See also* Politics/political action
    background on, 105–106
    explanation of, 106–107
    issue statement on, 108–109
    NASW involvement in, 107
    policy statement on, 109
Elementary and Secondary Education Act of 1965, 96
Elizabethan Poor Laws (England), 42
Emergencies. *See* Disasters
Emergency Assistance program, 180
Emergency contraception (EC), 128
Employee assistance
    background on, 111
    issue statement on, 112
    policy statement on, 113
Employee Assistance Professional Association (EAPA), 112
Employee Assistance Programs (EAPs), 89, 111–113
Employment. *See also* Workplace discrimination
    housing and, 193–194
    racism and, 282–283, 287
    women and, 113, 135, 157
Employment discrimination. *See* Affirmative action;
        Workplace discrimination
Employment Non-Discrimination Act (ENDA), 219
Empowerment, 71, 325
End-of-life care. *See also* Hospice care; Long-term care (LTC)
    definitions of, 114–116
    issue statement on, 117–118
    legislation related to, 116–117
    policy statement on, 118–119
English-only movement, 214–215
Environmental justice, 123
Environmental policy
    background on, 121–123
    issue statement on, 123–124
    policy statement on, 124–125
Environmental Protection Agency (EPA), 124
Environmental racism, 123
Equal Employment Opportunity Commission (EEOC), 155
Equal Pay Act of 1963, 154
Equal protection, access to, 51
Ethical issues
    in rural practice, 300
    in technology use, 340
Euthanasia, 115, 117
Executive Order No. 8808, 22
Executive Order No. 10925, 22

INDEX   401

Hispanics (*continued*)
    HIV/AIDS and, 33
    in hospice care, 188
    housing and, 283
    incarceration of, 327
    language use and, 214, 215
    statistics regarding, 214
    substance abuse and, 33
    workplace discrimination and, 154–156
HIV/AIDS
    adolescents and, 3
    background on, 171–172
    confidentiality and, 59–60, 64
    effects on individuals, families, and communities, 172
    foster care or adoption for children with, 148
    hospice care and, 188, 190
    issue statement on, 172–174
    policy statement on, 174–175
    political action and advocacy, 175
    prevention of, 174
    prostituted people and, 273–275
    substance abuse and, 33
    testing for, 171, 173–175
    treatment of, 172, 173, 175
    women and, 172, 173
Homeland Security Act, 50
Homelessness. *See also* Poverty
    background on, 177–181
    information sources on, 178
    issue statement on, 181
    policy on, 180–182
    policy statement on, 181–183
Homeless shelters, 179–180, 182
Home schooling, 98
Homicide
    adolescent, 3
    workplace, 112
Homosexuals. *See* Gays; Lesbian, gay, transgender and
    bisexual issues; Lesbians; Transgender identity
Hopkins, Harry, 105
Hospice care, 115. *See also* End-of-life care
    background on, 186–187
    explanation of, 186
    issue statement on, 187–189
    pharmaceutical costs and, 188
    policy statement on, 189–191
    reimbursement for, 187
Housing
    affordable, 181, 193
    background on, 192
    community infrastructure and, 193
    employment and, 193–194
    issue statement on, 192–194
    policy statement on, 194
    for populations with special needs, 193
    racism and, 283, 287
    social services and, 193
Housing Act of 1949, 193
Housing and Community Development Act Amendments
    of 1981, 23
Housing and Community Development Act of 1974, 23
Human Genome Education Model (HuGEM), 161
Human Genome Project, 161
Human rights
    history of, 202–203
    issue statement on, 204–205

    policy statement on, 205–206
    social work and, 203–204
Hurricane Katrina, 82

Illegal Immigration Reform and Immigrant Responsibility
    Act of 1996, 197
Illness. *See also* Health care; HIV/AIDS; Hospice care
    childhood trauma and, 44–45
    environmental degradation and, 122
    health care access and, 168
Immigrant Reform and Control Act of 1986, 196
Immigration. *See also* Slavery/human trafficking
    background on, 196–198
    imprisonment for offenses related to, 327
    issue statement on, 198
    language use and, 214, 215
    policy statement on, 199–200
    trends in, 135–136
Immigration Act of 1990, 196
Immigration and Nationality Act Amendments (1965), 196
Immigration and Naturalization Service, 197
Incarcerated individuals. *See also* Criminal justice system;
    Prison
    background on, 327
    for drug-related offenses, 327–328
    family issues for, 328
    health care needs of, 328
    for immigration-related offenses, 327
    issue statement on, 329–330
    juveniles as, 210, 211, 329
    mental health of, 328
    policy statement on, 330–331
    statistics regarding, 327, 329
    women as, 327–329
Incompetent, 116
Independent living (IL), 248
Indian Child Welfare Act (ICWA), 147
Indian General Allotment Act of 1887, 333
Indian Removal Act of 1830, 333
Indigenous peoples
    Alaska Natives, 334, 335 (*See also* American
        Indians/Alaska Natives)
    American Indians, 333, 335 (*See also* American
        Indians/Alaska Natives)
    American Samoans, 335
    Chamorus, 334, 335
    issue statement on, 335–336
    Kanaka Maoli, 333–334
    policy statement on, 336
    Taino Indians, 334, 335
Individualized education plan (IEP), 96
Individuals with Disabilities Education Act Amendments
    of 1997, 59
Individuals with Disabilities Education Act (IDEA), 96,
    230, 248
Individuals with Disabilities Education Improvement Act
    (2004), 97, 100
Infant mortality rate, 128
Information utilization
    background on, 59–60
    issue statement on, 60–61
    policy statement on, 61–64
Informed consent, 324
Institute of Medicine (IOM), 15, 167
Interethnic Adoption Provisions (Small Business Jobs
    Protection Act), 147

International Child Abduction Remedies Act, 239
International Classification of Diseases, 10th Revision (ICD-10), 229
International Covenant on Civil and Political Rights, 218
International Federation of Social Workers (IFSW), 113, 129, 245
International Policy on Human Rights (National Association of Social Workers), 202–206, 319. *See also* Human rights

Jackson, Jesse, 107
Jaffee v. Redmond (1996), 60
Job Opportunities and Basic Skill Training Program, 180
Johnson, Lyndon B., 22, 23, 96, 105, 127, 292
Joint Commission on Accreditation of Healthcare Organizations, 225
Joint Commission on Mental Illness and Health, 229
Journal of Technology in Human Services, 338
Justice. *See also* Civil liberties
    access to, 51
    economic, 242, 258–261
    environmental, 123
    social, 24, 40, 49–53
Juvenile justice
    background on, 208–209
    capital punishment and, 38–39
    incarceration and, 210, 211, 329
    issue statement on, 209–210
    policy statement on, 210–212
    racism and, 285
Juvenile Justice and Delinquency Prevention Act of 1974, 208

Kanaka Maoli, 333–334
Kendra's Law, 231–232
Kennedy, John F., 22, 127, 292
Kevorkian, Jack, 117
Know-Keene Health Care Service Plan Act of 1975, 112

Labor force. *See* Workplace
Latinos/Latinas. *See* Hispanics
Least-restrictive environment, 100
Lesbian, gay, transgender and bisexual issues
    adolescents in child welfare system and, 146–147
    background on, 218–219
    discrimination, 136, 218–220
    issue statement on, 219
    policy statement on, 220–221
    prostituted people and, 274
    youth suicide and, 375
Lesbians
    in families, 136
    same-sex marriage and, 218, 219
Life expectancy, 14
Life-sustaining treatment, 116
Linguistic competence, 70. *See also* Cultural/linguistic competence
Literacy, statistics regarding, 303
Living Wills, 114, 116
Long-term care (LTC). *See also* End-of-life care
    background on, 223–225
    explanation of, 223
    issue statement on, 225–226
    policy statement on, 226–227

Magna Carta, 202
Males
    adolescent pregnancy and, 9, 11
    contraception and, 129
Managed care. *See also* Health care
    long-term, 224–225
    substance abuse and, 31
Maternal and Child Health Block Grant, Title V, 5
Maternal wall, 361–362
McKinney-Vento Act, 97
Medicaid
    for children and adolescents, 5
    function of, 167, 168
    HIV/AIDS and, 172
    hospice care and, 187
    long-term care and, 224
Medical futility, 115
Medicare
    AIDS and, 172
    homelessness and, 181
    hospice care and, 187
    mental health care and, 231
Medicare Demonstration Project, 188
Mennonite Disaster Services, 82
Mental health
    background on, 229–232
    childhood trauma and, 44–45
    of incarcerated individuals, 328
    issue statement on, 232–234
    policy statement on, 234–235
    of social workers, 263–266
    substance abuse and, 32
Mental Health Act of 1946, 229
Mental Health Bill of Rights Act of 1985, 247
Mental health care
    for females, 371
    for transgender and transsexual individuals, 342–343, 347
Mental health education, 101–102
Mental health services
    access to, 5
    racism and, 283–284, 288
    sexual orientation and, 221
Mental Health Study Act of 1955, 229
Mental Retardation Facilities and Community Mental Health Centers Construction Act of 1963, 229–230
Meyer, Carol, 77
Migration. *See* Immigration
Military issues, 244
Miller, George, 44
Milliman Study, 188
Minors, 115
Model Cities Program, 54
Mortality rate, infant, 128
Mothers, adolescent. *See* Adolescent pregnancy and parenting
Mothers Against Drunk Driving, 66
Multiculturalism, 56
Multiethnic Placement Act (MEPA) of 1994, 147
Murder Victims' Families for Reconciliation (MVFR), 39

NASW Code of Ethics
    capital punishment and, 40–41
    client self-determination and, 187
    confidentiality and privacy and, 60, 63, 88, 340, 386–387
    cultural competence and, 73–74
    on culturally sensitive boundaries, 300

Racism (*continued*)
  housing and community and, 283, 287
  issue statement on, 285–286
  mental illness and, 234
  policy statement on, 286–289
  political activity and, 285, 289
  public welfare and, 284, 288
  research and, 285, 289
  social services and, 284, 288
  social work profession and, 289
  in United States, 244
Rand Institute for Civil Justice, 232
Randolph, A. Phillip, 22
Rankin, Jeanette, 105
Reagan, Ronald, 293
Reclassification. *See* Deprofessionalization/reclassification
Refugees. *See also* Immigration
  admissions of, 197
  background on, 196–198
  impact of terrorism on, 197
  issue statement on, 198
  policy statement on, 199
Regular Education Initiative, 96
Rehabilitation Act Amendments of 1992, 248
Rehabilitation Act of 1973, 88, 247
Report on Youth Violence (Office of the Surgeon General), 312
Reproductive choice
  abortion and, 128–129
  access to services for, 131
  background on, 127–128
  education and research and, 132
  emergency contraception and, 128
  issue statement on, 129–130
  legislation related to, 131–132
  men and contraception and, 129
  policy statement on, 130–132
  violence and, 129
Reproductive technology. *See* Contraception
Resilience, adolescent health and, 4
Revelle, Roger, 121
Reynolds, Bertha Capen, 111
Richmond. Mary, 338
Risk behaviors, in adolescents, 3–4
Risk factors
  school violence and, 312, 313
  for youth suicide, 375
Robert T, Stafford Disaster Relief and Emergency Assistance Act, 82, 84
Roe v. Wade (1973), 52, 131
Roggoveen, Jacob, 335
Roosevelt, Eleanor, 202
Roosevelt, Franklin, 22, 105
Rural social work
  background on, 297–299
  issue statement on, 299
  policy statement on, 299–301
Rust v. Sullivan (1991), 49

Safe from the Start: Taking Action on Children Exposed to Violence (Department of Justice), 309
Safeguarding Our Children: An Action Guide (Dwyer & Osher), 311, 313
Safe Schools Act, 311
Salvation Army, 82
Same-sex marriage, 218, 219
Same-sex relationships, violence within, 140

Samoa, 335
Sanger, Margaret, 127
Satcher, David, 312, 374
Schiavo, Terri, 117
School-based health centers (SBHCs), 4–5
Schools. *See also* Education
  alternative testing in, 100–101
  behavior management and code of conduct in, 313
  crisis intervention in, 314–315
  discipline in, 102
  function of, 99–100
  protective factors in, 4
  relationships between communities and, 98, 101
  safe and secure, 98
School social workers
  evaluation of services of, 103
  privacy and, 63–64
  role of, 99, 103
  violence prevention and, 314–315
School truancy/dropout prevention
  background on, 303–304
  issue statement on, 304–305
  policy statement on, 305–306
School violence
  background on, 309–311
  issue statement on, 311–313
  policy statement on, 313–315
Search Institute, 4
Self-care. *See* Professional self-care
Self-determination
  hospice care and, 186, 187
  importance of, 324
  individuals with disabilities and, 249
  in reproductive decisions, 129–130, 132
Self-help movement, 30
Self-sufficiency, 356
Seniors. *See* Elderly individuals
Sex education, 99, 174
Sexual abuse
  adolescent pregnancy and, 9
  health and childhood, 45
  prostitution and, 275
  of transgender individuals, 329
Sexual activity
  among adolescents, 3, 5, 9, 10
  HIV/AIDS and, 3
Sexual harassment, 362
Sexually transmitted diseases (STDs), 273. *See also* HIV/AIDS
Sexual orientation. *See also* Gays; Lesbians; Transgender identity
  cultural identity and, 70–71
  discrimination related to, 136, 218–219
Shalala, Donna, 312
Slavery/human trafficking. *See also* Prostituted people
  background of, 317–318
  issue statement on, 318–319
  policy statement on, 319–320
Small Business Jobs Protection Act of 1996, 147
Social justice. *See also* Civil liberties
  background on, 242–243
  civil liberties and, 49–53
  death penalty and, 40
  economic and military issues and, 244
  human rights and, 202, 203
  international cooperation and, 245

Survival sex, 274. *See also* Prostituted people
Sutherland, Bill, 214

Taino Indians, 334, 335
Tarasoff v. Regents of the University of California (1976), 62, 112
Task Force on Genetic Testing, 163
Technology
    background on, 338
    health care, 114
    human trafficking and, 318
    issue statement on, 338–340
    policy statement on, 340
    privacy issues and, 61
Temporary Assistance to Needy Families (TANF)
    background on, 355–356
    function of, 135, 180
    issue statement on, 356–357
    substance abuse and, 32
    women and, 370
    workforce entry of participants in, 91
Terminal and irreversible condition, 116
Terrorist attacks of September 11, 2001, 197, 242, 243
Thompson v. Thompson (1988), 239
Tobacco use, 3, 31. *See also* Substance abuse
Trade and Intercourse Acts, 333
Trafficking, 273, 317–320. *See also* Prostituted people;
    Slavery/human trafficking
Transgender identity. *See also* Lesbian, gay, transgender
    and bisexual issues; Sexual orientation
    background on, 342–344
    issue statement on, 344–345
    policy statement on, 345–348
Transgender people
    criminal justice policies and, 327, 329
    discrimination against, 173
Transsexual people, 342–343
Trauma, 269
Truancy. *See* School truancy/dropout prevention

Unaccompanied Refugee Minors Program, 197
Unemployment
    high school dropouts and, 303
    poverty and, 260
    trends in, 282–283
Uniform Child Custody Jurisdiction Act, 239
United Methodist church, 82
United Nations
    Commission for Human Rights, 130
    Convention on the Rights of the Child, 45
    Fourth World Conference on Women, 129
    human rights issues and, 202, 203
    on sexual trafficking, 273
United Way, 322
Universal Declaration of Human Rights (United Nations), 38, 198, 202–203
University of Albany, 78
U.S.A. Patriot Act, 50, 197

Vicarious traumatization, 268
Victim-offender mediation (VOM), 66
Victims. *See* Crime victim assistance; Crime victims
Victims' Bill of Rights, 65
Victims of Crime Act, 65
Victims of Crime Assistance (VOCA), 66

Violence. *See also* Child abuse and neglect; Crime
    effect on adolescents, 5, 312
    family, 44, 127–132, 136, 140–144
    mental health and, 231
    prostituted people and, 274
    reproductive health and, 129
    school, 309–315
    in United States, 242–243
    against women, 141, 368
    workplace, 112
Violence Against Women Act of 1990, 65, 197
Vocational education, 101
Volunteer Organizations Active in Disasters (VOAD), 82
Volunteers of America, 82
Voter participation. *See also* Politics/political action
    background on, 351–353
    issue statement on, 353
    policy statement on, 353–354
Voting rights, 351

War on Poverty, 96, 97, 127, 242, 243
Webdale, Kendra, 231–232
Welfare reform
    background on, 355–356
    effects of, 259
    issue statement on, 356–357
    policy statement on, 357–358
Welfare Reform Law of 1996, 356
Wellness
    adolescent, 4
    aging and, 14–18
Wheeler, Etta, 43
White House Conference on School Violence (1998), 311
White transparency, 281
Wilson, Mary Ellen, 42–43
Withdrawal of treatment, 116
Withholding of treatment, 116
Women
    compensation for, 137, 155, 157, 360–361
    elderly, 14
    HIV/AIDS and, 172, 173
    homeless, 182
    incarcerated, 327–329
    mental disorders in, 234
    poverty among, 15
    reproductive rights for, 49
    social justice and, 244
    violence against, 141, 368
    in workplace, 113, 135
    workplace death of, 112
    workplace discrimination and, 155–157, 370
Women in social work profession
    background on, 359–360
    glass ceilings and escalators for, 360–361
    issue statement on, 362–363
    maternal wall in, 361–362
    pay inequities of, 360
    policy statement on, 363–365
Women's issues
    background on, 367–369
    issue statement on, 369–370
    policy statement on, 370
    public assistance programs and, 370–371
Workplace
    drug testing in, 88–90